Advanced Dungeons & Dragons 2nd Edition

Player's Handbook

The revised and updated *Player's Handbook* for the AD&D® 2nd Edition game.

TSR, Inc.
POB 756
Lake Geneva
WI 53147 USA

TSR Ltd.
120 Church End, Cherry Hinton
Cambridge CB1 3LB
United Kingdom

Special Thanks To:

A vast work like the AD&D® 2nd Edition game doesn't spring into being from nothing. Especially not in this case, since this is the 2nd Edition of the game. The AD&D game owes its existence the efforts of many people.

The AD&D game probably never would have existed without the work of Gary Gygax and Dave Arneson. Together they introduced the world to the concept of role-playing games. Their efforts resulted in the DUNGEONS & DRAGONS® game, forerunner of the AD&D system. Gary Gygax then went on to be the principal creator and guiding force of the AD&D rules. His particular vision set the standards for what the ADVANCED DUNGEONS & DRAGONS® game was—and what it wasn't.

A game such as the AD&D game, or any role-playing game, is much more than the work of just one man. Many others have written rule books, contributed ideas, playtested, criticized, and added their own personal interpretations of what the game is. For their efforts, they too deserve credit. New rule books were written by David "Zeb" Cook (*Oriental Adventures*), Jeff Grubb (*Manual of the Planes*), Tracy Hickman (*DRAGONLANCE® Adventures*), Kim Mohan (*Wilderness Survival Guide*), Douglas Niles (*Dungeoneer's Survival Guide*), Jim Ward (*Legends and Lore*, *GREYHAWK® Adventures*), and Margaret Weis (*DRAGONLANCE® Adventures*).

Over the years, there have been many people who have written rules, edited manuscripts, offered suggestions, and playtested. With an undertaking as large as the AD&D game, this list is long, but each of these people deserves mention for his or her efforts. While there is not enough space to mention exactly what each person did, each has been important to the development of the game. Mark Acres, Peter Aronson, Jim Bambra, Brian Blume, Mike Breault, Mike Carr, Sean Cleary, Troy Denning, Michael Dobson, Jean-Louis Fiasson, Joe Fischer, Ed Greenwood, Ernie Gygax, Luke Gygax, Mary Gygax, Allen Hammack, Neal Healey, Kevin Hendryx, J. Eric Holmes, Tom Holsinger, Jake Jaquet, Harold Johnson, Timothy Jones, Tim Kask, Jeff Key, Tom Kirby, Rick Krebs, Rob Kuntz, Terry Kuntz, Dave LaForce, Len Lakofka, Jeff Leason, Alan Lucion, Francois Marcela-Froideval, Steve Marsh, Dave Megarry, Frank Mentzer, Tom Moldvay, Roger Moore, Mike Mornard, Graeme Morris, Bruce Nesmith, Schar Niebling, Will Niebling, Erol Otus, Jeff Perrin, Penny Petticord, Jon Pickens, Mike Price, Pat Price, Jean Rabe, Paul Reiche III, Gregory Rihn, Tom Robertson, Evan Robinson, John Sapienza, Lawrence Schick, Doug Schwegman, Carl Smith, Curtis Smith, Ed Sollers, Steve Sullivan, Dennis Sustare, Dave Sutherland, Dave Trampier, Don Turnbull, Jack Vance, Jean Wells, Tom Wham, Mike Williams, Skip Williams, and Steve Winter all deserve a share of the credit.

Even so, the list of those to thank is not complete. It can never be complete. The AD&D game is continually evolving—each player and each DM adds his own touch to the whole. No list of special thanks can be complete without recognizing the most important contributors of all—the millions of players who, over the years, have made the AD&D game what it is today.

Credits

2nd Edition design: David "Zeb" Cook
Development: Steve Winter and Jon Pickens
Playtest Coordination: Jon Pickens
Editing: Mike Breault
Proofreading: Jean Black, Curtis Smith, and James Ward
Typesetting: Kim Janke, Linda Bakk, Betty Elmore, and Angie Lokotz
Graphic Design: Linda Bakk
Cover Illustration: Jeff Easley
Interior Color Illustrations: Douglas Chaffee, Larry Elmore, Craig Farley, John & Laura Lakey, Erik Olson, and Jack Pennington
Interior Black & White Illustrations: Jeff Butler, Douglas Chaffee, Jeff Easley, John & Laura Lakey, Jean E. Martin, Dave Sutherland
Keylining: Colleen O'Malley and Paul Hanchette

Too numerous to mention by name are the hundreds of players who assisted us in playtesting the AD&D 2nd Edition game. Their efforts were invaluable in improving the manuscript.

Finally, credit must also be shared with anyone who has ever asked a question, offered a suggestion, written an article, or made a comment about the AD&D game.

This is a derivative work based on the original ADVANCED DUNGEONS & DRAGONS *Players Handbook* and *Dungeon Masters Guide* by Gary Gygax and *Unearthed Arcana* and other materials by Gary Gygax and others.

Foreword to the AD&D 2nd Edition Game

It has been a long time getting here. I don't mean the months, perhaps even years, you may have waited for a revised, expanded, and improved edition of the AD&D® game. I mean the long time it has taken me to reach this point, the writing of the foreword. Forewords are written last, so that you can summarize your feelings and experiences about the book you have written.

It's not accurate to say this is a book that I alone have written. First off, there are a lot of other names listed in the credits. They, especially the editors, contributed time and talents that I don't have. Improving the organization and readability was one of the reasons we started this project in the first place. These are tasks that can't be done without talented editors who play and care about the game. If you discover that it's easier to find rules during your gaming sessions and that everything seems to make more sense, thank the editors.

Even with the editors, this is not our work alone. None of this would ever have come into being without interested and involved players. The people who really decided what needed to be done for the AD&D 2nd Edition game are the players who mailed in questions, everyone who wrote an article for DRAGON® Magazine, and everyone who button-holed me (or other designers) at conventions. These were the people who decided what needed to be done, what needed fixing, what was unclear, and what they just didn't like. I didn't sit in a vacuum and make these decisions. As the designer and developer, I had to make the final choice, but those choices were based on your input. And your input is the most valuable asset we have going.

So how do I feel? Excited, exhausted, relieved, and nervous—all at once. It's a great bag of emotions. I'm excited to see this book come out. I've spent more time on this than I have on any other single work I've done. That leads to exhaustion. The AD&D 2nd Edition game has demanded and received hours upon months of attention. Now that it is finally coming out, the feeling of relief is beginning to set in. There were times when the task looked impossible, when it seemed it would never end, or when everything was going wrong. Only now, when it's in the final stages of polishing, am I beginning to realize that it really is done. And of course there is nervousness. The AD&D game is the granddaddy of all role-playing games. You've made it perfectly clear that you liked the original edition of the AD&D game, even with all its warts. I liked (and still like) it. So, now with the arrival of AD&D 2nd Edition, of course I'm nervous.

None of this comes as any surprise. I volunteered to prepare the this Edition because I wanted to do something for the game I liked. The ten years of experience I've had in game design has shown me what works and what doesn't and sometimes even why. At the very start, we outlined the goals: to make it easier to find things, to make the rules easier to understand, to fix the things that did not work, to add the best new ideas from the expansions and other sources, and, most important of all, to make sure the game was still the one you knew and enjoyed. Of them all, the last was the hardest and most demanding, conflicting as it did with my basic desire to design things. Fortunately, things didn't rest on me alone. Lots of eager eyes, from those of fellow designers to those of enthusiastic playtesters, minutely examined this book and restrained me from overzealousness. It hasn't always been easy to walk the fine line between "not enough" and "too much."

In the past two years, I've talked to interested players many times, hearing their concerns and sharing my ideas. It was at the end of one of these talks (at a convention in Missoula, Montana), just as I described some rules change, that one of the listeners smiled and said, "You know, we've been doing that for years." And that is what AD&D 2nd Edition is all about—collecting and organizing all those things that we, as players, have been doing for years.

David "Zeb" Cook
January, 1989

Table of Contents

Table of Contents

Table of Contents

Tables

You are reading the key to the most exciting hobby in the world—role-playing games.

These first few pages will introduce you to the second edition of the most successful role-playing game ever published. If you are a novice role-player, stop right here and read the section labeled *The Real Basics* (on the next page). When you understand what role-playing and the AD&D® game are all about, come back to this point and read the rest of the introduction. If you are an experienced role-player, skip *The Real Basics*.

Why a 2nd Edition?

Before answering that question, let's define what the second edition of the AD&D game is and is not.

This AD&D 2nd Edition game is a lot different from the original edition. The presentation of the game has been cleaned up. The rules are reorganized, clarified, and streamlined. Where necessary, things that didn't work have been fixed. Things that did work haven't been changed.

The AD&D 2nd Edition game is not a statement of what any one person thinks the game should be. It is the result of more than three years of discussion, thought, consultation, review, and playtesting.

Now to the question of "Why a second edition?" The AD&D game evolved over the course of 16 years. During that time, the game grew tremendously through play. Changes and improvements (and a few mistakes) were made. These were published in subsequent volumes. By 1988, the game consisted of 12 hardcover rule books. It was physically and intellectually unwieldy (but still a lot of fun). The time was right to reorganize and recombine all that information into a manageable package. That package is the second edition.

How the Rule Books are Organized

The AD&D game rule books are intended primarily as reference books. They are designed so any specific rule can be found quickly and easily during a game.

Everything a player needs to know is in the *Player's Handbook*. That's not to say that all the rules are in this book. But every rule that a player needs to know in order to play the game is in this book.

A few rules have been reserved for the *Dungeon Master's Guide (DMG)*. These either cover situations that very seldom arise or give the Dungeon Master (DM) information that players should not have beforehand. Everything else in the *DMG* is information that only the Dungeon Master needs. If the DM feels that players need to

know something that is explained in the *DMG*, he will tell them.

Like the *DMG*, the *Monstrous Compendium* is the province of the DM. This gives complete and detailed information about the monsters, people, and other creatures inhabiting the AD&D world. Some DMs don't mind if players read this information, but the game is more fun if players don't know everything about their foes—it heightens the sense of discovery and danger of the unknown.

Learning the Game

If you have played the AD&D game before, you know almost everything you need to play the 2nd Edition. We advise you to read the entire *Player's Handbook*, but the biggest changes are in these chapters: *Character Classes*, *Combat*, and *Experience*. Be sure to read at least those three chapters before sitting down to play.

If you come to a term you do not understand, look for it in the Glossary, which begins on page 11.

If you have never played the AD&D game before, the best way to learn to play the game is to find a group of experienced players and join them. They can get you immediately into the game and explain things as you need to know them. You don't need to read anything beforehand. In fact, it's best if you can play the game for several hours with experienced players before reading any of the rules. One of the truly marvelous things about a role-playing game is that even though the concept is difficult to explain, it is simple to demonstrate.

If none of your friends are involved in a game, the best place to find experienced players is through your local hobby store. Role-playing and general gaming clubs are common and are always eager to accept new members. Many hobby stores offer a bulletin board through which DMs can advertise for new players and new players can ask for information about new or ongoing games. If there is no hobby store in your area, check at the local library or school.

If you can't find anyone else who knows the AD&D game, you can teach yourself. Read the *Player's Handbook* and create some characters. Try to create a variety of character classes. Then pick up a prepackaged adventure module for low-level characters, round up two or three friends, and dive into it. You probably will make lots of mistakes and wonder constantly whether you are doing everything wrong. Even if you are, don't worry about it. The AD&D game is big, but eventually you'll bring it under control.

The AD&D Game 2nd Edition Line

Quite a few books and other products are published for the AD&D game. As a player, you need only one of them—this book. Every player and DM should have a copy of the *Player's Handbook*. Everything else is either optional or intended for the Dungeon Master.

The *Dungeon Master's Guide* is essential for the DM and it is for the DM only. Players who are not themselves DMs have no cause to read the *DMG*.

The *Monstrous Compendium* is not one, but several products. The book can be expanded whenever new compendiums are released. The first pack of monsters is essential to the game. It includes the most commonly encountered monsters, mythical beasts, and legendary creatures. Additional packs expand on these monsters and give the game more variety. Specialty compendiums—those for GRAYHAWK®, the FORGOTTEN REALMS®, Kara-Tur, etc.—are highly recommended for DMs who play in those settings.

Expanded character class books—*The Complete Fighter*, *The Complete Thief*, etc.—provide a lot more detail on these character classes than does the *Player's Handbook*. These books are entirely optional. They are for those players who really want a world of choice for their characters.

Adventure modules contain complete game adventures. These are especially useful for DMs who aren't sure how to create their own adventures and for DMs who need an adventure quickly and don't have time to write one of their own.

A Note About Pronouns

The male pronoun (he, him, his) is used exclusively throughout the second edition of the AD&D game rules. We hope this won't be construed by anyone to be an attempt to exclude females from the game or imply their exclusion. Centuries of use have neutered the male pronoun. In written material it is clear, concise, and familiar. Nothing else is.

Creating a Character

To create a character to play in the AD&D game, proceed, in order, through Chapters 1 through 6. (Chapter 5 is optional). These chapters will tell you how to generate your character's ability scores, race, and class, decide on his alignment, pick proficiencies, and buy equipment. Once you have done all this, your character is ready for adventure!

This section is intended for novice role-players. If you have played role-playing games before, don't be surprised if what you read here sounds familiar.

Games come in a wide assortment of types: board games, card games, word games, picture games, miniatures games. Even within these categories are subcategories. Board games, for example, can be divided into path games, real estate games, military simulation games, abstract strategy games, mystery games, and a host of others.

Still, in all this mass of games, role-playing games are unique. They form a category all their own that doesn't overlap any other category.

For that reason, role-playing games are hard to describe. Comparisons don't work because there isn't anything similar to compare them to. At least, not without stretching your imagination well beyond its normal, everyday extension.

But then, stretching your imagination is what role-playing is all about. So let's try an analogy.

Imagine that you are playing a simple board game, called Snakes and Ladders. Your goal is to get from the bottom to the top of the board before all the other players. Along the way are traps that can send you sliding back toward your starting position. There are also ladders that can let you jump ahead, closer to the finish space. So far, it's pretty simple and pretty standard.

Now let's change a few things. Instead of a flat, featureless board with a path winding from side to side, let's have a maze. You are standing at the entrance, and you know that there's an exit somewhere, but you don't know where. You have to find it.

Instead of snakes and ladders, we'll put in hidden doors and secret passages. Don't roll a die to see how far you move; you can move as far as you want. Move down the corridor to the intersection. You can turn right, or left, or go straight ahead, or go back the way you came. Or, as long as you're here, you can look for a hidden door. If you find one, it will open into another stretch of corridor. That corridor might take you straight to the exit or lead you into a blind alley. The only way to find out is to step in and start walking.

Of course, given enough time, eventually you'll find the exit. To keep the game interesting, let's put some other things in the maze with you. Nasty things. Things like vampire bats and hobgoblins and zombies and ogres. Of course, we'll give you a sword and a shield, so if you meet one of these things you can defend yourself. You do know how to use a sword, don't you?

And there are other players in the maze as well. They have swords and shields, too. How do you suppose another player would react if you chance to meet? He might attack, but he also might offer to team up.

After all, even an ogre might think twice about attacking two people carrying sharp swords and stout shields.

Finally, let's put the board somewhere you can't see it. Let's give it to one of the players and make that player the referee. Instead of looking at the board, you listen to the referee as he describes what you can see from your position on the board. You tell the referee what you want to do and he moves your piece accordingly. As the referee describes your surroundings, try to picture them mentally. Close your eyes and construct the walls of the maze around yourself. Imagine the hobgoblin as the referee describes it whooping and gamboling down the corridor toward you. Now imagine how you would react in that situation and tell the referee what you are going to do about it.

We have just constructed a simple role-playing game. It is not a sophisticated game, but it has the essential element that makes a role-playing game: The player is placed in the midst of an unknown or dangerous situation created by a referee and must work his way through it.

This is the heart of role-playing. The player adopts the role of a character and then guides that character through an adventure. The player makes decisions, interacts with other characters and players, and, essentially, "pretends" to be his character during the course of the game. That doesn't mean that the player must jump up and down, dash around, and act like his character. It means that whenever the character is called on to do something or make a decision, the player pretends that he is in that situation and chooses an appropriate course of action.

Physically, the players and referee (the DM) should be seated comfortably around a table with the referee at the head. Players need plenty of room for papers, pencils, dice, rule books, drinks, and snacks. The referee needs extra space for his maps, dice, rule books, and assorted notes.

The Goal

Another major difference between role-playing games and other games is the ultimate goal. Everyone assumes that a game must have a beginning and an end and that the end comes when someone wins. That doesn't apply to role-playing because no one "wins" in a role-playing game. The point of playing is not to win but to have fun and to socialize.

An adventure usually has a goal of some sort: protect the villagers from the monsters; rescue the lost princess; explore the ancient ruins. Typically, this goal can be attained in a reasonable playing time: four to eight hours is standard. This might require the players to get together for one,

two, or even three playing sessions to reach their goal and complete the adventure.

But the game doesn't end when an adventure is finished. The same characters can go on to new adventures. Such a series of adventures is called a campaign.

Remember, the point of an adventure is not to win but to have fun while working toward a common goal. But the length of any particular adventure need not impose an artificial limit on the length of the game. The AD&D® game embraces more than enough adventure to keep a group of characters occupied for years.

Required Materials

Aside from a copy of this book, very little is needed to play the AD&D game.

You will need some sort of character record. TSR publishes character record sheets that are quite handy and easy to use, but any sheet of paper will do. Blank paper, lined paper, or even graph paper can be used. A double-sized sheet of paper (11 x 17 inches), folded in half, is excellent. Keep your character record in pencil, because it will change frequently during the game. A good eraser is also a must.

A full set of polyhedral dice is necessary. A full set consists of 4-, 6-, 8-, 10-, 12-, and 20-sided dice. A few extra 6- and 10-sided dice are a good idea. Polyhedral dice should be available wherever you got this book.

Throughout these rules, the various dice are referred to by a code that is in the form: # of dice, followed by "d," followed by a numeral for the type of dice. In other words, if you are to roll one 6-sided die, you would see "roll 1d6." Five 12-sided dice are referred to as "5d12." (If you don't have five 12-sided dice, just roll one five times and add the results.)

When the rules say to roll "percentile dice" or "1d100," you need to generate a random number from 1 to 100. One way to do this is to roll two 10-sided dice of different colors. Before you roll, designate one die as the tens place and the other as the ones place. Rolling them together enables you to generate a number from 1 to 100 (a result of "0" on both dice is read as "00" or "100"). For example, if the blue die (representing the tens place) rolls an "8" and the red die (ones place) rolls a "5," the result is 85. Another, more expensive, way to generate a number from 1 to 100 is to buy one of the dice that actually have numbers from 1 to 100 on them.

At least one player should have a few sheets of graph paper for mapping the group's progress. Assorted pieces of scratch paper are handy for making quick notes, for passing secret messages to other players or the DM, or for keeping track of odd bits of information that you don't want cluttering up your character record.

Miniature figures are handy for keeping track of where everyone is in a confusing situation like a battle. These can be as elaborate or simple as you like. Some players use miniature lead or pewter figures painted to resemble their characters. Plastic soldiers, chess pieces, boardgame pawns, dice, or bits of paper can work just as well.

An Example of Play

To further clarify what really goes on during an AD&D® game, read the following example. This is typical of the sort of action that occurs during a playing session.

Shortly before this example begins, three player characters fought a skirmish with a wererat (a creature similar to a werewolf but which becomes an enormous rat instead of a wolf). The wererat was wounded and fled down a tunnel. The characters are in pursuit. The group includes two fighters and a cleric. Fighter 1 is the group's leader.

DM: You've been following this tunnel for about 120 yards. The water on the floor is ankle deep and very cold. Now and then you feel something brush against your foot. The smell of decay is getting stronger. The tunnel is gradually filling with a cold mist.

Fighter 1: I don't like this at all. Can we see anything up ahead that looks like a doorway, or a branch in the tunnel?

DM: Within the range of your torchlight, the tunnel is more or less straight. You don't see any branches or doorways.

Cleric: The wererat we hit had to come this way. There's nowhere else to go.

Fighter 1: Unless we missed a hidden door along the way. I hate this place; it gives me the creeps.

Fighter 2: We have to track down that wererat. I say we keep going.

Fighter 1: OK. We keep moving down the tunnel. But keep your eyes open for anything that might be a door.

DM: Another 30 or 35 yards down the tunnel, you find a stone block on the floor.

Fighter 1: A block? I take a closer look.

DM: It's a cut block, about 12 by 16 inches, and 18 inches or so high. It looks like a different kind of rock than the rest of the tunnel.

Fighter 2: Where is it? Is it in the center of the tunnel or off to the side?

DM: It's right up against the side.

Fighter 1: Can I move it?

DM (checking the character's Strength score): Yeah, you can push it around without too much trouble.

Fighter 1: Hmmm. This is obviously a marker of some sort. I want to check this area for secret doors. Spread out and examine the walls.

DM (rolls several dice behind his rule book, where players can't see the results): Nobody finds anything unusual along the walls.

Fighter 1: It has to be here somewhere. What about the ceiling?

DM: You can't reach the ceiling. It's about a foot beyond your reach.

Cleric: Of course! That block isn't a marker, it's a step. I climb up on the block and start prodding the ceiling.

DM (rolling a few more dice): You poke around for 20 seconds or so, then suddenly part of the tunnel roof shifts. You've found a panel that lifts away.

Fighter 1: Open it very carefully.

Cleric: I pop it up a few inches and push it aside slowly. Can I see anything?

DM: Your head is still below the level of the opening, but you see some dim light from one side.

Fighter 1: We boost him up so he can get a better look.

DM: OK, your friends boost you up into the room . . .

Fighter 1: No, no! We boost him just high enough to get his head through the opening.

DM: OK, you boost him up a foot. The two of you are each holding one of his legs. Cleric, you see another tunnel, pretty much like the one you were in, but it only goes off in one direction. There's a doorway about 10 yards away with a soft light inside. A line of muddy pawprints leads from the hole you're in to the doorway.

Cleric: Fine. I want the fighters to go first.

DM: As they're lowering you back to the block, everyone hears some grunts, splashing, and clanking weapons coming from further down the lower tunnel. They seem to be closing fast.

Cleric: Up! Up! Push me back up through the hole! I grab the ledge and haul myself up. I'll help pull the next guy up.

(All three characters scramble up through the hole.)

DM: What about the panel?

Fighter 1: We push it back into place.

DM: It slides back into its slot with a nice, loud "clunk." The grunting from below gets a lot louder.

Fighter 1: Great, they heard it. Cleric, get over here and stand on this panel. We're going to check out that doorway.

DM: Cleric, you hear some shouting and shuffling around below you, then there's a thump and the panel you're standing on lurches.

Cleric: They're trying to batter it open!

DM (to the fighters): When you peer around the doorway, you see a small, dirty room with a small cot, a table, and a couple of stools. On the cot is a wererat curled up into a ball. Its back is toward you. There's another door in the far wall and a

small gong in the corner.

Fighter 1: Is the wererat moving?

DM: Not a bit. Cleric, the panel just thumped again. You can see a little crack in it now.

Cleric: Do something quick, you guys. When this panel starts coming apart, I'm getting off it.

Fighter 1: OK already! I step into the room and prod the wererat with my shield. What happens?

DM: Nothing. You see blood on the cot.

Fighter 1: Is this the same wererat we fought before?

DM: Who knows? All wererats look the same to you. Cleric, the panel thumps again. That crack is looking really big.

Cleric: That's it. I get off the panel. I'm moving into the room with everybody else.

DM: There's a tremendous smash and you hear chunks of rock banging around out in the corridor, followed by lots of snarling and squeaking. You see flashes of torchlight and wererat shadows through the doorway.

Fighter 1: All right, the other fighter and I move up to block the doorway. That's the narrowest area, they can only come through it one or two at a time. Cleric, you stay in the room and be ready with your spells.

Fighter 2: At last, a decent, stand-up fight!

DM: As the first wererat appears in the doorway with a spear in his paws, you hear a slam behind you.

Cleric: I spin around. What is it?

DM: The door in the back of the room is broken off its hinges. Standing in the doorway, holding a mace in each paw, is the biggest, ugliest wererat you've ever seen. A couple more pairs of red eyes are shining through the darkness behind him. He's licking his chops in a way that you find very unsettling.

Cleric: Aaaaarrrgh! I scream the name of my deity at the top of my lungs and then flip over the cot with the dead wererat on it so the body lands in front of him. I've got to have some help here, guys.

Fighter 1 (to fighter 2): Help him, I'll handle this end of the room. (To DM): I'm attacking the wererat in the doorway.

DM: While fighter 2 is switching positions, the big wererat looks at the body on the floor and his jaw drops. He looks back up and says, "That's Ignatz. He was my brother. You killed my brother." Then he raises both maces and leaps at you.

At this point a ferocious melee breaks out. The DM uses the combat rules to play out the battle. If the characters survive, they can continue on whatever course they choose.

Ability - any of the six natural traits that represent the basic definition of a player character: Strength, Dexterity, Constitution, Intelligence, Wisdom, and Charisma. A player character's abilities are determined at the beginning of a game by rolling 6-sided dice (d6s). The scores continue to be used throughout the game as a means of determining success or failure of many actions.

Ability check - a 1d20 roll against one of your character's ability scores (modifiers may be added to or subtracted from the die roll). A result that is equal to or less than your character's ability score indicates that the attempted action succeeds.

AC - abbreviation for Armor Class (q.v.).

Alignment - a factor in defining a player character that reflects his basic attitude toward society and the forces of the universe. Basically there are nine categories demonstrating the character's relationship to order vs. chaos and good vs. evil. A player character's alignment is selected by the player when the character is created.

Area of effect - the area in which a magical spell or a breath weapon works on any creatures unless they make a saving throw.

Armor Class (abbr. **AC**) - a rating for the protective value of a type of armor, figured from 10 (no armor at all) to 0 or even −10 (the best magical armor). The higher the AC, the more vulnerable the character is to attack.

Attack roll - The 1d20 roll used to determine if an attack is successful.

Bend bars/lift gates roll - the roll of percentile dice to determine whether a character succeeds in bending metal bars, lifting a heavy portcullis, or similar task. The result needed is a function of Strength and can be found in Table 1.

Bonus spells - extra spells at various spell levels that a priest is entitled to because of high Wisdom; shown in Table 5.

Breath weapon - the ability of a dragon or other creature to spew a substance out of its mouth just by breathing, without making an attack roll. Those in the area of effect must roll a saving throw.

Cha - abbreviation for Charisma (q.v.).

Chance of spell failure - the percentage chance that a priest spell will fail when cast. Based on Wisdom, it is shown in Table 5.

Chance to know spell - the percentage chance for a wizard to learn a new spell. Based on Intelligence, it is shown in Table 4.

Charisma (abbr. **Cha**) - an ability score representing a character's persuasiveness, personal magnetism, and ability to lead.

Common - the language that all player characters in the AD&D® game world speak. Other languages may require the use of proficiency slots.

Con - abbreviation for Constitution (q.v.).

Constitution (abbr. **Con**) - an ability score that represents a character's general physique, hardiness, and state of health.

d - abbreviation for dice or die. A roll that calls for 2d6, for example, means that the player rolls two six-sided dice.

d3 - since there is no such thing as a three-sided die, a roll calling for d3 means to use a d6, making 1 and 2 be a 1, 3 and 4 be a 2, and 5 and 6 be a 3.

d4 - a four-sided die.

d6 - a six-sided die.

d8 - an eight-sided die.

d10 - a ten-sided die. Two d10s can be used as percentile dice (q.v.).

d12 - a twelve-sided die.

d20 - a twenty-sided die.

d100 - either an actual 100-sided die or two different-colored ten-sided dice to be rolled as percentile dice (q.v.).

DMG - a reference to the *Dungeon Master's Guide*.

Damage - the effect of a successful attack or other harmful situation, measured in hit points.

Demihuman - a player character who is not human: a dwarf, elf, gnome, half-elf, or halfling.

Dex - abbreviation for Dexterity (q.v.).

Dexterity (abbr. **Dex**) - an ability score representing a combination of a character's agility, reflexes, hand-eye coordination, and the like.

Dual-class character - a human who switches character class after having already progressed several levels. Only humans can be dual-classed.

Encumbrance - the amount, in pounds, that a character is carrying. How much he can carry and how being encumbered affects his movement rate are based on Strength and are shown in Tables 47 and 48. Encumbrance is an optional rule.

Energy drain - the ability of a creature, especially undead, to drain energy in the form of class levels from a character, in addition to the normal loss of hit points.

Experience points (abbr. **XP**) - points a character earns (determined by the Dungeon Master) for completing an adventure, for doing something related to his class particularly well, or for solving a major problem. Experience points are accumulated, enabling the character to rise in level in his class, as shown in Table 14 for warriors, Table 20 for wizards, Table 23 for priests, and Table 25 for rogues.

Follower - a non-player character who works for a character for money but is initially drawn to his reputation.

Gaze attack - the ability of a creature, such as a basilisk, to attack simply by making eye contact with the victim.

Henchmen - non-player characters who work for a character mainly out of loyalty and love of adventure. The number of henchmen a character can have is based on Charisma and is shown in Table 6. The DM and the player share control of the henchmen.

Hireling - non-player characters who work for a character just for money. Hirelings are completely under the control of the DM.

Hit dice - the dice rolled to determine a character's hit points. Up to a certain level, one or more new Hit Dice are rolled each time a character attains a new class level. A fighter, for example, has only one 10-sided Hit Die (1d10) at 1st level, but when he rises to the 2nd level, the player rolls a second d10, increasing the character's hit points.

Hit points - a number representing 1. how much damage a character can suffer before being killed, determined by Hit Dice (q.v.). The hit points lost to injury can usually be regained by rest or healing. 2. how much damage a specific attack does, determined by weapon or monster statistics, and subtracted from a player's total.

Infravision - the ability of certain character races or monsters to see in the dark. Infravision generally works up to 60 feet in the darkness.

Initiative - the right to attack first in a combat round, usually determined by the lowest roll of a 10-sided die. The initiative roll is eliminated if surprise (q.v.) is achieved.

Int - abbreviation for Intelligence (q.v.).

Intelligence (abbr. **Int**) - an ability score representing a character's memory, reasoning, and learning ability.

Italic type - used primarily to indicate spells and magical items.

Level - any of several different game factors that are variable in degree, especially: 1. class level, a measure of the character's power, starting at the 1st level as a beginning adventurer and rising through the accumulation of experience points to the 20th level or higher. At each level attained, the character receives new powers. 2. spell level, a measure of the power of a magical spell. A magic-using character can use only those spells for which his class level qualifies him. Wizard spells come in nine levels (Table 21); priest spells in seven (Table 24).

Loyalty base - a bonus added to or a penalty subtracted from the probability that henchmen are going to stay around when the going gets tough. Based on the character's Charisma, it is shown in Table 6.

M - abbreviation for material component (q.v.).

Magical defense adjustment - a bonus added to or a penalty subtracted from saving throws vs. spells that attack the mind. Based on Wisdom, it is shown in Table 5.

Maneuverability class - a ranking for flying creatures that reflects their ability to turn easily in aerial combat. Each class—from a top of A to a bottom rank of E—has specific statistical abilities in combat.

Material component (abbr. **M**) - any specific item that must be handled in some way during the casting of a magic spell.

Maximum press - the most weight a character can pick up and raise over his head. It is a function of Strength and may be found in Table 1.

Melee - combat in which characters are fighting in direct contact, such as with swords, claws, or fists, as opposed to fighting with missile weapons or spells.

Missile combat - combat involving the use of weapons that shoot missiles or items that can be thrown. Because the combat is not "toe-to-toe," the rules are slightly different than those for regular combat.

Movement rate - a number used in calculating how far and how fast a character can move in a round. This number is in units of *10 yards* per round outdoors, but it represents *10 feet* indoors. Thus, an MR of 6 is 60 yards per round in the wilderness, but only 60 feet per round in a dungeon.

MR - abbreviation for movement rate *(q.v.)*.

Multi-class character - a demihuman who improves in two or more classes at the same time by dividing experience points between the different classes. Humans cannot be multi-classed.

Mythos *(pl. mythoi)* - a complete body of belief particular to a certain time or place, including the pantheon of its gods.

Neutrality - a philosophical position, or alignment, of a character that is between belief in good or evil, order or chaos.

Non-player character - any character controlled by the DM instead of a player.

NPC - abbreviation for non-player character *(q.v.)*.

Open doors roll - the roll of a 20-sided die to see if a character succeeds in opening a heavy or stuck door or performing a similar task. The die roll at which the character succeeds can be found in Table 1.

Opposition school - a school of magic that is directly opposed to a specialist's school of choice, thus preventing him from learning spells from that school, as shown in Table 22.

PC - abbreviation for player character *(q.v.)*.

Percentage (or percent) chance - a number between 1 and 100 used to represent the probability of something happening. If a character is given an X percentage chance of an event occurring, the player rolls percentile dice *(q.v.)*.

Percentile dice - either a 100-sided die or two 10-sided dice used in rolling a percentage number. If 2d10 are used, they are of different colors, and one represents the tens digit while the other is the ones.

Player character *(abbr. PC)* - the characters in a role-playing game who are under the control of the players.

Poison save - a bonus or a penalty to a saving throw vs. poison. Based on Constitution, it is shown in Table 3.

Prime requisite - the ability score that is most important to a character class; for example, Strength to a fighter.

Proficiency - a character's learned skill not defined by his class but which gives him a greater percentage chance to accomplish a specific type of task during an adventure. Weapon and nonweapon proficiency slots are acquired as the character rises in level, as shown in Table 34. The use of proficiencies in the game is optional.

Proficiency check - the roll of a 20-sided die to see if a character succeeds in doing a task by comparing the die roll to the character's relevant ability score plus or minus any modifiers shown in Table 37 (the modified die roll must be equal to or less than the ability score for the action to succeed).

q.v. - "which see," or "turn to."

Race - a player character's species: human, elf, dwarf, gnome, half- elf, or halfling. Race puts some limitations on the PC's class.

Rate of fire *(abbr. ROF)* - number of times a missile-firing or thrown weapon can be shot in a round.

Reaction adjustment - a bonus added to or penalty subtracted from a die roll used in determining the success of a character's action. Such an adjustment is used especially in reference to surprise (shown on Table 2 as a function of Dexterity) and the reaction of other intelligence beings to a character (shown on Table 6 as a function of Charisma).

Regeneration - a special ability to heal faster than usual, based on an extraordinarily high Constitution, as shown in Table 3.

Resistance - the innate ability of a being to withstand attack, such as by magic. Gnomes, for example, have a magic resistance that adds bonuses to their saving throws against magic (Table 9).

Resurrection survival - the percentage chance a character has of being magically raised from death. Based on Constitution, it is shown in Table 3.

Reversible - of a magic spell, able to be cast "backwards," so that the opposite of the usual effect is achieved.

ROF - abbreviation for rate of fire *(q.v.)*.

Round - in combat, a segment of time approximately 1 minute long, during which a character can accomplish one basic action. Ten combat rounds equal one turn.

S - abbreviation for somatic component *(q.v.)*.

Saving throw - a measure of a character's ability to resist (to "save vs.") special types of attacks, especially poison, paralyzation, magic, and breath weapons. Success is usually determined by the roll of 1d20.

School of magic - One of nine different categories of magic, based on the type of magical energy utilized. Wizards who concentrate their work on a single school are called specialists. The specific school of

which a spell is a part is shown after the name of the spell in the spell section at the end of the book.

Somatic component *(abbr. S)* - the gestures that a spellcaster must use to cast a specific spell. A bound wizard cannot cast a spell requiring somatic components.

Specialist - a wizard who concentrates on a specific school of magic *(q.v.)*, as opposed to a mage, who studies all magic in general.

Spell immunity - protection that certain characters have against illusions or other specific spells, based on high Intelligence (Table 4) or Wisdom (Table 5).

Sphere of influence - any of sixteen categories of clerical spells to which a priest may have major access (he can eventually learn them all) or minor access (he can learn only the lower level spells). The relevant sphere of influence is shown as the first item in the list of characteristics in the priest spells.

Str - abbreviation for Strength *(q.v.)*.

Strength *(abbr. Str)* - an ability score representing a character's muscle power, endurance, and stamina.

Surprise roll - the roll of a ten-sided die by the Dungeon Master to determine if a character or group takes another by surprise. Successful surprise (a roll of 1, 2, or 3) cancels the roll for initiative on the first round of combat.

System shock - a percentage chance that a character survives major magical effects, such as being petrified. Based on Constitution, it is shown in Table 3.

THAC0 - an acronym for "To Hit Armor Class 0," the number that a character needs to roll in order to successfully hit a target with AC 0.

To-hit roll - another name for attack roll *(q.v.)*.

Turn - in game time, approximately 10 minutes; used especially in figuring how long various magic spells may last. In combat, a turn consists of 10 rounds.

Turn undead - a magical ability of a cleric or paladin to turn away an undead creature, such as a skeleton or a vampire.

V - abbreviation for verbal component *(q.v.)*.

Verbal component - specific words or sounds that must be uttered while casting a spell.

Weapon speed - an initiative modifier used in combat that accounts for the time required to get back into position to reuse a weapon.

Wis - abbreviation for Wisdom *(q.v.)*.

Wisdom *(abbr. Wis)* - an ability score representing a composite of a character's intuition, judgment, common sense, and will power.

XP - abbreviation for experience points *(q.v.)*.

To venture into the worlds of the AD&D® game, you first need to create a *character*. The character you create is your alter ego in the fantasy realms of this game, a make-believe person who is under your control and through whom you vicariously explore the world the Dungeon Master (DM) has created.

Each character in the AD&D game has six abilities: Strength, Dexterity, Constitution, Intelligence, Wisdom, and Charisma. The first three abilities represent the physical nature of the character, while the second three quantify his mental and personality traits.

In various places throughout these rules, the following abbreviations are used for the ability names: Strength—Str; Dexterity—Dex; Constitution—Con; Intelligence—Int; Wisdom—Wis; Charisma —Cha.

Rolling Ability Scores

Let's first see how to generate ability scores for your character, after which definitions of each ability will be given.

The six ability scores are determined randomly by rolling six-sided dice to obtain a score from 3 to 18. There are several methods for rolling up these scores.

• **Method I:** Roll three six-sided dice (3d6); the total shown on the dice is your character's Strength ability score. Repeat this for Dexterity, Constitution, Intelligence, Wisdom, and Charisma, in that order. This method gives a range of scores from 3 to 18, with most results in the 9 to 12 range. Only a few characters have high scores (15 and above), so you should treasure these characters.

Alternative Dice-Rolling Methods

Method I creates characters whose ability scores are usually between 9 and 12. If you would rather play a character of truly heroic proportions, ask your DM if he allows players to use optional methods for rolling up characters. These optional methods are designed to produce above-average characters.

• **Method II:** Roll 3d6 twice, noting the total of each roll. Use whichever result you prefer for your character's Strength score. Repeat this for Dexterity, Constitution, Intelligence, Wisdom, and Charisma. This allows you to pick the best score from each pair, generally ensuring that your character does not have any really low ability scores (but low ability scores are not all that bad anyway!).

• **Method III:** Roll 3d6 six times and jot down the total for each roll. Assign the scores to your character's six abilities however you want. This gives you the chance to custom-tailor your character, although you are not guaranteed high scores.

• **Method IV:** Roll 3d6 twelve times and jot down all twelve totals. Choose six of these rolls (generally the six best rolls) and assign them to your character's abilities however you want. This combines the best of methods II and III, but takes somewhat longer.

As an example, Joan rolls 3d6 twelve times and gets results of 12, 5, 6, 8, 10, 15, 9, 12, 6, 11, 10, and 7. She chooses the six best rolls (15, 12, 12, 11, 10, and 10) and then assigns them to her character's abilities so as to create the strengths and weaknesses that she wants her character to have (see the ability descriptions following this section for explanations of the abilities).

• **Method V:** Roll four six-sided dice (4d6). Discard the lowest die and total the remaining three. Repeat this five more times, then assign the six numbers to the character's abilities however you want. This is a fast method that gives you a good character, but you can still get low scores (after all, you could roll 1s on all four dice!).

• **Method VI:** This method can be used if you want to create a specific type of character. It does not guarantee that you will get the character you want, but it will improve your chances.

Each ability starts with a score of 8. Then roll seven dice. These dice can be added to your character's abilities as you wish. All the points on a die must be added to the same ability score. For example, if a 6 is rolled on one die, all 6 points must be assigned to one ability. You can add as many dice as you want to any ability, but no ability score can exceed 18 points. If you cannot make an 18 by exact count on the dice, you cannot have an 18 score.

The Ability Scores

The six character abilities are described below. Each description gives an idea of what that ability encompasses. Specific game effects are also given. At the end of each ability description is the table giving all modifiers and game information for each ability score. The unshaded area of these tables contains scores a player character can have naturally, without the aid of magical devices, spells, or divine intervention. The blue-shaded ability scores can be obtained only by extraordinary means, whether by good fortune (finding a magical book that raises a score) or ill fortune (an attack by a creature that lowers a score).

Strength

Strength (Str) measures a character's muscle, endurance, and stamina. This ability is the prime requisite of warriors because they must be physically powerful in order to wear armor and wield heavy weapons. A fighter with a score of 16 or more in Strength gains a 10 percent bonus to the experience points he earns.

Furthermore, any warrior with a Strength score of 18 is entitled to roll percentile dice (see Glossary) to determine exceptional Strength; exceptional Strength improves the character's chance to hit an enemy, increases the damage he causes with each hit, increases the weight the character is able to carry without a penalty for encumbrance (see below), and increases the character's ability to force open doors and similar portals.

The rest of this section on Strength consists of explanations of the columns in Table 1. Refer to the table as you read.

Hit Probability adjustments are added to or subtracted from the attack roll rolled on 1d20 (one 20-sided die) during combat. A bonus (positive number) makes the opponent easier to hit; a penalty (negative number) makes him harder to hit.

Damage Adjustment also applies to combat. The listed number is added to or subtracted from the dice rolled to determine the damage caused by an attack (regardless of subtractions, a successful attack roll can never cause less than 1 point of damage). For example, a short sword normally causes 1d6 points of damage (a range of 1 to 6). An attacker with Strength 17 causes one extra point of damage, for a range of 2 to 7 points of damage. The damage adjustment also applies to missile weapons, although bows must be specially made to gain the bonus; crossbows never benefit from the user's Strength.

Weight Allowance is the weight (in pounds) a character can carry without being encumbered (encumbrance measures how a character's possessions hamper his movement—see Glossary). These weights are expressed in pounds. A character carrying up to the listed weight can move his full movement rate.

Maximum Press is the heaviest weight a character can pick up and lift over his head. A character cannot walk more than a few steps this way. No human or humanoid creature without exceptional Strength can lift more than twice his body weight over his head. In 1987, the world record for lifting a weight overhead in a single move was 465 pounds. A heroic fighter with Strength 18/00 (see Table 1) can lift up to 480 pounds the same way and he can hold it overhead for a longer time!

Open Doors indicates the character's chance to force open a heavy or stuck door. When a character tries to force a door open, roll 1d20. If the result is equal to or less than the listed number, the door opens. A character can keep trying to open a door until it finally opens, but each attempt takes time (exactly how much is up to the DM) and makes a lot of noise.

Numbers in parentheses are the chances (on 1d20) to open a locked, barred, or magically held door, but only one attempt per door can ever be made. If it fails, no further attempts by that character can succeed.

Bend Bars/Lift Gates states the character's percentage chance (rolled on percentile dice) to bend normal, soft iron bars, lift a vertical gate (portcullis), or perform a similar feat of enormous strength. When the character makes the attempt, roll percentile dice. If the number rolled is equal to or less than the number listed on Table 1, the character bends the bar or lifts the gate. If the attempt fails, the character can never succeed at that task. A character can, however, try to bend the bars on a gate that he couldn't lift, and vice versa.

Table 1: STRENGTH

Ability Score	Hit Prob.	Damage Adj.	Weight Allow.	Max. Press	Open Doors	Bend Bars/ Lift Gates	Notes
1	−5	−4	1	3	1	0%	
2	−3	−2	1	5	1	0%	
3	−3	−1	5	10	2	0%	
4-5	−2	−1	10	25	3	0%	
6-7	−1	None	20	55	4	0%	
8-9	Normal	None	35	90	5	1%	
10-11	Normal	None	40	115	6	2%	
12-13	Normal	None	45	140	7	4%	
14-15	Normal	None	55	170	8	7%	
16	Normal	+1	70	195	9	10%	
17	+1	+1	85	220	10	13%	
18	+1	+2	110	255	11	16%	
18/01-50	+1	+3	135	280	12	20%	
18/51-75	+2	+3	160	305	13	25%	
18/76-90	+2	+4	185	330	14	30%	
18/91-99	+2	+5	235	380	15(3)	35%	
18/00	+3	+6	335	480	16(6)	40%	
19	+3	+7	485	640	16(8)	50%	Hill Giant
20	+3	+8	535	700	17(10)	60%	Stone Giant
21	+4	+9	635	810	17(12)	70%	Frost Giant
22	+4	+10	785	970	18(14)	80%	Fire Giant
23	+5	+11	935	1,130	18(16)	90%	Cloud Giant
24	+6	+12	1,235	1,440	19(17)	95%	Storm Giant
25	+7	+14	1,535	1,750	19(18)	99%	Titan

Dexterity

Dexterity (Dex) encompasses several physical attributes including hand-eye coordination, agility, reaction speed, reflexes, and balance. Dexterity affects a character's reaction to a threat or surprise, his accuracy with thrown weapons and bows, and his ability to dodge an enemy's blows. It is the prime requisite of rogues and affects their professional skills. A rogue with a Dexterity score of 16 or higher gains a 10 percent bonus to the experience points he earns.

Reaction Adjustment modifies the die roll to see if a character is surprised when he unexpectedly encounters NPCs. The more positive the modifier, the less likely the character is to be surprised.

Missile Attack Adjustment is used to modify a character's die roll whenever he uses a missile weapon (a bow or a thrown weapon). A positive number makes it easier for the character to hit with a missile, while a negative number makes it harder.

Defensive Adjustment applies to a character's saving throws (see Glossary) against attacks that can be dodged—lightning bolts, boulders, etc. It also modifies the character's Armor Class (see Glossary), representing his ability to dodge normal missiles and parry weapon thrusts. For example, Rath is wearing chain mail, giving him an Armor Class of 5. If his Dexterity score is 16, his Armor Class is modified by −2 to 3, making him harder to hit. If his Dexterity score is 5, his Armor Class is modified by +2 to 7, making him easier to hit. (In some situations, beneficial Dexterity modifiers to Armor Class do not apply. Usually this occurs when a character is attacked from behind or when his movement is restricted—attacked while prone, tied up, on a ledge, climbing a rope, etc.)

Table 2: DEXTERITY

Ability Score	Reaction Adj.	Missile Attack Adj.	Defensive Adj.
1	−6	−6	+5
2	−4	−4	+5
3	−3	−3	+4
4	−2	−2	+3
5	−1	−1	+2
6	0	0	+1
7	0	0	0
8	0	0	0
9	0	0	0
10-14	0	0	0
15	0	0	−1
16	+1	+1	−2
17	+2	+2	−3
18	+2	+2	−4
19	+3	+3	−4
20	+3	+3	−4
21	+4	+4	−5
22	+4	+4	−5
23	+4	+4	−5
24	+5	+5	−6
25	+5	+5	−6

Constitution

A character's Constitution (Con) score encompasses his physique, fitness, health, and physical resistance to hardship, injury, and disease. Since this ability affects the character's hit points and chances of surviving such tremendous shocks as being physically reshaped by magic or resurrected from death, it is vitally important to all classes. Some classes have minimum allowable Constitution scores.

A character's initial Constitution score is the absolute limit to the number of times the character can be raised or resurrected from death. Each such revival reduces the character's Constitution score by one. Magic can restore a reduced Constitution score to its original value or even higher, *but this has no effect on the number of times a character can be revived from death!* Once the character has exhausted his original Constitution, nothing short of divine intervention can bring him back, and divine intervention is reserved for only the bravest and most faithful heroes!

For example, Rath's Constitution score at the start of his adventuring career is 12. He can be revived from death 12 times. If he dies a 13th time, he cannot be *resurrected* or *raised*.

Hit Point Adjustment is added to or subtracted from each Hit Die rolled for the character. However, no Hit Die ever yields less than 1 hit point, regardless of modifications. If an adjustment would lower the number rolled to 0 or less, consider the final result to be 1. Always use the character's current Constitution to determine hit point bonuses and penalties.

Only warriors are entitled to a Constitution bonus of +3 or +4. Non-warrior characters who have Constitution scores of 17 or 18 receive only +2 per die.

The Constitution bonus ends when a character reaches 10th level (9th for warriors and priests)—neither the Constitution bonus nor Hit Dice are added to a character's hit points after he has passed this level (see the character class descriptions that start on page 25).

If a character's Constitution changes during the course of adventuring, his hit points may be adjusted up or down to reflect the change. The difference between the character's current hit point bonus (if any) and the new bonus is multiplied by the character's level (up to 10) and added to or subtracted from the character's total. If Delsenora's Constitution increased from 16 to 17, she would gain 1 hit point for every level she had, up to 10th level.

System Shock states the percentage chance a character has to survive magical effects that reshape or age his body: petrification (and reversing petrification), polymorph, magical aging, etc. It can also be used to see if the character retains consciousness in particularly difficult situations. For example, an evil mage polymorphs his dim-witted hireling into a crow. The hireling, whose Constitution score is 13, has an 85 percent chance to survive the change. Assuming he survives, he must successfully roll for system shock again when he is changed back to his original form or else he will die.

Resurrection Survival lists a character's percentage chance to be successfully resurrected or raised from death by magic. The player must roll the listed number or less on percentile dice for the character to be revived. If the dice roll fails, the character is dead, regardless of how many times he has previously been revived. Only divine intervention can bring such a character back again.

Poison Save modifies the saving throw vs. poison for humans, elves, gnomes, and half-elves. Dwarves and halflings do not use this adjustment, since they have special resistances to poison attacks. The DM has specific information on saving throws.

Regeneration enables those with specially endowed Constitutions (perhaps by a *wish* or magical item) to heal at an advanced rate, regenerating damage taken. The character heals 1 point of damage after the passage of the listed number of turns. However, fire and acid damage (which are more extensive than normal wounds) cannot be regenerated in this manner. These injuries must heal normally or be dealt with by magical means.

Table 3: CONSTITUTION

Ability Score	Hit Point Adjustment	System Shock	Resurrection Survival	Poison Save	Regeneration
1	-3	25%	30%	-2	Nil
2	-2	30%	35%	-1	Nil
3	-2	35%	40%	0	Nil
4	-1	40%	45%	0	Nil
5	-1	45%	50%	0	Nil
6	-1	50%	55%	0	Nil
7	0	55%	60%	0	Nil
8	0	60%	65%	0	Nil
9	0	65%	70%	0	Nil
10	0	70%	75%	0	Nil
11	0	75%	80%	0	Nil
12	0	80%	85%	0	Nil
13	0	85%	90%	0	Nil
14	0	88%	92%	0	Nil
15	+1	90%	94%	0	Nil
16	+2	95%	96%	0	Nil
17	+2 (+3)*	97%	98%	0	Nil
18	+2 (+4)*	99%	100%	0	Nil
19	+2 (+5)*	99%	100%	+1	Nil
20	+2 (+5)**	99%	100%	+1	1/6 turns
21	+2 (+6)***	99%	100%	+2	1/5 turns
22	+2 (+6)***	99%	100%	+2	1/4 turns
23	+2 (+6)****	99%	100%	+3	1/3 turns
24	+2 (+7)****	99%	100%	+3	1/2 turns
25	+2 (+7)****	100%	100%	+4	1/1 turn

* Parenthetical bonus applies to warriors only. All other classes receive maximum bonus of +2 per die.
** All 1s rolled for Hit Dice are automatically considered 2s.
*** All 1s and 2s rolled for Hit Dice are automatically considered 3s.
**** All 1s, 2s, and 3s rolled for Hit Dice are automatically considered 4s.

Intelligence

Intelligence (Int) represents a character's memory, reasoning, and learning ability, including areas outside those measured by the written word. Intelligence dictates the number of languages a character can learn. Intelligence is the prime requisite of wizards, who must have keen minds to understand and memorize magical spells. A wizard with an Intelligence score of 16 or higher gains a 10 percent bonus to experience points earned. The wizard's Intelligence dictates which spells he can learn and the number of spells he can memorize at one time. Only those of the highest Intelligence can comprehend the mighty magic of 9th-level spells.

This ability gives only a general indication of a character's mental acuity. A semi-intelligent character (Int 3 or 4) can speak (with difficulty) and is apt to react instinctively and impulsively. He is not hopeless as a player character (PC), but playing such a character correctly is not easy. A character with low Intelligence (Int 5-7) could also be called dull-witted or slow. A very intelligent person (Int 11 or 12) picks up new ideas quickly and learns easily. A highly intelligent character (Int 13 or 14) is one who can solve most problems without even trying very hard. One with exceptional intelligence (Int 15 or 16) is noticeably above the norm. A genius character is brilliant (Int 17 or 18). A character beyond genius is potentially more clever and more brilliant than can possibly be imagined.

However, the true capabilities of a mind lie not in numbers—I.Q., Intelligence score, or whatever. Many intelligent, even brilliant, people in the real world fail to apply their minds creatively and usefully, thus falling far below their own potential. Don't rely too heavily on your character's Intelligence score; you must provide your character with the creativity and energy he supposedly possesses!

Number of Languages lists the number of additional languages the character can speak beyond his native language. Every character can speak his native language, no matter what his Intelligence is. This knowledge extends only to speaking the language; it does not include reading or writing. The DM must decide if your character begins the game already knowing these additional languages or if the number shows only how many languages your character can possibly learn. The first choice will make communication easier, while the second increases your opportunities for role-playing (finding a tutor or creating a reason

Table 4: INTELLIGENCE

Ability Score	# of Lang.	Spell Level	Chance to Learn Spell	Max. # of Spells/Lvl	Spell Immunity
1	0*	—	—	—	—
2	1	—	—	—	—
3	1	—	—	—	—
4	1	—	—	—	—
5	1	—	—	—	—
6	1	—	—	—	—
7	1	—	—	—	—
8	1	—	—	—	—
9	2	4th	35%	6	—
10	2	5th	40%	7	—
11	2	5th	45%	7	—
12	3	6th	50%	7	—
13	3	6th	55%	9	—
14	4	7th	60%	9	—
15	4	7th	65%	11	—
16	5	8th	70%	11	—
17	6	8th	75%	14	—
18	7	9th	85%	18	—
19	8	9th	95%	All	1st-lvl illusions
20	9	9th	96%	All	2nd-lvl illusions
21	10	9th	97%	All	3rd-lvl illusions
22	11	9th	98%	All	4th-lvl illusions
23	12	9th	99%	All	5th-lvl illusions
24	15	9th	100%	All	6th-lvl illusions
25	20	9th	100%	All	7th-lvl illusions

* While unable to speak a language, the character can still communicate by grunts and gestures.

why you need to know a given language). Furthermore, your DM can limit your language selection based on his campaign. It is perfectly fair to rule that your fighter from the Frozen Wastes hasn't the tongues of the Southlands, simply because he has never met anyone who has been to the Southlands.

If the DM allows characters to have proficiencies, this column also indicates the number of extra proficiency slots the character gains due to his Intelligence. These extra proficiency slots can be used however the player desires. The character never needs to spend any proficiency slots to speak his native language.

Spell Level lists the highest level of spells that can be cast by a wizard with this Intelligence.

Chance to Learn Spell is the percentage probability that a wizard can learn a particular spell. A check is made as the wizard comes across new spells, not as he advances in level. To make the check, the wizard character must have access to a spell book containing the spell. If the player rolls the listed percentage or less, his character can learn the spell and copy it into his own spell book. If the wizard fails the roll, he cannot check that spell again until he advances to the next level (provided he still has access to the spell).

Maximum Number of Spells per Level (Optional Rule)

This number indicates the maximum number of spells a wizard can know from any particular spell level. Once a wizard has learned the maximum number of spells he is allowed in a given spell level, he cannot add any more spells of that level to his spell book (unless the optional spell research system is used). Once a spell is learned, it cannot be unlearned and replaced by a new spell.

For example, Delsenora the mage has an Intelligence of 14. She currently knows seven 3rd-level spells. During an adventure, she finds a musty old spell book on the shelves of a dank, forgotten library. Blowing away the dust, she sees a 3rd-level spell she has never seen before! Excited, she sits down and carefully studies the arcane notes. Her chance to learn the spell is 60 percent. Rolling the dice, Delsenora's player rolls a 37. She understands the curious instructions and can copy them into her own spell book. When she is finished, she has eight 3rd-level spells, only one away from her maximum number. If the die roll had been greater than 60, or she already had nine 3rd-level spells in her spell book, or the spell had been greater than 7th level (the maximum level her Intelligence allows her to learn), she could not have added it to her collection.

Spell Immunity is gained by those with exceptionally high Intelligence scores. Those with the immunity notice some inconsistency or inexactness in the illusion or phantasm, automatically allowing them to make their saving throws. All benefits are cumulative, thus a character with a 20 Intelligence is not fooled by 1st- or 2nd-level illusion spells.

Wisdom

Wisdom (Wis) describes a composite of the character's enlightenment, judgment, guile, willpower, common sense, and intuition. It can affect the character's resistance to magical attack. It is the prime requisite for priests; those with a Wisdom score of 16 or higher gain a 10 percent bonus to experience points earned. Clerics, druids, and other priests with Wisdom scores of 13 or higher also gain bonus spells over and above the number they are normally allowed to use.

Magical Defense Adjustment listed on Table 5 applies to saving throws against magical spells that attack the mind: *beguiling, charm, fear, hypnosis, illusions, possession, suggestion,* etc. These bonuses and penalties are applied automatically, without any conscious effort from the character.

Bonus Spells indicates the number of additional spells a priest (and only a priest) is entitled to because of his extreme Wisdom. Note that these spells are available only when the priest is entitled to spells of the appropriate level. Bonus spells are cumulative, so a priest with a Wisdom of 15 is entitled to two 1st-level bonus spells and one 2nd-level bonus spell.

Chance of Spell Failure states the percentage chance that any particular spell fails when cast. Priests with low Wisdom scores run the risk of having their spells fizzle. Roll percentile dice every time the priest casts a spell; if the number rolled is less than or equal to the listed chance for spell failure, the spell is expended with absolutely no effect whatsoever. Note that priests with Wisdom scores of 13 or higher don't need to worry about their spells failing.

Spell Immunity gives those extremely wise characters complete protection from certain spells, spell-like abilities, and magical items as listed. These immunities are cumulative, so that a character with a Wisdom of 23 is immune to all listed spells up to and including those listed on the 23 Wisdom row.

Table 5: WISDOM

Ability Score	Magical Defense Adjustment	Bonus Spells	Chance of Spell Failure	Spell Immunity
1	−6	—	80%	—
2	−4	—	60%	—
3	−3	—	50%	—
4	−2	—	45%	—
5	−1	—	40%	—
6	−1	—	35%	—
7	−1	—	30%	—
8	0	—	25%	—
9	0	0	20%	—
10	0	0	15%	—
11	0	0	10%	—
12	0	0	5%	—
13	0	1st	0%	—
14	0	1st	0%	—
15	+1	2nd	0%	—
16	+2	2nd	0%	—
17	+3	3rd	0%	—
18	+4	4th	0%	—
19	+4	1st, 4th	0%	*Cause fear, Charm person, Command, Friends, Hypnotism*
20	+4	2nd, 4th	0%	*Forget, Hold person, Ray of enfeeblement, Scare*
21	+4	3rd, 5th	0%	*Fear*
22	+4	4th, 5th	0%	*Charm monster, Confusion, Emotion, Fumble, Suggestion*
23	+4	5th, 5th	0%	*Chaos, Feeblemind, Hold monster, Magic jar, Quest*
24	+4	6th, 6th	0%	*Geas, Mass suggestion, Rod of rulership*
25	+4	6th, 7th	0%	*Antipathy/sympathy, Death spell, Mass charm*

Charisma

The Charisma (Cha) score measures a character's persuasiveness, personal magnetism, and ability to lead. It is not a reflection of physical attractiveness, although attractiveness certainly plays a role. It is important to all characters, but especially to those who must deal with non-player characters (NPCs), mercenary hirelings, retainers, and intelligent monsters. It dictates the total number of henchmen a character can retain and affects the loyalty of henchmen, hirelings, and retainers.

Maximum Number of Henchmen states the number of non-player characters who will serve as permanent retainers of the player character. It does not affect the number of mercenary soldiers, men-at-arms, servitors, or other persons in the pay of the character.

Loyalty Base shows the subtraction from or addition to the henchmen's and other servitors' loyalty scores (in the *DMG*). This is crucial during battles, when morale becomes important.

Reaction Adjustment indicates the penalty or bonus due to the character because of Charisma when dealing with non-player characters and intelligent creatures. For example, Rath encounters a centaur, an intelligent creature. Rath's Charisma is only 6, so he is starting off with one strike against him. He probably should try to overcome this slight handicap by making generous offers of gifts or information.

Table 6: CHARISMA

Ability Score	Maximum # of Henchmen	Loyalty Base	Reaction Adjustment
1	0	-8	-7
2	1	-7	-6
3	1	-6	-5
4	1	-5	-4
5	2	-4	-3
6	2	-3	-2
7	3	-2	-1
8	3	-1	0
9	4	0	0
10	4	0	0
11	4	0	0
12	5	0	0
13	5	0	+1
14	6	+1	+2
15	7	+3	+3
16	8	+4	+5
17	10	+6	+6
18	15	+8	+7
19	20	+10	+8
20	25	+12	+9
21	30	+14	+10
22	35	+16	+11
23	40	+18	+12
24	45	+20	+13
25	50	+20	+14

Optional Racial Adjustment. If your DM is using this rule, your character's apparent Charisma may be altered when dealing with beings of different races. These alterations are given in Chapter 2 (page 20), after the different player character races have been explained.

What the Numbers Mean

Now that you have finished creating the ability scores for your character, stop and take a look at them. What does all this mean?

Suppose you decide to name your character "Rath" and you rolled the following ability scores for him:

Strength	8
Dexterity	14
Constitution	13
Intelligence	13
Wisdom	7
Charisma	6

Rath has strengths and weaknesses, but it is up to you to interpret what the numbers mean. Here are just two different ways these numbers could be interpreted.

1) Although Rath is in good health (Con 13), he's not very strong (Str 8) because he's just plain lazy—he never wanted to exercise as a youth and now it's too late. His low Wisdom and Charisma scores (7, 6) show that he lacks the common sense to apply himself properly and projects a slothful,

"I'm not going to bother" attitude (which tends to irritate others). Fortunately, Rath's natural wit (Int 13) and Dexterity (14) keep him from being a total loss.

Thus you might play Rath as an irritating, smart-alecky twerp forever ducking just out of range of those who want to squash him.

2) Rath has several good points—he has studied hard (Int 13) and practiced his manual skills (Dex 14). Unfortunately, his Strength is low (8) from a lack of exercise (all those hours spent reading books). Despite that, Rath's health is still good (Con 13). His low Wisdom and Charisma (7, 6) are a result of his lack of contact and involvement with people outside the realm of academics.

Looking at the scores this way, you could play Rath as a kindly, naive, and shy professorial type who's a good tinkerer, always fiddling with new ideas and inventions.

Obviously, Rath's ability scores (often called "stats") are not the greatest in the world. Yet it is possible to turn these "disappointing" stats into a character who is both interesting and fun to play. Too often players become obsessed with "good" stats. These players immediately give up on a character if he doesn't have a majority of

above-average scores. There are even those who feel a character is hopeless if he does not have at least one ability of 17 or higher! Needless to say, these players would never consider playing a character with an ability score of 6 or 7.

In truth, Rath's survivability has a lot less to do with his ability scores than with your desire to role-play him. If you give up on him, of course he won't survive! But if you take an interest in the character and role-play him well, then even a character with the lowest possible scores can present a fun, challenging, and all-around exciting time. Does he have a Charisma of 5? Why? Maybe he's got an ugly scar. His table manners could be atrocious. He might mean well but always manage to say the wrong thing at the wrong time. He could be bluntly honest to the point of rudeness, something not likely to endear him to most people. His Dexterity is a 3? Why? Is he naturally clumsy or blind as a bat?

Don't give up on a character just because he has a low score. Instead, view it as an opportunity to role-play, to create a unique and entertaining personality in the game. Not only will you have fun creating that personality, but other players and the DM will have fun reacting to him.

After creating your character's ability scores, you must select a player character race. This is not a race in the true sense of the word: caucasian, black, asian, etc. It is actually a fantasy species for your character—human, elf, dwarf, gnome, half-elf, or halfling. Each race is different. Each possesses special powers and has different lists of classes to choose from.

All six of the standard races are described in detail in this chapter. In many cases, broad statements are made concerning the race in general. Players are not bound by these generalities. For example, the statement that "dwarves tend to be dour and taciturn" does not mean that your character cannot be a jolly dwarf. It means that the garden-variety dwarf is dour and taciturn. If player characters were just like everyone else, they wouldn't be adventurers. Make your character unique and he will be more fun to play.

Minimum and Maximum Ability Scores

All non-human PC races (also called "demihuman" races) have minimum and maximum requirements for their ability scores. If you want to have a demihuman character, the character's ability scores must be within the allowable range. The minimums and maximums for each race are listed on Table 7 (the minimums are listed before the slash; the maximums are listed after the slash). Your character's sex has no effect on these minimums or maximums.

Consult Table 7 *before* making any racial adjustments to your character's ability scores. If the basic scores that you rolled up meet the requirements for a particular race, your character can be of that race, even if later modifications change the ability scores so they exceed the maximums or don't meet the minimums. Once you satisfy the requirements at the start, you never have to worry about them again.

Table 7 gives the minimum and maximum scores a newly created character must have to be a member of a demihuman race. Any character can be a human, if the player so desires.

Racial Ability Adjustments

If you chose to make your character a dwarf, elf, gnome, or halfling, you now have to adjust some of your character's ability scores. The adjustments are mandatory; all characters of these races receive the adjustments. *Even if adjustments raise or lower your character's ability scores beyond the minimums and maximums shown on Table 7, you do **not** have to pick a new race.* The adjustments can also raise a score to 19 or lower it to 2.

Table 8: RACIAL ABILITY ADJUSTMENTS

Race	Adjustments
Dwarf	+1 Constitution; −1 Charisma
Elf	+1 Dexterity; −1 Constitution
Gnome	+1 Intelligence; −1 Wisdom
Halfling	+1 Dexterity; −1 Strength

Class Restrictions and Level Limits

The human race has one special ability in the AD&D® game: Humans can choose to be of any class—warrior, wizard, priest, or rogue—and can rise to great level in any class. The other races have fewer choices of character classes and usually are limited in the level they can attain. These restrictions reflect the natural tendencies of the races (dwarves like war and fighting and dislike magic, etc.). The limits are high enough so a demihuman can achieve power and importance in at least one class. A halfling, for example, can become the best thief in the land, but he cannot become a great fighter.

The limits also exist for play balance. The ability of humans to assume any role and reach any level is their only advantage. The demihuman races have other powers that make them entertaining to play—particularly the ability to be multi-classed (see Glossary). These powers balance the enjoyment of play against the ability to rise in level. Ask your DM for the level limits imposed on non-human characters.

Languages

Racial languages for demihumans can be handled in either of two ways, depending on whether or not your DM uses the optional proficiency system. Either way, your character automatically knows his native language.

Without the proficiency system, your character starts adventuring already knowing a number of additional languages (the number depends on his Int score, see Table 4). The additional languages must be chosen from among those listed in his race's description.

If you use the proficiency system, your character receives additional languages by using proficiency slots (see page 51) to determine how many languages he knows when he starts adventuring (his native language does not cost a slot). Demihumans must choose these languages from among those listed in the following racial descriptions.

Human PCs generally start the game knowing only their regional language—the language they grew up speaking. The DM may decide to allow beginning PCs additional languages (up to their Int score limit or proficiency slot limit), if he feels the PCs had the opportunity to learn these as they grew up. Otherwise, human PCs may learn additional languages as they adventure.

Dwarves

Dwarves are short, stocky fellows, easily identified by their size and shape. They average 4 to 4½ feet tall. They have ruddy cheeks, dark eyes, and dark hair. Dwarves generally live for 350 years.

Dwarves tend to be dour and taciturn. They are given to hard work and care little for most humor. They are strong and brave. They enjoy beer, ale, mead, and even stronger drink. Their chief love, however, is precious metal, particularly gold. They prize gems, of course, especially diamonds and opaque gems (except pearls, which they do not like). Dwarves like the earth and dislike the sea. Not overly fond of elves, they have a fierce hatred of orcs and goblins. Their short, stocky builds make them ill-suited for riding horses or other large mounts (although ponies present no difficulty, so they tend to be a trifle dubious and wary of these creatures). They are ill-disposed toward magic and have little talent for it, but revel in fighting, warcraft, and scientific arts such as engineering.

Though dwarves are suspicious and avaricious, their courage and tenacity more than compensate for these shortcomings.

Table 7: RACIAL ABILITY REQUIREMENTS

Ability	Dwarf	Elf	Gnome	Half-Elf	Halfling
Strength	8/18	3/18	6/18	3/18	7/18 *
Dexterity	3/17	6/18	3/18	6/18	7/18
Constitution	11/18	7/18	8/18	6/18	10/18
Intelligence	3/18	8/18	6/18	4/18	6/18
Wisdom	3/18	3/18	3/18	3/18	3/17
Charisma	3/17	8/18	3/18	3/18	3/18

* Halfling fighters do not roll for exceptional Strength.

Dwarves typically dwell in hilly or mountainous regions. They prefer life in the comforting gloom and solidness that is found underground. They have several special abilities that relate to their underground life, and they are noted for being particularly resistant to magics and poisons.

A character of the dwarven race can be a cleric, a fighter, or a thief. He can also choose to be a fighter/cleric or fighter/thief.

From living underground, dwarves have found it useful to learn the languages of several of their neighbors, both friendly and hostile. The initial languages a dwarf can learn are common, dwarf, gnome, goblin, kobold, orc, and any others your DM allows. The actual number of languages is limited by the Intelligence of the player character (see Table 4) or by the proficiency slots he allots to languages (if that optional system is used).

By nature, dwarves are nonmagical and never use magical spells (clerical spells are allowed however). This gives a bonus to dwarves' saving throws against attacks from magical wands, staves, rods, and spells. This bonus is +1 for every 3½ points of Constitution score. Thus, for example, if a dwarf has a Constitution score of 7 he gains +2 on saving throws. These bonuses are summarized on Table 9.

Table 9: CONSTITUTION SAVING THROW BONUSES

Constitution Score	Saving Throw Bonus
4-6	+1
7-10	+2
11-13	+3
14-17	+4
18-19	+5

Similarly, dwarves have exceptional resistance to toxic substances. All dwarven characters make saving throws against poison with the same bonuses that they get against magical attacks (see Table 9).

Also because of their nonmagical nature, however, dwarves have trouble using magical items. All magical items that are not specifically suited to the character's class have a 20 percent chance to malfunction when used by a dwarf. This check is made each time a dwarf uses a magical item. A malfunction affects only the current use; the item may work properly next time. For devices that are continually in operation, the check is made the first time the device is used during an encounter. If the check is passed, the device functions normally until it is turned off. Thus a dwarf would have to check upon donning a *robe of blending* but would not check again until he had taken the robe off and then put it on again. If a cursed item malfunctions, the character recognizes its cursed nature and can dispose of the item. Malfunction applies to rods, staves, wands, rings, amulets, potions, horns, jewels, and

all other magical items except weapons, shields, armor, gauntlets, and girdles. This penalty does not apply to dwarven clerics using clerical items.

In melee, dwarves add 1 to their dice rolls to hit orcs, half-orcs, goblins, and hobgoblins. When ogres, trolls, ogre magi, giants, or titans attack dwarves, these monsters must subtract 4 from their attack rolls because of the dwarves' small size and combat ability against these much bigger creatures.

Dwarven infravision enables them to see up to 60 feet in the dark.

Dwarves are miners of great skill. While underground, they can detect the following information when within 10 feet of the particular phenomenon (but they can determine their approximate depth below the surface at any time).

Detect grade or slope in passage	1-5 on 1d6
Detect new tunnel/passage construction	1-5 on 1d6
Detect sliding/shifting walls or rooms	1-4 on 1d6
Detect stonework traps, pits, and deadfalls	1-3 on 1d6
Determine approx. depth underground	1-3 on 1d6

Note that the dwarf must deliberately try to make these determinations; the information does not simply spring to mind unbidden.

Because of their sturdy builds, dwarves add 1 to their initial Constitution scores. Their dour and suspicious natures cause them to subtract 1 from their initial Charisma scores.

Elves

Elves tend to be somewhat shorter and slimmer than normal humans. Their features are finely chiseled and delicate, and they speak in melodic tones. Although they appear fragile and weak, as a race they are quick and strong. Elves often live to be over 1,200 years old, although long before this time they feel compelled to depart the realms of men and mortals. Where they go is uncertain, but it is an undeniable urge of their race.

Elves are often considered frivolous and aloof. In fact, they are not, although humans often find their personalities impossible to fathom. They concern themselves with natural beauty, dancing and frolicking, playing and singing, unless necessity dictates otherwise. They are not fond of ships or mines, but enjoy growing things and gazing at the open sky. Even though elves tend toward haughtiness and arrogance at times, they regard their friends and associates as equals. They do not make friends easily, but

a friend (or enemy) is never forgotten. They prefer to distance themselves from humans, have little love for dwarves, and hate the evil denizens of the woods.

Their humor is clever, as are their songs and poetry. Elves are brave but never foolhardy. They eat sparingly; they drink mead and wine, but seldom to excess. While they find well-wrought jewelry a pleasure to behold, they are not overly interested in money or gain. They find magic and swordplay (or any refined combat art) fascinating. If they have a weakness it lies in these interests.

There are five branches of the elven race: aquatic, gray, high, wood, and dark. Elf player characters are always assumed to be of the most common type—high elves—although a character can be another type of elf with the DM's permission (but the choice grants no additional powers). To the eye of outsiders, the differences between the groups are mostly cosmetic, but most elves maintain that there are important cultural differences between the various groups. Aquatic elves spend their lives beneath the waves and have adapted to these conditions. Gray elves are considered the most noble and serious-minded of this breed. High elves are the most common. Wood elves are considered to be wild, temperamental, and savage. All others hold that the subterranean dark elves are corrupt and evil, no longer part of the elven community.

A player character elf can be a cleric, fighter, mage, thief, or ranger. In addition, an elf can choose to be a multi-class fighter/mage, fighter/thief, fighter/mage/thief, or mage/thief. (The rules governing these combinations are explained under Multi-Class Characters, page 44.)

Elves have found it useful to learn the languages of several of the forest's children, both the good and the bad. As initial languages, an elf can choose common, elf, gnome, halfling, goblin, hobgoblin, orc, and gnoll. The number of languages an elf can learn is limited by his Intelligence (see Table 4) or the proficiency slots he allots to languages (if that optional system is used).

Elven characters have 90 percent resistance to *sleep* and all *charm*-related spells. (See Chapter 9: Combat for an explanation of magic resistance.) This is in addition to the normal saving throw allowed against a *charm* spell.

When employing a bow of any sort other than a crossbow, or when using a short or long sword, elves gain a bonus of +1 to their attack rolls.

An elf can gain a bonus to surprise opponents, but only if the elf is not in metal armor. Even then, the elf must either be alone, or with a party comprised only of elves or halflings (also not in metal armor), or 90 feet or more away from his party (the group of characters he is with) to gain this

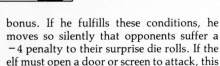

bonus. If he fulfills these conditions, he moves so silently that opponents suffer a −4 penalty to their surprise die rolls. If the elf must open a door or screen to attack, this penalty is reduced to −2.

Elven infravision enables them to see up to 60 feet in darkness.

Secret doors (those constructed so as to be hard to notice) and concealed doors (those hidden from sight by screens, curtains, or the like) are difficult to hide from elves. Merely passing within 10 feet of a concealed door gives an elven character a one-in-six chance (roll a 1 on 1d6) to notice it. If actively searching for such doors, elven characters have a one-in-three chance (roll a 1 or 2 on 1d6) to find a secret door and a one-in-two chance (roll a 1, 2, or 3 on 1d6) to discover a concealed portal.

As stated previously, elven characters add 1 to their initial Dexterity scores. Likewise, as elves are not as sturdy as humans, they deduct 1 from their initial Constitution scores.

Gnomes

Kin to dwarves, gnomes are noticeably smaller than their distant cousins. Gnomes, as they proudly maintain, are also less rotund than dwarves. Their noses, however, are significantly larger. Most gnomes have dark tan or brown skin and white hair. A typical gnome lives for 350 years.

Gnomes have lively and sly senses of humor, especially for practical jokes. They have a great love of living things and finely wrought items, particularly gems and jewelry. Gnomes love all sorts of precious stones and are masters of gem polishing and cutting.

Gnomes prefer to live in areas of rolling, rocky hills, well wooded and uninhabited by humans. Their diminutive stature has made them suspicious of the larger races—humans and elves—although they are not hostile. They are sly and furtive with those they do not know or trust, and somewhat reserved even under the best of circumstances. Dwelling in mines and burrows, they are sympathetic to dwarves, but find their cousins' aversion to surface dwellers foolish.

A gnome character can elect to be a fighter, a thief, a cleric, or an illusionist. A gnome can have two classes, but not three: fighter/thief, illusionist/thief, etc.

Due to his upbringing, a beginning gnome character can choose to know the following languages, in addition to any others allowed by the DM: common, dwarf, gnome, halfling, goblin, kobold, and the simple common speech of burrowing mammals (moles, badgers, weasels, shrews, ground squirrels, etc.). The actual number of languages a character begins with depends upon his In-

telligence score (see Table 4) or the proficiency slots he allots to languages (if that optional system is used).

Like their cousins the dwarves, gnomes are highly magic resistant. A gnome player character gains a bonus of +1 for every 3½ points of Constitution score, just as dwarves do (see Table 9). This bonus applies to saving throws against magical wands, staves, rods, and spells.

Gnomes also suffer a 20 percent chance for failure every time they use any magical item except weapons, armor, shields, illusionist items, and (if the character is a thief) items that duplicate thieving abilities. This check is made each time the gnome attempts to use the device or, in the case of continuous-use devices, each time the device is activated. Like dwarves, gnomes can sense a cursed item if the device fails to function.

In melee, gnome characters add 1 to their attack rolls to hit kobolds or goblins. When gnolls, bugbears, ogres, trolls, ogre magi, giants, or titans attack gnomes, these monsters must subtract 4 from their attack rolls because of the gnomes' small size and their combat skills against these much larger creatures.

Gnomish infravision enables them to see up to 60 feet in the dark.

Being tunnelers of exceptional merit, gnomes are able to detect the following within 10 feet (exception: They can determine their approximate depth or direction underground at any time.). They must stop and concentrate for one round to use any of these abilities.

Detect grade or slope in passage	1-5 on 1d6
Detect unsafe walls, ceiling, and floors	1-7 on 1d10
Determine approx. depth underground	1-4 on 1d6
Determine approx. direction underground	1-3 on 1d6

Gnome characters gain a +1 bonus to their Intelligence scores, to reflect their highly inquisitive natures. They suffer a −1 penalty to Wisdom because their curiosity often leads them unknowingly into danger.

Half-Elves

Half-elves are the most common mixed-race beings. The relationship between elf, human, and half-elf is defined as follows: 1) Anyone with both elven and human ancestors is either a human or a half-elf (elves have only elven ancestors). 2) If there are more human ancestors than elven, the person is human; if there are equal numbers or more elves, the person is half-elven.

Half-elves are usually much like their elven parent in appearance. They are hand-

some folk, with the good features of each of their races. They mingle freely with either race, being only slightly taller than the average elf (5 feet 6 inches on average) and weighing about 150 pounds. They typically live about 160 years. They do not have all the abilities of the elf, nor do they have the flexibility of unlimited level advancement of the human. Finally, in some of the less-civilized nations, half-elves are viewed with suspicion and superstition.

In general, a half-elf has the curiosity, inventiveness, and ambition of his human ancestors and the refined senses, love of nature, and artistic tastes of his elven ancestors.

Half-elves do not form communities among themselves; rather, they can be found living in both elven and human communities. The reactions of humans and elves to half-elves ranges from intrigued fascination to outright bigotry.

Of all the demihuman races, half-elves have the greatest range of choices in character class. They tend to make good druids and rangers. A half-elf can choose to be a cleric, druid, fighter, ranger, mage, specialist wizard, thief, or bard. In addition, a half-elf can choose from the following multi-class combinations: cleric (or druid)/fighter, cleric (or druid)/fighter/mage, cleric (or druid)/ranger, cleric (or druid)/mage, fighter/mage, fighter/thief, fighter/mage/thief, and mage/thief. The half-elf must abide by the rules for multi-class characters.

Half-elves do not have a language of their own. Their extensive contact with other races enables them to choose any of the following languages (plus any other allowed by the DM): common, elf, gnome, halfling, goblin, hobgoblin, orc, and gnoll. The actual number of languages the character knows is limited by his Intelligence (see Table 4) or by the number of proficiency slots he allots to languages (if that optional system is used).

Half-elven characters have a 30 percent resistance to *sleep* and all *charm*-related spells.

Half-elven infravision enables them to see up to 60 feet in darkness.

Secret or concealed doors are difficult to hide from half-elves, just as they are from elves. Merely passing within 10 feet of a concealed door (one hidden by obstructing curtains, etc.) gives the half-elven character a one-in-six chance (roll a 1 on 1d6) of spotting it. If the character is actively seeking to discover hidden doors, he has a one-in-three chance (roll a 1 or 2 on 1d6) of spotting a secret door (one constructed to be undetectable) and a one-in-two chance (roll a 1, 2, or 3 on 1d6) of locating a concealed door.

Halflings

Halflings are short, generally plump people, very much like small humans. Their faces are round and broad and often quite florid. Their hair is typically curly and the tops of their feet are covered with coarse hair. They prefer not to wear shoes whenever possible. Their typical life expectancy is approximately 150 years.

Halflings are sturdy and industrious, generally quiet and peaceful. Overall they prefer the comforts of home to dangerous adventuring. They enjoy good living, rough humor, and homespun stories. In fact, they can be a trifle boring at times. Halflings are not forward, but they are observant and conversational if in friendly company. Halflings see wealth only as a means of gaining creature comforts, which they love. Though they are not overly brave or ambitious, they are generally honest and hard working when there is need.

Halfling homes are well-furnished burrows, although most of their work is done on the surface. Elves generally like them in a patronizing sort of way. Dwarves cheerfully tolerate them, thinking halflings somewhat soft and harmless. Gnomes, although they drink more and eat less, like halflings best, feeling them kindred spirits. Because halflings are more open and outgoing than any of these other three, they get along with other races far better.

There are three types of halflings: Hairfeets, Tallfellows, and Stouts. Hairfeets are the most common type, but for player characters, any of the three is acceptable.

A halfling character can choose to be a cleric, fighter, thief, or a multi-class fighter/thief. The halfling must use the rules provided for multi-class characters.

Through their contact with other races, halfling characters are allowed to choose initial languages from common, halfling, dwarf, elf, gnome, goblin, and orc, in addition to any other languages the DM allows. The actual number of languages the character knows is limited by his Intelligence (see Table 4) or by the number of proficiency slots he allots to languages (if that optional system is used).

All halfling characters have a high resistance to magical spells, so for every 3½ points of Constitution score, the character gains a +1 bonus on saving throws vs. wands, staves, rods, and spells. These bonuses are summarized on Table 9.

Halflings have a similar resistance to poisons of all sorts, so they gain a Constitution bonus identical to that for saving throws vs. magical attacks when they make saving throws vs. poison (i.e., +1 to +5, depending on Constitution score).

Halflings have a natural talent with slings and thrown weapons. Rock pitching is a favorite sport of many a halfling child. All halflings gain a +1 bonus to their attack rolls when using thrown weapons and slings.

A halfling can gain a bonus to surprise opponents, but only if the halfling is not in metal armor. Even then, the halfling must either be alone, or with a party comprised only of halflings or elves, or 90 feet or more away from his party to gain this bonus. If he fulfills any of these conditions, he causes a −4 penalty to opponents' surprise rolls. If a door or other screen must be opened, this penalty is reduced to −2.

Depending on their lineage, certain halfling characters have infravision. Any halfling character has a 15 percent chance to have normal infravision (this means he is pure Stout), out to 60 feet; failing that chance, there is a 25 percent chance that he has limited infravision (mixed Stout/Tallfellow or Stout/Hairfeets lineage), effective out to 30 feet.

Similarly, halflings with any Stoutish blood can note if a passage is an up or down grade with 75 percent accuracy (roll a 1, 2, or 3 on 1d4). They can determine direction half the time (roll a 1, 2, or 3 on 1d6). These abilities function only when the character is concentrating on the desired information to the exclusion of all else, and only if the character is pure or partially Stout.

Halfling characters have a penalty of −1 to their initially generated Strength scores, and they gain a bonus of +1 to Dexterity.

Humans

Although humans are treated as a single race in the AD&D® game, they come in all the varieties we know on Earth. A human PC can have whatever racial characteristics the DM allows.

Humans have only one special ability: They can be of any character class and rise to any level in any class. Other PC races have limited choices in these areas.

Humans are also more social and tolerant than most other races, accepting the company of elves, dwarves, and the like with noticeably less complaint.

Because of these abilities and tendencies, humans have become significant powers within the world and often rule empires that other races (because of their racial tendencies) would find difficult to manage.

Other Characteristics

After you have selected a race, you may want to fill in the details of your character. You are not required to do so, but there are many situations in which this information is vital or useful to role-playing.

The sex and name of your character are up to you. Your character can be of the same sex as yourself or of the opposite sex.

Some people feel it is important to know whether their character is right- or left-handed. Actually, this has no bearing on the play of the game, since all characters are assumed to be reasonably competent with either hand (that doesn't mean everyone is trained to fight with two weapons). It is easiest to say that your character has the same handedness as you. This will result in the normal ratio of right- to left-handed people.

On occasion it may be useful to know your character's height and weight. The best way to determine height and weight is to choose the appropriate numbers, subject to your DM's approval. If you want a short, pudgy human fighter, you can select an appropriate height and weight. Otherwise, heights and weights can be generated randomly using Table 10 (next page). Take the appropriate base score and add the die roll modifier. As with all tables, this can create some ridiculous results (one of the problems with randomness) and, at the same time, cannot account for the full variety of mankind (or demihumankind). The table only reproduces a fairly average range for each race. Heights and weights for demihuman races not listed on the table must be decided by your DM.

> The tallest man on record stood 8 feet 11.1 inches, while the tallest woman was 8 feet 1.25 inches. The shortest man was only 26.5 inches tall and the shortest woman bettered this at only 24 inches in height. While the lightest humans are also among the shortest, the heaviest man weighed an estimated 1,400 pounds and stood only 6 feet 1 inch. The heaviest woman is thought to have weighed 880 pounds. Obviously, these figures indicate that there is a great deal of variety possible for player characters.

Players may also want to know their characters' starting ages. Human characters can start at any age that is agreeable to both the player and the DM. However, all beginning adventurers are assumed to be at least 16 years old, since they must grow physically, emotionally, and in practical experience before they are ready to undertake the rigors of an adventuring life. Table 11 can be used to give a starting age (add the variable die roll to the base starting age to get the character's starting age) and the possible life span of a character, assuming a quiet and peaceful life. Humans are also included on this list in case you want to determine their ages randomly. The maximum age for a character should be secretly determined and recorded by the DM. Player characters may have an idea of how long they expect to live, but do not know their true allotted life spans.

As a character ages, his ability scores are affected. Upon reaching one-half of his base maximum age (45 for a human), the character loses 1 point of Strength (or half of his exceptional Strength rating) and 1 point of Constitution, but gains 1 point each of Intelligence and Wisdom. At two-thirds of his base maximum age (60 for a human), the character loses 2 more points of Strength (or all his exceptional Strength and 1 point more), 2 points of Dexterity, and 1 more point of Constitution, but he gains 1 point of Wisdom. Upon reaching the base maximum age, the character loses 1 more point from each of Strength, Dexterity, and Constitution, while gaining 1 more point in both Intelligence and Wisdom. All aging adjustments are cumulative. See Table 12 for a summary of these effects.

> Although many people have claimed to live to great ages, the oldest human of verifiable age was 113 years old in 1988 and is still alive!

There may be times when a magical device or spell adds years to or subtracts years from a player character's life. This magical aging can have two different effects. Some magical aging physically affects the character. For example, a *haste* spell ages those it affects by one year. This aging is added directly to the player character's current age. He physically acquires the appearance of himself one year older (a few more wrinkles, etc.). Characters who increase in age from magical effects do not gain the benefits of increased Wisdom and Intelligence—these are a function of the passage of game time—but the character does suffer the physical losses to Strength, Dexterity, and Constitution associated with aging. These are breakdowns of the body's systems. Physical age can also be removed in the same manner. Some potions give years back to the character. In this case, the physical appearance of the character is restored. The character can regain lost vigor (Str, Dex, and Con) as his body is renewed but he does not lose any of the benefits of aging (Wis and Int).

Magical aging can also work to increase or decrease the life span of the character. In such a case, the actual age of the character is unaffected. All adjustments are made by the DM to the character's maximum age (which only the DM knows). For example, a human finds a magical fountain that bestows great longevity (10 to 60 years more). The DM has already determined the human will naturally live to 103 years (base 90 + 2d20, in this case 13). The water of the fountain bestows 40 more years so that, unless the character meets a violent end, he will live to 143 years. He still suffers the effects of aging at the usual ages (45, 60, and 90 years,

respectively), but the period in which he would be considered a venerable elder of his people is extended for 40 years.

There are a number of other personal characteristics your character has—hair and eye color, body shape, voice, noticeable features, and general personality. There are no tables for these things, nor should there be. Your job, as a player, is to add these details, thereby creating the type of character you want. You probably know some from the start (do you want to play a towering, robust warrior, or a slim, unassuming swordsman?); others, especially your character's personality, will grow and take form as you play. Remember, you are an actor and your character is your role!

Table 10: AVERAGE HEIGHT AND WEIGHT

	Height in Inches		Weight in Pounds	
Race	Base *	Modifier	Base *	Modifier
Dwarf	43/41	1d10	130/105	4d10
Elf	55/50	1d10	90/70	3d10
Gnome	38/36	1d6	72/68	5d4
Half-elf	60/58	2d6	110/85	3d12
Halfling	32/30	2d8	52/48	5d4
Human	60/59	2d10	140/100	6d10

* Females tend to be lighter and shorter than males. Thus, the base numbers for height and weight are divided into male/female values. Note that the modifier still allows for a broad range in each category.

Table 11: AGE

	Starting Age		Maximum Age Range
Race	Base Age	Variable	(Base + Variable)
Dwarf	40	5d6	250 + 2d100
Elf	100	5d6	350 + 4d100 *
Gnome	60	3d12	200 + 3d100
Half-elf	15	1d6	125 + 3d20
Halfling	20	3d4	100 + 1d100
Human	15	1d4	90 + 2d20

* Upon attaining this age, an elf does not die. Rather he feels compelled to migrate to some mysterious, other land, departing the world of men.

Table 12: AGING EFFECTS

	Middle Age*	Old Age**	Venerable***
Race	(½ Base Max.)	(⅔ Base Max.)	(Base Max.)
Dwarf	125 years	167 years	250 years
Elf	175 years	233 years	350 years
Gnome	100 years	133 years	200 years
Half-elf	62 years	83 years	125 years
Halfling	50 years	67 years	100 years
Human	45 years	60 years	90 years

* −1 Str/Con; +1 Int/Wis
** −2 Str/Dex, −1 Con; +1 Wis
*** −1 Str/Dex/Con; +1 Int/Wis

After choosing your character's race, you select his character class. A character class is like a profession or career. It is what your character has worked and trained at during his younger years. If you wanted to become a doctor, you could not walk out the door and begin work immediately. First you would have to get some training. The same is true of character classes in the AD&D® game. Your character is assumed to have some previous training and guidance before beginning his adventuring career. Now, armed with a little knowledge, your character is ready to make his name and fortune.

The character classes are divided into four groups according to general occupations: warrior, wizard, priest, and rogue. Within each group are several similar character classes. All classes within a group share the same Hit Dice, as well as combat and saving throw progressions. Each character class within a group has different special powers and abilities that are available only to that class. Each player must select a group for his character, then a specific class within that group.

Warrior	Wizard	Priest	Rogue
Fighter	Mage	Cleric	Thief
Ranger	*Illusionist*	*Druid*	*Bard*
Paladin	*Other*	*Other*	

Fighter, mage, cleric, and thief are the standard classes. They are historical and legendary archetypes that are common to many different cultures. Thus they are appropriate to any sort of AD&D game campaign. All of the other classes are optional. Your DM may decide that one or more of the optional classes are not appropriate to his campaign setting. Check with your DM before selecting an optional character class.

To help you choose your character's class, each group and its subordinate classes are described briefly. The groups and classes are described in detail later in this chapter.

Warrior: There are three different classes within the warrior group: fighter, paladin, and ranger. All are well-trained in the use of weapons and skilled in the martial arts.

The *fighter* is a champion, swordsman, soldier, and brawler. He lives or dies by his knowledge of weapons and tactics. Fighters can be found at the front of any battle, contesting toe-to-toe with monsters and villains. A good fighter needs to be strong and healthy if he hopes to survive.

The *paladin* is a warrior bold and pure, the exemplar of everything good and true. Like the fighter, the paladin is a man of combat. However, the paladin lives for the ideals of righteousness, justice, honesty, piety, and chivalry. He strives to be a living example of these virtues so that others might learn from him as well as gain by his actions.

The *ranger* is a warrior and a woodsman. He is skilled with weapons and is knowledgeable in tracking and woodcraft. The ranger often protects and guides lost travelers and honest peasant-folk. A ranger needs to be strong and wise to the ways of nature to live a full life.

Wizard: The wizard strives to be a master of magical energies, shaping them and casting them as spells. To do so, he studies strange tongues and obscure facts and devotes much of his time to magical research.

A wizard must rely on knowledge and wit to survive. Wizards are rarely seen adventuring without a retinue of fighters and men-at-arms.

Because there are different types (or schools) of magic, there are different types of wizards. The *mage* studies all types of magic and learns a wide variety of spells. His broad range makes him well suited to the demands of adventuring. The *illusionist* is an example of how a wizard can specialize in a particular school of magic, illusion in this case.

Priest: A priest sees to the spiritual needs of a community or location. Two types of priests—clerics and druids—are described in the *Player's Handbook*. Other types can be created by the DM to suit specific campaigns.

The *cleric* is a generic priest (of any mythos) who tends to the needs of a community. He is both protector and healer. He is not purely defensive, however. When evil threatens, the cleric is well-suited to seek it out on its own ground and destroy it.

The *druid* class is optional; it is an example of how the priest can be adapted to a certain type of setting. The druid serves the cause of nature and neutrality; the wilderness is his community. He uses his special powers to protect it and to preserve balance in the world.

Rogue: The rogue can be found throughout the world, wherever people gather and money changes hands. While many rogues are motivated only by a desire to amass fortune in the easiest way possible, some rogues have noble aims; they use their skills to correct injustice, spread good will, or contribute to the success of an adventuring group.

There are two types of rogues: thieves and bards.

To accomplish his goals, for good or ill, the *thief* is a skilled pilferer. Cunning, nimbleness, and stealth are his hallmarks. Whether he turns his talent against innocent passers-by and wealthy merchants or oppressors and monsters is a choice for the thief to make.

The *bard* is also a rogue, but he is very different from the thief. His strength is his pleasant and charming personality. With it and his wits he makes his way through the world. A bard is a talented musician and a walking storehouse of gossip, tall tales, and lore. He learns a little bit about everything that crosses his path; he is a jack-of-all-trades but master of none. While many bards are scoundrels, their stories and songs are welcome almost everywhere.

Class Ability Score Requirements

Each of the character classes has minimum scores in various abilities. A character must satisfy these minimums to be of that class. If your character's scores are too low for him to belong to any character class, ask your DM for permission to reroll one or more of your ability scores or to create an entirely new character. If you desperately want your character to belong to a particular class but have scores that are too low, your DM might allow you to increase these scores to the minimum needed. However, you must ask him first. Don't count on the DM allowing you to raise a score above 16 in any case.

Table 13: CLASS ABILITY MINIMUMS

Character Class	Str	Dex	Con	Int	Wis	Cha
Fighter	9	—	—	—	—	—
Paladin *	12	—	9	—	13	17
Ranger *	13	13	14	—	14	—
Mage	—	—	—	9	—	—
Specialist*	Var	Var	Var	Var	Var	Var
Cleric	—	—	—	—	9	—
Druid *	—	—	—	—	12	15
Thief	—	9	—	—	—	—
Bard *	—	12	—	13	—	15

* Optional character class. Specialist includes illusionist.

Class Descriptions

The complete character class descriptions that follow give the specific, detailed information you need about each class. These are organized according to groups. Information that applies to the entire group is presented at the start of the section. Each character class within the group is then explained.

The descriptions use game terms that may be unfamiliar to you; many of these are explained in this text (or you may look the terms up in the Glossary).

Experience Points measure what a character has learned and how he has improved his skill during the course of his adventures. Characters earn experience points by completing adventures and by doing things specifically related to their class. A fighter, for example, earns more experience for charging and battling a monster than does a thief, because the fighter's training emphasizes battle while the thief's emphasizes stealth and cleverness. Characters accumulate experience points from adventure to adventure. When they accumulate enough, they rise to the next level of experience, gaining additional abilities and powers. The experience level tables for each character group list the *total*, accumulated experience points needed to reach each level.

> Some DMs may require that a character spend a certain amount of time or money training before rising to the next experience level. Your DM will tell you the requirements for advancement when the time comes.

Level is a measure of the character's power. A beginning character starts at 1st level. To advance to the next level, the character must earn a requisite number of experience points. Different character classes improve at different rates. Each increase in level improves the character's survivability and skills.

Prime Requisite is the ability score or scores that are most important to a particular class. A fighter must be strong and a mage must be intelligent; their prime requisites, therefore, are Strength and Intelligence, respectively. Some character classes have more than one prime requisite. *Any character who has a score of 16 or more in* **all** *his prime requisites gains a 10 percent bonus to his experience point awards.*

Warrior

The warrior group encompasses the character classes of heroes who make their way in the world primarily by skill at arms: fighters, paladins, and rangers.

Warriors are allowed to use any weapon. They can wear any type of armor. Warriors

get 1 to 10 (1d10) hit points per level and can gain a special Constitution hit point bonus that is available only to warriors.

The disadvantage warriors have is that they are restricted in their selection of magical items and spells.

All warriors use Table 14 to determine their advancement in level as they earn experience points.

All warriors gain one 10-sided hit die per level from 1st through 9th. *After 9th level, warriors gain just 3 hit points per level and they no longer gain additional hit point bonuses for high Constitution scores.*

Table 14: WARRIOR EXPERIENCE LEVELS

Level	Fighter	Paladin/ Ranger	Hit Dice (d10)
1	0	0	1
2	2,000	2,250	2
3	4,000	4,500	3
4	8,000	9,000	4
5	16,000	18,000	5
6	32,000	36,000	6
7	64,000	75,000	7
8	125,000	150,000	8
9	250,000	300,000	9
10	500,000	600,000	9+3
11	750,000	900,000	9+6
12	1,000,000	1,200,000	9+9
13	1,250,000	1,500,000	9+12
14	1,500,000	1,800,000	9+15
15	1,750,000	2,100,000	9+18
16	2,000,000	2,400,000	9+21
17	2,250,000	2,700,000	9+24
18	2,500,000	3,000,000	9+27
19	2,750,000	3,300,000	9+30
20	3,000,000	3,600,000	9+33

All warriors gain the ability to make more than one melee attack per round as they rise in level. Table 15 shows how many melee attacks fighters, paladins, and rangers can make per round, as a function of their levels.

Table 15: WARRIOR MELEE ATTACKS PER ROUND

Warrior Level	Attacks/Round
1-6	1/round
7-12	3/2 rounds
13 & up	2/round

Fighter

Ability Requirements:	Strength 9
Prime Requisite:	Strength
Allowed Races:	All

The principal attribute of a fighter is Strength. To become a fighter, a character must have a minimum Strength score of 9. A good Dexterity rating is highly desirable.

A fighter who has a Strength score (his prime requisite) of 16 or more gains a 10 per-

cent bonus to the experience points he earns.

Also, high Strength gives the fighter a better chance to hit an opponent and enables him to cause more damage.

> The fighter is a warrior, an expert in weapons and, if he is clever, tactics and strategy. There are many famous fighters from legend: Hercules, Perseus, Hiawatha, Beowulf, Siegfried, Cuchulain, Little John, Tristan, and Sinbad. History is crowded with great generals and warriors: El Cid, Hannibal, Alexander the Great, Charlemagne, Spartacus, Richard the Lionheart, and Belisarius. Your fighter could be modeled after any of these, or he could be unique. A visit to your local library can uncover many heroic fighters.

Fighters can have any alignment: good or evil, lawful or chaotic, or neutral.

As a master of weapons, the fighter is the only character able to have weapon specialization (explained in Chapter 5). Weapon specialization enables the fighter to use a particular weapon with exceptional skill, improving his chances to hit and cause damage with that weapon. A fighter character is not required to specialize in a weapon; the choice is up to the player. No other character class—not even ranger or paladin—is allowed weapon specialization.

While fighters cannot cast magical spells, they can use many magical items, including potions, protection scrolls, most rings, and all forms of enchanted armor, weapons, and shields.

When a fighter attains 9th level (becomes a "Lord"), he can automatically attract men-at-arms. These soldiers, having heard of the fighter, come for the chance to gain fame, adventure, and cash. They are loyal as long as they are well-treated, successful, and paid well. Abusive treatment or a disastrous campaign can lead to grumbling, desertion, and possibly mutiny. To attract the men, the fighter must have a castle or stronghold and sizeable manor lands around it. As he claims and rules this land, soldiers journey to his domain, thereby increasing his power. Furthermore, the fighter can tax and develop these lands, gaining a steady income from them. Your DM has information about gaining and running a barony.

In addition to regular men-at-arms, the 9th-level fighter also attracts an elite bodyguard (his "household guards"). Although these soldiers are still mercenaries, they have greater loyalty to their Lord than do common soldiers. In return, they expect better treatment and more pay than the common soldier receives. Although the elite unit can be chosen randomly, it is better to ask your DM what unit your fighter attracts. This allows him to choose a troop consistent with the campaign.

Table 16: FIGHTER'S FOLLOWERS

Roll percentile dice on each of the following subtables of Table 16: once for the leader of the troops, once for troops, and once for a bodyguard (household guards) unit.

Die Roll	Leader (and suggested magical items)
01-40	5th-level fighter, plate mail, shield, *battle axe +2*
41-75	6th-level fighter, plate mail, *shield +1, spear +1, dagger +1*
76-95	6th-level fighter, *plate mail +1*, shield, *spear +1, dagger +1*, plus 3rd-level fighter, splint mail, shield, *crossbow of distance*
96-99	7th-level fighter, *plate mail +1, shield +1, broad sword +2*, heavy war horse with *horseshoes of speed*
00	DM's Option

Die Roll	Troops/Followers (all 0th-level)
01-50	20 cavalry with ring mail, shield, 3 javelins, long sword, hand axe; 100 infantry with scale mail, polearm *, club
51-75	20 infantry with splint mail, morning star, hand axe; 60 infantry with leather armor, pike, short sword
76-90	40 infantry with chain mail, heavy crossbow, short sword; 20 infantry with chain mail, light crossbow, military fork
91-99	10 cavalry with banded mail, shield, lance, bastard sword, mace; 20 cavalry with scale mail, shield, lance, long sword, mace; 30 cavalry with studded leather armor, shield, lance, long sword
00	DM's Option (Barbarians, headhunters, armed peasants, extra-heavy cavalry, etc.)

* Player selects type.

Die Roll	Elite Units
01-10	10 mounted knights: 1st-level fighters with field plate, large shield, lance, broad sword, morning star, and heavy war horse with full barding
11-20	10 1st-level elven fighter/mages with chain mail, long sword, long bow, dagger
21-30	15 wardens: 1st-level rangers with scale mail, shield, long sword, spear, long bow
31-40	20 berserkers: 2nd-level fighters with leather armor, shield, battle axe, broad sword, dagger (berserkers receive +1 bonus to attack and damage rolls)
41-65	20 expert archers: 1st-level fighters with studded leather armor, long bows or crossbows (+2 to hit, or bow specialization, if using that optional rule)
66-99	30 infantry: 1st-level fighters with plate mail, body shield, spear, short sword
00	DM's Option (pegasi cavalry, eagle riders, demihumans, siege train, etc.)

The DM may design other tables that are more appropriate to his campaign. Check with your DM upon reaching 9th level.

A fighter can hold property, including a castle or stronghold, long before he reaches 9th level. However, it is only when he reaches this level that his name is so widely known that he attracts the loyalty of other warriors.

Paladin

Ability Requirements:	Strength 12
	Constitution 9
	Wisdom 13
	Charisma 17
Prime Requisites:	Strength, Charisma
Races Allowed:	Human

The paladin is a noble and heroic warrior, the symbol of all that is right and true in the world. As such, he has high ideals that he must maintain at all times. Throughout legend and history there are many heroes who could be called paladins: Roland and the 12 Peers of Charlemagne, Sir Lancelot, Sir Gawain, and Sir Galahad are all examples of the class. However, many brave and heroic soldiers have tried and failed to live up to the ideals of the paladin. It is not an easy task!

Only a human may become a paladin. He must have minimum ability scores of Strength 12, Constitution 9, Wisdom 13, and Charisma 17. Strength and Charisma are the prime requisites of the paladin. A paladin must be lawful good in alignment and must always remain lawful good. A paladin who changes alignment, either deliberately or inadvertently, loses all his special powers—sometimes only temporarily and sometimes forever. He can use any weapon and wear any type of armor.

A paladin who has Strength and Charisma scores of 16 or more gains a 10 percent bonus to the experience points he earns.

Lawfulness and good deeds are the meat and drink of a paladin. If a paladin ever knowingly performs a chaotic act, he must seek a high-level (7th or more) cleric of lawful good alignment, confess his sin, and do penance as prescribed by the cleric. If a paladin should ever knowingly and willingly perform an evil act, he loses the status of paladinhood immediately and irrevocably. All benefits are then lost and no deed or magic can restore the character to paladinhood: He is ever after a fighter. The character's level remains unchanged when this occurs and experience points are adjusted accordingly. Thereafter the character is bound by the rules for fighters. He does not gain the benefits of weapon specialization (if this is used) since he did not select this for his character at the start.

If the paladin commits an evil act while enchanted or controlled by magic, he loses his paladin status until he can atone for the deed. This loss of status means the character loses all his special abilities and essentially functions as a fighter (without weapon specialization) of the same level. Regaining his status undoubtedly requires completion of some dangerous quest or important mission to once again prove his worth and assuage his own guilt. He gains no experience prior to or during the course of this mission, and regains his standing as a paladin only upon completing the quest.

A paladin has the following special benefits:

A paladin can detect the presence of evil intent up to 60 feet away by concentrating on locating evil in a particular direction. He can do this as often as desired, but each attempt takes one round. This ability detects evil monsters and characters.

A paladin receives a +2 bonus to all saving throws.

A paladin is immune to all forms of disease. (Note that certain magical afflictions—lycanthropy and mummy rot—are curses and not diseases.)

A paladin can heal by laying on hands. The paladin restores 2 hit points per experience level. He can heal himself or someone else, but only once per day.

A paladin can cure diseases of all sorts (though not cursed afflictions such as lycanthropy). This can be done only once per week for each five levels of experience (once per week at levels 1 through 5, twice per week at levels 6 through 10, etc.).

A paladin is surrounded by an aura of protection with a 10-foot radius. Within this radius, all summoned and specifically evil creatures suffer a −1 penalty to their attack rolls, regardless of whom they attack. Creatures affected by this aura can spot its source easily, even if the paladin is disguised.

A paladin using a *holy sword* projects a circle of power 30 feet in diameter when the sword is unsheathed and held. This power dispels hostile magic of a level up to the paladin's experience level. (A *holy sword* is a very special weapon; if your paladin acquires one, the DM will explain its other powers.)

A paladin gains the power to turn undead, devils, and demons when he reaches 3rd level. He affects these monsters the same as does a cleric two levels lower—e.g., at 3rd level he has the turning power of a 1st-level cleric. See the section on priests for more details on this ability.

A paladin may call for his war horse upon reaching 4th level, or anytime thereafter. This faithful steed need not be a horse; it may be whatever sort of creature is appropriate to the character (as decided by the DM). A paladin's war horse is a very special animal, bonded by fate to the warrior. The paladin does not really "call" the animal, nor does the horse instantly appear in front of him. Rather, the character must find his war horse in some memorable way, most frequently by a specific quest.

A paladin can cast priest spells once he reaches 9th level. He can cast only spells of the combat, divination, healing, and protective spheres. (Spheres are explained in the Priest section.) The acquisition and casting of these spells abide by the rules given for priests.

The spell progression and casting level are listed in Table 17. Unlike a priest, the paladin does *not* gain extra spells for a high Wisdom score. The paladin cannot cast spells from clerical or druidical scrolls nor can he use priest items unless they are allowed to the warrior group.

Table 17: PALADIN SPELL PROGRESSION

Paladin Level	Casting Level	Priest Spell Level 1	2	3	4
9	1	1	—	—	—
10	2	2	—	—	—
11	3	2	1	—	—
12	4	2	2	—	—
13	5	2	2	1	—
14	6	3	2	1	—
15	7	3	2	1	1
16	8	3	3	2	1
17	9 *	3	3	3	1
18	9 *	3	3	3	1
19	9 *	3	3	3	2
20 *	9 *	3	3	3	3

* Maximum spell ability

The following strictures apply to paladins.

A paladin may not possess more than 10 magical items. Furthermore, these may not exceed one suit of armor, one shield, four weapons (arrows and bolts are not counted), and four other magical items.

A paladin never retains wealth. He may keep only enough treasure to support himself in a modest manner, pay his henchmen, men-at-arms, and servitors a reasonable rate, and to construct or maintain a small castle or keep (funds can be set aside for this purpose). All excess must be donated to the church or another worthy cause. This money can never be given to another player character or NPC controlled by a player.

A paladin must tithe to whatever charitable, religious institution of lawful good alignment he serves. A tithe is 10 percent of the paladin's income, whether coins, jewels, magical items, wages, rewards, or taxes. It must be paid immediately.

A paladin does not attract a body of followers upon reaching 9th level or building a castle. However, he can still hire soldiers and specialists, although these men must be lawful good in comportment.

A paladin may employ only lawful good henchmen (or those who act in such a manner when alignment is unknown). A paladin will cooperate with characters of other alignments only as long as they behave themselves. He will try to show them the proper way to live through both word and deed. The paladin realizes that most people simply cannot maintain his high standards. Even thieves can be tolerated, provided they are not evil and are sincerely trying to reform. He will not abide the company of those who commit evil or unrighteous acts. Stealth in the cause of good is acceptable, though only as a last resort.

Ranger

Ability Requirements:	Strength 13
	Dexterity 13
	Constitution 14
	Wisdom 14
Prime Requisites:	Strength, Dexterity, Wisdom
Races Allowed:	Human, Elf, Half-elf

The ranger is a hunter and woodsman who lives by not only his sword, but also his wits. Robin Hood, Orion, Jack the giant killer, and the huntresses of Diana are examples of rangers from history and legend. The abilities of the ranger make him particularly good at tracking, woodcraft, and spying.

The ranger must have scores not less than 13 in Strength, 14 in Constitution, 13 in Dexterity, and 14 in Wisdom. The prime requisites of the ranger are Strength, Dexterity, and Wisdom. Rangers are always good, but they can be lawful, neutral, or chaotic. It is in the ranger's heart to do good, but not always by the rules.

A ranger who has Strength, Dexterity, and Wisdom scores of 16 or more gains a 10 percent bonus to the experience points he earns.

Although the ranger can use any weapon and wear any armor, several of his special abilities are usable only when he is wearing studded leather or lighter armor.

Although he has the basic skills of a warrior, the ranger also has several advantages. When wearing studded leather or lighter armor, a ranger can fight two-handed with no penalty to his attack rolls (see page 96). Obviously, the ranger cannot use a shield when fighting this way. A ranger can still fight with two weapons while wearing heavier armor than studded leather, but he suffers the standard attack roll penalties.

The ranger is a skilled woodsman. Even if the optional proficiency rules are not used, the ranger has Tracking proficiency. If the proficiency rules are used in your campaign, the ranger knows Tracking without expending any points. Furthermore, this skill

Table 18: RANGER ABILITIES

Ranger Level	Hide in Shadows	Move Silently	Casting Level	Priest Spell Levels 1	2	3
1	10%	15%	—	—	—	—
2	15%	21%	—	—	—	—
3	20%	27%	—	—	—	—
4	25%	33%	—	—	—	—
5	31%	40%	—	—	—	—
6	37%	47%	—	—	—	—
7	43%	55%	—	—	—	—
8	49%	62%	1	1	—	—
9	56%	70%	2	2	—	—
10	63%	78%	3	2	1	—
11	70%	86%	4	2	2	—
12	77%	94%	5	2	2	1
13	85%	99% *	6	3	2	1
14	93%	99%	7	3	2	2
15	99% *	99%	8	3	3	2
16	99%	99%	9	3	3**	3

* Maximum percentile score
** Maximum spell ability

improves by +1 for every three levels the ranger has earned (3rd to 5th level, +1; 6th to 8th level, +2, etc.). While wearing studded leather or lighter armor, the ranger can try to move silently and hide in shadows. His chance to succeed in natural surroundings is given on Table 18 (modified by the ranger's race and Dexterity, as given on Tables 27 and 28 on page 39). When attempting these actions in non-natural surroundings (a musty crypt or city streets) the chance of success is halved. Hiding in shadows and moving silently are not possible in any armor heavier than studded leather—the armor is inflexible and makes too much noise.

In their roles as protectors of good, rangers tend to focus their efforts against some particular creature, usually one that marauds their homeland. Before advancing to 2nd level, every ranger must select a species enemy. Typical enemies include giants, orcs, lizard men, trolls, or ghouls; your DM has final approval on the choice. Thereafter, whenever the ranger encounters that enemy, he gains a +4 bonus to his attack rolls. This enmity can be concealed only with great difficulty, so the ranger suffers a −4 penalty on all encounter reactions with creatures of the hated type. Furthermore, the ranger will actively seek out this enemy in combat in preference to all other foes unless someone else presents a much greater danger.

Rangers are adept with both trained and untamed creatures, having a limited degree of animal empathy. If a ranger carefully approaches or tends any natural animal, he can try to modify the animal's reactions. (A natural animal is one that can be found in the real world—a bear, snake, zebra, etc.)

When dealing with domestic or non-hostile animals, a ranger can approach the animal and befriend it automatically. He can easily discern the qualities of the creature (spotting the best horse in the corral or seeing that the runt of the litter actually has great promise).

When dealing with a wild animal or an animal trained to attack, the animal must roll a saving throw vs. rods to resist the ranger's overtures. (This table is used even though the ranger's power is non-magical.) The ranger imposes a −1 penalty on the die roll for every three experience levels he has earned (−1 at 1st to 3rd, −2 at 4th to 6th, etc.). If the creature fails the saving throw, its reaction can be shifted one category as the ranger chooses. Of course, the ranger must be at the front of the party and must approach the creature fearlessly.

For example, Beornhelm, a 7th-level ranger, is leading his friends through the woods. On entering a clearing, he spots a hungry black bear blocking the path on the other side. Signaling his friends to wait, Beornhelm approaches the beast, whispering soothing words. The DM rolls a saving throw vs. rods for the bear, modified by −3 for Beornhelm's level. The bear's normal reaction is unfriendly, but Beornhelm's presence reduces this to neutral. The party waits patiently until the bear wanders off to seek its dinner elsewhere.

Later, Beornhelm goes to the horse market to get a new mount. The dealer shows him a spirited horse, notorious for being vicious and stubborn. Beornhelm approaches it carefully, again speaking soothingly, and mounts the stallion with no difficulty. Ridden by Beornhelm, the horse is spirited but well-behaved. Approached by anyone else, the horse reverts to its old ways.

A ranger can learn priest spells, but only those of the plant or animal spheres (see page 34), when he reaches 8th level (see Table 18). He gains and uses his spells according to the rules given for priests (see page 32). He does not gain bonus spells for a high Wisdom score, nor is he ever able to use clerical scrolls or magical items unless specifically noted otherwise.

Rangers can build castles, forts, or strongholds, but do not gain any special followers by doing so.

At 10th level, a ranger attracts 2d6 followers. These followers might be normal humans, but they are often animals or even stranger denizens of the land. Table 19 can be used to determine these, or your DM may assign specific followers.

Table 19: RANGER'S FOLLOWERS

Die Roll	Follower
01-10	Bear, black
11-20	Bear, brown
21	Brownie *
22-26	Cleric (human)
27-38	Dog/wolf
39-40	Druid
41-50	Falcon
51-53	Fighter (elf)
54-55	Fighter (gnome)
56-57	Fighter (halfling)
58-65	Fighter (human)
66	Fighter/mage (elf)*
67-72	Great cat (tiger, lion, etc.) *
73	Hippogriff *
74	Pegasus *
75	Pixie *
76-80	Ranger (half-elf)
81-90	Ranger (human)
91-94	Raven
95	Satyr *
96	Thief (halfling)
97	Thief (human)
98	Treant *
99	Werebear/weretiger *
00	Other wilderness creature (chosen by the DM)

* If the ranger already has a follower of this type, ignore this result and roll again.

Of course, your DM can assign particular creatures, either choosing from the list above or from any other source. He can also rule that certain creatures are not found in the region—it is highly unlikely that a tiger would come wandering through a territory similar to western Europe!

These followers arrive over the course of several months. Often they are encountered during the ranger's adventures (allowing you and your DM a chance to role-play the initial meeting). While the followers are automatically loyal and friendly toward the ranger, their future behavior depends on the ranger's treatment of them. In all cases, the ranger does not gain any special method of communicating with his followers. He must either have some way of speaking to them or they simply mutely accompany him on his journeys. ("Yeah, this bear's been with me for years. Don't know why—he just seems to follow me around. I don't own him and can't tell him to do anything he don't want to do," said the grizzled old woodsman sitting outside the tavern.)

Of course, the ranger is not obligated to take on followers. If he prefers to remain independent, he can release his followers at any time. They reluctantly depart, but stand ready to answer any call for aid he might put out at a later time.

Like the paladin, the ranger has a code of behavior.

A ranger must always retain his good alignment. If the ranger intentionally commits an evil act, he automatically loses his ranger status. Thereafter he is considered a fighter of the same level (if he has more experience points than a fighter of his level, he loses all the excess experience points). His ranger status can never be regained. If the ranger involuntarily commits an evil act (perhaps in a situation of no choice), he cannot earn any more experience points until he has cleansed himself of that evil. This can be accomplished by correcting the wrongs he committed, revenging himself on the person who forced him to commit the act, or releasing those oppressed by evil. The ranger instinctively knows what things he must do to regain his status (i.e., the DM creates a special adventure for the character).

Furthermore, rangers tend to be loners, men constantly on the move. They cannot have henchmen, hirelings, mercenaries, or even servants until they reach 8th level. While they can have any monetary amount of treasure, they cannot have more treasure than they can carry. Excess treasure must either be converted to a portable form or donated to a worthy institution (an NPC group, not a player character).

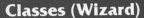

Wizard

The wizard group encompasses all spellcasters working in the various fields of magic—both those who specialize in specific schools of magic and those who study a broad range of magical theories. Spending their lives in pursuit of arcane wisdom, wizards have little time for physical endeavors. They tend to be poor fighters with little knowledge of weaponry. However, they command powerful and dangerous energies with a few simple gestures, rare components, and mystical words.

Spells are the tools, weapons, and armor of the wizard. He is weak in a toe-to-toe fight, but when prepared he can strike down his foes at a distance, vanish in an instant, become a wholly different creature, or even invade the mind of an enemy and take control of his thoughts and actions. No secrets are safe from a wizard and no fortress is secure. His quest for knowledge and power often leads him into realms where mortals were never meant to go.

Wizards cannot wear any armor, for several reasons. Firstly, most spells require complicated gestures and odd posturings by the caster and armor restricts the wearer's ability to do these properly. Secondly, the wizard spent his youth (and will spend most of his life) learning arcane languages, poring through old books, and practicing his spells. This leaves no time for learning other things (like how to wear armor properly and use it effectively). If the wizard had spent his time learning about armor, he would not have even the meager skills and powers he begins with. There are even unfounded theories that claim the materials in most armors disrupt the delicate fabric of a spell as it gathers energy; the two cannot exist side by side in harmony. While this idea is popular with the common people, true wizards know this is simply not true. If it were, how would they ever be able to cast spells requiring iron braziers or metal bowls?

For similar reasons, wizards are severely restricted in the weapons they can use. They are limited to those that are easy to learn or are sometimes useful in their own research. Hence, a wizard can use a dagger or a staff, items that are traditionally useful in magical studies. Other weapons allowed are darts, knives, and slings (weapons that require little skill, little strength, or both).

Wizards can use more magical items than any other characters. These include potions, rings, wands, rods, scrolls, and most miscellaneous magical items. A wizard can use a magical version of any weapon allowed to his class but cannot use magical armor, because no armor is allowed. Between their spells and magical items, however, wizards wield great power.

Finally, all wizards (whether mages or specialists) can create new magical items, ranging from simple scrolls and potions to powerful staves and magic swords. Once he reaches 9th level, a wizard can pen magical scrolls and brew potions. He can construct more powerful magical items only after he has learned the appropriate spells (or works with someone who knows them). Your DM should consult the Spell Research and Magical Items sections of the *DMG* for more information.

No matter what school of magic the wizard is involved in, Intelligence is his prime requisite (or one of several prime requisites). Characters must have an Intelligence score of at least 9 to qualify to be a wizard.

All wizards use Table 20 to determine their advancement in level as they earn experience points. They also use Table 21 to determine the levels and numbers of spells they can cast at each experience level.

All wizards gain one four-sided Hit Die (1d4) per level from 1st through 10th levels. *After 10th level, wizards earn 1 hit point per level and they no longer gain additional hit point bonuses for high Constitution scores.*

Table 20: WIZARD EXPERIENCE LEVELS

Level	Mage/Specialist	Hit Dice (d4)
1	0	1
2	2,500	2
3	5,000	3
4	10,000	4
5	20,000	5
6	40,000	6
7	60,000	7
8	90,000	8
9	135,000	9
10	250,000	10
11	375,000	10 + 1
12	750,000	10 + 2
13	1,125,000	10 + 3
14	1,500,000	10 + 4
15	1,875,000	10 + 5
16	2,250,000	10 + 6
17	2,625,000	10 + 7
18	3,000,000	10 + 8
19	3,375,000	10 + 9
20	3,750,000	10 + 10

Table 21: WIZARD SPELL PROGRESSION

Wizard Level	Spell Level 1	2	3	4	5	6	7	8	9
1	1	—	—	—	—	—	—	—	—
2	2	—	—	—	—	—	—	—	—
3	2	1	—	—	—	—	—	—	—
4	3	2	—	—	—	—	—	—	—
5	4	2	1	—	—	—	—	—	—
6	4	2	2	—	—	—	—	—	—
7	4	3	2	1	—	—	—	—	—
8	4	3	3	2	—	—	—	—	—
9	4	3	3	2	1	—	—	—	—
10	4	4	3	2	2	—	—	—	—
11	4	4	4	3	3	—	—	—	—
12	4	4	4	4	4	1	—	—	—
13	5	5	5	4	4	2	—	—	—
14	5	5	5	4	4	2	1	—	—
15	5	5	5	5	5	2	1	—	—
16	5	5	5	5	5	3	2	1	—
17	5	5	5	5	5	3	3	2	—
18	5	5	5	5	5	3	3	2	1
19	5	5	5	5	5	3	3	3	1
20	5	5	5	5	5	4	3	3	2

Learning and casting spells require long study, patience, and research. Once his adventuring life begins, a wizard is largely responsible for his own education; he no longer has a teacher looking over his shoulder and telling him which spell to learn next. This freedom is not without its price, however. It means that the wizard must find his own source for magical knowledge: libraries, guilds, or captured books and scrolls.

Whenever a wizard discovers instructions for a spell he doesn't know, he can try to read and understand the instructions. The player must roll percentile dice. If the result is equal to or less than the percentage chance to learn a new spell (listed on Table 4, page 16), the character understands the spell and how to cast it. He can enter the spell in his spell book (unless he has already learned the maximum number of spells allowed for that level). If this die roll is higher than the character's chance to learn the spell, he doesn't understand the spell. Once a spell is learned, it cannot be unlearned. It remains part of that character's repertoire forever. Thus a character cannot choose to "forget" a spell so as to replace it with another.

A wizard's spell book can be a single book, a set of books, a bundle of scrolls, or anything else your DM allows. The spell book is the wizard's diary, laboratory journal, and encyclopedia, containing a record of everything he knows. Naturally, it is his most treasured possession; without it he is almost helpless.

A spell book contains the complicated instructions for casting the spell—the spell's recipe, so to speak. Merely reading these instructions aloud or trying to mimic the instructions does not enable one to cast the spell. Spells gather and shape mystical energies; the procedures involved are very demanding, bizarre, and intricate. Before a wizard can actually cast a spell, he must memorize its arcane formula. This locks an energy pattern for that particular spell into his mind. Once he has the spell memorized, it remains in his memory until he uses the exact combination of gestures, words, and materials that triggers the release of this energy pattern. Upon casting, the energy of the spell is spent, wiped clean from the wizard's mind. The wizard cannot cast that spell again until he returns to his spell book and memorizes it again.

Initially the wizard is able to retain only a few of these magical energies in his mind at one time. Furthermore, some spells are more demanding and complex than others; these are impossible for the inexperienced wizard to memorize. With experience, the wizard's talent expands. He can memorize more spells and more complex spells. Still, he never escapes his need to study; the wizard must always return to his spell books to refresh his powers.

Another important power of the wizard is his ability to research new spells and construct magical items. Both endeavors are difficult, time-consuming, costly, occasionally even perilous. Through research, a wizard can create an entirely new spell, subject to the DM's approval. Likewise, by consulting with your DM, your character can build magical items, either similar to those already given in the rules or of your own design. Your DM has information concerning spell research and magical item creation.

Unlike many other characters, wizards gain no special benefits from building a fortress or stronghold. They can own property and receive the normal benefits, such as monthly income and mercenaries for protection. However, the reputations of wizards tend to discourage people from flocking to their doors. At best, a wizard may acquire a few henchmen and apprentices to help in his work.

Mage

Ability Requirements:	Intelligence 9
Prime Requisite:	Intelligence
Races Allowed:	Human, Elf, Half-elf

Mages are the most versatile types of wizards, those who choose not to specialize in any single school of magic. This is both an advantage and a disadvantage. On the positive side, the mage's selection of spells enables him to deal with many different situations. (Wizards who study within a single school of magic learn highly specialized spells, but at the expense of spells from other areas.) The other side of the coin is that the mage's ability to learn specialized spells is limited compared to the specialist's.

> Mages have no historical counterparts; they exist only in legend and myth. However, players can model their characters after such legendary figures as Merlin, Circe, or Medea. Accounts of powerful wizards and sorceresses are rare, since their reputations are based in no small part on the mystery that surrounds them. These legendary figures worked toward secret ends, seldom confiding in the normal folk around them.

A mage who has an Intelligence score of 16 or higher gains a 10 percent bonus to the experience points he earns.

The Schools of Magic

Spells are divided into nine different categories, or schools, according to the types of magical energy they utilize. Each school has its own special methods and practices.

Although they are called schools, schools of magic are not organized places where a person goes to study. The word "school" identifies a magical discipline. A school is an approach to magic and spellcasting that emphasizes a particular sort of spell. Practitioners of a school of magic may set up a magical university to teach their methods to beginners, but this is not necessary. Many powerful wizards learned their craft studying under reclusive masters in distant lands.

The nine schools of magic are **Abjuration, Alteration, Conjuration/Summoning, Enchantment/Charm, Greater Divination, Illusion, Invocation/Evocation, Necromancy, and Lesser Divination.**

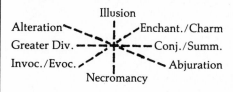

This diagram illustrates the schools that oppose each other. See Table 22 and its entry descriptions for more information.

Of these schools, eight are greater schools while the ninth, lesser divination, is a minor school. The minor school of lesser divination includes all divination spells of the 4th spell level or less (available to all wizards). Greater divinations are those divination spells of the 5th spell level or higher.

Specialist Wizards

A wizard who concentrates his effort in a single school of magic is called a specialist. There are specialists in each type of magic, although some are extremely rare. Not all specialists are well-suited to adventuring—the diviner's spells are limited and not generally useful in dangerous situations. On the other hand, player characters might want to consult an NPC diviner before starting an adventure.

Specialist wizards have advantages and disadvantages when compared to mages. Their chance to know spells of their school of magic is greatly increased, but the intensive study results in a smaller chance to know spells outside their school. The number of spells they can cast increases, but they lose the ability to cast spells of the school in opposition to their specialty (opposite it in the diagram). Their ability to research and create new spells within their specialty is increased, but the initial selection of spells in their school may be quite limited. All in all, players must consider the advantages and disadvantages carefully.

Not all wizards can become specialists. The player character must meet certain requirements to become a specialist. Most specialist wizards must be single-classed; multi-classed characters cannot become specialists, except for gnomes, who seem to have more of a natural bent for the school of illusion than characters of any other race. Dual-class humans *can* choose to become specialists. The dedication to the particular school of magic requires all the attention and concentration of the character. He does not have time for other class-related pursuits.

Table 22: WIZARD SPECIALIST REQUIREMENTS

Specialist	School	Race	Minimum Ability Score	Opposition School(s)
Abjurer	Abjuration	H	15 Wis	Alteration & Illusion
Conjurer	Conj./Summ.	H, ½ E	15 Con	Gr. Divin. & Invocation
Diviner	Gr. Divin.	H, ½ E, E	16 Wis	Conj./Summ.
Enchanter	Ench./Charm	H, ½ E, E	16 Cha	Invoc./Evoc. & Necromancy
Illusionist	Illusion	H, G	16 Dex	Necro., Invoc./Evoc., Abjur.
Invoker	Invoc./Evoc.	H	16 Con	Ench./Charm & Conj./Summ.
Necromancer	Necromancy	H	16 Wis	Illusion & Ench./Charm
Transmuter	Alteration	H, ½ E	15 Dex	Abjuration & Necromancy

In addition, each school has different restrictions on race, ability scores, and schools of magic allowed. These restrictions are given on Table 22. Note that lesser divination is not available as a specialty. The spells of this group, vital to the functioning of a wizard, are available to all wizards.

Race lists those races that, either through a natural tendency or a quirk of fate, are allowed to specialize in that art. Note that the gnome, though unable to be a regular mage, can specialize in illusions.

Minimum Ability score lists the ability minimums needed to study intensively in that school. All schools require at least the minimum Intelligence demanded of a mage and an additional prime requisite, as listed.

Opposition School(s) always includes the school directly opposite the character's school of study in the diagram on page 31. In addition, the schools to either side of this one may also be disallowed due to the nature of the character's school. For example, an invoker/evoker cannot learn enchantment/charm or conjuration/summoning spells and cannot use magical items that duplicate spells from these schools.

Being a specialist does have significant advantages to balance the trade-offs the character must make. These are listed here:

* A specialist gains one additional spell per spell level, provided the additional spell is taken in the specialist's school. Thus a 1st-level illusionist could have two spells—one being any spell he knows and the other limited to spells of the illusion school.

* Because specialists have an enhanced understanding of spells within their school, they receive a +1 bonus when making saving throws against those spells when cast by other wizards. Likewise, other characters suffer a −1 penalty when making saving throws against a specialist casting spells within his school. Both of these modifiers can be in effect at the same time—e.g., when an enchanter casts an enchantment spell at another enchanter, the modifiers cancel each other out.

* Specialists receive a bonus of +15 percent when learning spells from their school and a penalty of −15 percent when learning spells from other schools. The bonus or penalty is applied to the percentile dice roll the player must make when the character tries to learn a new spell (see Table 4).

* Whenever a specialist reaches a new spell level, he automatically gains one spell of his school to add to his spell books. This spell can be selected by the DM or he can allow the player to pick. No roll for learning the spell need be made. It is assumed that the character has discovered this new spell during the course of his research and study.

* When a specialist wizard attempts to create a new spell (using the rules given in the *DMG*), the DM should count the new

spell as one level less (for determining the difficulty) if the spell falls within the school of the specialist. An enchanter attempting to create a new enchantment spell would have an easier time of it than an illusionist attempting to do the same.

Illusionist

Ability Requirements: Dexterity 16
Prime Requisite: Intelligence
Races Allowed: Human, Gnome

The illusionist is an example of a specialist. The description of the illusionist given here can be used as a guide for creating wizards specializing in other magical schools.

First, the school of illusion is a very demanding field of study. To specialize as an illusionist, a wizard needs a Dexterity score of at least 16.

An illusionist who has an Intelligence of 16 or more gains a 10 percent bonus to the experience points he earns.

Because the illusionist knows far more about illusions than the standard wizard, he is allowed a +1 bonus when rolling saving throws against illusions; other characters suffer a −1 penalty when rolling saving throws against his illusions. (These modifiers apply only if the spell allows a saving throw.)

Through the course of his studies, the illusionist has become adept at memorizing illusion spells (though it is still an arduous process). He can memorize an extra illusion spell at each spell level. Thus as a 1st-level caster he can memorize two spells, although at least one of these must be an illusion spell.

Later, when he begins to research new spells for his collection, he finds it easier to devise new illusion spells to fill specialized needs. Research in other schools is harder and more time consuming for him.

Finally, the intense study of illusion magic prevents the character from mastering the other classes of spells that are totally alien to the illusion school (those diametrically opposite illusion on the diagram). Thus, the illusionist cannot learn spells from the schools of necromancy, invocation/evocation, or abjuration.

As an example, consider Joinville the illusionist. He has an Intelligence score of 15. In the course of his travels he captures an enemy wizard's spell book that contains an *improved invisibility* spell, a *continual light* spell, and a *fireball* spell, none of which are in Joinville's spell book. He has an 80 percent chance to learn the *improved invisibility* spell. *Continual light* is an alteration spell, however, so his chance to learn it is only 50 percent (consult Table 4 to see where these figures come from). He cannot learn the *fireball* spell, or even transcribe it into his spell book, because it is an evocation spell.

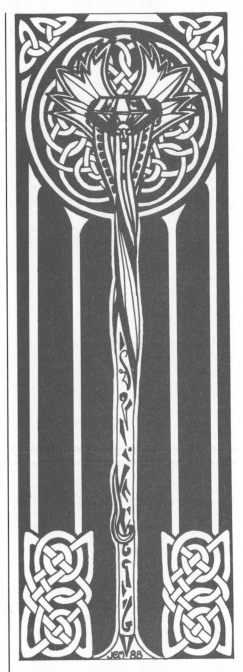

Priest

The priest is a believer and advocate of a god from a particular mythos. More than just a follower, he intercedes and acts on behalf of others, seeking to use his powers to advance the beliefs of his mythos.

All priests have certain powers: The ability to cast spells, the strength of arm to defend their beliefs, and special, deity-granted powers to aid them in their calling. While priests are not as fierce in combat as warriors, they are trained to use weaponry in the fight for their cause. They can cast spells, primarily to further their god's aims and protect its adherents. They have few offensive spells, but these are very powerful.

All priests use eight-sided Hit Dice (d8s). Only priests gain additional spells for having high Wisdom scores. All priests have a limited selection of weapons and armor, but the restrictions vary according to the mythos.

All priests use Table 23 to determine their advancement in level as they gain experience points. They also all use Table 24 to determine how many spells they receive at each level of experience.

All priest spells are divided into 16 categories called *spheres of influence*. Different types of priests have access to different spheres; no priest can cast spells from every sphere of influence. The 16 spheres of influence are as follows: All, Animal, Astral, Charm, Combat, Creation, Divination, Elemental, Guardian, Healing, Necromantic, Plant, Protection, Summoning, Sun, and Weather (see page 34).

In addition, a priest has either major or minor access to a sphere. A priest with major access to a sphere can (eventually) cast all spells in the sphere. A priest with minor access to a sphere can cast only 1st-, 2nd-, and 3rd-level spells from that sphere.

All priests gain one eight-sided Hit Die (1d8) per level from 1st through 9th. *After 9th level, priests earn 2 hit points per level and they no longer gain additional hit point bonuses for high Constitution scores.*

Table 23: PRIEST EXPERIENCE LEVELS

Level	Cleric	Druid	Hit Dice (d8)
1	0	0	1
2	1,500	2,000	2
3	3,000	4,000	3
4	6,000	7,500	4
5	13,000	12,500	5
6	27,500	20,000	6
7	55,000	35,000	7
8	110,000	60,000	8
9	225,000	90,000	9
10	450,000	125,000	9 + 2
11	675,000	200,000	9 + 4
12	900,000	300,000	9 + 6
13	1,125,000	750,000	9 + 8
14	1,350,000	1,500,000	9 + 10
15	1,575,000	3,000,000	9 + 12
16	1,800,000	3,500,000	9 + 14
17	2,025,000	500,000*	9 + 16
18	2,250,000	1,000,000	9 + 18
19	2,475,000	1,500,000	9 + 20
20	2,700,000	2,000,000	9 + 22

* See section on hierophant druids, page 37.

Table 24: PRIEST SPELL PROGRESSION

Priest Level	1	2	3	4	5	6*	7**
1	1	—	—	—	—	—	—
2	2	—	—	—	—	—	—
3	2	1	—	—	—	—	—
4	3	2	—	—	—	—	—
5	3	3	1	—	—	—	—
6	3	3	2	—	—	—	—
7	3	3	2	1	—	—	—
8	3	3	3	2	—	—	—
9	4	4	3	2	1	—	—
10	4	4	3	3	2	—	—
11	5	4	4	3	2	1	—
12	6	5	5	3	2	2	—
13	6	6	6	4	2	2	—
14	6	6	6	5	3	2	1
15	6	6	6	6	4	2	1
16	7	7	7	6	4	3	1
17	7	7	7	7	5	3	2
18	8	8	8	8	6	4	2
19	9	9	8	8	6	4	2
20	9	9	9	8	7	5	2

* Usable only by priests with 17 or greater Wisdom.

** Usable only by priests with 18 or greater Wisdom.

Cleric

Ability Requirement:	Wisdom 9
Prime Requisite:	Wisdom
Races Allowed:	All

The most common type of priest is the cleric. The cleric may be an adherent of any religion (though if the DM designs a specific mythos, the cleric's abilities and spells may be changed—see following). Clerics are generally good, but are not restricted to good; they can have any alignment acceptable to their order. A cleric must have a Wisdom score of 9 or more. High Constitution and Charisma are also particularly useful.

A cleric who has a Wisdom of 16 or more gains a 10 percent bonus to the experience points he earns.

The cleric class is similar to certain religious orders of knighthood of the Middle Ages: the Teutonic Knights, the Knights Templars, and Hospitalers. These orders combined military and religious training with a code of protection and service. Members were trained as knights and devoted themselves to the service of the church. These orders were frequently found on the outer edges of the Christian world, either on the fringe of the wilderness or in war-torn lands. Archbishop Turpin (of *The Song of Roland*) is an example of such a cleric. Similar orders can also be found in other lands, such as the sohei of Japan.

Clerics are sturdy soldiers, although their selection of weapons is limited. They can wear any type of armor and use any shield. Standard clerics, being reluctant to shed blood or spread violence, are allowed to use only blunt, bludgeoning weapons. They can use a fair number of magical items including clerical scrolls, most potions and rings, some wands and rods, staves, armor, shields, and magical versions of any weapons allowed by their order.

Spells are the main tools of the cleric, however, helping him to serve, fortify, protect, and revitalize those under his care. He has a wide variety of spells to choose from, suitable to many different purposes and needs. (A priest of a specific mythos probably has a more restricted range of spells— see page 34.) A cleric has major access to every sphere of influence except the plant, animal, weather, and elemental spheres (he has minor access to the elemental sphere and cannot cast spells of the other three spheres).

The cleric receives his spells as insight directly from his deity (the deity does not need to make a personal appearance to grant the spells the cleric prays for), as a sign of and reward for his faith, so he must take care not to abuse his power lest it be taken away as punishment.

The cleric is also granted power over undead—evil creatures that exist in a form of non-life, neither dead nor alive. The cleric is charged with defeating these mockeries of life. His ability to *turn undead* (see page 103) enables him to drive away these creatures or destroy them utterly (though a cleric of evil alignment can bind the creatures to his will). Some of the more common undead creatures are ghosts, zombies, skeletons, ghouls, and mummies. Vampires and liches (undead sorcerers) are two of the most powerful undead.

As a cleric advances in level, he gains additional spells, better combat skills, and a stronger turning ability. Upon reaching 8th level, the cleric automatically attracts a fanatically loyal group of believers, provided the character has established a place of worship of significant size. The cleric can build this place of worship at any time during his career, but he does not attract believers until he reaches 8th level. These followers are normal warriors, 0th-level soldiers, ready to fight for the cleric's cause. The cleric attracts 20 to 200 of these followers; they arrive over a period of several weeks. After the initial followers assemble, no new followers trickle in to fill the ranks of those who have fallen in service. The DM decides the exact number and types of followers attracted by the cleric. The character can hire other troops as needed, but these are not as loyal as his followers.

At 9th level, the cleric may receive official approval to establish a religious stronghold, be it a fortified abbey or a secluded convent.

Obviously, the stronghold must contain all the trappings of a place of worship and must be dedicated to the service of the cleric's cause. However, the construction cost of the stronghold is half the normal price, since the work has official sanction and much of the labor is donated. The cleric can hold property and build a stronghold anytime before reaching 9th level, but this is done without church sanction and does not receive the benefits described above.

Priests of Specific Mythoi

In the simplest version of the AD&D® game, clerics serve religions that can be generally described as "good" or "evil." Nothing more needs to be said about it; the game will play perfectly well at this level. However, a DM who has taken the time to create a detailed campaign world has often spent some of that time devising elaborate pantheons, either unique creations or adaptations from history or literature. If the option is open (and only your DM can decide), you may want your character to adhere to a particular mythos, taking advantage of the detail and color your DM has provided. If your character follows a particular mythos, expect him to have abilities, spells, and restrictions different from the generic cleric.

Priesthood in any mythos must be defined in five categories: requirements, weapons allowed, spells allowed, granted powers, and ethos.

Requirements

Before a character can become a priest of a particular mythos, certain requirements must be met. These usually involve minimum ability scores and mandatory alignments. All priests, regardless of mythos, must have Wisdom scores of at least 9. Beyond this, your DM can set other requirements as needed. A god of battle, for example, should require strong, healthy priests (13 Str, 12 Con). One whose sphere is art and beauty should demand high Wisdom and Charisma (16 or better). Most deities demand a specific type of behavior from their followers, and this will dictate alignment choices.

Weapons Allowed

Not all mythoi are opposed to the shedding of blood. Indeed, some require their priests to use swords, spears, or other specific weapons. A war deity might allow his priests to fight with spears or swords. An agricultural deity might emphasize weapons derived from farm implements—sickles and bills, for example. A deity of peace and harmony might grant only the simplest and least harmful weapons—perhaps only lassoes and nets. Given below are some suggested weapons, but many more are

possible (the DM *always* has the final word in this matter).

Deity	Weapon
Agriculture	Bill, flail, sickle
Blacksmith	War hammer
Death	Sickle
Disease	Scourge, whip
Earth	Pick
Healing	Man-catcher, quarterstaff
Hunt	Bow and arrows, javelin, light lance, sling, spear
Lightning	Dart, javelin, spear
Love	Bow and arrows, man-catcher
Nature	Club, scimitar, sickle
Oceans	Harpoon, spear, trident
Peace	Quarterstaff
Strength	Hammer
Thunder	Club, mace, war hammer
War	Battle axe, mace, morning star, spear, sword
Wind	Blowgun, dart

Of course there are many other reasons a deity might be associated with a particular weapon or group of weapons. These are often cultural, reflecting the weapons used by the people of the area. There may be a particular legend associated with the deity, tying it to some powerful artifact weapon (Thor's hammer, for example). The DM has the final choice in all situations.

Spells Allowed

A priest of a particular mythos is allowed to cast spells from only a few, related spheres. The priest's deity will have major and minor accesses to certain spheres, and this determines the spells available to the priest. (Each deity's access to spheres is determined by the DM as he creates the pantheon of his world.) The 16 spheres of influence are defined in the following paragraphs.

A priest whose deity grants major access to a sphere can choose from any spell within that sphere (provided he is high enough in level to cast it), while one allowed only minor access to the sphere is limited to spells of 3rd level or below in that sphere. The combination of major and minor accesses to spheres results in a wide variation in the spells available to priests who worship different deities.

All refers to spells usable by any priest, regardless of mythos. There are no Powers (deities) of the Sphere of All. This group includes spells the priest needs to perform basic functions.

Animal spells are those that affect or alter creatures. It does not include spells that affect people. Deities of nature and husbandry typically operate in this sphere.

Astral is a small sphere of spells that enable movement or communication between the different planes of existence. The

masters of a plane or particularly meddlesome Powers often grant spells from this sphere.

Charm spells are those that affect the attitudes and actions of people. Deities of love, beauty, trickery, and art often allow access to this sphere.

Combat spells are those that can be used to directly attack or harm the enemies of the priest or his mythos. These are often granted by deities of war or death.

Creation spells enable the priest to produce something from nothing, often to benefit his followers. This sphere can fill many different roles, from a provider to a trickster.

Divination enables the priest to learn the safest course of action in a particular situation, find a hidden item, or recover long-forgotten information. Deities of wisdom and knowledge typically have access to this sphere.

Elemental spells are all those that affect the four basic elements of creation—earth, air, fire, and water. Nature deities, elemental deities, those representing or protecting various crafts, and the deities of sailors would all draw spells from this sphere.

Guardian spells place magical sentries over an item or person. These spells are more active than protection spells because they create an actual guardian creature of some type. Protective, healing, and trickster deities may all grant spells of this sphere.

Healing spells are those that cure diseases, remove afflictions, or heal wounds. These spells cannot restore life or regrow lost limbs. Healing spells can be reversed to cause injury, but such use is restricted to evil priests. Protective and merciful deities are most likely to grant these spells, while nature deities may have lesser access to them.

Necromantic spells restore to a creature some element of its life-force that has been totally destroyed. It might be life, a limb, or an experience level. These spells in reverse are powerfully destructive, and are used only by extremely evil priests. Deities of life or death are most likely to act in this sphere.

Plant spells affect plants, ranging from simple agriculture (improving crops and the like) to communicating with plant-like creatures. Agricultural and nature Powers grant spells in this sphere.

Protection spells create mystical shields to defend the priest or his charges from evil attacks. War and protective deities are most likely to use these, although one devoted to mercy and kindness might also bestow these spells.

Summoning spells serve to call creatures from other places, or even other dimensions, to the service of the priest. Such service is often against the will of the creature, so casting these spells often involves great risk. Since creatures summoned often cause great harm and destruction, these spells are sometimes bestowed by war or death powers.

Sun spells are those dealing in the basic powers of the solar universe—the purity of light and its counterpart darkness. Sun spells are very common with nature, agricultural, or life-giving powers.

Weather spells enable the priest to manipulate the forces of weather. Such manipulation can be as simple as providing rain to parched fields, or as complex as unbridling the power of a raging tempest. Not surprisingly, these tend to be the province of nature and agricultural powers and appear in the repertoire of sea and ocean powers.

Additional spheres can be created by your DM. The listed spheres are typical of the areas in which deities concentrate their interest and power. Spells outside the deity's major and minor spheres of influence are not available to its priests.

Furthermore, the priest can obtain his spells at a faster or slower pace than the normal cleric. Should the character's ethos place emphasis on self-reliance, the spell progression is slower. Those deities associated with many amazing and wondrous events might grant more spells per level. Of course, your DM has final say on this, and he must balance the gain or loss of spells against the other powers, abilities, and restrictions of the character.

Granted Powers

Another aspect of a specific mythos is the special powers available to its priests. The cleric's granted power is the ability to turn undead. This ability, however, is not common to all priests. Other deities grant powers in accordance with their spheres. If your DM is using a specific mythos, he must decide what power is granted to your priest. Some possible suggestions are given below.

* *Incite Berserker Rage*, adding a +2 bonus to attack and damage rolls (War).

* *Soothing Word*, able to remove fear and influence hostile reactions (Peace, Mercy, Healing).

* *Charm or Fascination*, which could act as a *suggestion* spell (Love, Beauty, Art).

* *Inspire Fear*, radiating an aura of fear similar to the *fear* spell (Death).

These are only a few of the granted powers that might be available to a character. As with allowed weapons, much depends on the culture of the region and the tales and legends surrounding the Power and its priests.

Ethos

All priests must live by certain tenets and beliefs. These guide the priests' behavior. Clerics generally try to avoid shedding blood and try to aid their community. A war deity may order its priests to be at the forefront of battles and to actively crusade against all enemies. A harvest deity may want its priests to be active in the fields. The ethos may also dictate what alignment the priest must be. The nature of the mythos helps define the strictures the priest must follow.

Priest Titles

Priests of differing mythoi often go by titles and names other than priest. A priest of nature, for example (especially one based on Western European tradition) could be called a druid (see this page). Shamans and witch doctors are also possibilities. A little library research will turn up many more unique and colorful titles, a few of which are listed here:

Abbess, Abbot, Ayatollah, Bonze, Brother, Dom, Eye of the Law, Friar, Guru, Hajji, Imam, Mendicant, Metropolitan, Mullah, Pardoner, Patriarch, Prelate, Prior, Qadi, Rector, Vicar, and Yogi

Balancing It All

When creating a priest of a specific mythos, careful attention must be given to the balance of the character's different abilities. A priest strong in one area or having a wide range of choice must be appropriately weakened in another area so that he does not become too powerful compared to the other priests in the game. If a war deity allows a priest the use of all weapons and armor, the character should be limited in the spells allowed or powers granted. At the other extreme, a character who follows a deity of peace should have significant spells and granted powers to make up for his extremely limited or non-existent choice of weapons. A druid, for example, has more granted powers than a normal cleric to compensate for his limited armor and spell selection.

Druid

Ability Requirements: Wisdom 12
Charisma 15
Prime Requisites: Wisdom, Charisma
Races Allowed: Human, Half-elf

> Historically, druids lived among the Germanic tribes of Western Europe and Britain during the days of the Roman Empire. They acted as advisors to chieftains and held great influence over the tribesmen. Central to their thinking was the belief that the earth was the mother and source of all life. They revered many natural things—the sun, moon, and certain trees—as deities. Druids in the AD&D® game, however, are only loosely patterned after these historical figures. They are not required to behave like or follow the beliefs of historical druids.

The druid is an example of a priest designed for a specific mythos. His powers and beliefs are different from those of the cleric. The druid is a priest of nature and guardian of the wilderness, be it forest, plains, or jungle.

Requirements

A druid must be human or half-elven. He must have a Wisdom score of at least 12 and a Charisma score of 15 or more. Both of these abilities are prime requisites.

Weapons Allowed

Unlike the cleric, the druid is allowed to use only "natural" armors—leather armor and wooden shields, including those with magical enhancements. All other armors are forbidden to him. His weapons are limited to club, sickle, dart, spear, dagger, scimitar, sling, and staff.

Spells Allowed

Druids do not have the same range of spells as clerics. They have major access to the following spheres: all, animal, elemental, healing, plant, and weather. They have minor access to the divination sphere. Druids can use all magical items normally allowed priests, except for those that are written (books and scrolls) and armor and weapons not normally allowed for druids.

Granted Powers

A druid makes most saving throws as a priest, but he gains a bonus of +2 to all saving throws vs. fire or electrical attacks.

All druids can speak a secret language in addition to any other tongues they know. (If the optional proficiency rules are used, this language does not use a proficiency slot.) The vocabulary of this druidic language is limited to dealing with nature and natural events. Druids jealously guard this language; it is the one infallible method they have of recognizing each another.

Additional powers are granted as the druid reaches higher levels:

* He can identify plants, animals, and pure water with perfect accuracy after he reaches 3rd level.

* He can pass through overgrown areas (thick thorn bushes, tangled vines, briar patches, etc.) without leaving a trail and at his normal movement rate after he reaches 3rd level.

* He can learn the languages of woodland creatures. These include centaurs, dryads, elves, fauns, gnomes, dragons, giants, lizard men, manticores, nixies, pixies, sprites, and treants. The druid can add one language at 3rd level and one more every time he advances a level above 3rd. (If the optional proficiency rules are used, it is the druid's choice whether or not to spend a proficiency slot on one or more of these languages.)

* He is immune to *charm* spells cast by woodland creatures (dryads, nixies, etc.) after he reaches 7th level.

* He gains the ability to shapechange into a reptile, bird, or mammal up to three times per day after he reaches 7th level. Each animal form (reptile, bird, or mammal) can be used only once per day. The size can vary from that of a bullfrog or small bird to as large as a black bear. Upon assuming a new form, the druid heals 10 to 60 percent (1d6 x 10%) of all damage he has suffered (round fractions down). The druid can only assume the form of a normal (real world) animal in its normal proportions, but by doing so he takes on all of that creature's characteristics—its movement rate and abilities, its Armor Class, number of attacks, and damage per attack.

Thus, a druid could change into a wren to fly across a river, transform into a black bear on the opposite side and attack the orcs gathered there, and finally change into a snake to escape into the bushes before more orcs arrive.

The druid's clothing and one item held in each hand also become part of the new body; these reappear when the druid resumes his normal shape. The items cannot be used while the druid is in animal form.

*A druid *cannot* turn undead.

Ethos

As protectors of nature, druids are aloof from the complications of the temporal world. Their greatest concern is for the continuation of the orderly and proper cycles of nature—birth, growth, death, and rebirth. Druids tend to view all things as cyclic and thus the battles of good and evil are only the rising and falling tides of time. Only when the cycle and balance are disrupted does the druid become concerned. Given this view of things, the druid must be neutral in alignment.

Druids are charged with protecting wilderness—in particular trees, wild plants, wild animals, and crops. By association, they are also responsible for their followers and their animals. Druids recognize that all creatures (including humans) need food, shelter, and protection from harm. Hunting, farming, and cutting lumber for homes are logical and necessary parts of the natural cycle. However, druids do not tolerate unnecessary destruction or exploitation of nature for profit. Druids often prefer subtle and devious methods of revenge against those who defile nature. It is well known that druids are both very unforgiving and very patient.

Mistletoe is an important holy symbol to druids and it is a necessary part of some spells (those requiring a holy symbol). To be fully effective, the mistletoe must be gathered by the light of the full moon using a golden or silver sickle specially made for the purpose. Mistletoe gathered by other means halves the effectiveness of a given spell, if it causes damage or has an area of effect, and grants the target a +2 bonus to his saving throw if a saving throw is applicable.

Druids as a class do not dwell permanently in castles, cities, or towns. All druids prefer to live in sacred groves, where they build small sod, log, or stone cottages.

Druid Organization

Druids have a worldwide structure. At their upper levels (12th and above), only a few druids can hold each level.

Druids, Archdruids, and the Great Druid

At 12th level, the druid character acquires the official title of "druid" (all druid characters below 12th level are officially known as "initiates"). There can be only nine 12th-level druids in any geographic region (as defined by oceans, seas, and mountain ranges; a continent may consist of three or four such regions). A character cannot reach 12th level unless he takes his place as one of the nine druids. This is possible only if there are currently fewer than nine druids in the region, or if the character defeats one of the nine druids in magical or hand-to-hand combat, thereby assuming the defeated druid's position. If such combat is not mortal, the loser drops experience points so that he has exactly 200,000 remaining—just enough to be 11th level.

The precise details of each combat are worked out between the two combatants in advance. The combat can be magical, non-magical, or a mixture of both. It can be fought to the death, until only one character is unconscious, until a predetermined number of hit points is lost, or even until the first blow is landed, although in this case both players would have to be supremely confident of their abilities. Whatever can be agreed upon between the characters is legitimate, so long as there is some element of skill and risk.

When a character becomes a 12th-level druid, he gains three underlings. Their level depends on the character's position among the nine druids. The druid with the most experience points is served by three initiates of 9th level; the second-most experienced druid is served by three initiates of 8th level; and so on, until the least experienced druid is served by three 1st-level initiates.

Only three archdruids (13th level) can operate in a geographical region. To become an archdruid, a 12th-level druid must defeat one of the reigning archdruids or advance into a vacant position. Each of the three archdruids is served by three initiates of 10th level. From among the archdruids of the entire world, three are chosen to serve the Grand Druid (see "The Grand Druid and Hierophant Druids" section). These three retain their attendees but are themselves servants of the Grand Druid.

The great druid (14th level) is unique in his region. He, too, won his position from the previous great druid. He is served by three initiates of 11th level.

The ascendance of a new great druid usually sets off shock waves of turmoil and chaos through the druidical hierarchy. The advancement of an archdruid creates an opening that is fiercely contested by the druids, and the advancement of a druid creates an opening in their ranks.

The Grand Druid and Hierophant Druids

The highest ranking druid in the world is the Grand Druid (15th level). Unlike great druids (several of whom can operate simultaneously in different lands), only one person in a world can ever hold this title at one time. Consequently, only one druid can be 15th level at any time.

The Grand Druid knows six spells of each level (instead of the normal spell progression) and also can cast up to six additional spell levels, either as a single spell or as several spells whose levels total to six (e.g., one 6th-level spell, six 1st-level spells, three 2nd-level spells, etc.).

The Grand Druid is attended by nine other druids who are subject only to him and have nothing to do with the hierarchy of any specific land or area. Any druid character of any level can seek the Grand Druid and ask to serve him. Three of these nine are archdruids who roam the world, acting as his messengers and agents. Each of them receives four additional spell levels. The remainder are normally druids of 7th to 11th level, although the Grand Druid can request a druid of any level to serve him and often considers applications from humble aspirants.

The position of Grand Druid is not won through combat. Instead, the Grand Druid selects his successor from the acting great druids. The position is demanding, thankless, and generally unexciting for anyone except a politician. After a few hundred thousand experience points of such stuff, any adventurer worthy of the name probably is ready to move on to something else.

For this reason, the Grand Druid reaches 16th level after earning only 500,000 more experience points. After reaching 16th level, the Grand Druid can step down from his position at any time, provided he can find a suitable successor (another druid with 3,000,000 experience points).

Upon stepping down, the former Grand Druid must relinquish the six bonus spell levels and all of his experience points but 1 (he keeps the rest of his abilities). He is now a 16th-level hierophant druid, and begins advancing anew (using the progression given in Table 23). The character may rise as high as 20th level as a hierophant druid (almost always through self training).

Beyond 15th level, a druid never gains any new spells (ignore the Priest Spell Progression table from this point on). Casting level continues to rise with experience. Rather than spells, spell-like powers are acquired.

16th level: At 16th level, the hierophant druid gains four powers:

* Immunity to all natural poisons. Natural poisons are ingested or insinuated animal or vegetable poisons, including monster poisons, but not mineral poisons or poison gas.

* Vigorous health for a person of his age. The hierophant is no longer subject to the ability score adjustments for aging.

* The ability to alter his appearance at will. Appearance alteration is accomplished in one round. A height and weight increase or decrease of 50 percent is possible, with an apparent age from childhood to extreme old age. Body and facial features can resemble any human or humanoid creature. This alteration is not magical, so it cannot be detected by any means short of *true seeing*.

17th Level: The character gains the biological ability to hibernate. His body functions slow to the point where the character may appear dead to a casual observer; aging ceases. The character is completely unconscious during hibernation. He awakens either at a preordained time ("I will hibernate for 20 days") or when there is a significant change in his environment (the weather turns cold, someone hits him with a stick, etc.).

A 17th-level hierophant druid can also enter the elemental plane of Earth at will. The transference takes one round to complete. This ability also provides the means to survive on that plane, move around, and return to the Prime Material plane at will. It does not confer similar abilities or immunities on the Prime Material plane.

18th level: The character gains the ability to enter and survive in the elemental plane of Fire.

19th level: The character gains the ability to enter and survive in the elemental plane of Water.

20th level: The character gains the ability to enter and survive in the elemental plane of Air.

Rogue

Rogues are people who feel that the world (and everyone in it) somehow owes them a living. They get by day by day, living in the highest style they can afford and doing as little work as possible. The less they have to toil and struggle like everyone else (while maintaining a comfortable standard of living), the better off they think they are. While this attitude is neither evil nor cruel, it does not foster a good reputation. Many a rogue has a ques-

tionable past or a shady background he'd prefer was left uninvestigated.

Rogues combine a few of the qualities of the other character classes. They are allowed to use a wide variety of magical items, weapons, and armor.

Rogues have some special abilities that are unique to their group. All rogues tend to be adept at languages and thus have a percentage chance to read strange writings they come across. All are skilled in climbing and clinging to small cracks and outcroppings—even more skilled than the hardy men of the mountains. They are alert and attentive, hearing things that others would miss. Finally, they are dextrous (and just a little bit light-fingered), able to perform tricks and filch small items with varying degrees of success.

Rogues have a number of special abilities, such as picking pockets and detecting noise, for which they are given a percentage chance of success (this chance depends on the class, level, Dexterity score, and race of the rogue). When a rogue tries to use a special ability, a percentile dice roll determines whether the attempt succeeds or fails. If the dice roll is equal to or less than the special ability score, the attempt succeeds. Otherwise, it fails. (See this page and page 39 for more details.)

All rogues use Table 25 to determine their advancement in levels as they gain experience points.

All rogues gain one six-sided Hit Die (1d6) per level from 1st through 10th. *After 10th level, rogues earn 2 hit points per level and no longer receive additional hit point bonuses for high Constitution scores.*

Table 25: ROGUE EXPERIENCE LEVELS

Level	Thief/Bard	Hit Dice (d6)
1	0	1
2	1,250	2
3	2,500	3
4	5,000	4
5	10,000	5
6	20,000	6
7	40,000	7
8	70,000	8
9	110,000	9
10	160,000	10
11	220,000	10 + 2
12	440,000	10 + 4
13	660,000	10 + 6
14	880,000	10 + 8
15	1,100,000	10 + 10
16	1,320,000	10 + 12
17	1,540,000	10 + 14
18	1,760,000	10 + 16
19	1,980,000	10 + 18
20	2,200,000	10 + 20

Thief

Ability Requirement: Dexterity 9
Prime Requisite: Dexterity
Races Allowed: All

Thieves come in all sizes and shapes, ready to live off the fat of the land by the easiest means possible. In some ways they are the epitome of roguishness.

> The profession of thief is not honorable, yet it is not entirely dishonorable, either. Many famous folk heroes have been more than a little larcenous—Reynard the Fox, Robin Goodfellow, and Ali Baba are but a few. At his best, the thief is a romantic hero fired by noble purpose but a little wanting in strength of character. Such a person may truly strive for good but continually run afoul of temptation.

The thief's prime requisite is Dexterity; a character must have a minimum score of 9 to qualify for the class. While high numbers in other scores (particularly Intelligence) are desirable, they are not necessary. The thief can have any alignment except lawful good. Many are at least partially neutral.

A thief with a Dexterity score of 16 or more gains a 10 percent bonus to the experience points he earns.

Thieves have a limited selection of weapons. Most of their time is spent practicing thieving skills. The allowed weapons are club, dagger, dart, hand crossbow, knife, lasso, short bow, sling, broad sword, long sword, short sword, and staff. A thief can wear leather, studded leather, padded leather, or elven chain armor. When wearing any allowed armor other than leather, the thief's abilities are penalized (see Table 29).

To determine the initial value of each skill, start with the base scores listed on Table 26. To these base scores, add (or subtract) any appropriate modifiers for race, Dexterity, and armor worn (given on Tables 27, 28, and 29, respectively).

The scores arrived at in the preceding paragraph do not reflect the effort a thief has spent honing his skills. To simulate this extra training, all thieves at 1st level receive 60 discretionary percentage points that they can add to their base scores. No more than 30 points can be assigned to any single skill. Other than this restriction, the player can distribute the points however he wants.

Each time the thief rises a level in experience, the player receives another 30 points to distribute. No more than 15 points per level can be assigned to a single skill, and no skill can be raised above 95 percent, including all adjustments for Dexterity, race, and armor. As an option, the DM can rule that some portion of the points earned must be applied to skills used during the course of the adventure.

Table 26: THIEVING SKILL BASE SCORES

Skill	Base Score
Pick Pockets	15%
Open Locks	10%
Find/Remove Traps	5%
Move Silently	10%
Hide in Shadows	5%
Detect Noise	15%
Climb Walls	60%
Read Languages	0%

In addition to the base percentages listed above, demihuman characters and characters with high or low Dexterity scores have adjustments to their base numbers. Some characters may find that, after adjustments, they have negative scores. In this case, the character must spend points raising his skill percentage to at least 1% before he can use the skill. (Some races just aren't very good at certain things!)

A thief character uses the "No Armor" column if wearing *bracers of defense* or a cloak without large or heavy protective clothing.

Skill Explanations

Pick Pockets: The thief uses this skill when filching small items from other peoples' pockets, sleeves, girdles, packs, etc., when palming items (such as keys), and when performing simple sleight of hand.

A failed attempt means the thief did not get an item, but it does not mean that his attempt was detected. To determine whether the victim noticed the thief's indiscretion, subtract three times the victim's level from 100. If the thief's pick pockets roll was equal to or greater than this number, the attempt is detected. A 0th-level victim, for example, notices the attempt only if the roll was 00 (100), while a 13th-level character notices the attempt on a dice roll of 61 or more. In some cases, the attempt may succeed and be noticed at the same time.

> If the DM wishes, he can rule that a thief of higher level than his victim is less likely to be caught pilfering. The chance that the victim notices the attempt can be modified by subtracting the victim's level from the thief's level, and then adding this number to the percentage chance the

> thief is detected. For example, Ragnar, a 15th-level thief, tries to pick the pocket of Horace, a 9th-level fighter. Normally, Ragnar would be detected if his pick pockets roll was 73 or more (100-[3 × 9] = 73). Using this optional system, since Ragnar is six levels higher than Horace, this number is increased by six to 79 (73 + 6 = 79). This option only applies if the thief is higher level than his victim.

A thief can try to pick someone's pocket as many times as he wants. Neither failure nor success prevents additional attempts, but getting caught might!

Open Locks: A thief can try to pick padlocks, finesse combination locks (if they exist), and solve puzzle locks (locks with sliding panels, hidden releases, and concealed keyholes). Picking a padlock requires tools. Using typical thief's tools grants normal chances for success. Using improvised tools (a bit of wire, a thin dirk, a stick, etc.) imposes a penalty on the character's chance for success. The DM sets the penalty based on the situation; penalties can range from −5 for an improvised but suitable tool, to −60 for an awkward and unsuitable item (like a stick). The amount of time required to pick a lock is 1d10 rounds. A thief can try to pick a particular lock only once per experience level. If the attempt fails, the lock is simply too difficult for the character until he learns more about picking locks (goes up a level).

Find/Remove Traps: The thief is trained to find small traps and alarms. These include poisoned needles, spring blades, deadly gases, and warning bells. This skill is not effective for finding deadfall ceilings, crushing walls, or other large, mechanical traps.

To find the trap, the thief must be able to touch and inspect the trapped object. Normally, the DM rolls the dice to determine whether the thief finds a trap. If the DM says, "You didn't find any traps," it's up to the player to decide whether that means there are no traps or there are traps but the thief didn't see them. If the thief finds a trap, he knows its general principle but not its exact nature. A thief can check an item for traps once per experience level. Searching for a trap takes 1d10 rounds.

Once a trap is found, the thief can try to remove it or disarm it. This also requires 1d10 rounds. If the dice roll indicates success, the trap is disarmed. If the dice roll indicates failure, the trap is beyond the thief's current skill. He can try disarming the trap again when he advances to the next experience level. If the dice roll is 96-100, the thief accidentally triggers the trap and suffers the consequences. Sometimes (usually because his percentages are low) a thief will deliberately spring a trap rather than

Table 27: THIEVING SKILL RACIAL ADJUSTMENTS

Skill	Dwarf	Elf	Gnome	Half-elf	Halfling
Pick Pockets	—	+5%	—	+10%	+5%
Open Locks	+10%	−5%	+5%	—	+5%
Find/Remove Traps	+15%	—	+10%	—	+5%
Move Silently	—	+5%	+5%	—	+10%
Hide in Shadows	—	+10%	+5%	+5%	+15%
Detect Noise	—	+5%	+10%	—	+5%
Climb Walls	−10%	—	−15%	—	−15%
Read Languages	−5%	—	—	—	−5%

Table 28: THIEVING SKILL DEXTERITY ADJUSTMENTS

Dexterity	Pick Pockets	Open Locks	Find/Remove Traps	Move Silently	Hide in Shadows
9	−15%	−10%	−10%	−20%	−10%
10	−10%	−5%	−10%	−15%	−5%
11	−5%	—	−5%	−10%	—
12	—	—	—	−5%	—
13-15	—	—	—	—	—
16	—	+5%	—	—	—
17	+5%	+10%	—	+5%	+5%
18	+10%	+15%	+5%	+10%	+10%
19	+15%	+20%	+10%	+15%	+15%

Table 29: THIEVING SKILL ARMOR ADJUSTMENTS

Skill	No Armor	Elven Chain*	Padded or Studded Leather
Pick Pockets	+5%	−20%	−30%
Open Locks	—	−5%	−10%
Find/Remove Traps	—	−5%	−10%
Move Silently	+10%	−10%	−20%
Hide in Shadows	+5%	−10%	−20%
Detect Noise	—	−5%	−10%
Climb Walls	+10%	−20%	−30%
Read Languages	—	—	—

* Bards (only) in non-elven chain mail suffer an additional −5% penalty.

have unpleasant side effects if the trap doesn't work quite the way the thief thought, and he triggers it while standing in the wrong place.

This skill is far less useful when dealing with magical or invisible traps. Thieves can attempt to remove these traps, but their chances of success are half their normal percentages.

Move Silently: A thief can try to move silently at any time simply by announcing that he intends to do so. While moving silently, the thief's movement rate is reduced to 1/3 normal. The DM rolls percentile dice to determine whether the thief is moving silently; the thief always *thinks* he is being quiet. Successful silent movement improves the thief's chance to surprise a victim, avoid discovery, or move into position to stab an enemy in the back. Obviously, a thief moving silently but in plain view of his enemies is wasting his time.

Hide in Shadows: A thief can try to disappear into shadows or any other type of concealment—bushes, curtains, crannies, etc. A thief can hide this way only when no one is looking at him; he remains hidden only as long as he remains virtually motionless. (The thief can make small, slow, careful movements: draw a weapon, uncork a potion, etc.) A thief can never become hidden while a guard is watching him, no matter what his dice roll is—his position is obvious to the guard. However, trying to hide from a creature that is locked in battle with another is possible, as the enemy's attention is fixed elsewhere. The DM rolls the dice and keeps the result secret, but the thief always *thinks* he is hidden.

Hiding in shadows cannot be done in total darkness, since the talent lies in fooling the eye as much as in finding real concealment (camouflage, as it were). However, hidden characters are equally concealed to those with or without infravision. Spells, magical items, and special abilities that reveal invisible objects can reveal the location of a hidden thief.

Detect Noise: A good thief pays attention to every detail, no matter how small, including faint sounds that most others miss. His ability to hear tiny sounds (behind heavy doors, down long hallways, etc.) is much better than the ordinary person's. Listening is not automatic; the thief must stand still and concentrate on what he's hearing for one round. He must have silence in his immediate surroundings and must remove his helmet or hat. Sounds filtering through doors or other barriers are unclear at best.

Climb Walls: Although everyone can climb rocky cliffs and steep slopes, the thief is far superior to others in this ability. Not only does he have a better climbing percentage than other characters, he can also climb most surfaces without tools, ropes, or devices. Only the thief can climb smooth and very smooth surfaces without climbing gear. Of course, the thief is very limited in his actions while climbing—he is unable to fight or effectively defend himself.

Read Languages: Out of necessity, thieves tend to learn odd bits of information. Among these is the ability to read various languages, particularly as they apply to treasure maps, deeds, secret notes, and the like. At 4th level, the thief has enough exposure to languages that he has a chance to read most nonmagical writing. This ability naturally improves with more experience. However, your DM can rule that some languages (those the thief has never encountered) are indecipherable to the thief.

The die roll to read a language must be made every time the character tries to read a document (not just once per language). A successful die roll means the thief puzzled out the meaning of the writing. His understanding of the document is roughly equal to his percentage chance for success: a 20 percent chance means that, if the thief understands it at all, he gets about 20 percent of the meaning. A different document in the same language requires another die roll (it probably contains different words). It isn't necessary to keep notes about what languages the thief has read in the past, since each document is handled individually.

Only one die roll can be made for any particular document at a given experience level. If the die roll fails, the thief can try again after gaining a new experience level.

If the character knows how to read a given language because he spent a proficiency slot on it, this dice roll is unnecessary for documents in that language.

Thieves have other abilities not listed on Table 26:

Backstab: Thieves are weak in toe-to-toe hacking matches, but they are masters of the knife in the back. When attacking someone by surprise and from behind, a thief can improve his chance to successfully hit (+4 modifier for rear attack and negate the target's shield and Dexterity bonuses) and greatly increase the amount of damage his blow causes.

To use this ability, the thief must be behind his victim and the victim must be unaware that the thief intends to attack him. If an enemy sees the thief, hears him approach from a blind side, or is warned by another, he is not caught unaware, and the backstab is handled like a normal attack (although bonuses for a rear attack still apply). Opponents in battle will often notice a thief trying to maneuver behind them—the first rule of fighting is to never turn your back on an enemy! However, someone who isn't expecting to be attacked (a friend or ally, perhaps) can be caught unaware even if he knows the thief is behind him.

The multiplier given in Table 30 applies to the amount of damage before modifiers for Strength or weapon bonuses are added. The weapon's standard damage is multiplied by the value given in Table 30. Then strength and magical weapon bonuses are added.

Backstabbing does have limitations. First, the damage multiplier applies only to the first attack made by the thief, even if multiple attacks are possible. Once a blow is struck, the initial surprise effect is lost. Second, the thief cannot use it on every creature. The victim must be generally humanoid. Part of the skill comes from knowing just where to strike. A thief could backstab an ogre, but he wouldn't be able to do the same to a beholder. The victim must also have a definable back (which leaves out most slimes, jellies, oozes, and the like). Finally, the thief has to be able to reach a significant target area. To backstab a giant, the thief would have to be standing on a ledge or window balcony. Backstabbing him in the ankle just isn't going to be as effective.

Table 30: BACKSTAB DAMAGE MULTIPLIERS

Thief's Level	Damage Multiplier
1-4	× 2
5-8	× 3
9-12	× 4
13 +	× 5

The ogre marches down the hallway, peering into the gloom ahead. He fails to notice the shadowy form of Ragnar the thief hidden in an alcove. Slipping into the hallway, Ragnar creeps up behind the monster. As he sets himself to strike a mortal blow, his foot scrapes across the stone. The hairy ears of the ogre perk up. The beast whirls around, ruining Ragnar's chance for a backstab and what remains of his day. If Ragnar had made a successful roll to move silently, he could have attacked the ogre with a +4 bonus on his chance to hit and inflicted five times his normal damage (since he is 15th level).

Thieves' Cant: Thieves' cant is a special form of communication known by all thieves and their associates. It is not a distinct language; it consists of slang words and implied meanings that can be worked into any language. The vocabulary of thieves' cant limits its use to discussing things that interest thieves: stolen loot, easy marks, breaking and entering, mugging, confidence games, and the like. It is not a language, however. Two thieves cannot communicate via thieves' cant unless they know a common language. The cant is useful, however, for identifying fellow cads and bounders by slipping a few tidbits of lingo into a normal conversation.

The concept of thieves' cant is historical (the cant probably is still used today in one form or another), although in the AD&D® game it has an ahistorically broad base. A few hours of research at a large library should turn up actual examples of old thieves' cant for those who want to learn more about the subject.

Use Scrolls: At 10th level, a thief gains a limited ability to use magical and clerical scrolls. A thief's understanding of magical writings is far from complete, however. The thief has a 25 percent chance to read the scroll incorrectly and reverse the spell's effect. This sort of malfunction is almost always detrimental to the thief and his party. It could be as simple as accidentally casting the reverse of the given spell or as complex as a foul-up on a *fireball* scroll, causing the ball of flame to be centered on the thief instead of its intended target. The exact effect is up to the DM (this is the sort of thing DMs enjoy, so expect the unexpected).

Thieves do not build castles or fortresses in the usual sense. Instead, they favor small, fortified dwellings, especially if the true purpose of the building can easily be disguised. A thief might, for example, construct a well-protected den in a large city behind the facade of a seedy tavern or old warehouse. Naturally, the true nature of the place will be a closely guarded secret! Thieves almost always build their strongholds in or near cities, since that is where they ply their trades most lucratively.

This, of course, assumes that the thief is interested in operating a band of thieves out of his stronghold. Not all thieves have larceny in their hearts, however. If a character devoted his life to those aspects of thieving that focus on scouting, stealth, and the intricacies of locks and traps, he could build an entirely different sort of stronghold—one filled with the unusual and intriguing objects he has collected during his adventurous life. Like any thief's home, it should blend in with its surroundings; after all, a scout never advertises his whereabouts. It might be a formidable maze of rooms, secret passages, sliding panels, and mysterious paraphernalia from across the world.

Once a thief reaches 10th level, his reputation is such that he can attract followers—either a gang of scoundrels and scalawags or a group of scouts eager to learn from a reputed master. The thief attracts 4d6 of these fellows. They are generally loyal to him, but a wise thief is always suspicious of his comrades. Table 31 can be used to determine the type and level of followers, or the

DM can choose followers appropriate to his campaign.

Table 31: THIEF'S FOLLOWERS

D100 Roll	Follower	Level Range
01-03	Dwarf fighter/thief	1-4
04-08	Dwarf thief	1-6
09-13	Elf thief	1-6
14-15	Elf thief/fighter/mage	1-3
16-18	Elf thief/mage	1-4
19-24	Gnome thief	1-6
25-27	Gnome thief/fighter	1-4
28-30	Gnome thief/illusionist	1-4
31-35	Half-elf thief	1-6
36-38	Half-elf thief/fighter	1-4
39-41	Half-elf thief/fighter/mage	1-3
42-46	Halfling thief	1-8
47-50	Halfling thief/fighter	1-6
51-98	Human thief	1-8
99	Human dual-class thief/?	1-8/1-4
00	Other (DM selection)	—

Thieves tend to be very jealous of their territory. If more than one thief starts a gang in the same area, the result is usually a war. The feud continues until one side or the other is totally eliminated or forced to move its operation elsewhere.

Bard

Ability Requirements:	Dexterity 12
	Intelligence 13
	Charisma 15
Prime Requisite:	Dexterity, Charisma
Races Allowed:	Human, Half-elf

The bard is an optional character class that can be used if your DM allows. He makes his way in life by his charm, talent, and wit. A good bard should be glib of tongue, light of heart, and fleet of foot (when all else fails).

In precise historical terms, the title "bard" applies only to certain groups of Celtic poets who sang the history of their tribes in long, recitative poems. These bards, found mainly in Ireland, Wales, and Scotland, filled many important roles in their society. They were storehouses of tribal history, reporters of news, messengers, and even ambassadors to other tribes. However, in the AD&D® game, the bard is a more generalized character. Historical and legendary examples of the type include Alan-a-Dale, Will Scarlet, Amergin, and even Homer. Indeed, every culture has its storyteller or poet, whether he is called bard, skald, fili, jongleur, or something else.

To become a bard, a character must have a Dexterity of 12 or more, an Intelligence of 13 or more, and a Charisma of 15 or more. The prime requisites are Dexterity and Charisma. A bard can be lawful, neutral or chaotic, good or evil, but must always be partially neutral. Only by retaining some amount of detachment can he successfully fulfill his role as a bard.

A bard, by his nature, tends to learn many different skills. He is a jack-of-all-trades but master of none. Although he fights as a rogue, he can use any weapon. He can wear any armor up to, and including, chain mail, but he cannot use a shield.

All bards are proficient singers, chanters,

or vocalists and can play a musical instrument of the player's choice (preferably one that is portable). Additional instruments can be learned if the optional proficiency rules are used—the bard can learn two instruments for every proficiency slot spent.

In his travels, a bard also manages to learn a few wizard spells. Like a wizard, a bard's Intelligence determines the number of spells he can know and the chance to know any given spell. These he keeps in his spell book, abiding by all the restrictions on memorization and spell use that bind a mage, especially in the prohibition of armor. Hence, a bard will tend to use his spells more to entertain and impress than to fight. Table 32 lists the number of spells a bard can cast at each level.

Since bards are dabblers rather than full-time wizards, their spells tend to be gained by serendipity and happenstance. In no case can a bard choose to specialize in a school of magic. Beginning bards do not have a selection of spells. A 2nd-level bard begins with one to four spells, chosen either randomly or by the DM. (An Intelligence check must still be made to see if the bard can learn a given spell.) The bard is not guaranteed to know *read magic*, as this is not needed to read the writings in a spell book. The bard can add new spells to his spell book as he finds them, but he does not automatically gain additional spells as he advances in level. All spells beyond those he starts with must be found during the course of adventuring. The bard's casting level is equal to his current level.

Table 32: BARD SPELL PROGRESSION

Bard Level	Spell Level					
	1	2	3	4	5	6
1	—	—	—	—	—	—
2	1	—	—	—	—	—
3	2	—	—	—	—	—
4	2	1	—	—	—	—
5	3	1	—	—	—	—
6	3	2	—	—	—	—
7	3	2	1	—	—	—
8	3	3	1	—	—	—
9	3	3	2	—	—	—
10	3	3	2	1	—	—
11	3	3	3	1	—	—
12	3	3	3	2	—	—
13	3	3	3	2	1	—
14	3	3	3	3	1	—
15	3	3	3	3	2	—
16	4	3	3	3	2	1
17	4	4	3	3	3	1
18	4	4	4	3	3	2
19	4	4	4	4	3	2
20	4	4	4	4	4	3

Combat and spells, however, are not the main strength of the bard. His expertise is in dealing and communicating with others. To this end, the bard has a number of special powers. The base percentage for each power

is listed on Table 33. This base percentage must be adjusted for the race and Dexterity of the bard as given in the Thief description. After all adjustments are made, the player must distribute (however he chooses) 20 additional percentage points to the various special abilities. Thereafter, each time the character advances a level, he receives an additional 15 points to distribute.

Table 33: BARD ABILITIES

Climb Walls	Detect Noise	Pick Pockets	Read Languages
50%	20%	10%	5%

Bard abilities are subject to modifiers for situation and armor as per the thief (see page 39 for a complete explanation).

Climb Walls enables the bard to climb near sheer surfaces without the aid of tools, just like the thief.

Detect Noise improves the bard's chances of hearing and interpreting sounds. He may be able to overhear parts of a conversation on the other side of a door or pick up the sound of something stalking the party. To use the ability, the bard must stand unhelmeted and concentrate for one round (one minute). During this time, all other party members must remain silent. The DM secretly makes the check and informs the player of the result.

Pick Pockets enables the bard not only to filch small purses, wallets, keys, and the like, but also to perform small feats of sleight-of-hand (useful for entertaining a crowd). Complete details on pickpocketing (and your character's chances of getting caught) can be found in the Thief description.

Read Languages is an important ability, since words are the meat and drink of bards. They have some ability to read documents written in languages they do not know, relying on words and phrases they have picked up in their studies and travels. The Read Languages column in Table 33 gives the base percentage chance to puzzle out a foreign tongue. It also represents the degree of comprehension the bard has if he is successful. The DM can rule that a language is too rare or unfamiliar, especially if it has never been previously encountered by the bard, effectively foiling his attempts to translate it. At the other extreme, the bard need not make the dice roll for any language he is proficient in. Success is assumed to be automatic in such cases.

The bard can also influence reactions of groups of NPCs. When performing before a group that is not attacking (and not intending to attack in just seconds), the bard can try to alter the mood of the listeners. He can try to soften their mood or make it uglier. The method can be whatever is most suitable to the situation at the moment—a fiery speech, collection of jokes, a sad tale, a fine

tune played on a fiddle, a haunting lute melody, or a heroic song from the old homeland. Everyone in the group listening must roll a saving throw vs. paralyzation (if the crowd is large, make saving throws for groups of people using average hit dice). The die roll is modified by −1 for every three experience levels of the bard (round fractions down). If the saving throw fails, the group's reaction can be shifted one level (see the Reactions section in the *DMG*), toward either the friendly or hostile end of the scale, at the player's option. Those who make a successful saving throw have their reaction shifted one level toward the opposite end of the scale.

Cwell the Fine has been captured by a group of bandits and hauled into their camp. Although they are not planning to kill him on the spot, any fool can plainly see that his future may be depressingly short. In desperation, Cwell begins spinning a comic tale about Duke Dunderhead and his blundering knights. It has always been a hit with the peasants, and he figures it's worth a try here. Most of the bandits have 1 Hit Die, but the few higher level leaders raise the average level to 3. Cwell is only 2nd level so he gains no modifier. A saving throw is rolled and the group fails (Cwell succeeds!). The ruffians find his tale amusing. The player shifts their reaction from hostile to neutral. The bandits decide not to kill Cwell but to keep him around, under guard, to entertain them. If the bandits' saving throw had succeeded, the bandits would have been offended by the story (perhaps some of them served under Duke Dunderhead!), and their reaction would have shifted from hostile to violent. They probably would have roasted Cwell immediately.

This ability cannot affect people in the midst of battle; it is effective only when the audience has time to listen. If Cwell tried telling his tale while the bandits were attacking his group, the bandits would have quickly decided that Cwell was a fool and carried on with their business. Furthermore, the form of entertainment used must be appropriate to the audience. Cwell might be able to calm (or enrage) a bear with music, but he won't have much luck telling jokes to orcs unless he speaks their language.

The music, poetry, and stories of the bard can also be inspirational, rallying friends and allies. If the exact nature of an impending threat is known, the bard can heroically inspire his companions (immortalizing them in word and song), granting a +1 bonus to attack rolls, or a +1 bonus to saving throws, or a +2 bonus to morale (particularly useful in large battles) to those involved in melee. The bard must spend at least three full rounds singing or reciting before the battle begins. This affects those

within a range of 10 feet per experience level of the bard.

The effect lasts one round per level. Once the effect wears off, it can't be renewed if the recipients are still in battle. However, troops who have withdrawn from combat can be reinspired by the bard's words. A troop of soldiers, inspired by Cwell, could charge into battle. After fighting a fierce fight, they retreat and the enemy does not pursue. Cwell, seeing them crestfallen and dispirited, once again rouses their will to fight. Reinvigorated, they charge back into battle with renewed spirit.

Bards are also able to counter the effects of songs and poetry used as magical attacks. Characters within 30 feet of the bard are immune to the attack as long as the bard sings a counter song (or recites a poem, etc.). While doing this, the bard can perform no other action except a slow walk. Furthermore, if he is struck or fails a saving throw, his effort is ruined. Success is checked by having the bard make a saving throw vs. spell. Success blocks the attack, failure means the attack has its normal effect (everyone affected rolls saving throws, normal damage is inflicted, etc.). The bard can use this ability once per encounter or battle. This power does not affect verbal spell components or command words; it is effective against spells that involve explanations, commands, or suggestions.

Finally, bards learn a little bit of everything in their studies and travels. Thus all bards can read and write their native tongue (if a written language exists) and all know local history (without cost if the optional proficiency rules are used). Furthermore, bards have a 5 percent chance per experience level to identify the general purpose and function of any magical item. The bard need not handle the item but must examine it closely. Even if successful, the exact function of the item is not revealed, only its general nature.

Since Cwell the Fine is 2nd level, he has a 10 percent chance to know something about a magical *sword +1*. If he succeeds, he knows whether the sword is cursed and whether it has an alignment ("This sword was used by the evil warrior Lurdas. I wouldn't touch it if I were you!"). This ability does not enable him to identify the sword's exact properties, only its history and background. He has no idea of its bonuses or penalties or any special magical powers, except as can be inferred from the histories.

Being something of a warrior, a bard can build a stronghold and attract followers upon reaching 9th level. The bard attracts 10d6 0th-level soldiers into his service. They arrive over a period of time, but they are not automatically replaced if lost in battle. Of course, a bard can build a stronghold any time, but no followers arrive until he reaches 9th level.

Upon reaching 10th level, a bard can attempt to use magical devices of written nature—scrolls, books, etc. However, his understanding of magic is imperfect (although better than that of a thief), so there is a 15% chance that any written item he uses is read incorrectly. When this happens, the magical power works the opposite of what is intended, generally to the detriment of the bard or his friends. The DM will tell you what happens to your character, based on the situation and particular magical item. The result may be unpleasant, deadly, or embarrassing. (Deciding these things is part of the DM's fun!)

Multi-Class and Dual-Class Characters

A multi-class character improves in two or more classes simultaneously. His experience is divided equally between each class. The available class combinations vary according to race. The character can use the abilities of both classes at any time, with only a few restrictions. Only demihumans can be multi-class characters.

A dual-class character is one who starts with a single class, advances to moderate level, and then changes to a second character class and starts over again. The character retains the benefits and abilities of the first class but never again earns experience for using them. There are some limitations on combining the abilities of the two classes but, as long as minimum ability and alignment requirements are met, there are no restrictions on the possible character class combinations. Only humans can be dual-class characters.

Multi-Class Combinations

All of the standard demihuman races are listed here, along with their allowable multi-class combinations. Note that the character class names (not group names) are used below.

Dwarf	Halfling
Fighter/Thief	Fighter/Thief
Fighter/Cleric	

Elf	Half-elf
Fighter/Mage	Fighter/Cleric
Fighter/Thief	Fighter/Thief
Mage/Thief	Fighter/Druid
Fighter/Mage/Thief	Fighter/Mage
	Cleric/Ranger
Gnome	Cleric/Mage
Fighter/Cleric	Thief/Mage
Fighter/Illusionist	Fighter/Mage/Cleric
Fighter/Thief	Fighter/Mage/Thief
Cleric/Illusionist	
Cleric/Thief	
Illusionist/Thief	

As stated earlier in their description, specialist wizards cannot be multi-class (gnome illusionists are the single exception to this rule). The required devotion to their single field prevents specialist wizards from applying themselves to other classes. Priests of a specific mythos might be allowed as a multi-class option; this will depend on the nature of the mythos as determined by the DM.

Multi-Class Benefits and Restrictions

A multi-class character always uses the most favorable combat value and the best saving throw from his different classes.

The character's hit points are the average of all his Hit Dice rolls. When the character is first created, the player rolls hit points for each class separately, totals them up, then divides by the number of dice rolled (round fractions down). Any Constitution bonus is then added to the character's hit points. If one of the character's classes is fighter and he has a Constitution of 17 or 18, then he gains the +3 or +4 Constitution bonus available only to warriors (instead of the +2 maximum available to the other character classes).

Later the character is likely to gain levels in different classes at different times. When this happens, roll the appropriate Hit Die and divide the result by the number of classes the character has (round fractions down, but a Hit Die never yields less than 1 hit point). The character's Constitution bonus is split between his classes; thus a fighter/mage gets 1/2 of his Con bonus when he goes up a level as a fighter and the other 1/2 of the Con bonus when he goes up a level as a mage. A fighter/mage/thief would get 1/3 of his bonus when he goes up as a fighter, 1/3 when he goes up as a mage, and the other 1/3 when he goes up as a thief.

If the optional proficiency system is used, the character starts with the largest number of proficiency slots of the different classes. Thereafter, he gains new proficiency slots at the fastest of the given rates. To determine the character's initial money, roll according to the most generous of the character's different classes.

Rupert's character, Morrison the Multi-Faceted, is a half-elf fighter/mage/thief. At 1st level, Morrison rolls three dice for hit points: 1d10 (fighter), 1d6 (thief), and 1d4 (mage). The results are 6, 5, and 2. Their sum (13) is divided by three and rounded down to equal 4 (13/3 = 4 1/3 = 4). Morrison begins the game with 4 hit points. Later, Morrison reaches 2nd level as a thief before he reaches 2nd level as a fighter or a mage. He rolls 1d6 for additional hit points and the result is 4. He divides this by 3 (because he has three classes) and rounds down. Morrison gets 1 more hit point when he becomes a

2nd-level thief. (He will also roll 1d10 and 1d4 [both rolls divided by 3] when he reaches 2nd level as a fighter and as a mage, respectively.)

Multi-class characters can combine abilities from their different classes with the following restrictions:

Warrior: A multi-classed warrior can use all of his abilities without restriction. The warrior abilities form the base for other character classes.

Priest: Regardless of his other classes, a multi-classed priest must abide by the weapon restrictions of his mythos. Thus, a fighter/cleric can use only bludgeoning weapons (but he uses the warrior combat value). He retains all his normal priest abilities.

Wizard: A multi-classed wizard can freely combine the powers of the wizard with any other class allowed, although the wearing of armor is restricted. Elves wearing elven chain can cast spells in armor, as magic is part of the nature of elves. However, elven chain is extremely rare and can never be purchased. It must be given, found, or won.

Thief: A multi-classed thief cannot use any thieving abilities other than open locks or detect noise if he is wearing armor that is normally not allowed to thieves. He must remove his gauntlets to open locks and his helmet to detect noise.

Dual-Class Benefits and Restrictions

Only humans can be dual-classed characters. To be dual-classed, the character must have scores of 15 or more in the prime requisites of his first class and scores of 17 or more in the prime requisites of any classes he switches to. The character selects one class to begin his adventuring life. He can advance in this class as many levels as he desires before switching to another class; there is no cut-off point beyond which a character cannot switch. However, he must attain at least 2nd level in his current class before changing to another class. There is no limit to the number of classes a character can acquire, as long as he has the ability scores and wants to make the change. (Certain character classes have alignment restrictions that the character must meet, however.)

Any time after reaching 2nd level, a human character can enter a new character class, provided he has scores of 17 or better in the prime requisites of the new class. After switching to a new class, the character no longer earns experience points in his previous character class and he can no longer advance in level in that class. Nor can he switch back to his first class at a later date, hoping to resume his advancement where he left off. Once he leaves a class he has fin-

ished his studies in it. Instead, he starts over in a new class, at 1st level with 0 experience points, but he does retain his previous Hit Dice and hit points. He gains the abilities, and must abide by all of the restrictions, of the new class. He does not gain or lose any points on his ability scores (e.g., an 18 Strength mage who changes to fighter does not gain the percentile Strength bonus, but likewise a fighter changing to a mage would not lose it). The character uses the combat and saving throw tables appropriate to his new class and level.

This is not to imply that a dual-class human forgets everything he knew before; he still has, at his fingertips, all the knowledge, abilities, and proficiencies of his old class. *But if he uses any of his previous class's abilities during an encounter, he earns no experience for that encounter and only half experience for the adventure.* The only values that can be carried over from the previous class without restriction are the character's Hit Dice and hit points. The character is penalized for using his old attack or saving throw numbers, weapons or armor that are now prohibited, and any special abilities of the old class that are not also abilities of the new class. (The character is trying to learn new ways to do things; by slipping back to his old methods, he has set back his learning in his new character class.)

In addition, the character earns no additional Hit Dice or hit points while advancing in his new class.

The restrictions in the previous two paragraphs last until the character reaches a *higher* level in his new class than his maximum level in any of his previous classes. At that point, both restrictions are dropped: the character gains the abilities of his previous classes without jeopardizing his experience points for the adventure, and he earns additional Hit Dice (those of his new class) and hit points for gaining experience levels in his new class.

Once these restrictions are lifted, the character must still abide by the restrictions of whichever class he is using at the moment. A dual-class fighter/mage, for example, cannot cast spells while wearing armor.

Tarus Blood-heart begins his career as a cleric with a Wisdom of 16. He rises to 3rd level and then decides to become a fighter, since his Strength is 17. He keeps his 14 hit points (rolled on 3d8), but in all other ways he is treated as a 1st-level fighter. Upon reaching 4th level, Tarus is allowed to roll 1d10 for additional hit points. He can now cast spells as a 3rd-level cleric and fight as a 4th-level fighter. For the rest of his career, Tarus advances as a fighter but retains his minor clerical powers—a useful advantage when the situation gets ugly!

When a dual-class or multi-class character is struck by a level-draining creature, he first loses levels in the class in which he has advanced the highest. When his different classes are equal in level, the class level requiring the most experience points is lost first.

The player character is allowed to regain levels lost by level draining, but until he regains all of his former levels, he must select which class he will use prior to any particular adventure. Using abilities of the other class then subjects him to the experience penalties given earlier. When he regains all of his former levels, he is then free to use all the abilities of all his classes once again. Of course, he cannot raise his earlier class(es) above the level(s) he was at when he switched class.

Tarus is a 4th-level cleric/3rd-level fighter. He is struck by a wight and loses one level from his cleric class, since it is his highest level. If struck again, he would lose one level from his fighter class. Thereafter he could regain his lost levels, but would have to choose to act as either a fighter or cleric. Once he earned enough experience to regain his previous fighter level, he would not be allowed to advance further in it (restoring himself to his previous level only). But he could still advance as a cleric and use his 3rd-level fighter abilities.

After all other steps toward creating a character have been completed, the player must choose an alignment for the character. In some cases (especially the paladin), the choice of alignment may be limited.

The character's alignment is a guide to his basic moral and ethical attitudes toward others, society, good, evil, and the forces of the universe in general. Use the chosen alignment as a guide to provide a clearer idea of how the character will handle moral dilemmas. Always consider alignment as a tool, not a straitjacket that restricts the character. Although alignment defines general attitudes, it certainly doesn't prevent a character from changing his beliefs, acting irrationally, or behaving out of character.

Alignment is divided into two sets of attitudes: order and chaos, and good and evil. By combining the different variations within the two sets, nine distinct alignments are created. These nine alignments serve well to define the attitudes of most of the people in the world.

Law, Neutrality, and Chaos

Attitudes toward order and chaos are divided into three opposing beliefs. Picture these beliefs as the points of a triangle, all pulling away from each other. The three beliefs are law, chaos, and neutrality. One of these represents each character's ethos—his understanding of society and relationships.

Characters who believe in law maintain that order, organization, and society are important, indeed vital, forces of the universe. The relationships between people and governments exist naturally. Lawful philosophers maintain that this order is not created by man but is a natural law of the universe. Although man does not create orderly structures, it is his obligation to function within them, lest the fabric of everything crumble. For less philosophical types, lawfulness manifests itself in the belief that laws should be made and followed, if only to have understandable rules for society. People should not pursue personal vendettas, for example, but should present their claims to the proper authorities. Strength comes through unity of action, as can be seen in guilds, empires, and powerful churches.

Those espousing neutrality tend to take a more balanced view of things. They hold that for every force in the universe, there is an opposite force somewhere. Where there is lawfulness, there is also chaos; where there is neutrality, there is also partisanship. The same is true of good and evil, life and death. What is important is that all these forces remain in balance with each other. If one factor becomes ascendant over its oppo-

site, the universe becomes unbalanced. If enough of these polarities go out of balance, the fabric of reality could pull itself apart. For example, if death became ascendant over life, the universe would become a barren wasteland.

Philosophers of neutrality not only presuppose the existence of opposites, but they also theorize that the universe would vanish should one opposite completely destroy the other (since nothing can exist without its opposite). Fortunately for these philosophers (and all sentient life), the universe seems to be efficient at regulating itself. Only when a powerful, unbalancing force appears (which almost never happens) need the defenders of neutrality become seriously concerned.

The believers in chaos hold that there is no preordained order or careful balance of forces in the universe. Instead they see the universe as a collection of things and events, some related to each other and others completely independent. They tend to hold that individual actions account for the differences in things and that events in one area do not alter the fabric of the universe halfway across the galaxy. Chaotic philosophers believe in the power of the individual over his own destiny and are fond of anarchistic nations. Being more pragmatic, nonphilosophers recognize the function of society in protecting their individual rights. Chaotics can be hard to govern as a group, since they place their own needs and desires above those of society.

Good, Neutrality, and Evil

Like law and order, the second set of attitudes is also divided into three parts. These parts describe, more or less, a character's moral outlook; they are his internal guideposts to what is right or wrong.

Good characters are just that. They try to be honest, charitable, and forthright. People are not perfect, however, so few are good all the time. There are always occasional failings and weaknesses. A good person, however, worries about his errors and normally tries to correct any damage done.

Remember, however, that goodness has no absolute values. Although many things are commonly accepted as good (helping those in need, protecting the weak), different cultures impose their own interpretations on what is good and what is evil.

Those with a neutral moral stance often refrain from passing judgment on anything. They do not classify people, things, or events as good or evil; what is, is. In some cases, this is because the creature lacks the capacity to make a moral judgment (animals fall into this category). Few normal creatures do anything for good or evil reasons. They kill because they are hungry or

threatened. They sleep where they find shelter. They do not worry about the moral consequences of their actions—their actions are instinctive.

Evil is the antithesis of good and appears in many ways, some overt and others quite subtle. Only a few people of evil nature actively seek to cause harm or destruction. Most simply do not recognize that what they do is destructive or disruptive. People and things that obstruct the evil character's plans are mere hindrances that must be overcome. If someone is harmed in the process...well, that's too bad. Remember that evil, like good, is interpreted differently in different societies.

Alignment Combinations

Nine different alignments result from combining these two sets. Each alignment varies from all others, sometimes in broad, obvious ways, and sometimes in subtle ways. Each alignment is described in the following paragraphs.

Lawful Good: Characters of this alignment believe that an orderly, strong society with a well-organized government can work to make life better for the majority of the people. To ensure the quality of life, laws must be created and obeyed. When people respect the laws and try to help one another, society as a whole prospers. Therefore, lawful good characters strive for those things that will bring the greatest benefit to the most people and cause the least harm. An honest and hard-working serf, a kindly and wise king, or a stern but forthright minister of justice are all examples of lawful good people.

Lawful Neutral: Order and organization are of paramount importance to characters of this alignment. They believe in a strong, well-ordered government, whether that government is a tyranny or benevolent democracy. The benefits of organization and regimentation outweigh any moral questions raised by their actions. An inquisitor determined to ferret out traitors at any cost or a soldier who never questions his orders are good examples of lawful neutral behavior.

Lawful Evil: These characters believe in using society and its laws to benefit themselves. Structure and organization elevate those who deserve to rule as well as provide a clearly defined hierarchy between master and servant. To this end, lawful evil characters support laws and societies that protect their own concerns. If someone is hurt or suffers because of a law that benefits lawful evil characters, too bad. Lawful evil characters obey laws out of fear of punishment. Because they may be forced to honor an unfavorable contract or oath they have made, lawful evil characters are usually very careful about giving their word. Once given, they break their word only if they can find a way to do it legally, within the laws of the society. An iron-fisted tyrant and a devious, greedy merchant are examples of lawful evil beings.

Neutral Good: These characters believe that a balance of forces is important, but that the concerns of law and chaos do not moderate the need for good. Since the universe is vast and contains many creatures striving for different goals, a determined pursuit of good will not upset the balance; it may even maintain it. If fostering good means supporting organized society, then that is what must be done. If good can only come about through the overthrow of existing social order, so be it. Social structure itself has no innate value to them. A baron who violates the orders of his king to destroy something he sees as evil is an example of a neutral good character.

True Neutral: True neutral characters believe in the ultimate balance of forces, and they refuse to see actions as either good or evil. Since the majority of people in the world make judgments, true neutral characters are extremely rare. True neutrals do their best to avoid siding with the forces of either good or evil, law or chaos. It is their duty to see that all of these forces remain in balanced contention.

True neutral characters sometimes find themselves forced into rather peculiar alliances. To a great extent, they are compelled to side with the underdog in any given situation, sometimes even changing sides as the previous loser becomes the winner. A true neutral druid might join the local barony to put down a tribe of evil gnolls, only to drop out or switch sides when the gnolls were brought to the brink of destruction. He would seek to prevent either side from becoming too powerful. Clearly, there are very few true neutral characters in the world.

Neutral Evil: Neutral evil characters are primarily concerned with themselves and their own advancement. They have no particular objection to working with others or, for that matter, going it on their own. Their only interest is in getting ahead. If there is a quick and easy way to gain a profit, whether it be legal, questionable, or obviously illegal, they take advantage of it. Although neutral evil characters do not have the every-man-for-himself attitude of chaotic characters, they have no qualms about betraying their friends and companions for personal gain. They typically base their allegiance on power and money, which makes them quite receptive to bribes. An unscrupulous mercenary, a common thief, and a double-crossing informer who betrays people to the authorities to protect and advance himself are typical examples of neutral evil characters.

Chaotic Good: Chaotic good characters are strong individualists marked by a streak of kindness and benevolence. They believe in all the virtues of goodness and right, but they have little use for laws and regulations. They have no use for people who "try to push folk around and tell them what to do." Their actions are guided by their own moral compass which, although good, may not always be in perfect agreement with the rest of society. A brave frontiersman forever moving on as settlers follow in his wake is an example of a chaotic good character.

Chaotic Neutral: Chaotic neutral characters believe that there is no order to anything, including their own actions. With this as a guiding principle, they tend to follow whatever whim strikes them at the moment. Good and evil are irrelevant when making a decision. Chaotic neutral characters are extremely difficult to deal with. Such characters have been known to cheerfully and for no apparent purpose gamble away everything they have on the roll of a single die. They are almost totally unreliable. In fact, the only reliable thing about them is that they cannot be relied upon! This alignment is perhaps the most difficult to play. Lunatics and madmen tend toward chaotic neutral behavior.

Chaotic Evil: These characters are the bane of all that is good and organized. Chaotic evil characters are motivated by the desire for personal gain and pleasure. They see absolutely nothing wrong with taking whatever they want by whatever means possible. Laws and governments are the tools of weaklings unable to fend for themselves. The strong have the right to take what they want, and the weak are there to be exploited. When chaotic evil characters band together, they are not motivated by a desire to cooperate, but rather to oppose powerful enemies. Such a group can be held together only by a strong leader capable of bullying his underlings into obedience. Since leadership is based on raw power, a leader is likely to be replaced at the first sign of weakness by anyone who can take his position away from him by any method. Bloodthirsty buccaneers and monsters of low Intelligence are fine examples of chaotic evil personalities.

Non-Aligned Creatures

In addition to the alignments above, some things—particularly unintelligent monsters (killer plants, etc.) and animals—never bother with moral and ethical concerns. For these creatures, alignment is simply not applicable. A dog, even a well-trained one, is neither good nor evil, lawful nor chaotic. It is simply a dog. For these creatures, alignment is always detected as neutral.

Playing the Character's Alignment

Aside from a few minimal restrictions required for some character classes, a player is free to choose whatever alignment he wants for his character. However, before rushing off and selecting an alignment, there are a few things to consider.

First, alignment is an aid to role-playing and should be used that way. Don't choose an alignment that will be hard to role play or that won't be fun. A player who chooses an unappealing alignment probably will wind up playing a different alignment anyway. In that case, he might as well have chosen the second alignment to begin with. A player who thinks that lawful good characters are boring goody-two-shoes who don't get to have any fun should play a chaotic good character instead. On the other hand, a player who thinks that properly role-playing a heroic, lawful good fighter would be an interesting challenge is encouraged to try it. No one should be afraid to stretch his imagination. Remember, selecting an alignment is a way of saying, "My character is going to act like a person who believes this."

Second, the game revolves around cooperation among everyone in the group. The character who tries to go it alone or gets everyone angry at him is likely to have a short career. Always consider the alignments of other characters in the group. Certain combinations, particularly lawful good and any sort of evil, are explosive. Sooner or later the group will find itself spending more time arguing than adventuring. Some of this is unavoidable (and occasionally amusing), but too much is ultimately destructive. As the players argue, they get angry. As they get angry, their characters begin fighting among themselves. As the characters fight, the players continue to get more angry. Once anger and hostility take over a game, no one has fun. And what's the point of playing a game if the players don't have fun?

Third, some people choose to play evil alignments. Although there is no specific prohibition against this, there are several reasons why it is not a good idea. First, the AD&D® game is a game of heroic fantasy. What is heroic about being a villain? If an evilly aligned group plays its alignment correctly, it is as much a battle for the characters to work together as it is to take on the outside world. Neutral evil individuals would be paranoid (with some justification) that the others would betray them for profit or self-aggrandizement. Chaotic evil characters would try to get someone else to take all the risks so that they could become (or remain) strong and take over. Although lawful evil characters might have some code of conduct that governed their party, each member would look for ways to twist the rules to his own favor. A group of players who play a harmonious party of evil characters simply are not playing their alignments correctly. By its nature, evil alignments call for disharmony and squabbling, which destroys the fun.

Imagine how groups of different alignments might seek to divide a treasure trove. Suppose the adventuring party contains one character of each alignment (a virtually impossible situation, but useful for illustration). Each is then allowed to present his argument:

The lawful good character says, "Before we went on this adventure, we agreed to split the treasure equally, and that's what we're going to do. First, we'll deduct the costs of the adventure and pay for the resurrection of those who have fallen, since we're sharing all this equally. If someone can't be raised, then his share goes to his family."

"Since we agreed to split equally, that's fine," replies the lawful evil character thoughtfully. "But there was nothing in this deal about paying for anyone else's expenses. It's not my fault if you spent a lot on

equipment! Furthermore, this deal applies only to the surviving partners; I don't remember anything about dead partners. I'm not setting aside any money to raise that klutz. He's someone else's problem."

Flourishing a sheet of paper, the lawful neutral character breaks in. "It's a good thing for you two that I've got things together, nice and organized. I had the foresight to write down the exact terms of our agreement, and we're all going to follow them."

The neutral good character balances the issues and decides, "I'm in favor of equal shares—that keeps everybody happy. I feel that expenses are each adventurer's own business: If someone spent too much, then he should be more careful next time. But raising fallen comrades seems like a good idea, so I say we set aside money to do that."

After listening to the above arguments, the true neutral character decides not to say anything yet. He's not particularly concerned with any choice. If the issue can be solved without his becoming involved, great. But if it looks like one person is going to get everything, that's when he'll step in and cast his vote for a more balanced distribution.

The neutral evil character died during the adventure, so he doesn't have anything to say. However, if he could make his opinion known, he would gladly argue that the group ought to pay for raising him and set aside a share for him. The neutral evil character would also hope that the group doesn't discover the big gem he secretly pocketed during one of the encounters.

The chaotic good character objects to the whole business. "Look, it's obvious that the original agreement is messed up. I say we scrap it and reward people for what they did. I saw some of you hiding in the background when the rest of us were doing all the real fighting. I don't see why anyone should be rewarded for being a coward! As far as raising dead partners, I say that's a matter of personal choice. I don't mind chipping in for some of them, but I don't think I want everyone back in the group."

Outraged at the totally true but tactless accusation of cowardice, the chaotic evil character snaps back, "Look, I was doing an important job, guarding the rear! Can I help it if nothing tried to sneak up behind us? Now, it seems to me that all of you are pretty beat up—and I'm not. So, I don't think there's going to be too much objection if I take all the jewelry and that wand. And I'll take anything interesting those two dead guys have. Now, you can either work with me and do what I say or get lost—permanently!"

The chaotic neutral character is also dead (after he tried to charge a gorgon), so he doesn't contribute to the argument. However, if he were alive, he would join forces with whichever side appealed to him the most at the moment. If he couldn't decide, he'd flip a coin.

Clearly, widely diverse alignments in a group can make even the simplest task impossible. It is almost certain that the group in the example would come to blows before they could reach a decision. But dividing cash is not the only instance in which this group would have problems. Consider the battle in which they gained the treasure in the first place.

Upon penetrating the heart of the ruined castle, the party met its foe, a powerful gorgon commanded by a mad warrior. There, chained behind the two, was a helpless peasant kidnapped from a nearby village.

The lawful good character unhesitatingly (but not foolishly) entered the battle; it was the right thing to do. He considered it his duty to protect the villagers. Besides, he could not abandon an innocent hostage to such fiends. He was willing to fight until he won or was dragged off by his friends. He had no intention of fighting to his own death, but he would not give up until he had tried his utmost to defeat the evil creatures.

The lawful evil character also entered the battle willingly. Although he cared nothing

for the peasant, he could not allow the two fiends to mock him. Still, there was no reason for him to risk all for one peasant. If forced to retreat, he could return with a stronger force, capture the criminals, and execute them publicly. If the peasant died in the meantime, their punishment would be that much more horrible.

The lawful neutral character was willing to fight, because the villains threatened public order. However, he was not willing to risk his own life. He would have preferred to come back later with reinforcements. If the peasant could be saved, that is good, because he is part of the community. If not, it would be unfortunate but unavoidable.

The neutral good character did not fight the gorgon or the warrior, but he tried to rescue the peasant. Saving the peasant was worthwhile, but there was no need to risk injury and death along the way. Thus, while the enemy was distracted in combat, he tried to slip past and free the peasant.

The true neutral character weighed the situation carefully. Although it looked like the forces working for order would have the upper hand in the battle, he knew there had been a general trend toward chaos and destruction in the region that must be combatted. He tried to help, but if the group failed, he could work to restore the balance of law and chaos elsewhere in the kingdom.

The neutral evil character cared nothing about law, order, or the poor peasant. He figured that there had to be some treasure around somewhere. After all, the villain's lair had once been a powerful temple. He could poke around for cash while the others did the real work. If the group got into real trouble and it looked like the villains would attack him, then he would fight. Unfortunately, a stray magical arrow killed him just after he found a large gem.

The chaotic good character joined the fight for several reasons. Several people in the group were his friends, and he wanted to fight at their sides. Furthermore, the poor, kidnapped peasant deserved to be rescued. Thus, the chaotic good character fought to aid his companions and save the peasant. He didn't care if the villains were killed, captured, or just driven away. Their attacks against the village didn't concern him.

The chaotic neutral character decided to charge, screaming bloodthirsty cries, straight for the gorgon. Who knows? He might have broken its nerve and thrown it off guard. He discovered that his plan was a bad one when the gorgon's breath killed him.

The chaotic evil character saw no point in risking his hide for the villagers, the peasant, or the rest of the party. In fact, he thought of several good reasons not to. If the party was weakened, he might be able to take over. If the villains won, he could probably make a deal with them and join their

side. If everyone was killed, he could take everything he wanted and leave. All these sounded a lot better than getting hurt for little or no gain. So he stayed near the back of the battle, watching. If anyone asked, he could say he was watching the rear, making sure no one came to aid the enemy.

The two preceding examples of alignment are extreme situations. It's not very likely that a player will ever play in a group of alignments as varied as those given here. If such a group ever does form, players should seriously reconsider the alignments of the different members of the party! More often, the adventuring party will consist of characters with relatively compatible alignments. Even then, players who role-play their characters' alignments will discover small issues of disagreement.

Changing Alignment

Alignment is a tool, not a straitjacket. It is possible for a player to change his character's alignment after the character is created, either by action or choice. However, changing alignment is not without its penalties.

Most often the character's alignment will change because his actions are more in line with a different alignment. This can happen if the player is not paying attention to the character and his actions. The character gradually assumes a different alignment. For example, a lawful good fighter ignores the village council's plea for help because he wants to go fight evil elsewhere. This action is much closer to chaotic good, since the character is placing his desire over the need of the community. The fighter would find himself beginning to drift toward chaotic good alignment.

All people have minor failings, however, so the character does not instantly become chaotic good. Several occasions of lax behavior are required before the character's alignment changes officially. During that time, extremely lawful good activities can swing the balance back. Although the player may have a good idea of where the character's alignment lies, only the DM knows for sure.

Likewise, the character cannot wake up one morning and say, "I think I'll become lawful good today." (Well, he can say it, but it won't have any effect.) A player can choose to change his character's alignment, but this change is accomplished by deeds, not words. Tell the DM of the intention and then try to play according to the new choice.

Finally, there are many magical effects that can change a character's alignment. Rare and cursed magical items can instantly alter a character's alignment. Powerful artifacts may slowly erode a character's determination and willpower, causing subtle

shifts in behavior. Spells can compel a character to perform actions against his will. Although all of these have an effect, none are as permanent or damaging as those choices the character makes of his own free will.

Changing the way a character behaves and thinks will cost him experience points and slow his advancement. Part of a character's experience comes from learning how his own behavior affects him and the world around him. In real life, for example, a person learns that he doesn't like horror movies only by going to see a few of them. Based on that experience, he learns to avoid certain types of movies. Changing behavior means discarding things the character learned previously. Relearning things takes time. This costs the character experience.

There are other, more immediate effects of changing alignment. Certain character classes require specific alignments. A paladin who is no longer lawful good is no longer a paladin. A character may have magical items usable only by specific alignments (intelligent swords, etc.). Such items don't function (and may even prove dangerous) in the hands of a differently aligned character.

News of a character's change in behavior will certainly get around to friends and acquaintances. Although some people he never considered friendly may now warm to him, others may take exception to his new attitudes. A few may even try to help him "see the error of his ways." The local clergy, on whom he relies for healing, may look askance on his recent behavior, denying him their special services (while at the same time sermonizing on his plight). The character who changes alignment often finds himself unpopular, depending on the attitudes of the surrounding people. People do not understand him. If the character drifts into chaotic neutral behavior in a highly lawful city, the townspeople might decide that the character is afflicted and needs close supervision, even confinement, for his own good!

Ultimately, the player is advised to pick an alignment he can play comfortably, one that fits in with those of the rest of the group, and he should stay with that alignment for the course of the character's career. There will be times when the DM, especially if he is clever, creates situations to test the character's resolve and ethics. But finding the right course of action within the character's alignment is part of the fun and challenge of role-playing.

Most of what a player character can do is defined by his race, class, and ability scores. These three characteristics don't cover everything, however. Characters can have a wide range of talents, from the potent (and intricate) arts of magic to the simple and mundane knowledge of how to build a good fire. The character's magical ability (or lack thereof) is defined by his class. Lesser abilities, such as fire building, are defined by proficiencies.

A proficiency is a learned skill that isn't essential to the character's class. A ranger, for example, may find it useful to know something about navigation, especially if he lives near an ocean or sea coast. On the other hand, he isn't likely to suffer if he doesn't know how to navigate; he is a ranger, not a sailor.

Proficiencies are divided into two groups: weapon proficiencies (those related to weapons and combat) and nonweapon proficiencies (those related to everything else).

All proficiency rules are additions to the game. Weapon proficiencies are tournament-level rules, optional in regular play, and nonweapon proficiencies are completely optional. Proficiencies are not necessary for a balanced game. They add an additional dimension to characters, however, and anything that enriches characterization is a bonus. If weapon proficiencies are used in your game, expect them to apply to all characters, including NPCs. Nonweapon proficiencies may be used by players who enjoy them and ignored by those who don't without giving unfair advantages to anyone (provided your DM allows this; he's the one who must deal with any problems).

Once a proficiency slot is filled, it can never be changed or reassigned.

Acquiring Proficiencies

Even newly created, 1st-level characters have proficiencies. The number of proficiency slots that a character starts with is determined by his group, as shown in Table 34. Each proficiency slot is empty until the player "fills" it by selecting a proficiency. If your DM allows nonweapon proficiencies, the character's Intelligence score can modify the number of slots he has, granting him more proficiencies (see page 16). In both cases, new proficiencies are learned the same way.

Consider the case of Rath, a dwarf fighter. Table 34 gives him four weapon proficiency slots (he is a warrior). If nonweapon proficiencies are used, he has three slots and his Intelligence of 11 gives him two additional proficiency slots (according to Table 4, page 16) for a total of five nonweapon proficiency slots. The player must assign weapon or nonweapon proficiencies to all of these slots before the character goes on his first adventure. These represent what the character has learned before beginning his adventuring career.

Table 34: PROFICIENCY SLOTS

Group	Weapon Proficiencies Initial	#Levels	Penalty	Nonweapon Proficiencies Initial	#Levels
Warrior	4	3	−2	3	3
Wizard	1	6	−5	4	3
Priest	2	4	−3	4	3
Rogue	2	4	−3	3	4

Thereafter, as the character advances in experience levels, he gains additional proficiency slots. The rate at which he gains them depends on the group he belongs to. Table 34 lists how many weapon and nonweapon proficiency slots the character starts with, and how many levels the character must gain before he earns another slot.

Initial Weapon Proficiencies is the number of weapon proficiency slots received by characters of that group at 1st level.

#Levels (for both weapon and nonweapon proficiencies) tells how quickly a character gains additional proficiency slots. A new proficiency slot is gained at every experience level that is evenly divisible by the number listed. Rath (a warrior), for example, gains one weapon proficiency slot at every level evenly divisible by 3. He gets one new slot at 3rd level, another at 6th, another at 9th, and so on. (Note that Rath also gains one nonweapon proficiency at 3rd, 6th, 9th, etc.)

Penalty is the modifier to the character's attack rolls when he fights using a weapon he is not proficient with. Rath, a dwarf, chose to be proficient with the warhammer. Finding himself in a desperate situation, he snatches up a flail, even though he knows little about it (he is not proficient with it). Using the weapon awkwardly, he has a −2 penalty to his chance to hit.

Initial Nonweapon Proficiencies is the number of nonweapon proficiency slots that character has at 1st level. Even if you are playing with weapon proficiencies, nonweapon proficiencies are optional.

Training

Like all skills and abilities, proficiencies do not leap unbidden and fully realized into a character's mind. Instead, a character must train, study, and practice to learn a new proficiency. However, role-playing the training time needed to learn a new skill is not much fun. Thus there are no training times or study periods associated with any proficiency. When a character chooses a proficiency, it is assumed that he had been studying it in his spare time.

Consider just how much spare time the character has. The player is not role-playing every second of his character's life. The player may decide to have his character spend a night in town before setting out on the long journey the next day. Perhaps the character must wait around for several days while his companions heal from the last adventure. Or he might spend weeks on an uneventful ocean voyage. What is he doing during that time?

Among other things, he is studying whatever new proficiencies he will eventually learn. Using this "down time" to handle the unexciting aspects of a role-playing campaign lets players concentrate on more important (or more interesting) matters.

Another part of training is finding a teacher. Most skills are easier to learn if someone teaches the character. The DM can handle this in several ways. For those who like simplicity, ignore the need for teachers—there are self-taught people everywhere in the world. For those who want more complexity, make the player characters find someone to teach them any new proficiency they want to learn. This can be another player character or an NPC. Although this adds realism, it tends to limit the PC's adventuring options, especially if he is required to stay in regular contact with his instructor. Furthermore, most teachers want payment. While a barter arrangement might be reached, the normal payment is cash. The actual cost of the service depends on the nature of the skill, the amount of training desired, the availability of tutors, the greed of the instructor, and the desire of the DM to remove excess cash from his campaign.

Weapon Proficiencies

A weapon proficiency measures a character's knowledge and training with a specific weapon. When a character is created, the player checks Table 34 to see how many weapon proficiency slots the character has. These initial slots must be filled immediately, before the character embarks on his first adventure. Any slots that aren't filled by then are lost.

Each weapon proficiency slot must be assigned to a particular weapon, not just a class of weapons. Each weapon listed in Table 44 (Weapons) requires its own proficiency; each has its own special tricks and quirks that must be mastered before the weapon can be handled properly and effectively. A fencer who is master of the epee, for example, is not necessarily skilled with a saber; the two weapons look similar, but the

Table 35: SPECIALIST ATTACKS PER ROUND

Fighter Level	Melee Weapon	Light X-bow	Heavy X-bow	Thrown Dagger	Thrown Dart	Other (Non-bow) Missiles
1-6	3/2	1/1	1/2	3/1	4/1	3/2
7-12	2/1	3/2	1/1	4/1	5/1	2/1
13+	5/2	2/1	3/2	5/1	6/1	5/2

fighting styles they are designed for are entirely different. A player character could become proficient with a long bow or a short bow, but not with all bows in general (unless he devotes a proficiency slot to each individually). Furthermore, a character can assign weapon proficiency slots only to those weapons allowed to his character class.

As a character reaches higher experience levels, he also earns additional weapon proficiencies. The rate at which proficiencies are gained depends on the character's class. Warriors, who concentrate on their martial skills, learn to handle a great number of weapons. They gain weapon proficiencies quickly. Wizards, who spend their time studying forgotten magical arts, have little time to practice with weapons. They gain additional weapon proficiencies very slowly. Multi-class characters can use the most beneficial line on Table 34 to determine their initial proficiencies and when they gain new proficiencies.

Effects of Weapon Proficiencies

A character who has a specific weapon proficiency is skilled with that weapon and familiar with its use. A character does not gain any bonuses for using a weapon he is proficient with; the combat rules and attack chances assume that everyone uses a weapon he is proficient with. This eliminates the need to add a modifier to every die roll during battle.

When a character uses a weapon that he is not proficient with, however, he suffers a penalty on his chance to hit. The size of this penalty depends on the character's class. Warriors have the smallest penalty because they are assumed to have passing familiarity with all weapons. Wizards, by comparison, are heavily penalized because of their limited study of weapons. The modifiers for each class (which are taken as penalties to the attack die roll) are listed on Table 34.

Related Weapons Bonus

When a character gains a weapon proficiency, he is learning to use a particular weapon effectively. However, many weapons have similar characteristics. A long sword, bastard sword, and broad sword, while all different, are all heavy, slashing swords. A character who is trained with one can apply some of his skill to the others. He is not fully proficient with

the weapon, but he knows more about it than someone who picks it up without any skill in similar weapons.

When a character uses a weapon that is similar to a weapon he is proficient with, his attack penalty is only one-half the normal amount (rounded up). A warrior, for example, would have a −1 penalty with a related weapon instead of −2. A wizard would have a −3 penalty instead of −5.

Specific decisions about which weapons are related are left to the DM. Some likely categories are:

hand axe, battle axe;
short bow, long bow, composite bow;
heavy and light crossbows;
dagger, knife;
glaive, halberd, bardiche, voulge, guisarme, glaive-guisarme, guisarme-voulge;
harpoon, spear, trident, javelin;
footman's mace, horseman's mace, morning star, flail, hammer, club;
military fork, ranseur, spetum, partisan;
scimitar, bastard sword, long sword, broad sword;
sling, staff sling

Weapon Specialization

Knowing how to use a weapon without embarrassing yourself is very different from being a master of that weapon. There are warriors, and then there are martial artists. An Olympic fencer is more than just an athlete; he can do things with his weapon that astound most fencers.

In the AD&D® game, part of your character's skill is reflected in the bonuses he earns as he reaches higher levels. As your character advances, he becomes a wiser, more dangerous fighter. Experience has taught him to anticipate his opponents and to pounce on any advantage that presents itself. But this is a general, overall improvement, brought about by the warrior's sharpening senses and timing. It applies equally to all types of fighting.

Weapon specialization is an optional rule that enables a fighter (only) to choose a single weapon and specialize in its use. Any weapon may be chosen. Specialization is normally announced (and paid for with weapon proficiency slots) when the character is created. But even after a player character earns experience, he can still choose to specialize in a weapon, provided he

has the weapon proficiency slots available.

In one way, a weapon specialist is like a wizard specialist. The specialization requires a single-minded dedication and training. Thus multi-class characters cannot use weapon specialization; it is available only to single-class fighters.

Cost of Specialization

Weapon specialization is obtained by devoting extra weapon proficiency slots to the chosen weapon. To specialize in any sort of melee weapon or crossbow, the character must devote two slots—one slot to become proficient with it, and then a second slot to specialize in it. Any bow (other than a crossbow) requires a total of three proficiency slots: one for proficiency and two to specialize. Assume, for the moment, that Rath the dwarf decided to specialize with the warhammer. Two of his four proficiency slots are thus devoted to the warhammer. With the two remaining, he can become proficient with the short sword and short bow (for example).

Effects of Specialization

When a character specializes with a *melee* weapon, he gains a +1 bonus to all his attack rolls with that weapon and a +2 bonus to all damage rolls (in addition to bonuses for Strength and magic). The attack bonuses are not magical and do not enable the character to affect a creature that can be injured only by magical weapons.

Bow and *crossbow* specialists gain an additional range category: point blank. Point-blank range for bows is from six feet to 30 feet. Point-blank range for crossbows is from six feet to 60 feet. At point-blank range, the character gains a +2 modifier on attack rolls. No additional damage is caused, but Strength (for bows) and magical bonuses apply. Furthermore, if the character has an arrow nocked and drawn, or a bolt loaded and cocked, and has his target in sight, he can fire at the beginning of the round before any initiative rolls are made.

Fighters who specialize also gain extra attacks earlier than those who don't specialize. Bonus attacks for specialists are listed on Table 35. The use of this table is explained in Chapter 9: Combat. Bow specialists do not gain any additional attacks per round.

Nonweapon Proficiencies

A player character is more than a collection of combat modifiers. Most people have a variety of skills learned over the years. Consider yourself as an example—how many skills do you possess? If you have gone through 12 years of school, were moderately active in after-school programs, and did fairly well on your grades, the following might be a partial list of your skills:

    English reading and writing
    Geometry, algebra, and trigonometry
    Basic chemistry
    Basic physics
    Music (playing an instrument, singing, or both)
    Spanish reading and writing (or French, German, etc.)
    Basic Shop or Home Economics
    Typing
    Driving
    History
    Basic biology

In addition to the things learned in school, you have also learned things from your parents, friends, scouts, or other groups. You might be able to add any of the following to your list.

    Swimming
    Hunting
    Fishing
    Canoeing
    Sailing
    Horseback riding
    First aid
    Animal training
    Cooking
    Sewing
    Embroidery
    Dancing

If you consider all your hobbies and all the things you have done, you probably know many more skills. In fact, if you make a list, you probably will be surprised by the large number of basic skills you have. And, at this point, you are (or were) still young!

Now, having graduated from school, you get a job. Are you just a carpenter, mechanic, electrician, salesman, or secretary? Of course not; you are a lot more than just your job. All those things you learned in school and elsewhere are part of what you are. Shouldn't it be the same for your player character?

For a really complete role-playing character, you should know what your character can do. There are three different ways to do this: using what you know, using secondary skills, and using nonweapon proficiencies. Each of these is optional, but each increases the amount of detail that rounds out your character.

Using What You Know

If your DM decides not to use secondary skills or nonweapon proficiencies, situations will arise in which you'll have to determine whether your character has certain skills. For example, Delsenora the mage slips at the edge of a steep riverbank and tumbles into the water. The current sweeps her into the middle of the river. To escape, she must swim to

safety. But does Delsenora know how to swim?

One way to answer this is to pretend that your character knows most of the things that you know. Do you know how to swim? If you do, then your character can swim. If you know a little about mountain climbing, horseback riding, carpentry, or sewing, your character knows these things, too. This also applies to things your character might want to build. Perhaps your character decides he wants to build a catapult. If you can show your DM how to make such a device, then the DM may allow your character the same knowledge. Indeed, you might visit the local library just to gain this information.

There are real advantages to this method. You can learn something at the library or school and bring it into your game. Also, there are fewer rules to get in the way of your fun. Since there are fewer rules, your DM has a lot of flexibility and can play out all the drama inherent in a scene.

There are also problems with this method. First, you probably know a lot of things your character should not—basic electronics, the components of gunpowder, or calculus, for instance. You have a lot of knowledge that is just not available to someone in a medieval world (even a fantasy medieval world). Likewise, there are things that a typical person in a medieval world would know that you, as a modern person, have never needed to learn. Do you know how to make armor? Skin a deer? Salt meat away for the winter? Turn flax into linen? Thatch a roof? Read heraldry? You might, but there is no way you can consider these common skills anymore. But in a medieval world they would be common.

Also, knowing something about a skill or trade doesn't mean you know a lot, and there is a big difference between the two. When Delsenora fell into the raging river, she had to swim out. But was she a strong enough swimmer to pull free of the current? The DM must make up a rule on the spot to handle the situation. Perhaps you can swim, but can you swim well enough to escape a raging torrent?

The biggest drawback to this method is that there are no rules to resolve tricky situations. The DM must make it up during play. Some players and DMs enjoy doing this. They think up good answers quickly. Many consider this to be a large part of the fun. This method is perfect for them, and they should use it.

Other players and DMs like to have clear rules to prevent arguments. If this is the case in your group, it is better to use secondary skills or nonweapon proficiencies.

Secondary Skills

The second method for determining what your character knows is to assign secondary skills. Secondary skills are broad areas of expertise. Most correspond to occupations that your character may have been apprenticed in or otherwise picked up before beginning his adventuring life. Secondary skills are much more general than nonweapon proficiencies. They should not be used in combination with nonweapon proficiencies, which are explained later.

Every player character has a chance at a secondary skill. Either choose one from Table 36 or take a chance and roll randomly. A random roll may result in one, two, or no secondary skills.

Table 36: SECONDARY SKILLS

D100 Roll	Secondary Skill
01-02	Armorer (make, repair, & evaluate armor and weapons)
03-04	Bowyer/Fletcher (make, repair, & evaluate bows and arrows)
05-10	Farmer (basic agriculture)
11-14	Fisher (swimming, nets, and small boat handling)
15-20	Forester (basic wood lore, lumbering)
21-23	Gambler (knowledge of gambling games)
24-27	Groom (animal handling)
28-32	Hunter (basic wood lore, butchering, basic tracking)
33-34	Jeweler (appraisal of gems and jewelry)
35-37	Leather worker (skinning, tanning)
38-39	Limner/Painter (map making, appraisal of art objects)
40-42	Mason (stone-cutting)
43-44	Miner (stone-cutting, assaying)
45-46	Navigator (astronomy, sailing, swimming, navigation)
47-49	Sailor (sailing, swimming)
50-51	Scribe (reading, writing, basic math)
52-53	Shipwright (sailing, carpentry)
54-56	Tailor/Weaver (weaving, sewing, embroidery)
57-59	Teamster/Freighter (animal handling, wagon-repair)
60-62	Trader/Barterer (appraisal of common goods)
63-66	Trapper/Furrier (basic wood lore, skinning)
67-68	Weaponsmith (make, repair, & evaluate weapons)
69-71	Woodworker/Carpenter (carpentry, carving)
72-85	No skill of measureable worth
86-00	Roll twice (reroll any result of 86-00)

Once a character has a secondary skill, it is up to the player and the DM to determine just what the character can do with it. The items in parentheses after each skill describe some of the things the character knows. Other knowledge may be added with the DM's approval. Thus, a hunter might know the basics of finding food in the wilderness, how to read animal signs to identify the types of creatures in the area, the habits of dangerous animals, and how to stalk wild animals.

Like the previous method ("Using What You Know"), this method has strengths and weaknesses. Secondary skills do not provide any rules for determining whether a character succeeds when he uses a skill to do something difficult. It is safe to assume that simple jobs succeed automatically. (A hunter could find food for himself without any difficulty.) For more complicated tasks, the DM must assign a chance for success. He can assign a percentage chance, have the character make a saving throw, or require an Ability check (see Glossary). The DM still has a lot of flexibility.

This flexibility means the DM must sometimes make up the rule to cover the situation, however. As mentioned earlier, some DMs enjoy this; others do not, their strengths being elsewhere. While secondary skills define and limit the player's options, they do not greatly simplify the DM's job.

Nonweapon Proficiencies

The most detailed method for handling character skills is that of nonweapon proficiencies. These are much like weapon proficiencies. Each character starts with a specific number of nonweapon proficiency slots and then earns additional slots as he advances. Initial slots must be assigned immediately; they cannot be saved or held in reserve.

Nonweapon proficiencies are the most detailed way to handle the question of what the player character knows. They allow the player to choose from a broad selection and define the effects of each choice. Like the other methods, however, this system is not without drawbacks. First, nonweapon proficiencies are rigid. Being so defined, they limit the options of both the player and DM. At the same time, there will still be questions unanswered by these proficiencies. Whereas before such questions were broad, they will now tend to be more precise and detailed. Secondly, using this system increases the amount of time needed to create a character. While the end result is a more complete, well-rounded person, set-up time can take up to two or three hours. Novice players especially may be overwhelmed by the number of choices and rules.

Unlike weapon proficiencies, in which some weapons are not available to certain character classes, all nonweapon proficiencies are available to all characters. Some nonweapon proficiencies are easier for certain character classes to learn, however.

Table 37 lists all nonweapon proficiencies. They are divided into categories that correspond to character groups. The proficiencies listed under each group can be learned easily by characters of that group. A fifth category—"General"—contains proficiencies that can be learned easily by any character.

Refer to Table 38. When a player selects a nonweapon proficiency from those categories listed under "Proficiency Groups" for his character's group, it requires the number of proficiency slots listed in Table 37. When a player selects a proficiency from any other category, it requires one additional proficiency slot beyond the number listed.

Table 37: NONWEAPON PROFICIENCY GROUPS

GENERAL

Proficiency	# of Slots Required	Relevant Ability	Check Modifier
Agriculture	1	Intelligence	0
Animal Handling	1	Wisdom	−1
Animal Training	1	Wisdom	0
Artistic Ability	1	Wisdom	0
Blacksmithing	1	Strength	0
Brewing	1	Intelligence	0
Carpentry	1	Strength	0
Cobbling	1	Dexterity	0
Cooking	1	Intelligence	0
Dancing	1	Dexterity	0
Direction Sense	1	Wisdom	+1
Etiquette	1	Charisma	0
Fire-building	1	Wisdom	−1
Fishing	1	Wisdom	−1
Heraldry	1	Intelligence	0
Languages, Modern	1	Intelligence	0
Leatherworking	1	Intelligence	0
Mining	2	Wisdom	−3
Pottery	1	Dexterity	−2
Riding, Airborne	2	Wisdom	−2
Riding, Land-based	1	Wisdom	+3
Rope Use	1	Dexterity	0
Seamanship	1	Dexterity	+1
Seamstress/Tailor	1	Dexterity	−1
Singing	1	Charisma	0
Stonemasonry	1	Strength	−2
Swimming	1	Strength	0
Weather Sense	1	Wisdom	−1
Weaving	1	Intelligence	−1

PRIEST

Proficiency	# of Slots Required	Relevant Ability	Check Modifier
Ancient History	1	Intelligence	−1
Astrology	2	Intelligence	0
Engineering	2	Intelligence	−3
Healing	2	Wisdom	−2
Herbalism	2	Intelligence	−2
Languages, Ancient	1	Intelligence	0
Local History	1	Charisma	0
Musical Instrument	1	Dexterity	−1
Navigation	1	Intelligence	−2
Reading/Writing	1	Intelligence	+1
Religion	1	Wisdom	0
Spellcraft	1	Intelligence	−2

ROGUE

Proficiency	# of Slots Required	Relevant Ability	Check Modifier
Ancient History	1	Intelligence	−1
Appraising	1	Intelligence	0
Blind-fighting	2	NA	NA
Disguise	1	Charisma	−1
Forgery	1	Dexterity	−1
Gaming	1	Charisma	0
Gem Cutting	2	Dexterity	−2
Juggling	1	Dexterity	−1
Jumping	1	Strength	0
Local History	1	Charisma	0
Musical Instrument	1	Dexterity	−1
Reading Lips	2	Intelligence	−2
Set Snares	1	Dexterity	−1
Tightrope Walking	1	Dexterity	0
Tumbling	1	Dexterity	0
Ventriloquism	1	Intelligence	−2

WARRIOR

Proficiency	# of Slots Required	Relevant Ability	Check Modifier
Animal Lore	1	Intelligence	0
Armorer	2	Intelligence	−2
Blind-fighting	2	NA	NA
Bowyer/Fletcher	1	Dexterity	−1
Charioteering	1	Dexterity	+2
Endurance	2	Constitution	0
Gaming	1	Charisma	0
Hunting	1	Wisdom	−1
Mountaineering	1	NA	NA
Navigation	1	Intelligence	−2
Running	1	Constitution	−6
Set Snares	1	Dexterity	−1
Survival	2	Intelligence	0
Tracking	2	Wisdom	0
Weaponsmithing	3	Intelligence	−3

WIZARD

Proficiency	# of Slots Required	Relevant Ability	Check Modifier
Ancient History	1	Intelligence	−1
Astrology	2	Intelligence	0
Engineering	2	Intelligence	−3
Gem Cutting	2	Dexterity	−2
Herbalism	2	Intelligence	−2
Languages, Ancient	1	Intelligence	0
Navigation	1	Intelligence	−2
Reading/Writing	1	Intelligence	+1
Religion	1	Wisdom	0
Spellcraft	1	Intelligence	−2

Table 38: NONWEAPON PROFICIENCY GROUP CROSSOVERS

Character Class	Proficiency Groups
Fighter	Warrior, General
Paladin	Warrior, Priest, General
Ranger	Warrior, Wizard, General
Cleric	Priest, General
Druid	Priest, Warrior, General
Mage	Wizard, General
Illusionist	Wizard, General
Thief	Rogue, General
Bard	Rogue, Warrior, Wizard, General

Using Nonweapon Proficiencies

When a character uses a proficiency, either the attempt is automatically successful or the character must roll a proficiency check. If the task is simple or the proficiency has only limited game use (such as cobbling or carpentry), a proficiency check is generally not required. If the task the character is trying to perform is difficult or subject to failure, a proficiency check is required. Read the descriptions of the proficiencies for details about how and when each can be used.

If a proficiency check is required, Table 37 lists which ability is used with each proficiency. Add the modifier (either positive or negative) listed in Table 37 to the appropriate ability score. Then the player rolls 1d20. If the roll is equal to or less than the character's adjusted ability score, the character accomplished what he was trying to do. If the roll is greater than the character's ability score, the character fails at the task. (A roll of 20 *always* fails.) The DM determines what effects, if any, accompany failure.

Of course, to use a proficiency, the character must have any tools and materials needed to do the job. A carpenter can do very little without his tools, and a smith is virtually helpless without a good forge. The character must also have enough time to do the job. Certainly, carpentry proficiency enables your character to build a house, but not in a single day! Some proficiency descriptions state how much time is required for certain jobs. Most, however, are left to the DM's judgment.

The DM can raise or lower a character's chance of success if the situation calls for it. Factors that can affect a proficiency check include availability and quality of tools, quality of raw material used, time spent doing the job, difficulty of the job, and how familiar the character is with the task. A positive modifier is added to the ability score used for the check. A negative modifier is subtracted from the ability score.

Rath, skilled as a blacksmith, has been making horseshoes for years. Because he is so familiar with the task and has every tool he needs, the DM lets him make horseshoes automatically, without risk of failure. However, Delsenora has persuaded Rath to make an elaborate wrought-iron cage (she needs it to create a magical item). Rath has never done this before and the work is very intricate, so the DM imposes a penalty of −3 on Rath's ability check.

When two proficient characters work together on the same task, the highest ability score is used (the one with the greatest chance of success). Furthermore, a +1 bonus is added for the other character's assistance. The bonus can never be more than +1, as having too many assistants is sometimes worse than having none.

Nonweapon proficiencies can also be improved beyond the ability score the character starts with. For every additional proficiency slot a character spends on a nonweapon proficiency, he gains a +1 bonus to those proficiency checks. Thus, Rath (were he not an adventurer) might spend his additional proficiency slots on blacksmithing, to become a very good blacksmith, gaining a +1, +2, +3, or greater bonus to his ability checks.

Many non-player craftsmen are more accomplished in their fields than player characters, having devoted all their energies to improving a single proficiency. Likewise, old masters normally have more talent than young apprentices—unless the youth has an exceptional ability score! However, age is no assurance of talent. Remember that knowing a skill and being good at it are two different things. There are bad potters, mediocre potters, and true craftsmen. All this has much less to do with age than with dedication and talent.

Nonweapon Proficiency Descriptions

The following proficiency descriptions are arranged alphabetically, not according to character class. Each description gives a general outline of what a character with the proficiency knows and can do. Furthermore, some descriptions include rules to cover specific uses or situations, or exact instructions on the effects of the proficiency.

Agriculture: The character has a knowledge of the basics of farming. This includes planting, harvesting, storing crops, tending animals, butchering, and other typical farming chores.

Ancient History: The character has learned the legends, lore, and history of some ancient time and place. The knowledge must be specific, just as a historian would specialize today in the English Middle Ages, the Italian Renaissance, or the Roman Republic before Caesar. (The DM either can have ancient periods in mind for his game or can allow the players to name and designate them.) Thus, a player character could know details about the Age of Thorac Dragonking or the Time of the Sea-Raiders or whatever else was available.

The knowledge acquired gives the character familiarity with the principal legends, historical events, characters, locations, battles, breakthroughs (scientific, cultural, and magical), unsolved mysteries, crafts, and oddities of the time. The character must roll a proficiency check to identify places or things he encounters from that age. For example, Rath knows quite a bit about the Coming of the Trolls, a particularly dark period of dwarven history. Moving through some deep caverns, he and his companions stumble across an ancient portal, sealed for untold ages. Studying the handiwork, he realizes (rolls a successful proficiency check) that it bears several seals similar to those he has seen on "banned" portals from the time of Angnar, doorways to the legendary realm of Trolhel.

Animal Handling: Proficiency in this area enables a character to exercise a greater-than-normal degree of control over pack animals and beasts of burden. A successful proficiency check indicates that the character has succeeded in calming an excited or

agitated animal; in contrast, a character without this proficiency has only a 20% chance of succeeding in the attempt.

Animal Lore: This proficiency enables a character to observe the actions or habitat of an animal and interpret what is going on. Actions can show how dangerous the creature is, whether it is hungry, protecting its young, or defending a nearby den. Furthermore, careful observation of signs and behaviors can even indicate the location of a water hole, animal herd, predator, or impending danger, such as a forest fire. The DM will secretly roll a proficiency check. A successful check means the character understood the basic actions of the creature. If the check fails by 4 or less, no information is gained. If the check fails by 5 or more, the character misinterprets the actions of the animal.

A character may also imitate the calls and cries of animals that he is reasonably familiar with, based on his background. This ability is limited by volume. The roar of a tyrannosaurus rex would be beyond the abilities of a normal character. A successful proficiency check means that only magical means can distinguish the character's call from that of the true animal. The cry is sufficient to fool animals, perhaps frightening them away or

luring them closer. A failed check means the sound is incorrect in some slight way. A failed call may still fool some listeners, but creatures very familiar with the cry automatically detect a false call. All other creatures and characters are allowed a Wisdom check to detect the fake.

Finally, animal lore increases the chance of successfully setting snares and traps (for hunting) since the character knows the general habits of the creature hunted.

Animal Training: Characters with this proficiency can train one type of creature (declared when the proficiency is chosen) to obey simple commands and perform tricks. A character can spend additional proficiencies to train other types of creatures or can improve his skill with an already chosen type. Creatures typically trained are dogs, horses, falcons, pigeons, elephants, ferrets, and parrots. A character can choose even more exotic creatures and monsters with animal intelligence (although these are difficult to control).

A trainer can work with up to three creatures at one time. The trainer may choose to teach general tasks or specific tricks. A general task gives the creature the ability to react to a number of nonspecific commands to do its job. Examples of tasks include guard and attack, carry a rider, perform heavy labor, hunt, track, or fight alongside soldiers (such as a war horse or elephant). A specific trick teaches the trained creature to do one specific action. A horse may rear on command, a falcon may pluck a designated object, a dog may attack a specific person, or a rat may run through a particular maze. With enough time, a creature can be trained to do both general tasks and specific tricks.

Training for a general task requires three months of uninterrupted work. Training for a specific trick requires 2d6 weeks. At the end of the training time, a proficiency check is made. If successful, the animal is trained. If the die roll fails, the beast is untrainable. An animal can be trained in 2d4 general tasks or specific tricks, or any combination of the two.

An animal trainer can also try to tame wild animals (preparing them for training later on). Wild animals can be tamed only when they are very young. The taming requires one month of uninterrupted work with the creature. At the end of the month, a proficiency check is made. If successful, the beast is suitable for training. If the check fails, the creature retains enough of its wild behavior to make it untrainable. It can be kept, though it must be leashed or caged.

Appraising: This proficiency is highly useful for thieves, as it allows characters to estimate the value and authenticity of antiques, art objects, jewelry, cut gemstones, or other crafted items they find (although the DM can exclude those items too exotic or rare to be well known). The character must have the item in hand to examine. A successful proficiency check (rolled by the DM) enables the character to estimate the value of the item to the nearest 100 or 1,000 gp and to identify fakes. On a failed check, the character cannot estimate a price at all. On a roll of 20, the character wildly misreads the value of the item, always to the detriment of the character.

Armorer: This character can make all of the types of armor listed in the *Player's Handbook*, given the proper materials and facilities. When making armor, the proficiency check is rolled at the end of the normal construction time.

The time required to make armor is equal to two weeks per level of AC below 10. For example, a shield would require two weeks of work, whereas a suit of full plate armor would require 18 weeks of work.

If the proficiency check indicates failure but is within 4 of the amount needed for success, the armorer has created usable, but flawed, armor. Such armor functions as 1 AC worse than usual, although it looks like the armor it was intended to be. Only a character with armorer proficiency can detect the flaws, and this requires careful and detailed inspection.

If the flawed armor is struck in melee combat with a natural die roll of 19 or 20, it breaks. The character's AC immediately worsens by 4 additional classes (although never above 10), and the broken armor hampers the character's movement. Until the character can remove the broken armor (a process requiring 1d4 rounds), the character moves at 1/2 of his normal rate and suffers a −4 penalty to all of his attack rolls.

If an armorer is creating a suit of field plate or full plate armor, the character who will use the armor must be present at least once a week during the creation of the armor, since such types of armor require very exact fitting.

Artistic Ability: Player characters with artistic ability are naturally accomplished in various forms of the arts. They have an inherent understanding of color, form, space, flow, tone, pitch, and rhythm. Characters with artistic ability must select one art form (painting, sculpture, composition, etc.) to be proficient in. Thereafter they can attempt to create art works or musical compositions in their given field. Although it is not necessary to make a proficiency check, one can be made to determine the quality of the work. If a 1 is rolled on the check, the artist has created a work with some truly lasting value. If the check fails, the artist has created something aesthetically unpleasing or just plain bad.

Artistic ability also confers a +1 bonus to all proficiency checks requiring artistic skill—music or dance—and to attempts to appraise objects of art.

Astrology: This proficiency gives the character some understanding of the supposed influences of the stars. Knowing the birth date and time of any person, the astrologer can study the stars and celestial events and then prepare a forecast of the future for that person. The astrologer's insight into the future is limited to the next 30 days, and his knowledge is vague at best. If a successful proficiency check is made, the astrologer can foresee some general event—

a great battle, a friend lost, a new friendship made, etc. The DM decides the exact prediction (based on his intentions for the next few gaming sessions). Note that the prediction does not guarantee the result—it only indicates the potential result. If the proficiency check is failed, no information is gained unless a 20 is rolled, in which case the prediction is wildly inaccurate.

Clearly this proficiency requires preparation and advance knowledge on the part of the DM. Because of this, it is permissible for the DM to avoid the question, although this shouldn't be done all the time. Players who want to make their DM's life easier (always a good idea) should consider using this proficiency at the end of a gaming session, giving the DM until the next session to come up with an answer. The DM can use this proficiency as a catalyst and guide for his adventures—something that will prompt the player characters to go to certain places or to try new things.

Characters with the astrology proficiency gain a +1 bonus to all navigation proficiency checks, provided the stars can be seen.

Blacksmithing: A character with blacksmithing proficiency is capable of making tools and implements from iron. Use of the proficiency requires a forge with a coal-fed fire and bellows, as well as a hammer and anvil. The character cannot make armor or most weapons, but can craft crowbars, grappling hooks, horseshoes, nails, hinges, plows, and most other iron objects.

Blind-fighting: A character with blind-fighting is skilled at fighting in conditions of poor or no light (but this proficiency does not allow spell use). In total darkness, the character suffers only a −2 penalty to his attack roll (as compared to a −4 penalty without this proficiency). Under starlight or moonlight, the character incurs only a −1 penalty. The character suffers no penalties to his AC because of darkness.

Furthermore, the character retains special abilities that would normally be lost in darkness, although the effectiveness of these are reduced by one-half (proficiency checks are made at half the normal score, etc.). This proficiency is effective only against opponents or threats within melee distance of the character. Blind-fighting does not grant any special protection from missile fire or anything outside the immediate range of the character's melee weapon. Thus AC penalties remain for missile fire. (By the time the character hears the whoosh of the arrow, for example, it is too late for him to react.)

While moving in darkness, the character suffers only half the normal movement penalty of those without this proficiency.

Furthermore, this skill aids the character when dealing with invisible creatures, reducing the attack penalty to −2. However, it does not enable the character to dis-

cover invisible creatures; he has only a general idea of their location and cannot target them exactly.

Bowyer/Fletcher: This character can make bows and arrows of the types given in Table 44, page 68.

A weaponsmith is required to fashion arrowheads, but the bowyer/fletcher can perform all other necessary functions. The construction time for a long or short bow is one week, while composite bows require two weeks, and 1d6 arrows can be made in one day.

When the construction time for the weapon is completed, the player makes a proficiency check. If the check is successful, the weapon is of fine quality and will last for many years of normal use without breaking. If the check fails, the weapon is still usable, but has a limited life span: An arrow breaks on the first shot; a bow breaks if the character using it rolls an unmodified 1 on his 1d20 attack roll.

Option: If a character wishes to create a weapon of truly fine quality and the DM allows it, the player can opt to use the following alternative procedure for determining the success of his attempt. When the proficiency check is made, any failure means that the weapon is useless. However, a successful check means that the weapon enables the character to add Strength bonuses to attack and damage rolls. Additionally, if the proficiency check is a natural 1, the range of the bow is increased 10 yards for all range classes or is of such fine work that it is suitable for enchantment.

Brewing: The character is trained in the art of brewing beers and other strong drink. The character can prepare brewing formulas, select quality ingredients, set up and manage a brewery, control fermentation, and age the finished product.

Carpentry: The carpentry proficiency enables the character to do woodworking jobs: building houses, cabinetry, joinery, etc. Tools and materials must be available. The character can build basic items from experience, without the need for plans. Unusual and more complicated items (a catapult, for example) require plans prepared by an engineer. Truly unusual or highly complex items (wooden clockwork mechanisms, for example) require a proficiency check.

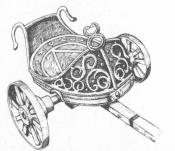

Charioteering: A character with proficiency in this skill is able to safely guide a chariot, over any type of terrain that can normally be negotiated, at a rate 1/3 faster than the normal movement rate for a chariot driven by a character without this proficiency. Note that this proficiency does not impart the ability to move a chariot over terrain that it cannot traverse; even the best charioteer in the world cannot take such a vehicle into the mountains.

Cobbling: The character can fashion and repair shoes, boots, and sandals.

Cooking: Although all characters have rudimentary cooking skills, the character with this proficiency is an accomplished cook. A proficiency check is required only when attempting to prepare a truly magnificent meal worthy of a master chef.

Dancing: The character knows many styles and varieties of dance, from folk dances to formal court balls.

Direction Sense: A character with this proficiency has an innate sense of direction. By concentrating for 1d6 rounds, the character can try to determine the direction the party is headed. If the check fails but is less than 20, the character errs by 90 degrees. If a 20 is rolled, the direction chosen is exactly opposite the true heading. (The DM rolls the check.)

Furthermore, when traveling in the wilderness, a character with direction sense has the chance of becoming lost reduced by 5%.

Disguise: The character with this skill is trained in the art of disguise. He can make himself look like any general type of person of about the same height, age, weight, and race. A successful proficiency check indicates that the disguise is successful, while a failed roll means the attempt was too obvious in some way.

The character can also disguise himself as a member of another race or sex. In this case, a −7 penalty is applied to the proficiency check. The character may also attempt to disguise himself as a specific person, with a −10 penalty to the proficiency check. These modifiers are cumulative, thus it is extremely difficult for a character to disguise himself as a specific person of another race or sex (a −17 penalty to the check).

Endurance: A character with endurance proficiency is able to perform continual strenuous physical activity for twice as long as a normal character before becoming subject to the effects of fatigue and exhaustion. In those cases where extreme endurance is required, a successful proficiency check must be made. Note that this proficiency does not enable a character to extend the length of time that he can remain unaffected by a lack of food or water.

Engineering: The character is trained as a builder of both great and small things. Engineers can prepare plans for everything from simple machines (catapults, river locks, grist mills) to large buildings (fortresses, dams). A proficiency check is required only when designing something particularly complicated or unusual. An engineer must still find talented workmen to carry out his plan, but he is trained to supervise and manage their work.

An engineer is also familiar with the principles of siegecraft and can detect flaws in the defenses of a castle or similar construction. He knows how to construct and use siege weapons and machines, such as catapults, rams, and screws.

Etiquette: This proficiency gives the character a basic understanding of the proper forms of behavior and address required in many different situations, especially those involving nobility and persons of rank. Thus, the character will know the correct title to use when addressing a duke, the proper steps of ceremony to greet visiting diplomats, gestures to avoid in the presence of dwarves, etc. For extremely unusual occurrences, a proficiency check must be made for the character to know the proper etiquette for the situation (an imperial visit, for example, is a sufficiently rare event).

However, having the character know what is correct and actually do what is correct are two different matters. The encounters must still be role-played by the character. Knowledge of etiquette does not give the character protection from a gaffe or faux pas; many people who know the correct thing still manage to do the exact opposite.

Fire-building: A character with fire-building proficiency does not normally need a tinderbox to start a fire. Given some dry wood and small pieces of tinder, he can start a fire in 2d20 minutes. Flint and steel are not required. Wet wood, high winds, or other adverse conditions increase the time to 3d20, and a successful proficiency check must be rolled to start a fire.

Fishing: The character is skilled in the art of fishing, be it with hook and line, net, or spear. Each hour the character spends fishing, roll a proficiency check. If the roll is failed, no fish are caught that hour. Otherwise, a hook and line or a spear will land fish equal to the difference between the die roll and the character's Wisdom score. A net will catch three times this amount.

Of course, no fish can be caught where no fish are found. On the other hand, some areas teem with fish, such as a river or pool during spawning season. The DM may modify the results according to the situation.

Forgery: This proficiency enables the character to create duplicates of documents and handwriting and to detect such forgeries created by others. To forge a document (military orders, local decrees, etc.) where the handwriting is not specific to a person, the character needs only to have seen a similar document before. To forge a name, an autograph of that person is needed, and a proficiency check with a −2 penalty must be successfully rolled. To forge a longer document written in the hand of some particular person, a large sample of his handwriting is needed, with a −3 penalty to the check.

It is important to note that the forger always *thinks* he has been successful; the DM rolls the character's proficiency check in secret and the forger does not learn of a failure until it is too late.

If the check succeeds, the work will pass examination by all except those intimately familiar with that handwriting or by those with the forgery proficiency who examine the document carefully. If the check is failed, the forgery is detectable to anyone familiar with the type of document or handwriting—if he examines the document closely. If the die roll is a 20, the forgery is immediately detectable to anyone who normally handles such documents without close examination. The forger will not realize this until too late.

Furthermore, those with forgery proficiency may examine a document to learn if it is a forgery. On a successful proficiency roll, the authenticity of any document can be ascertained. If the die roll is failed but a 20 is not rolled, the answer is unknown. If a 20 is rolled, the character reaches the incorrect conclusion.

Gaming: The character knows most common games of chance and skill, including cards, dice, bones, draughts, and chess. When playing a game, the character may either play out the actual game (which may take too much time for some) or make a proficiency check, with success indicating victory. If two proficient characters play each other, the one with the highest successful die roll wins. A character with gaming proficiency can also attempt to cheat, thus gaining a +1 bonus to his ability score. If the proficiency check for the game is 17 to 20, however, the character has been caught cheating (even if he won the game).

Gem Cutting: A character with this proficiency can finish the rough gems that are discovered through mining at a rate of 1d10 stones per day. A gem cutter derives no benefit from the assistance of nonproficient characters. A gem cutter must work with a good light source and must have an assortment of chisels, small hammers, and specially hardened blades.

Uncut gems, while still of value, are not nearly as valuable as the finished product. If the cutting is successful (as determined by a proficiency check), the gem cutter increases the value of a given stone to the range appropriate for its type. If a 1 is rolled, the work is exceptionally brilliant and the value of the gem falls into the range for the next most valuable gem (the DM has the relevant tables).

Healing: A character proficient in healing knows how to use natural medicines and basic principles of first aid and doctoring. If the character tends another within one round of wounding (and makes a successful proficiency check), his ministrations restore 1d3 hit points (but no more hit points can be restored than were lost in the previous round). Only one healing attempt can be made on a character per day.

If a wounded character remains under the care of someone with healing proficiency, that character can recover lost hit points at the rate of 1 per day even when traveling or engaging in nonstrenuous activity. If the wounded character gets complete rest, he can recover 2 hit points per day while under such care. Only characters with both healing and herbalism proficiencies can help others recover at the rate of 3 hit points per day of rest. This care does not require a proficiency check, only the regular attention of the proficient character. Up to six patients can be cared for at any time.

A character with healing proficiency can also attempt to aid a poisoned individual, provided the poison entered through a wound. If the poisoned character can be tended to immediately (the round after the character is poisoned) and the care continues for the next five rounds, the victim gains a +2 bonus to his saving throw (delay his saving throw until the last round of tending). No proficiency check is required, but the poisoned character must be tended to immediately (normally by sacrificing any other action by the proficient character) and cannot do anything himself. If the care and rest are interrupted, the poisoned character must immediately roll a normal saving throw for the poison. This result is unalterable by normal means (i.e., more healing doesn't help). Only characters with both healing and herbalism proficiencies can attempt the same treatment for poisons the victim has swallowed or touched (the character uses his healing to diagnose the poison and his herbalist knowledge to prepare a purgative).

A character with healing proficiency can also attempt to diagnose and treat diseases. When dealing with normal diseases, a successful proficiency check automatically reduces the disease to its mildest form and shortest duration. Those who also have herbalism knowledge gain an additional +2 bonus to this check. A proficient character can also attempt to deal with magical diseases, whether caused by spells or creatures. In this case, a successful proficiency check diagnoses the cause of the disease. However, since the disease is magical in nature, it can be treated only by magical means.

Heraldry: The knowledge of heraldry enables the character to identify the different crests and symbols that denote different persons and groups. Heraldry comes in many forms and is used for many different purposes. It can be used to identify noblemen, families, guilds, sects, legions, political factions, and castes. The symbols may appear on flags, shields, helmets, badges, embroidery, standards, clothing, coins, and more. The symbols used may include geometric patterns, calligraphed lines of script, fantastic beasts, religious symbols, and magical seals (made for the express purpose of identification). Heraldry can vary from the highly formalized rules and regulations of late medieval Europe to the knowledge of different shield patterns and shapes used by African tribesmen.

The character automatically knows the different heraldic symbols of his homeland and whom they are associated with. In addition, if the character makes a successful proficiency check, he can correctly identify the signs and symbols of other lands, provided he has at least a passing knowledge of the inhabitants of that land. His heraldry skill is of little use upon first entering a foreign land.

Herbalism: Those with herbalist knowledge can identify plants and fungus and prepare nonmagical potions, poultices, powders, balms, salves, ointments, infusions, and plasters for medical and pseudo-medical purposes. They can also prepare natural plant poisons and purgatives. The DM must decide the exact strength of such poisons based on the poison rules in the *DMG*. A character with both herbalism and healing proficiencies gains bonuses when using his healing talent (see the Healing proficiency).

Hunting: When in wilderness settings, the character can attempt to stalk and bring down game. A proficiency check must be made with a −1 penalty to the ability score for every nonproficient hunter in the party. If the die roll is successful, the hunter (and those with him) have come within 101 to 200 yards (100 + 1d100) of an animal. The group can attempt to close the range, but a proficiency check must be made for each 20 yards closed. If the stalking is successful, the hunter automatically surprises the game. The type of animal stalked depends on the nature of the terrain and the whim of the DM.

Juggling: The character can juggle, a talent useful for entertainments, diversions, and certain rare emergencies. When juggling normally (to entertain or distract), no proficiency check is required. A check is made when trying spectacular tricks ("Watch me eat this apple in mid-air!"). However, juggling also enables the character to attempt desperate moves. On a successful attack roll vs. AC 0 (not a proficiency check), the character can catch small items thrown to harm him (as opposed to items thrown for him to catch).

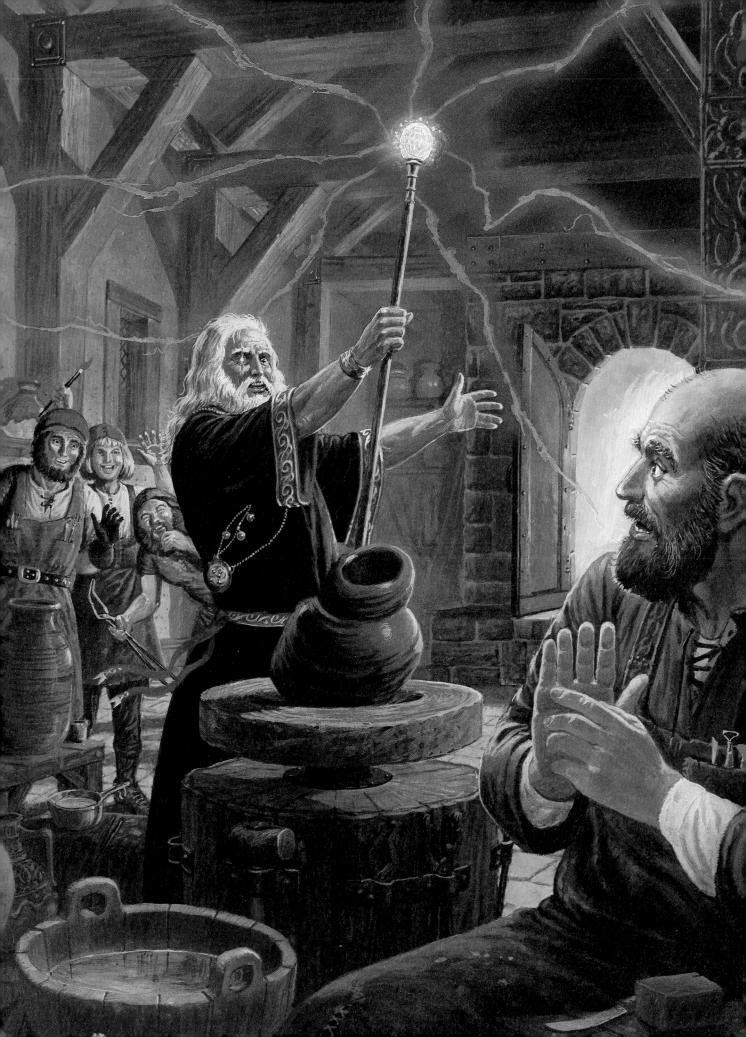

Thus the character could catch a dagger or a dart before it hits. If this attack roll fails, however, the character automatically suffers damage (sticking your hand in the path of a dagger is likely to hurt).

Jumping: The character can attempt exceptional leaps both vertically and horizontally. If the character has at least a 20-foot running start, he can leap (broad jump) 2d6 + his level in feet. No character can broad jump more than six times his height, however. With the same start, he can leap vertically (high jump) 1d3 plus half his level in feet. No character can high jump more than 1½ times his own height.

From a standing start, a character with this proficiency can broad jump 1d6 plus half his level in feet and high jump only three feet.

The character can also attempt vaults using a pole. A vault requires at least a 30-foot running start. If a pole is used, it must be four to 10 feet longer than the character's height. The vault spans a distance equal to 1½ times the length of the pole. The character can clear heights equal to the height of the pole. He can also choose to land on his feet if the vault carries him over an obstacle no higher than ½ the height of his pole. Thus, using a 12-foot pole, the character could either vault through a window 12 feet off the ground (tumbling into the room beyond), land on his feet in an opening six feet off the ground, or vault across a moat 18 feet wide. In all cases, the pole is dropped at the end of the vault.

Languages, Ancient: The character has mastered a difficult and obscure tongue, now primarily found in the writings of pedantic sages and sorcerers. The main use of the language is to read tomes of ancient secrets written by long-dead mystics. This proficiency enables the character to either read and write or speak the language (his choice).

Languages, Modern: The character has learned to speak a language of the known world. To do so, there must be a teacher available. This could be another player character, an NPC hireling, or simply a local townsman.

Leatherworking: This proficiency enables a character to tan and treat leather and to make clothing and other leather objects. The character can make leather armor, as well as backpacks, saddlebags, saddles, and all sorts of harnesses.

Local History: The character is a storehouse of facts about the history of a region the size of a large county or a small province. The character knows when the ruined tower on the hill was built and who built it (and what happened to him), what great heroes and villains fought and fell at the old battlefield, what great treasure is supposed to be kept in a local temple, how the mayor of the next town miraculously grew hair on his balding pate, and more.

The DM will provide information about local sites and events as the character needs to know them. Furthermore, the character can try to retell these events as entertaining stories. Once the subject is chosen, he can either make a proficiency check and, if successful, add that tale to his repertoire, or actually tell the story to other characters. If the character succeeds in entertaining them, the player need not make a proficiency roll for the character, since he has succeeded. The character can tell these stories to entertain others, granting him a +2 bonus to his Charisma for the encounter. But telling stories to hostile beings is probably not going to do any good.

Mining: A character with mining proficiency is needed to site and supervise the operations of any mine. First, the character can attempt to determine what types of ores or gems can be found in a given area. To do this, he must spend at least a week searching a four-square-mile area. The DM may rule that more area must be searched to find anything of value and may thus increase the amount of time required. At the end of the search, the character can say what is likely to be found in this area. After this, the character can site the mine. On a successful proficiency check (made secretly by the DM), the character has found a good site to begin mining for any minerals that may be in the area. The check does not guarantee a successful mine, only that a particular site is the best choice in a given area. The DM must determine what minerals, if any, are to be found in the region of the mine. On a failed check, the character only thinks he has found a good site. Much effort is spent before the character is proved wrong, of course.

Once the mine is in operation, a character with mining proficiency must remain onsite to supervise all work. Although this is a steady job, most player characters will find it better to hire an NPC for this purpose.

Mountaineering: A character with this proficiency can make difficult and dangerous climbs up steep slopes and cliffs with the aid of spikes, ropes, etc. If a character with mountaineering proficiency leads a party, placing the pitons (spikes) and guiding the others, all in the party can gain the benefit of his knowledge. A mountaineer can guide a party up a cliff face it could not otherwise climb. A character with this proficiency gains a 10 percent bonus per proficiency slot spent to his chance to climb any surface. Note that mountaineering is not the same as the thief's climbing ability, since the latter does not require aids of any sort.

Musical Instrument: The character can play a specific musical instrument. An additional instrument can be added for every extra slot devoted to this proficiency. The character plays quite well, and no proficiency check is normally required. The DM may direct the character to make a proficiency check in what he feels are extraordinary circumstances.

Navigation: The character has learned the arts of navigating by the stars, studying currents, and watching for telltale signs of land, reefs, and hidden danger. This is not particularly useful on land. At sea, a successful proficiency check by the navigator reduces the chance of getting lost by 20 percent.

Pottery: A character with this proficiency can create any type of clay vessel or container commonly used in the campaign world. The character requires a wheel and a kiln, as well as a supply of clay and glaze. The character can generally create two small- or medium-sized items or one large-sized item per day. The pieces of pottery must then be fired in the kiln for an additional day.

The raw materials involved cost three cp to make a small item, five cp to make a medium-sized item, and one sp to make a large item.

Reading Lips: The character can understand the speech of those he can see but not hear. When this proficiency is chosen, the player must specify what language the character can lip read (it must be a language the character can already speak). To use the proficiency, the character must be within 30 feet of the speaker and be able to see him speak. A proficiency check is made. If the check fails, nothing is learned. If the check is successful, 70 percent of the conversation is understood. Since certain sounds are impossible to differentiate, the understanding of a lip-read conversation is never better than this.

Reading/Writing: The character can read and write a modern language he can speak, provided there is someone available to teach the character (another PC, a hireling, or an NPC). This proficiency does not enable the character to learn ancient languages (see Languages, Ancient).

Religion: Characters with religion proficiency know the common beliefs and cults of their homeland and the major faiths of neighboring regions. Ordinary information (type of religious symbol used, basic attitude of the faith, etc.) of any religion is automatically known by the character. Special information, such as how the clergy is organized or the significance of particular holy days, requires a proficiency check.

Additional proficiencies spent on religion enable the character either to expand his general knowledge into more distant regions (using the guidelines above) or to gain precise information about a single faith. If the latter is chosen, the character is no longer required to make a proficiency check when answering questions about that religion. Such expert knowledge is highly

useful to priest characters when dealing with their own and rival faiths.

Riding, Airborne: The character is trained in handling a flying mount. The particular creature must be chosen when the proficiency is chosen. Additional proficiency slots can be used to learn how to handle other types of mounts. Unlike land-based riding, a character must have this proficiency (or ride with someone who does) to handle a flying mount. In addition, a proficient character can do the following:

* Leap onto the saddle of the creature (when it is standing on the ground) and spur it airborne as a single action. This requires no proficiency check.

* Leap from the back of the mount and drop 10 feet to the ground or onto the back of another mount (land-based or flying). Those with only light encumbrance can drop to the ground without a proficiency check. In all other situations, a proficiency check is required. A failed roll means the character takes normal falling damage (for falling flat on his face) or misses his target (perhaps taking large amounts of damage as a result). A character who is dropping to the ground can attempt an immediate melee attack, if his proficiency check is made with a −4 penalty to the ability roll. Failure has the consequences given above.

* Spur his mount to greater speeds on a successful check, adding 1d4 to the move-ment rate of the mount. This speed can be maintained for four consecutive rounds. If the check fails, an attempt can be made again the next round. If two checks fail, no attempt can be made for a full turn. After the rounds of increased speed, its movement drops to ²/₃ its normal rate and its Maneu-verability Class (see Glossary) becomes one class worse. These conditions last until the mount lands and is allowed to rest for at least one hour.

* The rider can guide the mount with his knees and feet, keeping his hands free. A proficiency check is made only after the character suffers damage. If the check is failed, the character is knocked from the saddle. A second check is allowed to see if the character manages to catch himself (thus hanging from the side by one hand or in some equally perilous position). If this fails, the rider falls. Of course a rider can strap himself into the saddle, although this could be a disadvantage if his mount is slain and plummets toward the ground.

Riding, Land-Based: Those skilled in land riding are proficient in the art of riding and handling horses or other types of ground mounts. When the proficiency slot is filled, the character must declare which type of mount he is proficient in. Possibilities include griffons, unicorns, dire wolves, and virtually any creatures used as mounts by humans, demihumans, or humanoids.

A character with riding proficiency can perform all of the following feats. Some of them are automatic, while others require a proficiency check for success.

* The character can vault onto a saddle whenever the horse or other mount is stand-ing still, even when the character is wearing armor. This does not require a proficiency check. The character must make a check, however, if he wishes to get the mount mov-ing during the same round in which he lands in its saddle. He must also make a proficien-cy check if he attempts to vault onto the sad-dle of a moving mount. Failure indicates that the character falls to the ground— presumably quite embarrassed.

* The character can urge the mount to jump tall obstacles or leap across gaps. No check is required if the obstacle is less than three feet tall or the gap is less than 12 feet wide. If the character wants to roll a profi-ciency check, the mount can be urged to leap obstacles up to seven feet high, or jump across gaps up to 30 feet wide. Success means that the mount has made the jump. Failure indicates that it balks, and the char-acter must make another proficiency check to see whether he retains his seat or falls to the ground.

* The character can spur his steed on to great speeds, adding 6 feet per round to the animal's movement rate for up to four turns. This requires a proficiency check

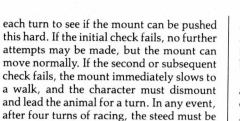

each turn to see if the mount can be pushed this hard. If the initial check fails, no further attempts may be made, but the mount can move normally. If the second or subsequent check fails, the mount immediately slows to a walk, and the character must dismount and lead the animal for a turn. In any event, after four turns of racing, the steed must be walked by its dismounted rider for one turn.

* The character can guide his mount with his knees, enabling him to use weapons that require two hands (such as bows and two-handed swords) while mounted. This feat does not require a proficiency check unless the character takes damage while so riding. In this case, a check is required and failure means that the character falls to the ground and sustains an additional 1d6 points of damage.

* The character can drop down and hang alongside the steed, using it as a shield against attack. The character cannot make an attack or wear armor while performing this feat. The character's Armor Class is lowered by 6 while this maneuver is performed. Any attacks that would have struck the character's normal Armor Class are considered to have struck the mount instead. No proficiency check is required.

* The character can leap from the back of his steed to the ground and make a melee attack against any character or creature within 10 feet. The player must roll a successful proficiency check with a −4 penalty to succeed. On a failed roll, the character fails to land on his feet, falls clumsily to the ground, and suffers 1d3 points of damage.

Rope Use: This proficiency enables a character to accomplish amazing feats with rope. A character with rope use proficiency is familiar with all sorts of knots and can tie knots that slip, hold tightly, slide slowly, or loosen with a quick tug. If the character's hands are bound and held with a knot, he can roll a proficiency check (with a −6 penalty) to escape the bonds.

This character gains a +2 bonus to all attacks made with a lasso. The character also receives a +10 percent bonus to all climbing checks made while he is using a rope, including attempts to belay (secure the end of a climbing rope) companions.

Running: The character can move at twice his normal movement rate for a day. At the end of the day he must sleep for eight hours. After the first day's movement, the character must roll a proficiency check for success. If the die roll succeeds, the character can continue his running movement the next day. If the die roll fails, the character cannot use his running ability the next day. If involved in a battle during a day he spent running, he suffers a −1 penalty to his attack rolls.

Seamanship: The character is familiar with boats and ships. He is qualified to work as a crewman, although he cannot

actually navigate. Crews of trained seamen are necessary to manage any ship, and they improve the movement rates of inland boats by 50 percent.

Seamstress/Tailor: The character can sew and design clothing. He can also do all kinds of embroidery and ornamental work. Although no proficiency check is required, the character must have at least needle and thread to work.

Set Snares: The character can make simple snares and traps, primarily to catch small game. These can include rope snares and spring traps. A proficiency check must be rolled when the snare is first constructed and every time the snare is set. A failed proficiency check means the trap does not work for some reason. It may be that the workmanship was bad, the character left too much scent in the area, or he poorly concealed the finished work. The exact nature of the problem does not need to be known. The character can also attempt to set traps and snares for larger creatures: tiger pits and net snares, for example. A proficiency check must be rolled, this time with a −4 penalty to the ability score. In both cases, setting a successful snare does not ensure that it catches anything, only that the snare works if triggered. The DM must decide if the trap is triggered.

Thief characters (and only thieves) with this proficiency can also attempt to rig man-traps. These can involve such things as crossbows, deadfalls, spiked springboards, etc. The procedure is the same as that for setting a large snare. The DM must determine the amount of damage caused by a man-trap.

Setting a small snare or trap takes one hour of work. Setting a larger trap requires two to three people (only one need have the proficiency) and 2d4 hours of work. Setting a man-trap requires one or more people (depending on its nature) and 1d8 hours of work. To prepare any trap, the character must have appropriate materials on hand.

Characters with animal lore proficiency gain a +2 bonus to their ability score when attempting to set a snare for the purposes of catching game. Their knowledge of animals and the woods serves them well for this purpose. They gain no benefit when attempting to trap monsters or intelligent beings.

Singing: The character is an accomplished singer and can use this ability to entertain others and perhaps earn a small living (note that bards can do this automatically). No proficiency check is required to sing. The character can also create choral works on a successful proficiency check.

Spellcraft: Although this proficiency does not grant the character any spellcasting powers, it does give him familiarity with the different forms and rites of spellcasting. If he observes and overhears someone who is casting a spell, or if he examines the material

components used, he can attempt to identify the spell being cast. A proficiency check must be rolled to make a correct identification. Wizard specialists gain a +3 bonus to the check when attempting to identify magic of their own school. Note that since the spellcaster must be observed until the very instant of casting, the spellcraft proficiency does not grant an advantage against combat spells. The proficiency is quite useful, however, for identifying spells that would otherwise have no visible effect.

Those talented in this proficiency also have a chance (equal to 1/2 of their normal proficiency check) of recognizing magical or magically endowed constructs for what they are.

Stonemasonry: A stonemason is able to build structures from stone so that they last many years. He can do simple stone carvings, such as lettering, columns, and flourishes. The stone can be mortared, carefully fitted without mortar, or loosely fitted and chinked with rocks and earth. A stonemason equipped with his tools (hammers, chisels, wedges, block and tackle) can build a plain section of wall one foot thick, ten feet long, and five feet high in one day, provided the stone has already been cut. A stonemason can also supervise the work of unskilled laborers to quarry stone; one stonemason is needed for every five laborers. Dwarves are among the most accomplished stonemasons in the world; they receive a +2 bonus when using this skill.

Survival: This proficiency must be applied to a specific environment—i.e., a specific type of terrain and weather factors. Typical environments include arctic, woodland, desert, steppe, mountain, or tropical. The character has basic survival knowledge for that terrain type. Additional proficiency slots can be used to add more types of terrain.

A character skilled in survival has a basic knowledge of the hazards he might face in that land. He understands the effects of the weather and knows the proper steps to lessen the risk of exposure. He knows the methods to locate or gather drinkable water. He knows how to find basic, not necessarily appetizing, food where none is apparent, thus staving off starvation. Furthermore, a character with survival skill can instruct and aid others in the same situation. When using the proficiency to find food or water, the character must roll a proficiency check. If the check is failed, no more attempts can be made that day.

The survival skill in no way releases the player characters from the hardships and horrors of being lost in the wilderness. At best it alleviates a small portion of the suffering. The food found is barely adequate, and water is discovered in miniscule amounts. It is still quite possible for a character with survival knowledge to die in the wilderness. Indeed, the little knowledge the character has may lead to overconfidence and doom!

Swimming: A character with swimming proficiency knows how to swim and can move according to the rules given in the Swimming section (page 120). Those without this proficiency cannot swim. They can hold their breath and float, but they cannot move themselves about in the water.

Tightrope Walking: The character can attempt to walk narrow ropes or beams with greater than normal chances of success. He can negotiate any narrow surface not angled up or down greater than 45 degrees. Each round the character can walk 60 feet. One proficiency check is made every 60 feet (or part thereof), with failure indicating a fall. The check is made with a −10 penalty to the ability score if the surface is one inch or less in width (a rope), a −5 penalty if two inches to six inches wide, and unmodified if seven inches to 12 inches wide. Wider than one foot requires no check for proficient characters under normal circumstances. Every additional proficiency spent on tightrope walking reduces these penalties by 1. Use of a balancing rod reduces the penalties by 2. Winds or vibrations in the line increases the penalties by 2 to 6.

The character can attempt to fight while on a tightrope, but he suffers a −5 penalty to his attack roll and must roll a successful proficiency check at the beginning of each round to avoid falling off. Since the character cannot maneuver, he gains no adjustments to his Armor Class for Dexterity. If he is struck while on the rope, he must roll an immediate proficiency check to retain his balance.

Tracking: Characters with tracking proficiency are able to follow the trail of creatures and characters across most types of terrain. Characters who are not rangers roll a proficiency check with a −6 penalty to their ability scores; rangers have no penalty to their ability scores. In addition, other modifiers are also applied to the attempt, according to Table 39.

Table 39: TRACKING MODIFIERS

Terrain	Mod.
Soft or muddy ground	+4
Thick brush, vines, or reeds	+3
Occasional signs of passage, dust	+2
Normal ground, wood floor	0
Rocky ground or shallow water	−10
Every two creatures in the group	+1
Every 12 hours since trail was made	−1
Every hour of rain, snow, or sleet	−5
Poor lighting (moon or starlight)	−6
Tracked party attempts to hide trail	−5

The modifiers in Table 39 are cumulative—total the modifiers for all conditions that apply and combine that with the tracker's Wisdom score to get the modified chance to track.

For example, if Thule's Wisdom score is 16 and he is trying to track through mud (+4), at night (−6), during a sleet storm (−5), his chance to track is 9 (16 + 4 −6 −5). (Thule is a ranger, so he does not suffer the −6 penalty for non-rangers tracking.)

For tracking to succeed, the creature tracked must leave some type of trail. Thus it is virtually impossible to track flying or noncorporeal creatures. The DM may allow this in rare instances, but he should also assign substantial penalties to the attempt.

To track a creature, the character must first find the trail. Indoors, the tracker must have seen the creature in the last 30 minutes and must begin tracking from the place last seen. Outdoors, the tracker must either have seen the creature, have eyewitness reports of its recent movement ("Yup, we saw them orcs just high-tail it up that trail there not but yesterday."), or must have obvious evidence that the creature is in the area (such as a well-used game trail). If these conditions are met, a proficiency check is rolled. Success means a trail has been found. Failure means no trail is found. Another attempt cannot be made until the above conditions are met again under different circumstances.

Once the trail is found, additional proficiency checks are rolled for the following situations:

* The chance to track decreases (terrain, rain, creatures leaving the group, darkness, etc.).
* A second track crosses the first.
* The party resumes tracking after a halt (to rest, eat, fight, etc.).

Once the tracker fails a proficiency check, another check can be rolled after spending at least one hour searching the area for new signs. If this check is failed, no further attempts can be made. If several trackers are following a trail, a +1 bonus is added to the ability score of the most adept tracker. Once he loses the trail, it is lost to all.

If the modifiers lower the chance to track below 0 (e.g., the modifiers are −11 and the character's Wisdom is 10), the trail is totally lost to that character and further tracking is impossible (even if the chance later improves). Other characters may be able to continue tracking, but that character cannot.

A tracking character can also attempt to identify the type of creatures being followed and the approximate number by rolling a proficiency check. All the normal tracking modifiers apply. One identifying check can be rolled each time a check is rolled to follow the trail. A successful check identifies the creatures (provided the character has some knowledge of that type of creature) and gives a rough estimate of their numbers. Just how accurate this estimate is depends on the DM.

When following a trail, the character (and those with him) must slow down, the speed depending on the character's modified chance to track as found from Table 39.

Table 40: MOVEMENT WHILE TRACKING

Chance to Track	Movement Rate
1-6	1/4 normal
7-14	1/2 normal
14 or greater	3/4 normal

In the earlier example, Thule has a modified tracking chance of 9, so he moves at 1/2 his normal movement rate.

Tumbling: The character is practiced in all manner of acrobatics—dives, rolls, somersaults, handstands, flips, etc. Tumbling can only be performed while burdened with light encumbrance or less. Aside from entertaining, the character with tumbling proficiency can improve his Armor Class by 4 against attacks directed solely at him in any round of combat, provided he has the initiative and foregoes all attacks that round. When in unarmed combat he can improve his attack roll by 2.

On a successful proficiency check, he suffers only one-half the normal damage from falls of 60 feet or less and none from falls of 10 feet or less. Falls from greater heights result in normal damage.

Ventriloquism: The character has learned the secrets of "throwing his voice." Although not actually making sound come from somewhere else (like the spell), the character can deceive others into believing this to be so. When using ventriloquism, the supposed source of the sound must be relatively close to the character. The nature of the speaking object and the intelligence of those watching can modify the character's chance of success. If the character makes an obviously inanimate object talk (a book, mug, etc.), a −5 penalty is applied to his ability score. If a believable source (a PC or NPC) is made to appear to speak, a +2 bonus is added to his ability score. The observer's intelligence modifies this as follows:

Intelligence	Modifier
less than 3	+6
3-5	+4
6-8	+2
9-14	0
15-16	−1
17-18	−2
19+	−4

A successful proficiency check means the character has successfully deceived his audience. One check must be made for every sentence or response. The character is limited to sounds he could normally make (thus the roar of a lion is somewhat beyond him).

Since ventriloquism relies on deception, people's knowledge of speech, and assumptions about what should and shouldn't talk, it is effective only on intelligent creatures. Thus it has no effect on animals and the like. Furthermore, the audience must be watching the character since part of the deception is visual ("Hey, his lips don't move!"). Using ventriloquism to get someone to look behind him does not work, since the voice is not actually behind him (this requires the *ventriloquism* spell). All but those with the gullibility of children realize what is truly happening. They may be amused—or they may not be.

Weaponsmithing: This highly specialized proficiency enables a character to perform the difficult and highly exacting work involved in making metal weapons, particularly those with blades. The character blends some of the skill of the blacksmith with an ability to create blades of strength and sharpness. A fully equipped smithy is necessary to use this proficiency.

The time and cost to make various types of weapons are listed on Table 41.

Table 41: WEAPON CONSTRUCTION

Weapon	Construction Time	Material Cost
Arrowhead	10/day	1 cp
Battle Axe	10 days	10 sp
Hand Axe	5 days	5 sp
Dagger	5 days	2 sp
H. Crossbow	20 days	10 sp
L. Crossbow	15 days	5 sp
Fork, Trident	20 days	10 sp
Spear, Lance	4 days	4 sp
Short Sword	20 days	5 sp
Long Sword	30 days	10 sp
2-hd Sword	45 days	2 gp

Weather Sense: This proficiency enables the character to make intelligent guesses about upcoming weather conditions. A successful proficiency check means the charac-

ter has correctly guessed the general weather conditions in the next six hours. A failed check means the character read the signs wrong and forecast the weather incorrectly. The DM should roll the check secretly. A proficiency check can be made once every six hours. However, for every six hours of observation, the character gains a +1 bonus to his ability score (as he watches the weather change, the character gets a better sense of what is coming). This modifier is cumulative, although sleep or other activity that occupies the attention of the character for a long period negates any accumulated bonus.

Sometimes impending weather conditions are so obvious that no proficiency check is required. It is difficult not to notice the tornado funnel tearing across the plain or the mass of dark clouds on the horizon obviously headed the character's way. In these cases, the player should be able to deduce what is about to happen to his character anyway.

Weaving: A character with weaving proficiency is able to create garments, tapestries, and draperies from wool or cotton. The character requires a spinning apparatus and a loom. A weaver can create two square yards of material per day.

Although your character has some impressive abilities and skills, he really isn't going to be effective without the equipment necessary for adventuring. To get this equipment, he needs money. Not only does he need money to outfit himself, but your character also has to cover his living expenses.

Although there are many different types of coins and currencies in the world, all prices and treasures in the AD&D® rules are given in standard coinage. Your DM may have specific names for different coins and may have different rates of exchange, but this is material particular to his campaign. He will tell you if there are differences from the coins listed here. The standard rate of exchange for each coin is given in Table 42.

The basic coins are the copper piece (cp) and the silver piece (sp). These form the backbone of the monetary system and are the coins most frequently found in the hands of the common folk. Above these two coins is the much rarer gold piece (gp). This coin is seldom found in common use and mainly exists on paper as the standard money of account. This means it is used to measure the value of property and goods. Land values, ship cargoes, gemstones, and penalty bonds (royal court fines) are normally calculated in gold pieces, although payment of such vast sums normally takes other forms.

In addition to these coins, there are other unusual metals used in exchange. Most of these come from failed currencies. As such, they are viewed with skepticism by many honest folk. Principal among these coins are the electrum (ep) and platinum pieces (pp). These coins are rarely circulated, and most are hidden away in ancient treasure hoards.

The value of each coin can also be figured by the following: 10 cp = 1 sp; 5 sp = 1 ep; 2 ep = 1 gp; 5 gp = 1 pp.

However, remember that not all wealth is measured by coins. Wealth can take many forms—land, livestock, the right to collect taxes or customs, and jewelry are all measures of wealth. Coins have no guaranteed value. A gold piece can buy a lot in a small village but won't go very far in a large city. This makes other forms of wealth, land for instance, all the more valuable. Indeed, many a piece of jewelry is actually a way of carrying one's wealth. Silver armbands can be traded for goods, a golden brooch can buy a cow, etc. In your adventures, wealth and riches may take many different forms.

Furthermore, in your DM's campaign, there may be special situations or considerations to bear in mind. The Kingdom of Gonfli may be at war with the neighboring Principality of Boosk. Patriotic Gonflians might refuse Boosk coins (probably because they think the coins are worthless). Practical Booskites might accept the Gonfli florin at half normal value (so they can melt them down and mint new Boosk drachmas). Of course, both groups would send your character to the local money changer (if there is one), who would cheerfully convert your foreign coins to the local tender. He will, of course, charge a small commission (10-30%) for this service.

Situations such as these can affect the value of any coin. If your characters start flashing about a lot of gold, pumping it into the local economy, merchants will quickly raise prices. As another example, the local lord may commandeer most of the region's horses for his knights, making those left all that much more expensive.

Starting Money

All player characters begin with some amount of cash. This nest egg may be your character's life savings. It may be a gift from his parents to start him out in the world. It may be his booty from an army campaign. Perhaps he stumbled across a small treasure chest, whetting his appetite for greater and more dangerous prizes. How he came by his money is not important (although it may be fun to know). You are free to create any explanation you want.

To learn your character's starting funds, roll the dice indicated for his group in Table 43. This is the number of gold pieces your character has to obtain equipment. If you are creating a character starting out at a level above 1st level, check with the DM to see if you can increase your character's funds beyond the amounts given here.

Multi-class characters use the most advantageous die range of their classes.

Table 43: INITIAL CHARACTER FUNDS

Character Group	Die Range
Warrior	5d4 × 10 gp
Wizard	(1d4 + 1) × 10 gp
Rogue	2d6 × 10 gp
Priest *	3d6 × 10 gp

* Priest characters can use their money only to purchase equipment and goods. Once all purchases are made, the priest character must return all but two or three of his remaining gold pieces to his superiors (since his equipment is supplied by his organization). Priests cannot lend any of their initial funds to other characters.

Table 42: STANDARD EXCHANGE RATES

			Exchange Value		
Coin	CP	SP	EP	GP	PP
Copper Piece (CP) =	1	$1/10$	$1/50$	$1/100$	$1/500$
Silver Piece (SP) =	10	1	$1/5$	$1/10$	$1/50$
Electrum Piece (EP) =	50	5	1	$1/2$	$1/10$
Gold Piece (GP) =	100	10	2	1	$1/5$
Platinum Piece (PP) =	500	50	10	5	1

Equipment Lists

The following lists include much of the equipment your character needs for adventuring. The most basic of these are weapons, armor, clothing, and outfitting gear. The other lists provide goods and services your character may need during the course of his many adventures. While most items are always available, your DM may add to or delete from these lists. What you want may not be available or, if your DM has set his game in a specific time period, may not have been discovered or invented yet! While he should tell you which items are and aren't available, you should ask if you have any doubts, particularly on large purchases.

Many of the uncommon items in these lists are explained in the following pages.

The price given for each item in the lists is its average price, the amount you can expect the item to cost in a normal economy. However, large cities, barren wildernesses, and places with brave adventurers carrying bags full of gold are not normal economies. In these places you may find yourself paying more (very rarely less) than the amount listed. You can also haggle with merchants over prices, although to speed up the game it's recommended that you save this for your important purchases. If you wind up haggling over the cost of every tankard of ale, your character is going to spend more time being a pennypincher than an adventurer!

Table 44: EQUIPMENT

Clothing

Item	Cost
Belt	3 sp
Boots	—
Riding	3 sp
Soft	1 gp
Breeches	2 gp
Cap, hat	1 sp
Cloak	—
Good cloth	8 sp
Fine fur	50 gp
Girdle	3 gp
Gloves	1 gp
Gown, common	12 sp
Hose	2 gp
Knife sheath	3 cp
Mittens	3 sp
Pin	6 gp
Plain brooch	10 gp

Item	Cost
Robe	—
Common	9 sp
Embroidered	20 gp
Sandals	5 cp
Sash	2 sp
Shoes	1 gp
Silk jacket	80 gp
Surcoat	6 sp
Sword scabbard, hanger, baldric	4 gp
Tabard	6 sp
Toga, coarse	8 cp
Tunic	8 sp
Vest	6 sp

Daily Food and Lodging

Item	Cost
Ale (per gallon)	2 sp
Banquet (per person)	10 gp
Bread	5 cp
Cheese	4 sp
City rooms (per month)	—
Common	20 gp
Poor	6 sp
Common wine (pitcher)	2 sp
Egg or fresh vegetables	1 cp
Grain and stabling for horse (daily)	5 sp
Honey	5 sp
Inn lodging (per day/week)	—
Common	5 sp/3 gp
Poor	5 cp/2 sp
Meat for one meal	1 sp
Meals (per day)	—
Good	5 sp
Common	3 sp
Poor	1 sp
Separate latrine for rooms (per month)	2 gp
Small beer (per gallon)	5 cp
Soup	5 cp

Household Provisioning

Item	Cost
Barrel of pickled fish	3 gp
Butter (per lb.)	2 sp
Coarse sugar (per lb.)	1 gp
Dry rations (per week)	10 gp
Eggs (per 100)	8 sp
(per two dozen)	2 sp
Figs (per lb.)	3 sp
Firewood (per day)	1 cp
Herbs (per lb.)	5 cp
Nuts (per lb.)	1 gp
Raisins (per lb.)	2 sp
Rice (per lb.)	2 sp
Salt (per lb.)	1 sp
Salted herring (per 100)	1 gp
Spice (per lb.)	—
Exotic (e.g., saffron, clove)	15 gp
Rare (e.g., pepper, ginger)	2 gp
Uncommon (cinnamon)	1 gp
Tun of cider (250 gal.)	8 gp
Tun of good wine (250 gal.)	20 gp

Tack and Harness

Item	Cost	Wgt (lb.)
Barding	—	—
Chain	500 gp	70
Full plate	2,000 gp	85
Full scale	1,000 gp	75
Half brigandine	500 gp	45
Half padded	100 gp	25
Half scale	500 gp	50
Leather or padded	150 gp	60
Bit and bridle	15 sp	3
Cart harness	2 gp	10
Halter	5 cp	*
Horseshoes & shoeing	1 gp	10
Saddle	—	—
Pack	5 gp	15
Riding	10 gp	35
Saddle bags	—	—
Large	4 gp	8
Small	3 gp	5
Saddle blanket	3 sp	4
Yoke	—	—
Horse	5 gp	15
Ox	3 gp	20

* These items weigh little individually. Ten of these items weigh one pound.

Transport *

Item	Cost
Barge	500 gp
Canoe	—
Small	30 gp
War	50 gp
Caravel	10,000 gp
Carriage	—
Common	150 gp
Coach, ornamented	7,000 gp
Chariot	—
Riding	200 gp
War	500 gp
Coaster	5,000 gp
Cog	10,000 gp
Curragh	500 gp
Drakkar	25,000 gp
Dromond	15,000 gp
Galleon	50,000 gp
Great galley	30,000 gp
Knarr	3,000 gp
Longship	10,000 gp
Oar	—
Common	2 gp
Galley	10 gp
Raft or small keelboat	100 gp
Sail	20 gp
Sedan chair	100 gp
Wagon or cart wheel	5 gp

* Movement rates for this equipment are given in the *DMG*.

Miscellaneous Equipment

Item	Cost	Wgt (lb)
Backpack	2 gp	2
Barrel, small	2 gp	30
Basket	—	—
Large	3 sp	1
Small	5 cp	*
Bell	1 gp	—
Belt pouch	—	—
Large	1 gp	1
Small	7 sp	1/2
Block and tackle	5 gp	5
Bolt case	1 gp	1
Bucket	5 sp	3
Chain (per ft.)	—	—
Heavy	4 gp	3
Light	3 gp	1
Chest	—	—
Large	2 gp	25
Small	1 gp	10
Cloth (per 10 sq. yds.)	—	—
Common	7 gp	10
Fine	50 gp	10
Rich	100 gp	10
Candle	1 cp	*
Canvas (per sq. yard)	4 sp	1
Chalk	1 cp	*
Crampons	4 gp	2
Fishhook	1 sp	**
Fishing net, 10 ft. sq.	4 gp	5
Flint and steel	5 sp	*
Glass bottle	10 gp	*
Grappling hook	8 sp	4
Holy item (symbol, water, etc.)	25 gp	*
Hourglass	25 gp	1
Iron pot	5 sp	2
Ladder, 10 ft.	5 cp	20
Lantern	—	—
Beacon	150 gp	50
Bullseye	12 gp	3
Hooded	7 gp	2
Lock	—	—
Good	100 gp	1
Poor	20 gp	1
Magnifying glass	100 gp	*
Map or scroll case	8 sp	1/2
Merchant's scale	2 gp	1
Mirror, small metal	10 gp	*
Musical instrument	5-100 gp	1/2-3
Oil (per flask)	—	—
Greek fire	10 gp	2
Lamp	6 cp	1
Paper (per sheet)	2 gp	**
Papyrus (per sheet)	8 sp	**
Parchment (per sheet)	1 gp	**
Perfume (per vial)	5 gp	*
Piton	3 cp	1/2
Quiver	8 sp	1
Rope (per 50 ft.)	—	—
Hemp	1 gp	20
Silk	10 gp	8
Sack	—	—
Large	2 sp	1/2
Small	5 cp	*

Sealing/candle wax
  (per lb.) 1 gp 1
Sewing needle 5 sp **
Signal whistle 8 sp *
Signet ring or
  personal seal 5 gp *
Soap (per lb.) 5 sp 1
Spyglass 1,000 gp 1
Tent — —
  Large 25 gp 20
  Pavilion 100 gp 50
  Small 5 gp 10
Thieves' picks 30 gp 1
Torch 1 cp 1
Water clock 1,000 gp 200
Whetstone 2 cp 1
Wineskin 8 sp 1
Winter blanket 5 sp 3
Writing ink (per vial) 8 gp *

  * These items weigh little individually. Ten of these items weigh one pound.
  ** These items have no appreciable weight and should not be considered for encumbrance unless hundreds are carried.

Animals

Animal	Cost
Boar	10 gp
Bull	20 gp
Calf	5 gp
Camel	50 gp
Capon	3 cp
Cat	1 sp
Chicken	2 cp
Cow	10 gp
Dog	—
Guard	25 gp
Hunting	17 gp
War	20 gp
Donkey, mule, or ass	8 gp
Elephant	—
Labor	200 gp
War	500 gp
Falcon (trained)	1,000 gp
Goat	1 gp
Goose	5 cp
Guinea hen	2 cp
Horse	—
Draft	200 gp
Heavy war	400 gp
Light war	150 gp
Medium war	225 gp
Riding	75 gp
Hunting cat (jaguar, etc.)	5,000 gp
Ox	15 gp
Partridge	5 cp
Peacock	5 sp
Pig	3 gp
Pigeon	1 cp
Pigeon, homing	100 gp
Pony	30 gp
Ram	4 gp
Sheep	2 gp
Songbird	10 sp
Swan	5 sp

Weapons

Item	Cost	Weight (lb.)	Size	Type†	Speed Factor	Damage S-M	L
Arquebus ***	500 gp	10	M	P	15	1d10	1d10
Battle axe	5 gp	7	M	S	7	1d8	1d8
Blowgun	5 gp	2	L	—	5	—	—
Barbed Dart	1 sp	‡	S	P	—	1d3	1d2
Needle	2 cp	‡	S	P	—	1	1
Bow	—	—	—	—	—	—	—
Composite long bow	100 gp	3	L	—	7	—	—
Composite short bow	75 gp	2	M	—	6	—	—
Flight arrow	3sp/12	‡	S	P	—	1d6	1d6
Long bow	75 gp	3	L	—	8	—	—
Sheaf arrow	3 sp/6	‡	S	P	—	1d8	1d8
Short bow	30 gp	2	M	—	7	—	—
Club	—	3	M	B	4	1d6	1d3
Crossbow	—	—	—	—	—	—	—
Hand quarrel	1 gp	‡	S	P	—	1d3	1d2
Hand crossbow	300 gp	3	S	—	5	—	—
Heavy quarrel	2 sp	‡	S	P	—	1d4+1	1d6+1
Heavy crossbow	50 gp	14	M	—	10	—	—
Light quarrel	1 sp	‡	S	P	—	1d4	1d4
Light crossbow	35 gp	7	M	—	7	—	—
Dagger or dirk	2 gp	1	S	P	2	1d4	1d3
Dart	5 sp	½	S	P	2	1d3	1d2
Footman's flail	15 gp	15	M	B	7	1d6+1	2d4
Footman's mace	8 gp	10	M	B	7	1d6+1	1d6
Footman's pick	8 gp	6	M	P	7	1d6+1	2d4
Hand or throwing axe	1 gp	5	M	S	4	1d6	1d4
Harpoon	20 gp	6	L	P	7	2d4	2d6
Horseman's flail	8 gp	5	M	B	6	1d4+1	1d4+1
Horseman's mace	5 gp	6	M	B	6	1d6	1d4
Horseman's pick	7 gp	4	M	P	5	1d4+1	1d4
Javelin	5 sp	2	M	P	4	1d6	1d6
Knife	5 sp	½	S	P/S	2	1d3	1d2
Lance @	—	—	—	—	—	—	—
Heavy horse lance	15 gp	15	L	P	8	1d8+1	3d6
Light horse lance	6 gp	5	L	P	6	1d6	1d8
Jousting lance	20 gp	20	L	P	10	1d3-1	1d2-1
Medium horse lance	10 gp	10	L	P	7	1d6+1	2d6
Mancatcher **	30 gp	8	L	—	7	—	—
Morning star	10 gp	12	M	B	7	2d4	1d6+1
Polearm	—	—	—	—	—	—	—
Awl pike #	5 gp	12	L	P	13	1d6	1d12
Bardiche	7 gp	12	L	S	9	2d4	2d6
Bec de corbin	8 gp	10	L	P/B	9	1d8	1d6
Bill-guisarme	7 gp	15	L	P/S	10	2d4	1d10
Fauchard	5 gp	7	L	P/S	8	1d6	1d8
Fauchard-fork	8 gp	9	L	P/S	8	1d8	1d10
Glaive *	6 gp	8	L	S	8	1d6	1d10

Services

Service	Cost
Bath	3 cp
Clerk (per letter)	2 sp
Doctor, leech, or bleeding	3 sp
Guide, in city (per day)	2 sp
Lantern or torchbearer (per night)	1 sp
Laundry (by load)	1 cp
Messenger, in city (per message)	1 sp
Minstrel (per performance)	3 gp
Mourner (per funeral)	2 sp
Teamster w/wagon	1 sp/mile

Weapons

Item	Cost	Weight (lb.)	Size	Type†	Speed Factor	Damage S-M	L
Glaive-guisarme *	10 gp	10	L	P/S	9	2d4	2d6
Guisarme	5 gp	8	L	S	8	2d4	1d8
Guisarme-voulge	8 gp	15	L	P/S	10	2d4	2d4
Halberd	10 gp	15	L	P/S	9	1d10	2d6
Hook fauchard	10 gp	8	L	P/S	9	1d4	1d4
Lucern hammer #	7 gp	15	L	P/B	9	2d4	1d6
Military fork *	5 gp	7	L	P	7	1d8	2d4
Partisan #	10 gp	8	L	P	9	1d6	1d6 + 1
Ranseur #	6 gp	7	L	P	8	2d4	2d4
Spetum #	5 gp	7	L	P	8	1d6 + 1	2d6
Voulge	5 gp	12	L	S	10	2d4	2d4
Quarterstaff	—	4	L	B	4	1d6	1d6
Scourge	1 gp	2	S	—	5	1d4	1d2
Sickle	6 sp	3	S	S	4	1d4 + 1	1d4
Sling	5 cp.	‡	S	—	6	—	—
Sling bullet	1 cp.	1/2	S	B	—	1d4 + 1	1d6 + 1
Sling stone	—	1/2	S	B	—	1d4	1d4
Spear	8 sp	5	M	P	6	1d6	1d8
Staff sling	2 sp	2	M	—	11	—	—
Sword	—	—	—	—	—	—	—
Bastard sword	—	—	—	—	—	—	—
One-handed	25 gp	10	M	S	6	1d8	1d12
Two-handed	25 gp	10	M	S	8	2d4	2d8
Broad sword	10 gp	4	M	S	5	2d4	1d6 + 1
Khopesh	10 gp	7	M	S	9	2d4	1d6
Long sword	15 gp	4	M	S	5	1d8	1d12
Scimitar	15 gp	4	M	S	5	1d8	1d8
Short sword	10 gp	3	S	P	3	1d6	1d8
Two-hand. sword	50 gp	15	L	S	10	1d10	3d6
Trident	15 gp	5	L	P	7	1d6 + 1	3d4
Warhammer	2 gp	6	M	B	4	1d4 + 1	1d4
Whip	1 sp	2	M	—	8	1d2	1

* This weapon inflicts double damage against charging creatures of L or greater size.

** This weapon can dismount a rider on a successful hit.

*** This weapon available only if allowed by DM.

@ This weapon inflicts double damage when used from the back of a charging mount.

This weapon inflicts double damage when firmly set to receive a charge.

† The "Type" category is divided into Bludgeoning (B), Piercing (P), and Slashing (S). This indicates the type of attack made, which may alter the weapon's effectiveness against different types of armor. See the optional rule on page 90.

‡ These items weigh little individually. Ten of these weigh one pound.

Armor*

Type	Cost	Wgt (lb.)
Banded mail	200 gp	35
Brigandine	120 gp	35
Bronze plate mail	400 gp	45
Chain mail	75 gp	40
Field plate	2000 gp	60
Full plate	4,000-10,000 gp	70
Helmet	—	—
Great helm	30 gp	10
Basinet	8 gp	5
Hide	15 gp	30
Leather	5 gp	15
Padded	4 gp	10
Plate mail	600 gp	50
Ring mail	100 gp	30
Scale mail	120 gp	40
Shield	—	—
Body	10 gp	15
Buckler	1 gp	3
Medium	7 gp	10
Small	3 gp	5
Splint mail	80 gp	40
Studded leather	20 gp	25

* See page 75 for the Armor Class ratings of various armor types.

Table 45: MISSILE WEAPON RANGES

Weapon	ROF	Range S	M	L
Arquebus	1/3	5	15	21
Blowgun	2/1	1	2	3
Comp. long bow, flight arrow	2/1	6	12	21
Comp. long bow, sheaf arrow	2/1	4	8	17
Comp. short bow	2/1	5	10	18
Longbow, flight arrow	2/1	7	14	21
Longbow, sheaf arrow	2/1	5	10	17
Short bow	2/1	5	10	15
Club	1	1	2	3
Hand crossbow	1	2	4	6
Heavy crossbow	1/2	8	16	24
Light crossbow	1	6	12	18
Dagger	2/1	1	2	3
Dart	3/1	1	2	4
Hammer	1	1	2	3
Hand axe	1	1	2	3
Harpoon	1	1	2	3
Javelin	1	2	4	6
Knife	2/1	1	2	3
Sling bullet	1	5	10	20
Sling stone	1	4	8	16
Spear	1	1	2	3
Staff sling bullet	2/1	—	3-6	9
Staff sling stone	2/1	—	3-6	9

"ROF" is the rate of fire—how many shots that weapon can fire off in one round. This is independent of the number of melee attacks a character can make in a round.

Range is given in *tens of yards*. Each range category (Short, Medium, or Long) includes attacks from distances equal to or less than the given range. Thus a heavy crossbow fired at a target 136 yards away uses the medium-range modifier.

The modifiers for range are −2 for medium range and −5 for long range.

Arquebuses (if allowed) double all range modifiers.

Equipment Descriptions

Not every piece of equipment is described here. The vast majority of things found on the equipment lists need no description, as their functions, forms, and purposes are obvious. Only those items whose use is obscure or appearance is unusual are described below. Specific game effects of equipment are given in the appropriate sections of the rules.

Tack and Harness

Barding: A war horse, or any animal trained for combat, is a considerable investment for the average warrior. Therefore it behooves the owner to see that his mount is as well-protected as possible. Other than avoiding risks, the best nonmagical protection is horse armor or barding. Barding is simply some type of armor fitted to be worn by the mount. Full barding covers the neck, chest, and body of the beast, while half barding covers the head, neck, chest, and front quarters. Barding can be made from many different materials; stouter types provide increasing protection according to the Armor Class of the construction. All of this, however, is at the expense of increased weight and lowered maneuverability of the mount. Plate barding, for example, is the equivalent of a warrior's field plate and is made of carefully interlocked plates and joints. It provides an Armor Class of 2 to the mount. It weighs at least 80 to 100 pounds at the lightest and thus a fully equipped war horse with this armor can manage little more than a steady trot at top speed.

Barded animals also require special attention. Care must be taken to prevent chafing and sores. The mount cannot wear the armor indefinitely. It must be removed at night and ideally should not be worn except in preparation for a battle or tournament. Removing horse barding takes 15 minutes for leather and 30 minutes for metal armors. Fitting it on takes twice as long. The weight of barding is carefully distributed to account for the weight of the armor and the rider, so barded animals cannot be used as pack animals! It is normal practice to have a second mount for carrying gear and supplies.

When barding is fitted over a mount whose natural Armor Class is better than the barding, some protection is still gained. This is explained under Armor on page 76.

In addition to horses and elephants, it may be possible to fit barding on more fantastic mounts. Flying steeds can wear only leather or magical barding. Aquatic creatures cannot wear normal barding although extremely rare magical pieces may exist. Other land creatures can certainly be barded, provided your DM rules that they are sturdy enough to carry the weight of armor and rider. Camels, for instance, are seldom barded for this reason. A huge ostrich would not be able to carry barding, since its legs would not support the weight.

Saddles: There two basic saddles—riding and pack. Riding saddles take many forms, but their basic purpose is to carry a person. If your DM has set his campaign in an ancient or early Medieval setting, saddles may be without stirrups. Ask your DM to be sure. Pack saddles are special frames designed to carry supplies and equipment. The only practical limit to how much a well-stowed pack saddle can carry is the carrying ability of the animal.

Transport

Caravel: This ship was sailed in late Medieval/early Renaissance times and was the type of ship Columbus used to reach the New World. (It should be used only in late Medieval settings.) It normally has two or three masts and square sails. No oars are used. The typical caravel is 70 feet long and 20 feet wide. The normal crew is from 30 to 40 men. The average cargo displacement is 150-200 tons.

Coaster: Also called a round ship, this is a small merchant ship that hugs the coasts. This is a sailing ship, fitted with two masts and triangular sails. The average size is 60 to 70 feet long and 20 feet wide. The rudder hangs from one side. The crew is 20 to 30 men, and the cargo capacity is about 100 tons. Normally there is only a small sterncastle. A coaster is slow and not tremendously seaworthy, but it can carry large amounts of cargo with smaller crews than galleys.

Cog: This ship is a larger, improved version of the coaster, able to make ventures into the open sea. Like the coaster, it is a sailing ship with one or two masts, but the cog employs square sails. It is about 75 to 90 feet long and 20 feet wide. The crew is only 18 to 20 men. There is normally one deck and fore- and sterncastles. The cargo capacities of cogs vary greatly, but the average is 100 to 200 tons.

Currach: This ship is an early, primitive vessel. It is made from thick hides stretched over a wood-and-wicker frame. A single mast carries a small square sail, but the curragh is usually worked by oars. It is normally 20 to 40 feet long. The crew is approximately six to eight and the cargo space is limited—no more than five tons.

Drakkar: The largest of the Viking longships is known as a drakkar or dragonship. Built for war, this ship stretches about 100 feet in length. Although a single mast can be raised, oars provide the main source of power. The crew of 60 to 80 men rows, one man to an oar. Up to 160 additional men can be carried for boarding and raiding. Due to its great size, a drakkar is not very seaworthy. This and the fact that there is no space on board for many supplies (certainly not enough for 240 men) or sleeping quarters keep the drakkar close to the coast where it can put in for the night. Because of its cost and limited use, a drakkar is usually built by kings and rulers and is not used for the mundane task of shipping cargo.

Dromond: This ship is the largest of the Byzantine galleys. Although it boasts one or two masts and triangular sails, the main power comes from the 100 oars, 50 to a side. These oars are divided into an upper and lower bank, with one man per oar on the lower bank and three men on the upper bank. Thus, the total crew is about 200 men. The dromond is about 130 to 175 feet long and 15 feet wide, making it a very slender ship. The cargo capacity is around 70 to 100 tons.

A dromond can be used both for shipping and war. As a warship, a ram projects from the front just above the water line. Castles are built fore, aft, and amidships as firing platforms. The cargo space is then taken up by marines. With such numbers of men, it is a very dangerous ship to attack. A dromond is not a seaworthy craft, however, and usually sails in sight of shore. They beach at night like all galleys, since supplies and sleeping accommodations are very limited.

Galleon: This is the largest and most advanced sailing ship that might be available in the AD&D® game. It should appear only in Renaissance-period settings. It is a sail-driven ship with three or four masts. There are normally three through decks (running the length of the ship), while the castles fore and aft have two decks. The average size is about 130 feet long and 30 feet wide. Crews average about 130 men. Although cargo capacity is about 500 tons, a galleon is mainly used as a warship. (In the real world they were fitted with cannon, something beyond the standard AD&D® game rules.) They can easily carry men equal to their tonnage, making capture by pirates nearly impossible.

Great Galley: Built during the Late Middle Ages, the great galley is an improved version of the dromond. It is slightly smaller than the dromond, about 130 feet long and 20 feet wide. The main power comes from 140 rowers, one man to an oar but is supplemented by three masts; this combination gives it better speed and handling. The cargo capacity is 150 tons. When outfitted as a warship, the front end is built as a ram and marines are carried instead of cargo. Like all galleys, the great galley is a coastal vessel, rarely venturing into open water. It is not seaworthy in heavy storms and waits in port for these to pass.

Knarr: This small ship was a common cargo ship of the Scandinavian region. It is 50 to 75 feet long and 15 to 20 feet wide. It has a single mast and a square sail. In times of poor wind, a few oars at the bow and stern can provide more power. The crew ranges from eight to 14 men. The cargo capacity is small, anywhere from ten to 50 tons. The ship is, however, relatively seaworthy and can be used to make long sea voyages (although it cannot be called comfortable). Its flat bottom makes it useful for sailing up rivers and estuaries, and it can be beached easily.

Longship: This is the standard Viking warship. It is more substantial than the knarr but not nearly as massive as the drakkar. An average longship is 75 feet long with 20 to 25 oars per side. Each oar is worked by a single man for a total crew of 40 to 50 men. There is also a single mast and

a square sail. In addition to the crew, the ship can carry an additional 120 to 150 men. A longship can be used for shipping, but its cargo capacity is only about 50 tons. It is, however, fairly seaworthy and can sail across the open sea when necessary.

Miscellaneous Equipment

Holy Item: Holy items are small representations of all those things revered by religions—stars, crosses, hammers, rosaries, anointed oils, blessed wine, sacred teachings, and more. Just what constitutes a holy item depends on the campaign your character is in. All good holy items have similar effects on undead and other evil creatures, provided they are wielded by a follower of a belief associated with these items. Thus, rules that refer to holy symbols and holy water apply to all similar items, provided these items are specially prepared by the cleric's order.

Because of their special nature, holy items cannot normally be purchased. Different sects tend to protect the symbols of their faith to prevent their misuse or corruption. Therefore such items must be obtained through the auspices of a local congregation. This is not difficult for sincere followers of that faith, although requests for rare or unusual items must always be justified. Nonbelievers are given holy items only

if there is a clear and present danger to the faith.

Lanterns: A *hooded lantern* (30-foot radius of light) is a standard lantern with shuttered or hinged sides. It is not directional, as its light is cast equally in all directions. A *bullseye lantern* (60-foot radius of light) has only a single shutter, the other sides being highly polished to reflect the light in a single direction. Both hooded and bullseye lanterns can be carried in one hand. A single flask of oil (one pint) burns for six hours in either.

The *beacon lantern* (240-foot radius of light) is a much larger affair and must be mounted on the prow of a ship, the bed of a wagon, or other large structure. It operates like the bullseye lantern but illuminates to a greater distance. The beacon goes through oil quickly, burning a flask every two hours.

Locks: Locks are still fairly primitive affairs (except for those complicated by the use of magic). All are worked with a large bulky key. Combination locks are virtually unknown at this time. As with most things, there are good, very complex locks as well as bad, easily opened locks.

Magnifying Glass: This simple lens is more an oddity than a useful tool. It does not greatly enhance viewing, especially since many are unevenly ground, creating distortion. It is useful as a substitute for tinder and steel when starting fires.

Merchant's Scale: This is a small balance and pans along with a suitable assortment of weights. Its main use is to weigh coins—a common method of settling a transaction. Merchants are well aware that coins can be undersized, shaved, or plated. The only sound protection is to check the coins against a set of established weights. It is also needed when using foreign coins to make a purchase or exchange. Of course, merchants are no more noble than anyone else and may use sets of false weights—one set heavier than normal for selling an item (causing the customer to pay more) and another set lighter than usual for buying items (letting the merchant pay less). In well-regulated areas, officials verify the accuracy of weights and measures, but this in itself is no protection. Players may wish to have a scale and weights for their own protection.

Oil: *Greek fire* is a general name given to all highly flammable oils used in combat. (Historically, Greek fire was a special combination of oil and chemicals that was sticky and difficult to extinguish.) These oils are highly flammable and a little dangerous to carry. *Lamp oil* is used for lamps and lanterns. It is not particularly explosive although it can be used to feed an existing blaze.

Spyglass: Like the magnifying glass, the spyglass is more of an oddity than a useful item. Objects viewed through it are a little closer, although not much. For better results, magical items are preferred. The spyglass gives from two to three times magnification.

Thieves' Picks: This is a small collection of tools useful to burglars. The kit includes one or more skeleton keys, long metal picks, a long-nosed clamp, a small hand saw, and a small wedge and hammer. These combined with some common tools (such as a crowbar) make up most of the special equipment a thief needs to perform his trade.

Water Clock: This bulky item is good for giving the time accurate to a half-hour. Activated by a regulated flow of drops, the water clock is not something you carry in your pocket. For it to work at all, it must have a source of water and be left undisturbed. A very uncommon item, it is primarily an amusement for the wealthy and a tool for the student of arcane lore. The vast majority of society is not concerned with exact time.

Weapons

The Weapons Table lists more than just the price of each item. It also gives other game information. Since each weapon is different, you should note this information separately for each weapon your character purchases or finds.

Weapon Size: All weapons are classed according to a size category—S, M, L, G, or H. Small (S) weapons are approximately two feet or less in size; medium (M) weapons are two to five feet long; large (L) weapons are generally six feet or greater in length. Giant (G) and huge (H) weapons are not found on the lists, since these are items normally used by ogres, giants, and even greater creatures. They are not items of equipment a PC can normally buy!

A character can always wield a weapon equal to his own size or less. Normally this requires only one hand, except for some missile weapons (bows and crossbows in particular). A character can also use a weapon one size greater than himself although it must be gripped with two hands. Beyond this size limit, the weapon is not usable without special means (most often magical).

Drelb the halfling (size S) can use a short sword with no difficulty (a size S weapon), or a long sword with two hands (a size M weapon), but a glaive (size L) is just too large for him to wield. Likewise, he can use a short bow but is unable to handle a long bow.

Type: Weapons are classified according to types—bludgeoning (B), piercing (P), and slashing (S). These types are used to determine armor type modifiers (if these are used). Weapons vs. Armor Type is explained in Chapter 9: Combat (page 89).

Speed Factor: Weapon speed is a relative measure of the clumsiness of the weapon. The lower the number, the quicker and easier the weapon is to use. Weapon speed is explained in Chapter 9: Combat.

Damage: All weapons are rated for the amount of damage they can cause to small- and medium-sized creatures (S-M) and larger-than-man-sized creatures (L).

Arquebus: This weapon may be disallowed by your DM and you must check with him before you purchase it. An arquebus is an early form of the musket, almost as dangerous to its user as it is to the target. To use an arquebus, you must have a supply of powder and shot and a piece of slow-burning match or cord. These items may or may not be commonly available. (Powder is treated as a magical item in these rules.) The weapon can be fired only once every three rounds, and then only if the character is not attacked while loading. When firing an arquebus, all penalties for range are doubled.

If the attack roll for the arquebus is a 1 or 2, the weapon backfires, causing 1d6 points of damage to the firer. It is also fouled and cannot be used again until it has been cleaned, which takes about 30 minutes. When a arquebus scores a hit, it normally does 1 to 9 points of damage on 1d10. When a 10 is rolled, the die is rolled again and this amount is added to 10. Each time a 10 is rolled, the die is rolled again and added to the previous total. Thus, in a rare instance, a single shot could inflict 37 points, for example, if three consecutive 10s were rolled, followed by a 7. The damage caused by an arquebus is never modified for a high Strength score.

Bows: Bows come in various shapes and sizes. The power of a bow is measured by its pull. The greater the pull, the more Strength needed to work the bow. Thus it is possible for characters to have bows that grant them damage bonuses for high Strength (it is assumed the character has chosen a bow that has a greater pull). Likewise, characters with low Strengths suffer their usual penalties when using a bow (they are forced to use weaker bows or simply cannot draw back as far). The pull of a bow seldom prevents a character from using the weapon, only from gaining the full effect. The true test of a character's Strength comes in stringing a bow—the bow of a strong hero may simply be unstringable by a lesser man (as was Odysseus's).

Heavier pull bows are not normally any more expensive than standard bows. The exceptions to this are those bows that enable the fighter to gain bonuses for exceptional Strength (18/01 or greater). These bows must be custom crafted and cost three to five times the normal price. These bows are also difficult to string or use effectively for those without exceptional Strength. These characters must roll a successful bend bars/lift gates roll to string or use such weapons (again, think of the test of the suitors in Odysseus's household).

Arrows for long bows of all types are divided between light-weight flight arrows and heavier sheaf arrows. Flight arrows have longer ranges and are normally used in hunting. Sheaf arrows have a stronger metal head but a reduced range. They are often used in times of war.

Crossbow: Strength bonuses or penalties do not apply to crossbows, since these are purely mechanical devices. The hand crossbow is easily held in one hand and cocked with the other. The light crossbow, also called latches, must be braced against an object to be cocked with a lever mounted on the stock. The heavy crossbow, also called arbalest, has a powerful pull and must be cocked with a cranequin (a simple winch or lever) that comes with the weapon. One foot is placed in a stirrup at the end of the crossbow while the cranequin is worked. All crossbows fire quarrels or bolts and the correct size must be used with each weapon.

Lance: The different lances are rated according to size and sturdiness. Each type can be used only if the rider is on the same type of horse or a greater one. A man on a light war horse could not use a heavy horse lance, if only because the impact would

bowl him and the horse right over! Furthermore, the heavy and jousting lances require that the rider is firmly in a saddle and using stirrups. The jousting lance is a heavy horse lance modified for use in tournaments, in which the desire is not to kill the opponent. The end of the lance is fitted with a special blunted tip intended to lessen the chance of wounds. Of course, good intentions often go awry, so there is still a chance of injury during a joust.

Mancatcher: This item is a highly specialized type of polearm designed to capture without killing a victim. It consists of a long pole with a spring-loaded set of sharpened jaws at the end. The victim is caught between the arms, which then snap shut. The mancatcher is effective only on man-sized creatures. The target is always treated as AC 10, modified for Dexterity. If a hit is scored, the character is caught. The caught victim loses all shield and Dexterity bonuses and can be pushed and pulled about. This causes an automatic 1d2 points of damage per round and gives a 25% chance of pulling the victim to the ground. The victim can escape on a successful bend bars/lift gates roll, although this results in 1d2 points more damage. A common tactic is to use the weapon to pull horsemen off their mounts, then pin them to the ground.

Polearms: A popular group of weapons during the ancient and Medieval periods were the polearms. Their length was a distinct advantage and, for the peasant, they were a relatively easy weapon to make. Thus there came to be an abundance of polearms of different sizes and shapes. Due to their numbers, there is no standard system for naming polearms. The names used in the AD&D® game might possibly be applied to other weapons elsewhere.

Because of their length, all polearms are infantry weapons and require two hands to use. They are almost always the weapon of the common peasant and soldier, who, lacking a horse and heavy armor, needs some weapon to keep the enemy's knights at bay. Thus most polearms are intended to be used in close-packed formations that present a forest of sharp points and wicked blades to any knight foolish enough to charge.

Awl Pike: Essentially this is a long spear 12 to 20 feet long ending in a spike point of tapered spear head. It was a popular weapon during the Renaissance. Since the pike stuck out in front, men could be packed side-by-side in dense formations, and several rows of men could fight. Large blocks of pikemen made formidable troops. However, once the pikemen engaged in close combat, they normally dropped their clumsy awl pikes and fought hand-to-hand with short swords.

Bardiche: One of the simplest of polearms, the bardiche is an elongated battle axe. A large curving axe-head is mounted on the end of a five- to eight-foot-long shaft. It probably grew out of common peasant tools and was popular with them. One relative disadvantage is that the bardiche required more space to wield than a pike or a spear.

Bec de corbin: This was a highly specialized weapon of the upper classes during the Late Middle Ages and the early Renaissance. It is an early can-opener designed specifically to deal with plate armor. The pick or beak is made to punch through plate, while the hammer side can be used to give a stiff blow. The end is fitted with a short blade for dealing with unarmored or helpless foes. The weapon is about eight feet long. Since the weapon relies on impact, a great deal of swinging space is needed.

Bill-guisarme: A particularly bizarre-looking combination weapon, the bill-guisarme is an outgrowth of the common bill hook. Mounted on a seven- to eight-foot-long pole, it has a combination of a heavy, cleaver blade, a jutting back spike, and a hook or spike on the end. Thus, it can be used in several different ways. Like most polearms, it requires lots of room to use.

Fauchard: An outgrowth of the sickle and scythe, the fauchard is a long, inward curving blade mounted on a shaft six to eight feet long. It can slash or thrust, although the inward curving point makes thrusting rather ineffective. Its advantage is that a peasant can easily convert his common scythe into this weapon of war.

Fauchard-fork: This is an attempted improvement on the fauchard, adding a long spike or fork to the back of the blade. Supposedly this improves the thrusting ability of the weapon. It is still an inefficient weapon.

Glaive: One of the most basic polearms, the glaive is a single-edged blade mounted on a eight- to ten-foot-long shaft. While not the most efficient weapon, it is relatively easy to make and use. Normally the blade turns outward to increase the cutting area until it almost resembles a cleaver or axe.

Glaive-guisarme: Another combination weapon, this one takes the basic glaive and adds a spike or hook to the back of the blade. In theory, this increases the usefulness of the weapon although its actual application is somewhat questionable.

Guisarme: Thought to have derived from a pruning hook, this is an elaborately curved heavy blade. While convenient and handy, it is not very effective.

Guisarme-voulge: This weapon has a modified axe blade mounted on an eight-foot-long shaft. The end of the blade tapers to a point for thrusting and a back spike is fitted for punching through armor. Sometimes this spike is replaced by a sharpened hook for dismounting riders.

Halberd: After the awl pike and the bill, this was one of the most popular weapons of the Middle Ages. Fixed on a shaft five to eight feet long is a large axe blade, angled for maximum impact. The end of the blade tapers to a long spear point or awl pike. On the back is a hook for attacking armor or dismounting riders. Originally intended to defeat cavalry, it is not tremendously successful in that role since it lacks the reach of the pike and needs considerable room to swing. It found new life against blocks of pikemen. Should the advance of the main attack stall, halberdiers issue out of the formation and attack the flanks of the enemy. The pikemen with their overlong weapons are nearly defenseless in such close combat.

Hook fauchard: This combination weapon is another attempted improvement to the fauchard. A back hook is fitted to the back of the blade, supposedly to dismount horsemen. Like the fauchard, this is not a tremendously successful weapon.

Lucern hammer: This weapon is similar to the bec de corbin. Fitted with a shaft up to ten feet long, it is usually found in the hands of the common soldier. Like the bec de corbin, its main purpose is to punch through armor. The end is fitted with the long point of an awl pike to hold off enemy cavalry.

Military fork: This is one of the simplest modifications of a peasant's tool since it is little more than a pitchfork fixed to a longer shaft. With tines strengthened and straightened, the military fork serves well. The need for cutting and cleaving eventually often results in combining the fork with other weapons.

Partisan: Shorter than the awl pike but longer than the spear, the partisan is a broad spear-head mounted on an eight-foot-long shaft. Two smaller blades project out from the base of the main blade, just to increase damage and trap weapons. Since it is a thrusting weapon, it can be used in closely packed formations.

Ranseur: Very much like the partisan, the ranseur differs in that the main blade is thinner and the projecting blades extended more like tines of a fork. These can trap a weapon and sometimes punch through armor.

Spetum: The spetum is a modification of the normal spear. The shaft increases to eight to ten feet and side blades are added. Some have blades that angle back, increasing the damage when pulling the weapon out of a wound. These blades can also trap and block weapons or catch and hold an opponent.

Voulge: The voulge, like the bardiche, is a variation on the axe and the cleaver. The voulge is little more than a cleaver on the end of a long (seven- to eight-foot) pole. It is a popular weapon, easy to make and simple to learn. It is also called the Lochaber axe.

Scourge: This wicked weapon is a short whip with several thongs or tails. Each thong is studded with metal barbs, resulting in a terrible lash. It is sometimes used as an instrument of execution.

Sword, Bastard: This sword is similar to a long sword in size and weight, but has a longer hilt. It can be used one- or two-handed. Use the speed factor and damage appropriate to the grip. If it is used two-handed, your character cannot employ a shield.

Sword, Khopesh: This is an Egyptian weapon. A khopesh has about six inches of handle and quillons. Its blade is then straight from the quillons for about two feet. The blade becomes sickle-shaped at this point, being about two additional feet long but effectively extending the overall length of the sword by only 1¹/₂ feet. This makes the khopesh both heavy and unwieldy, difficult to employ properly, and slow to recover, particularly after a badly missed blow. Its sickle-like portion can snag an opponent or an opposing weapon.

Armor

You are going to want your player character to buy armor, if he is allowed to use any. Armor is the easiest and cheapest way to improve your character's chance of surviving the more violent dangers of the adventuring life. Clearly, the better the armor the character possesses, the less likely he is to be hurt. **Armor protection is measured by Armor Class (AC), a number rating; the lower the Armor Class number, the better the protection.** Table 46 lists the values for all the types of armor found in the equipment lists.

Table 46: ARMOR CLASS RATINGS

Type of Armor	AC Rating
None	10
Shield only	9
Leather or padded armor	8
Leather or padded armor + shield, studded leather, or ring mail armor	7
Studded leather or ring mail + shield, brigandine, scale mail, or hide armor	6
Scale mail or hide + shield, chain mail	5
Chain mail + shield, splint mail, banded mail, bronze plate mail	4
Splint mail, banded mail, or bronze plate mail + shield, plate mail	3
Plate mail + shield, field plate	2
Field plate armor + shield, full plate	1
Full plate armor + shield	0

Note: See this page for more information on the defensive benefits of various shields.

Although there is some controversy historically over the different types of armor, all known or suspected types are included here. However, not all armor may be available if your DM has chosen to set his campaign in a particular historical era or locale. For example, full plate armor is not available to characters adventuring in an ancient Greek setting.

Banded: This armor is made of overlapping strips of metal sewn to a backing of leather and chain mail. Generally the strips cover only the more vulnerable areas, while the chain and leather protect the joints where freedom of movement must be ensured. Through straps and buckles, the weight is more or less evenly distributed.

Brigandine: This armor is made from small metal plates sewn or riveted to a layer of canvas or leather and protected by an outer layer of cloth. It is rather stiff and does not provide adequate protection to the joints where the metal plates must be spaced widely or left off.

Bronze plate mail: This is a plate mail armor—a combination of metal plates, chain mail or brigandine, leather and padding—made of softer bronze. It is easier and cheaper to make than steel armor, but it does not protect as well. A large breastplate and other metal plates cover areas of the body, but the other materials must protect the joints and movable parts of the body. It is not the full plate armor of the heavy knight of the Late Middle Ages and the Renaissance.

Chain mail: This armor is made of interlocking metal rings. It is always worn with a layer of quilted fabric padding underneath to prevent painful chafing and to cushion the impact of blows. Several layers of mail are normally hung over vital areas. The links yield easily to blows, absorbing some of the shock. Most of the weight of this armor is carried on the shoulders and it is uncomfortable to wear for long periods of time.

Field plate armor: This is the most common version of full plate armor, consisting of shaped and fitted metal plates riveted and interlocked to cover the entire body. It includes gauntlets, boots, and a visored helmet. A thick layer of padding must be worn underneath. However, the weight of the suit is well-distributed over the whole body. Such armor hampers movement only slightly. Aside from its expense, the main disadvantages are the lack of ventilation and the time required to put it on and take it off (see the "Getting Into and Out of Armor" section). Each suit of field plate must be individually fitted to its owner by a master armorer, although captured pieces can be resized to fit the new owner (unless such is patently absurd, such as a human trying to resize a halfling's armor).

Full Plate: This is the impressive, high Gothic-style armor of the Late Middle Ages and Renaissance. It is perfectly forged and fitted. All the plates are interlocking and carefully angled to deflect blows. The surfaces are normally highly ornamented with etching and inlaid metals. Each suit must be carefully custom-fitted to the owner and there is only a 20% chance that a captured suit can be refitted to a new owner of approximately the same size. The metal plates are backed by padding and chain mail. The weight is well-distributed. The armor is hot, slow to don, and extremely expensive. Due to these factors, it tends to be used more for parades and triumphs than actual combat.

Hide: This is armor prepared from the extremely thick hide of a creature (such as an elephant) or from multiple layers of regular leather. It is stiff and hard to move in.

Leather: This armor is made of leather hardened in boiling oil and then shaped into breastplate and shoulder protectors. The remainder of the suit is fashioned from more flexible, somewhat softer materials.

Padded: This is the simplest type of armor, fashioned from quilted layers of cloth and batting. It tends to get hot and after a time becomes foul with sweat, grime, lice, and fleas.

Plate mail: This armor is a combination of chain or brigandine with metal plates (curiass, epaulettes, elbow guards, gauntlets, tassets, and greaves) covering vital areas. The weight is distributed over the whole body and the whole thing is held together by buckles and straps. This is the most common form of heavy armor.

Ring mail: This is an early (and less effective) form of chain mail in which metal rings are sewn directly to a leather backing instead of being interlaced. (Historians still debate whether this armor ever existed.)

Scale mail: This is a coat and leggings (and perhaps a separate skirt) of leather covered with overlapping pieces of metal, much like the scales of a fish.

Shields: All shields improve a character's Armor Class by 1 or more against a specified number of attacks. A shield is useful only to protect the front and flanks of the user. Attacks from the rear or rear flanks cannot be blocked by a shield (exception: a shield slung across the back does help defend against rear attacks). The reference to the size of the shield is relative to the size of the character. Thus a human's small shield would have all the effects of a medium shield when used by a gnome.

A *buckler* (or target) is a very small shield that fastens on the forearm. It can be worn by crossbowmen and archers with no hindrance. Its small size enables it to protect against only one attack per melee round (of the user's choice), improving the character's Armor Class by 1 against that attack.

A *small shield* is carried on the forearm and gripped with the hand. Its light weight permits the user to carry other items in that hand (although he cannot use weapons). It can be used to protect against two frontal attacks of the user's choice.

The *medium shield* is carried in the same manner as the small shield. Its weight prevents the character from using his shield hand for other purposes. With a medium shield, a character can protect against any frontal or flank attacks.

The *body shield* is a massive shield reaching nearly from chin to toe. It must be firmly fastened to the forearm and the shield hand must grip it at all times. It provides a great deal of protection, improving the Armor Class of the character by 1 against melee attacks and by 2 against missile attacks, for attacks from the front or front flank sides. It is very heavy; the DM may wish to use the optional encumbrance system if he allows this shield.

Splint Mail: The existence of this armor has been questioned. It is claimed that the armor is made of narrow vertical strips riveted to a backing of leather and cloth padding. Since this is not flexible, the joints are protected by chain mail.

Studded leather: This armor is made from leather (not hardened as with normal leather armor) reinforced with close-set metal rivets. In some ways it is very similar to brigandine, although the spacing between each metal piece is greater.

In addition to the types of armor listed above, your DM may have special armors prepared from rare or exotic materials. Since it is highly unlikely that your character can afford these at the start, the DM will tell you when you need to know about such items.

Armor Sizes

The equipment list reflects the price of a suit of armor (including an appropriate helmet) made for any normal player character race. Although a halfling is much smaller than a human and needs a smaller suit, there are fewer armorers available to meet such specialized needs. Thus the armor for a halfling is as expensive as that for a human. Armor for nonstandard sizes and shapes is going to cost significantly more and must be custom-made. This is not the kind of thing one can pick up at the local store!

When armor is found during the course of an adventure, the players should note the creature who wore the armor previously. While a human-sized character might be able to wear the armor of a gnoll, it will do little good for a halfling. Likewise, the armor of a giant is of little use to anyone.

Armor size also affects the weight of the armor, if the optional encumbrance system is used. The weights listed on the table are for human-sized (Medium) armors. Small armor weighs half the amount listed, while large armor weighs 50% more.

Getting Into and Out of Armor

There are times when it is important to know how quickly a character can get into or out of his armor. Accidents and unforeseen events happen all the time. The party is attacked at night. Those sleeping around the campfire may want to don their armor before rushing into battle. A character slips and falls into the river where his heavy armor pulls him down like a stone. He greatly desires to get it off before he drowns. Just how long does it take him?

The time required to don armor depends on its make. Those armors that are a single piece—leather tunics, robes, chain mail—take one round (two for metal items) to don with slight assistance. Without aid, the time is doubled. Armor that is made of separate pieces requires 1d6 + 4 rounds, again with assistance. Without help, the time required is tripled. In all cases, the times given assume that the proper undergarments and padding are also worn.

Sometimes characters need to get into armor in a hurry and thus they dress hastily. This assumes that some buckles aren't fastened, seatings adjusted, etc. Single suits can be hastily donned in one round at the cost of 1 worse AC (though never worse than 8). Thus, a fighter could hastily pull on his brigandine jack (AC 6) and charge into a fray with an AC of 7. Hastily donning piece armor (plate mail for example) improves the character's AC by 1 (from a base of 10) for every round spent dressing. A fighter could choose to spend three rounds fitting on parts of his plate mail, giving him an AC of 7, before going into battle.

Removing armor is a much quicker matter. Most can be shed in a single round. Piece armor (particularly full plate) requires 1d4 + 1 rounds. However, if the character is willing to cut straps and bend pins, such armors can be removed in half the time (roll 1d4 +1, divide by 2, then round fractions up).

Creatures with Natural Armor Classes

Some creatures possess a natural Armor Class already superior to some of the armor types (for example, the horse is AC 7). However, these creatures can still benefit from wearing armor of a quality worse than their natural Armor Class. If the AC of armor is equal to or worse than the AC of the creature, the AC of the creature improves by 1.

For example, a horse has a natural AC of 7. The AC of leather armor is 8, worse than the horse's natural AC. However, if a horse is fitted with leather barding, its AC drops to 6 since it gains the benefit of the additional protection.

Encumbrance (Optional Rule)

A natural desire is to have your character own one of everything. Thus equipped, your character could just reach into his pack and pull out any item he wants whenever he needs it. Sadly, there are limits to how much your character, his horse, his mule, his elephant, or his whatever can carry. These limits are determined by *encumbrance*.

Encumbrance is measured in pounds. To calculate encumbrance, simply total the pounds of gear carried by the creature or character. Add five pounds for clothing, if any is worn. This total is then compared to the carrying capacity of the creature to determine the effects. In general, the more weight carried, the slower the movement and the worse the character is at fighting.

Table 47: CHARACTER ENCUMBRANCE

Character Strength	Unencum.	Light	Encumbrance Moderate	Heavy	Severe	Max. Carried Weight
2	0-1	2	3	4	5-6	6
3	0-5	6	7	8-9	10	10
4-5	0-10	11-13	14-16	17-19	20-25	25
6-7	0-20	21-29	30-38	39-46	47-55	55
8-9	0-35	36-50	51-65	66-80	81-90	90
10-11	0-40	41-58	59-76	77-96	97-110	110
12-13	0-45	46-69	70-93	94-117	118-140	140
14-15	0-55	56-85	86-115	116-145	146-170	170
16	0-70	71-100	101-130	131-160	161-195	195
17	0-85	86-121	122-157	158-193	194-220	220
18	0-110	111-149	150-188	189-227	228-255	255
18/01-50	0-135	136-174	175-213	214-252	253-280	280
18/51-75	0-160	161-199	200-238	239-277	278-305	305
18/76-90	0-185	186-224	225-263	264-302	303-330	330
18/91-99	0-235	236-274	275-313	314-352	353-380	380
18/00	0-335	336-374	375-413	414-452	453-480	480

Basic Encumbrance (Tournament Rule)

Encumbrance is divided into five categories: Unencumbered, Light, Moderate, Heavy, and Severe Encumbrance.

To calculate your character's encumbrance category, first figure out the total weight he is carrying (including five pounds for clothing). Then look across the row corresponding to your character's Strength on Table 47 until you come to the column that includes your character's carried weight. The heading at the top of that column shows his level of encumbrance.

Use Table 49 to figure out the encumbrance category of your character's mount or beast of burden.

The Max. Carried Wgt. column lists the most weight (in pounds) your character can carry and still move. But movement is limited to 10 feet per round, as your character staggers under the heavy load.

Specific Encumbrance (Optional Rule)

The maximum total weight your character can carry is determined by his Strength, as listed on Table 47.

The basic encumbrance rule gives general categories of encumbrance but does not allow for fine distinctions. Some players and DMs may take exception to the idea that adding one more pound to a character suddenly shifts that character to the next (and drastically worse) encumbrance category. They may want to use the following optional table; Table 48 reduces a character's movement rating 1 factor at a time.

To determine your character's movement rate (see "Movement," page 119) for a given load, find the row on Table 48 with his Strength score. Read across it until you find the first column in which the number of pounds listed is *greater* than your character's current load. At the top of that column are two rows for base movement rates. Characters with a base movement rate of 12 use the top row; those with a base movement rate of 6 use the bottom row. The number in the appropriate upper row is your character's modified movement rate.

Tarus (a human with a base movement of 12) has a Strength of 17 and is carrying a 140-pound load. Looking across on the 17 row shows that 140 falls between 133 and 145 on the table. Looking at the top

Table 48: MODIFIED MOVEMENT RATES

Strength Score	Base Move 12 / 6	11 / 5	10 / 5	9 / 4	8 / 4	7 / 3	6 / 3	5 / 2	4 / 2	3 / 1	2 / 1	1 / 1
2	1	—	2	—	—	3	—	—	4	—	—	5
3	5	—	6	—	7	—	—	8	—	9	—	—
4-5	10	11	12	13	14	15	16	17	18	19	20	21
6-7	20	23	26	29	32	35	38	41	44	47	50	53
8-9	35	40	45	50	55	60	65	70	75	80	85	89
10-11	40	46	52	58	64	70	76	82	88	94	100	106
12-13	45	53	61	69	77	85	93	101	109	117	125	133
14-15	55	65	75	85	95	105	115	125	135	145	155	165
16	70	80	90	100	110	120	130	140	150	160	170	180
17	85	97	109	121	133	145	157	169	181	193	205	217
18	110	123	136	149	162	175	188	201	214	227	240	253
18/01-50	135	148	161	174	187	200	213	226	239	252	265	278
18/51-75	160	173	186	199	212	225	238	251	264	277	290	303
18/76-90	185	198	211	224	237	250	263	276	289	302	315	328
18/91-99	235	248	261	274	287	300	313	326	339	352	365	378
18/00	335	348	361	374	387	400	413	426	439	452	465	478

Table 49: CARRYING CAPACITIES OF ANIMALS

Mount	Base Move	2/3 Move	1/3 Move
Camel	0-330 lbs.	331-500 lbs.	501-660 lbs.
Dog	0-15 lbs.	16-20 lbs.	21-30 lbs.
Elephant	0-500 lbs.	501-750 lbs.	751-1,000 lbs.
Horse, draft	0-260 lbs.	261-390 lbs.	391-520 lbs.
Horse, heavy	0-260 lbs.	261-390 lbs.	391-520 lbs.
Horse, light	0-170 lbs.	171-255 lbs.	256-340 lbs.
Horse, medium	0-220 lbs.	221-330 lbs.	331-440 lbs.
Horse, riding	0-180 lbs.	181-270 lbs.	271-360 lbs.
Mule	0-250 lbs.	251-375 lbs.	376-500 lbs.
Ox	0-220 lbs.	221-330 lbs.	331-440 lbs.
Yak	0-220 lbs.	221-330 lbs.	331-440 lbs.

Aside from knowing the weight limits, your character needs to have ways to hold all his gear. The capacities of different containers are given in Table 50.

Table 50: STOWAGE CAPACITY

Item	Weight Cap.	Volume
Backpack	50 lbs.	3' × 2' × 1'
Basket, large	20 lbs.	2' × 2' × 2'
Basket, small	10 lbs.	1' × 1' × 1'
Belt pouch, large	8 lbs.	6" × 8" × 2"
Belt pouch, small	5 lbs.	4" × 6" × 2"
Chest, large	100 lbs.	3' × 2' × 2'
Chest, small	40 lbs.	2' × 1' × 1'
Sack, large	30 lbs.	2' × 2' × 1'
Sack, small	15 lbs.	1' × 1' × 8"
Saddle bags, large	30 lbs.	18" × 1' × 6"
Saddle bags, small	20 lbs.	1' × 1' × 6"

of the 145 column shows that Tarus has a modified movement rate of 7. He can carry five more pounds of gear (total 145 pounds) and maintain his speed, or drop seven pounds of equipment (to 133 pounds) and increase his speed to 8.

Encumbrance and Mounts (Tournament Rule)

The "Base Move" column in Table 49 lists the maximum amount an animal can carry and maintain its normal movement rate. Animals can be loaded greater than this, up to a maximum of twice their normal load. However, this causes a drop in the animal's movement rate (as indicated by the column headings). When calculating a mount's load, be sure to include the weight of the rider!

The values listed in Table 50 are for standard-sized items. It is certainly possible for sacks, chests, and backpacks to be larger or smaller than the sizes listed. The weight capacity, however, lists the maximum weight the item can carry, regardless of size. Beyond this point, the material used to construct the item will fail, sooner or later. The volume gives the length, width, and height or depth of the item. Items that exceed the capacity of a container cannot be stored in it.

Since all player characters are adventurers, it is assumed they know the best methods for packing and stowing equipment. Blankets are rolled into bedrolls, small items are carefully arranged, rope is properly coiled, weapons are slung in the most comfortable manner, etc. While small items can be easily stuffed into a pack, large bulky things may encumber more than their actual weight would indicate. The DM has the right to rule that an object is more encumbering than it actually appears.

For example, Tarus Bloodheart finds a 5' × 9' flying carpet. He carefully rolls it into a thick cylinder and wisely ties it closed. Even though he has taken this sensible precaution, the carpet is still a large and awkward thing. The DM rules that although the carpet weighs only 20 pounds, its encumbrance is equal to that of an item weighing 50 pounds. Tarus must increase his current encumbrance level by 50 pounds, adding the awkwardness of the rolled carpet slung over his shoulder to his already carefully packed backpack.

Magical Armor and Encumbrance

One of the special properties of magical armor is its effect on encumbrance. Although magical armor appears to weigh as much as normal armor, the weight of magical armor applies only toward the weight limit of the character. It does not apply when determining the effects of encumbrance on movement and combat. In essence, the armor appears to weigh as much as normal armor but does not restrict or hamper the character.

For example, Cwell the bard finds a suit of chain mail +1. Lifting it up, he finds it weighs 60 pounds. Cwell is already carrying 50 pounds of gear. Donning the chain mail, he is now carrying 110 lbs. of gear. Cwell's Strength is 12, which means that he can carry only 30 more pounds of equipment. However, when calculating the effect of all this weight on his movement, Cwell is considered to only be carrying 50 pounds of gear—the magical armor doesn't count. Furthermore, he does not suffer any combat penalties for the chain mail's weight.

Effects of Encumbrance

Encumbrance has two basic effects. First, it reduces your character's movement rate. If encumbrance categories are used, Unencumbered has no effect on movement, Light reduces the movement rate by $1/3$ (round fractions down), Moderate reduces it by $1/2$, Heavy reduces it by $2/3$, and Severe lowers the movement rate to 1. If the optional system is used, the character's movement rate is reduced to the amount found by using Table 48. The movement rate determines how far your character can move in a round, turn, hour, and day. As his movement rate gets lower, your character moves slower and slower. See "Movement," on page 119, for more details.

Encumbrance also reduces your character's combat abilities. If encumbrance reduces your character to $1/2$ of his normal movement rate, he suffers a −1 penalty to his attack roll. If he is reduced to $1/3$ or less of his normal movement rate, the attack penalty is −2 and there is an additional AC penalty of +1. If your character's movement is reduced to 1, the attack roll penalty is −4 and the AC penalty is +3. Clearly, the wise thing for a heavily encumbered character to do is to quickly drop most of his gear before entering battle.

Some of the most powerful weapons player characters have at their disposal in the AD&D® game are magical spells. Through spells a player character can control earthquakes, call lightning out of the sky, heal grievous injuries, hurl explosive balls of fire, create barriers of stone, fire, and ice, and learn secrets long forgotten. These are only a few of the things player characters can do once they master the strange lore of spells.

Not every character is capable of casting spells, however. This ability requires a certain amount of aptitude, depending on the type of spells cast. Wizard spells are best mastered by those with keen intelligence and patience for the long years of study that are required. Priest spells call for inner peace and faith and an intense devotion to one's calling.

The vast majority of people in a fantasy campaign lack these traits or have never had the opportunity to develop them. The baker may be a bright and clever fellow, but, following in his father's footsteps, he has spent his life learning the arts of bread making. There has simply been no time in his life for the study of old books and crumbling scrolls. The hard-working peasant may be pious and upright in his faith, but he lacks the time for the contemplative and scholarly training required of a priest. So it is only a fortunate few who have the ability and opportunity to learn the arcane lore of spellcasting.

A few character classes have a limited ability to cast spells. The ranger, through his close association with nature, is able to cast a few spells, though his choices are limited to his natural inclinations. The paladin, through his devotion and humility, can use some of the spells of the priest. The bard, through luck, happenstance, curiosity, and perseverance, can manage a few wizard spells, perhaps by persuading a lonely mage to reveal his secrets.

Regardless of their source, all spells fall into the general categories of wizard or priest. Although some spells appear in both categories, in general the categories differ in how spells are acquired, stored, and cast.

Wizard Spells

Wizard spells range from spells of simple utility to great and powerful magics. The wizard spell group has no single theme or purpose. The vast majority of wizard spells were created by ancient mages for many different purposes. Some are to serve the common man in his everyday needs. Others provide adventurers with the might and firepower they need to survive. Some are relatively simple and safe to use (as safe as magic can be); others are complicated, filled with hazards and snares for the rash and unwary. Perhaps the greatest of all wizard spells is the powerful and tricky *wish*. It represents the epitome of spell-casting—causing things to happen simply because the mage desires it to be so. But it is a long and difficult task to attain the mastery needed to learn this spell.

Although some characters can use spells, the workings of magic are dimly understood at best. There are many theories about where the power comes from. The most commonly accepted idea is that the mysterious combination of words, gestures, and materials that make up a spell somehow taps an extradimensional source of energy that in turn causes the desired effect. Somehow the components of the spells—those words, gestures and materials—route this energy to a specific and desired result. Fortunately, how this happens is not very important to the majority of wizards. It is enough to know that "when you do this, that happens."

Casting a wizard spell is a very complicated ordeal. The process of learning the correct procedure to cast a spell is difficult and taxing to the mind. Thus a wizard must check to see if he learns each new spell (according to his Intelligence—see Table 4). Furthermore, there is a limit to just how much of this strangeness—illogical mathematics, alchemical chemistry, structuralist linguistics—a wizard's mind can compre-

hend, and so he must also live with a limit to the number of spells he can know.

As the wizard learns spells, he records their arcane notes into his spell books. Without spell books, a wizard cannot memorize new spells. Within them are all his instructions for memorizing and casting all the spells he knows. As the wizard successfully learns a new spell, he carefully enters its formula into his spell books. A wizard can never have a spell in his books that he does not know, because if he doesn't understand it, he cannot write the formula. Likewise, he cannot enter a spell into his books that is higher in level than he can cast. If he finds an ancient tome with spells of higher power, he must simply wait until he advances to a level at which he can use them.

The exact shape and size of a character's spell books is a detail your DM will provide. They may be thick tomes of carefully inked parchment, crackling scrolls in bulky cases, or even weighty clay tablets. They are almost never convenient to carry around. Their exact form depends on the type and setting of the campaign world your DM has created.

Ultimately, it is the memorization that is important. To draw on magical energy, the wizard must shape specific mental patterns in his mind. He uses his spell books to force his mind through mental exercises, preparing it to hold the final, twisted patterns. These patterns are very complicated and alien to normal thought, so they don't register in the mind as normal learning. To shape these patterns, the wizard must spend time memorizing the spell, twisting his thoughts and recasting the energy patterns each time to account for subtle changes—planetary motions, seasons, time of day, and more.

Once a wizard memorizes a spell, it remains in his memory (as potential energy) until he uses the prescribed components to trigger the release of the energy patterns. The mental patterns apparently release the energy while the components shape and guide it. Upon casting, the energy of the spell is spent, wiped clean from the wizard's mind. The mental patterns are lost until the wizard studies and memorizes that spell again.

The number of spells a wizard can memorize is given by his level (see Table 21); he can memorize the same spell more than once, but each memorization counts as one spell toward his daily memorization limit. Part of a wizard's intelligence can be seen in the careful selection of spells he has memorized.

Memorization is not a thing that happens immediately. The wizard must have a clear head gained from a restful night's sleep and then has to spend time studying his spell books. The amount of study time needed is 10 minutes per level of the spell being mem-

orized. Thus, a 9th-level spell (the most powerful) would require 90 minutes of careful study. Clearly, high-level spellcasters do not lightly change their memorized spells.

Spells remain memorized until they are cast or wiped from the character's mind by a spell or magical item. A wizard cannot choose to forget a memorized spell to replace it with another one. He can, however, cast a spell just to cleanse his mind for another spell. (The DM must make sure that the wizard does not get experience for this.)

Schools of Magic

Although all wizard spells are learned and memorized the same way, they fall into nine different schools of magic. A school of magic is a group of related spells.

Abjuration spells are a group of specialized protective spells. Each is used to prevent or banish some magical or nonmagical effect or creature. They are often used to provide safety in times of great danger or when attempting some other particularly dangerous spell.

Alteration spells cause a change in the properties of some already existing thing, creature, or condition. This is accomplished by magical energy channeled through the wizard.

Conjuration/summoning spells bring something to the caster from elsewhere. Conjuration normally produces matter or items from some other place. Summoning enables the caster to compel living creatures and powers to appear in his presence or to channel extraplanar energies through himself.

Enchantment/charm spells cause a change in the quality of an item or the attitude of a person or creature. Enchantments can bestow magical properties on ordinary items, while charms can unduly influence the behavior of beings.

Greater divinations are more powerful than lesser divinations (see below). These spells enable the wizard to learn secrets long forgotten, to predict the future, and to uncover things hidden or cloaked by spells.

Illusions deal with spells to deceive the senses or minds of others. Spells that cause people to see things that are not there, hear noises not made, or remember things that never happened are all illusions.

Invocation/Evocation spells channel magical energy to create specific effects and materials. Invocation normally relies on the intervention of some higher agency (to whom the spell is addressed), while evocation enables the caster to directly shape the energy.

Lesser divination spells are learnable by all wizards, regardless of their affiliation. This school includes the most basic and vital spells of the wizard—those he needs to prac-

tice other aspects of his craft. Lesser divinations include *read magic* and *detect magic*.

Necromancy is one of the most restrictive of all spell schools. It deals with dead things or the restoration of life, limbs, or vitality to living creatures. Although a small school, its spells tend to be powerful. Given the risks of the adventuring world, necromantic spells are considered quite useful.

Learning Spells

Whether a character chooses to be a mage or a specialist in one of the schools of magic, he must learn his spells from somewhere. While it might be possible for the exceptional wizard to learn the secrets of arcane lore entirely on his own, it isn't very likely. It is far more likely that your character was apprenticed to another wizard as a lad. This kindly (severe), loving (callous), understanding (ill-tempered), generous (mean-spirited), and upright (untrustworthy) master taught your character everything he knows at the start of the game. Then, when it was time, the master sent him into the world (threw him out) with a smile and a pat on the back (snarling with his foot on your character's behind).

Or perhaps your character studied at a proper academy for wizards (if your DM has such things). There he completed his lessons under the eye of a firm (mean) but patient (irritable) tutor who was ready with praise for good work (a cane for the slightest fault). But alas, your character's parents were impoverished and his studies had to end (fed up with this treatment, your youthful character fled during the night).

As you can see, there are a number of ways your character might have learned his spells.

The one good thing that comes from your character's studies is his initial spell book. It may have been a gift from his school or he may have stolen it from his hated master. Whatever the case, your character begins play with a spell book containing up to a few 1st-level spells. Your DM will tell you the exact number of spells and which spells they are. As your character adventures, he will have the opportunity to add more spells to his collection.

When your character attains a new level, he may or may not receive new spells. This is up to your DM. He may allow your character to return to his mentor (provided he departed on good terms!) and add a few spells to his book. It may be possible for your character to copy spells from the spell book of another player character (with his permission, of course). Or he may have to wait until he can find a spell book with new spells. How he gets his spells is one of the things your DM decides.

In all cases, before he can add a new spell

to his spell book, you have to check to see if your character learns that spell. The chance of learning a spell depends on your wizard's Intelligence, as given in Table 4. This chance may be raised or lowered if your character is a specialist.

Illusions

Of all spells, those of the illusion school cause the most problems. Not that they are more difficult for your player character to cast, but these spells are more difficult for you to role-play and for your DM to adjudicate. Illusions rely on the idea of believability, which in turn relies on the situation and the state of mind of the victim. Your DM must determine this for NPCs, which is perhaps an easier job. You must role-play this for your character.

Spells of this school fall into two basic groups. *Illusions* are creations that manipulate light, color, shadow, sound, and sometimes even scent. Higher level illusions tap energy from other planes, and are actually quasi-real, being woven of extradimensional energies by the caster. Common illusions create appearances; they cannot make a creature or object look like nothing (i.e., invisible), but they can conceal objects by making them look like something else.

Phantasms exist only in the minds of their victims; these spells are never even quasi-real. (The exceptions to this are the *phantasmal force* spells, which are actually illusions rather than phantasms.) Phantasms act upon the mind of the victim to create an intense reaction—fear being most common.

The key to successful illusions or phantasms is believability, which depends on three main factors: what the caster attempts, what the victim expects, and what is happening at the moment the spell is cast. By combining the information from these three areas, the player and the DM should be able to create and adjudicate reasonable illusions and phantasms.

When casting an illusion or phantasm, the caster can attempt to do anything he desires within the physical limits of the spell. Prior knowledge of the illusion created is not necessary but is extremely useful.

For example, suppose Delsenora decides to cast a phantasmal force *spell and can choose between creating the image of a troll (a creature she has seen and battled) or that of a beholder (a creature she has never seen but has heard terrifying descriptions of). She can either use her memory to create a realistic troll or use her imagination to create something that may or may not look like a real beholder. The troll, based on her first-hand knowledge of these creatures, is going to have lots of little details—a big nose, warts, green, scabby skin, and even a shambling troll-like walk. Her illusion of a beholder will be much less precise, just a floating ball with one big eye and eyestalks. She doesn't know its color, size, or behavior.*

The type of image chosen by the caster affects the reaction of the victim. If the victim in the above case has seen both a troll and a beholder, which will be more believable? Almost certainly it will be the troll, which looks and acts the way the victim thinks a troll should. He might not even recognize the other creature as a beholder since it doesn't look like any beholder he's ever seen. Even if the victim has never seen a troll or a beholder, the troll will still be more believable; it acts in a realistic manner, while the beholder does not. Thus spellcasters are well-advised to create images of things they have seen, for the same reason authors are advised to write about things they know.

The next important consideration is to ask if the spell creates something that the victim expects. Which of these two illusions would be more believable—a huge dragon rising up behind a rank of attacking kobolds (puny little creatures) or a few ogres forming a line behind the kobolds? Most adventurers would find it hard to believe that a dragon would be working with kobolds. The dragon is far too powerful to associate with such little shrimps. Ogres, however, could very well work with kobolds—bossing them around and using them as cannon fodder. The key to a good illusion is to create something the victim does not expect but can quickly accept.

The most believable illusion may be that of a solid wall in a dungeon, transforming a passage into a dead end. Unless the victim is familiar with these hallways, he has no reason not to believe that the wall is there.

Of course, in a fantasy world many more things can be believed than in the real world. Flames do not spring out of nowhere in the real world, but this can happen in a fantasy world. The presence of magic in a fantasy world makes victims more willing to accept things our logic tells us cannot happen. A creature appearing out of nowhere could be an illusion or it could be summoned. At the same time, you must remember that a properly role-played character is familiar with the laws of his world. If a wall of flames appears out of nowhere, he will look for the spellcaster. A wall blocking a corridor may cause him to check for secret doors. If the illusion doesn't conform to his idea of how things work, the character should become suspicious. This is something you have to provide for your character and something you must remember when your character attempts to use illusions.

This then leads to the third factor in the believability of an illusion, how appropriate the illusion is for the situation. As mentioned before, the victim is going to have certain expectations about any given encounter. The best illusions reinforce these expectations to your character's advantage. Imagine that your group runs into a war party of orcs in the local forest. What could you do that would reinforce what the orcs might already believe? They see your group, armed and ready for battle. They do not know if you are alone or are the advance guard for a bigger troop. A good illusion could be the glint of metal and spear points coming up behind your party. Subtlety has its uses. The orcs will likely interpret your illusion as reinforcements to your group, enough to discourage them from attacking.

However, the limitations of each spell must be considered when judging appropriateness. A *phantasmal force* spell creates vision only. It does not provide sound, light, or heat. In the preceding situation, creating a troop of soldiers galloping up behind you would not have been believable. Where is the thunder of hooves, the creak of saddle leather, the shouts of your allies, the clank of drawn metal, or the whinny of horses? Orcs may not be tremendously bright, but they are not fooled that easily. Likewise, a dragon that suddenly appears without a thunderous roar and dragonish stench isn't likely to be accepted as real. A wise spellcaster always considers the limitations of his illusions and finds ways to hide their weaknesses from the enemy.

An illusion spell, therefore, depends on its believability. Believability is determined by the situation and a saving throw. Under normal circumstances, those observing the illusion are allowed a saving throw vs. spell if they actively disbelieve the illusion. For player characters, disbelieving is an action in itself and takes a round. For NPCs and monsters, a normal saving throw is made if the DM deems it appropriate. The DM can give bonuses or penalties to this saving throw as he thinks appropriate. If the caster has cleverly prepared a realistic illusion, this certainly results in penalties on the victim's saving throw. If the victim were to rely more on scent than sight, on the other hand, it could gain bonuses to its saving throw. If the saving throw is passed, the victim sees the illusion for what it is. If the saving throw is failed, the victim believes the illusion. A good indication of when player characters should receive a positive modifier to their saving throws is when they say they don't believe what they see, especially if they can give reasons why.

There are rare instances when the saving throw may automatically succeed or fail. There are times when the illusion created is either so perfect or so utterly fantastic as to be impossible even in a fantasy world. Be warned, these occasions are very rare and you should not expect your characters to benefit from them more than once or twice.

In many encounters, some party members will believe an illusion while others see it for what it really is. In these cases, revealing the truth to those deluded by the spell is not a simple matter of telling them. The magic of the spell has seized their minds. Considered from their point of view, they see a horrible monster (or whatever) while a friend is telling them it isn't real. They know magic can affect people's minds, but whose mind has been affected in this case? At best, having an illusion pointed out grants another saving throw with a +4 bonus.

Illusions do have other limitations. The caster must maintain a show of reality at all times when conducting an illusion. (If a

squad of low-level fighters is created, the caster dictates their hits, misses, damage inflicted, apparent wounds, and so forth, and the referee decides whether the bounds of believability have been exceeded.) Maintaining an illusion normally requires concentration on the part of the caster, preventing him from doing other things. Disturb him and the illusion vanishes.

Illusions are spells of trickery and deceit, not damage and destruction. Thus, illusions cannot be used to cause real damage. When a creature is caught in the blast of an illusionary fireball or struck by the claws of an illusionary troll, he thinks he takes damage. The DM should record the illusionary damage (but tell the player his character has taken real damage). If the character takes enough damage to "die," he collapses in a faint. A system shock roll should be made for the character. (His mind, believing the damage to be real, may cause his body to cease functioning!) If the character survives, he regains consciousness after 1d3 turns with his illusionary damage healed. In most cases, the character quickly realizes that it was all an illusion.

When an illusion creates a situation of inescapable death, such as a giant block dropping from the ceiling, all those believing the illusion must roll for system shock. If they fail, they die—killed by the sheer terror of the situation. If they pass, they are allowed a new saving throw with a +4 bonus. Those who pass recognize the illusion for what it is. Those who fail faint for 1d3 turns.

Illusions do not enable characters to defy normal physical laws. A illusionary bridge cannot support a character who steps on it, even if he believes the bridge is real. A illusionary wall does not actually cause a rock thrown at it to bounce off. However, affected creatures attempt to simulate the reality of what they see as much as possible. A character who falls into an illusionary pit drops to the ground as if he had fallen. A character may lean against an illusionary wall, not realizing that he isn't actually putting his weight on it. If the same character were suddenly pushed, he would find himself falling through the very wall he thought was solid!

Illusions of creatures do not automatically behave like those creatures, nor do they have those creatures' powers. This depends on the caster's ability and the victim's knowledge of the creatures. Illusionary creatures fight using the caster's combat ability. They take damage and die when their caster dictates it. An illusory orc could continue to fight, showing no damage, even after it had been struck a hundred or a thousand times. Of course, long before this its attackers will become suspicious. Illusionary creatures can have whatever special abilities the caster can make appear (i.e., a

dragon's fiery breath or a troll's regeneration), but they do not necessarily have unseen special abilities. There is no way a caster can create the illusion of a basilisk's gaze that turns people to stone. However, these abilities might be manifested through the fears of the victims. For example, Rath the fighter meets an illusionary basilisk. Rath has fought these beasties before and knows what they can do. His gaze accidentally locks with that of the basilisk. Primed by his own fears, Rath must make a system shock roll to remain alive. But if Rath had never seen a basilisk and had no idea that the creature's gaze could turn him to stone, there is no way his mind could generate the fear necessary to kill him. Sometimes ignorance is bliss!

Priest Spells

The spells of a priest, while sometimes having powers similar to those of the wizard, are quite different in their overall tone. The priest's role, more often than not, is as defender and guide for others. Thus the majority of his spells work to aid others or provide some service to the community in which he lives. Few of his spells are truly offensive, but many can be used cleverly to protect or defend.

Like the wizard, the priest's level determines how many spells he retains. He must select these spells in advance, demonstrating his wisdom and far-sightedness by choosing those spells he thinks will be most useful in the trials that lurk ahead.

Unlike the wizard, the priest needs no spell book and does not roll to see if he learns spells. Priest spells are obtained in an entirely different manner. To obtain his spells, a priest must be faithful to the cause of his deity. If the priest feels confident in this (and most do), he can pray for his spells. Through prayer, the priest humbly and politely requests those spells he wishes to memorize. Under normal circumstances, these spells are then granted.

A priest's spell selection is limited by his level and by the different spheres of spells. (The spheres of influence, into which priest spells are divided, can be found on page 34.) Within the major spheres of his deity, a priest can use any spell of a given level when he is able to cast spells of that level. Thus, a druid is able to cast any 2nd-level plant sphere spells when he is able to cast 2nd-level spells. For spells belonging to the minor spheres of the priest's deity, he can cast spells only up to 3rd level. The knowledge of what spells are available to the priest becomes instantly clear as soon as he advances in level. This, too, is bestowed by his deity.

Priests must pray to obtain spells, as they are requesting their abilities from some greater power, be it their deity or some intermediary agent of this power. The conditions for praying are identical to those needed for the wizard's studying. Clearly then, it behooves the priest to maintain himself in good standing with this power, through word and deed. Priests who slip in their duties, harbor indiscreet thoughts, or neglect their beliefs, find that their deity has an immediate method of redress. If the priest has failed in his duties, the deity can deny him spells as a clear message of dissatisfaction. For minor infractions, the deity can deny minor spells. Major failings result in the denial of major spells or, even worse, all spells. These can be regained if the character immediately begins to make amends for his errors. Perhaps the character only needs to be a little more vigilant, in the case of a minor fault. A serious transgression could require special service, such as a quest or some great sacrifice of goods. These are things your DM will decide, should your character veer from the straight and narrow path of his religion.

Finally, your DM may rule that not all deities are equal, so that those of lesser power are unable to grant certain spells. If this optional rule is used, powers of demigod status can only grant spells up to the 5th spell level. Lesser deities can grant 6th-level spells, while the greater deities have all spell levels available to them. You should inquire about this at the time you create your character (and decide which deity he worships), to prevent any unwelcome surprises later on.

Casting Spells

Both wizards and priests use the same rules for casting spells. To cast a spell, the character must first have the spell memorized. If it is not memorized, the spell cannot be cast. The caster must be able to speak (not under the effects of a *silence* spell or gagged) and have both arms free. (Note that the optional spell component rule [following section] can modify these conditions.) If the spell is targeted on a person, place, or thing, the caster must be able to see the target. It is not enough to cast a fireball 150 feet ahead into the darkness; the caster must be able to see the point of explosion and the intervening distance. Likewise, a magic missile (which always hits its target) cannot be fired into a group of bandits with the instruction to strike the leader; the caster must be able to identify and see the leader.

Once the casting has begun, the character must stand still. Casting cannot be accomplished while riding a roughly moving beast or a vehicle, unless special efforts are made to stabilize and protect the caster. Thus a spell cannot be cast from the back of a galloping horse under any conditions, nor can a wizard or priest cast a spell on the deck of

a ship during a storm. However, if the caster were below decks, protected from the wind and surging waves, he could cast a spell. While it is not normally possible to cast a spell from a moving chariot, a character who was steadied and supported by others could do so. Your DM will have to make a ruling in these types of extraordinary conditions.

During the round in which the spell is cast, the caster cannot move to dodge attacks. Therefore, no AC benefit from Dexterity is gained by spellcasters while casting spells. Furthermore, if the spellcaster is struck by a weapon or fails to make a saving throw before the spell is cast, the caster's concentration is disrupted. The spell is lost in a fizzle of useless energy and is wiped clean from the memory of the caster until it can be rememorized. Spellcasters are well advised not to stand at the front of any battle, at least if they want to be able to cast any spells!

Spell Components (Optional Rule)

When your character casts a spell, it is assumed that he is doing something to activate that spell. He may utter a few words, wave his hand around a couple of times, wiggle his toes, swallow a live spider, etc. But, under the standard rules, you don't have to know exactly what he does to activate the spell. Some of this can be answered if your DM uses the rules for spell components.

The actions required to cast a spell are divided into three groups: verbal, somatic (gestures), and material. Each spell description (starting on page 131) lists what combination of these components is needed to cast a spell. Verbal components require the caster to speak clearly (not be silenced in any way);

somatic components require free gestures (thus the caster cannot be bound or held); material components must be tossed, dropped, burned, eaten, broken, or whatever for the spell to work. While there is no specific description of the words and gestures that must be performed, the material components are listed in the spell descriptions. Some of these are common and easy to obtain. Others represent items of great value or scarcity. Whatever the component, it is automatically destroyed or lost when the spell is cast, unless the spell description specifically notes otherwise.

If the spell components optional rule is used in your campaign, your wizard or priest must have these items to cast the spell. Without them, he is helpless, even if the spell is memorized. For simplicity of play, it is best to assume that any spellcaster with any sense has a supply of the common items he is likely to need—wax, feathers, paint, sand, sticks, and fluff, for example. For expensive and rare items, it is perfectly proper for your DM to insist that special efforts be made to obtain these items. After all, you simply cannot assume your character has a valuable pearl handy whenever he needs one!

The three different aspects of spell components also change the conditions under which your character can cast his spells. No longer does he need to be able to speak, move, and use some item. He only needs to fulfill the required components. Thus a spell with only a verbal component could be used by a naked, bound spellcaster. One requiring only gestures could be cast even within the radius of a *silence* spell. Most spells require a combination of components, but clever spellcasters often create new spells that need only a word or a gesture, enabling them to take their enemies by surprise.

Magical Research

One oft-ignored asset of both wizards and priests is magical research. While the spell lists for both groups offer a wide variety of tools and effects, the clever player character can quickly get an edge by researching his own spells. Where other spellcasters may fall quickly into tired and predictable patterns ("Look, it's a mage! Get ready for the fireball, guys!"), an enterprising character can deliver sudden (and nasty) surprises!

Although your DM has the rules for handling spell research, there are some things you should know about how to proceed. First and foremost, research means that you and your DM will be working together to expand the game. This is not a job he does for you! Without your input, nothing happens. Second, whatever your character researches, it cannot be more powerful than the spells he is already able to cast. If it is, you must wait until your character can cast spells of an equal power. (Thus, as a 1st-level wizard, you cannot research a spell that is as powerful as a fireball. You must wait until your character can cast a fireball.) Finally, you will have to be patient and willing to have your character spend some money. He won't create the spell immediately, as research takes time. It also takes money, so you can expect your DM to use this opportunity to relieve your character of some of that excess cash. But, after all, how better for a spellcaster to spend his money?

Knowing these things, you should first write up a description of the spell you want to create. Be sure to include information on components, saving throws, range, duration, and all the other entries you find in the normal spell listings. When you give your DM the written description, tell him what you want the spell to do. (Sometimes what you write isn't really what you mean, and talking to your DM is a good way to prevent confusion.) After this, he will either accept or reject your spell. This is his choice and not all DMs will have the same answer. Don't kick and complain; find out what changes are needed to make the spell acceptable. You can probably iron out the differences.

Once all these things are done, your character can research the spell. Be ready for this to take some time. Eventually he will succeed, although the spell may not do quite what he expected. Your DM may revise the spell, perhaps reducing the area of effect or damage inflicted. Finally, all you have to do is name your spell. This should be something suitably pompous, such as "Delsenora's Malevolent Steamroller." After all, you want something to impress the locals!

Spell Descriptions

The spells are organized according to their group (priest or wizard) and level, starting on page 131. Within each level, the spells are arranged alphabetically. At the start of each spell description is the following important game information:

Name: Each spell is identified by name. In parentheses after the name is the school (for wizard spells) to which that spell belongs. When more than one is listed, that spell is common to all schools given.

Some spells are reversible (they can be cast for an effect opposite to that of the standard spell). This is noted after the spell name. Priests with reversible spells must memorize the desired version. For example, a priest who desires a *cause light wounds* spell must petition for this form of the *cure light wounds* spell when meditating and praying. Note that severe penalties can result if the spell choice is at variance with the priest's alignment (possible penalties include denial of specific spells, entire spell levels, or even all spells for a certain period). The exact result (if any) depends on the reaction of the priest's patron deity, as determined by the DM.

Reversible wizard spells operate similarly. When the spell is learned, both forms are recorded in the wizard's spell books. However, the wizard must decide which version of the spell he desires to cast when memorizing the spell, unless the spell description specifically states otherwise. For example, a wizard who has memorized *stone to flesh* and desires to cast *flesh to stone* must wait until the latter form of the spell can be memorized (i.e., rest eight hours and study). If he could memorize two 6th-level spells, he could memorize each version once or one version twice.

School: In parentheses after the spell name is the name of the school of magic to which the spell belongs. For wizard spells, this defines which spells a wizard specialist can learn, depending on the wizard's school of specialization. For priest spells, the school notation is used only for reference purposes, to indicate which school the spell is considered to belong to, in case the DM needs to know for spell resistance (e.g., elves' resistance to charm spells).

Sphere: This entry appears only for priest spells and identifies the sphere or spheres into which that spell falls.

Range: This lists the distance from the caster at which the spell effect occurs or begins. A "0" indicates the spell can be used on the caster only, with the effect embodied within or emanating from him. "Touch" means the caster can use the spell on others if he can physically touch them. Unless otherwise specified, all other spells are centered on a point visible to the caster and within the range of the spell. The point can be a creature or object if desired. In general, a spell that affects a limited number of creatures within an area affects those closest to the center of the area first, unless there are other parameters operating (such as level or Hit Dice). Spells can be cast through narrow openings only if both the caster's vision and the spell energy can be directed simultaneously through the opening. A wizard standing behind an arrow slit can cast through it; sending a fireball through a small peephole he is peering through is another matter.

Components: This lists the category of components needed, V for verbal, S for somatic, and M for material. When material components are required, these are listed in the spell description. Spell components are expended as the spell is cast, unless otherwise noted. Clerical holy symbols are not lost when a spell is cast. For cases in which material components are expended at the end of the spell (*free action, shapechange,* etc.), premature destruction of the components ends the spell.

Duration: This lists how long the magical energy of the spell lasts. Spells of instantaneous duration come and go the moment they are cast, although the results of these spells may be permanent and unchangeable by normal means. Spells of permanent duration last until the effects are negated by some means, usually by a *dispel magic.* Some spells have a variable duration. In most cases, the caster cannot choose the duration of spells. Spells with set durations (e.g., 3 rounds/level) must be kept track of by the player. Spells of variable duration (e.g., 3 + 1d4 rounds) are secretly rolled and recorded by the DM. Your DM may warn you when spell durations are approaching expiration, but there is usually no sign that a spell is going to expire; check with your DM to determine exactly how he handles this issue.

Certain spells can be ended at will by the caster. In order to dismiss these spells, the original caster must be within range of the spell's center of effect—within the same range at which the spell can be cast. The caster also must be able to speak words of dismissal. Note that only the original caster can dismiss his spells in this way.

Casting Time: This entry is important, if the optional casting time rules are used. If only a number is given, the casting time is added to the caster's initiative die rolls. If the spell requires a round or number of rounds to cast, it goes into effect at the end of the last round of casting time. If Delsenora casts a spell that takes one round, it goes into effect at the end of the round in which she begins casting. If the spell requires three rounds to cast, it goes into effect at the end of the third round. Spells requiring a turn or more go into effect at the end of the stated turn.

Area of Effect: This lists the creatures, volume, dimensions, weight, etc., that can be affected by the spell. Spells with an area or volume that can be shaped by the caster will have a minimum dimension of 10 feet in any direction, unless the spell description specifically states otherwise. Thus a cloud that has a 10-foot cube per caster level might, when cast by a 12th-level caster, have dimensions 10′ × 10′ × 120′, 20′ × 20′ × 30′, or any similar combination that totals twelve 10-foot cubes. Combinations such as 5′ × 10′ × 240′ are not possible unless specifically allowed.

Some spells (such as *bless*) affect the friends or enemies of the caster. In all cases, this refers to the perception of the caster at the time the spell is cast. For example, a chaotic good character allied with a lawful neu-

tral cleric would receive the benefits of the latter's *bless* spell.

Saving Throw: This lists whether the spell allows the target a saving throw and the effect of a successful save: "Neg." results in the spell having no effect; "1/2" means the character suffers half the normal amount of damage; "none" means no saving throw is allowed.

Wisdom adjustments to saving throws apply to enchantment/charm spells.

Solid physical barriers provide saving throw bonuses and damage reduction. Cover and concealment may affect saving throws and damage (the DM has additional information about this).

A creature that successfully saves against a spell with no apparent physical effect (such as a *charm, hold,* or *magic jar*) may feel a definite force or tingle that is characteristic of a magical attack, if the DM desires. But the exact hostile spell effect or creature ability used cannot be deduced from this tingle.

A being's carried equipment and possessions are assumed to make their saving throws against special attacks if the creature makes its saving throw, unless the spell specifically states otherwise. If the creature fails its saving throw, or if the attack form is particularly potent, the possessions may require saving throws using either item saving throws (see the *DMG*) or the being's saving throw. The DM will inform you when this happens.

Any character can voluntarily forgo a saving throw. This allows a spell or similar attack that normally grants a saving throw to have full effect on the character. Likewise, any creature can voluntarily lower its magic resistance allowing a spell to automatically function when cast on it. Forgoing a saving throw or magic resistance roll need not always be voluntary. If a creature or

character can be tricked into lowering its resistance, the spell will have full effect, even if it is not the spell the victim believed he was going to receive. The victim must consciously choose to lower his resistance; it is not sufficient that he is caught off guard. For example, a character would receive a saving throw if a mage in the party suddenly attacked him with a fireball, even if the mage had been friendly to that point. However, the same character would not receive a saving throw if the mage convinced him that he was about to receive a *levitation* spell but cast a fireball instead. Your DM will decide when NPCs have lowered their resistances. You must tell your DM when your character is voluntarily lowering his resistance.

Spell Description: The text provides a complete description of how the spell functions and its game effects. It covers most typical uses of the spell, if there are more than one, but cannot deal with every possible application players might find. In these cases, the spell information in the text should provide guidance on how to adjudicate the situation.

Spells with multiple functions enable the caster to select which function he wants to use at the time of casting. Usually a single function of a multiple-function spell is weaker than a single-function spell of the same level.

Spell effects that give bonuses or penalties to abilities, attack rolls, damage rolls, saving throws, etc., are not usually cumulative with each other or with other magic: the strongest single effect applies. For example, a fighter drinks a *potion of giant strength* and then receives the 2nd-level wizard spell *strength.* Only the strongest magic (the potion) is effective. When the potion's duration ends, however, the *strength* spell is still in effect, until its duration also expires.

After a player's character has bravely set out and survived his first adventure, the player will have experienced the entertainment of role-playing games. But what will the character have gained? If the character never improves, he will never be able to survive, let alone overcome the powerful dangers that fill the AD&D® game worlds.

Fortunately, this isn't the case. Every time a character goes on an adventure he learns something. He may learn a little more about his physical limits, encounter a creature he has never seen before, try a spell as yet unused, or discover a new peculiarity of nature. Indeed, not all his learning experience need be positive. After blowing up half his party with a poorly placed fireball, a wizard may (though there is no guarantee) learn to pay more attention to ranges and areas of effect. After charging a basilisk, a fighter may learn that caution is a better tactic for dealing with the beast (provided the other characters can change him from stone back to flesh). Regardless of the method, the character has managed to learn something.

Some of the information and skills learned in the game can be applied directly in play. When a wizard toasts his friends with a badly cast fireball, the player learns to pay more attention to the area of effect of a fireball. Though the player made the mistake and his character only carried out the actions, the player's friends will also learn to keep their characters well away from his.

The reward for this type of learning is direct and immediate. The characters benefit because each of the players has a better understanding of what to do or where to go.

However, a character also improves by increasing his power. Although the player can improve his play, he cannot arbitrarily give his character more hit points, more spells, or a better chance to hit with an attack. These gains are made by earning experience points (XP).

An experience point is a concrete measure of a character's improvement. It represents a host of abstract factors: increased confidence, physical exercise, insight, and on-the-job training. When a character earns enough experience points to advance to the next experience level, these abstract factors translate into a measurable improvement in the abilities of the character. Just what areas improve and how quickly improvement occurs all depend on the character's class.

Group Experience Awards

Experience points are earned through the activities of the characters, which generally relate to their adventuring goals. Thus all characters on an adventure receive some experience points for overcoming their enemies or obstacles. Since group cooperation is important, experience points for defeating foes are given to all members of the group, regardless of their actions. Who is to say that the wizard, standing ready with a spell just in case things got ugly, might not have been necessary? Or that the bard who covered the party's escape route wasn't doing something important? A character who never hefts a sword may still have good advice or important suggestions on better tactics. Furthermore, the wizard and the bard can also learn from the actions of others.

Individual Experience Awards

Player characters also earn experience points for individual deeds, as determined by their class. Generally, each character earns points for doing actions appropriate to his group. Warriors earn additional experience points for defeating creatures. The more difficult the battle, the greater the number of experience points. Wizards earn points for using their spells for specific purposes. The wizard who walks into the woods and casts his spells for no reason doesn't gain experience points; the wizard who casts a lightning bolt at a beholder has used his spell for a purpose. He gains experience points. Wizards also earn experience points for researching new spells and creating magical items. Priests can earn experience points by spreading their beliefs and using their powers in service of their deity. Rogues, who tend to have a larcenous streak, earn experience points by using their special abilities and finding or earning gold.

A character can also earn experience for the player's actions, such as playing the game well. When a player does a good job creating and pretending to be his character, the DM may give the character experience points for good role-playing. If the player is really involved and takes a major part in the game, the DM can give the player's character extra experience points. If the player uses his head to come up with a really good idea, the DM can give the character experience points for his contribution.

Finally, a character can earn experience points for successfully completing an adventure or achieving a goal the DM has set. Although a player may have a pretty good idea of what his character is supposed to accomplish, he won't know if he'll be awarded experience points for it until his character actually receives them. However, there is no rule that the DM must be consistent in these awards, or even that he must give a character anything at all.

Training

Even when a character has earned enough experience to attain the next level, the DM may not allow immediate advancement. He may require the character to receive training to advance. When training, a character studies his skills under a tutor, taking the raw knowledge he has gained and honing it into measurable improvement. On the average, this takes a few weeks (depending on the tutor's ability), and it is normally done during the character's nonadventuring time.

A DM can also rule that the circumstances are not appropriate for the character to advance in level. For instance, if the game session ends with the characters deep in an abandoned mine complex. The party has just finished a battle with a band of gnolls and faces more such encounters before it can reach the surface. The DM rules that the characters receive no experience until they leave the mines, because he doesn't want them to increase in level in the middle of the adventure. He is perfectly justified in doing this. And if the characters live through the adventure, they will undoubtedly profit from it, either in experience points or knowledge gained.

Where's the Specific Info?

The preceding text has covered general guidelines as to how and why characters receive experience points. Since the DM actually determines how many XP each character actually receives, the detailed rules for awarding experience are given in the *Dungeon Master's Guide*.

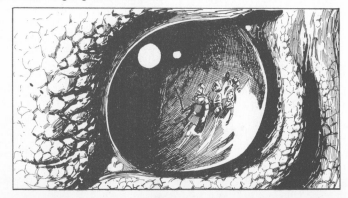

The AD&D® game is an adventure game designed to give players a feeling of excitement and danger. Characters brave the unknown perils of moldering dungeons and thorn-covered wilderness, facing off against hideous monsters and evil villains. Thus, it is important for all players to know the basic rules for handling combat.

To create the proper sense of danger and excitement, the rules for combat must be thorough, but they must also be playable and exciting enough to create a vivid picture in the minds of the players. Combat in the AD&D game has to allow many different actions and outcomes—as many as the imagination can produce. Knowing that anything could happen next (because the rules allow it) creates excitement for everyone.

More Than Just Hack-and-Slash

As important as fighting is to the AD&D game, it isn't the be-all and end-all of play. It's just one way for characters to deal with situations. If characters could do nothing but fight, the game would quickly get boring—every encounter would be the same. Because there is more to the game than fighting, we'll cover much more than simple hack-and-slash combat in this chapter.

In addition to explaining the basic mechanics of hitting and missing, there are rules here for turning undead, special ways to attack and defend, poison, heroic feats, and more.

Definitions

Many game terms are used throughout the combat rules. To understand the rules, players must understand these terms, so brief explanations appear below. Further details are provided throughout this chapter.

Armor Class (AC) is the protective rating of a type of armor. In some circumstances, AC is modified by the amount of protection gained or lost because of the character's situation. For instance, crouching behind a boulder improves a character's Armor Class, while being attacked from behind worsens his AC.

Armor provides protection by reducing the chance that a character is attacked successfully (and suffers damage). Armor does not absorb damage, it prevents it. A fighter in full plate mail may be a slow-moving target, but penetrating his armor to cause any damage is no small task.

Armor Class is measured on a scale from 10, the worst (no armor), to −10, the best (very powerful magical armors). *The lower the number, the more effective the armor.* Shields can also improve the AC of a character (see page 75).

Abilities and situations can also affect a character's Armor Class. High Dexterity gives a bonus to Armor Class, for example. But even a character with a Dexterity bonus can have this bonus negated if he is attacked from the rear.

Damage is what happens to a character when an opponent attacks him successfully. Damage can also occur as a result of poison, fire, falling, acid, and anything even remotely dangerous in the real world. Damage from most attacks is measured in *hit points*. Each time a character is hit, he suffers points of damage. It could be as little as 1 point to as many as 80 or more. These points are subtracted from the character's current hit point total. When this reaches 0, the character is dead.

Initiative determines the order in which things happen in a combat round. Like so many things in the world, initiative is determined by a combination of ability, situation, and chance.

At the start of each round of a battle, an initiative roll is made by both sides. This roll can be modified by the abilities of the combatants and by the situation. The person or side with the lower modified die roll acts first.

Melee is any situation in which characters are battling each other hand-to-hand, whether with fists, teeth, claws, swords, axes, pikes, or something else. Strength and Dexterity are valuable assets in melee.

Missile combat is defined as any time a weapon is shot, thrown, hurled, kicked, or otherwise propelled. Missile and melee combat have the same basic rules, but there are special situations and modifiers that apply only to missile combat.

Saving throws are measures of a character's resistance to special types of attacks—poisons, magic, and attacks that affect the whole body or mind of the character. The ability to make successful saving throws improves as the character increases in level; Dexterity and general mental fortitude aid in honing combat senses. Experience makes saving throws easier.

Surprise can happen any time characters meet another group unexpectedly (monsters, evil knights, peasants, etc.). Surprise is simply what happens when one side—a person or party—is taken unawares, unable to react until they gather their wits. Their opponents, if unsurprised, are allowed a bonus round of action while the surprised characters recover. It's entirely possible for both sides in a given situation to be surprised!

Attacking with surprise gives bonuses to the attack roll (see Table 51). A surprised character also has a decreased chance of rolling a successful saving throw, if one is needed.

Surprise is determined by a die roll and is normally checked at the beginning of an encounter. Surprise is very unpredictable,

so there are very few modifiers to the roll.

THAC0 is an acronym for "To Hit Armor Class 0." This is the number a character, NPC, or monster needs to attack an Armor Class 0 target successfully. THAC0 depends on a character's group and level (see Table 53 on page 91). The THAC0 number can be used to calculate the number needed to hit any Armor Class. THAC0 is refigured each time a character increases in level. Using THAC0 speeds the play of combat greatly.

The Attack Roll

At the heart of the combat system is the attack roll. This is the die roll that determines whether an attack succeeds or fails. The number a player needs in order to make a successful attack roll is also called the "to-hit" number.

Attack rolls are used for attacks with swords, bows, rocks, and other weapons, as well as blows from fists, tackling, and other hand-to-hand attacks. Attack rolls are also used to resolve a variety of potentially injury-causing actions that require accuracy (e.g., throwing a rock at a small target or tossing a sword to a party member in the middle of a fight).

Figuring the To-Hit Number

The first step in making an attack roll is to find the number needed to hit the target. Subtract the Armor Class of the target from the attacker's THAC0. (Remember that if the Armor Class is a negative number, you *add* it to the attacker's THAC0.) The character has to roll the resulting number, or higher, on 1d20 to hit the target.

Here's a simple example: Rath has reached 7th level as a fighter. His THAC0 is 14 (found on Table 53), meaning he needs to roll a 14 or better to hit a character or creature of Armor Class 0. In combat, Rath, attacking an orc wearing chainmail armor (AC 6), needs to roll an 8 (14−6 = 8) to hit the orc. An 8 or higher on 1d20 will hit the orc. If Rath hits, he rolls the appropriate dice (see Table 44) to determine how much damage he inflicts.

The example above is quite simple—in a typical AD&D® game combat situation, THAC0 is modified by weapon bonuses, Strength bonuses, and the like (the next section "Modifiers to the Attack Roll," lists the specifics of these modifiers). Figure Strength and weapon modifiers, subtract the total from the base THAC0, and record this modified THAC0 with each weapon on the character sheet. Subtract the target's Armor Class from this modified THAC0 when determining the to-hit number.

Here's the same example, with some common modifiers thrown in: Rath is still a 7th-level fighter. He has a Strength of 18/80 (which gives him a +2 bonus to his attack roll). He fights with a long sword +1. His THAC0 is 14, modified to 12 by his Strength and to 11 by his weapon. If attacking the orc from the earlier example, Rath would have to roll a 5 or higher on 1d20 in order to hit (11-6 = 5). Again, Table 44 would tell him how much damage he inflicts with his weapon (this information should also be written on his character sheet).

The DM may also throw in situational modifiers, (e.g., a bonus if the target is struck from behind, or a penalty if the target is crouching behind a boulder). If the final, modified die roll on 1d20 is equal to or greater than the number needed to hit the target, the attack succeeds. If the roll is lower than that needed, the attack fails.

Modifiers to the Attack Roll

In combat, many factors can modify the number a character needs for a successful hit. These variables are reflected in modifiers to the to-hit number or to the attack roll.

Strength Modifiers: A character's Strength can modify the die roll, altering both the chance to hit and the damage caused. This modifier is always applied to melees and attacks with hurled missile weapons (a spear or an axe).

A positive Strength modifier can be applied to bows if the character has a special bow made for him, designed to take advantage of his high Strength. Characters with Strength penalties always suffer them when using a bow weapon. They simply are not able to draw back the bowstring far enough. Characters never have Strength modifiers when using crossbows—the power of the shot is imparted by a machine, not the player character.

Magical items: The magical properties of a weapon can also modify combat. Items that impart a bonus to the attack roll or Armor Class are identified by a plus sign. For example, a *sword +1* improves a character's chance to hit by one. A suit of *chain mail +1* improves the Armor Class of the character by one (which means you *subtract* one from the character's AC, changing an AC of 5 to an AC of 4, for example). Cursed items have a negative modifier (a penalty), resulting in a subtraction from the attack roll or an addition to Armor Class.

There is no limit to the number of modifiers that can be applied to a single die roll. Nor is there a limit to the positive or negative number (the total of all modifiers) that can be applied to a die roll.

Table 51 lists some standard combat modifiers. Positive numbers are bonuses for the attacker; negative numbers are penalties.

Table 51: COMBAT MODIFIERS

Situation	Attack Roll Modifier
Attacker on higher ground	+1
Defender invisible	-4
Defender off-balance	+2
Defender sleeping or held	Automatic*
Defender stunned or prone	+4
Defender surprised	+1
Missile fire, long range	-5
Missile fire, medium range	-2
Rear attack	+2

*If the defender is attacked during the course of a normal melee, the attack automatically hits and causes normal damage. If no other fighting is going on (i.e., all others have been slain or driven off), the defender can be slain automatically.

Weapon Type vs. Armor Modifiers

(Optional Rule)

Not all weapons perform the same. If they did, there would be no need for the wide variety of weapons that exists. Only one form of each weapon-type, the most useful one, would be used throughout the world. This is obviously not the case.

Aside from the differences in size, weight, length, and shape, certain types of weapons are more useful against some types of armor than others. Indeed, the different armors and weapons of the world are the result of an ancient arms race. Every new weapon led to the development of a new type of armor designed to counter it. This led to new weapons, which led to new armor, and so on.

The Various Types of Weapons

In the AD&D® game, weapons fall into several categories, based on how they are used. The basic categories are slashing, piercing, and bludgeoning.

Slashing weapons include swords, axes, and knives. Damage is caused by the combination of weight, muscle, and a good sharp edge.

Piercing weapons (some swords, spears, pikes, arrows, javelins, etc.) rely on the penetrating power of a single sharp point and much less on the weight of the weapon.

Bludgeoning weapons (maces, hammers, and flails) depend almost entirely on the impact caused by weight and muscle.

A few weapons, particularly some of the more exotic polearms, fall into more than one of these categories. A halberd can be used as a pole-axe (a slashing weapon) or as a short pike (a piercing weapon). The versatility of these weapons provides the user with a combat advantage, in that the mode most favorable to the attacker can be used, depending upon the situation.

Natural weapons can also be classified according to their attack type. Claws are slashing weapons; a bite pierces; a tail-attack bludgeons. The DM must decide which is most appropriate to the creature and method of attack.

Armor types, in turn, have different qualities. Field plate is more effective, overall, than other armors by virtue of the amount and thickness of the metal, but it still has specific weaknesses against certain classes of weapons.

Table 52 lists the weapon vs. armor modifiers applied to the attacker's THAC0, if this optional system is used. To use this table, the actual armor type of the target must be known in addition to the target's Armor Class. The bonuses of magical armor do not change the type of armor, only the final Armor Class.

This system is used only when attacking creatures in armor. The modifiers are not used when attacking creatures with a natural Armor Class.

Table 52: WEAPON TYPE VS. ARMOR MODIFIERS

Armor Type	Slash	Pierce	Bludgeon
Banded mail	+2	0	+1
Brigandine	+1	+1	0
Chain mail*	+2	0	-2
Field Plate	+3	+1	0
Full Plate	+4	+3	0
Leather armor**	0	-2	0
Plate mail	+3	0	0
Ring mail	+1	+1	0
Scale mail	0	+1	0
Splint mail	0	+1	+2
Studded leather	+2	+1	0

* Includes bronze chain mail
** Includes padded armor and hides

Impossible To-Hit Numbers

Sometimes the attacker's to-hit number seems impossible to roll. An attack may be so difficult it requires a roll greater than 20 (on a 20-sided die!), or so ridiculously easy it can be made on a roll less than 1. In both cases, an attack roll is still required!

The reason is simple: With positive die roll modifiers (for magic, Strength, situation, or whatever), a number greater than 20 can be rolled. Likewise, die roll penalties can push the attack roll below 0.

No matter what number a character needs

to hit, a roll of 20 is *always* considered a hit and a roll of 1 is *always* a miss, unless the DM rules otherwise. Under most circumstances, a natural 20 hits and a natural 1 misses, regardless of any modifiers applied to the die roll.

Thus, even if a character's chance to hit a monster is 23 and the character has a −3 penalty applied to the die roll, he might be able to score a hit—but only if the die roll is a 20 before any modifiers are applied. Likewise, a character able to hit a monster on a 3 or better, waving a *sword +4*, could still miss if a 1 is rolled on the die.

There are no sure things, good or bad, in the unpredictable chaos of combat situations.

Calculating THAC0

To make an attack roll, the character's THAC0 must be known. This depends on the group and level, if the attacker is a player character or NPC, or the Hit Dice if the attacker is a monster or an animal. All 1st-level characters have THAC0s of 20, regardless of class.

For a character of level 1 through level 20, consult Table 53. This table lists the THAC0 number of each group through 20th level, so players don't have to perform any calculations.

For a character higher than 20th level, find the Improvement Rate for the character's group in Table 54. There you'll find the number of levels a character must advance to reduce his THAC0 by 1 (or more) points. Calculate the character's THAC0 according to his level.

The *DMG* contains the information on monster THAC0s.

Combat and Encounters

Encounters are the heart of the AD&D® game. Since encounters with monsters and NPCs often lead to combat, an understanding of what happens during battles is vital for everyone. There are several factors the DM will consider in any combat, most of which arise from the circumstances of the encounter. Is anyone surprised? How far apart are the opponents? How many of them are there? Answers to these questions are found in the Encounter section of the *DMG*. These are questions common to all encounters, whether combat occurs or not.

The Combat Round

If an encounter escalates into a combat situation, the time scale of the game automatically goes to *rounds* (also called melee rounds or combat rounds). Rounds are used to measure the actions of characters in combat (or other intensive actions in which time is important).

A round is approximately one minute long. Ten combat rounds equal a *turn* (or, put another way, a turn equals 10 minutes of game time). This is particularly important to remember for spells that last for turns, rather than rounds.

But these are just approximations—precise time measurements are impossible to make in combat. An action that might be ridiculously easy under normal circumstances could become an undertaking of truly heroic scale when attempted in the middle of a furious, chaotic battle.

Imagine the simple act of imbibing a healing potion. First, a character decides to drink the potion before retiring for the night. All he has to do is get it out of his backpack, uncork it, and drink the contents. No problem.

Now imagine the same thing in the middle of a fight. The potion is safely stowed in the character's backpack. First, he takes stock of the situation to see if anyone else can get the potion out for him, but, not surprisingly, everyone is rather busy. So, sword in one hand, he shrugs one strap of the pack off his shoulder. Then, just as two orcs leap toward him, the other strap threatens to slip down, entangling his sword arm. Already the loose strap keeps him from fully using his shield.

Holding the shield as best as possible in front of him, he scrambles backward to avoid the monsters' first wild swings. He gets pushed back a few more feet when a companion shoulders past to block their advance. His companion bought him a little time, so he kneels, lays down his sword, and slips the backpack all the way off. Hearing a wild cry, he instinctively swings his shield up just in time to ward off a glancing blow.

Table 53: CALCULATED THAC0S

								Level												
Group	1	2	3	4	5	6	7	8	9	10	11	12	13	14	15	16	17	18	19	20
Priest	20	20	20	18	18	18	16	16	16	14	14	14	12	12	12	10	10	10	8	8
Rogue	20	20	19	19	18	18	17	17	16	16	15	15	14	14	13	13	12	12	11	11
Warrior	20	19	18	17	16	15	14	13	12	11	10	9	8	7	6	5	4	3	2	1
Wizard	20	20	20	19	19	19	18	18	18	17	17	17	16	16	16	15	15	15	14	14

Table 54: THAC0 ADVANCEMENT

Group	Improvement Rate Points/Level
Priest	2/3
Rogue	1/2
Warrior	1/1
Wizard	1/3

Rummaging through the pack, he finally finds the potion, pulls it out, and, huddling behind his shield, works the cork free. Just then there is a flash of flame all around him—a fireball! He grits his teeth against the heat, shock, and pain and tries to remember not to crush or spill the potion vial. Biting back the pain of the flames, he is relieved to see the potion is still intact.

Quickly, he gulps it down, reclaims his sword, kicks his backpack out of the way, and runs back up to the front line. In game terms, the character withdrew, was missed by one attacker, made a successful saving throw vs. spell (from the fireball), drank a potion, and was ready for combat the next round.

What You Can Do in One Round

Whatever the precise length of a combat round, a character can accomplish only one basic action in that round, be it making an attack, casting a spell, drinking a potion, or tending to a fallen comrade. The basic action, however, may involve several lesser actions.

When making an attack, a character is likely to close with his opponent, circle for an opening, feint here, jab there, block a thrust, leap back, and perhaps finally make a telling blow. A spellcaster may fumble for his components, dodge an attacker, mentally review the steps of the spell, intone the spell, and then move to safety when it is all done. It has already been shown what drinking a potion might entail. All of these things might happen in a bit less than a minute or a bit more, but the standard is one minute and one action to the round.

Some examples of the actions a character can accomplish include the following:
- Make an attack (make attack rolls up to the maximum number allowed the character class at a given level)
- Cast one spell (if the casting time is one round or less)
- Drink a potion
- Light a torch
- Use a magical item
- Move to the limit of his movement rate
- Attempt to open a stuck or secret door
- Bind a character's wounds
- Search a body
- Hammer in a spike
- Recover a dropped weapon

There are also actions that take a negligible amount of time, things the character does without affecting his ability to perform a more important task. Examples of these include the following:
- Shout warnings, brief instructions, or demands for surrender, but not conversations where a reply is expected.
- Change weapons by dropping one and drawing another.

- Drop excess equipment, such as backpacks, lanterns, or torches.

The Combat Sequence

In real life, combat is one of the closest things to pure anarchy. Each side is attempting to harm the other, essentially causing disorder and chaos. Thus combats are filled with unknowns—unplanned events, failed attacks, lack of communication, and general confusion and uncertainty. However, to play a battle in the game, it is necessary to impose some order on the actions that occur. Within a combat round, there is a set series of steps that must be followed. These steps are:

1. The DM decides what actions the monsters or NPCs will take, including casting spells (if any).
2. The players indicate what their characters will do, including casting spells (if any).
3. Initiative is determined.
4. Attacks are made in order of initiative.

These steps are followed until the combat ends—either one side is defeated, surrenders, or runs away.

NPC/Monster Determination: In the first step, the DM secretly decides in general terms what each opponent will do—attack, flee, or cast a spell. He does not announce his decisions to the players. If a spell is to be cast, the DM picks the spell before the players announce their characters' actions.

Player Determination: Next, the players give a general indication of what their characters are planning to do. This does not have to be perfectly precise and can be changed somewhat, if the DM decides circumstances warrant.

If the characters are battling goblins, a player can say, "My fighter will attack" without having to announce which goblin he will strike. If the characters are battling a mixed group of goblins and ogres, the player has to state whether his character is attacking goblins or ogres.

Spells to be cast must also be announced at this time and cannot be changed once the initiative die is rolled.

Before moving on, the DM will make sure he has a clear idea of not only what the player characters are doing, but also what actions any hirelings and henchmen are taking. Once he has a clear view of everything that's likely to happen, the DM can overrule any announced action that violates the rules (or in the case of an NPC, is out of character).

He is not required to overrule an impossible action, but he can let a character attempt it anyway, knowing full well the character cannot succeed. It is not the DM's position to advise players on the best strate-

gies, most intelligent actions, or optimum maneuvers for their characters.

Initiative: In the third step, dice are rolled to determine initiative, according to the rules for initiative (this page).

Resolution: In the last step, PCs, NPCs, and monsters make their attacks, spells occur, and any other actions are resolved according to the order of initiative.

The above sequence is not immutable. Indeed, some monsters violate the standard sequence, and some situations demand the application of common sense. In these cases the DM's word is final.

Here's an example of the combat sequence in action: Rath is leading a party through the corridors of a dungeon. Right behind him are Rupert and Delsenora. Rounding a bend, they see a group of orcs and trolls about 20 feet away. No one is surprised by the encounter.

The DM has notes telling him the orcs are hesitant. He secretly decides that they will fall back and let the trolls fight. The trolls, able to regenerate, are naturally overconfident and step forward to the front rank (cursing the orcs at the same time) and prepare to attack. Turning to the players, the DM asks, "What are you going to do?"

Harry (playing Rath, a dwarf who hates orcs): "Orcs?—CHARGE!"

Anne (playing Delsenora the Mage): "Uh—what!? Wait—don't do that...I was going to...now I can't use a fireball."

DM: "Rath is charging forward. Quick—what are you doing?"

Jon (playing Rupert, the half-elf, to Anne): "Cast a spell! (To DM) Can I fire my bow over him?"

DM: "Sure, he's short."

Jon: "OK, I'll shoot at orcs."

DM: "Anne, tell me what Delsenora's doing or she'll lose the round trying to make up her mind!"

Anne: "Got it!—Acid arrow spell at the lead troll."

DM: "Fine. Harry, Rath is in front. Roll for initiative."

Initiative

The initiative roll determines who acts first in any given combat round. Initiative is not set, but changes from round to round (combat being an uncertain thing, at best). A character never knows for certain if he will get to act before another.

Initiative is normally determined with a single roll for each side in a conflict. This tells whether all the members of the group get to act before or after those of the other side(s).

There are also two optional methods that can be used to determine initiative. Each of these optional methods breaks the group action down into more individual initiatives. However, the general method of determining initiative remains the same in all cases.

Standard Initiative Procedure

To determine the initiative order for a round of combat, roll 1d10 for each side in the battle. Normally, this means the DM rolls for the monsters (or NPCs), while one of the players rolls for the PC party. Low roll wins initiative. If more than two sides are involved in combat, the remaining sides act in ascending order of initiative.

If both (or all) sides roll the same number for initiative, everything happens simultaneously—all attack rolls, damage, spells, and other actions are completed before any results are applied. It is possible for a mage to be slain by goblins who collapse from his *sleep* spell at the end of the round.

Initiative Modifiers

Situational factors can affect who has initiative. To reflect this, modifiers are added to or subtracted from the initiative die roll.

Table 55: STANDARD MODIFIERS TO INITIATIVE

Specific Situation	Modifier
Hasted	−2
Slowed	+2
On higher ground	−1
Set to receive a charge	−2
Wading or slippery footing	+2
Wading in deep water	+4
Foreign environment*	+6
Hindered (tangled, climbing, held)	+3
Waiting (see p. 112)	+1

* This applies to situations in which the party is in a completely different environment (swimming underwater without the aid of a *ring of free movement*, for example).

Everyone in the party who will be involved in the round's action must qualify for the modifier. For example, all members of a party must be on higher ground than the opposition in order to get the higher ground modifier. The DM will probably ask each player where his character is standing in order to clarify this.

The side with the *lowest* modified roll on 1d10 has the initiative and acts first.

Continuing the example above, the DM decides that one initiative roll is sufficient for each group and no modifiers are needed for either group. (Although Rath is charging, the orcs and trolls are too busy rearranging their lines to be set to receive his

charge and so the −2 to receive charge is not used.)

Harry, rolling for the player characters, gets a 7 on a 10-sided die. The DM rolls a 10. The player characters, having the lowest number, act first.

Delsenora's acid arrow strikes one of the trolls just as Rath takes a swing at the last of the fleeing orcs. A bowshot from Rupert drops another one of the creatures as it takes its position in the second rank. Now the monsters strike back.

The orcs manage to finish forming their line. Enraged by the acid, the lead troll tears into Rath, hurting him badly. The others swarm around him, attempting to tear him limb from limb.

see p. 112

Group Initiative (Optional Rule)

Some people believe that using a single initiative roll for everyone on the same side is too unrealistic. It is, admittedly, a simplification, a way to keep down the number of die rolls required in a single round, allowing for much faster combat. However, the actions of different characters, the types of weapons they use, and the situation can all be factors in determining initiative.

Using this optional method, one initiative die roll is still made for each side in the fight. However, more modifiers are applied to this roll, according to the actions of individual characters. These modifiers are listed on Table 56.

Table 56: OPTIONAL MODIFIERS TO INITIATIVE

Specific Situation	Modifier
Attacking with weapon	Weapon speed
Breath weapon	+1
Casting a spell	Casting time
Creature size (Monsters attacking with natural weapons only)*	
Tiny	0
Small	+3
Medium	+3
Large	+6
Huge	+9
Gargantuan	+12
Innate spell ability	+3
Magical Items**	
Miscellaneous Magic	+3
Potion	+4
Ring	+3
Rods	+1
Scroll	Casting time of spell
Stave	+2
Wand	+3

* This applies only to creatures fighting with natural weapon—claws, bites, etc. Creatures using weaponry use the speed factor of the weapon, regardless of the creature's size.

** Use the initiative modifier listed unless the item description says otherwise.

Some of the modifiers depend on ability, spell, and weapon. Characters casting spells (but not monsters using innate abilities) must add the spellcasting time to the die roll. Characters attacking with weapons add the weapons' speed factors to the die roll (see pages 68 and 69). All other modifiers are applied according to each individual's situation.

Example: In the second round of the combat, the DM decides to use the modified group initiative. Rath is surrounded by trolls and not in the best of health. The rest of the party has yet to close with the monsters.

The DM decides that one troll will continue attacking Rath, with the help of the orcs, while the other trolls move to block reinforcements. In particular, the troll burned by the acid arrow is looking for revenge. The DM then turns to the players for their actions.

Players (all at once): "I'm going to..." "Is he going?..." "I'm casting a..."
DM (shouting): "One at time! Rath?"
Harry: "I'll blow my horn of blasting."
DM: "It'll take time to dig it out."
Harry: "I don't care, I'm doing it."
Jon: "Draw my sword and attack one of the trolls!"
DM: "Anne?"
Anne (not paying attention to the other two): "Cast a fireball."
Harry and Jon: "NO! DON'T!"
DM: "Well, is that what you're doing? Quickly!"
Anne: "No, I'll cast a haste spell! Centered on me, so Rupert and Rath are just at the edge."
DM: "Okay. Harry, roll initiative and everyone modify for your actions."

Harry rolls 1d10 and gets a 6. The DM rolls for the monsters and gets a 5. Each person's initiative is modified as follows:

Rath is using a miscellaneous magical item (modifier +3). His modified initiative is 9 (6 + 3 = 9).

Rupert is using a bastard sword +1 with two hands (weapon speed 7 instead of 8 because of the +1). His modified initiative is 13 (6 + 7 = 13).

Delsenora is casting a spell (haste spell, casting time 3). Her modified initiative is the same as Rath's, 9.

The trolls are attacking with their claws and bites (large creatures attacking with natural weapons +6). Their modified initiative is 11 (5 + 6 = 11).

The orcs are using long swords (weapon speed 5). Their modified initiative is 10 (5 + 5 = 10).

After all modified initiatives are figured, the combat round goes as follows: Delsenora (initiative 9) completes her spell at the same time that Rath (9) brings the house down on the orcs with his horn of blasting.

The orcs (initiative 10) would have gone next, but all of them have been crushed under falling rock.

The three trolls (initiative 11) are unfazed and attack, one at Rath and the other two springing forward, hitting Delsenora and missing Rupert.

Finally, Rupert (initiative 13) strikes back. He moved too slowly to block one troll's path to Delsenora, but manages to cut off the second. Things look very grim for the player characters.

Individual Initiative (Optional Rule)

This method of determining initiative is the same as that just given earlier, except that each PC, NPC, and monster involved in the fight rolls and then modifies his own initiative roll. This gives combat a more realistic feel, but at the expense of quick play.

To players, it may not seem like too much for each to roll a separate initiative die, but consider the difficulties: Imagine a combat between six player characters (each controlled by a player) and five hirelings and henchmen against 16 hobgoblins and five ogres (all of which must be rolled by the DM).

Furthermore, each die roll must be modified according to each individual's actions. The resulting rolls make every combat round a major calculation.

This method is not recommended for large-scale combats. It is best used with small battles in which characters on the same side have vastly different speeds.

Example: In the third round of combat, the DM decides to use individual initiatives. Each character is involved in his own fight and there aren't too many to deal with. Cut off from retreat by fallen rock, the trolls attack. The DM asks the players their intentions.

Harry: "Hit him with my hammer +4!"
Rupert: "Chop him up."
Anne (now in serious trouble): "Cast a burning hands spell."

Each character or monster now rolls 1d10. The rolls and modified results are:

Rath rolls a 2 and is attacking with his hammer (weapon speed 0 instead of 4 due to +4) and is hasted (−2), so his modified initiative is 0.

Rath's troll rolls a 1 and is attacking with natural weapons (+6 modifier) for a total of 7 (1 + 6 = 7).

Rupert rolls a 2 and has a weapon speed of 7 and is hasted (−2) for a modified initiative of 7 (2 + 7−2 = 7).

Rupert's troll rolls a 5 and modifies this by +6 for an 11 (5 + 6 = 11).

Delsenora is very unlucky and rolls a 9. Since she is casting a spell, she gains no benefit from the haste spell this round. She has a casting time of 1 for a total of 10 (9 + 1 = 10).

The troll fighting Delsenora is very quick and rolls a 1, modified to 7 (1 + 6 = 7.)

The order of attacks is: Rath (initiative 0) strikes with his hammer. Rupert and the two trolls (attacking Rath and Delsenora, all initiative 7) attack immediately after. Rupert hits. The troll attacking Rath misses, but Delsenora is hit. Delsenora's spell (initiative 10) would normally happen next, but instead it fizzles, her concentration ruined by the blow from the troll. Next, Rupert's troll attacks and misses. Because of the haste spell, Rath and Rupert now attack again (in order of initiative), Rath first, then Rupert.

Multiple Attacks and Initiative

Often combat involves creatures or characters able to attack more than once in a single round. This may be due to multiple attack forms (claws and bite), skill with a weapon, or character level. No matter what the reason, all multiple attacks are handled by one of two methods.

When multiple attacks are the result of different attack forms—claws and a bite or bite and tail or a ranger with his two-weapon combat ability for example—the attacks all occur at the same time. The creature resolves all of its attacks in initiative order.

When the attacks are true multiples—using the same weapon more than once—as in the case of a highly skilled fighter, the attacks are staggered. Everyone involved in the combat completes one action before the second (or subsequent) attack roll is made.

Take, for example, a fighter who can attack twice per round, and say he's battling creatures that can only make one attack. The fighter wins initiative. He makes his first attack according to the rolled initiative order. Then each creature gets its attack. Finally, the fighter gets his second attack.

If fighters on both sides in a battle were able to attack twice in the round, their first attacks would occur according to the initiative roll. Their second attacks would come after all other attacks, and would then alternate according to the initiative roll.

Spellcasting and Initiative

Casting times for spells can modify initiative rolls, creating a realistic delay for the spellcaster. When a spell's "Casting Time" parameter is given as a number without any units (e.g., rounds or turns), then that number is added to the caster's initiative roll to determine his modified initiative. When a spell requires a round or more to cast, a normal initiative roll is not made—a spell requiring one round to cast takes effect at the end of the current round, after all other actions are completed.

Spells that require more than one round to cast involve some bookkeeping. The DM or one of the players must keep track of the rounds spent in casting. If the spellcasting character is disturbed during this time, the spell is lost. If all goes well, the spell takes effect at the very end of the last round of the required casting time. Thus, a spell requiring 10 minutes to cast would require 10 combat rounds, and wouldn't take effect until the very end of the 10th round.

Weapon Speed and Initiative (Optional Rule)

Each time a character swings a weapon, he places himself out of position to make his next attack. Swinging a hammer is not as simple as tapping in a nail. A war hammer is heavy. Swing it in one direction and it pulls in that direction. It has to be brought under control and repositioned before it can be swung again. The user must regain his balance and plant his feet firmly. Only after doing all this is he ready for his next attack.

Compare how quickly someone can throw a punch to the amount of time required to swing a chair to get a good idea of what weapon speed factors are about.

Weapon speed factors slow the speed of a character's attack. The higher the weapon speed factor, the heavier, clumsier, or more limited the weapon is. For the most part, weapon speed factors apply to all creatures using manufactured weapons. The speed factor of a weapon is added to the initiative roll of the character to get his modified initiative roll.

Thus, if the DM decides to use weapon speed factors for player characters, they should also be used for giants, orcs, centaurs, and the like. Otherwise the DM isn't being fair to the players. However, creatures with natural weapons are not affected by weapon speed. Their attacks are natural extensions of their bodies, giving them much faster recovery and reaction times.

Magical Weapon Speeds

Magical weapons are easier to wield in combat than ordinary ones. Maybe the weapon is lighter or better balanced than normal; maybe it just pulls the character into the proper position of its own volition. Whatever the cause, each bonus point conferred by a magical weapon reduces the speed factor of that weapon by 1. (A *sword +3* reduces the weapon speed factor by 3, for example.) When a weapon has two bonuses, the lesser one is used. No weapon can have a speed factor of less than 0.

Attacking with Two Weapons

A tricky fighting style available only to warriors and rogues is that of fighting with two weapons simultaneously. The character chooses not to use a shield in favor of another weapon, granting him a greater number of attacks, with a penalty to his attack rolls (rangers are exempt from the attack roll penalty).

When using a second weapon in his off-hand, a character is limited in his weapon choice. His principal weapon can be whatever he chooses, provided it can be wielded with one hand. The second weapon must be smaller in size and weight than the character's main weapon (though a dagger can always be used as a second weapon, even if the primary weapon is also a dagger). A fighter can use a long sword and a short sword, or a long sword and a dagger, but he cannot use two long swords. Nor can the character use a shield, unless it is kept strapped onto his back.

When attacking, all characters but rangers suffer penalties to their attack rolls. Attacks made with the main weapon suffer a −2 penalty, and attacks made with the second weapon suffer a −4 penalty. The character's Reaction Adjustment (based on his Dexterity, see Table 2) modifies this penalty. A low Dexterity score will worsen the character's chance to hit with each attack. A high Dexterity can negate this particular penalty, although it *cannot* result in a positive modifier on the attack rolls for either weapon (i.e., the Reaction Adjustment can, at best, raise the attack roll penalties to 0).

The use of two weapons enables the character to make one additional attack each combat round, with the second weapon. The character gains only one additional attack each round, regardless of the number of attacks he may normally be allowed. Thus a warrior able to attack 3/2 (once in the first round and twice in the second) can attack 5/2 (twice in the first round and three times in the second).

Movement in Combat

Since a round is roughly a minute long, it should be easy for a character to move just about anywhere he wants during the course of the round. After all, Olympic-class sprinters can cover vast amounts of ground in a minute.

However, a character in an AD&D® game is not an Olympic sprinter running in a straight line. He is trying to maneuver through a battle without getting killed. He is keeping his eyes open for trouble, avoiding surprise, watching his back, watching the backs of his partners, and looking for a good opening, while simultaneously planning his next move, sometimes through a haze of pain. He may be carrying a load of equipment that slows him down significantly. Because of all these things, the distance a character can move is significantly less than players generally think.

In a combat round, a being can move up to 10 times its movement rating (see Chapter 14) in feet. Thus, if a character has a movement rating of 9, he can move up to 90 feet in a round. However, the types of moves a character can make during combat are somewhat limited.

Movement in Melee

The basic move is to get closer for combat—i.e., move close enough to an enemy to attack. This is neither a blind rush nor a casual stroll. Instead, the character approaches quickly but with caution. When closing for combat, a character can move up to half his allowed distance and still make a melee attack.

Movement and Missile Combat

Rather than slug it out toe to toe with an opponent, a character can move up to one-half his normal movement rate and engage in missile fire at half his normal rate of fire. Thus a man capable of moving 120 feet and armed with a long bow (two shots per round, under normal circumstances) could move 60 feet and still fire one shot. The same man, armed with a heavy crossbow (one shot every other round) would be able to shoot only once every four rounds while on the move.

Charging an Opponent

A character can also charge a foe. A charge increases the character's movement rate by 50% and enables the character to make an attack at the end of his movement. A charging character also gains a +2 bonus to his attack roll, mainly from momentum. Certain weapons (such as a lance) inflict double the rolled damage in a charge.

However, charging gives the opponents several advantages. First, they gain a −2 bonus to their initiative rolls. Second, charging characters gain no Dexterity bonuses to Armor Class and they suffer an AC penalty of 1. Finally, if the defender is using a spear or polearm weapon and sets it against the charge (bracing the butt against a stone or his foot), he inflicts double damage on a successful hit.

Retreat

To get out of a combat, characters can make a careful withdrawal or they can simply flee.

Withdrawing: When making a withdrawal, a character carefully backs away from his opponent (who can choose to follow). The character moves up to 1/3 his normal movement rate.

If two characters are fighting a single opponent and one of them decides to withdraw, the remaining character can block the advance of the opponent. This is a useful method for getting a seriously injured man out of a combat.

Fleeing: To flee from combat, a character simply turns and runs up to his full movement rate. However, the fleeing character drops his defenses and turns his back to his opponent.

The enemy is allowed a free attack (or multiple attacks if the creature has several attacks per round) at the rear of the fleeing character. This attack is made the instant the character flees: It doesn't count against the number of attacks that opponent is allowed during the round, and initiative is irrelevant.

The fleeing character can be pursued, unless a companion blocks the advance of the enemy.

Attacking Without Killing

There are times when a character wants to defeat another being without killing it. A companion may have been charmed into attacking his friends (and his friends don't want to kill him to save themselves!); an enemy may have information the PCs can get only by subduing him; characters may simply see the monetary value of bringing back a real, live monster. Whatever the case, sooner or later characters are going to try.

There are three types of nonlethal attacks—punching, wrestling, and overbearing. Punching is basic bare-fisted fighting. Wrestling is the classic combination of grappling, holds, and throws. Overbearing is simply trying to pull down an opponent by sheer mass or weight of numbers, pinning him to the ground.

Punching and Wrestling

These are the most basic of combat skills, unknowingly practiced by almost all children as they rough and tumble with each other. Thus all characters, regardless of class, are assumed to be somewhat proficient in both these forms of fighting.

Punching occurs when a character attacks with his fists. No weapons are used, although the character can wear an iron gauntlet or similar item. Wrestling requires both hands free, unencumbered by shields and the like.

When punching or wrestling, a normal attack roll is made. The normal Armor Class of the target is used. If a character is attempting to wrestle in armor, the modifiers on Table 57 are used (these are penalties to the attacker's attack roll). Normal modifiers to the attack roll are also applied.

Penalties for being held or attacking a held opponent do not apply to wrestlers.

Wrestling involves a lot of holding and twisting as it is, and the damage resolution system for punching and wrestling takes this into account.

Table 57: ARMOR MODIFIERS FOR WRESTLING

Armor	Modifier
Studded leather	−1
Chain, ring, and scale mail	−2
Banded, splint, and plate mail	−5
Field plate armor	−8
Full plate armor	−10

If the attack roll is successful, consult Table 58 to find the result of the attack: Cross-index the character's modified attack roll with the proper attack form. If, for example, a character successfully punched with an 18, the result would be a rabbit punch (if he rolled an 18 on a successful wrestling attempt, the result would be a kick). Punching and wrestling attacks *can* succeed on attack rolls of 1 or less (exceptions to the general rule).

Table 58: PUNCHING AND WRESTLING RESULTS

Attack Roll	Punch	Damage	% KO	Wrestle
20+	Haymaker	2	10	Bear hug*
19	Wild swing	0	1	Arm twist
18	Rabbit punch	1	3	Kick
17	Kidney punch	1	5	Trip
16	Glancing blow	1	2	Elbow smash
15	Jab	2	6	Arm lock*
14	Uppercut	1	8	Leg twist
13	Hook	2	9	Leg lock
12	Kidney punch	1	5	Throw
11	Hook	2	10	Gouge
10	Glancing blow	1	3	Elbow smash
9	Combination	1	10	Leg lock*
8	Uppercut	1	9	Headlock*
7	Combination	2	10	Throw
6	Jab	2	8	Gouge
5	Glancing blow	1	3	Kick
4	Rabbit punch	2	5	Arm lock*
3	Hook	2	12	Gouge
2	Uppercut	2	15	Headlock*
1	Wild swing	0	2	Leg twist
Less than 1	Haymaker	2	25	Bearhug*

* Hold can be maintained from round to round, until broken.

Punch: This is the type of blow landed. In game terms, the type of blow has little effect, but using the names adds spice to the battle and makes the DM's job of describing the action easier.

Damage: Bare-handed attacks cause only 1 or 2 points of damage. Metal gauntlets, brass knuckles, and the like cause 1d3 points of damage. A character's Strength bonus, if any, *does* apply to punching attacks.

Punching damage is handled a little differently than normal damage. Only 25% of the damage caused by a bare-handed attack is normal damage. The remaining 75% is temporary. For the sake of convenience, record punching damage separately from other damage and calculate the percentage split at the end of all combat.

If a character reaches 0 hit points due to punching attacks (or any combination of punching and normal attacks), he immediately falls unconscious.

A character can voluntarily pull his punch, not causing *any* hit point damage, provided he says so before the damage is applied to his enemy. There is still a chance of a knockout.

% K.O.: Although a punch does very little damage, there is a chance of knocking an opponent out. This chance is listed on the table as "% K.O." If this number or less is rolled on percentile dice, the victim is stunned for 1d10 rounds.

Wrestle: This lists the action or type of grip the character managed to get. Wrestling moves marked with an asterisk (*) are holds maintained from round to round, unless they are broken. A hold is broken by a throw, a gouge, the assistance of another person, or the successful use of a weapon. (Penalties to the attack roll apply to weapon attacks by a character who is in a hold.)

All wrestling moves inflict 1 point of damage plus Strength bonus (if the attacker desires), while continued holds cause cumulatively 1 more point of damage for each round they are held. A head lock held for six rounds would inflict 21 points of damage total (1 + 2 + 3 + 4 + 5 + 6). Remember, this is the equivalent of pressing hard on a full-nelson headlock for roughly six minutes!

Overbearing

Sometimes the most effective attack is simply to pull an opponent down by sheer numbers. No attempt is made to gain a particular hold or even to harm the victim. The only concern is to pin and restrain him.

To overbear an opponent, a normal attack roll is made. For every level of size difference (1 if a Large attacker takes on a Medium defender, for example), the attack roll is modified by 4 (+4 if the attacker is larger; −4 if the defender is larger).

The defender also gains a benefit if it has more than two legs: a −2 penalty to the attacker's roll for every leg beyond two. There is no penalty to the defender if it has no legs. A lone orc attempting to pull down a horse and rider would have at least a −8 penalty applied to the attack roll (−4 for size and −4 for the horse's four legs).

If the attack succeeds, the opponent is pulled down. A character can be pinned if further successful overbearing attacks are rolled each round. For pinning purposes, do not use the prone modifier to combat (from Table 51).

If multiple attackers are all attempting to pull down a single target, make only one attack roll with a +1 bonus for each attacker beyond the first. Always use the to-hit number of the weakest attacker to figure the chance of success, since cooperation always depends on the weakest link. Modifiers for size should be figured for the largest attacker of the group.

A giant and three pixies attempting to pull down a man would use the pixies' attack roll, modified by +3 for three extra attackers and +8 for the size difference of the giant (Huge) and the man (Medium).

Weapons in Non-Lethal Combat

As you might expect, weapons have their place in non-lethal combat, whether a character is defending or pressing the attack.

Weapons in Defense: A character attempting to punch, wrestle, or overbear an armed opponent can do so only by placing himself at great risk. Making matters worse, an armed defender is automatically allowed to strike with his weapon before the unarmed attack is made, regardless of the initiative die roll. Furthermore, since his opponent must get very close, the defender gains a +4 bonus to his attack and damage rolls. If the attacker survives, he can then attempt his attack.

Those involved in a wrestling bout are limited to weapons of small size after the first round of combat—it's very difficult to use a sword against someone who is twisting your sword arm or clinging to your back, trying to break your neck. For this reason, nearly all characters will want to carry a dagger or a knife.

Non-Lethal Weapon Attacks: It is possible to make an armed attack without causing serious damage (striking with the flat of the blade, for example). This is not as easy as it sounds, however.

First, the character must be using a weapon that enables him to control the damage he inflicts. This is impossible with an arrow or sling. It isn't even feasible with a war hammer or mace. It can be done with swords and axes, as long as the blade can be turned so it doesn't cut.

Second, the character has a −4 penalty to his attack roll, since handling a weapon in this way is clumsier than usual. The damage from such an attack is 50% normal; one-half of this damage is temporary.

Non-Lethal Combat and Creatures

When dealing with non-humanoid opponents, a number of factors must be considered.

First, unintelligent creatures, as a rule, never try to grapple, punch, or pull down an opponent. They cheerfully settle for tearing him apart, limb by limb. This, to their small and animalistic minds, is a better solution.

Second, the natural weapons of a creature are always usable. Unlike men with swords, a lion or a carnivorous ape doesn't lose the use of its teeth and fangs just because a character is very close to it.

Finally, and of greatest importance, creatures tend to be better natural fighters than humans. All attacks for a tiger are the same as punching or wrestling. It's just that the tiger has claws! Furthermore, a tiger can use all of its legs effectively—front and back.

Touch Spells and Combat

Many spells used by priests and wizards take effect only when the target is touched by the caster. Under normal circumstances, this is no problem—the spellcaster reaches out and touches the recipient. However, if the target is unwilling, or the spell is used in the midst of a general melee, the situation is much different.

Unwilling Targets: The spellcaster must make a successful attack roll for the spell to have any effect. The wizard or priest calculates his to-hit number normally, according to the intended victim's Armor Class and other protections. The DM can modify the roll if the victim is unprepared for or unaware of the attack. If the roll succeeds, the spellcaster touches the target and the normal spell effect occurs.

Willing Targets: When attempting to cast a spell on a willing target, the casting is automatic as long as both characters are not engaged in combat. For example, if a fighter withdraws from melee, a cleric could heal him the next round.

If the recipient of the spell attempts to do anything besides waiting for the spell to take effect, an attack roll against AC 10 must be made. However, no AC modifiers for Dexterity are applied, since the target is not trying to avoid the spell!

Whenever a touch spell is successful, the spellcaster suffers from any special defenses of his target, if they are continually in operation. A successful touch to a vampire would not result in energy drain, since the power only works when the vampire wills it, but touching a fire elemental would result in serious burns.

When a touch spell is cast, it normally remains effective only for that round. However, certain spells do specify special conditions or durations. Be sure to check each spell description carefully.

Missile Weapons in Combat

In general, missile combat is handled identically to standard melee. Intentions are announced, initiative is rolled, and attack rolls are made. However, there are some special rules and situations that apply only to missile combat.

Missile weapons are divided into two general categories. The first includes all standard, direct-fire, single-target missiles —slings, arrows, quarrels, spears, throwing axes, and the like.

The second category includes all grenade-like missiles that have an area effect, no matter how small. Thus an attack with these weapons does not have to hit its target directly to have a chance of affecting it. Included in this group are small flasks of oil, acid, poison, holy water, potions, and boulders. Hurled boulders are included because they bounce and bound along after they hit, leaving a swath of destruction.

Range

The first step in making a missile attack is to find the range from the attacker to the target. This is measured in yards from one point to the other. This distance is compared to the range categories for the weapon used (see Table 45 in Chapter 6).

If the distance is greater than the long range given, the target is out of range; if the distance is between the long- and medium-range numbers, the target is at long range; when between the medium- and short-range numbers, medium range is used; when equal to or less than the short-range distance, the target is at short range.

Short-range attacks suffer no range modifier. Medium-range attacks suffer a −2 penalty to the attack roll. Long-range attacks suffer a −5 penalty. Some weapons have no short range since they must arc a certain distance before reaching their target. These attacks are always made with an attack roll penalty.

Rate of Fire

Bows, crossbows, and many other missile weapons have different rates of fire (ROF)—the number of missiles they can shoot in a single round.

Small, light weapons can be thrown very quickly, so up to three darts can be thrown in a single round. Arrows can be nocked and let loose almost as quickly, so up to two shots can be fired in a single round.

Some weapons (such as heavy crossbows) take a long time to load and can be fired only every other round.

Whatever the ROF, multiple missile shots are handled the same way as other multiple attacks for the purposes of determining initiative. The ROF of each missile weapon is listed in table 45 in Chapter 6.

Ability Modifiers in Missile Combat

Attack roll and damage modifiers for Strength are always used when an attack is made with a hurled weapon. Here the power of the character's arm is a significant factor in the effectiveness of the attack.

When using a bow, the attack roll and damage Strength modifiers apply only if the character has a properly prepared bow (see Chapter 6: Money and Equipment). Characters never receive Strength bonuses when using crossbows or similar mechanical devices.

Dexterity modifiers to the attack roll are applied when making a missile attack with a hand-held weapon. Thus, a character adds his Dexterity modifier when using a bow, crossbow, or axe but not when firing a trebuchet or other siege engine.

Firing into a Melee

Missile weapons are intended mainly as long-range weapons. Ideally, they are used before the opponents reach your line. However, ideal situations are all too rare, and characters often discover that the only effective way to attack is to shoot arrows (or whatever) at an enemy already in melee combat with their companions. While possible, and certainly allowed, this is a risky proposition.

When missiles are fired into a melee, the DM counts the number of figures in the immediate area of the intended target. Each Medium figure counts as 1. Small (S) figures count as ½, Large as 2, Huge as 4, and Gargantuan as 6. The total value is compared to the value of each character or creature in the target melee. Using this ratio, the DM rolls a die to determine who (or what) will be the target of the shot.

For example, Tarus Bloodheart (man-size, or 1 point) and Rath (also man-size, or 1 point) are fighting a giant (size G, 6 points) while Thule fires a long bow at the giant. The total value of all possible targets is 8 (6+1+1). There's a 1 in 8 chance that Rath is the target; a 1 in 8 chance that Tarus is hit; and a 6 in 8 chance the shot hits the giant.

The DM could roll an 8-sided die to determine who gets hit, or he could reduce the ratios to a percentage (75% chance the giant is hit, etc.) and roll percentile dice.

Taking Cover Against Missile Fire

One of the best ways to avoid being hit and injured is to hide behind something—a wall, a tree, a building corner, a heap of boulders, or whatever happens to be available. Professional adventurers, wishing to make this sound heroic, call this taking cover.

Taking cover doesn't work particularly well in a melee, since the cover hampers defender and attacker equally. However, it is quite an effective tactic against missile fire.

There are two types of protection a character can have. The first is *concealment*, also called soft cover. A character hiding behind a clump of bushes is concealed. He can be seen, but only with difficulty, and it's no easy task to determine exactly where he is. The bushes cannot stop an arrow, but they do make it less likely that the character is hit. Other types of concealment include curtains, tapestries, smoke, fog, and brambles.

The other type of protection is *cover*, sometimes called, more precisely, hard cover. It is, as its name implies, something a character can hide behind that will block a missile. Hard cover includes stone walls, the corner of a building, tables, doors, earth embankments, tree trunks, and magical walls of force.

Cover helps a potential target by giving the attacker a negative modifier to his attack roll. The exact modifier for concealment or cover depends on the degree to which it is being used as shelter. A character who stands behind a two-foot wall is a pretty obvious target, especially when compared to the character who lies down behind that wall and carefully peers over it. Table 59 lists the different modifiers for varying degrees of cover and concealment.

Table 59: COVER AND CONCEALMENT MODIFIERS

Target is:	Cover	Concealment
25% hidden	−2	−1
50% hidden	−4	−2
75% hidden	−7	−3
90% hidden	−10	−4

Cover also has an affect on saving throws, granting the character the modifier listed on Table 59 as a bonus to his saving throws against spells that cause physical damage (e.g., *fireball, lightning bolt*, etc.).

Furthermore, a character who has 90% cover (or more) suffers one-half normal damage on a failed save and no damage at all if a saving throw is successful. This assumes, of course, that the fireball, lightning bolt, or whatever, hit the cover—a man crouching behind a stone wall would be protected if a fireball exploded in front of the wall, but would not be protected by cover if the blast occurred behind him, on his side of the wall.

Grenade-Like Missiles

Unlike standard missiles, which target a specific creature, a grenade-like missile is aimed at a point, whether this point is a creature or a spot on the ground. When the attack is announced, the player indicates where he wants the missile to land. This then becomes the target point and is used to determine the direction and distance of any scatter.

Most grenade-like missiles are items of opportunity or necessity—rocks, flasks of oil, vials of holy water, or beakers of acid. As such, these items are not listed on the equipment tables for range, ROF, and damage. The range each can be thrown varies with the Strength of the character and the weight of the object.

A missile of five pounds or less can be thrown about 30 feet. Short range is 10 feet, medium range is 20 feet, and everything beyond is maximum range. Heavier items have reduced ranges. Just how far an object can be thrown is decided by the DM.

Exceptionally heavy items can be thrown only if the character rolls a successful bend bars/lift gates check. In no case can a character throw an item heavier than his Strength would allow him to lift. Thus, the DM can rule that a character would have little trouble chucking a half-empty backpack across a ten-foot chasm, but the character would need to make a check in order to heave an orc ten feet through the air into the faces of his orcish friends.

Once a container hits, it normally breaks immediately. However, this is not always true. Some missiles, like soft leather flasks or hard pottery, are particularly resistant. If there's some doubt about whether or not a thrown object will break, the DM can require an item saving throw (this information is in the *DMG*) to see if it shatters or rips, spewing its contents everywhere.

The *DMG* contains information on how to resolve the inevitable situations in which grenade-like missiles miss their targets.

Types of Grenade-Like Missiles

Acid damage is particularly grim. Aside from the possibility of scarring (which is left to the DM), acid damage cannot be healed by regeneration. It must be healed normally. Thus it is very useful against regenerating creatures such as trolls. Acid is very rare.

Holy Water affects most forms of undead and creatures from the lower planes. It has no effect against a creature in gaseous form or undead without material form.

Unholy water (essentially holy water used by evil priests) affects paladins, creatures whose purpose is to defend good (lammasu, shedu, etc.), and creatures and beings from the upper planes.

Holy (or unholy) water affects creatures as does acid, causing damage that cannot be regenerated but must be healed normally.

Oil causes damage only when it is lit. This normally requires a two-step process—first soaking the target in flammable oil and then setting it afire. Thus using flaming oil often requires two successful attacks.

A direct hit from flaming oil burns for two rounds, causing 2d6 points of damage in the first round and 1d6 points in the second round.

Poison is generally not very effective as a missile weapon. Most poisons take effect only if the missile scores a direct hit, and even then only if it drops into the gaping maw of some huge creature. Contact poisons have normal poison effects on a direct hit. The DM has information about specific poison effects in the *DMG*.

Special Defenses

So far, the bulk of this chapter has dealt with ways to attack. Now, it's time to turn to defense. There are several ways to avoid taking damage. Two of the most common are the *saving throw* and *magic resistance*. Somewhat less common, because its use is limited to clerics and paladins, is the ability to *turn undead*.

Parrying (Optional Rule)

During a one-minute combat round, each character is assumed to block many attempted attacks and see many of his own attacks blocked. In normal combat, characters parry all the time—there's no need to single out each parry.

When a character deliberately chooses not to parry (a mage casting a spell, for instance), his chance of being hit increases. Thus, choosing to parry, in and of itself, is not a separate option under the AD&D® game rules.

At the same time, the assumption is that characters in combat are constantly exposing themselves to some risk—trying to get a clear view of a target or looking for the opening to make an attack. There are times, however, when this is not the case. Sometimes, the only thing a character wants to do is avoid being hit.

In order to make himself harder to hit, a character can parry—forfeit all actions for the round—he can't attack, move, or cast spells. This frees the character to concentrate solely on defense. At this point, all characters but warriors gain an AC bonus equal to half their level. A 6th-level wizard would have a +3 bonus to his AC (lowering his AC by 3). A warrior gets a bonus equal to half his level plus one. A 6th-level fighter would gain a +4 AC bonus.

Note that the benefit is not a perfect all-around defense, and it's not effective against rear or missile attacks. It applies only to those characters attacking the defender with frontal melee attacks. This optional defense has no effect against magical attacks, so it wouldn't do anything to protect a character from the force of a lightning bolt or fireball, for example.

The Saving Throw

The *saving throw* is a die roll that gives a chance, however slim, that the character or creature finds some way to save himself from certain destruction (or at least lessen the damage of a successful attack).

More often than not, the saving throw represents an instinctive act on the part of the character—diving to the ground just as a fireball scorches the group, blanking the mind just as a mental battle begins; blocking the worst of an acid spray with a shield. The exact action is not important—DMs and players can think of lively and colorful explanations of why a saving throw succeeded or failed. Explanations tailored to the events of the moment enhance the excitement of the game.

Rolling Saving Throws

To make a saving throw, a player rolls a 20-sided die (1d20). The result must be equal to or greater than the character's saving throw number. The number a character needs to roll varies depending upon the character's group, his level, and what the character is trying to save himself from. A character's saving throw numbers can be found in Table 60.

Saving throws are made in a variety of situations: For attacks involving paralyzation, poison, or death magic; petrification or polymorph; rod, staff, or wand; breath weapon; and spells. The type of saving throw a character must roll is determined by the specific spell, monster, magical item, or situation involved.

Monsters also use Table 60. The DM has specific information about monster saving throws.

Table 60: CHARACTER SAVING THROWS

Character Class and Experience Level		Paralyzation, Poison, or Death Magic	Rod, Staff, or Wand	Petrification or Polymorph*	Breath Weapon**	Spell***
				Attack to be Saved Against		
Priests	1-3	10	14	13	16	15
	4-6	9	13	12	15	14
	7-9	7	11	10	13	12
	10-12	6	10	9	12	11
	13-15	5	9	8	11	10
	16-18	4	8	7	10	9
	19+	2	6	5	8	7
Rogues	1-4	13	14	12	16	15
	5-8	12	12	11	15	13
	9-12	11	10	10	14	11
	13-16	10	8	9	13	9
	17-20	9	6	8	12	7
	21+	8	4	7	11	5
Warriors	0	16	18	17	20	19
	1-2	14	16	15	17	17
	3-4	13	15	14	16	16
	5-6	11	13	12	13	14
	7-8	10	12	11	12	13
	9-10	8	10	9	9	11
	11-12	7	9	8	8	10
	13-14	5	7	6	5	8
	15-16	4	6	5	4	7
	17+	3	5	4	4	6
Wizards	1-5	14	11	13	15	12
	6-10	13	9	11	13	10
	11-15	11	7	9	11	8
	16-20	10	5	7	9	6
	21+	8	3	5	7	4

* Excluding *polymorph wand* attacks.
** Excluding those that cause petrification or polymorph.
*** Excluding those for which another saving throw type is specified, such as death, petrification, polymorph, etc.

Saving Throw Priority

Sometimes the type of saving throw required by a situation or item isn't clear, or more than one category of saving throw may seem appropriate. For this reason, the saving throw categories in Table 60 are listed in order of importance, beginning with paralyzation, poison, and death magic, and ending with spells.

Imagine that Rath is struck by the ray from a *wand of polymorphing*. Both a saving throw vs. wands and a saving throw vs. polymorph would be appropriate. But Rath must roll a saving throw vs. wands because that category has a higher priority than polymorph.

The categories of saving throws are as follows:

Save vs. Paralyzation, Poison, and Death Magic: This is used whenever a character is affected by a paralyzing attack (regardless of source), poison (of any strength), or certain spells and magical items that otherwise kill the character outright (as listed in their descriptions). This saving throw can also be used in situations in which exceptional force of will or physical fortitude are needed.

Save vs. Rod, Staff, or Wand: As its name implies, this is used whenever a character is affected by the powers of a rod, staff, or wand, provided another save of higher priority isn't called for. This saving throw is sometimes specified for situations in which a character faces a magical attack from an unusual source.

Save vs. Petrification or Polymorph: This is used any time a character is turned to stone (petrified) or polymorphed by a monster, spell, or magical item (other than a wand). It can also be used when the character must withstand some massive physical alteration of his entire body.

Save vs. Breath Weapon: A character uses this save when facing monsters with breath weapons, particularly the powerful blast of a dragon. This save can also be used in situations where a combination of physical stamina and Dexterity are critical factors in survival.

Save vs. Spell: This is used whenever a character attempts to resist the effects of a magical attack, either by a spellcaster or from a magical item, provided no other type

of saving throw is specified. This save can also be used to resist an attack that defies any other classification.

Voluntarily Failing Saving Throws

No save is made if the target voluntarily chooses not to resist the effect of a spell or special attack. This is the case even if the character was duped as to the exact nature of the spell. When a character announces that he is not resisting the spell's power, that spell (or whatever) has its full effect.

The intention not to resist must be clearly stated or set up through trickery, however. If a character is attacked by surprise or caught unawares, he is normally allowed a saving throw. The DM can modify this saving throw, making the chance of success worse, if the situation warrants it. Only in extreme cases of trickery and deception should an unwitting character be denied a saving throw.

Ability Checks as Saving Throws

When a character attempts to avoid danger through the use of one of his abilities, an ability check can be used in lieu of a saving throw.

For example, Ragnar the thief has broken into someone's home when he hears a grating noise from the ceiling above him. He looks up to find a five-ton block of the ceiling headed straight for him! He is going to need speedy reactions to get out of the way, so a Dexterity ability check should be rolled to see if he avoids the trap.

Modifying Saving Throws

Saving throws can be modified by magical items, specific rules, and special situations. These modifiers can increase or decrease the chance of a successful saving throw.

Modifiers that increase the chance are given as a number preceded by a plus sign. Modifiers that make success more difficult are given as a number preceded by a minus sign (−1, −2, etc.).

Saving throw modifiers affect a character's die roll, not the saving throw number needed. Thus, if Delsenora needed an 11 for a successful saving throw vs. petrification and had a +1 bonus to her save, she would still need to roll an 11 or higher after all adjustments were made (but the +1 bonus would be added to her die roll, so that effectively she needs to roll only a 10 on the die to reach her saving throw number of 11).

High ability scores in Dexterity and Wisdom sometimes give saving throw bonuses. A high Wisdom protects against illusions, charms, and other mental attacks. Dexterity, if high enough, can give a character a

slightly higher chance of avoiding the effects of fireballs, lightning bolts, crushing boulders, and other attacks where nimbleness may be a help. (See Tables 2 and 5.)

Magical items like cloaks and rings of protection give bonuses to a character's saving throw (these are listed in the item descriptions in the *DMG*).

Magical armor allows a saving throw bonus only when the save is made necessary by something physical, whether normal or magical; magical armor never gives a saving throw bonus against gas (which it cannot block), poison (which operates internally), and spells that are mental in nature or that cause no physical damage.

For example, magical armor would not help a character's saving throw against the sting of a giant scorpion, the choking effects of a *stinking cloud* spell, or the transformation effect of a *polymorph others* spell. Magical armor does extend its protective power to saving throws against acid sprays or splashes, disintegration, magical and normal fires, spells that cause damage, and falls (if any saving throw is allowed in this case). Other situations must be handled on a case-by-case basis by the DM.

Specific spells and magical items have effects, both good and ill, on a character's saving throws. Often, spells force the victim to save with a penalty, which makes even the most innocuous spell quite dangerous. (Specific information can be found in the spell descriptions, for spells, or in the *DMG*'s Magical Items section, for magical items.)

Minor poisons of verminous creatures such as giant centipedes, while dangerous, are weak and unlikely to bring about death in a healthy man. To recreate this effect in the game, a saving throw bonus is allowed for anyone affected by these poisons. The DM has this information.

Unpredictable situations are sure to crop up. When this happens, the DM must determine whether saving throw modifiers are appropriate. As a guideline, modifiers for situations should range from −4 to +4. An evil cleric attacked in his shrine could very well have a +3 bonus to all his saving throws and a −3 penalty applied to those of his enemies. The powerful evil of the place could warrant the modifier.

Magic Resistance

Some creatures or items strongly resist the effects of magic (or impart such resistance to others). This makes them more difficult to affect with magical energy than ordinary creatures or items.

A rare few creatures are extremely antimagical—magic rolls off them like water off a duck's back. More common are creatures, especially from the outer planes of existence, that live in enchanted or sorcerous lands and are filled with powerful magical energies. These creatures eat and breathe the vapors of wizardry, and they have a high tolerance against arcane power.

Magic resistance is an innate ability—that is, the possessor does not have to do anything special to use it. The creature need not even be aware of the threat for his magic resistance to operate. Such resistance is part of the creature or item and cannot be separated from it. (Creatures, however, can voluntarily lower their magic resistance at will.)

Magic resistance is also an individual ability. A creature with magic resistance *cannot* impart this power to others by holding their hands or standing in their midst. Only the rarest of creatures and magical items have the ability to bestow magic resistance upon another.

Magic resistance is given as a percentile number. For a magical effect to have any chance of success, the magic resistance must be overcome. The target (the one with the magic resistance) rolls percentile dice. If the roll is higher than the creature's magic resistance, the spell has a normal effect. If the roll is equal to or less than the creature's magic resistance, the spell has absolutely no effect on the creature.

Effects of Magic Resistance

Magic resistance enables a creature to ignore the effects of spells and spell-like powers. It does not protect the creature from magical weapon attacks or from natural forces that may be a direct or accidental result of a spell. Nor does it prevent the protected creature from using his own abilities or from casting spells and using magical items. It can be effective against both individually targeted spells and, within limits, area-effect spells.

If a magic resistance roll fails, and the spell has normal effect, the target can make all saving throws normally allowed against the spell.

When Magic Resistance Applies

Magic resistance applies only if the successful casting of a spell would directly affect the resistant creature or item. Thus, magic resistance is effective against *magic missile* (targeted at a creature or item) or *fireball* (damaging the area the creature or item is in) spells.

Magic resistance is not effective against an earthquake caused by a spell. While the creature may suffer injury or death falling into a chasm the spell opens under its feet, the magical energy of the spell was directed at the ground, not the creature. Magic resistant creatures are not immune to events that occur as the consequence of spells, only to the direct energy created or released by a spell.

Player characters do not normally have magic resistance (though they still get saving throws vs. magical spells and such); this ability is reserved mainly for special monsters.

Successful Magic Resistance Rolls

A successful magic resistance check can have four different results, depending on the nature of the spell being resisted:

Individually Targeted Spells: By definition, these spells affect just one creature, and only the targeted creature rolls for magic resistance (if it has any). If a spell of this type is directed at several targets, each rolls independently of the others. (An example of this would be a *hold person* spell aimed at four creatures, with each creature getting a magic resistance roll, if they have magic resistance.)

If the magic resistance roll is successful, the spell has no effect on that creature. If the spell is targeted only at the creature, the spell fails completely and disappears. If several targets are involved, the spell may still affect others who fail their magic resistance roll.

Area-Effect Spells: These spells are not targeted on a single creature, but on a point. The spell's effect encompasses everything within a set distance of that point. A successful magic resistance check enables the creature to ignore the effect of the spell. However, the spell is not negated and still applies to all others in the area of effect.

In-Place Spells: These spells operate continuously in a particular place or on a particular creature, character, or item. *Protection from evil* is one example of this kind of spell.

Magic resistance comes into play only if a creature or item finds himself (or itself) in the place where the spell is in operation. Even then, magic resistance may not come into play—nothing happens if the spell isn't of a type that affects the character. Thus, a *part water* spell would not collapse simply because a magic resistant creature walked through the area. A *protection from evil* spell, which could affect the creature, would be susceptible to magic resistance.

If the DM determines that a magic resistance roll is appropriate, and the roll succeeds, the in-place spell collapses (usually with a dramatic thunderclap and puff of smoke).

Permanent Spells: Magic resistance is insufficient to destroy a permanent spell. Instead, the spell is negated (within the same guidelines given for in-place spells) for as long as the magic resistant creature is in the area of effect.

Thus, a magic-resistant creature might be

able to step through a permanent wall of force as if it weren't there. However, the wall would spring back into existence as soon as the creature passed through (i.e., no one else can pass through).

Turning Undead

One important, and potentially life-saving, combat ability available to priests and paladins is the ability to turn undead. This is a special power granted by the character's deity. Druids *cannot* turn undead; priests of specific mythoi may be able to at the DM's option.

Through the priest or paladin, the deity manifests a portion of its power, terrifying evil, undead creatures or blasting them right out of existence. However, since the power must be channeled through a mortal vessel, success is not always assured.

When encountering undead, a priest or paladin can attempt to turn the creatures (remember that the paladin turns undead as if he was two levels lower—a 5th-level paladin uses the level 3 column in Table 61). Only one attempt can be made per character per encounter, but several different charac-

To resolve a turning attempt, look on Table 61. Cross-index the Hit Dice or type of the undead with the level of the character (two levels lower for a paladin). If there is a number listed, roll 1d20. If the number rolled is equal to or greater than that listed, the attempt is successful. If the letter "T" (for "turned") appears, the attempt is automatically successful without a die roll. If the letter "D" (for "dispel") is given, the turning utterly destroys the undead. A dash (—) means that a priest or paladin of that level cannot turn that type of undead. *A successful turn or dispel affects 2d6 undead. If the undead are a mixed group, the lowest Hit Dice creatures are turned first.*

Only one die is rolled regardless of the number of undead the character is attempting to turn in a given round. The result is read individually for each type of undead.

For example, Gorus, a 7th-level priest, and his party are attacked by two skeletons led by a wight and a spectre. The turning attempt is made, resulting in a roll of 12.

Gorus's player reads the table for all three types of undead *using the same roll—12—* for all three. The skeletons are destroyed (as Gorus knew they would be). The wight is

If the character forces the free-willed undead to come closer than ten feet (by pressing them into a corner, for example) the turning is broken and the undead attack normally.

Evil Priests and Undead

Evil priests are normally considered to be in league with undead creatures, or at least to share their aims and goals. Thus, they have no ability to turn undead. However, they can attempt to command these beings.

This is resolved in the same way as a turning attempt. Up to 12 undead can be commanded. A "T" result means the undead automatically obey the evil priest, while a "D" means the undead become completely subservient to the evil priest. They follow his commands (to the best of their ability and understanding) until turned, commanded, or destroyed by another.

Evil priests also have the ability to affect paladins, turning them as if they were undead. However, since the living spirit of a paladin is far more difficult to quell and subvert, paladins are vastly more difficult to turn.

An evil priest attempting to turn a paladin does so as if the priest were three levels lower than he actually is. Thus, a 7th-level evil priest would turn paladins on the 4th-level column. He would have only a slim chance of turning a 7th-level paladin (7 HD) and would not be able to turn one of 8th level at all (using the level of the paladin as the HD to be turned). All "D" results against paladins are treated as "T" results.

Injury and Death

Sometimes, no degree of luck, skill, ability, or resistance to various attacks can prevent harm from coming to a character. The adventuring life carries with it unavoidable risks. Sooner or later a character is going to be hurt.

To allow characters to be heroic (and for ease of play), damage is handled abstractly in the AD&D® game. All characters and monsters have a number of hit points. The more hit points a creature has, the harder it is to defeat.

Damage is subtracted from a character's (or creature's) hit points. Should one of the player characters hit an ogre in the side of the head for 8 points of damage, those 8 points are subtracted from the ogre's total hit points. The damage isn't applied to the head, or divided among different areas of the body.

Hit point loss is cumulative until a character dies or has a chance to heal his wounds.

Cwell the Fine, with 16 hit points, is injured by an orc that causes 3 points of damage. Fifteen minutes later, Cwell runs into a

Table 61: TURNING UNDEAD

Type or Hit Dice of Undead	Level of Priest†											
	1	2	3	4	5	6	7	8	9	10-11	12-13	14+
Skeleton or 1 HD	10	7	4	T	T	D	D	D*	D*	D*	D*	D*
Zombie	13	10	7	4	T	T	D	D	D*	D*	D*	D*
Ghoul or 2 HD	16	13	10	7	4	T	T	D	D	D*	D*	D*
Shadow or 3-4 HD	19	16	13	10	7	4	T	T	D	D	D*	D*
Wight or 5 HD	20	19	16	13	10	7	4	T	T	D	D	D*
Ghast	—	20	19	16	13	10	7	4	T	T	D	D
Wraith or 6 HD	—	—	20	19	16	13	10	7	4	T	T	T
Mummy or 7 HD	—	—	—	20	19	16	13	10	7	4	T	T
Spectre or 8 HD	—	—	—	—	20	19	16	13	10	7	4	T
Vampire or 9 HD	—	—	—	—	—	20	19	16	13	10	7	4
Ghost or 10 HD	—	—	—	—	—	—	20	19	16	13	10	7
Lich or 11 + HD	—	—	—	—	—	—	—	20	19	16	13	10
Special**	—	—	—	—	—	—	—	—	20	19	16	13

*An additional 2d4 creatures of this type are turned.

**Special creatures include unique undead, free-willed undead of the Negative Material plane, certain Greater and Lesser Powers, and those undead that dwell in the outer planes.

† Paladins turn undead as priests who are two levels lower.

ters can make attempts at the same time (with the results determined individually).

Attempting to turn counts as an action, requiring one round and occurring during the character's turn in the initiative order (thus the undead may get to act before the character can turn them). The mere presence of the character is not enough—a touch of drama from the character is important. Speech and gestures are important, so the character must have his hands free and be in a position to speak. However, turning is not like spellcasting and is not interrupted if the character is attacked during the attempt.

turned (a 4 or better was needed) and flees. The spectre, however, continues forward undaunted (since a 16 was needed to turn the spectre).

Turned undead bound by the orders of another (e.g., skeletons) simply retreat and allow the character and those with him to pass or complete their actions.

Free-willed undead attempt to flee the area of the turning character, until out of his sight. If unable to escape, they circle at a distance, no closer than ten feet to the character, provided he continues to maintain his turning (no further die rolls are needed).

bugbear that inflicts 7 points of damage, Cwell has suffered 10 points of points of damage. This 10 points of damage remains until Cwell heals, either naturally or through magical means.

Wounds

When a character hits a monster, or vice versa, damage is suffered by the victim. The amount of damage depends on the weapon or method of attack. In Table 44 of Chapter 6, all weapons are rated for the amount of damage they inflict to Small, Medium, and Large targets. This is given as a die range (1d8, 2d6, etc.).

Each time a hit is scored, the appropriate dice are rolled and the damage is subtracted from the current hit points of the target. An orc that attacks with a sword, for example, causes damage according to the information given for the type of sword it uses. A troll that bites once and rends with one of its clawed hands causes 2d6 points of damage with its bite and 1d4 + 4 points with its claw. (The DM gets this information from the *Monstrous Compendium*.)

Sometimes damage is listed as a die range along with a bonus of +1 or more. The troll's claw attack, above, is a good example. This bonus may be due to high Strength, magical weapons, or the sheer ferocity of the creature's attack. The bonus is added to whatever number comes up on the die roll, assuring that some minimum amount of damage is caused. Likewise, penalties can also be applied, but no successful attack can result in less than 1 point of damage.

Sometimes an attack has both a die roll and a damage multiplier. The number rolled on the dice is multiplied by the multiplier to determine how much damage is inflicted. This occurs mainly in backstabbing attempts. In cases where damage is multiplied, only the base damage caused by the weapon is multiplied. Bonuses due to Strength or magic are not multiplied; they are added after the rolled damage is multiplied.

Special Damage

Getting hit by weapons or monsters isn't the only way a character can get hurt. Indeed, the world is full of dangers for poor, hapless player characters, dangers the DM can occasionally spring on them with glee. Some of the nastier forms of damage are described below.

Falling

Player characters have a marvelous (and, to the DM, vastly amusing) tendency to fall off things, generally from great heights and almost always

onto hard surfaces. While the falling is harmless, the abrupt stop at the end tends to cause damage.

When a character falls, he suffers 1d6 points of damage for every 10 feet fallen, to a maximum of 20d6 (which for game purposes can be considered terminal velocity).

This method is simple and it provides all the realism necessary in the game. It is not a scientific calculation of the rate of acceleration, exact terminal velocity, mass, impact energy, etc., of the falling body.

The fact of the matter is that physical laws may describe the exact motion of a body as it falls through space, but relatively little is known about the effects of impact. The distance fallen is not the only determining factor in how badly a person is hurt. Other factors may include elasticity of the falling body and the ground, angle of impact, shock wave through the falling body, dumb luck, and more.

People have actually fallen from great heights and survived, albeit very rarely. The current record-holder, Vesna Vulovic, survived a fall from a height of 33,330 feet in 1972, although she was severely injured. Flight-Sergeant Nicholas S. Alkemade actually fell 18,000 feet—almost 3.5 miles—without a parachute and landed uninjured!

The point of all this is roll the dice, as described above, and don't worry too much about science.

Paralysis

A character or creature affected by paralysis becomes totally immobile for the duration of the spell's effect. The victim can breathe, think, see, and hear, but he is unable to speak or move in any manner. Coherent thought needed to trigger magical items or innate powers is still possible.

Paralysis affects only the general motor functions of the body and is not the ultimate destroyer of powerful creatures. It can be particularly potent on flying creatures, however.

An Example of Paralysis: The adventurers encounter a beholder, a fearsome creature with magical powers that emanate from its many eyes.

After several rounds of combat, the party's priest casts a *hold monster* spell, paralyzing the creature. The paralyzed beholder can still use the spell-like powers of its eyes and can still move about (since it levitates at will). But, on the other hand, it is not able to move its eyestalks to aim. Since all of its eyes were most likely facing forward at the moment of paralysis, the adventurers cleverly spread out in a ring around the creature. To attack one or two of them with its powers, the beholder must turn its back on the rest.

Energy Drain

This is a feature of powerful undead (and other particularly nasty monsters). The energy drain is a particularly horrible power, since it causes the loss of one or more experience levels!

When a character is hit by an energy-draining creature, he suffers normal damage from the attack. In addition, the character loses one or more levels (and thus Hit Dice and hit points). For each level lost, roll the Hit Dice appropriate to the character's class and subtract that number of hit points from the character's total (subtract the Constitution bonus also, if applicable). If the level(s) lost was one in which the character received a set number of hit points rather than a die roll, subtract the appropriate number of hit points. The adjusted hit point total is now the character's maximum (i.e., hit points lost by energy drain are not taken as damage but are lost permanently).

The character's experience points drop to halfway between the minimum needed for his new (post-drain) level and the minimum needed for the next level above his new level.

Multi-class and dual-class characters lose their highest level first. If both levels are equal, the one requiring the greater number of experience points is lost first.

All powers and abilities gained by the player character by virtue of his former level are immediately lost, including spells. The character must instantly forget any spells that are in excess of those allowed for his new level. In addition, a wizard loses all understanding of spells in his spell books that are of higher level than he can now cast. Upon regaining his previous level, the spellcaster must make new rolls to see if he can relearn a spell, regardless of whether he knew it before.

If a character is drained to 0th level but still retains hit points (i.e., he is still alive), that character's adventuring career is over. He cannot regain levels and has lost all benefits of a character class. The adventurer has become an ordinary person. A *restoration* or *wish* spell can be used to allow the character to resume his adventuring career. If a 0th-level character suffers another energy drain, he is slain instantly, regardless of the number of hit points he has remaining.

If the character is drained to less than 0 levels (thereby slain by the undead), he returns as an undead of the same type as his slayer in 2d4 days. The newly risen undead has the same character class abilities it had in normal life, but with only half the experience it had at the beginning of its encounter with the undead who slew it.

The new undead is automatically an NPC! His goals and ambitions are utterly opposed to those he held before. He possesses great hatred and contempt for his former colleagues, weaklings who failed him in his time of need. Indeed, one of his main ambitions may be to destroy his former companions or cause them as much grief as possible.

Furthermore, the newly undead NPC is under the total control of the undead who slew it. If this master is slain, its undead minions gain one level for each level they drain from victims until they reach the maximum Hit Dice for their kind. Upon reaching full Hit Dice, these undead are able to acquire their own minions (by slaying characters).

Appropriate actions on the part of the other player characters can prevent a drained comrade from becoming undead. The steps necessary vary with each type of undead and are explained in the monster descriptions in the *Monstrous Compendium*.

Poison

This is an all-too frequent hazard faced by player characters. Bites, stings, deadly potions, drugged wines, and bad food all await characters at the hands of malevolent wizards, evil assassins, hideous monsters, and incompetent innkeepers. Spiders, snakes, centipedes, scorpions, wyverns, and certain giant frogs all have poisons deadly to characters. Wise PCs quickly learn to respect and fear such creatures.

The strength of different poisons varies wildly and is frequently overestimated. The bite of the greatly feared black widow spider kills a victim in the United States only once every other year. Only about 2% of all rattlesnake bites prove fatal.

At the other extreme, there are natural poisons of intense lethality. Fortunately, such poisons tend to be exotic and rare—the golden arrow-poison frog, the western taipan snake, and the stonefish all produce highly deadly poisons.

Furthermore, the effect of a poison depends on how it is delivered. Most frequently, it must be injected into the bloodstream by bite or sting. Other poisons are only effective if swallowed; assassins favor these for doctoring food. By far the most deadly variety, however, is contact poison, which need only touch the skin to be effective.

Paralytic poisons leave the character unable to move for 2d6 hours. His body is limp, making it difficult for others to move him. The character suffers no other ill effects from the poison, but his condition can lead to quite a few problems for his companions.

Debilitating poisons weaken the character for 1d3 days. All of the character's ability scores are reduced by half during this time. All appropriate adjustments to attack rolls, damage, Armor Class, etc., from the lowered ability scores are applied during the course of the illness. Furthermore, the character moves at one-half his normal movement rate. Finally, the character cannot heal by normal or magical means until the poison is neutralized or the duration of the debilitation is elapsed.

Treating Poison Victims

Fortunately, there are many ways a character can be treated for poison. Several spells exist that either slow the onset time, enabling the character the chance to get further treatment, or negate the poison entirely. However, cure spells (including *heal*) do not negate the progress of a poison, and *neutralize poison* doesn't recover hit points already lost to the effects of poison. In addition, characters with herbalism proficiency can take steps to reduce the danger poison presents to player characters.

Healing

Once a character is wounded, his player will naturally want to get him healed. Characters can heal either by natural or magical means. Natural healing is slow, but it's available to all characters, regardless of class. Magical healing may or may not be available, depending on the presence (or absence) of spellcasters or magical devices.

The only limit to the amount of damage a character can recover through healing is the total hit points the character has. A character cannot exceed this limit until he gains a new level, whereupon another Hit Die (or a set number of points) is added to his total. Healing can never restore more hit points to a character than his maximum hit point total.

Natural Healing

Characters heal naturally at a rate of 1 hit point per day of rest. Rest is defined as low activity—nothing more strenuous than riding a horse or traveling from one place to another. Fighting, running in fear, lifting a heavy boulder, or any other physical activity, prevents resting, since it strains old wounds and may even reopen them.

If a character has complete bed rest (doing nothing for an entire day), he can regain 3 hit points for the day. For each complete week of bed rest, the character can add any Constitution hit point bonus he might have to the base of 21 points (3 points per day) he regained during that week.

In both cases above, the character is assumed to be getting adequate food, water, and sleep. If these are lacking, the character does not regain any hit points that day.

Magical Healing

Healing spells, potions, and magical devices can speed the process of healing considerably. The specifics of such magical healing methods are described in the spell descriptions in this book and in the *DMG* (for magical items). By using these methods, wounds close instantly and vigor is restored. The effects are immediate.

Magical healing is particularly useful in the midst of combat or in preparation for a grievous encounter. Remember, however that the characters' opponents are just as likely to have access to magical healing as the player characters—an evil high priest is likely to carry healing spells to bestow on his own followers and guards. Healing is not, of itself, a good or evil act.

Remember that under no circumstances can a character be healed to a point greater than his original hit point total. For example, say a character has 30 hit points, but suffers 2 points of damage in a fight. A while later, he takes an additional point of damage, bringing his current hit point total to 27. A spellcaster couldn't restore more than 3 points to him, regardless of the healing method used. Any excess points are lost.

Herbalism & Healing Proficiencies

Characters can also gain minor healing benefits from those proficient in the arts of herbalism and healing. These talents are explained in Chapter 5.

Character Death

When a character reaches 0 hit points, that character is slain. The character is immediately dead and unable to do anything unless some specialized magical effect takes precedence.

Death From Poison

Poison complicates this situation, somewhat. A character who dies as a result of poisoning may still have active venom in his system.

Poisons remain effective for 2d6 hours after the death of the victim. If the character is raised during this time, some method must be found to neutralize the poison before the character is restored to life. If this is not done, then after the character rolls the resurrection survival check as given in "Raising the Dead" on page 106 (and assuming the roll is successful), he must immediately roll a successful saving throw vs. poison or suffer all the effects of the poison in his body, as per the normal rules. This may only injure some characters, but it may kill other characters seconds after being raised!

Death From Massive Damage

In addition to dying when hit points reach 0, a character also runs the risk of dying abruptly when he suffers massive amounts of damage. A character who suffers 50 or more points of damage from a single attack must roll a successful saving throw vs. death, or he dies.

This applies only if the damage was done by a single attack. Multiple attacks totaling 50 points in a single round don't require a saving throw.

For example, a character would be required to make a check if a dragon breathed on him for 72 points of damage. He wouldn't have to do so if eight orcs hit him for a total of 53 points of damage in that round.

If the saving throw is successful, the character remains alive (unless of course the 50-hit-point loss reduced his hit points to 0 or below!). If the saving throw fails, the character immediately dies from the intense shock his body has taken. His hit points are reduced to 0.

The character may still be raised in the normal ways, however.

Inescapable Death

There are occasions when death is unavoidable, no matter how many hit points a character has.

A character could be locked in a room with no exits, with a 50-ton ceiling descending to crush him. He could be trapped in an escape-proof box filled completely with acid. These examples are extreme (and extremely grisly), but they could happen in a fantasy world.

Raising the Dead

Curative and healing spells have no effect on a dead character—he can only be returned to life with a *raise dead* or *resurrection* spell (or a device that accomplishes one of these effects). Each time a character is returned to life, the player must make a resurrection survival roll based on his current Constitution (see Table 3). If the die roll is successful (i.e., the player rolls equal to or less than his resurrection survival percentage), the character is restored to life in whatever condition is specified by the spell or device.

A character restored to life in this way has his Constitution permanently lowered by 1 point. This can affect hit points previously earned. Should the character's Constitution bonus go down, the character's hit point total is reduced by the appropriate number of hit points (the amount of hit point bonus lost is multiplied by the number of levels for which the character gained extra hit points from that bonus). When the character's Constitution drops to 0, that character can no longer be raised. He is permanently removed from play.

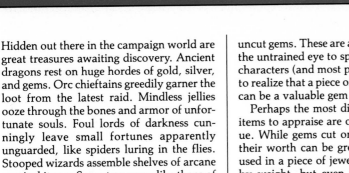

Hidden out there in the campaign world are great treasures awaiting discovery. Ancient dragons rest on huge hordes of gold, silver, and gems. Orc chieftains greedily garner the loot from the latest raid. Mindless jellies ooze through the bones and armor of unfortunate souls. Foul lords of darkness cunningly leave small fortunes apparently unguarded, like spiders luring in the flies. Stooped wizards assemble shelves of arcane magical items. Some treasures, like those of dragons, are gathered and horded for reasons fully understood only by their collectors. Others are gathered for more mundane purposes—power, luxury, and security. A rare few troves date from eons before, their owners long dead and forgotten. Some treasure hordes are small, such as the pickings of a yellow mold. Others are enormous, such as the Tyrant King's treasury. Treasures may be free for the taking or fiercely trapped and watched over.

Treasure Types

Treasure comes in many different forms and sizes, ranging from the mundane to the exotic. There are of course coins of copper, silver, gold, electrum, and platinum. But precious metals can also be shaped into gilded cups, etched bowls, or even silverware. Characters know the value of coins and will have no difficulty establishing their worth in most cases. However, ancient treasure hordes may contain coins no longer used. It may be that these can be sold only by their weight. Objects made of valuable metal are even more difficult to appraise. Either the characters must find a goldsmith who can value the item and a buyer willing to pay a fair price, or these too must be melted down for their metal. In large cities this is not too difficult. There are always appraisers and fences handy, although getting full value might be difficult. (Accusations of theft are another small problem.) Characters must be aware of cheats and counterfeiters though. An apparently valuable bowl could actually be base metal plated in silver. The metal of coins could be debased with copper or brass. Weights could be rigged to give false prices. Characters must find merchants they can trust.

Gems are another common form of treasure and here player characters are even more dependent on others. Unless the party has a skilled appraiser of precious stones, they're going to have to trust others. After all, those red stones they found in the last treasure could be cheap glass, richly colored but only marginally valuable quartz, semiprecious garnets, or valuable rubies. Again, the player characters are going to have to find a jeweler they can trust and be watchful for cheats and scams. However, truly tricky DMs might present your characters with uncut gems. These are almost impossible for the untrained eye to spot or appraise. Most characters (and most players) are not going to realize that a piece of unremarkable stone can be a valuable gem when properly cut.

Perhaps the most difficult of all treasure items to appraise are objects of artistic value. While gems cut or uncut are valuable, their worth can be greatly increased when used in a piece of jewelry. Gold is valuable by weight, but even more so when fashioned into a cup or pin. Dwarven craftsmen from hidden communities practice the finest arts of gem-cutting, while gnomish artisans in earthen burrows labor away on elaborate gold and silver filigrees. Ancient elven carvings, done in exquisitely grained woods, stand side by side with the purest of statues chiseled by man. All of these have a value that goes far beyond their mere materials.

But artistic creations seldom have a fixed value. Their price depends on the player characters finding a buyer and that person's willingness to buy. A few large cities may have brokers in arts, merchants who know the right people and are willing to act as go-betweens. Most of the time, however, the player characters have to go to the effort of peddling their wares personally. This requires tact and delicacy, for such items are seldom bought by any but the wealthy and the wealthy often do not like stooping to business negotiations. Player characters must carefully avoid giving insult to the barons, dukes, counts, and princes they might deal with.

Finally, there are the truly unusual things your character can find—furs, exotic animals, spices, rare spell components, or even trade goods. As with art objects, the values of these items are highly subjective. First the player characters have to find a buyer. This is not too difficult for everyday things, such as furs or trade goods, but it can be a tremendous enterprise if you have a spell component that is useful only to the most powerful of wizards. Next the PCs must haggle about the price. Furriers and merchants do this as a matter of course. Others haggle because they hope the PCs do not know the true value of what they hold or because they themselves do not know. After all this, the PCs might be able to sell their goods. However, if you enter into this in the true spirit of role-playing and see it as part of the adventure, the whole process is enjoyable.

Magical Items

The treasures mentioned thus far are all monetary. Their usefulness is immediate and obvious. They give characters wealth, and with wealth comes power and influence. However, there are other treasures, very desirable ones, that your characters will not want to sell or give away. These are the magical items that your characters find and use.

Although priests and wizards can make magical items (according to the guidelines your DM has for magical research), it is far more common for characters to find these items during the course of adventures. Magical items are powerful aids for characters. With them, characters can gain bonuses in combat, cast spells with the mere utterance of a word, withstand the fiercest fire, and perform feats impossible by any other known means. Not all magical items are beneficial, however. Some are cursed, the result of faulty magical construction or, very rarely, the deliberate handiwork of some truly mad or evil wizard.

A very few magical items are *artifacts*—items created by beings more powerful than the greatest player characters. These are perilously dangerous items to use. There are only three methods to determine how to use artifacts—dumb luck, trial and error, and diligent research.

There are many different magical items your character can find, but they all fall into a few basic categories. Each type of magical item has properties you should be aware of.

Magical Weapons: There can be a magical version of nearly any type of normal weapon, although there are admittedly few magical bardiches or guisarme-voulges. By far the most common magical weapons are swords and daggers. A magical weapon typically gives a +1 or greater bonus to attack rolls, increasing a character's chance to hit and cause damage. Perhaps magical swords are quicker on the attack, or maybe they're sharper than normal steel—the explanation can be whatever the DM desires. Whatever the reason, magical weapons give results far beyond those of even the finest-crafted nonmagical blade.

A rare few weapons have even greater powers. These may allow your character to sense danger, heal wounds, float in mid-air, or have the most amazing luck. The rarest of the rare can actually communicate with your character and are imbued with an other-worldly intelligence. While the most powerful of magical weapons, these clever instruments of destruction sometimes seek to impose their wills on their owners.

When you find a magical weapon, more than likely you do not know its properties. Some functions, such as the advantage it gives you in combat, can be learned by trial and error. Other properties must be learned through research and spells. Ancient histories and *legend lore* spells can provide information on the properties of your weapon. On rare occasions, properties are discovered through blind luck. Simply commanding the weapon to activate one power after another (hoping it will suddenly spring to life) works only for the most minor abilities—detecting danger, spotting secret doors, or locating treasure. Greater abilities require that specific commands be uttered, perhaps in long-forgotten languages.

Magical Armor: Enchanted armors are the complements to magical weapons. These armors have a +1 or better bonus to their normal Armor Class, being made of stuff stronger and finer than nonmagical armor. Furthermore, these armors grant some measure of protection against attacks that normal armors would not stop. *Chain mail +1*, for instance, improves the character's saving throw against the fiery breath of a dragon by 1, thus providing more than just a physical shield. In rare instances, armor may possess extraordinary powers. Although such armors are generally finely made and elaborately engraved, characters can discover the armors' powers only by the same methods they use to discover the powers of magical weapons.

Potions and Oils: Magical potions and oils are easily found but hard to identify. They come in small bottles, jugs, pots, or vials and clearly radiate magic if a detection spell is used. However, the effect of any potion is unknown until some brave soul tries a small sample. The results can be quite varied. The imbiber may discover he can float or fly, resist great heat or cold, heal grievous wounds, or fearlessly face the greatest dangers. He may also find himself hopelessly smitten by the first creature he

sees or struck dead by a powerful poison. It is a risk that must be taken to learn the nature of the potion.

Scrolls: Scrolls are a convenience and luxury for spellcasters. By reading the incantation written on the pages, the priest or wizard can instantly cast that spell. He does not need to memorize it, have the material components handy, or do any of the things normal spellcasting requires. Experienced and powerful wizards normally spend their evenings preparing such scrolls for their own adventuring use.

Some scrolls are usable by all characters, granting special but temporary protections from various dangers—evil creatures, werewolves, powerful beings from other planes, etc. Other scrolls bear hideous or humorous curses, brought into effect at the mere reading of their titles. Unfortunately, the only way to know what a scroll contains is to silently scan its contents. For scrolls containing wizard spells, this requires the use of a *read magic* spell. Other scrolls can be read by all. This scan does not cast the spell written on the scroll, but it tells the character what is written there (and exposes him to the effects of curses). Once the scroll is read, it can be used at any time in the future by that character.

Rings: Magical rings are usable by many different classes and bestow a wide range of powers, from pyrotechnic displays to wish-

es. While the aura of a magical ring can be detected, its properties cannot be discovered until it is worn and the command word is uttered. (The command word is most commonly found inscribed on the inside of the band.) As with all magical items, some rings can harm your character. Worse still, cursed rings can be removed only with the aid of spells!

Wands, Staves, and Rods: These are among the most powerful of standard magical items. Wands are commonly used by wizards, allowing them to cast powerful spells with the flick of a wrist. Staves can be used by either a wizard or a priest. Staves can be truly destructive, dwarfing even the potential of a wand. Rods are the rarest of all, the accouterments of witch-kings and great lords. With rods come dominance and power.

Fortunately for your character, few of these items are cursed or dangerous to handle. But all must be operated by a command word—a specific word or phrase that triggers the power within. No wand, stave, or rod shows any indication of its powers by mere sight or handling. Careful research and probing are most often needed to tap the potential stored within.

Wands, staves, and rods are not limitless in their power. Each use drains them slightly, using up a charge. There is no power gauge or meter showing what is left. A char-

acter discovers his wand is drained only when it no longer functions or suddenly crumbles into useless dust.

Miscellaneous Magic: Miscellaneous magical items are where the true variety of magical treasures lies. Each item possesses some unique power. There are horseshoes to make your horse go faster, brooms to ride, sacks that hold more than they should, paints that create real things, girdles that grant great strength, caps to make your character smarter, books that increase ability scores, and much, much more. Each item is different and not all can be identified in the same way. The effects of some become obvious the instant the item is handled, donned, or opened. Others require research and questioning to learn the command word needed to activate them. All are quite valuable and rare.

Artifacts and Relics: Finally, there are artifacts and relics. Don't count on your PC ever finding one of these rarest of all magical items. Even if your character does find one, think carefully before you decide to let him keep it permanently. Artifacts are the most powerful magical items in the game. Indeed, many are powerful enough to alter the course of history! They are all unique and have unique histories. You can never find more than one *Hand of Vecna* in a world. Because it is so unique, each artifact has special and significant powers. Artifacts never appear by accident; they are always placed by the DM.

Finding artifacts is always the result of a very special adventure. Your DM has placed that artifact for a reason. It is not likely that he really intends for your characters to keep it. Instead, he has something arranged in which you need that artifact for a specific purpose. The problem with keeping artifacts is that they are too powerful. Not only do they unbalance your character in the short run, they also eventually corrupt and destroy him. The magical power of artifacts is such that they destroy their owners sooner or later. There is a price to be paid for power, and it is not a cheap one.

Dividing and Storing Treasure

Once your group completes a successful adventure, it is almost certain to have collected some treasure. Therefore, it helps to have some prearranged agreement about how this treasure is to be divided among the different player characters and their henchmen. This is a true role-playing decision that must be reached among all the players at the table. There are no rules about how your characters should divide treasures.

However, there are some suggested methods and reasons to make or not make some agreements. If you bear these in mind, you will have fewer arguments and bad feelings between the different players and their characters in your group.

Cash treasure is the easiest. The most direct and simplest method is equal shares for all player characters and full or half shares for all henchmen. A player may argue that his character's contribution was greater than that of other characters, but these things average out in the long run. Besides, that player has no real idea of the contribution of others. A character who guarded the rear may have discouraged hidden opponents from springing an ambush on the group, something that only the DM knows.

Additional considerations include extraordinary costs. Some adventuring groups establish a special fund to pay the costs (if there are any) of healing, resurrecting, or restoring fellow player characters. Again this works on the principle that all faced the danger and therefore all should share equally in the expenses. Other groups make allowances for differing character levels (higher level characters assumedly shouldered more of the burden of the adventure, and so should be rewarded proportionately.) Some parties give special rewards to those who took greater chances or saved others. These encourage everyone in the group to take part.

Magical treasure is more difficult to divide up, since there is rarely enough to give a useful item to every character, nor are all items of equal value or power. Here you must rely more on your sense of fairness if you wish to maintain party harmony. Since magical items are worthwhile to a party only if they can be used, your first concern should normally be to get the right item into the right hands. A magical sword in the possession of a wizard is not nearly as useful as it would be in the hands of a fighter. Likewise, a wand does a fighter little good but could be a potent addition to a wizard. Therefore it is a good idea to match items to characters.

Alternatively, your party could determine the price an item would sell for, and then make it available to any PC who is willing to give the rest of the party that amount of money. If more than one player is willing to pay the price, the interested players could roll dice to see who gets the item. Or, for items that several characters could all use equally well (such as a *potion of healing* that is useful to all), the characters can bargain with each other and roll dice for choices. A player character may relinquish a claim on one magical item in exchange for another. A character who has already received a magical item may not be allowed another choice if there are not enough pieces to go around. If no other agreement can be reached, the players can roll dice and have their characters pick in descending order. It is a fair method (since people cannot rightfully complain about a random roll), but it can create imbalances. One or two characters could wind up with the bulk of the magical items over the course of several adventures. At this point, they would be wise to voluntarily withdraw from the selection process.

There are tactical issues to think about when distributing treasure. It is simply not wise for one or two characters to carry the bulk of the party's magical items. Successful adventurers spread their gear throughout their party. (This holds true even for explorers and special forces in the real world.) This way, if one character falls off the cliff and disappears forever or is spirited away by an invisible stalker, the party has not lost everything. To illustrate another consideration, you are better off to have the fighters, thieves, and mages carry the healing potions rather than let the cleric do it, since he has healing spells. If he has both the healing spells and the potions and should disappear into the mist, your party has lost all its healing ability. If it is spread around through the group, at worst you might lose the potions or the spells, but not both (unless disaster really strikes, in which case there is no way to prevent it anyway). In the end, you will find that it does not pay to be too greedy.

Once your characters have assembled a sizeable amount of treasure, they have to find some place to keep it. If your DM is running a fairly medieval campaign, one thing PCs are not going to find is a bank like today's. Instead, your characters must find other ways to keep their money secure. Chests with strong locks are a good start, but there are still better methods. One choice is to make the treasure small enough that you can carry it with you at all times. (Of course, one good mugging and you're broke.) There is also the difficulty of buying a drink with a 1,000-gp gem. A second choice is to place your money in the hands of someone you think you can trust. We all know what the risks are there. You could have your character give his fortune to a local lord or church and then hope to call in favors at a future date. This is not quite as foolish as it sounds. If the beneficiary of your largess refuses to honor your agreement, you'll never give him money again and neither will anyone else, most likely. If no one gives him any money, where will he find the funds to support his life-style? No, such a person must seriously try to honor his commitments. Of course, he may not do as much as you would like. The best solution is that used throughout history—buy goods and chattels. Land, livestock, and trade goods are harder to steal and harder to lose. If you must keep a large fortune, it is best to keep it in something that can be carried easily and is unlikely to be stolen.

Whenever a player character meets an NPC (non-player character), fights a monster, or even discovers a mysterious fountain in the woods, he is having an encounter. An encounter is any significant thing a character meets, sees, or interacts with during the course of a game. When a player character discovers the fountain of blue flame in the midst of the forest, its very strangeness forces the character to react and the player to think. Why is it here? Does it have a purpose? Is it beneficial or dangerous? Few characters are going to pass this by as just another flaming fountain in the forest.

Encounters are vital to the AD&D® game, for without them nothing can really happen to the player character. An adventure without encounters is like sitting in a room all day with no one to talk to and little to look at. It certainly wouldn't be very exciting. And who wants to play an unexciting roleplaying game? Encounters provide danger, risk, mystery, information, intrigue, suspense, humor, and more.

For an encounter to provide excitement, it must also have an element of danger. A good deal of this comes from the fact that player characters don't know how the encountered beings will react to them. Your DM is not going to say, "You meet a group of peasants and they are friendly." (If he does say this, you ought to be suspicious.) Instead, he will say something like, "As you ride around the bend, you come upon an ox-cart lumbering down the road. A young man in rough clothes is leading the cart. Peering over the sides are a woman and several dirty children. When the man sees you he nods, smiles, and says, 'Hail, strangers. Have you news of Thornhampton-on-the-Hill?' " You can probably guess they are peasants and they seem friendly, but your DM didn't come out and said so. Not knowing for sure is what keeps you on your toes. They could be anything!

When your character travels or explores a dungeon, your DM will have prepared two general types of encounters. The first are *specific* (planned) *encounters*. These are meetings, events, or things the DM has chosen to place in the adventure to build on the story of the adventure.

For example, upon sneaking into the bugbear stronghold, your characters find a squalid cell filled with humans and elves. Your DM has placed them here for your character to rescue. Of course, he could also be playing a trick and the prisoners could actually be evil dopplegangers (creatures able to change their appearances at will).

Later, while in the hallway, your group bumps into a bugbear patrol. This is the second type of encounter, a *random encounter*, also called a *wandering encounter*. In this case, your DM has made die rolls to see if you come upon something and, if so, just what that something is.

Specific encounters generally have more choices of action—your DM may want you to discover some important information or set up a particularly difficult battle. Specific encounters usually yield greater treasures and more magical items. Creatures may be placed by the DM to guard the armory or prevent the characters from reaching the throne room.

Random encounters normally involve simple choices—run away, fight, or ignore. Sometimes characters can talk to creatures in random encounters and learn valuable information, but not often. Random encounters also tend to have little or no treasure. A patrol of city guardsmen does not carry as many valuable items on its rounds as it would have in its barracks. Random encounters are most often used to weaken PCs, raise an unexpected alarm, hurry them along, or just make their lives difficult.

Sometimes encounters are not with people or monsters but with things. The fountain in the forest is an encounter, but your characters cannot fight it or talk to it (well, maybe not). So what are you supposed to do? In these cases, the encounter is more of a puzzle. You have to figure out why this fountain is here, what it can do, and if it is important to your adventure. It may be a red herring—something placed there just to confuse you; it may be a set up for a future adventure—later on your characters may learn that the flaming fountain they saw is important to their latest mission. It may be a deadly trap. To find out, though, you will have to deal with the thing in some way. You could throw stones into the pool, drink the glowing water, try to walk through the flames, or use spells to learn more. By doing these things, you may get more information from your DM. Of course, you may not like the answer! ("You drank the water? Oh, dear. Tsk, tsk, tsk.")

The Surprise Roll

Sometimes an encounter, either random or planned by the DM, catches one of the two groups involved totally off guard. This is called *surprise* and is determined by rolling 1d10 for each side (or only one side if the DM has decided that one of the sides cannot be surprised, for some reason). If the die roll is a 1, 2, or 3, that group or character is surprised (for effects, see the "Effects of Surprise" section). Naturally, surprise does not happen all the time. There are many easy and intelligent ways it can be prevented. The most obvious is if the player characters can see those they are about to encounter well before getting close. For example the characters may see the dust of a group of horsemen coming their way, or notice the lanterns of a group of peasants coming through the woods, or

hear the grunting barks of a gnoll war party closing through the trees. In these cases there is no way the characters are going to be surprised by the encounter. But if a leopard leaped upon one of the group while he was intently watching the approaching riders, or if a group of goblins suddenly sprang from the darkness, then the characters would have to roll to see if they were surprised. They were unprepared for these threats and so could be taken off guard.

The DM decides when a check for surprise must be made. He can require that one roll be made for the entire party, that a separate check be made for each character, or that only specific characters check. This depends entirely upon the situation.

For example, the entire party is intently watching the band of approaching riders. Then a leopard leaps from the branches of a tree overhead. The DM knows that no one in the group was particularly paying attention to the treetops, so he has one person in the group roll the surprise die for the entire party. The roll is a 2, the PCs are surprised, the leopard gets a free round of attacks, and there is mass confusion as the clawing, biting creature lands in their midst! If two of the characters had been on a general watch, the DM could have had these characters roll for surprise instead of the entire group. If both were surprised, the entire group would have been unprepared for the leopard's attack. Otherwise, one or both of the guards might have noticed the creature before it pounced. Experienced player characters quickly learn the value of having someone on watch at all times.

The surprise roll can also be modified by Dexterity, race, class, cleverness, and situation. The DM has the listing of modifiers that apply to given situations. Modifiers can affect either your character's chance of being surprised or his chance of surprising others. A plus to your die roll reduces the odds that you are surprised; a minus increases those odds. Likewise, a minus to the enemy's die roll means that the modifier is in your favor, while a plus means that things are going his way. High Dexterity characters are virtually unsurpriseable, caught off guard only in unusual situations.

It is important to bear in mind that surprise and ambush are two different things. Surprise works as explained above. An ambush is prepared by one group to make an unexpected attack on another group and works only if the DM decides the other group cannot detect the ambush. A properly set ambush gives the attackers the opportunity to use spells and normal attacks before the other side reacts. If the ambush succeeds, the ambushing group gets its initial attack *and* the other group must roll for surprise in the next round, so the ambushing group may get two rounds of attacks before the other group can reply.

Effects of Surprise

Characters and monsters that are surprised all suffer the same penalty. They are caught off guard and thus cannot react quickly. The surprising group receives one round of attacks with melee, missile, or magical items. They cannot use these moments of surprise to cast spells.

A ranger on the unsurprised side could fire his long bow twice (two attacks per round) before his opponents could even hope to react. A fighter able to attack twice per round could attempt both hits before any initiative dice are rolled. A mage could unleash a bolt from his *wand of lightning* before the enemy knew he was there. Of course, what applies to player characters also applies to monsters, so that the leopard in the earlier example could claw and bite before the characters even knew what was happening.

The second effect of surprise is that the surprised characters lose all AC bonuses for high Dexterity during that instant of surprise. The surprised characters are dumbfounded by the attack. Instead of ducking and countering, they're just standing there rather flat-footed (maybe even with dumb expressions on their faces). Since they don't grasp the situation, they cannot avoid the hazards and dangers very well.

Surprise can also be used to avoid an encounter. Unsurprised characters can attempt to flee from a surprised group before the other group reacts. Of course, this is not always successful, since escape is greatly dependent upon the movement rates of the different creatures.

If both groups manage to surprise each other, the effects of surprise are cancelled. For example, Rath runs around the corner straight into some lounging guardsmen. Taken by surprise, he stops suddenly and frantically looks for someplace else to run. The guardsmen in turn look up rather stupidly, trying to figure out why this dwarf just raced around the corner. The surprise passes. Rath spots another alley and the guards decide that since he's running, Rath must be a criminal. Initiative rolls are now made to see who acts first.

Encounter Distance

Once your character or party has an encounter and it has been determined whether or not anyone was surprised, your DM will tell you the range of the encounter—the distance separating you from the other group. Many factors affect encounter distance. These include the openness of the terrain, the weather conditions, whether surprise occurred, and the time of day, to name a few. Although you do not know the exact distance until your DM tells you, surprise, darkness, or close terrain

(woods, city streets, or narrow dungeons) usually results in shorter encounter distances, while open ground (deserts, plains, or moors), good light, or advance warning results in greater encounter distances (see Chapter 13).

Encounter Options

Once an encounter occurs, there is no set sequence for what happens next. It all depends on just what your characters have encountered and what they choose to do. That's the excitement of a role-playing game—once you meet something, almost anything could happen. There are some fairly common results of encounters, however.

Evasion: Sometimes all you want is for your characters to avoid, escape, or otherwise get away from whatever it is you've met. Usually this is because you realize your group is seriously outmatched. Perhaps returning badly hurt from an adventure, your group spots a red dragon soaring overhead. You know it can turn your party to toast if it wants. Rather than take that risk, your group hides, waiting for it to pass. Or, topping a ridge, you see the army of Frazznargth the Impious, a noted warlord. There are 5,000 of them and six of you. Retreat seems like the better part of valor, so you turn your horses and ride.

Sometimes you want to avoid an encounter simply because it will take too much time. While riding with an urgent message for his lord, your character rides into a group of wandering pilgrims. Paying them no mind, he lashes his horse and gallops past.

Evading or avoiding an encounter is not always successful. Some monsters pursue, others do not. In the examples above, Frazznargth the Impious (being a prudent commander) orders a mounted patrol to chase the characters and bring them in for questioning. The pilgrims, on the other hand, shout a few oaths as your galloping horse splashes mud on them and then continue on their way. Your character's success at evading capture will depend on movement rates, determination of pursuit, terrain, and just a little luck. Sometimes when he really should be caught, your character gets lucky. At other times, well, he just has to stand his ground.

Talk: Your character doesn't run from encounters all the time, and attacking everything you meet eventually leads to problems. Sometimes the best thing to do is talk, whether it's casual conversation, hardball negotiation, jovial rumor-swapping, or intimidating threats. In fact, talking is often better than fighting. To solve the problems your DM has created for your character, you need information. Asking the right questions, developing contacts, and putting

out the word are all useful ways to use an encounter. Not everything you meet, human or otherwise, is out to kill your character. Help often appears in the most surprising forms. Thus it often pays to take the time to talk to creatures.

Fight: Of course, there are times when you don't want to or can't run away. (Running all the time is not that heroic.) And there are times when you know talking is not a good idea. Sooner or later, your character will have to fight. The real trick is knowing when to fight and when to talk or run. If you attack every creature you meet, the first thing that will happen is that nobody will want to meet with your character. Your character will also manage to kill or chase off everyone who might want to help him. Finally, sooner or later your DM is going to get tired of this and send an incredibly powerful group of monsters after your character. Given the fact that you've been killing everything in sight, he's justified in doing this.

So it is important always to know who you are attacking and why. As with the best police in the world today, the trick is to figure out who are the bad guys and who are the good guys. Make mistakes and you pay. You may kill an NPC who has a vital clue, or unintentionally anger a baron far more powerful than yourself. NPCs will be reluctant to associate with your character, and the law will find fewer and fewer reasons to protect him. It is always best to look on combat as a last resort.

Wait: Sometimes when you encounter another group, you don't know what you should do. You don't want to attack them in case they are friendly, but you don't want to say anything to provoke them. What you can do is wait and see how they react. Waiting is a perfectly sensible option. However, there is the risk that in waiting, you lose the advantage should the other side suddenly decide to attack. Waiting for a reaction so that you can decide what to do causes a +1 penalty to the first initiative roll for your group, if the other side attacks.

Of course, in any given encounter, there may be many other options open to your character. The only limit is your imagination (and common sense). Charging a band of orcs to break through their lines and flee may work. Talking them down with an elaborate bluff about the army coming up behind you might scare them off. Clever use of spells could end the encounter in sudden and unexpected ways. The point is, this is a role-playing game and the options are as varied as you wish to make them.

Player characters cannot fight, survive, wheel, deal, plot, or scheme without interacting with non-player characters (NPCs). Indeed, the very heart of the AD&D® game is the relationship between player characters and non-player characters. How the player characters react to and treat NPCs determines the type of game the group plays. Although many choices are possible, players quickly find that consideration and good treatment of NPCs is the most frequently successful route.

An NPC is any person, creature, or monster that is controlled by the DM. Most NPCs are either people (intelligent races that live in local society) or monsters (intelligent and unintelligent creatures that aren't normally found in towns and villages). The term "monster" is only a convenient label. It doesn't mean the creature is automatically dangerous or hostile. Likewise, NPCs who are people aren't uniformly helpful and cooperative. As with all things, the range of possible reactions of NPCs to PCs covers the entire spectrum.

In the course of their adventures, player characters will be most concerned with three groups of NPCs: hirelings, followers, and henchmen. It is their aid that helps player characters vanquish deadly monsters and accomplish mighty deeds. As their names imply, these NPCs can be persuaded in various ways to join the player characters in their adventures. The most common methods of persuasion are money and loyalty.

Hirelings

The most frequently employed NPC is the *hireling*. A hireling is a person who works for money. Most hirelings have fairly ordinary skills, while others are masters of a craft or art, and a few are experts of specialized adventuring skills. Typical hirelings include the following:

Archer	Architect
Armorer	Assassin
Baker	Blacksmith
Bladesmith	Foot Soldier
Jeweler	Laborer
Messenger	Minstrel
Sage	Sailor
Spy	Thief

Hirelings are always employed for a stated term of service or for the performance of a specific task. Thus a mercenary contracts to serve for a season. A thief can be hired to steal a named item. A sage works to answer a single question. A blacksmith may indenture himself for a term of years. A sailor works for a single voyage. Quite often these contracts can be renewed without difficulty, but the only thing that binds a hireling to the player character is regular pay and good treatment. Hirelings do not serve a PC out of any great loyalty.

Thus there are some things hirelings will not do. Most hirelings do not foolishly risk their lives. There are soldiers willing to take their chances on the field of battle, but even these courageous (or foolish) few do not willingly undertake the greater hazards of adventuring. They man castle walls, guard caravans, collect taxes, and charge the massed foe well enough, but they often refuse to accompany a PC on an adventure. Even a hireling who regularly undertakes dangerous missions (a thief or an assassin, for example) normally refuses to join player character parties. These hirelings are loners. They contract to do a job and get it done in their own way, without interference from anyone else.

Hirelings are no more loyal than human nature allows. For the most part, if paid and treated well, with opportunities to realize their ambitions, working for a charismatic leader, hirelings can be relied on to do their jobs faithfully. But poor pay, injustice, discrimination, threats, abuse, and humiliation at the hands of their masters make them somewhat less than reliable. A smart leader sees to the comfort and morale of his men before his own concerns. With less savory characters—those hired to perform dark deeds—the player character takes even greater chances, especially given the questionable morals of such characters.

Whatever their personalities, hirelings generally need to make morale checks (explained in the *DMG*) whenever they are faced with a particularly dangerous situation or are offered a bribe or other temptation.

Finding hirelings is not difficult. People need jobs. It is simply a matter of advertising. Under normal circumstances, applicants respond to ads. Only when trying to employ vast numbers or hire those with unusual specialties (such as spies) does the process become complicated. Just what

needs to be done in this situation depends entirely upon the DM's campaign. Your character may have to skulk through the unsavory bars of the waterfront, rely on questionable go-betweens, or pay a visit to the thieves' guild (if there is one). Just employing one of these characters can be a small adventure in itself.

Employment costs of hirelings vary from a few gold pieces a month to thousands of gold pieces for an especially dangerous task. The skill and experience of a hireling has a great effect on his salary. A learned sage researching some obscure piece of lore can charge hefty sums. Costs can also be affected by the conditions of the campaign—the setting, the recent events of the world, and the reputations of the player characters (if any). Most hirelings sign on for what they think is fair. While few will turn down more money, most will drive the best bargain they can. Your DM has more information about employment costs, since he may need to alter these to fit his campaign.

Followers

More reliable than those who are motivated purely by money are those characters who, while they expect pay, were originally drawn into service by the reputation of the player character. These are *followers*, usually a unit of soldiers of one type or another. Followers serve only those of significant power and reputation, thus the construction of a stronghold is necessary to attract followers.

Followers have the same needs and limitations of hirelings. Most must be paid and well-treated. They also do not accompany the player characters on group adventures. They have some advantages over hirelings, however. Followers do not serve for a specific term of contract. They remain with the player character as long as their basic needs are met. They are more loyal than the average hireling and are treated as elite troops. Unlike most hirelings, followers can increase in level (although this occurs very slowly since they act only as soldiers). All followers in a unit advance to the next level at the same time. Finally, the player character need not seek out followers—they come to him, seeking positions within his illustrious household.

Followers appear only once. Replacements do not arrive to fill the ranks of the fallen. (Massive losses of followers in combat only gives the character a bad reputation, discouraging others from flocking to his banner.) Player characters should take care of their followers, perhaps treating them as an elite bodyguard.

Some characters attract unique followers such as animals or magical beings. Although termed followers, these creatures are more properly treated as henchmen in terms of loyalty and what they will and will not do. They do not count against the character's limit on henchmen, however, since they are technically followers.

Henchmen

Henchmen are much that hirelings are not. They are adventurers who serve out of loyalty. They are willing to risk their lives for those they respect. They are also hard to find.

Henchmen are powerful allies to a player character. Unlike hirelings, they have the nerve and ability to become powerful adventurers. Although they expect their share of treasure, they do not usually join a player character for money. They are attracted to the PC because of his reputation or other qualities he possesses. As such, henchmen cannot be expected to flock to the banner of a neophyte adventurer. He may gain himself one or two companions, but others come only when he has earned a greater reputation, met more people, and proven himself a true friend and ally to these NPCs.

Henchmen can come from any source. Most often they are at first mere hirelings or followers who, through distinctive actions, come to the attention of the player character. Some may be higher level, more skilled hirelings who develop a bond to the player character through long employment. Others may be followers who have sound advice for the player character.

A henchman is always of lower level than the PC. Should he ever equal or surpass the PC's level, the henchman leaves forever; it is time for him to try his luck in the real world. In some ways, the player character is the mentor and the henchman his student. When the student has learned as much as the teacher, it is time for him to go out on his own.

Henchmen are more than just loyal followers; they are friends and allies. Naturally they expect to be treated as such. They have little need for those who do not trust them or treat them coldly. Abusiveness or taking advantage of the friendship quickly ends the relationship. Just as players must come with their own friends, player characters must be sensitive to the needs and feelings of their henchmen. Furthermore, henchmen attach themselves to a particular player character, not a group of player characters. Thus it is only under the direst of circumstances that a henchman accepts the orders of another PC. Should his friend (the player character) fall, the henchman sees to his needs. He doesn't abandon him and continue on with the other player characters unless this is clearly the only way to aid his friend.

A PC's Charisma determines the maximum number of henchmen he can have. This is a lifetime limit, not just a maximum possible at any given time. In a world where the fallen can be restored to life, it is expected that a man would make this effort for his dearest friends, both player characters and henchmen. For example, Rupert the half-elf has had seven henchmen, but all have fallen for one reason or another. Rupert's Charisma is 15, so with the death of his latest henchman, no more come to join him. (Word has obviously gotten around that Rupert's friends tend to meet unpleasant ends, and he doesn't even have the decency to bring them back to life! Even if he had tried to raise his henchmen and failed, Rupert would still be viewed as a jinx, bad luck for those around him.)

Attracting a henchman is fairly difficult. One cannot advertise for friends with any great success. They grow and develop from other relationships. A henchman can be found by placing trust in a skilled hireling. Heroic deeds (saving the life of an NPC) can create a strong and instant bond. Love certainly can form this bond. The player and the DM must trust their own judgment to determine when an NPC becomes a henchman. There is no clear line an NPC must cross to make the transition from hireling to henchman. Instead, it is a slide from one status to the other.

Once an NPC becomes a henchman, the player gains a high degree of control over the character. He should be responsible for the record keeping for that character. It is almost, but not quite, like having a new PC for the player. If the DM allows it, the player can have all information regarding the abilities of the henchman, although the DM may choose not to reveal this information. The player is allowed to make nearly all decisions for the NPC, but the DM can overrule any action as being out of character.

There are certain things henchmen do not do. They do not give away or loan out magical items. They do not allow others free access to their spell books. They do not tolerate spell use that questions their loyalty (*detect lie* or *know alignment* cast upon them). They do not accept less than their due share. In general, within these limits, henchman do what is desired of them. The DM can at any time dictate the actions of a henchman, since the character is still an NPC.

If a PC is not attentive to the wishes and needs of his henchmen, or if he abuses and humiliates them, he can expect the worst. This is the stuff mutinies and rebellions are made of. Should an abusive player character fall at the hands of a once-loyal henchman, he has only himself to blame.

On the other hand, not all henchmen are paragons of loyalty. The player character must always be aware that henchmen are sometimes not what they seem. They can be a means to get at the player character. Throughout history, many a cruel and cunning villain has posed as a true companion, waiting his chance to strike or spy on his friend.

Player Character Obligations

Whenever a player character takes on a hireling, follower, or henchman, he has committed himself to certain obligations and customs that surround such agreements. Some of these are obvious, having been worked out between the player character and the NPC in advance. Usually the wage and term of service are settled upon before any agreement is reached. For hirelings and followers, this is a set amount of money each day, week, or month, or a fee for a specific task. Henchmen commonly receive a portion (1/2 a normal share) of all treasure and magic found on adventures. A player character is normally expected to contribute a little more from his own funds, however.

Other obligations of the player character are varied. Some must always be considered, while others almost never come into effect. A player character is expected to provide meals and boarding (unless the NPC has a home nearby). This is the most common obligation and applies to NPCs of all walks of life. For those engaged in more dangerous pursuits, however, additional concessions must be granted. Since horses are expensive, player characters should be ready to cover the cost of mounts lost in combat or on campaign. It is unreasonable to expect a mercenary to buy a new mount from his meager savings. Likewise, other items of war craft—weapons and armor—must be replaced by the player character. All soldiers are expected to provide their own equipment when they are first employed, but the player character must replace all losses. Certainly all player characters are expected to pay the cost of special transport—securing passage on ships and arranging wagons for baggage. Of the grimmer duties, player characters are expected to pay for a decent (though hardly lavish) interment.

One of the more unusual obligations of a player character is to ransom his men. This is especially true of men lost during a campaign. The greater number of soldiers lost in a battle are not slain but captured. Common practice of the medieval period was to officially ransom these prisoners for well-established prices. A common yeoman footman might ransom for 2 gp, a minor priest for 80 gp, a knight's squire for 200 gp, and a king's man for 500 gp. These are paid for by the lord of the prisoner. A player character (as a lord and master) is expected

to do the same. Of course, the player character can pass much of this cost on to his own subjects and the relatives of the prisoner. Thus men might languish for long periods in the hands of the enemy before their ransom was raised. Furthermore, should a player character ransom a hireling, follower, or henchman, he has every reason to expect loyal service from that man in the future. After all, he has demonstrated his willingness to save that NPC from hardship and death.

In a fantasy world, a player character is also expected to bear the cost of magical spells cast to the benefit of his men. He may arrange to have his men blessed before battle or healed after it. He shouldn't grumble about the expense, because the spells also make good tactical sense. The *bless* spell

increases the success of his army in the field. Magical cures get his army back on its feet quicker. All these things can make him very successful while also making him popular with his hired men.

Finally, the player character is expected to make an effort to raise or restore slain henchmen. This is not a normal expectation of hirelings or followers (although it can happen in extreme cases). The effort should be honest and true. A player character shouldn't fool himself into thinking no one will notice if he doesn't do his utmost. The player character who returns from an adventure minus his henchman is automatically under a cloud of suspicion, despite his most vehement protests. A player character must take great care to maintain his reputation as a good and upright employer.

Before a character can do anything in the dungeon or the wilderness, he has to be able to see what he is doing. If a character can't see a target, his chances of hitting it are very small. If he can't see, he can't read a scroll or a large "Keep Out" sign on the wall. In the AD&D® game, characters can see set distances and often by fantastic means that defy logic.

Limits of Vision

The first limitation on vision is how far away an object can be before it cannot been seen clearly. Size and weather have a great effect on this. Mountains can be seen from great distances, 60 to 100 miles or more, yet virtually no detail can be seen. On level ground, the horizon is about five to 12 miles away, but a character usually cannot see a specific object that far away. The limit of vision for seeing and identifying man-sized objects is much less than this.

Under optimum conditions, the maximum range at which a man-sized object can be seen is about 1,500 yards, if it is moving. If the object doesn't move, it usually cannot

Table 62: VISIBILITY RANGES

Condition	Movement	Spotted	Type	ID	Detail
Clear sky	1,500	1,000	500	100	10
Fog, dense or blizzard	10	10	5	5	3
Fog, light or snow	500	200	100	30	10
Fog, moderate	100	50	25	15	10
Mist or light rain	1,000	500	250	30	10
Night, full moon	100	50	30	10	5
Night, no moon	50	20	10	5	3
Twilight	500	300	150	30	10

be seen at this distance. Even if it is moving, all that can be seen is a moving object. The character cannot tell what it is or what it is doing.

At 1,000 yards, both moving and stationary man-sized objects can be spotted. General size and shape can be determined, but exact identifications are impossible. It is not likely that creature type can be identified at this range, unless the creature has a very unique shape.

At 500 yards, general identifications can be made. Size, shape, color, and creature type are all distinguishable. Individuals still cannot be identified, unless they are distinctively dressed or separated from the rest of

the group. Livery and heraldic symbols or banners can seen if large and bold. Most coats of arms cannot be distinguished at this distance. General actions can be ascertained with confidence.

At 100 yards, individuals can be identified (unless, of course, their features are concealed). Coats of arms are clear. Most actions are easily seen, although small events are unclear.

At 10 yards, all details but the smallest are clear. Emotions and actions are easily seen, including such small actions as pickpocketing (if it is detectable).

Of course, conditions are seldom perfect. There are a number of factors that can reduce visibility and alter the ranges at which things can be spotted and identified. Table 62 lists the effects of different types of conditions.

All ranges are given in yards.

"Movement" indicates the maximum distance at which a moving figure can be seen. "Spotted" is the maximum distance a moving or a stationary figure can be seen. "Type" gives the maximum distance at which the general details of a figure can be seen—species or race, weapons, etc. "ID" range enables exact (or reasonably exact) identification. "Detail" range means small actions can be seen clearly.

There are many factors other than weather that affect viewing. Size is an important factor. When looking at a small creature (size S), all categories are reduced to the next lower category (except the "detail" range, which remains unchanged). Thus, under clear conditions, the ranges for seeing a small creature are "movement" at 1,000 yards, "spotted" at 500 yards, "type" at 100 yards, and "ID" and "detail" at 10 yards.

When sighting large creatures, the "movement," "spotting," and "type" ranges are doubled. Exceptionally large creatures can be seen from even greater distances. Large groups of moving creatures can be seen at great distances. Thus it is easy to see a herd of buffalo or an army on the march.

The ranges given in Table 62 do not take terrain into account. All ranges are based on flat, open ground. Hills, mountains, tall grass, and dense woods all drastically reduce the chances of seeing a creature. (The terrain does not alter sighting ranges, only the chances of seeing a creature.) Thus, even

though on a clear day woods may hide a bear until he is 30 yards away, it is still a clear day for visibility. The bear, once seen, can be quickly and easily identified as a bear. The DM has more information on specific terrain effects on sighting.

As a final caveat, the ranges in Table 62 assume Earth-like conditions. Sighting conditions on one of the Lower Planes, or the horizon distance on another world, could be entirely different. If your DM feels he must take this into account, he will have to learn more about the subject at his local library or make it up.

Light

Most characters cannot see much without light. Some night conditions (those for the outdoors) are given in Table 62. But all of these assume some small amount of light. In totally lightless conditions, normal vision is impossible, unless a source of light is carried by the party.

Light sources vary in the area they affect. Table 63 gives the radius of light and burning time for the most common types of light sources.

Table 63: LIGHT SOURCES

Source	Radius	Burning time
Beacon lantern	240 ft.*	30 minutes/pint
Bonfire	50 ft.	1/2 hour/armload
Bullseye lantern	60 ft.*	2 hours/pint
Campfire	35 ft.	1 hour/armload
Candle	5 ft.	10 minutes/inch
Continual light	60 ft.	Indefinite
Hooded lantern	30 ft.	2 hours/pint
Light spell	20 ft.	Variable
Torch	15 ft.	30 minutes
Weapon**	5 ft.	As desired

* Light from these is not cast in a radius, but a rather in a cone-shaped beam. At its far end, the cone of light from a beacon lantern is 90 feet wide. A bullseye lantern has a beam 20 feet wide at its far end.

** Magical weapons shed light if your DM allows this optional rule.

Of course, while a lantern or fire enables characters to see, it does have some disadvantages. The greatest of these is that it is hard to sneak up on someone if he can see you coming. It is hard to remain inconspicuous when you have the only campfire on the plain, or you are carrying the only torch in the dungeon. Furthermore, not only do creatures know you are coming, they can generally see you before you see them (since the light source illuminates the area around you, those outside this area can see into the area). Characters should always bear these risks in mind.

Infravision

Some characters and monsters have the power of *infravision*. This can mean one of two things, depending on whether the standard or the optional rule is used (this is discussed in detail in the *Dungeon Master's Guide*). The choice is left to the DM and he must tell the players how he wants infravision to work. Regardless of how the power functions, the range of infravision is at most 60 feet unless otherwise noted.

Using Mirrors

At times it is useful for characters to look at objects or creatures via reflections in a mirror. This is particularly true of those creatures so hideous (such as a medusa) that gazing directly upon them might turn the viewer to stone. When using a mirror, a light source must be present. Second, attempting to direct your actions by looking in a mirror is very disorienting (try it and see). Thus, all actions requiring an ability or proficiency check or an attack roll suffer a −2 penalty. The character also loses all Dexterity bonuses to Armor Class if fighting an opponent seen only in a mirror.

As in the real world, time passes in all AD&D® game worlds. Weeks slip away as wizards research spells. Days go by as characters ride across country. Hours pass while exploring ruins. Minutes flash by during battles. All of these are passages of time.

There are two different types of time that are talked about in these rules. *Game time* is the imaginary time that passes for the characters in the game. *Real time* is the time in the real world, the time that passes for the players and DM as they play the AD&D game. The two times are very different; players and DMs should be careful to distinguish game time from real time.

For example, when the character Delsenora researches a spell for three weeks, this is three weeks of game time. Delsenora is out of action as three weeks passes in the campaign world. Since nothing interesting at all happens to Delsenora during this research time, it should require only a minute or two of real time to handle the situation. The exchange in real time is something like this:

Louise (Delsenora's player): "Delsenora's going to research her new spell."
DM: "Okay, it'll take three weeks. Nothing happens to her. While she's doing that, the rest of you get a chance to heal your wounds and do some stuff that you've been ignoring. Johann [pointing at another player], you'd better spend some time at the church. The patriarch's been a little upset that you haven't been attending ceremonies."
Jon (Johann's player): "Can't I go out and earn some more experience?"
DM (Not wanting to deal with a split-up group): "The patriarch mumbles something about failing in your duties to your deity, and he rubs his holy symbol a lot. You know, it's not very often that low levels like you have personal audiences with the patriarch. What do you think?"
Jon: "Marvelous. Subtle hint. I'll stay and be a good boy."
DM: "Well, great! The three weeks pass. Nothing happens. Del, make your roll for the spell research."

And so three weeks of game time flash by in brief minutes of real time.

The importance of game time is that as a campaign progresses, characters tend to become involved in different time-consuming projects. Three characters may set off on a four-week overland journey, while a mage researches for six weeks. At the inn, a fighter rests and heals his wounds for two weeks. It is important to note how much time passes on different tasks, so the activities of different characters can be followed.

Campaign time is measured just as it is in real life: years, months, weeks, days, hours, minutes, and seconds. But, since this is a fantasy game, the DM can create entirely different calendars for his world. There may be only ten months in the year or 63 days to a month. When beginning play, these things are not tremendously important, so players need not worry about them right away. With continued adventuring, players eventually become familiar with the calendar of the campaign.

Rounds and *turns* are units of time that are often used in the AD&D game, particularly for spells and combat. A round is approximately equal to a minute (it is not exactly one minute, so as to grant the DM some flexibility during combat). A turn is equal to ten minutes of game time. Turns are normally used to measure specific tasks (such as searching) and certain spells. Thus a spell that lasts ten turns is equal to 100 minutes or 1²/₃ hours.

Movement

Closely related to time is movement. Clearly your character is able to move, otherwise adventures would be rather static and boring. But how fast can he move? If a large, green carrion crawler is scuttling after Rath, is the redoubtable dwarf fast enough to escape? Could Rath outrun an irritated but heavily loaded elf? Sooner or later these considerations become important to player characters.

All characters have movement rates that are based on their race. Table 64 lists the movement rates for unencumbered characters of different races.

Table 64: BASE MOVEMENT RATES

Race	Rate
Human	12
Dwarf	6
Elf	12
Half-elf	12
Gnome	6
Halfling	6

A character can normally walk his movement rate in *tens of yards* in a single round. An unencumbered human can walk 120 yards (360 feet), slightly more than a football field, in one minute. A dwarf, similarly equipped, can walk 60 yards in the same time. This walk is at a fairly brisk, though not strenuous, pace that can be kept up for long periods of time.

However, a character may have to move slower than this pace. If the character is carrying equipment, he may move slower because of the encumbrance (see page 76), if this optional rule is used. As the character carries more gear, he gradually slows down until he reaches the point where he can barely move at all.

When a character is moving through a dungeon or similar setting, his movement rate corresponds to *tens of feet* per round (rather than the tens of yards per round of outside movement). It is assumed that the character is moving more cautiously, paying attention to what he sees and hears while avoiding traps and pitfalls. Again, this rate can be lowered if the optional encumbrance system is used.

Characters can also move faster than the normal walking pace. In the dungeon (or anytime the character is using his dungeon movement rate) the character can automatically increase his movement to that of his normal walking pace. In doing so, however, he suffers a −1 penalty to his chance of being surprised and gives a +1 bonus to others on their chance of being surprised by him (the rapidly moving character is not taking care to conceal the noise of his passage in the echoing confines of the underground). Furthermore the character does not notice traps, secret doors, or other unusual features.

It is also certainly possible for a character to jog or run—an especially useful thing when being chased by creatures tougher than he cares to meet. The simplest method for handling these cases is to roll an initiative die. If the fleeing character wins, he increases the distance between himself and his pursuers by 10 times the difference in the two dice (in feet or yards, whichever the DM feels is most appropriate). This is repeated each turn until the character escapes or is captured. (If this seems unrealistic, remember that fear and adrenaline can do amazing things!)

Jogging and Running (Optional Rule)

If your DM wants greater precision in a chase, the speeds of those involved in the chase can be calculated exactly. (But this is time-consuming and can slow down an exciting chase.) Using this optional rule, a character can always double his normal movement rate (in yards) to a jog. Thus a character with a movement rate of 12 can jog 240 yards in a round. While jogging, a character can automatically keep going for the number of rounds equal to his Constitution. After this limit has been reached, the player must roll a successful Constitution check at the end of each additional round spent jogging. There are no modifiers to this check. Once a Constitution check is failed, the character must stop and rest for as many rounds as he spent jogging. After this, he can resume his jogging pace with no penalties (although the same limitations on duration apply).

If a jogging pace isn't fast enough, a character can also run. If he rolls a successful Strength check, he can move at three times his normal rate; if he rolls a Strength check with a −4 penalty, he can quadruple his normal rate; if he rolls a Strength check with a −8 penalty, he can quintuple his normal rate. Failing a Strength check means only that the char-

acter cannot increase his speed to the level he was trying to reach, but he can keep running at the pace he was at before the failed Strength check. Once a character fails a Strength check to reach a level of running, he cannot try to reach that level again in the same run.

Continued running requires a Constitution check every round, with penalties that depend on how long and how fast the character has been running. There is a −1 penalty for each round of running at triple speed, a −2 penalty for each round of running at quadruple speed, and a −3 penalty for each round of running at quintuple speed (these penalties are cumulative). If the check is passed, the character can continue at that speed for the next round. If the check is failed, the character has exhausted himself and must stop running. The character must rest for at least one turn.

For example, Ragnar the thief has a Strength of 14, a Constitution of 15, and a movement rate of 12. Being pursued by the city guard, he starts jogging at 240 yards a round. Unfortunately, so do they. His Constitution is a 14, so he can keep going for at least 14 rounds. He decides to speed up. The player rolls a Strength check, rolling a 7. Ragnar pours on the speed, increasing up to 360 yards per round (triple speed). Some of the guardsmen drop out of the race, but a few hold in there. Ragnar now has a −1 penalty to his Constitution check. A 13 is rolled, so he just barely passes.

But one of the blasted guardsmen is still on his tail! In desperation, Ragnar tries to go faster (trying for four times walking speed). The Strength check is an 18: Ragnar just doesn't have any more oomph in him; he can't run any faster, but he is still running three times faster than his walking speed. The player now must roll a Constitution check with a −2 penalty (for two rounds of running at triple speed). The player rolls the die and gets a 4—no problem! And just then the last guardsman drops out of the race. Ragnar takes no chances and keeps running. Next round another Constitution check is necessary, with a −3 penalty. The player rolls an 18. Exhausted, Ragnar collapses in a shadowy alley, taking care to get out of sight.

Cross-Country Movement

A normal day's marching lasts for ten hours, including reasonable stops for rest and meals. Under normal conditions, a character can walk twice his movement rate in miles in those ten hours. Thus an unencumbered man can

walk 24 miles across clear terrain.

Characters can also *force march*, intentionally hurrying along, at the risk of exhaustion. Force marching enables a character to travel 2 1/2 times his movement rate in miles (thus a normal man could force march 30 miles in a day). At the end of each day of the march, the character or creature must roll a Constitution check. Large parties (such as army units) make the check at the average Constitution of the group (weaker members are supported, encouraged, and goaded by their peers). Creatures must roll a saving throw vs. death at the end of each day's force marching (since they lack Constitution scores). A −1 penalty is applied to the check for each consecutive day spent force marching. If the check is passed, the force marching pace can be continued the next day. If the check fails, no more force marching attempts can be made until the characters have completely recovered from the ordeal. Recovery requires 1/2 day per day of force marching.

Even if the Constitution check fails, the character can continue overland movement at his normal rate.

One drawback of force marching is that each day of force marching results in a −1 penalty to all attack rolls. This modifier is cumulative. Half a day's rest is required to remove one day's worth of force marching penalty. Characters who have managed to force march for eight straight days suffer a −8 penalty to their attack rolls; it takes four days of rest to return to no attack roll penalty.

Overland movement rates can be increased or decreased by many factors. Terrain can speed or slow movement. Well-tended roads allow faster marching, while trackless mountains slow marches to a snail's pace. Lack of food, water, and sleep weaken characters. Poor weather slows their pace. All these factors are detailed in the *DMG*.

Swimming

All characters are either untrained swimmers or proficient swimmers.

When the DM determines the swimming ability of characters, the decision should be based on his campaign. If the campaign is centered around a large body of water, or if a character grew up near the sea, chances are good that the character knows how to swim. However, being a sailor does not guarantee that a character can swim. Many a medieval mariner or black-hearted pirate never learned how to swim and so developed a morbid fear of the water! This is one of the things that made "walking the plank" such a fearful punishment. Furthermore, some character races are normally suspicious of water and swimming. While these may vary from campaign to campaign,

dwarves and halflings often don't know how to swim.

Untrained swimmers are a fairly hapless lot. When they are unencumbered, they can manage a rough dog-paddle in relatively calm waters. If the waters are rough, the current strong, or the depth excessive (at sea or far out on a lake), untrained swimmers may panic and sink. If weighed down with enough gear to reduce their movement rate, they sink like stones, unable to keep their heads above water. In no way do they make any noticeable progress (unless, of course, the object is to sink beneath the surface).

Proficient swimmers are able to swim, dive, and surface with varying degrees of success. All proficient characters are able to swim $1/2$ their current land movement rate times 10 in yards, provided they are not wearing metal armor. A character with a movement rate of 12 could swim 60 yards (180 feet) in a round. Characters whose movement rates have been reduced to $1/3$ or less of normal (due to gear) or who are wearing metal armor cannot swim—the weight of the gear pulls the character under. They can still walk on the bottom, however, at $1/3$ their current movement rate.

Proficient swimmers can double their swimming speed, if a successful Strength check is rolled (vs. $1/2$ the character's normal Strength score). For a character with a movement rate of 12, a successful check means he can swim 120 yards in one round, an Olympic-class performance.

Like running, swimming is not something that a character can do indefinitely. There are several different speeds a character can choose to swim at, thus moving in either short sprints or a slower, but longer-lasting, pace.

* If swimming at $1/2$ normal speed or treading water, the character can maintain this for a number of hours equal to his Constitution score (although he will have to abandon most of his gear). After a character

swims for a number of hours equal to his Constitution, a Constitution check must be made for each additional hour. For each extra hour of swimming, 1 Constitution point is temporarily lost (regaining lost ability points is explained in the next column).

Each hour spent swimming causes a cumulative penalty of −1 to all attack rolls.

All this assumes calm water. If the seas are choppy, a Constitution check should be made every hour spent swimming, regardless of the character's Constitution. Rough seas can require more frequent checks; heavy seas or storms may require a check every round. The DM may decide that adverse conditions cause a character's Constitution score to drop more rapidly than 1 point per hour.

If a swimming character fails a Constitution check, he must tread water for $1/2$ hour before he can continue swimming (this counts as time spent swimming, for purposes of Constitution point loss).

A character drowns if his Constitution score drops to 0.

As an example, a freak wave sweeps Fiera (an elf) overboard during the night. Fortunately she can swim and knows that land is nearby. Bravely, she sets out through calm water. Her Constitution score is 16. After 14 hours of steady swimming, she makes out an island on the horizon. Two hours later she is closer, but still has some way to go. During the next hour (her 17th in the water), her Constitution drops to 15 (her attack penalty is −17!) and she must make a Constitution check. A 12 is rolled—she passes. In the last hour, the 18th, the seas become rough. Her Constitution is now 13 (the DM ruled that the heavy seas made her lose 2 points of Constitution this hour), and the DM decides she must pass an extra Constitution check to reach shore. She rolls a 5 and flops onto shore, exhausted.

* Characters can also swim long distances at a faster pace, although at increasing risk. Swimming at the character's normal movement rate (instead of the usual swimming speed of $1/2$ the normal movement rate) requires a Constitution check every hour, reduces Strength and Constitution by 1 point every hour, and results in a −2 cumulative attack penalty for each hour of swimming. Characters can swim at twice this speed (quadruple normal swimming speed), but they must roll a check every turn and suffer the above penalties for every turn spent swimming. Again, when an ability score reaches 0, the character sinks and drowns.

* Upon reaching shore, characters can recover lost ability score points and negate attack penalties by resting. Each day of rest recovers 1d6 ability points (if both Strength and Constitution points were lost, roll 1d3 for each ability to determine points recovered) and removes 2d6 points of attack penalties. Rest assumes adequate food and water. Characters need not be fully rested before undertaking any activity, although the adjusted ability scores are treated as the character's current scores until the character has rested enough to fully recover from the swim.

To continue the earlier example with Fiera, after a bad last hour in the water, she reaches shore. Her Constitution is 13 and she has a −18 penalty to her attack roll. Exhausted, she finds some ripe fruit and collapses in the shade of a palm tree. All the next day she rests. At the end of the day she rolls a 4 on 1d6 and regains 4 points of Constitution, restoring it to normal. An 8 is rolled to reduce her attack penalty, so the next day she suffers only a −10 penalty to her attack roll. The next day of rest lowers this by 6 to −4 and the third day erases it completely. So in three days she has fully recovered from her 18-hour ordeal in the water.

Holding Your Breath

Under normal circumstances (with a good gulp of air and not performing strenuous feats), a character can hold his breath up to 1/3 his Constitution score in rounds (rounded up). If the character is exerting himself, this time is halved (again rounded up). Characters reduced to 1/3 or less of their normal movement because of encumbrance are always considered to be exerting themselves. If unable to get a good gulp of air, these times are reduced by 1/2. All characters are able to hold their breath for one round, regardless of circumstances.

While attempting to hold his breath beyond this time, the character must roll a Constitution check each round. The first check has no modifiers, but each subsequent check suffers a −2 cumulative penalty. Once a check is failed, the character must breathe (if he cannot reach the surface, he drowns).

Diving: All characters can dive to a depth of 20 feet in a single round. For each encumbrance category above unencumbered (or for each point of movement below the character's normal rate, if this optional system is used—see page 76), two feet is added to this depth (the additional weight helps pull the character down). A short run or a few feet of height adds 10 feet of depth to the first round of a dive. For every 10 feet of height above the water, an additional five feet of depth is added, up to a maximum addition of 20 feet. Thus, with a run and from a height of 40 feet or more, an unencumbered man can dive 50 feet in a single round.

Surfacing: A character can normally rise at the rate of 20 feet per round. This rate is reduced by two feet for every encumbrance category above unencumbered or for every point of current movement below the character's normal rate (if this optional system is used). Note that, under the optional encumbrance system, heavily loaded characters (those who have lost 10 or more points off their normal movement rate because of their current encumbrance) cannot even swim to the surface. Those simply floating to the surface (unconscious characters, for example) rise at a rate that is five feet per round slower than someone similarly encumbered who is actively swimming up to the surface.

It is quite possible for a moderately weighed-down character to sink if he makes no effort to stay on the surface.

Climbing

Although thieves have specialized climbing abilities, all characters are able to climb to some degree or another. Climbing ability is divided into three categories: thief, mountaineer, and unskilled.

Thieves are the most skilled at climbing. They are the only characters who can climb very smooth, smooth, and rough surfaces without the use of ropes or other equipment. They are the fastest of all climbers and have the least chance of falling.

Mountaineers are characters with mountaineering proficiency or those the DM deems to possess this skill. They have a better climbing percentage than unskilled characters. Mountaineers with proper equipment can climb very smooth, smooth, and rough surfaces. They can assist unskilled characters in all types of climbs.

Unskilled climbers are the vast majority of characters. While they are able to scramble over rocks, they cannot use climbing equipment or negotiate very smooth, smooth, and rough surfaces. They have the lowest climbing success rate of all characters.

Calculating Success

The chance of success of a climb is calculated by taking the character's skill level (given as a percentage) and modifying it for his race, the condition of the surface, and situational modifiers. Table 65 lists the percentages for the different categories of climbers.

The chance of success given in Table 65 is modified by many factors. Some of these remain the same from climb to climb (such as a character's race) and can be figured into the character's base score. Others depend on the conditions of a given climb. All of these are listed on Table 66.

Table 66: CLIMBING MODIFIERS

Situation	Modifier
Abundant handholds (brush, trees, ledges)	+40%
Rope and wall **	+55%
Sloped inward	+25%
Armor	
Banded, splint	−25%
Plate armors (all types)	−50%
Scale, chain	−15%
Studded leather, padded	−5%
Character race *	
Dwarf	−10%
Gnome	−15%
Halfling	−15%
Encumbrance	−5%/†
Surface condition:	
Slightly slippery (wet or crumbling)	−25%
Slippery (icy, slimy)	−40%
Climber wounded below 1/2 hp	−10%

* These are the same as the modifiers given in Table 27. Make sure that thief characters are not penalized twice for race.

** Rope and wall applies in most climbing situations in which the character is able to brace his feet against the surface being climbed and use a rope to assist in the task.

† This is −5% per encumbrance category above unencumbered, or per movement rate point lost off normal movement rate.

The final result of Tables 65 and 66 is the number the character uses for Climbing checks. A Climbing check is made by rolling percentile dice. If the number rolled is equal to or less than the number found from Tables 65 and 66, the character succeeds with the Climbing check. Rolls above this number indicate failure.

A Climbing check must be made any time a character tries to climb a height of 10 feet or more. This check is made before the character ascends the first 10 feet of the climb. If the check is passed, the character can continue climbing. If the check is failed, the character is unable to find a route and cannot even attempt the climb. No further attempts can be made by that character until a change occurs. This is either a significant change in location (a half mile or more along the face of a cliff) or an improvement in the character's chance of success.

For example, Brondvrouw the gnome is an unskilled climber. Her normal chance of success is 25% (40% − 15% for being a gnome). She has been cut off from the rest of the party by a rugged cliff, 50 feet high. Fortunately, the cliff is dry and the rock seems solid. She makes an attempt, but a 49 is rolled on the percentile dice. She cannot climb the cliff. Then one of her friends up above remembers to lower a rope. With the rope, Brondvrouw can again try the climb, since her percentage chance is now 80%. A 27 is rolled and she makes the ascent.

Table 65: BASE CLIMBING SUCCESS RATES

Category	Success Rate
Thief with mountaineering proficiency *	Climb walls % + 10%
Thief	Climb walls %
Mountaineering proficiency *	40% + 10% per proficiency slot
Mountaineer (decided by DM)	50%
Unskilled climber	40%

* Only if optional proficiency system is used.

On particularly long climbs—those greater than 100 feet or requiring more than one turn (10 minutes) of climbing time—the DM may require additional checks. The frequency of these checks is for the DM to decide. Characters who fail a check could fall a very long way, so it is wise to carry ropes and tools.

Climbing Rates

Climbing is different from walking or any other type of movement a character can do. The rate at which a character moves varies greatly with the different types of walls and surfaces that must be climbed. Refer to Table 67. Cross-reference the type of surface to be climbed with the surface condition. Multiply the appropriate number from the table by the character's current movement rate. The result is the rate of climb for the character, in feet per round, in any direction (up, down, or sideways).

All the movement rates given on Table 67 are for non-thief characters. Thief characters are able to climb at double the movement rate for normal characters.

Ragnar the thief and his companion Rupert (a half-elf) are climbing a cliff with rough ledges. A recent rain has left the surface slightly slippery. Ragnar has a movement rate of 12 and Rupert's is 8. Ragnar can cover 12 feet per round (12 × 1 since he is a thief), but Rupert struggles along at the pace of 4 feet per round (8 × 1/2). If Ragnar had gone up first and lowered a rope to Rupert, the half-elf could have climbed at the rate of 8 feet per round using rope and wall (8 × 1).

Table 67: RATES OF CLIMBING

| | Surface Condition | | |
Type of Surface	Dry	Slightly Slippery	Slippery
Very smooth *	1/4	— **	— **
Smooth, cracked *	1/2	1/3	1/4
Rough *	1	1/3	1/4
Rough w/ledges	1	1/2	1/3
Ice wall	—	—	1/4
Tree	4	3	2
Sloping wall	3	2	1
Rope and wall	2	1	1/2

* Non-thief characters must be mountaineers and have appropriate tools (pitons, rope, etc.) to climb these surfaces.

** Thief characters can climb very smooth, slightly slippery surfaces at 1/4. Even thieves cannot climb very smooth, slippery surfaces.

Types of Surfaces

Very smooth surfaces include expanses of smooth, uncracked rock, flush-fitted wooden walls, and welded or bolted metal walls. Completely smooth walls, unbroken by any feature, cannot be climbed by anyone without tools.

Smooth and cracked walls include most types of well-built masonry, cavern walls, maintained castle walls, and slightly eroded cliff faces.

Rough faces are most natural cliffs, poorly maintained or badly built masonry, and typical wooden walls or stockades. Any natural stone surface is a rough face.

Rough with ledges is similar to rough faces but is dotted with grips three inches or more wide. Frost-eroded cliffs and natural chimneys are in this category, as are masonry buildings falling into ruin.

Ice walls are cliffs or faces made entirely of frozen ice. These are different from very smooth and smooth surfaces in that there are still many natural cracks and protrusions. They are extremely dangerous to climb, so a Climbing check should be made every round for any character attempting it without tools.

Trees includes climbs with an open framework, such as a scaffold, as well as trees.

Sloping walls means not quite cliff-like but too steep to walk up. If a character falls while climbing a sloping wall, he suffers damage only if he fails a saving throw vs. petrification. If the save is made, the character slides a short distance but is not harmed.

Rope and wall require that the character uses a rope and is able to brace himself against a solid surface.

Actions While Climbing

Although it is possible to perform other actions while climbing, such as spellcasting or fighting, it is not easy. Spellcasters can use spells only if they are in a steady, braced position, perhaps with the aid of other characters.

Climbing characters lose all Armor Class bonuses for Dexterity and shield and most often have rear attack modifiers applied against them also. Their own attack, damage, and saving throw rolls suffer −2 penalties. Those attacking from above gain a +2 bonus to their attack rolls, while those attacking from below suffer an additional −2 penalty to their attack rolls. A climbing

character cannot use a two-handed weapon while climbing. The DM can overrule these penalties if he feels the player character has reached a place of secure footing. If struck while climbing (for any amount of damage), the character must make an immediate Climbing check. Failure for a roped character means he spends a round regaining his balance; an unroped character falls if he fails this check.

Climbing Tools

Tools are an integral part of any mountaineer's equipment and all climbs can profit from the use of tools. Mountaineering tools include rope, pitons (spikes), and ice axes. However, it is a mistaken belief that the main function of tools is to aid in a climb. The main purpose of pitons, rope, and the like is to prevent a disastrous fall. Climbers must rely on their own skills and abilities, not ropes and spikes, when making a climb. Accidents happen when people forget this basic rule and trust their weight to their ropes and pitons.

Therefore, aside from ropes, other tools do not increase the chance of climbing success. However, in the case of a fall, climbing tools can reduce the distance fallen. When a character falls, he can fall only as far as the rope allows, if being belayed, or as far as twice the distance to the last piton set (if the piton holds—a piton pulls free 15% of the time when a sudden stress occurs). The distance fallen depends on how far apart the pitons have been set. Falling characters fall twice the distance to the last spike that holds.

For example, Rath is 15 feet above his last piton. Suddenly he slips. He falls the 15 feet to his piton, plus another 15 feet past his piton since there's 15 feet of rope between him and the piton, for a total of 30 feet fallen and 3d6 points of falling damage.

Roping characters together increases individual safety, but it also increases the chance that more than one person falls. When a character falls, the character(s) on either side of the falling climber must roll Climbing checks (a penalty of −10 is applied for each falling character after the first one to fall). If all checks are successful, the fall is stopped and no one suffers any damage. If a check is failed, that character also falls and Climbing checks must be repeated as before. Climbing checks are made until either the fall is stopped (the climbers on either side of the falling character[s] successfully roll Climbing checks or the last nonfalling climber succeeds with his check), or all the roped-together characters fall.

For example, a party of five is roped together as they go up the cliff. Suddenly Johann falls. Megarran, immediately above him, and Drelb, following him, must roll Climbing checks. Megarran passes her check. But Drelb fails and is snapped off the wall. Now Megarran must make another check with a −10 penalty (for two falling characters), and Targash, who's bringing up the rear, must also roll a check with a −10 penalty. Both succeed on their rolls and the fall is stopped.

Getting Down

Aside from jumping or flying, the quickest way to get down from a height is to rappel. This requires a rope attached at the top of the climb and a skilled mountaineer to set up the rappel and to hold the rope at the bottom. When rappeling down a surface, a Climbing check with a +50 bonus must be rolled. Free rappels (the end of the rope unsupported at the bottom) can also be done, but the modifier is only +30. Of course, a failed check results in a slip sometime during the rappel (the DM decides on the damage suffered). A character can rappel at a speed equal to his normal dungeon movement (120 feet/round for an unencumbered human). One other thing to bear in mind is that there must be a landing point at the end of the rope. Rappelling 60 feet down a 100-foot cliff means the character is either stranded at the end of the rope or, worse still, rappels right off the end and covers the last 40 feet much faster than he did the first 60!

Wizard Spells

1st Level	2nd Level	3rd Level	4th Level
1 Affect Normal Fires	Alter Self	Blink	Charm Monster
2 Alarm	Bind	Clairaudience	Confusion
3 Armor	Blindness	Clairvoyance	Contagion
4 Audible Glamer	Blur	Delude	Detect Scrying
5 Burning Hands	*Continual Light*	Dispel Magic	Dig
6 Cantrip	Darkness, 15' Radius	Explosive Runes	Dimension Door
7 Change Self	Deafness	Feign Death	Emotion
8 Charm Person	Deeppockets	Fireball	Enchanted Weapon
9 Chill Touch	*Detect Evil*	Flame Arrow	Enervation
10 Color Spray	Detect Invisibility	Fly	Evard's Black Tentacles
11 *Comprehend Languages*	ESP	Gust of Wind	Extension I
12 Dancing Lights	Flaming Sphere	Haste	Fear
13 Detect Magic	Fog Cloud	Hold Person	Fire Charm
14 Detect Undead	Fools' Gold	Hold Undead	Fire Shield
15 *Enlarge*	Forget	Illusionary Script	Fire Trap
16 Erase	Glitterdust	Infravision	Fumble
17 Feather Fall	Hypnotic Pattern	Invisibility, 10' Radius	Hallucinatory Terrain
18 Find Familiar	Improved Phantasmal Force	Item	Ice Storm
19 Friends	Invisibility	Leomund's Tiny Hut	Illusionary Wall
20 Gaze Reflection	Irritation	Lightning Bolt	Improved Invisibility
21 Grease	*Knock*	Melf's Minute Meteors	Leomund's Secure Shelter
22 Hold Portal	*Know Alignment*	Monster Summoning I	Magic Mirror
23 Hypnotism	Leomund's Trap	Non-Detection	Massmorph
24 Identify	Levitate	Phantom Steed	Minor Creation
25 Jump	*Locate Object*	*Protection From Evil, 10' Radius*	Minor Globe of Invulnerability
26 Light	Magic Mouth	Protection From Normal Missiles	Monster Summoning II
27 Magic Missile	Melf's Acid Arrow	Secret Page	Otiluke's Resilient Sphere
28 Mending	Mirror Image	Sepia Snake Sigil	Phantasmal Killer
29 Message	Misdirection	Slow	Plant Growth
30 Mount	Protection From Cantrips	Spectral Force	Polymorph Other
31 Nystul's Magical Aura	Pyrotechnics	Suggestion	Polymorph Self
32 Phantasmal Force	Ray of Enfeeblement	*Tongues*	Rainbow Pattern
33 *Protection From Evil*	Rope Trick	Vampiric Touch	Rary's Mnemonic Enhancer
34 Read Magic	Scare	*Water Breathing*	*Remove Curse*
35 Shield	Shatter	Wind Wall	Shadow Monsters
36 Shocking Grasp	Spectral Hand	Wraithform	Shout
37 Sleep	Stinking Cloud		Solid Fog
38 Spider Climb	Strength		Stoneskin
39 Spook	Summon Swarm		Vacancy
40 Taunt	Tasha's Uncontrollable Hideous		Wall of Fire
41 Tenser's Floating Disc	Laughter		Wall of Ice
42 Unseen Servant	Web		Wizard Eye
43 Ventriloquism	Whispering Wind		
44 Wall of Fog	Wizard Lock		
45 Wizard Mark			

* *Italicized* spells are reversible.

5th Level

Advanced Illusion
Airy Water
Animal Growth
Animate Dead
Avoidance
Bigby's Interposing Hand
Chaos
Cloudkill
Cone of Cold
Conjure Elemental
Contact Other Plane
Demi-Shadow Monsters
Dismissal
Distance Distortion
Domination
Dream
Extension II
Fabricate
False Vision
Feeblemind
Hold Monster
Leomund's Lamentable
   Belaborment
Leomund's Secret Chest
Magic Jar
Major Creation
Monster Summoning III
Mordenkainen's Faithful
   Hound
Passwall
Seeming
Sending
Shadow Door
Shadow Magic
Stone Shape
Summon Shadow
Telekinesis
Teleport
Transmute Rock to Mud
Wall of Force
Wall of Iron
Wall of Stone

6th Level

Anti-Magic Shell
Bigby's Forceful Hand
Chain Lightning
Conjure Animals
Contingency
Control Weather
Death Fog
Death Spell
Demi-Shadow Magic
Disintegrate
Enchant an Item
Ensnarement
Extension III
Eyebite
Geas
Glassee
Globe of Invulnerability
Guards and Wards
Invisible Stalker
Legend Lore
Lower Water
Mass Suggestion
Mirage Arcana
Mislead
Monster Summoning IV
Mordenkainen's Lucubration
Move Earth
Otiluke's Freezing Sphere
Part Water
Permanent Illusion
Programmed Illusion
Project Image
Reincarnation
Repulsion
Shades
Stone to Flesh
Tenser's Transformation
Transmute Water to Dust
True Seeing
Veil

7th Level

Banishment
Bigby's Grasping Hand
Charm Plants
Control Undead
Delayed Blast Fireball
Drawmij's Instant Summons
Duo-Dimension
Finger of Death
Forcecage
Limited Wish
Mass Invisibility
Monster Summoning V
Mordenkainen's Magnificent
   Mansion
Mordenkainen's Sword
Phase Door
Power Word, Stun
Prismatic Spray
Reverse Gravity
Sequester
Shadow Walk
Simulacrum
Spell Turning
Statue
Teleport Without Error
Vanish
Vision

8th Level

Antipathy-Sympathy
Bigby's Clenched Fist
Binding
Clone
Demand
Glassteel
Incendiary Cloud
Mass Charm
Maze
Mind Blank
Monster Summoning VI
Otiluke's Telekinetic Sphere
Otto's Irresistible Dance
Permanency
Polymorph Any Object
Power Word, Blind
Prismatic Wall
Screen
Serten's Spell Immunity
Sink
Symbol
Trap the Soul

9th Level

Astral Spell
Bigby's Crushing Hand
Crystalbrittle
Energy Drain
Foresight
Gate
Imprisonment
Meteor Swarm
Monster Summoning VII
Mordenkainen's Disjunction
Power Word, Kill
Prismatic Sphere
Shape Change
Succor
Temporal Stasis
Time Stop
Weird
Wish

* *Italicized* spells are reversible.

Priest Spells

1st Level	2nd Level	3rd Level	4th Level
1 Animal Friendship	Aid	Animate Dead	Abjure
2 *Bless*	Augury	Call Lightning	Animal Summoning I
3 Combine	Barkskin	*Continual Light*	Call Woodland Beings
4 Command	Chant	Create Food & Water	*Cloak of Bravery*
5 *Create Water*	Charm Person or Mammal	*Cure Blindness or Deafness*	Control Temperature, 10' Radius
6 *Cure Light Wounds*	*Detect Charm*	*Cure Disease*	*Cure Serious Wounds*
7 *Detect Evil*	Dust Devil	Dispel Magic	*Detect Lie*
8 Detect Magic	Enthrall	Feign Death	Divination
9 Detect Poison	Find Traps	Flame Walk	Free Action
10 Detect Snares & Pits	Fire Trap	Glyph of Warding	*Giant Insect*
11 Endure Heat/Endure Cold	Flame Blade	Hold Animal	*Hallucinatory Forest*
12 Entangle	*Goodberry*	*Locate Object*	Hold Plant
13 Faerie Fire	*Heat Metal*	Magical Vestment	Imbue With Spell Ability
14 Invisibility to Animals	Hold Person	Meld Into Stone	*Lower Water*
15 Invisibility to Undead	*Know Alignment*	Negative Plane Protection	*Neutralize Poison*
16 *Light*	Messenger	Plant Growth	Plant Door
17 Locate Animals or Plants	Obscurement	Prayer	*Produce Fire*
18 Magical Stone	Produce Flame	Protection From Fire	*Protection From Evil, 10' Radius*
19 Pass Without Trace	Resist Fire/Resist Cold	Pyrotechnics	Protection From Lightning
20 *Protection From Evil*	Silence, 15' Radius	*Remove Curse*	Reflecting Pool
21 *Purify Food & Drink*	Slow Poison	Remove Paralysis	Repel Insects
22 *Remove Fear*	Snake Charm	Snare	Speak With Plants
23 Sanctuary	Speak With Animals	Speak With Dead	Spell Immunity
24 Shillelagh	Spiritual Hammer	Spike Growth	*Sticks to Snakes*
25	Trip	Starshine	*Tongues*
26	*Warp Wood*	Stone Shape	
27	Withdraw	Summon Insects	
28	Wyvern Watch	Tree	
29		*Water Breathing*	
30		Water Walk	

5th Level	6th Level	7th Level
1 Air Walk	Aerial Servant	Animate Rock
2 *Animal Growth*	Animal Summoning III	Astral Spell
3 Animal Summoning II	Animate Object	Changestaff
4 Anti-Plant Shell	Anti-Animal Shell	Chariot of Sustarre
5 Atonement	Blade Barrier	Confusion
6 Commune	Conjure Animals	*Conjure Earth Elemental*
7 Commune With Nature	*Conjure Fire Elemental*	Control Weather
8 Control Winds	*Find the Path*	Creeping Doom
9 *Cure Critical Wounds*	Fire Seeds	Earthquake
10 *Dispel Evil*	Forbiddance	Exaction
11 Flame Strike	*Heal*	*Fire Storm*
12 Insect Plague	Heroes' Feast	Gate
13 Magic Font	Liveoak	*Holy Word*
14 Moonbeam	Part Water	*Regenerate*
15 Pass Plant	Speak With Monsters	Reincarnate
16 Plane Shift	Stone Tell	*Restoration*
17 Quest	*Transmute Water to Dust*	*Resurrection*
18 Rainbow	Transport Via Plants	*Succor*
19 *Raise Dead*	Turn Wood	Sunray
20 Spike Stones	Wall of Thorns	Symbol
21 *Transmute Rock to Mud*	Weather Summoning	Transmute Metal to Wood
22 *True Seeing*	Word of Recall	Wind Walk
23 Wall of Fire		

* *Italicized* spells are reversible.

Spell Descriptions

The spells are organized according to their group (Priest or Wizard) and level, starting on page 131. Within each level, the spells are arranged alphabetically. At the start of each spell description are the following important game statistics:

Name: Each spell is identified by name. In parentheses after the name is the school (for wizard spells) to which that spell belongs. When more than one is listed, that spell is common to all schools given.

Some spells are reversible (they can be cast for an effect opposite to that of the standard spell). This is noted after the spell name. Priests with reversible spells must memorize the desired version. For example, a priest who desires a *cause light wounds* spell must petition for this form of the spell when meditating and praying. Note that severe penalties can result if the spell choice is at variance with the priest's alignment (possible penalties include denial of specific spells, entire spell levels, or even all spells for a certain period. The exact result (if any) depends on the reaction of the priest's patron deity, as determined by the DM.

Reversible wizard spells operate similarly. When the spell is learned, both forms are recorded in the wizard's spell books. However, the wizard must decide which version of the spell he desires to cast when memorizing the spell, unless the spell description specifically states otherwise. For example, a wizard who has memorized *stone to flesh* and desires to cast *flesh to stone* must wait until the latter form of the spell can be memorized (i.e., rest eight hours and study). If he can memorize two 6th-level spells, he could memorize each version once or one version twice.

School: In parentheses after the spell name is the name of the school of magic to which the spell belongs. For wizard spells, this defines which spells a wizard specialist can learn, depending on the wizard's school of specialization. For priest spells, the school notation is used only for reference purposes, to indicate which school the spell is considered to belong to, in case the DM needs to know for spell resistance (e.g., elves' resistance to charm spells).

Sphere: This entry appears only for priest spells and identifies the sphere or spheres into which each spell falls.

Range: This lists the distance from the caster at which the spell effect occurs or begins. A "0" indicates the spell can be used on the caster only, with the effect embodied within or emanating from him. "Touch" means the caster can use the spell on others if he can physically touch them. Unless otherwise specified, all other spells are centered on a point visible to the caster and within the range of the spell. The point can be a

creature or object if desired. In general, a spell that affects a limited number of creatures within an area affects those closest to the center first, unless there are other parameters operating (such as level or Hit Dice). Spells can be cast through narrow openings only if both the caster's vision and the spell energy can be directed simultaneously through the opening. A wizard standing behind an arrow slit can cast through it; sending a fireball through a small peephole he is peering through is another matter.

Components: This lists the category of components needed, V for verbal, S for somatic, and M for material. When material components are required, these are listed in the spell description. Spell components are expended as the spell is cast, unless otherwise noted. Clerical holy symbols are not lost when a spell is cast. For cases in which material components are expended at the end of the spell (*free action, shapechange,* etc.), premature destruction of the components ends the spell.

Duration: This lists how long the magical energy of the spell lasts. Spells of instantaneous duration come and go the moment they are cast, although the results of these spells may be permanent and unchangeable by normal means. Spells of permanent duration last until the effects are negated by some means, usually by a *dispel magic.* Some spells have a variable duration. The caster cannot choose the duration of spells, in most cases. Spells with set durations (e.g., 3 rounds/level of the wizard) must be kept track of by the player. Spells of variable duration (e.g., 3 + 1d4 rounds) are secretly recorded by the DM. Your DM may warn you when spell durations are approaching expiration, but there is usually no sign that a spell is going to expire; check with your DM to determine exactly how he handles this issue.

Certain spells can be ended at will by the caster. In order to dismiss these spells, the original caster must be within range of the spell's center of effect—within the same range at which the spell can be cast. The caster also must be able to speak words of dismissal. Note that only the original caster can dismiss his spells in this way.

Casting Time: This entry is important, if the optional casting time modifier to initiative is used. If only a number is given, the casting time is added to the caster's initiative die rolls. If the spell requires a round or number of rounds to cast, it goes into effect at the end of the last round of casting time. If Delsenora casts a spell that takes one round, it goes into effect at the end of the round in which she begins casting. If the spell requires three rounds to cast, it goes into effect at the end of the third round. Spells requiring a turn or more go into effect at the end of the stated turn.

Area of Effect: This lists the creatures,

volume, dimensions, weight, etc., that can be affected by the spell. Spells with an area or volume that can be shaped by the caster will, unless the spell description specifically states otherwise, have a minimum dimension of 10 feet in any direction. Thus a cloud that has a 10-foot cube per caster level might, when cast by a 12th-level caster, have dimensions 10' × 10' × 120', 20' × 20' × 30', or any similar combination that totals 12 10-foot cubes. Combinations such as 5' × 10' × 240' are not possible unless specifically stated.

Some spells (such as *bless*) affect the friends or enemies of the caster. In all cases, this refers to the perception of the caster at the time the spell is cast. For example, a chaotic good character allied with a lawful neutral cleric would receive the benefits of the latter's *bless* spell.

Saving Throw: This lists whether the spell allows the target a saving throw and explains the effect of a successful save: "Neg." results in the spell having no effect; "¹/₂" means the character suffers half the normal amount of damage; "none" means no saving throw is allowed. Wisdom adjustments to saving throws apply only to enchantment/charm spells.

Solid physical barriers provide saving throw bonuses and damage reduction. Cover and concealment may affect saving throws and damage (the DM has additional information about this).

A creature that successfully saves against a spell with no apparent physical effect (such as a *charm, hold,* or *magic jar*) may feel a definite force or tingle that is characteristic of a magical attack, if the DM desires. But the exact hostile spell effect or creature ability used cannot be deduced from this tingle.

A being's carried equipment and possessions are assumed to make their saving throws against special attacks if the creature makes its saving throw, unless the spell specifically states otherwise. If the creature fails its saving throw, or if the attack form is particularly potent, saving throws may have to be rolled to see if any possessions survive, using either item saving throws (see the *DMG*) or the being's saving throw. The DM will inform you when this happens.

Any character can voluntarily forgo a saving throw. This allows a spell or similar attack that normally grants a saving throw to have full effect on the character. Likewise, any creature can voluntarily lower its magic resistance allowing a spell to automatically function when cast on it. Foregoing a saving throw or magic resistance roll need not always be voluntary. If a creature or character can be tricked into lowering its resistance, the spell will have full effect, even if it is not the spell the victim believed he was going to receive. The victim must consciously choose to lower his resistance;

it is not sufficient that he is caught off guard. For example, a character would receive a saving throw if a mage in the party suddenly attacked him with a fireball, even if the mage had been friendly to that point. However, the same character would not receive a saving throw if the mage convinced him that he was about to receive a *levitation* spell but cast a fireball instead. Your DM will decide when NPCs have lowered their resistances. You must tell your DM when your character is lowering his resistance.

Spell Description: The text provides a complete description of how the spell functions and its game effects. It covers most typical uses of the spell, if there are more than one, but cannot deal with every possible application players might find. In these cases, the spell information in the text should provide guidance on how to adjudicate the situation.

Spells with multiple functions enable the caster to select which function he wants to use at the time of casting. Usually a single function of a multiple-function spell is weaker than a single-function spell of the same level.

Spell effects that give bonuses or penalties to abilities, attack rolls, damage rolls, saving throws, etc., are not usually cumulative with each other or with other magic: the strongest single effect applies. For example, a fighter drinks a *potion of giant strength* and then receives the 2nd-level wizard spell *strength*. Only the strongest magic (the potion) is effective. When the potion's duration ends, however, the *strength* spell is still in effect, until its duration also expires.

Adjudicating Illusions

All illusions are cases of DM adjudication; each depends upon the exact situational factors deemed significant by the DM. All of the following points are only subsidiary guidelines to help the DM maintain consistency.

Intrinsically Deadly Illusions: "Instant kill" illusions that are automatically fatal regardless of level, Hit Dice, or saving throws: collapsing ceilings, inescapable lava pits, etc. The absolute maximum effect of these is to force a system shock check. Surviving characters are not further affected by that illusion.

Spell Effects: Illusions that duplicate spell effects are keyed to the caster's level (e.g., a 10th-level illusionist casting a fireball can create a convincing 10-die fireball). Exceeding this limit creates a fatal flaw in the illusion that negates its effect.

Monster Special Attacks: Before the caster can effectively duplicate a monster's special attack, the wizard must have undergone it (a wizard cannot conjure up the twinkle in a medusa's eye correctly without actually experiencing it—i.e., having been

turned to stone by one).

Option: Illusionary monsters attack using the wizard's attack values. This would be a subtle clue that the monsters are fake.

Option: Extend the spell level control to monsters—the caster can create monsters only if the total monster Hit Dice are equal to or less than the caster's level (an 8th-level caster could convincingly do one hill giant, two ogres, or four 2nd-level fighters).

Illusion spells require a higher degree of DM-player interaction than other wizard spells. The timing and staging of such spells by the caster are extremely important. Effects that appear out of nowhere are not believed unless the caster takes this into account. On the other hand, an illusionary fireball cast after a wizard has cast a real one could have devastating effects.

The caster must maintain a show of realism at all times when conducting an illusion (if a squad of low-level fighters is created, the caster dictates their hits, misses, damage inflicted, apparent wounds, and so forth; the DM decides whether the bounds of believability have been exceeded).

NPC illusions require careful preparation by the DM, including clues to their nature.

Intelligence is the best defense against illusions. Low and non-intelligent creatures are more vulnerable to illusions, unless the illusion is completely outside their experience or the illusion touches on an area of the creatures' particular competence. Undead are generally immune to illusions, but they are vulnerable to quasi-real effects, most of which start to appear in the 4th-level spell list.

Illusions usually cease to affect a character if they are actively disbelieved. Disbelief must be stated by the player, based on clues provided by the DM. Players stating disbelief must give a reason for disbelief based on sensory information available to the character. Failure to give such a reason results in failure to disbelieve. The DM can impose additional requirements or delays in recognizing illusions (such as Intelligence checks) as needed, such as when one player is obviously parroting a discovery made by another. Disbelief automatically forfeits a saving throw if the effect is real.

For NPCs, a saving throw, Intelligence check, or DM adjudication can be used to determine disbelief, whichever the DM deems appropriate.

First-Level Spells

Affect Normal Fires (Alteration)

Range: 5 yards/level
Components: V, S
Duration: 2 rounds/level
Casting Time: 1
Area of Effect: 10-foot radius
Saving Throw: None

This spell enables the wizard to cause nonmagical fires—from as small as a torch or lantern to as large as the area of effect—to reduce in size and brightness to become mere coals or increase in light to become as bright as full daylight and increase the illumination to double the normal radius. Note that this does not affect either fuel consumption or damage caused by the fire. The caster can affect any or all fires in the spell's area. He can alter their intensities with a single gesture as long as the spell is in effect. The spell lasts until the caster cancels it, all fuel is burned, or the duration expires. The caster can also extinguish all flames in the area, which expends the spell immediately. The spell does not affect fire elementals or similar creatures.

Alarm (Abjuration, Evocation)

Range: 10 yards
Components: V, S, M
Duration: 4 hours + 1/2 hour/level
Casting Time: 1 round
Area of Effect: Up to a 20-foot cube
Saving Throw: None

When an *alarm* spell is cast, the wizard causes a selected area to react to the presence of any creature larger than a normal rat—anything larger than about one-half cubic foot in volume or more than about three pounds in weight. The area of effect can be a portal, a section of floor, stairs, etc. As soon as any creature enters the warded area, touches it, or otherwise contacts it without speaking a password established by the caster, the *alarm* spell lets out a loud ringing that can be heard clearly within a 60-foot radius. (Reduce the radius by 10 feet for each interposing door and by 20 feet for each substantial interposing wall.) The sound lasts for one round and then ceases. Ethereal or astrally projected creatures do not trigger an alarm, but flying or levitating creatures, invisible creatures, or incorporeal or gaseous creatures do. The caster can dismiss the alarm with a single word.

The material components of this spell are a tiny bell and a piece of very fine silver wire.

Armor (Conjuration)

Range: Touch
Components: V, S, M
Duration: Special
Casting Time: 1 round
Area of Effect: 1 creature
Saving Throw: None

By means of this spell, the wizard creates a magical field of force that serves as if it were scale mail armor (AC 6). The spell has no effect on a person already armored or a creature with Armor Class 6 or better. It is not cumulative with the *shield* spell, but it is cumulative with Dexterity and, in the case of fighter/mages, with the shield bonus. The *armor* spell does not hinder movement, adds no weight or encumbrance, nor does it prevent spellcasting. It lasts until successfully dispelled or until the wearer sustains cumulative damage totaling greater than 8 points +1 per level of the caster. (It is important to note that the armor does *not* absorb this damage. The armor merely grants an AC of 6; the wearer still suffers full damage from any successful attacks.) Thus, the wearer might suffer 8 points from an attack, then several minutes later sustain an additional 1 point of damage. Unless the spell were cast by a wizard of 2nd level or higher, it would be dispelled at this time. Until it is dispelled, the *armor* spell grants the wearer full benefits of the Armor Class gained.

The material component is a piece of finely cured leather that has been blessed by a priest.

Audible Glamer (Illusion/Phantasm)

Range: 60 yards + 10 yards/level
Components: V, S, M
Duration: 3 rounds/level
Casting Time: 1
Area of Effect: Hearing range
Saving Throw: Special

When the *audible glamer* spell is cast, the wizard causes a volume of sound to arise, at whatever distance he desires (within range), and seem to recede, approach, or remain at a fixed place as desired. The volume of sound created, however, is directly related to the level of the spellcaster. The volume is based upon the lowest level at which the spell can be cast, 1st level. The noise of the *audible glamer* at this level is that of four men, maximum. Each additional experience level of the wizard adds a like volume, so that at 2nd level the wizard can have the spell cause sound equal to that of eight men. Thus, talking, singing, shouting, walking, marching, or running sounds can be created. The auditory illusion created by an *audible glamer* spell can be virtually any type of sound, but the relative volume must be commensurate with the level of the wizard casting the spell. A horde of rats running and squeaking is about the same volume as eight men running and shouting. A roaring lion is equal to the noise volume of 16 men, while a roaring dragon is equal to the noise volume of no fewer than 24 men.

A character stating that he does not believe the sound receives a saving throw, and if it succeeds, the character then hears a faint and obviously false sound, emanating from the caster's direction. Note that this spell can enhance the effectiveness of the *phantasmal force* spell.

The material component of the spell is a bit of wool or a small lump of wax.

Burning Hands (Alteration)

Range: 0
Components: V, S
Duration: Instantaneous
Casting Time: 1
Area of Effect: The caster
Saving Throw: 1/2

When the wizard casts this spell, a jet of searing flame shoots from his fingertips. His hands must be held so as to send forth a fan-like sheet of flames: the wizard's thumbs must touch each other and fingers must be spread. The burning hands send out flame jets of five-foot length in a horizontal arc of about 120 degrees in front of the wizard. Any creature in the area of the flames suffers 1d3 hit points of damage, plus 2 points for each level of experience of the spellcaster, to a maximum of 1d3 + 20 points of fire damage. Those successfully saving vs. spell receive half damage. Flammable materials touched by the fire burn (e.g., cloth, paper, parchment, thin wood, etc.). Such materials can be extinguished in the next round if no other action is taken.

Cantrip (All Schools)

Range: 10 feet
Components: V, S
Duration: 1 hour/level
Casting Time: 1
Area of Effect: Special
Saving Throw: None

Cantrips are minor spells studied by wizards during their apprenticeship, regardless of school. The *cantrip* spell is a practice method for the apprentice, teaching him how to tap minute amounts of magical energy. Once cast, the *cantrip* spell enables the caster to create minor magical effects for the duration of the spell. So minor are these effects that they have severe limitations. They are completely unable to cause a loss of hit points, cannot affect the concentration of spellcasters, and can only create small, obviously magical materials. Furthermore, materials created by a cantrip are extremely fragile and cannot be used as tools of any sort. Lastly, a cantrip lacks the power to duplicate any other spell effects.

Whatever manifestation the cantrip takes, it remains in effect only as long as the wizard concentrates. Wizards typically use cantrips to impress common folk, amuse children, and brighten dreary lives. Common tricks with cantrips include tinklings of ethereal music, brightening faded flowers, glowing balls that float over the caster's hand, puffs of wind to flicker candles, spicing up aromas and flavors of bland food, and little whirlwinds to sweep dust under rugs. Combined with the *unseen servant* spell, these are the tools to make housekeeping and entertaining simpler for the wizard.

Change Self (Illusion/Phantasm)

Range: 0
Components: V, S
Duration: 2d6 rounds + 2 rounds/level
Casting Time: 1
Area of Effect: The caster
Saving Throw: None

This spell enables the wizard to alter the appearance of his form—including clothing and equipment—to appear one foot shorter or taller; thin, fat, or in between; human, humanoid, or any other generally manshaped bipedal creature. The caster cannot duplicate a specific individual. The spell does not provide the abilities or mannerisms of the chosen form. The duration of the spell is 2d6 rounds plus two additional rounds per level of experience of the spellcaster. The DM may allow a saving throw for disbelief under certain circumstances: for example, if the caster acts in a manner obviously inconsistent with his chosen role. The spell does not alter the perceived tactile (i.e., touch) properties of the caster or his equipment, and the ruse can be discovered in this way.

Charm Person (Enchantment/Charm)

Range: 120 yards
Components: V, S
Duration: Special
Casting Time: 1
Area of Effect: 1 person
Saving Throw: Neg.

This spell affects any single person it is cast upon. The term *person* includes any bipedal human, demihuman, or humanoid of man-size or smaller, such as brownies, dryads, dwarves, elves, gnolls, gnomes, goblins, half-elves, halflings, half-orcs, hobgoblins, humans, kobolds, lizard men, nixies, orcs, pixies, sprites, troglodytes, and others. Thus, a 10th-level fighter could be charmed, but an ogre could not.

The person receives a saving throw vs. spell to avoid the effect, with any adjustment due to Wisdom (see Table 5). If the person receives damage from the caster's group in the same round the *charm* is cast, an additional bonus of +1 per hit point of damage received is added to the victim's saving throw.

If the spell recipient fails his saving throw, he regards the caster as a trusted friend and ally to be heeded and protected. The spell does not enable the caster to control the charmed creature as if it were an automaton, but any word or action of the caster is viewed in the most favorable way. Thus, a charmed person would not obey a suicide command, but he might believe the caster if assured that the only chance to save the caster's life is for the person to hold back an onrushing red dragon for "just a round or two." Note also that the spell does not endow the caster with linguistic capabilities beyond those he normally possesses (i.e., he must speak the victim's language to communicate his commands).

The duration of the spell is a function of the charmed person's Intelligence and is tied to the saving throw. The spell may be broken if a successful saving throw is rolled, and this saving throw is checked on a periodic basis, according to the creature's Intelligence (see the following table). If the caster harms, or attempts to harm, the charmed person by some overt action, or if a *dispel magic* spell is successfully cast upon the charmed person, the *charm* spell is broken.

If two or more *charm* effects simultaneously affect a creature, the result is decided by the DM. This could range from one effect being clearly dominant, to the subject being torn by conflicting desires, to new saving throws that could negate both spells.

Note that the subject has full memory of the events that took place while he was charmed.

Intelligence Score	Time Between Checks
3 or less	3 months
4 to 6	2 months
7 to 9	1 month
10 to 12	3 weeks
13 to 14	2 weeks
15 to 16	1 week
17	3 days
18	2 days
19 or more	1 day

Note: The period between checks is the time period during which the check occurs. When to roll the check during this time is determined (randomly or by selection) by the DM. The roll is made secretly.

Chill Touch (Necromancy)

Range: 0
Components: V, S
Duration: 3 rounds + 1 round/level
Casting Time: 1
Area of Effect: The caster
Saving Throw: Neg.

When the caster completes this spell, a blue glow encompasses his hand. This energy attacks the life force of any living creature upon which the wizard makes a successful melee attack. The touched creature must roll a successful saving throw vs. spell or suffer 1d4 points of damage and lose 1 point of Strength. If the save is successful, the creature remains unharmed. Creatures not rated for Strength suffer a −1 penalty to their attack rolls for every other successful touch. Lost Strength returns at the rate of 1 point per hour. Damage must be cured magically or healed naturally.

This spell has a special effect on undead creatures. Undead touched by the caster suffer no damage or Strength loss, but they must successfully save vs. spell or flee for 1d4 rounds + 1 round per level of the caster.

Color Spray (Alteration)

Range: 0
Components: V, S, M
Duration: Instantaneous
Casting Time: 1
Area of Effect: 5' x 20' x 20' wedge
Saving Throw: Special

Upon casting this spell, the wizard causes a vivid, fan-shaped spray of clashing colors to spring forth from his hand. From one to six creatures (1d6) within the area are affected in order of increasing distance from the wizard. All creatures above the level of the spellcaster and all those of 6th level or 6 Hit Dice or more are entitled to a saving throw vs. spell. Blind or unseeing creatures are not affected by the spell.

Creatures not allowed or failing saving throws, and whose Hit Dice or levels are less than or equal to the spellcaster's level, are struck unconscious for 2d4 rounds; those with Hit Dice or levels 1 or 2 greater than the wizard's level are blinded for 1d4 rounds; those with Hit Dice or levels 3 or more greater than that of the spellcaster are stunned (reeling and unable to think or act coherently) for one round.

The material components of this spell are a pinch each of powder or sand that is colored red, yellow, and blue.

Comprehend Languages (Alteration)
Reversible

Range: Touch
Components: V, S, M
Duration: 5 rounds/level
Casting Time: 1 round
Area of Effect: 1 speaking creature or
          written object
Saving Throw: None

When this spell is cast, the wizard is able to understand the spoken words of a creature or read an otherwise incomprehensible written message (such as writing in another language). In either case, the wizard must touch the creature or the writing. Note that the ability to read does not necessarily impart understanding of the material, nor does the spell enable the caster to speak or write an unknown language. Written material can be read at the rate of one page or equivalent per round. Magical writing cannot be read, other than to know it is magical, but the spell is often useful when deciphering treasure maps. This spell can be foiled by certain warding magics (the 3rd-level *secret page* and *illusionary script* spells) and it does not reveal messages concealed in otherwise normal text.

The material components of this spell are a pinch of soot and a few grains of salt.

The reverse of this spell, *confuse languages*, cancels a *comprehend languages* spell or renders a writing or a creature's speech incomprehensible, for the same duration as above.

Dancing Lights (Alteration)

Range: 40 yards + 10 yards/level
Components: V, S, M
Duration: 2 rounds/level
Casting Time: 1
Area of Effect: Special
Saving Throw: None

When a *dancing lights* spell is cast, the wizard creates, at his option, from one to four lights that resemble either torches or lanterns (and cast that amount of light), glowing spheres of light (such as evidenced by will-o-wisps), or one faintly glowing, vaguely man-like shape, somewhat similar to that of a creature from the elemental plane of Fire. The dancing lights move as the spellcaster desires, forward or back, straight or turning corners, without concentration upon such movement by the wizard. The spell cannot be used to cause blindness (see 1st-level *light* spell), and it winks out if the range or duration is exceeded.

The material component of this spell is either a bit of phosphorus or wychwood, or a glowworm.

Detect Magic (Divination)

Range: 0
Components: V, S
Duration: 2 rounds/level
Casting Time: 1
Area of Effect: 10' path, 60' long
Saving Throw: None

When the *detect magic* spell is cast, the wizard detects magical radiations in a path 10 feet wide and up to 60 feet long, in the direction he is facing. The intensity of the magic can be determined (dim, faint, moderate, strong, overwhelming), and the wizard has a 10% chance per level to recognize if a certain type of magic (alteration, conjuration, etc.) is present. The caster can turn, scanning a 60-degree arc per round. A stone wall of one foot or more thickness, solid metal of one inch thickness, or a yard or more of solid wood blocks the spell. Magical areas, multiple types of magic, or strong local magical emanations may confuse or conceal weaker radiations. Note that this spell does not reveal the presence of good or evil, or reveal alignment. Other-planar creatures are not necessarily magical.

Detect Undead
(Divination, Necromancy)

Range: 0
Components: V, S, M
Duration: 3 turns
Casting Time: 1 round
Area of Effect: 60' + 10'/level
Saving Throw: None

This spell enables the caster to detect all undead creatures out to the range of the spell. The area of effect extends in a path 10 feet wide and 60 feet long (plus 10 feet longer per level of the wizard), in the direction the caster is facing. Scanning a direction requires one round, and the caster must be motionless. While the spell indicates direction, it does not give specific location or distance. It detects undead through walls and obstacles but is blocked by one foot of solid stone, one yard of wood or loose earth, or a thin coating of metal. The spell does not indicate the type of undead detected, only that undead are present.

The material component for this spell is a bit of earth from a grave.

Enlarge (Alteration)
Reversible

Range: 5 yards/level
Components: V, S, M
Duration: 5 rounds/level
Casting Time: 1
Area of Effect: 1 creature or object
Saving Throw: Neg.

This spell causes instant growth of a creature or object, increasing both size and weight. It can be cast only upon a single creature (or a symbiotic or community entity) or upon a single object that does not exceed ten cubic feet in volume per caster level. The object or creature must be seen to be affected. It grows by up to 10% per level of experience of the wizard, increasing this amount in height, width, and weight.

All equipment worn or carried by a creature is enlarged by the spell. Unwilling victims are entitled to a saving throw vs. spell. A successful saving throw means the spell fails. If insufficient room is available for the desired growth, the creature or object attains the maximum possible size, bursting weak enclosures in the process, but it is constrained without harm by stronger materials—the spell cannot be used to crush a creature by growth.

Magical properties are not increased by this spell—a huge *sword +1* is still only +1, a staff-sized wand is still only capable of its normal functions, a giant-sized potion merely requires a greater fluid intake to make its magical effects operate, etc. Weight, mass, and strength are affected, though. Thus, a table blocking a door would be heavier and more effective, a hurled stone would have more mass (and cause more damage), chains would be more massive, doors thicker, a thin line turned to a sizeable, longer rope, and so on. A creature's hit points, Armor Class, and attack rolls do not change, but damage rolls increase proportionately with size. For example, a fighter at 160% normal size hits with his long sword and rolls a 6 for damage. The adjusted damage roll is 10 (that is, 6 x 1.6 = 9.6, rounded up). Bonuses due to Strength, class, and magic are not altered.

The reverse spell, *reduce*, negates the *enlarge* spell or makes creatures or objects smaller. The creature or object loses 10% of its original size for every level of the caster, to a minimum of 10% of the original size. Thereafter, the size shrinks by one-foot increments to less than one foot, by one-inch increments to one inch, and by 1/10-inch increments to a minimum of 1/10 of an inch—the recipient cannot dwindle away to nothingness. For example, a 16-foot-tall giant reduced by a 15th-level wizard (15 steps) would be reduced to 1.6 feet (in nine steps), then to 6/10 of a foot or 7.2 inches (in one step), and finally to 2.2 inches (in the last five steps). A shrinking object may damage weaker materials affixed to it, but an object will shrink only as long as the object itself is not damaged. Unwilling creatures are allowed a saving throw vs. spell.

The material component of this spell is a pinch of powdered iron.

Erase (Alteration)

Range: 30 yards
Components: V, S
Duration: Permanent
Casting Time: 1
Area of Effect: 1 scroll or 2 pages
Saving Throw: Special

The *erase* spell removes writings of either magical or mundane nature from a scroll or from one to two pages of paper, parchment, or similar surfaces. It removes *explosive runes*, *glyphs of warding*, *sepia snake sigils*, and *wizard marks*, but it does not remove *illusory script* or *symbols* (see these spells). Nonmagical writings are automatically erased if the caster is touching them, otherwise the chance for success is 90%. Magical writings must be touched, and are only 30% likely to be erased, plus 5% per caster level, to a maximum of 90% (e.g., 35% for a 1st-level caster, 40% for a 2nd-level caster, etc.).

Feather Fall (Alteration)

Range: 10 yards/level
Components: V
Duration: 1 round/level
Casting Time: 1
Area of Effect: Special
Saving Throw: None

When this spell is cast, the creature(s) or object(s) affected immediately assumes the mass of a piece of down. Rate of falling is instantly changed to a mere two feet per second (120 feet per round), and no damage is incurred upon landing while the spell is in effect. However, when the spell duration ceases, normal rate of fall occurs. The spell can be cast upon the wizard or some other creature or object up to the maximum range and lasts for one round for each level of the wizard. The *feather fall* affects one or more objects or creatures in a 10-foot cube, as long as the maximum weight of the creatures or objects does not exceed a combined total of 200 pounds plus 200 pounds per level of the spellcaster.

For example, a 2nd-level wizard has a range of 20 yards, a duration of two rounds, and a weight limit of 600 pounds when casting this spell. The spell works only upon free-falling, flying, or propelled objects (such as missiles). It does not affect a sword blow or a charging creature. Note that the spell can be effectively combined with *gust of wind* and similar spells.

Find Familiar (Conjuration/Summoning)

Range: 1 mile/level
Components: V, S, M
Duration: Special
Casting Time: 2d12 hours
Area of Effect: 1 familiar
Saving Throw: Special

This spell enables the caster to attempt to summon a familiar to act as his aide and companion. Familiars are typically small creatures, such as cats, frogs, ferrets, crows, hawks, snakes, owls, ravens, toads, weasels, or even mice. A creature acting as a familiar can benefit a wizard, conveying its sensory powers to its master, conversing with him, and serving as a guard/scout/spy as well. A wizard can have only one familiar at a time, however, and he has no control over what sort of creature answers the summoning, if any at all come.

The creature is always more intelligent than others of its type (typically 2 or 3 Int points), and its bond with the wizard confers upon it an exceptionally long life. The wizard receives the heightened senses of his familiar, which grants the wizard a +1 bonus to all surprise die rolls. Normal familiars have 2-4 hit points plus 1 hit point per caster level, and an Armor Class of 7 (due to size, speed, etc.).

The wizard has an empathic link with the familiar and can issue it mental commands at a distance of up to one mile. Note that empathic responses from the familiar are generally fairly basic—while able to communicate simple thoughts, these are often overwhelmed by instinctual responses. Thus a ferret familiar spying on a band of orcs in the woods might lose its train of thought upon sighting a mouse. Certainly its communications to its master would be tinged with fear of the "big ones" it was spying on! The caster cannot see through the familiar's eyes.

If separated from the caster, the familiar loses 1 hit point each day, and dies if reduced to 0 hit points. When the familiar is in physical contact with its wizard, it gains the wizard's saving throws against special attacks. If a special attack would normally cause damage, the familiar suffers no damage if the saving throw is successful and half damage if the saving throw is failed. If the familiar dies, the wizard must successfully roll an immediate system shock check or die. Even if he survives this check, the wizard loses 1 point from his Constitution when the familiar dies.

The power of the conjuration is such that it can be attempted but once per year. When the wizard decides to find a familiar, he must load a brass brazier with charcoal. When this is burning well, he adds 1,000 gp worth of incense and herbs. The spell incantation is then begun and must be continued

until the familiar comes or the casting time is finished. The DM secretly determines all results. Note that most familiars are not inherently magical, nor does a *dispel magic* spell send them away.

Deliberate mistreatment, failure to feed and care for the familiar, or continuous unreasonable demands have adverse effects on the familiar's relationship with its master. Purposely arranging the death of one's own familiar incurs great disfavor from certain powerful entities, with dire results.

D20 Roll	Familiar *	Sensory Powers
1-5	Cat, black	Excellent night vision & superior hearing
6-7	Crow	Excellent vision
8-9	Hawk	Very superior distance vision
10-11	Owl	Night vision equals human daylight vision, superior hearing
12-13	Toad	Wide-angle vision
14-15	Weasel	Superior hearing & very superior olfactory power
16-20	No familiar available within spell range	

* The referee can substitute other small animals suitable to the area.

Friends (Enchantment/Charm)

Range: 0
Components: V, S, M
Duration: 1d4 rounds + 1 round/level
Casting Time: 1
Area of Effect: 60-foot radius
Saving Throw: Special

A *friends* spell causes the wizard to temporarily gain 2d4 points of Charisma. Intelligent creatures within the area of effect at the time the spell is cast must make immediate reaction checks based on the character's new Charisma. Those with favorable reactions tend to be very impressed with the spellcaster and make an effort to be his friends and help him, as appropriate to the situation. Officious bureaucrats might decide to become helpful; surly gate guards might wax informative; attacking orcs might spare the caster's life, taking him captive instead. When the spell wears off, the creatures realize that they have been influenced, and their reactions are determined by the DM.

The components for this spell are chalk (or white flour), lampblack (or soot), and vermilion applied to the face before casting the spell.

Gaze Reflection (Alteration)

Range: 0
Components: V, S
Duration: 2 rounds + 1 round/level
Casting Time: 1
Area of Effect: Special
Saving Throw: None

The *gaze reflection* spell creates a shimmering, mirror-like area of air before the wizard that moves with the caster. Any gaze attack, such as that of a basilisk, *eyes of charming*, a vampire's gaze, the 6th-level *eyebite* spell, and so on, is reflected back upon the gazer if the gazer tries to make eye contact with the spellcaster (the spellcaster suffers no effects from the gaze attack). Such creatures receive a saving throw vs. their own gaze effect. The spell does not affect vision or lighting and is not effective against creatures whose effect comes from being gazed upon (such as a medusa). Only active gaze attacks are blocked by this spell.

Grease (Conjuration)

Range: 10 yards
Components: V, S, M
Duration: 3 rounds + 1 round/level
Casting Time: 1
Area of Effect: 10' × 10' square area
Saving Throw: Special

A *grease* spell covers a material surface with a slippery layer of a fatty, greasy nature. Any creature entering the area or caught in it when the spell is cast must save vs. spell or slip, skid, and fall. Those who successfully save can reach the nearest non-*greased* surface by the end of the round. Those who remain in the area are allowed a saving throw each round until they escape the area. The DM should adjust saving throws by circumstance; for example, a creature charging down an incline that is suddenly *greased* has little chance to avoid the effect, but its ability to exit the affected area is almost assured! The spell can also be used to create a greasy coating on an item—a rope, ladder rungs, weapon handle, etc. Material objects not in use are always affected by this spell, while creatures wielding or employing items receive a saving throw vs. spell to avoid the effect. If the initial saving throw is failed, the creature immediately drops the item. A saving throw must be made each round the creature attempts to use the *greased* item. The caster can end the effect with a single utterance; otherwise it lasts for three rounds plus one round per level.

The material component of the spell is a bit of pork rind or butter.

Hold Portal (Alteration)

Range: 20 yards/level
Component: V
Duration: 1 round/level
Casting Time: 1
Area of Effect: 20 square feet/level
Saving Throw: None

This spell magically bars a door, gate, or valve of wood, metal, or stone. The magical closure holds the portal fast, just as if it were securely closed and locked. Any extraplanar creature (djinn, elemental, etc.) with 4 or more Hit Dice can shatter the spell and burst open the portal. A wizard of 4 or more experience levels higher than the spellcaster can open the held portal at will. A *knock* spell or a successful *dispel magic* spell can negate the *hold portal*. Held portals can be broken or physically battered down.

Hypnotism (Enchantment/Charm)

Range: 5 yards
Components: V, S
Duration: 1 round + 1 round/level
Casting Time: 1
Area of Effect: 30-foot cube
Saving Throw: Neg.

The gestures of the wizard, along with his droning incantation, cause 1d6 creatures within the area to become susceptible to a suggestion—a brief and reasonable-sounding request (see the 3rd-level wizard *suggestion* spell). The request must be given after the *hypnotism* spell is cast. Until that time the success of the spell is unknown. Note that the subsequent suggestion is not a spell, but simply a vocalized urging (the caster must speak a language the creature understands for this spell to work). Creatures that successfully roll their saving throws are not under hypnotic influence. Those who are exceptionally wary or hostile save with +1 to +3 bonuses. If the spell is cast at an individual creature that meets the caster's gaze, the saving throw is made with a penalty of −2. A creature that fails its saving throw does not remember that the caster enspelled it.

Identify (Divination)

Range: 0
Components: V, S, M
Duration: 1 round/level
Casting Time: Special
Area of Effect: 1 item/level
Saving Throw: None

When an *identify* spell is cast, magical items subsequently touched by the wizard can be identified. The eight hours immediately preceding the casting of the spell must be spent purifying the items and removing influences that would corrupt and blur their magical auras. If this period is interrupted, it must be begun again. When the spell is cast, each item must be handled in turn by the wizard. Any consequences of this handling fall fully upon the wizard and may end the spell, although the wizard is allowed any applicable saving throw.

The chance of learning a piece of information about an item is equal to 10% per level of the caster, to a maximum of 90%, rolled by the DM. Any roll of 96-00 indicates a false reading (91-95 reveals nothing). Only one function of a multi-function item is discovered per handling (i.e., a 5th-level wizard could attempt to determine the nature of five different items, five different functions of a single item, or any combination of the two). If any attempt at reading fails, the caster cannot learn any more about that item until he advances a level. Note that some items, such as special magical tomes, cannot be identified with this spell.

The item never reveals its exact attack or damage bonuses, although the fact that it has few or many bonuses can be determined. If it has charges, only a general indication of the number of charges remaining is learned: powerful (81%-100% of the total possible charges), strong (61%-80%), moderate (41%-60%), weak (6%-40%), or faint (five charges or less). The faint result takes precedence, so a fully charged *ring of three wishes* always appears to be only faintly charged.

After casting the spell and determining what can be learned from it, the wizard loses 8 points of Constitution. He must rest for one hour to recover each point of Constitution. If the 8-point loss drops the spellcaster below a Constitution of 1, he falls unconscious. Consciousness is not regained until full Constitution is restored, which takes 24 hours (one point per three hours for an unconscious character).

The material components of this spell are a pearl (of at least 100 gp value) and an owl feather steeped in wine, with the infusion drunk prior to spellcasting. If a *luckstone* is powdered and added to the infusion, the divination becomes much more potent: exact bonuses or charges can be determined, and the functions of a multi-functional item can be learned from a single reading. At the DM's option, certain properties of an artifact or relic might also be learned.

Jump (Alteration)

Range: Touch
Components: V, S, M
Duration: 1d3 rounds + 1 round/level
Casting Time: 1
Area of Effect: Creature touched
Saving Throw: None

The individual touched when this spell is cast is empowered to leap once per round for the duration of the spell. Leaps can be up to 30 feet forward or straight upward or 10 feet backward. Horizontal leaps forward or backward have only a slight arc—about two feet per 10 feet of distance traveled. The *jump* spell does not ensure safety in landing or grasping at the end of the leap.

The material component of this spell is a grasshopper's hind leg, to be broken by the caster when the spell is cast.

Light (Alteration)

Range: 60 yards
Components: V, M
Duration: 1 turn/level
Casting Time: 1
Area of Effect: 20-foot-radius globe
Saving Throw: Special

This spell creates a luminous glow, equal to torchlight, within a fixed radius of the spell's center. Objects in darkness beyond this sphere can be seen, at best, as vague and shadowy shapes. The spell is centered on a point selected by the caster, and he must have a line of sight and unobstructed path for the spell when it is cast. *Light* can spring from air, rock, metal, wood, or almost any similar substance.

The effect is immobile unless it is specifically centered on a moveable object or mobile creature. If this spell is cast upon a creature, the applicable magic resistance and saving throw rolls must be made. Successful resistance negates the spell, while a successful saving throw indicates that the spell is centered immediately behind the creature, rather than upon the creature itself. *Light* taken into an area of magical darkness does not function, but if cast directly against magical darkness negates it (but only for the duration of the *light* spell, if the darkness effect is continual).

Light centered on the visual organs of a creature blinds it, reducing its attack rolls and saving throws by 4 and worsening its Armor Class by 4. The caster can end the spell at any time by uttering a single word.

The material component is a firefly or a piece of phosphorescent moss.

Magic Missile (Evocation)

Range: 60 yards + 10 yards/level
Components: V, S
Duration: Instantaneous
Casting Time: 1
Area of Effect: 1 or more creatures
in a 10-foot cube
Saving Throw: None

Use of the *magic missile* spell creates up to five missiles of magical energy that dart forth from the wizard's fingertip and unerringly strike their target. This includes enemy creatures in a melee. The target creature must be seen or otherwise detected to be hit, however, so near-total concealment, such as

that offered by arrow slits, can render the spell ineffective. Likewise, the caster must be able to identify the target. He cannot direct a magic missile to "Strike the commander of the legion," unless he can single out the commander from the rest of the soldiers. Specific parts of a creature cannot be singled out. Inanimate objects (locks, etc.) cannot be damaged by the spell, and any attempt to do so wastes the missiles to no effect. Against creatures, each missile inflicts 1d4 + 1 points of damage.

For every two extra levels of experience, the wizard gains an additional missile—he has two at 3rd level, three at 5th level, four at 7th level, etc., up to a total of five missiles at 9th level. If the wizard has multiple missile capability, he can have them strike a single target creature or several creatures, as desired.

Mending (Alteration)

Range: 30 yards
Components: V, S, M
Duration: Permanent
Casting Time: 1
Area of Effect: 1 object
Saving Throw: None

This spell repairs small breaks or tears in objects. It will weld a broken ring, chain link, medallion, or slender dagger, providing but one break exists. Ceramic or wooden objects with multiple breaks can be invisibly rejoined to be as strong as new. A hole in a leather sack or wineskin is completely healed over by a *mending* spell. This spell does not, by itself, repair magical items of any type. One turn after the spell is cast, the magic of the joining fades, and the effect cannot be magically dispelled. The maximum volume of material the caster can mend is one cubic foot per level.

The material components of this spell are two small magnets of any type (lodestone in all likelihood) or two burrs.

Message (Alteration)

Range: 0
Components: V, S, M
Duration: 5 rounds/level
Casting Time: 1
Area of Effect: Special
Saving Throw: None

When this spell is cast, the wizard can whisper messages and receive replies with little chance of being overheard. When the spell is cast, the wizard secretly or openly points his finger at each creature to be included in the spell effect. Up to one creature per level can be included. When the wizard whispers, the whispered message travels in a straight line and is audible to all of the involved creatures within 30 feet, plus 10 feet per level of the caster. The creatures

who receive the message can whisper a reply that is heard by the spellcaster. Note that there must be an unobstructed path between the spellcaster and the recipients of the spell. The message must be in a language the caster speaks; this spell does not by itself confer understanding upon the recipients. This spell is most often used to conduct quick and private conferences when the caster does not wish to be overheard.

The material component of the spell is a short piece of copper drawn fine.

Mount (Conjuration/Summoning)

Range: 10 yards
Components: V, S, M
Duration: 2 hours + 1 hour/level
Casting Time: 1 turn
Area of Effect: 1 mount
Saving Throw: None

By means of this spell, the caster conjures a normal animal to serve him as a mount. The animal serves willingly and well, but at the expiration of the spell duration it disappears, returning to its own place. The type of mount gained by this spell depends on the level of the caster; of course, a caster can choose a lesser mount if desired. Available mounts include the following:

Caster Level	Mount
1st-3rd level	Mule or light horse
4th-7th level	Draft horse or war horse
8th-12th level	Camel
13th-14th level	Elephant (and howdah at 18th level)
15th level & up	Griffon (and saddle at 18th level)

The mount does not come with any riding gear, unless it is of a class lower than the caster would normally be entitled to; thus a 4th-level wizard can gain a war horse without saddle and harness, or a light horse with saddle and harness. The statistics of the animal gained are typical of all creatures of the same class. The mount disappears when slain.

The material component of the spell is a bit of hair from the type of animal to be conjured.

Nystul's Magical Aura
(Illusion/Phantasm)

Range: Touch
Components: V, S, M
Duration: 1 day/level
Casting Time: 1 round
Area of Effect: Special
Saving Throw: Special

By means of this spell, any one item of no more than five pounds weight per level of the spellcaster can be given an aura that is noticed by someone using magic detection. Furthermore, the caster can specify the type of magical aura that is detected (alteration, conjuration, etc.) and this effectively masks the item's actual aura, if any, unless the item's own aura is exceptionally powerful (if it is an artifact, for instance). If the object bearing *Nystul's magical aura* has an *identify* spell cast on it or is similarly examined, the examiner has a 50% chance of recognizing that the aura has been placed to mislead the unwary. Otherwise, the aura is believed and no amount of testing reveals what the true magic is.

The component for this spell is a small square of silk, which must be passed over the object that receives the aura.

Phantasmal Force (Illusion/Phantasm)

Range: 60 yards + 10 yards/level
Components: V, S, M
Duration: Special
Casting Time: 1
Area of Effect: 400 sq. ft. + 100 sq. ft./level
Saving Throw: Special

This spell creates the illusion of any object, creature, or force, as long as it is within the boundaries of the spell's area of effect. The illusion is visual and affects all believing creatures (undead are immune) that view it. It does not create sound, smell, or temperature. Effects that depend on these senses usually fail. The illusion lasts until struck by an opponent—unless the spellcaster causes the illusion to react appropriately—or until the wizard ceases concentration upon the spell (due to desire, moving, or a successful attack that causes damage). Saving throws for illusions are explained under Illusion in the Magic chapter (page 80) and on page 130. Creatures that disbelieve the illusion see it for what it is and add +4 to associates' saving throws if this knowledge can be communicated effectively. Creatures believing the illusion are subject to its effects, again as explained under Illusions.

The illusionary effect can be moved by the caster within the limits of the area of effect. The DM has to rule on the effectiveness of this spell; detailed guidelines are outlined on page 130 and in Chapter 7: Magic.

The material component of the spell is a bit of fleece.

Protection From Evil (Abjuration)
Reversible

Range: Touch
Components: V, S, M
Duration: 2 rounds/level
Casting Time: 1
Area of Effect: Creature touched
Saving Throw: None

When this spell is cast, it creates a magical barrier around the recipient at a distance of one foot. The barrier moves with the recipient and has three major effects:

First, all attacks made by evil (or evilly enchanted) creatures against the protected creature suffer −2 penalties to attack rolls; any saving throws caused by such attacks are made with +2 bonuses.

Second, any attempt to possess (as by a *magic jar* attack) or to exercise mental control over (as by a vampire's *charm* ability) the protected creature is blocked by this spell. Note that the protection does not prevent a vampire's *charm* itself, but it does prevent the exercise of mental control through the barrier. Likewise, a possessing life force is merely kept out. It would not be expelled if in place before the protection is cast.

Third, the spell prevents bodily contact by creatures of an extraplanar or conjured nature (such as aerial servants, elementals, imps, invisible stalkers, salamanders, water weirds, xorn, and others). This causes the natural (body) weapon attacks of such creatures to fail and the creatures to recoil, if such attacks require touching the protected being. Animals or monsters summoned or conjured by spells or similar magic are likewise hedged from the character.

This protection ends if the protected character makes a melee attack against or tries to force the barrier against the blocked creature.

To complete this spell, the wizard must trace a three-foot-diameter circle on the floor (or ground) with powdered silver.

This spell can be reversed to become *protection from good*; the second and third benefits remaining unchanged. The material component for the reverse is a circle of powdered iron.

Read Magic (Divination)

Range: 0
Components: V, S, M
Duration: 2 rounds/level
Casting Time: 1 round
Area of Effect: Special
Saving Throw: None

By means of a *read magic* spell, the wizard is able to read magical inscriptions on objects—books, scrolls, weapons, and the like—that would otherwise be totally unintelligible. (The personal books of the wiz-

ard, and works already magically read, are intelligible.) This deciphering does not normally invoke the magic contained in the writing, although it may do so in the case of a cursed scroll. Furthermore, once the spell is cast and the wizard has read the magical inscription, he is thereafter able to read that particular writing without recourse to the use of the *read magic* spell. The duration of the spell is two rounds per level of experience of the spellcaster; the wizard can read one page or its equivalent per round.

The wizard must have a clear crystal or mineral prism, which is not expended, to cast the spell.

Shield (Evocation)

Range: 0
Components: V, S
Duration: 5 rounds/level
Casting Time: 1
Area of Effect: Special
Saving Throw: None

When this spell is cast, an invisible barrier comes into being in front of the wizard. This shield totally negates magic missile attacks. It provides the equivalent protection of AC 2 against hand-hurled missiles (axes, darts, javelins, spears, etc.), AC 3 against small device-propelled missiles (arrows, bolts, bullets, manticore spikes, sling stones, etc.), and AC 4 against all other forms of attack. The shield also adds a +1 bonus to the wizard's saving throws against attacks that are basically frontal. Note that these benefits apply only if the attacks originate from in front of the wizard, where the shield can move to interpose itself.

Shocking Grasp (Alteration)

Range: Touch
Components: V, S
Duration: Special
Casting Time: 1
Area of Effect: Creature touched
Saving Throw: None

When the wizard casts this spell, he develops a powerful electrical charge that gives a jolt to the creature touched. The spell remains in effect for one round per level of the caster or until it is discharged by the caster touching another creature. The shocking grasp delivers 1d8 points of damage, plus 1 point per level of the wizard (e.g., a 2nd-level wizard would discharge a shock causing 1d8 + 2 points of damage). While the wizard must come close enough to his opponent to lay a hand on the opponent's body or upon an electrical conductor that touches the opponent's body, a like touch from the opponent does not discharge the spell.

Sleep (Enchantment/Charm)

Range: 30 yards
Components: V, S, M
Duration: 5 rounds/level
Casting Time: 1
Area of Effect: Special
Saving Throw: None

When a wizard casts a *sleep* spell, he causes a comatose slumber to come upon one or more creatures (other than undead and certain other creatures specifically excluded from the spell's effects). All creatures to be affected by the *sleep* spell must be within 30 feet of each other. The number of creatures that can be affected is a function of Hit Dice or levels. The spell affects 2d4 Hit Dice of monsters. Monsters with 4 + 3 Hit Dice (4 Hit Dice plus 3 hit points) or more are unaffected. The center of the area of effect is determined by the spellcaster. The creatures with the least Hit Dice are affected first, and partial effects are ignored.

For example, a wizard casts *sleep* at three kobolds, two gnolls, and an ogre. The roll (2d4) result is 4. All the kobolds and one gnoll are affected ($\frac{1}{2} + \frac{1}{2} + \frac{1}{2} + 2 = 3\frac{1}{2}$ Hit Dice). Note that the remainder is not enough to affect the last gnoll or the ogre.

Slapping or wounding awakens affected creatures but normal noise does not. Awakening requires one entire round. Magically sleeping opponents can be attacked with substantial bonuses (see Combat, page 90).

The material component for this spell is a pinch of fine sand, rose petals, or a live cricket.

Spider Climb (Alteration)

Range: Touch
Components: V, S, M
Duration: 3 rounds + 1 round/level
Casting Time: 1
Area of Effect: Creature touched
Saving Throw: Neg.

A *spider climb* spell enables the recipient to climb and travel upon vertical surfaces as well as a giant spider, or even hang upside down from ceilings. Unwilling victims must be touched and are then allowed a saving throw vs. spell to negate the effect. The affected creature must have bare hands and feet in order to climb in this manner, at a movement rate of 6 (3 if at all encumbered). During the course of the spell, the recipient cannot handle objects that weigh less than a dagger (one pound), for such objects stick to his hands and feet. Thus a wizard will find it virtually impossible to cast spells if under a *spider climb* spell. Sufficient force can pull the recipient free; the DM can assign a saving throw based on circumstances, the strength of the force, and so on. For example, a creature with a Strength of 12 might pull the subject free if the subject fails a sav-

ing throw vs. paralyzation (a moderately difficult saving throw). The caster can end the spell effect with a word.

The material components of this spell are a drop of bitumen and a live spider, both of which must be eaten by the spell recipient.

Spook (Illusion/Phantasm)

Range: 0
Components: V, S
Duration: Special
Casting Time: 1
Area of Effect: 1 creature within 30 feet
Saving Throw: Neg.

A *spook* spell enables the wizard to play upon natural fears to cause the target creature to perceive the spellcaster as someone or something inimical. Without actually knowing what this is, the wizard merely advances threateningly upon the creature. If a successful saving throw vs. spell is not made, the creature turns and flees at maximum speed as far from the wizard as possible, though items carried are *not* dropped. The creature has a saving throw penalty of −1 for every two experience levels of the the caster, to a maximum of −6 at 12th level. Note that a natural (unmodified) roll of 20 automatically succeeds, regardless of saving throw penalties. Although the caster does not actually pursue the fleeing creature, a phantasm from its own mind does. Each round after the initial casting, the creature receives another saving throw, without penalty, until it successfully saves and the spell is broken. In any event, the spell functions only against creatures with Intelligences of 2 or more, and undead are not affected at all.

Taunt (Enchantment)

Range: 60 yards
Components: V, S, M
Duration: 1 round
Casting Time: 1
Area of Effect: 30-foot radius
Saving Throw: Neg.

A *taunt* spell enables the caster to jape and jeer effectively at a single type of creature with an Intelligence of 2 or greater. The caster need not speak the language of the creatures. His words and sounds have real meaning for the subject creature or creatures: challenging, insulting, and generally irritating and angering the listeners. Those failing to save vs. spell rush forth in fury to do battle with the spellcaster. All affected creatures attack the spellcaster in melee if physically capable of doing so, seeking to use body or hand-held weapons rather than missile weapons or spells. Separation of the caster from the victim by an impenetrable or uncrossable boundary (a wall of fire, a deep chasm, a formation of set pikemen)

causes the spell to break. If the caster taunts a mixed group, he must choose the type of creature to be affected. Creatures commanded by a strong leader (i.e., with a Charisma bonus, with higher Hit Dice, etc.) might gain a saving throw bonus of +1 to +4, at the DM's discretion. If used in conjunction with a *ventriloquism* spell, the creatures may attack the apparent source, depending upon their Intelligence, a leader's presence, and so on.

The material component is a slug, which is hurled at the creatures to be taunted.

Tenser's Floating Disc (Evocation)

Range: 20 yards
Components: V, S, M
Duration: 3 turns + 1 turn/level
Casting Time: 1
Area of Effect: Special
Saving Throw: None

With this spell, the caster creates the slightly concave, circular plane of force known as Tenser's floating disc (after the famed wizard whose greed and ability to locate treasure are well known). The disc is three feet in diameter and holds 100 pounds of weight per level of the wizard casting the spell. The disc floats at approximately three feet above the ground at all times and remains level. It floats along horizontally within its range of 20 yards at the command of the caster, and will accompany him at a movement rate of no more than 6. If unguided, it maintains a constant interval of six feet between itself and the wizard. If the spellcaster moves beyond range (by moving faster, or by such means as a *teleport* spell, or by trying to take it more than three feet from the surface beneath it), or if the spell duration expires, the floating disc winks out of existence and whatever it was supporting crashes to the surface beneath it.

The material component of the spell is a drop of mercury.

Unseen Servant
(Conjuration/Summoning)

Range: 0
Components: V, S, M
Duration: 1 hour + 1 turn/level
Casting Time: 1
Area of Effect: 30-foot radius
Saving Throw: None

The unseen servant is a non-visible, mindless, and shapeless force, used to step and fetch, open unstuck doors, and hold chairs, as well as to clean and mend. It is not strong, but unfailingly obeys the command of the wizard. It can carry out only one activity at a time and can move only lightweight items—carry a maximum of 20 pounds or push or pull 40 pounds across a smooth surface. It can open only normal doors, drawers, lids, etc. The unseen servant cannot fight, nor can it be killed, as it is a force rather than a creature. It can be magically dispelled, or eliminated after receiving 6 points of damage from area-effect spells, breath weapons, or similar attacks. If the caster attempts to send it beyond the allowed radius, the spell ends immediately.

The material components of the spell are a piece of string and a bit of wood.

Ventriloquism (Illusion/Phantasm)

Range: 10 yards/level, maximum 90 yards
Components: V, M
Duration: 4 rounds + 1 round/level
Casting Time: 1
Area of Effect: 1 creature or object
Saving Throw: Special

This spell enables the wizard to make his voice—or someone else's voice—or a similar sound seem to issue from someplace else, such as from another creature, a statue, from behind a door, down a passage, etc. The spellcaster can speak in any language that he knows, or make any sound that he can normally make. With respect to such voices and sounds, anyone rolling a successful saving throw vs. spell with a −2 penalty detects the ruse. If cast in conjunction with other illusions, the DM may rule greater penalties or disallow an independent saving throw against this spell in consideration of its contribution to the total effect of the combined illusion.

The material component of this spell is a parchment rolled up into a small cone.

Wall of Fog (Evocation)

Range: 30 yards
Components: V, S, M
Duration: 2d4 rounds + 1 round/level
Casting Time: 1
Area of Effect: 20' cube + 10' cube/level
Saving Throw: None

By casting this spell, the wizard creates a billowing wall of misty vapors in any area within the spell range. The wall of fog obscures all sight, normal and infravision, beyond two feet. The caster may create less vapor if he wishes. The wall must be a roughly cubic or rectangular mass, at least ten feet wide in its smallest dimension. The misty vapors persist for three or more rounds. Their duration can be halved by a moderate wind, and they can be blown away by a strong wind.

The material component is a pinch of split dried peas.

Wizard Mark (Alteration)

Range: Touch
Components: V, S, M
Duration: Permanent
Casting Time: 1
Area of Effect: Up to 1 square foot
Saving Throw: None

When this spell is cast, the wizard is able to inscribe, visibly or invisibly, his personal rune or mark, as well as up to six additional characters of smaller size. A *wizard mark* spell enables the caster to etch the rune upon stone, metal, or any softer substance without harm to the material upon which the mark is placed. If an invisible mark is made, a *detect magic* spell will cause it to glow and be visible (though not necessarily understandable). *Detect invisibility*, *true seeing*, a *gem of seeing*, or a *robe of eyes* will likewise expose an invisible wizard mark. A *read magic* spell will reveal the maker's words, if any. The mark cannot be dispelled, but it can be removed by the caster or by an *erase* spell. If cast on a living being, normal wear gradually causes the mark to fade.

The material components for this spell are a pinch of diamond dust (about 100 gp worth) and a pigment or pigments for the coloration of the mark. If the mark is to be invisible, the pigments are still used, but the caster uses a stylus of some sort rather than his finger.

Second-Level Spells

Alter Self (Alteration)

Range: 0
Components: V, S
Duration: 3d4 rounds + 2 rounds/level
Casting Time: 2
Area of Effect: The caster
Saving Throw: None

When this spell is cast, the wizard can alter his appearance and form—including clothing and equipment—to appear taller or shorter; thin, fat, or in between; human, humanoid, or any other generally man-shaped bipedal creature. The caster's body can undergo a limited physical alteration and his size can be changed up to 50%. If the form selected has wings, the wizard can actually fly, but at only 1/3 the speed of a true creature of that type, and with a loss of two maneuverability classes (to a minimum of E). If the form has gills, the caster can breathe underwater as long as the spell lasts. However, any multiple attack routines or additional damage allowed to an assumed form are not gained by the caster.

The caster's attack rolls, Armor Class, and saving throws do not change. The spell does not confer special abilities, attack forms, or defenses. Once the new form is chosen, it remains for the duration of the spell. The caster can change back into his own form at will; this ends the spell immediately. A caster who is slain automatically returns to his normal form.

Bind (Enchantment)

Range: 30 yards
Components: V, S, M
Duration: 1 round/level
Casting Time: 2
Area of Effect: Special
Saving Throw: None

When this spell is employed, the wizard can command any non-living ropelike object, including string, yarn, cord, line, rope, or even a cable. The spell affects 50 feet of normal rope (one-inch diameter), plus five feet per caster level. This length is reduced by 50% for every additional inch of thickness and increases by 50% for each 1/2 inch less. The possible commands are Coil (form a neat, coiled stack), Coil & Knot, Loop, Loop & Knot, Tie & Knot, and the reverses of all of the above (Uncoil, etc.). One command can be given each round.

The rope can only enwrap a creature or an object within one foot of it—it does not snake outward—so it must be thrown or hurled near the intended target. Note that the rope itself, and any knots tied in it, are not magical. A typical rope might be AC 6 and take 4 points of slashing damage before breaking. The rope does not inflict damage of any type, but it can be used as a trip line or to entangle a single opponent who fails a saving throw vs. spell.

Blindness (Illusion/Phantasm)

Range: 30 yards + 10 yards/level
Component: V
Duration: Special
Casting Time: 2
Area of Effect: 1 creature
Saving Throw: Neg.

The *blindness* spell causes the victim to become blind, able to see only a grayness before its eyes. Various *cure* spells will not remove this effect, and only a *dispel magic* or the spellcaster can do away with the blindness if the creature fails its initial saving throw vs. spell. A blinded creature suffers a −4 penalty to its attack rolls, and its opponents gain a +4 bonus to their attack rolls.

Blur (Illusion/Phantasm)

Range: 0
Components: V, S
Duration: 3 rounds + 1 round/level
Casting Time: 2
Area of Effect: The caster
Saving Throw: None

When a *blur* spell is cast, the wizard causes the outline of his form to become blurred, shifting and wavering. This distortion causes all missile and melee combat attacks against the caster to be made with −4 penalties on the first attempt and −2 penalties on all successive attacks. It also grants the wizard a +1 bonus to his saving throw for any direct magical attack. A *detect invisibility* spell will not counter this effect, but the 5th-level clerical spell *true seeing* and similar magic will.

Continual Light (Alteration)
Reversible

Range: 60 yards
Components: V, S
Duration: Permanent
Casting Time: 2
Area of Effect: 60-foot radius
Saving Throw: Special

This spell is similar to a *light* spell, except that it is as bright as full daylight and lasts until negated by magical darkness or by a *dispel magic* spell. Creatures who suffer penalties in bright light suffer them in this spell's area of effect. As with the *light* spell, it can be cast into the air, onto an object, or at a creature. In the third case, the spell affects the space about one foot behind a creature that successfully rolls its saving throw vs. spell. Note that this spell can also blind a creature if it is successfully cast upon the

creature's attack rolls, saving throws, and Armor Class by 4. If the spell is cast on a small object that is then placed in a light-proof covering, the spell's effects are blocked until the covering is removed.

A *continual light* brought into an area of magical darkness (or vice versa) is temporarily negated so that the otherwise prevailing light conditions exist in the overlapping areas of effect. A direct casting of *continual light* against a similar or weaker magical darkness cancels both.

This spell eventually consumes the material it is cast upon, but the process takes far longer than the time in the typical campaign. Extremely hard and expensive materials can last hundreds or even thousands of years.

Darkness, 15' Radius (Alteration)

Range: 10 yards/level
Components: V, S, M
Duration: 1 turn + 1 round/level
Casting Time: 2
Area of Effect: 15-foot radius
Saving Throw: None

This spell causes total, impenetrable darkness in the area of effect. Infravision is useless. Neither normal nor magical light works unless a *light* or *continual light* spell is used. In the former event, the *darkness* spell is negated by the *light* spell and vice versa.

The material components of this spell are a bit of bat fur and either a drop of pitch or a piece of coal.

Deafness (Illusion/Phantasm)

Range: 60 yards
Components: V, S, M
Duration: Special
Casting Time: 2
Area of Effect: 1 creature
Saving Throw: Neg.

The *deafness* spell causes the recipient to become totally deaf and unable to hear any sounds. The victim is allowed a saving throw vs. spell. An affected creature has a −1 penalty to its surprise rolls unless its other senses are unusually keen. Deafened spellcasters have a 20% chance to miscast any spell with a verbal component. This *deafness* can be done away with only by means of a *dispel magic* spell or by the spellcaster.

The material component of this spell is beeswax.

Deeppockets (Alteration, Enchantment)

Range: Touch
Components: V, S, M
Duration: 12 hours + 1 hour/level
Casting Time: 1 turn
Area of Effect: 1 garment
Saving Throw: None

This spell enables the wizard to specially prepare a garment so as to hold far more than it normally could. A finely sewn gown or robe of high-quality material (at least 50 gp value) is fashioned so as to contain numerous hand-sized pockets. One dozen is the minimum number. The *deeppockets* spell then enables these pockets to hold a total of 100 pounds (five cubic feet in volume) as if it were only 10 pounds of weight. Furthermore, there are no discernible bulges where the special pockets are. At the time of casting, the caster can instead chose to have 10 pockets each holding 10 pounds (1/2 cubic foot volume each). If the robe or like garment is sewn with 100 or more pockets (200 gp minimum cost), 100 pockets can be created to contain one pound of weight and 1/6 cubic foot volume each. Each special pocket is actually an extradimensional holding space.

If the spell duration expires while there is material within the enchanted pockets, or if a successful *dispel magic* is cast upon the enchanted garment, all the material suddenly appears around the wearer and immediately falls to the ground. The caster can also cause all the pockets to empty with a single command.

In addition to the garment, which is reusable, the material components of this spell are a tiny golden needle and a strip of fine cloth given a half-twist and fastened at the ends.

Detect Evil (Divination)
Reversible

Range: 60 yards
Components: V, S
Duration: 5 rounds/level
Casting Time: 2
Area of Effect: 10-foot path
Saving Throw: None

This spell discovers emanations of evil (or of good in the case of the reverse spell) from any creature, object, or area. Character alignment is *not* revealed under most circumstances: characters who are strongly aligned, do not stray from their faith, and who are at least 9th level might radiate good or evil if they are intent upon appropriate actions. Powerful monsters, such as ki-rin, send forth emanations of evil or good, even if polymorphed. Aligned undead radiate evil, for it is this power and negative force that enable them to continue existing. An evilly cursed object or unholy water radiates evil, but a hidden trap or an unintelligent viper does not. The degree of evil (faint, moderate, strong, overwhelming) can be noted. Note that priests have a more powerful version of this spell.

The spell has a path of detection ten feet wide in the direction in which the mage is facing. The wizard must concentrate—stop, have quiet, and intently seek to detect the aura—for at least one round to receive a reading.

Detect Invisibility (Divination)

Range: 10 yards/level
Components: V, S, M
Duration: 5 rounds/level
Casting Time: 2
Area of Effect: 10-foot path
Saving Throw: None

When the wizard casts a *detect invisibility* spell, he is able to see clearly any objects or beings that are invisible, as well as any that are astral, ethereal, or out of phase. In addition, it enables the wizard to detect hidden or concealed creatures (e.g., thieves in shadows, halflings in underbrush, and so on). It does not reveal the method of concealment or invisibility, except in the case of astral travelers (where the silver cord can be seen). It does not reveal illusions or enable the caster to see through physical objects. Detection is in the wizard's line of sight along a ten-foot-wide path to the range limit.

The material components of this spell are a pinch of talc and a small sprinkling of powdered silver.

ESP (Divination)

Range: 5 yards/level, 90 yards maximum
Components: V, S, M
Duration: 1 round/level
Casting Time: 2
Area of Effect: 1 creature per probe
Saving Throw: None

When an *ESP* spell is used, the caster is able to detect the surface thoughts of any creatures in range—except for those of undead and creatures without minds (as we know them). The ESP is stopped by two or more feet of rock, two or more inches of any metal other than lead, or a thin sheet of lead foil. The wizard employing the spell is able to probe the surface thoughts of one creature per round, getting simple instinctual thoughts from lower order creatures. Probes can continue on the same creature from round to round or can move on to other creatures. The caster can use the spell to help determine if a creature lurks behind a door, for example, but the ESP does not always reveal what sort of creature it is. If used as part of a program of interrogation,

an intelligent and wary subject receives an initial saving throw. If successful, the creature successfully resists and the spell reveals no additional information. If the saving throw is failed, the caster may learn additional information, according to the DM's ruling. The creature's Wisdom adjustment applies, as may additional bonuses up to +4, based on the sensitivity of the information sought.

The material component of this spell is a copper piece.

Flaming Sphere (Evocation)

Range: 10 yards
Components: V, S, M
Duration: 1 round/level
Casting Time: 2
Area of Effect: 3-foot-radius sphere
Saving Throw: Neg.

A *flaming sphere* spell creates a burning globe of fire within ten yards of the caster. This sphere rolls in whichever direction the wizard points, at a rate of 30 feet per round. It rolls over barriers less than four feet tall, such as furniture, low walls, etc. Flammable substances are set afire by contact with the sphere. Creatures in contact with the globe must successfully save vs. spell or suffer 2d4 points of fire damage. Those within five feet of the sphere's surface must also save or suffer 1d4 points of heat damage. A successful saving throw means no damage is suffered. The DM may adjust the saving throws if there is little or no room to dodge the sphere.

The sphere moves as long as the spellcaster actively directs it, otherwise it merely stays at rest and burns. It can be extinguished by the same means as any normal fire of its size. The surface of the sphere has a spongy, yielding consistency and so does not cause damage except by its flame. It cannot push unwilling creatures aside or batter down large obstacles.

The material components are a bit of tallow, a pinch of sulphur, and a dusting of powdered iron.

Fog Cloud (Alteration)

Range: 10 yards
Components: V, S
Duration: 4 rounds + 1 round/level
Casting Time: 2
Area of Effect: Special
Saving Throw: None

The *fog cloud* spell can be cast in either one of two ways, at the caster's option: as a large, stationary bank of normal fog, or as a harmless fog that resembles the 5th-level wizard spell, *cloudkill*.

As a fog bank, this spell creates a fog of any size and shape up to a maximum 20-foot cube per caster level. The fog obscures all

sight, normal and infravision, beyond two feet.

As a cloudkill-like fog, this is a billowing mass of ghastly, yellowish-green vapors, measuring 40' x 20' x 20'. This moves away from the caster at ten feet per round. The vapors are heavier than air and sink to the lowest level, even pouring down sinkholes and den openings. Very thick vegetation breaks up the fog after it has moved 20 feet into the vegetation.

The only effect of either version is to obscure vision. A strong breeze will disperse either effect in one round, while a moderate breeze will reduce the spell duration by 50%. The spell cannot be cast underwater.

Fools' Gold (Alteration, Illusion)

Range: 10 yards
Components: V, S, M
Duration: 1 hour/level
Casting Time: 1 round
Area of Effect: 10 cu. in./level
Saving Throw: Special

Copper coins can temporarily be changed to gold pieces, or brass items turned to solid gold, for the spell duration by means of this magic. The area of effect is ten cubic inches per level—i.e., a 1" x 1" x 10" volume or equivalent, equal to about 150 gold coins. Any creature viewing the "gold" is entitled to a saving throw vs. spell, which can be modified by the creature's Wisdom; for every level of the wizard, the creature must subtract 1 from his dice roll. Thus it is unlikely that fools' gold will be detected if it was created by a high-level caster. If the "gold" is struck hard by an object of cold-wrought iron, there is a slight chance it will revert to its natural state, depending on the material component used to create the "gold." If a 25-gp citrine is powdered and sprinkled over the metal as this spell is cast, the chance that cold iron will return it to its true nature is 30%; if a 50-gp amber stone is powdered and used, there is a 25% chance that iron will dispel the magic; if a 250-gp topaz is powdered, the chance drops to 10%; if a 500-gp oriental (corundum) topaz is powdered, there is only a 1% chance that the cold iron will reveal that it is fools' gold.

Forget (Enchantment/Charm)

Range: 30 yards
Components: V, S
Duration: Permanent
Casting Time: 2
Area of Effect: 20-foot cube
Saving Throw: Neg.

By means of this spell, the spellcaster causes creatures within the area of effect to forget the events of the previous round (the one minute of time previous to the utterance of the spell). For every three levels of experience of the spellcaster, another minute of past time is forgotten. This does not negate *charm, suggestion, geas, quest,* or similar spells, but it is possible that the being who placed such magic upon the recipient could be forgotten. From one to four creatures can be affected, at the discretion of the caster. If only one is to be affected, the recipient saves vs. spell with a −2 penalty; if two, they save with −1 penalties; if three or four are to be affected, they save normally. All saving throws are adjusted by Wisdom. A priest's *heal* or *restoration* spell, if specially cast for this purpose, will restore the lost memories, as will a *limited wish* or *wish,* but no other means will do so.

Glitterdust (Conjuration/Summoning)

Range: 10 yards/level
Components: V, S, M
Duration: Special
Casting Time: 2
Area of Effect: 20-foot cube
Saving Throw: Special

This spell creates a cloud of glittering golden particles within the area of effect. Those in the area must roll a successful saving throw vs. spell or be blinded (−4 penalties to attack rolls, saving throws, and Armor Class) for 1d4+1 rounds. In addition, all within the area are covered by the dust, which cannot be removed and continues to sparkle until it fades. Note that this reveals invisible creatures. The dust fades in 1d4 rounds plus one round per caster level. Thus glitterdust cast by a 3rd-level wizard lasts for four to seven rounds.

The material component is ground mica.

Hypnotic Pattern (Illusion/Phantasm)

Range: 30 yards
Components: S, M
Duration: Special
Casting Time: 2
Area of Effect: 30-foot cube
Saving Throw: Neg.

When this spell is cast, the wizard creates a weaving, twisting pattern of subtle colors in the air. This pattern causes any creature looking at it to become fascinated and stand gazing at it as long as the spellcaster maintains the display, plus two rounds thereafter. The spell can captivate a maximum of 24 levels, or Hit Dice, of creatures (e.g., 24 creatures with 1 Hit Die each, 12 with 2 Hit Dice, etc). All creatures affected must be within the area of effect, and each is entitled to a saving throw vs. spell. A damage-inflicting attack on an affected creature frees it from the spell immediately.

The mage need not utter a sound, but he must gesture appropriately while holding a glowing stick of incense or a crystal rod filled with phosphorescent material.

Improved Phantasmal Force (Illusion/Phantasm)

Range: 60 yards + 10 yards/level
Components: V, S, M
Duration: Special
Casting Time: 2
Area of Effect: 200 sq. ft./ + 50 sq.ft./level
Saving Throw: Special

Like the 1st-level *phantasmal force* spell, this spell creates the illusion of any object, creature, or force, as long as it is within the spell's area of effect. The spellcaster can maintain the illusion with minimal concentration, thus he can move at half normal speed (but not cast other spells). Some minor sounds are included in the effects of the spell, but not understandable speech. Also, the improved phantasm continues for two rounds after the wizard ceases to concentrate upon it.

The material component is a bit of fleece.

Invisibility (Illusion/Phantasm)

Range: Touch
Components: V, S, M
Duration: Special
Casting Time: 2
Area of Effect: Creature touched
Saving Throw: None

This spell causes the creature touched to vanish from sight and be undetectable by normal vision or even infravision. Of course, the invisible creature is not magically silenced, and certain other conditions can render the creature detectable. Even allies cannot see the invisible creature or his gear, unless these allies can normally see invisible things or employ magic to do so. Items dropped or put down by the invisible creature become visible, items picked up disappear if tucked into the clothing or pouches worn by the creature. Note, however, that light never becomes invisible, although a source of light can become so (thus the effect is that of a light with no visible source).

The spell remains in effect until it is magically broken or dispelled, until the wizard or recipient cancels it, until the recipient attacks any creature, or until 24 hours have passed. Thus the invisible being can open doors, talk, eat, climb stairs, etc., but if he attacks, he immediately becomes visible, although the invisibility enables him to attack first. Note that the clerical *bless, chant,* and *prayer* spells are not attacks for this purpose. All highly Intelligent (Int 13 or more) creatures with 10 or more Hit Dice or levels of experience have a chance to detect invisible objects (they roll saving throws vs. spell; success means they noticed the invisible object).

The material components of the *invisibility* spell are an eyelash and a bit of gum arabic, the former encased in the latter.

Irritation (Alteration)

Range: 10 yards/level
Components: V, S, M
Duration: Special
Casting Time: 2
Area of Effect: 1 to 4 creatures in a 15-foot-radius area
Saving Throw: Neg.

An *irritation* spell affects the epidermis of the subject creatures. Creatures with very thick or insensitive skins (such as buffalo, elephants, scaled creatures, etc.) are basically unaffected by this. There are two versions of the spell, either of which can be cast from the standard preparation:

Itching. When cast, this causes each subject to feel an instant itching sensation on some portion of its body. If one round is not immediately spent scratching the irritated area, the creature is so affected that the next three rounds are spent squirming and twisting, effectively worsening its Armor Class by 4 and its attack rolls by 2 during this time. Spell preparations are ruined in the first round this spell is in effect, but not in the following three rounds. Doing nothing but scratching the itch for a full round prevents the rest of the effect. If cast at one creature, the saving throw has a −3 penalty; if cast at two creatures, the saving throw has a −1 penalty; and if cast at three or four creatures, the saving throw is normal.

Rash. When a rash is cast, the subject notices nothing for 1d4 rounds, but thereafter its entire skin breaks out in red welts that itch. The rash persists until either a *cure disease* or *dispel magic* spell is cast upon it. It lowers Charisma by 1 point per day for each of four days (i.e., maximum Charisma loss is 4 points). After one week, Dexterity is lowered by 1 point also. Symptoms vanish immediately upon the removal of the rash, and all statistics return to normal. This can be cast at one creature only, with a saving throw penalty of −2.

The material component for this spell is a leaf from poison ivy, oak, or sumac.

Knock (Alteration)
Reversible

Range: 60 yards
Component: V
Duration: Special
Casting Time: 1
Area of Effect: 10 square feet/level
Saving Throw: None

The *knock* spell opens stuck, barred, locked, held, or wizard-locked doors. It opens secret doors, as well as locked or trick-opening boxes or chests. It also loosens welds, shackles, or chains. If used to open a wizard-locked door, the spell does not remove the former spell, but simply suspends its functioning for one turn. In all other cases, it permanently opens locks or welds—although the former could be closed and locked again later. It does not raise barred gates or similar impediments (such as a portcullis), nor does it affect ropes, vines, and the like. Note that the effect is limited by the area; a 3rd-level wizard can knock a door of 30 square feet or less (e.g., a standard 4' x 7' door). Each spell can undo up to two means of preventing egress through a portal. Thus if a door is locked, barred, and held, or triple locked, opening it requires two *knock* spells. In all cases, the location of the door or item must be known—the spell cannot be used against a wall in hopes of discovering a secret door.

The reverse spell, *lock*, closes and locks a door or similar closure, provided there is a physical mechanism. It does not create a weld, but it locks physically operated locking mechanisms, set bars, and so on, up to two functions. It cannot affect a portcullis.

Know Alignment (Divination)
Reversible

Range: 10 yards
Components: V, S
Duration: 1 round/level
Casting Time: 1 round
Area of Effect: 1 creature or object
            per 2 rounds
Saving Throw: Neg.

A *know alignment* spell enables the wizard to read the aura of a creature or an aligned object (unaligned objects reveal nothing). The caster must remain stationary and concentrate on the subject for two full rounds. A creature is allowed a saving throw vs. spell and, if successful, the caster learns nothing about that particular creature from the casting. If a creature or object is concentrated on for only one round, only its alignment with respect to law and chaos can be learned. Certain magical devices negate the *know alignment* spell.

The reverse, *undetectable alignment*, conceals the alignment of an object or creature for 24 hours—even from a *know alignment* spell.

Leomund's Trap (Illusion/Phantasm)

Range: Touch
Components: V, S, M
Duration: Permanent
Casting Time: 3 rounds
Area of Effect: Object touched
Saving Throw: None

This false trap is designed to fool a thief or other character attempting to pilfer the spellcaster's goods. The wizard places the spell upon any small mechanism or device, such as a lock, hinge, hasp, screw-on cap, ratchet, etc. Any character able to detect traps, or who uses any spell or device enabling trap detection, is 100% certain a real trap exists. Of course, the spell is illusory and nothing happens if the trap is sprung; its primary purpose is to frighten away thieves or make them waste precious time.

The material component of the spell is a piece of iron pyrite touched to the object to be trapped while the object is sprinkled with a special dust requiring 200 gp to prepare. If another *Leomund's trap* is within 50 feet when the spell is cast, then the casting fails.

Levitate (Alteration)

Range: 20 yards/level
Components: V, S, M
Duration: 1 turn/level
Casting Time: 2
Area of Effect: 1 creature or object
Saving Throw: Neg.

When a *levitate* spell is cast, the wizard can place it upon his person, upon an object, or upon a single creature, subject to a maximum weight limit of 100 pounds per level of experience (e.g., a 3rd-level wizard can *levitate* up to 300 pounds maximum). If the spell is cast upon the wizard, he can move vertically up or down at a movement rate of 2 per round. If cast upon an object or another creature, the wizard can *levitate* it at the same speed according to his command. Horizontal movement is not empowered by this spell, but the recipient could push along the face of a cliff, for example, to move laterally. The spellcaster can cancel the spell as desired. If the subject of the spell is unwilling, or the object is in the possession of a creature, a saving throw vs. spell is allowed to determine if the *levitate* spell affects it.

Once cast, the spell requires no concentration, except when changing height. A levitating creature attempting to use a missile weapon finds himself increasingly unstable; the first attack has an attack roll penalty of −1, the second −2, and the third −3, etc., up to a maximum of −5. A full round spent stabilizing allows the creature to begin again at −1. Lack of leverage makes it impossible to cock a medium or heavy crossbow.

The material component of this spell is either a small leather loop or a piece of golden wire bent into a cup shape with a long shank on one end.

Locate Object (Divination)
Reversible

Range: 20 yards/level
Components: V, S, M
Duration: 1 round/level
Casting Time: 2
Area of Effect: Special
Saving Throw: None

This spell aids in locating a known or familiar object. The wizard casts the spell, slowly turns, and senses when he is facing in the direction of the object to be located, provided the object is within range, i.e., 60 yards for 3rd-level mages, 80 yards for 4th, 100 yards for 5th, etc. The spell can locate such objects as apparel, jewelry, furniture, tools, weapons, or even a ladder or stairway. Note that attempting to find a specific item such as jewelry or a crown, requires an accurate mental image; if the image is not close enough to the actual, the spell does not work. Desired but unique objects cannot be located by this spell unless they are known by the caster. The spell is blocked by lead. Creatures cannot be found by this spell.

The material component is a forked twig.

The reversal, *obscure object*, hides an object from location by spell, crystal ball, or similar means for eight hours. Creatures cannot be affected by this spell. The material component is a chameleon skin.

Magic Mouth (Alteration)

Range: 10 yards
Components: V, S, M
Duration: Special
Casting Time: 2
Area of Effect: 1 object
Saving Throw: None

When this spell is cast, the wizard imbues the chosen object with an enchanted mouth that suddenly appears and speaks his message when a specified event occurs. The message, which must be of 25 words or less, can be in any language known by the spellcaster, and can be delivered over a one-turn period. The mouth cannot speak magical spells or use command words. It does, however, move to the words articulated—if it is placed upon a statue, the mouth of the statue would actually move and appear to speak. Of course, the magic mouth can be placed upon a tree, rock, door, or any other object, excluding intelligent members of the animal or vegetable kingdoms.

The spell functions when specific conditions are fulfilled, according to the command of the spellcaster. Some examples are to speak "to the first creature that touches you," or "to the first creature that passes within 30 feet." Commands can be as general or as detailed as desired, although only visual and audible triggers can be used, such as the following: "Speak only when a venerable female human carrying a sack of groat clusters sits crosslegged within one foot." Such visual triggers can react to a character using the *disguise* ability. Command range is five yards per level of the wizard, so a 6th-level wizard can command the *magic mouth* to speak at a maximum encounter range of 30 yards ("Speak when a winged creature comes within 30 yards."). The spell lasts until the speak command can be fulfilled, thus the spell duration is variable. A *magic mouth* cannot distinguish invisible creatures, alignments, level, Hit Dice, or class, except by external garb. If desired, the effect can be keyed to a specific noise or spoken word.

The material component of this spell is a small bit of honeycomb.

Melf's Acid Arrow (Conjuration)

Range: 180 yards
Components: V, S, M
Duration: Special
Casting Time: 2
Area of Effect: 1 target
Saving Throw: Special

By means of this spell, the wizard creates a magical arrow that speeds to its target as if fired from the bow of a fighter of the same level as the wizard. No modifiers for range, non-proficiency, or specialization are used. The arrow has no attack or damage bonus, but it inflicts 2d4 points of acid damage (with saving throws for items on the target). (There is no splash damage.) For every three levels that the caster has achieved, the acid lasts for another round, unless somehow neutralized, inflicting another 2d4 points of damage each round. So at 3rd-5th level, the acid lasts two rounds, at 6th-8th level, the acid lasts for three rounds, etc.

The material components of the spell are a dart, powdered rhubarb leaf, and an adder's stomach.

Mirror Image (Illusion/Phantasm)

Range: 0
Components: V, S
Duration: 3 rounds/level
Casting Time: 2
Area of Effect: 6-foot radius
Saving Throw: None

When a *mirror image* spell is invoked, the spellcaster causes from two to eight exact duplicates of himself to come into being around him. These images do exactly what the wizard does. Since the spell causes a blurring and slight distortion when it is cast, it is impossible for opponents to be certain which are the illusions and which is the actual wizard. When an image is struck by a melee or missile attack, magical or otherwise, it disappears, but any other existing images remain intact until struck. The images seem to shift from round to round, so that if the actual wizard is struck during one round, he cannot be picked out from among his images the next. To determine the number of images that appear, roll 1d4 and add 1 for every three levels of experience the wizard has achieved, to a maximum of eight images. At the end of the spell duration, all surviving images wink out.

Misdirection (Illusion/Phantasm)

Range: 30 yards
Components: V, S
Duration: 8 hours
Casting Time: 2
Area of Effect: 1 creature or object
Saving Throw: Neg.

By means of this spell, the wizard misdirects the information from a detection spell (*detect charm, detect evil, detect invisibility, detect lie, detect magic, detect snares and pits*, etc.). While the detection spell functions, it indicates the wrong area, creature, or the opposite of the truth with respect to *detect evil* or *detect lie*. The wizard directs the spell effect upon the object of the detection spell. If the caster of the detection spell fails his saving throw vs. spell, the misdirection takes place. Note that this spell does not affect other types of divination (*know alignment, augury, ESP, clairvoyance*, etc.).

Protection From Cantrips (Abjuration)

Range: Touch
Components: V, S
Duration: 5 hours + 1 hour/level
Casting Time: 1 round
Area of Effect: Creature or object touched
Saving Throw: None

By casting this spell, the wizard receives immunity to the effects of cantrips cast by other wizards, apprentices, or creatures that use the *cantrip* spell. The spell protects the caster, or one item or person that he touches (such as a spell book or a drawer containing spell components). Any cantrip cast against the protected person or item dissipates with an audible popping sound. This spell is often used by a wizard who has mischievous apprentices, or one who wishes apprentices to clean or shine an area using elbow grease rather than magic. Any unwilling target of this spell must be touched (via an attack roll) and is allowed a saving throw vs. spell to escape the effect.

Pyrotechnics (Alteration)

Range: 120 yards
Components: V, S, M
Duration: Special
Casting Time: 2
Area of Effect: 1 fire source (special)
Saving Throw: None

A *pyrotechnics* spell draws on an existing fire source to produce either of two effects, at the option of the caster. First, it can produce a flashing and fiery burst of glowing, colored aerial fireworks that lasts one round. This effect temporarily blinds those creatures in, under, or within 120 feet of the area and that have an unobstructed line of sight to the burst. Creatures viewing this are blinded for 1d4 + 1 rounds unless they successfully save vs. spell. The fireworks fill a volume ten times greater than that of the original fire source.

This spell can also cause a thick, writhing stream of smoke to arise from the source and form a choking cloud that lasts for one round per experience level of the caster. This covers a roughly spherical volume from the ground or floor up (or conforming to the shape of a confined area) that totally obscures vision beyond two feet. The smoke fills a volume 100 times that of the fire source. All within the cloud must roll successful saving throws vs. spell or suffer −2 penalties to all combat rolls and Armor Class.

The spell uses one fire source within a 20-foot cube, which is immediately extinguished. An extremely large fire used as a source might be only partially extinguished. Magical fires are not extinguished, although a fire-based creature (such as a fire elemental) used as a source suffers 1 point of damage per caster level.

Ray of Enfeeblement (Enchantment/Charm)

Range: 10 yards + 5 yards/level
Components: V, S
Duration: 1 round/level
Casting Time: 2
Area of Effect: 1 creature
Saving Throw: Neg.

By means of a *ray of enfeeblement*, a wizard weakens an opponent, reducing its Strength and thereby the attacks that rely upon it. Humans, demihumans, and humanoids of man-size or less are reduced to an effective Strength of 5, losing all Strength bonuses and suffering an attack roll penalty of −2 and a −1 penalty to damage. Other creatures suffer a penalty of −2 on attack rolls. Furthermore, they have a −1 penalty for each die of damage they inflict. (But no damage roll can inflict less than 1 point per die of damage.) Your DM will determine any other effects appropriate to the affected creature. If the target creature makes its saving throw, the spell has no effect. This spell does not affect combat bonuses due to magical items, and those conferring increased Strength function normally.

Rope Trick (Alteration)

Range: Touch
Components: V, S, M
Duration: 2 turns/level
Casting Time: 2
Area of Effect: Special
Saving Throw: None

When this spell is cast upon a piece of rope from five to 30 feet long, one end of the rope rises into the air until the whole hangs perpendicular, as if affixed at the upper end. The upper end is, in fact, fastened to an extradimensional space. The spellcaster and up to seven others can climb up the rope and disappear into this place of safety where no creature can find them. The rope can be taken into the extradimensional space if fewer than eight persons have climbed it, otherwise it simply stays hanging in the air (extremely strong creatures might be able to remove it, at the DM's option). Spells cannot be cast across the interdimensional interface, nor can area effects cross it. Those in the extradimensional space can see out of it as if there is a 3′ x 5′ window centered on the rope. The persons in the extradimensional space must climb down prior to the end of the spell, or they are dropped from the height at which they entered the extradimensional space. The rope can be climbed by only one person at a time. Note that the *rope trick* spell enables climbers to reach a normal place if they do not climb all the way to the extradimensional space. Also note

that creating or taking extradimensional spaces into an existing extradimensional space is hazardous.

The material components of this spell are powdered corn extract and a twisted loop of parchment.

Scare (Enchantment/Charm)

Range: 30 yards + 10 yards/level
Components: V, S, M
Duration: 1d4 rounds + 1 round/level
Casting Time: 2
Area of Effect: 15-foot radius
Saving Throw: Special

This spell causes creatures with fewer than 6 Hit Dice or levels of experience to fall into fits of trembling and shaking. The frightened creatures have a −2 reaction adjustment and may drop items held if encumbered. If cornered, they fight, but with −1 penalties to attack and damage rolls, and to saving throws as well.

Only elves, half-elves, and priests are allowed saving throws against this spell. Note that this spell has no effect on the undead (skeletons, zombies, ghouls, and so on), or on upper or lower planar creatures of any sort.

The material component used for this spell is a bit of bone from an undead skeleton, zombie, ghoul, ghast, or mummy.

Shatter (Alteration)

Range: 30 yards + 10 yards/level
Components: V, S, M
Duration: Instantaneous
Casting Time: 2
Area of Effect: 3-foot radius
Saving Throw: Neg.

The *shatter* spell is a sound-based attack that affects nonmagical objects of crystal, glass, ceramic, or porcelain, such as vials, bottles, flasks, jugs, windows, mirrors, etc. All such objects within a three-foot radius of the center of the spell effect are smashed into dozens of pieces by the spell. Objects weighing more than one pound per level of the caster are not affected, but all other objects of the appropriate composition must save vs. crushing blow or be shattered. Alternatively, the spell can be focused against a single item of up to 10 pounds per caster level. Crystalline creatures usually suffer 1d6 points of damage per caster level to a maximum of 6d6, with a saving throw vs. spell for half damage.

The material component of this spell is a chip of mica.

Spectral Hand (Necromancy)

Range: 30 yards + 5 yards/level
Components: V, S
Duration: 2 rounds/level
Casting Time: 2
Area of Effect: 1 opponent
Saving Throw: None

This spell causes a ghostly, glowing hand, shaped from the caster's life force, to materialize within the spell range and move as the caster desires. Any touch attack spell of 4th level or less that is subsequently cast by the wizard can be delivered by the spectral hand. The spell gives the caster a +2 bonus to his attack roll. The caster cannot perform any other actions when attacking with the hand; the hand returns to the caster and hovers if the caster takes other actions. The hand lasts the full spell duration unless dismissed by the caster, and it is possible to use more than one touch attack with it. The hand receives flank and rear attack bonuses if the caster is in a position to do so. The hand is vulnerable to magical attack (but it has an Armor Class of −2). Any damage to the hand ends the spell and inflicts 1d4 points of damage to the caster.

Stinking Cloud (Evocation)

Range: 30 yards
Components: V, S, M
Duration: 1 round/level
Casting Time: 2
Area of Effect: 20-foot cube
Saving Throw: Special

When a *stinking cloud* is cast, the wizard creates a billowing mass of nauseous vapors up to 30 yards away from his position. Any creature caught within the cloud must roll a successful saving throw vs. poison or be reeling and unable to attack because of nausea, for 1d4 + 1 rounds after leaving the cloud. Those who make successful saving throws can leave the cloud without suffering any ill effects, although those remaining in the cloud must continue to save each round. These poisonous effects can be slowed or neutralized by appropriate magic. The cloud duration is halved in a moderate breeze (8-18 m.p.h) and is dispersed in one round by a stronger breeze.

The material component of the spell is a rotten egg or several skunk cabbage leaves.

Strength (Alteration)

Range: Touch
Components: V, S, M
Duration: 1 hour/level
Casting Time: 1 turn
Area of Effect: Person touched
Saving Throw: None

Application of this spell increases the Strength of the character by a number of points—or tenths of points after 18 Strength is attained (only if the character is a warrior). Benefits of the *strength* spell last for the duration of the magic. The amount of added Strength depends upon the spell recipient's group and is subject to all restrictions on Strength due to race and class. Multi-class characters use the best die.

Class	Strength Gain
Priest	1d6 points
Rogue	1d6 points
Warrior	1d8 points
Wizard	1d4 points

If a warrior has an 18 Strength already, from 10% to 80% is added to his extraordinary Strength roll. The spell cannot confer a Strength of 19 or more, nor is it cumulative with other magic that adds to Strength. Beings without Strength scores (kobolds, lizard men, etc.) receive a +1 to attack and damage rolls.

The material component of this spell is a few hairs, or a pinch of dung, from a particularly strong animal—ape, bear, ox, etc.

Summon Swarm (Conjuration/Summoning)

Range: 60 yards
Components: V, S, M
Duration: Special
Casting Time: 2
Area of Effect: 10-foot cube
Saving Throw: Neg.

The swarm of small animals (roll on following table to determine type, or the DM can assign an appropriate creature) drawn by the *summon swarm* spell will viciously attack all creatures in the area chosen by the caster. Creatures actively defending against the swarm to the exclusion of other activities suffer 1 point of damage for each round spent in the swarm. Those taking other actions, including leaving the swarm, receive damage equal to 1d4 points + 1 point per three levels of the caster, every round. Note that spellcasting within the swarm is impossible.

Dice Roll	Swarm Type
01-40	Rats
41-70	Bats
71-80	Spiders
81-90	Centipedes/beetles
91-100	Flying insects

The swarm cannot be fought effectively with weapons, but fire and area effects can force it to disperse by inflicting damage. The swarm disperses when it has taken a total of 2 hit points per caster level from these attacks. A *protection from evil* spell keeps the swarm at bay, and certain area-effect spells, such as *gust of wind* and *stinking cloud*, disperse a swarm immediately, if appropriate to the swarm summoned (e.g., only flyers are affected by a *gust of wind*). The caster must remain stationary and undisturbed to control the swarm; if his concentration lapses or is broken, the swarm disperses in two rounds. The swarm is stationary once conjured.

The material component is a square of red cloth.

Tasha's Uncontrollable Hideous Laughter (Enchantment/Charm)

Range: 60 yards
Components: V, S, M
Duration: 1 round/level
Casting Time: 2
Area of Effect: 1 or more creatures in a 30-foot cube
Saving Throw: Neg.

The victim of this spell perceives everything as hilariously funny. The effect is not immediate, and the creature feels only a slight tingling on the round the spell is cast. On the round immediately following, the victim begins smiling, then giggling, chuckling, tittering, snickering, guffawing, and finally collapsing into gales of uncontrollable, hideous laughter. Although this magical mirth lasts only a single round, the affected creature must spend the next round regaining its feet, and it loses 2 points from its Strength (or −2 to attack and damage rolls) for all remaining rounds of the spell.

The saving throw vs. spell is modified by the Intelligence of the creature. Creatures with Intelligences of 4 or less (semi-intelligent) are totally unaffected. Those with Intelligences of 5-7 (low) save with −6 penalties. Those with Intelligences of 8-12 (average to very) save with −4 penalties. Those with Intelligences of 13-14 (high) save with −2 penalties. Those with Intelligences of 15 or greater (exceptional) have unmodified saving throws.

The caster can affect one creature for every three levels attained—e.g., one at 3rd level, two at 6th level, three at 9th level, etc. All affected beings must be within 30 feet of each other.

The material components are a small feather and minute tarts. The tarts are hurled at the subjects, while the feather is waved in one hand.

Web (Evocation)

Range: 5 yards/level
Components: V, S, M
Duration: 2 turns/level
Casting Time: 2
Area of Effect: Special
Saving Throw: Neg. or ½

A *web* spell creates a many-layered mass of strong, sticky strands similar to spider webs but far larger and tougher. These masses must be anchored to two or more solid and diametrically opposed points—floor and ceiling, opposite walls, etc., or the web collapses upon itself and disappears.

The *web* spell covers a maximum area of eight 10' x 10' x 10' cubes and the webs must be at least 10 feet thick, so a mass 40 feet high, 20 feet wide, and 10 feet deep may be cast. Creatures caught within webs, or simply touching them, become stuck among the gluey fibers.

Anyone in the area when the spell is cast must roll a saving throw vs. spell with a −2 penalty. If the saving throw is successful, two things may have occurred. If the creature has room to escape the area, then it is assumed to have jumped free. If there is no room to escape, then the webs are only half strength. Creatures with less than 13 Strength (7 if the webs are half strength) are stuck until freed by another or until the spell wears off. Missile fire is generally ineffective against creatures trapped in webs.

Creatures with Strengths between 13 and 17 can break through one foot of webs per round. Creatures with 18 or greater Strength can break through two feet of webs per round. If the webs are at half strength, these rates are doubled. (Great mass equates to great strength in this case, and creatures of large mass hardly notice webs.) Strong and huge creatures can break through 10 feet of webs per round.

Furthermore, the strands of a *web* spell are flammable. A magical *flaming sword* can slash them away as easily as a hand brushes away cobwebs. Any fire—torch, flaming oil, flaming sword, etc.—can set them alight and burn them away in a single round. All creatures within flaming webs suffer 2d4 points of damage from the flames, but those free of the strands are not harmed.

The material component of this spell is a bit of spider web.

Whispering Wind
(Alteration, Phantasm)

Range: 1 mile/level
Components: V, S
Duration: Special
Casting Time: 1
Area of Effect: 2-foot radius
Saving Throw: None

By means of this spell, the wizard is able to either send a message or cause some desired sound effect. The whispering wind can travel as many miles above ground as the spellcaster has levels of experience, to a specific location within range that is familiar to the wizard. The whispering wind is as gentle and unnoticed as a zephyr until it reaches the location. It then delivers its whisper-quiet message or other sound. Note that the message is delivered regardless of whether anyone is present to hear it. The wind then dissipates. The wizard can prepare the spell to bear a message of up to 25 words, cause the spell to deliver other sounds for one round, or merely have the whispering wind seem to be a faint stirring of the air that has a susurrant sound. He can likewise cause the whispering wind to move as slowly as a mile per hour or as quickly as a mile every turn. When the spell reaches its objective, it swirls and remains until the message is delivered. As with the *magic mouth* spell, no spells may be cast via the *whispering wind*.

Wizard Lock (Alteration)

Range: Touch
Components: V, S
Duration: Permanent
Casting Time: 2
Area of Effect: 30 square feet/level
Saving Throw: None

A *wizard lock* spell cast upon a door, chest, or portal magically locks it. The caster can freely pass his own lock without affecting it; otherwise, the wizard-locked door or object can be opened only by breaking in, a successful *dispel magic*, or *knock* spell, or by a wizard four or more levels higher than the one casting the spell. Note that the last two methods do not remove the wizard lock, they only negate it for a brief duration, about one turn. Creatures from other planes cannot burst a wizard lock as they can a held portal (see the *hold portal* spell).

Third-Level Spells

Blink (Alteration)

Range: 0
Components: V, S
Duration: 1 round/level
Casting Time: 1
Area of Effect: The caster
Saving Throw: None

By means of this spell, the wizard causes his material form to "blink" directly from one point to another at a random time and in a random direction. This means that melee attacks against the wizard automatically miss if initiative indicates they fall after he has blinked.

Each round the spell is in effect, the wizard rolls 2d8 to determine the timing of the blink—the result of the dice roll is used as the wizard's initiative for that round. The wizard disappears and instantaneously reappears 10 feet distant from his previous position. (Direction is determined by roll of 1d8: 1 = right ahead, 2 = right, 3 = right behind, 4 = behind, 5 = left behind, 6 = left, 7 = left ahead, 8 = ahead.) The caster cannot blink into a solid object; if such is indicated, reroll the direction. Movable objects of size and mass comparable to the caster are shoved aside when the caster blinks in. If blinking is impossible except into a fixed, solid object, the caster is then trapped on the Ethereal plane.

During each round that he blinks, the spellcaster can be attacked only by opponents who win initiative or by those who are able to strike both locations at once (e.g., with a breath weapon, fireball, or similar wide-area attack forms). Opponents with multiple attacks, or those operating under haste or similar effects, can often strike early enough to have at least one attack against the caster.

If the spellcaster holds off his attack (if any) until after the blink, the 2d8 delay until the blink is added to his normal 1d10 initiative roll (thus he probably attacks last in the round). Or the spellcaster can try to get his attack in before he blinks (he must announce his intent before rolling the 2d8 for blink timing and the 1d10 for initiative). In this case, the caster compares the two dice rolls, hoping that his initiative roll is lower than his blink roll (the two rolls are *not* added if he is trying to attack before he blinks). If so, he attacks according to his initiative roll, then blinks according to the blink roll. If his blink roll is lower than his initiative roll, however, he blinks out, then he attacks in whatever direction he's facing (he must go through with his attack, even if he is facing in the wrong direction to affect anyone).

Clairaudience (Divination)

Range: Special
Components: V, S, M
Duration: 1 round/level
Casting Time: 3
Area of Effect: Special
Saving Throw: None

The *clairaudience* spell enables the wizard to concentrate upon some locale and hear in his mind any noise within a 60-foot radius of the spell's casting point. Distance is not a factor, but the locale must be known—a place familiar to the spellcaster or an obvious one (such as behind a door, around a corner, in a copse of trees, etc.). Only sounds that are normally detectable by the wizard can be heard by use of this spell. Lead sheeting or magical protections prevent the operation of the spell, and the wizard has some indication that the spell is so blocked. Note that it functions only on the wizard's current plane of existence. The spell creates an invisible sensor that can be magically dispelled.

The material component of the spell is a small horn of at least 100 gp value.

Clairvoyance (Divination)

Range: Special
Components: V, S, M
Duration: 1 round/level
Casting Time: 3
Area of Effect: Special
Saving Throw: None

Similar to the *clairaudience* spell, the *clairvoyance* spell empowers the wizard to see in his mind whatever is within sight range from the spell locale chosen. Distance from the wizard is not a factor, but the locale must be known—familiar or obvious. Furthermore, light is a factor, as the spell does not enable the use of infravision or magical enhancements. If the area is magically dark, only darkness is seen; if naturally pitch dark, only a 10-foot radius from the center of the spell's area of effect can be seen. Otherwise, the seeing extends to the normal vision range according to the prevailing light. Lead sheeting or magical protection foils a *clairvoyance* spell, and the wizard has some indication that it is so blocked. The spell creates an invisible sensor, similar to that created by a *crystal ball* spell, that can be dispelled. The spell functions only on the wizard's current plane of existence.

The material component is a pinch of powdered pineal gland.

Delude (Alteration)

Range: 0
Components: V, S
Duration: 1 turn/level
Casting Time: 3
Area of Effect: The caster
Saving Throw: Neg.

By means of a *delude* spell, the wizard conceals his own alignment with that of any creature within a 30-foot radius at the time the spell is cast. The creature must be of higher than animal intelligence for the spell to work; its own alignment remains unchanged. The creature receives a saving throw vs. spell and, if successful, the *delude* spell fails. If the spell is successful, any *know alignment* spell used against the caster discovers only the assumed alignment. Note that a *detect good* or *detect evil* also detects the assumed aura, if the aura is strong enough. The creature whose aura has been assumed radiates magic, but the wizard radiates magic only to the creature whose alignment has been assumed. If a *delude* spell is used in conjunction with a *change self* or *alter self* spell, the class of the wizard can be totally hidden, if he is clever enough to carry off the disguise.

Dispel Magic (Abjuration)

Range: 120 yards
Components: V, S
Duration: Instantaneous
Casting Time: 3
Area of Effect: 30-foot cube
Saving Throw: None

When a wizard casts this spell, it has a chance to neutralize or negate magic it comes in contact with, as follows:

First, it removes spells and spell-like effects (including device effects and innate abilities) from creatures or objects. Second, it disrupts the casting or use of these in the area of effect at the instant the dispel is cast. Third, it destroys magical potions (which are treated as 12th level for purposes of this spell).

Each effect or potion in the spell's area is checked to determine if it is dispelled. The caster can always dispel his own magic; otherwise the chance to dispel depends on the difference in level between the magical effect and the caster. The base chance is 50% (11 or higher on 1d20 to dispel). If the caster is higher level than the creator of the effect to be dispelled, the difference is subtracted from the number needed on 1d20 to dispel (thus making it more likely that the dispel succeeds); if the caster is of lower level, then the difference is added to the number needed on 1d20 to dispel (making it less likely that the dispel succeeds). A roll of 20 always succeeds and a roll of 1 always fails. Thus, if a caster is 10 levels higher, only a roll of 1 prevents the effect from being dispelled.

A *dispel magic* spell does not affect a specially enchanted item, such as a magical scroll, ring, wand, rod, staff, miscellaneous item, weapon, shield, or armor, unless it is cast directly upon the item. This renders the item nonoperational for 1d4 rounds. An item possessed and carried by a creature gains the creature's saving throw against this effect, otherwise it is automatically rendered nonoperational. An interdimensional interface (such as a *bag of holding*) rendered nonoperational would be temporarily closed. Note that an item's physical properties are unchanged: a nonoperational magical sword is still a sword.

Artifacts and relics are not subject to this spell; however, some of their spell-like effects may be, at the DM's option.

Note that this spell can be very effective when used upon charmed and similarly beguiled creatures. Certain spells or effects cannot be dispelled; these are listed in the spell descriptions.

Explosive Runes (Alteration)

Range: Touch
Components: V, S
Duration: Special
Casting Time: 3
Area of Effect: 10-foot radius
Saving Throw: None or 1/2

By tracing these mystic runes upon a book, map, scroll, or similar object bearing written information, the wizard prevents unauthorized persons from reading his material. The explosive runes are difficult to detect—5% chance per level of magic use experience of the reader; thieves have only a 5% chance. But trap detection by spell or magical device always finds these runes.

When read, the explosive runes detonate, delivering 6d4 + 6 points of damage to the reader, who gets no saving throw. A like amount, or half that if saving throws are made, is suffered by each creature within the blast radius. The wizard who cast the spell, as well as any he instructs, can read the protected writing without triggering the runes. Likewise, the wizard can remove the runes whenever desired. Others can remove them only with a successful *dispel magic* or *erase* spell. Explosive runes otherwise last until the spell is triggered. The item upon which the runes are placed is destroyed when the explosion takes place, unless it is not normally subject to destruction by magical fire (see the Item Saving Throws in the *Dungeon Master's Guide*).

Summary of *Dispel Magic* Effects

Source of Effect	Resists As	Result of Dispel
Caster	None	Dispel automatic
Other caster/innate ability	Level/HD of other caster	Effect negated
Wand	6th level	*
Staff	8th level	*
Potion	12th level	Potion destroyed
Other magic	12th, unless special	*
Artifact	DM discretion	DM discretion

* Effect negated; if cast directly on item, item becomes nonoperational for 1d4 rounds.

Feign Death (Necromancy)

Range: Touch
Components: V, S
Duration: 1 hour + 1 turn/level
Casting Time: 1
Area of Effect: Creature touched
Saving Throw: None

By means of this spell, the caster (or any other creature whose levels of experience or Hit Dice do not exceed the wizard's own level) can be put into a cataleptic state that is impossible to distinguish from death. Although the person or creature affected by the *feign death* spell can smell, hear, and know what is going on, no feeling or sight of any sort is possible. Thus any wounding or mistreatment of the body is not felt and no reaction occurs; damage is only ½ normal. In addition, paralysis, poison, or energy-level drain cannot affect an individual under the influence of this spell. Poison injected or otherwise introduced into the body takes effect when the spell recipient is no longer under the influence of this spell, although a saving throw is permitted.

Note that only a willing individual can be affected by feign death. The spellcaster can end the spell effects at any time desired, as will a successful dispel, but a full round is required for bodily functions to begin again.

Fireball (Evocation)

Range: 10 yards + 10 yards/level
Components: V, S, M
Duration: Instantaneous
Casting Time: 3
Area of Effect: 20-foot radius
Saving Throw: ½

A fireball is an explosive burst of flame, which detonates with a low roar and delivers damage proportional to the level of the wizard who cast it—1d6 points of damage for each level of experience of the spellcaster (up to a maximum of 10d6). The burst of the fireball creates little pressure and generally conforms to the shape of the area in which it occurs. The fireball fills an area equal to its normal spherical volume (roughly 33,000 cubic feet—thirty-three 10′ x 10′ x 10′ cubes). Besides causing damage to creatures, the fireball ignites all combustible materials within its burst radius, and the heat of the fireball melts soft metals such as gold, copper, silver, etc. Exposed items require saving throws vs. magical fire to determine if they are affected, but items in the possession of a creature that rolls a successful saving throw are unaffected by the fireball.

The wizard points his finger and speaks the range (distance and height) at which the fireball is to burst. A streak flashes from the pointing digit and, unless it impacts upon a material body or solid barrier prior to attaining the prescribed range, blossoms into the fireball (an early impact results in an early detonation). Creatures failing their saving throws each suffer full damage from the blast. Those who roll successful saving throws manage to dodge, fall flat, or roll aside, each receiving half damage (the DM rolls the damage and each affected creature suffers either full damage or half damage [round fractions down], depending on whether the creature saved or not).

The material component of this spell is a tiny ball of bat guano and sulphur.

Flame Arrow (Conjuration/Summoning)

Range: 30 yards + 10 yards/level
Components: V, S, M
Duration: 1 round
Casting Time: 3
Area of Effect: Special
Saving Throw: None

This spell has two effects. First, the wizard can cause normal arrows or crossbow bolts to become magical flaming missiles for one round. The missiles must be nocked and drawn (or cocked) at the completion of the spell. If they are not loosed within one round, they are consumed by the magic. For every five levels the caster has achieved, up to 10 arrows or bolts can be affected. The arrows inflict normal damage, plus 1 point of fire damage to any target struck. They may also cause incendiary damage. This version of the spell is used most often in large battles.

The second version of this spell enables the caster to hurl fiery bolts at opponents within range. Each bolt inflicts 1d6 points of piercing damage, plus 4d6 points of fire damage. Only half of the fire damage is inflicted if the creature struck saves vs. spell. The caster receives one bolt for every five experience levels (two bolts at 10th level, three bolts at 15th level, etc.). Bolts must be used on creatures within 20 yards of each other and in front of the wizard.

The material components for this spell are a drop of oil and a small piece of flint.

Fly (Alteration)

Range: Touch
Components: V, S, M
Duration: 1 turn/level + 1d6 turns
Casting Time: 3
Area of Effect: Creature touched
Saving Throw: None

This spell enables the wizard to bestow the power of magical flight. The creature affected is able to move vertically and horizontally at a rate of 18 (half that if ascending, twice that if descending in a dive). The maneuverability class of the creature is B. Using the *fly* spell requires as much concentration as walking, so most spells can be cast while hovering or moving slowly (movement of 3). Possible combat penalties while flying are known to the DM (in the "Aerial Combat" section of the *DMG*). The exact duration of the spell is always unknown to the spellcaster, as the variable addition is determined secretly by the DM.

The material component of the *fly* spell is a wing feather of any bird.

Gust of Wind (Alteration)

Range: 0
Components: V, S, M
Duration: 1 round
Casting Time: 3
Area of Effect: 10-foot wide path, 10 yards/level long
Saving Throw: None

When this spell is cast, a strong puff of air originates from the wizard and moves in the direction he is facing. The force of this gust of wind (about 30 m.p.h) is sufficient to extinguish candles, torches, and similar unprotected flames. It causes protected flames—such as those of lanterns—to dance wildly and has a 5% chance per level of experience of the spellcaster to extinguish even such lights. It also fans large fires outward 1d6 feet in the direction of the wind's movement. It forces back small flying creatures 1d6 × 10 yards and causes man-sized beings to be held motionless if attempting to move against its force. It slows larger-than-man-sized flying creatures by 50% for one round. It blows over light objects, disperses most vapors, and forces away gaseous or unsecured levitating creatures. Its path is 10 feet wide by 10 yards long per level of experience of the caster (e.g., an 8th-level wizard causes a gust of wind that travels 80 yards).

The material component of the spell is a legume seed.

Haste (Alteration)

Range: 60 yards
Components: V, S, M
Duration: 3 rounds + 1 round/level
Casting Time: 3
Area of Effect: 40′ cube, 1 creature/level
Saving Throw: None

When this spell is cast, each affected creature functions at double its normal movement and attack rates. A hasted creature gains a −2 initiative bonus. Thus, a creature moving at 6 and attacking once per round would move at 12 and attack twice per round. Spellcasting and spell effects are *not* sped up. The number of creatures that can be affected is equal to the caster's experience level; those creatures closest to the center of effect are affected first. All affected by haste must be in the designated area of effect. Note that this spell negates the effects of a *slow* spell. Additionally, this spell ages the recipient by one year, because of sped-up metabolic processes. This spell is not cumulative with itself or with other similar magic.

Its material component is a shaving of licorice root.

Hold Person (Enchantment/Charm)

Range: 120 yards
Components: V, S, M
Duration: 2 rounds/level
Casting Time: 3
Area of Effect: 1 to 4 persons in a
20-foot cube
Saving Throw: Neg.

This spell holds 1d4 humans, demihumans, or humanoid creatures rigidly immobile for five or more rounds.

The *hold person* spell affects any bipedal human, demihuman or humanoid of man-size or smaller, including brownies, dryads, dwarves, elves, gnolls, gnomes, goblins, half-elves, halflings, half-orcs, hobgoblins, humans, kobolds, lizard men, nixies, orcs, pixies, sprites, troglodytes, and others.

The spell is centered on a point selected by the caster; it affects persons selected by the caster within the area of effect. If the spell is cast at three or four people, each gets an unmodified saving throw. If only two people are being enspelled, each makes his saving throw with a −1 penalty. If the spell is cast at only one person, the saving throw suffers a −3 penalty. Saving throws are adjusted for Wisdom. Those succeeding on their saving throws are unaffected by the spell. Undead creatures cannot be held.

Held beings cannot move or speak, but they remain aware of events around them and can use abilities not requiring motion or speech. Being held does not prevent the worsening of the subjects' condition due to wounds, disease, or poison. The caster can end the spell with a single utterance at any time; otherwise the duration is 10 rounds at 5th level, 12 rounds at 6th level, 14 rounds at 7th level, etc.

The spellcaster needs a small, straight piece of iron as the material component of this spell.

Hold Undead (Necromancy)

Range: 60'
Components: V, S, M
Duration: 1d4 rounds +1 round/level
Casting Time: 5
Area of Effect: 1d3 undead
Saving Throw: Neg.

When cast, this spell renders immobile 1d3 undead creatures whose total Hit Dice are equal to or less than the caster's level. No more than three undead can be affected by a single spell. To cast, the wizard aims the spell at a point within range and the three undead closest to this are considered to be in the area of effect, provided all are within the field of vision and spell range of the caster. Undead of a mindless nature (skeletons, zombies, or ghouls) are automatically affected. Other forms of undead are allowed a saving throw to negate the effect. If the spell is successful, it renders the undead immobile for the duration of the spell.

The material component for this spell is a pinch of sulphur and powdered garlic.

Illusionary Script (Illusion/Phantasm)

Range: Touch
Components: V, S, M
Duration: 1 day/level
Casting Time: Special
Area of Effect: Creature reading the script
Saving Throw: Special

This spell enables the wizard to write instructions or other information on parchment, paper, etc. The illusionary script appears to be some form of foreign or magical writing. Only the person (or people) who the wizard desires to read the writing can do so. An illusionist recognizes it for illusionary script.

Unauthorized creatures glancing at the script must roll saving throws vs. spell. A successful save means the creature can look away with only a mild sense of disorientation. Failure means the creature is subject to a suggestion implanted in the script by the caster at the time the illusionary script was cast. The suggestion cannot require more than three turns to carry out. The suggestion could be to close the book and leave, or to forget the existence of the book, for example. A successful *dispel magic* spell will remove the illusionary script, but an unsuccessful attempt erases all of the writing. The hidden writings can be read by a combination of the *true seeing* spell and either the *read magic* or *comprehend languages* spell, as applicable.

The material component is a lead-based ink that requires special manufacture by an alchemist, at a cost of not less than 300 gp per usage.

Infravision (Alteration)

Range: Touch
Components: V, S, M
Duration: 2 hours + 1 hour/level
Casting Time: 1 round
Area of Effect: Creature touched
Saving Throw: None

By means of this spell, the wizard enables the recipient to see in normal darkness up to 60 feet without light. Note that strong sources of light (fire, lanterns, torches, etc.) tend to blind this vision, so infravision does not function efficiently in the presence of such light sources. Invisible creatures are not detectable by infravision.

The material component of this spell is either a pinch of dried carrot or an agate.

Invisibility, 10' Radius (Illusion/Phantasm)

Range: Touch
Components: V, S, M
Duration: Special
Casting Time: 3
Area of Effect: 10-foot radius of
creature touched
Saving Throw: None

This spell confers invisibility upon all creatures within 10 feet of the recipient. Gear carried and light sources are included, but any light emitted is still visible. The center of the effect is mobile with the recipient. Those affected by this spell cannot see each other. Any affected creature moving out of the area becomes visible, but creatures moving into the area after the spell is cast do not become invisible. Affected creatures (other than the recipient) that attack negate the invisibility only for themselves. If the spell recipient attacks, the *invisibility, 10' radius* spell is broken for all.

The material components are the same as for the *invisibility* spell.

Item (Alteration)

Range: Touch
Components: V, S, M
Duration: 4 hours/level
Casting Time: 3
Area of Effect: 2 cu. ft./level
Saving Throw: Special

By means of this spell, the wizard is able to shrink one nonmagical item (if it is within the size limit) to 1/12 of its normal size. Optionally, the caster can also change its now-shrunken composition to a cloth-like one. An object in the possession of another creature is allowed a saving throw vs. spell. Objects changed by an *item* spell can be returned to normal composition and size merely by tossing them onto any solid surface or by a word of command from the original spellcaster. Note that even a burning fire and its fuel can be shrunk by this spell.

Leomund's Tiny Hut (Alteration)

Range: 0
Components: V, S, M
Duration: 4 hours + 1 hour/level
Casting Time: 3
Area of Effect: 15-foot-diameter sphere
Saving Throw: None

When this spell is cast, the wizard creates an unmoving, opaque sphere of force of any desired color around his person. Half of the sphere projects above the ground, and the lower hemisphere passes through the ground. Up to seven other man-sized creatures can fit into the field with its creator, and these can freely pass into and out of the hut without harming it, but if the spellcaster removes himself from it, the spell dissipates.

The temperature inside the hut is 70° F, if the exterior temperature is between 0° and 100° F. An exterior temperature below 0° or above 100° lowers or raises, respectively, the interior temperature on a 1°-for-1° basis. The tiny hut also provides protection against the elements, such as rain, dust, sandstorms, and the like. The hut can withstand any wind of less than hurricane force without being harmed, but wind force greater than that destroys it.

The interior of the hut is a hemisphere; the spellcaster can illuminate it dimly upon command, or extinguish the light as desired. Note that although the force field is opaque from the outside, it is transparent from within. Missiles, weapons, and most spell effects can pass through the hut without affecting it, although the occupants cannot be seen from outside the hut. The hut can be dispelled.

The material component for this spell is a small crystal bead that shatters when the spell duration expires or the hut is dispelled.

Lightning Bolt (Evocation)

Range: 40 yards + 10 yards/level
Components: V, S, M
Duration: Instantaneous
Casting Time: 3
Area of Effect: Special
Saving Throw: ½

Upon casting this spell, the wizard releases a powerful stroke of electrical energy that inflicts 1d6 points of damage per level of the spellcaster (maximum damage of 10d6) to each creature within its area of effect. A successful saving throw vs. spell reduces this damage to half (round fractions down). The bolt begins at a range and height decided by the caster and streaks outward in a direct line from the casting wizard (e.g., if a 40-foot bolt was started at 180 feet from the wizard, the far end of bolt would reach 220 feet (180 + 40). The lightning bolt may set fire to combustibles, sunder wooden doors, splinter up to ½ foot thickness of stone, and melt metals with a low melting point (lead, gold, copper, silver, bronze). Saving throws must be rolled for objects that withstand the full force of a stroke (see the *fireball* spell). If the damage caused to an interposing barrier shatters or breaks through it (i.e., the saving throw fails), the bolt continues. A bolt can breach one inch of wood or ½ inch of stone per caster level up to a maximum of one foot of wood or ½ foot of stone.

The lightning bolt's area of effect is chosen by the spellcaster: either a forked bolt 10 feet wide and 40 feet long or a single bolt five feet wide and 80 feet long. If a bolt cannot reach its full length, because of an unyielding barrier (such as a stone wall), the lightning bolt rebounds from the barrier toward its caster, ending only when it reaches its full length.

Example: An 80-foot-long stroke is begun at a range of 40 feet, but it hits a stone wall at 50 feet. The bolt travels 10 feet, hits the wall, and rebounds for 70 feet back toward its creator (who is only 50 feet from the wall, and so is caught in his own lightning bolt!).

The DM might allow reflecting bolts. When this type of lightning bolt strikes a solid surface, the bolt reflects from the surface at an angle equal to the angle of incidence (like light off a mirror). A creature crossed more than once by the bolt must roll a saving throw for every time it is crossed, but it still suffers either full damage (if one saving throw is missed) or half damage (if all saving throws are made).

The material components of the spell are a bit of fur and an amber, crystal, or glass rod.

Melf's Minute Meteors (Evocation, Alteration)

Range: 70 yards + 10 yards/level
Components: V, S, M
Duration: Special
Casting Time: 3
Area of Effect: 1 target per meteor
Saving Throw: None

This spell enables the wizard to cast small globes of fire (one for each experience level he has attained), each of which bursts into a one-foot-diameter sphere upon impact, inflicting 1d4 points of damage to the creature struck. It can also ignite combustible materials (even solid planks). The meteors are treated as missiles hurled by the wizard with a +2 bonus to the attack rolls and with no penalty for range. Misses are treated as grenade-like missiles that inflict 1 point of damage to creatures within three feet.

The spell can be cast in either of two ways:

A) The wizard discharges five meteors every round (see the "Multiple Attacks and Initiative" section, page 95). Note that this carries over into at least the following round.

B) The wizard discharges only one meteor per round. In addition to releasing the missile, the caster can perform other actions in the round, including spellcasting, melee, or device use. Spells requiring concentration force the wizard to forgo the rest of the missiles to maintain concentration. Also, if the wizard fails to maintain an exact mental count of the number of missiles he has remaining, he has involuntarily lost the remaining portion of the spell.

The spell ends when the caster has fired off as many meteors as he has experience levels, when he forgoes casting any still remaining, or when a successful *dispel magic* spell is thrown upon the caster.

The components necessary for the casting of this spell are nitre and sulphur formed into a bead by the addition of pine tar. The caster must also have a small hollow tube of minute proportion, fashioned from gold. The tube costs no less than 1,000 gp to construct, so fine is its workmanship and magical engraving, and it can be reused.

Monster Summoning I (Conjuration/Summoning)

Range: 30 yards
Components: V, S, M
Duration: 2 rounds + 1 round/level
Casting Time: 3
Area of Effect: Special
Saving Throw: None

Within one round of casting this spell, the wizard magically conjures 2d4 1st-level monsters (selected by the DM, from his 1st-level encounter tables). The monsters appear in an area within the spell range, as desired by the wizard. They attack the spell user's opponents to the best of their ability until either he commands that the attacks cease, the spell duration expires, or the monsters are slain. These creatures do not check morale, but they vanish when slain. Note that if no opponent exists to fight, summoned monsters can, if the wizard can communicate with them and if they are physically able, perform other services for the summoning wizard.

In rare cases, adventurers have been known to disappear, summoned by powerful spellcasters using this spell. Those summoned recall all the details of their trip.

The material components of this spell are a tiny bag and a small (not necessarily lit) candle.

Non-Detection (Abjuration)

Range: Touch
Components: V, S, M
Duration: 1 hour/level
Casting Time: 3
Area of Effect: 1 creature or item
Saving Throw: None

By casting this spell, the wizard makes the creature or object touched undetectable by divination spells such as *clairaudience*, *clairvoyance*, *locate object*, *ESP*, and detect spells. It also prevents location by such magical items as *crystal balls* and *ESP medallions*. It does not affect the *know alignment* spell or the ability of intelligent or high-level beings to detect invisible creatures. If a divination is attempted, the *non-detection* caster must roll a saving throw vs. spell. If this is successful, the divination fails.

The material component of the spell is a pinch of diamond dust worth 300 gp.

Phantom Steed (Conjuration, Phantasm)

Range: Touch
Components: V, S
Duration: 1 hour/level
Casting Time: 1 turn
Area of Effect: Special
Saving Throw: None

When this spell is cast, the wizard creates a quasi-real, horse-like creature. The steed can be ridden only by the wizard who created it, or by any person for whom the wizard specifically creates such a mount. A phantom steed has a black head and body, gray mane and tail, and smoke-colored, insubstantial hooves that make no sound. Its eyes are milky-colored. It does not fight, but all normal animals shun it and only monstrous ones will attack. The mount has an Armor Class of 2 and 7 hit points, plus 1 per level of the caster. If it loses all of its hit points, the phantom steed disappears. A phantom steed moves at a movement rate of 4 per level of the spellcaster, to a maximum movement rate of 48. It has what seems to be a saddle and a bit and bridle. It can bear its rider's weight, plus up to 10 pounds per caster level.

These mounts gain certain powers according to the level of the wizard who created them:

8th Level: The ability to pass over sandy, muddy, or even swampy ground without difficulty.

10th Level: The ability to pass over water as if it were firm, dry ground.

12th Level: The ability to travel in the air as if it were firm land, so chasms and the like can be crossed without benefit of a bridge. Note, however, that the mount cannot casually take off and fly; the movement must be between points of similar altitude.

14th Level: The ability to perform as if it were a pegasus; it flies at a rate of 48 per round upon command.

Note that a mount's abilities include those of lower levels; thus a 12th-level mount has the 8th-, 10th-, and 12th-level abilities.

Protection From Evil, 10' Radius (Abjuration)
Reversible

Range: Touch
Components: V, S, M
Duration: 2 rounds/level
Casting Time: 3
Area of Effect: 10-foot-radius sphere around creature touched
Saving Throw: None

The globe of protection of this spell is identical in all respects to a *protection from evil* spell, except that it encompasses a much larger area and its duration is greater. The effect is centered on and moves with the creature touched. Any protected creature within the circle can break the warding against enchanted or summoned monsters by meleeing them. If a creature too large to fit into the area of effect is the recipient of the spell, the spell acts as a normal *protection from evil* spell for that creature only.

To complete this spell, the caster must trace a circle 20 feet in diameter using powdered silver. The material component for the reverse is powdered iron.

Protection From Normal Missiles (Abjuration)

Range: Touch
Components: V, S, M
Duration: 1 turn/level
Casting Time: 3
Area of Effect: Creature touched
Saving Throw: None

By means of this spell, the wizard bestows total invulnerability to hurled and projected missiles such as arrows, axes, bolts, javelins, small stones, and spears. Furthermore, it causes a reduction of 1 from each die of damage (but no die inflicts less than 1 point of damage) inflicted by large or magical missiles, such as ballista missiles, catapult stones, hurled boulders, and magical arrows, bolts, javelins, etc. Note, however, that this spell does not convey any protection from such magical attacks as fireballs, lightning bolts, or magic missiles.

The material component of this spell is a piece of tortoise or turtle shell.

Secret Page (Alteration)

Range: Touch
Components: V, S, M
Duration: Until dispelled
Casting Time: 1 turn
Area of Effect: 1 page of any size, up to 2 ft. square
Saving Throw: None

When cast, a *secret page* spell alters the actual contents of a page so that they appear to be something entirely different. Thus a map can be changed to become a treatise on burnishing ebony walking sticks. The text of a spell can be altered to show a ledger page or even another form of spell. *Confuse languages* and *explosive runes* spells may be cast upon the secret page, but a *comprehend languages* spell cannot reveal the secret page's contents. The caster is able to reveal the original contents by speaking a command word, perusing the actual page, and then returning it to its secret page form. The caster can also remove the spell by double repetition of the command word. Others noting the dim magic of a page with this spell cloaking its true contents can attempt to dispel magic, but if it fails, the page is destroyed. A *true seeing* spell does not reveal the contents unless cast in combination with a *comprehend languages* spell. An *erase* spell can destroy the writing.

The material components are powdered herring scales and either will o' wisp or boggart essence.

Sepia Snake Sigil (Conjuration/Summoning)

Range: 5 yards
Components: V, S, M
Duration: Special
Casting Time: 3
Area of Effect: 1 sigil
Saving Throw: None

When this spell is cast, a small written symbol appears in the text of any written work. When read, the so-called sepia snake springs into being and strikes at the nearest living creature (but does not attack the wizard who cast the spell). Its attack is made as if it were a monster with Hit Dice equal to the level of the wizard who cast the spell. If it strikes successfully, the victim is engulfed in a shimmering amber field of force, frozen and immobilized until released, either at the caster's command, by a successful *dispel magic* spell, or until a time equal to 1d4 days + 1 day per caster level has elapsed. Until then, nothing can get at the victim, move the shimmering force surrounding him, or otherwise affect him. The victim does not age, grow hungry, sleep, or regain spells while in this state. He is not aware of his surroundings.

If the sepia snake misses its target, it dissipates in a flash of brown light, with a loud noise and a puff of dun-colored smoke that is 10 feet in diameter and lasts for one round.

The spell cannot be detected by normal observation, and *detect magic* reveals only that the entire text is magical. A *dispel magic* can remove it; an *erase* spell destroys the entire page of text. It can be cast in combination with other spells that hide or garble text.

The components for the spell are 100 gp worth of powdered amber, a scale from any snake, and a pinch of mushroom spores.

Slow (Alteration)

Range: 90 yards + 10 yards/level
Components: V, S, M
Duration: 3 rounds + 1 round/level
Casting Time: 3
Area of Effect: 40' cube, 1 creature/level
Saving Throw: Neg.

A *slow* spell causes affected creatures to move and attack at ½ of their normal rates. It negates a *haste* spell or equivalent, but does not otherwise affect magically speeded or slowed creatures. Slowed creatures have an Armor Class penalty of +4 AC, an attack penalty of −4, and all Dexterity combat bonuses are negated. The magic affects a number of creatures equal to the spellcaster's level, if they are within the area of effect chosen by the wizard (i.e., a 40-foot cubic volume centered as called for by the caster). The creatures are affected from the center of the spell outward. Saving throws against the spell suffer a −4 penalty.

The material component of this spell is a drop of molasses.

Spectral Force (Illusion/Phantasm)

Range: 60 yards + 1 yard/level
Components: V, S
Duration: Special
Casting Time: 3
Area of Effect: 40' cube + a 10' cube/level
Saving Throw: Special

The *spectral force* spell creates an illusion in which sound, smell, and thermal illusions are included. It is otherwise similar to the *improved phantasmal force* spell. The spell last for three rounds after concentration ceases.

Suggestion (Enchantment/Charm)

Range: 30 yards
Components: V, M
Duration: 1 hour + 1 hour/level
Casting Time: 3
Area of Effect: 1 creature
Saving Throw: Neg.

When this spell is cast by the wizard, he influences the actions of the chosen recipient by the utterance of a few words—phrases or a sentence or two—suggesting a course of action desirable to the spellcaster. The creature to be influenced must, of course, be able to understand the wizard's suggestion—it must be spoken in a language that the spell recipient understands.

The suggestion must be worded in such a manner as to make the action sound reasonable; asking the creature to stab itself, throw itself onto a spear, immolate itself, or do some other obviously harmful act automatically negates the effect of the spell. However, a suggestion that a pool of acid was actually pure water and that a quick dip would be refreshing is another matter. Urging a red dragon to stop attacking the wizard's party so that the dragon and party could jointly loot a rich treasure elsewhere is likewise a reasonable use of the spell's power.

The course of action of a suggestion can continue in effect for a considerable duration, such as in the case of the red dragon mentioned above. Conditions that will trigger a special action can also be specified; if the condition is not met before the spell expires, then the action will not be performed. If the target successfully rolls its saving throw, the spell has no effect. Note that a very reasonable suggestion causes the saving throw to be made with a penalty (such as −1, −2, etc.) at the discretion of the Dungeon Master. Undead are not subject to suggestion.

The material components of this spell are a snake's tongue and either a bit of honeycomb or a drop of sweet oil.

Tongues (Alteration)
Reversible

Range: 0
Components: V, M
Duration: 1 round/level
Casting Time: 3
Area of Effect: 30-foot radius
Saving Throw: None

This spell enables the wizard to speak and understand additional languages, whether they are racial tongues or regional dialects. This does not enable the caster to speak with animals. The spell enables the caster to be understood by all creatures of that type within hearing distance, usually 60 feet.

This spell does not predispose the subject toward the caster in any way.

The wizard can speak one additional tongue for every three levels of experience. The reverse of the spell cancels the effect of the *tongues* spell or confuses verbal communication of any sort within the area of effect.

The material component is a small clay model of a ziggurat, which shatters when the spell is pronounced.

Vampiric Touch (Necromancy)

Range: 0
Components: V, S
Duration: One touch
Casting Time: 3
Area of Effect: The caster
Saving Throw: None

When the caster touches an opponent in melee with a successful attack roll, the opponent loses 1d6 hit points for every two caster levels, to a maximum drain of 6d6 for a 12th-level caster. The spell is expended when a successful touch is made or one turn passes. The hit points are added to the caster's total, with any hit points over the caster's normal total treated as temporary additional hit points. Any damage to the caster is subtracted from the temporary hit points first. After one hour, any extra hit points above the caster's normal total are lost. The creature originally losing hit points through this spell can regain them by magical or normal healing. Undead creatures are unaffected by this spell.

Water Breathing (Alteration)
Reversible

Range: Touch
Components: V, S, M
Duration: 1 hour/level + 1d4 hours
Casting Time: 3
Area of Effect: Creature touched
Saving Throw: None

The recipient of a *water breathing* spell is able to breathe water freely for the duration of the spell. The caster can touch more than one creature with a single casting; in this case the duration is divided by the number of creatures touched. The reverse, *air breathing*, enables water-breathing creatures to comfortably survive in the atmosphere for an equal duration.

The material component of the spell is a short reed or piece of straw.

Wind Wall (Alteration)

Range: 10 yards/level
Components: V, S, M
Duration: 1 round/level
Casting Time: 3
Area of Effect: A 10' wide × 5' high area per caster level
Saving Throw: Special

This spell brings forth an invisible vertical curtain of wind two feet thick and of considerable strength—a strong breeze sufficient to blow away any bird smaller than an eagle or to tear papers and like materials from unsuspecting hands. (If in doubt, a saving throw vs. spell determines whether the subject maintains its grasp.) Normal insects cannot pass such a barrier. Loose materials, even cloth garments, fly upward when caught in a wind wall. Arrows and bolts are deflected upward and miss, while sling stones and other missiles under two pounds in weight receive a −4 penalty to a first shot and −2 penalties thereafter. Gases, most breath weapons, and creatures in gaseous form cannot pass this wall, although it is no barrier to noncorporeal creatures.

The material components are a tiny fan and a feather of exotic origin.

Wraithform (Alteration, Illusion)

Range: 0
Components: S, M
Duration: 2 rounds/level
Casting Time: 1
Area of Effect: The caster
Saving Throw: None

When this spell is cast, the wizard and all of his gear become insubstantial. The caster is subject only to magical or special attacks, including those by weapons of +1 or better, or by creatures otherwise able to affect those struck only by magical weapons. Undead of most sorts will ignore an individual in wraithform, believing him to be a wraith or spectre, though a lich or special undead may save vs. spell with a −4 penalty to recognize the spell.

The wizard can pass through small holes or narrow openings, even mere cracks, with all he wears or holds in his hands, as long as the spell persists. Note, however, that the the caster cannot fly without additional magic. No form of attack is possible when in wraithform, except against creatures that exist on the Ethereal plane, where all attacks (both ways) are normal. A successful *dispel magic* spell forces the wizard in wraithform back to normal form. The spellcaster can end the spell with a single word.

The material components for the spell are a bit of gauze and a wisp of smoke.

Fourth-Level Spells

Charm Monster (Enchantment/Charm)

Range: 60 yards
Components: V, S
Duration: Special
Casting Time: 4
Area of Effect: 1 or more creatures in a 20-foot radius
Saving Throw: Neg.

This spell is similar to a *charm person* spell, but it can affect any living creature—or several low-level creatures. The spell affects 2d4 Hit Dice or levels of creatures, although it only affects one creature of 4 or more Hit Dice or levels, regardless of the number rolled.

All possible subjects receive saving throws vs. spell, adjusted for Wisdom. Any damage inflicted by the caster or his allies in the round of casting grants the wounded creature another saving throw at a bonus of +1 per point of damage received. Any affected creature regards the spellcaster as friendly, an ally or companion to be treated well or guarded from harm. If communication is possible, the charmed creature follows reasonable requests, instructions, or orders most faithfully (see the *suggestion* spell). If communication is not possible, the creature does not harm the caster, but others in the vicinity may be subject to its intentions, hostile or otherwise. Any overtly hostile act by the caster breaks the spell, or at the very least allows a new saving throw against the charm. Affected creatures eventually come out from under the influence of the spell. This is a function of the creature's level (i.e., its Hit Dice).

Monster Level or Hit Dice	Percent Chance/ Week of Breaking Spell
1st or up to 2	5%
2nd or up to 3 + 2	10%
3rd or up to 4 + 4	15%
4th or up to 6	25%
5th or up to 7 + 2	35%
6th or up to 8 +4	45%
7th or up to 10	60%
8th or up to 12	75%
9th or over 12	90%

The exact day of the week and time of day is secretly determined.

Confusion (Enchantment/Charm)

Range: 120 yards
Components: V, S, M
Duration: 2 rounds + 1 round/level
Casting Time: 4
Area of Effect: Up to 60-foot cube
Saving Throw: Special

This spell causes confusion in one or more creatures within the area, creating indecision and the inability to take effective action. The spell affects 1d4 creatures, plus one creature per caster level. These creatures are allowed saving throws vs. spell with −2 penalties, adjusted for Wisdom. Those successfully saving are unaffected by the spell. Confused creatures react as follows (roll 1d10):

1	Wander away (unless prevented) for duration of spell
2-6	Stand confused one round (then roll again)
7-9	Attack nearest creature for one round (then roll again)
10	Act normally for one round (then roll again)

The spell lasts for two rounds plus one round for each level of the caster. Those who fail are checked by the DM for actions each round for the duration of the spell, or until the "wander away for the duration of the spell" result occurs.

Wandering creatures move as far from the caster as possible, according to their most typical mode of movement (characters walk, fish swim, bats fly, etc.). Saving throws and actions are checked at the beginning of each round. Any confused creature that is attacked perceives the attacker as an enemy and acts according to its basic nature.

If there are many creatures involved, the DM may decide to assume average results. For example, if there are 16 orcs affected and 25% could be expected to make the saving throw, then four are assumed to have succeeded. Out of the other 12, one wanders away, four attack the nearest creature, six stand confused, and the last acts normally but must check next round. Since the orcs are not near the party, the DM decides that two attacking the nearest creature attack each other, one attacks an orc that saved, and one attacks a confused orc, which strikes back. The next round, the base is 11 orcs, since four originally saved and one wandered off. Another one wanders off, five stand confused, four attack, and one acts normally.

The material component is a set of three nut shells.

Contagion (Necromancy)

Range: 30 yards
Components: V, S
Duration: Permanent
Casting Time: 4
Area of Effect: 1 creature
Saving Throw: Neg.

This spell causes a major disease and weakness in a creature. The afflicted individual is immediately stricken with painful and distracting symptoms: boils, blotches, lesions, seeping abscesses, and so on. Strength, Dexterity, and Charisma are reduced by 2. Attack rolls are decreased by 2. The effect persists until the character receives a *cure disease* spell or spends 1d3 weeks taking a complete rest to recover. Characters ignoring the contagion for more than a day or so may be susceptible to worse diseases at the discretion of the DM.

Detect Scrying (Divination)

Range: 0
Components: V, S, M
Duration: 1d6 turns + 1 turn/level
Casting Time: 3
Area of Effect: 120-foot radius
Saving Throw: Special

By means of this spell, the wizard immediately becomes aware of any attempt to observe him by means of clairvoyance, clairaudience, or magic mirror. This also reveals the use of crystal balls or other magical scrying devices, provided the attempt is within the area of effect of the spell. Since the spell is centered on the spellcaster, it moves with him, enabling him to "sweep" areas for the duration of the spell.

When a scrying attempt is detected, the scryer must immediately roll a saving throw. If this is failed, the identity and general location of the scryer immediately become known to the wizard who cast this spell. The general location is a direction and significant landmark close to the scryer. Thus, the caster might learn, "The wizard Sniggel spies on us from east, under the stairs," or, "You are watched by Asquil in the city of Samarquol."

The material components for this spell are a small piece of mirror and a miniature brass hearing trumpet.

Dig (Evocation)

Range: 30 yards
Components: V, S, M
Duration: 1 round/level
Casting Time: 4
Area of Effect: 5-foot cube/level
Saving Throw: Special

A *dig* spell enables the caster to excavate 125 cubic feet of earth, sand, or mud per round (i.e., a cubic hole five feet on a side). In later rounds the caster can expand an existing hole or start a new one. The material thrown from the excavation scatters evenly around the pit. If the wizard continues downward past 20 feet in earth, there is a 15% chance that the pit collapses. This check is made for every five feet dug beyond 20 feet. Sand tends to collapse after 10 feet, mud fills in and collapses after five feet, and quicksand fills in as rapidly as it is dug.

Any creature at the edge (within one foot) of a pit must roll a successful Dexterity check or fall into the hole. Creatures moving rapidly toward a pit dug immediately before them must roll a saving throw vs. spell to avoid falling in. Any creature in a pit being excavated can climb out at a rate decided by the DM. A creature caught in a collapsing pit must roll a saving throw vs. death to avoid being buried; it escapes the pit if successful. Tunneling is possible with this spell as long as there is space available

for the material removed. Chances for collapse are doubled and safe tunneling distance is half of the safe excavation depth unless such construction is most carefully braced and supported.

The spell is also effective against creatures of earth and rock, particularly clay golems and those from the elemental plane of Earth. When cast upon such a creature, it suffers 4d6 points of damage. A successful saving throw vs. spell reduces this damage to half.

To activate the spell, the spellcaster needs a miniature shovel and tiny bucket and must continue to hold them while each pit is excavated. These items disappear at the conclusion of the spell.

Dimension Door (Alteration)

Range: 0
Components: V
Duration: Instantaneous
Casting Time: 1
Area of Effect: The caster
Saving Throw: None

By means of a *dimension door* spell, the wizard instantly transfers himself up to 30 yards distance per level of experience. This special form of teleportation allows for no error, and the wizard always arrives at exactly the spot desired—whether by simply visualizing the area (within spell transfer distance, of course) or by stating direction such as, "300 yards straight downward," or, "upward to the northwest, 45 degree angle, 420 yards." If the wizard arrives in a place that is already occupied by a solid body, he remains trapped in the Astral plane. If distances are stated and the spellcaster arrives with no support below his feet (i.e., in midair), falling and damage result unless further magical means are employed. All that the wizard wears or carries, subject to a maximum weight equal to 500 pounds of nonliving matter, or half that amount of living matter, is transferred with the spellcaster. Recovery from use of a *dimension door* spell requires one round.

Emotion (Enchantment/Charm)

Range: 10 yards/level
Components: V, S
Duration: Special
Casting Time: 4
Area of Effect: 20-foot cube
Saving Throw: Neg.

When this spell is cast, the wizard can create a single emotional reaction in the subject creatures. The following are typical:

1. *Courage:* This emotion causes the creatures affected to become berserk, fighting with a +1 bonus to the attack dice, causing +3 points of damage, and temporarily gaining 5 hit points. The recipients fight without shield, and regardless of life, never

checking morale. This spell counters (and is countered by) *fear*.

2. *Fear*: The affected creatures flee in panic for 2d4 rounds. It counters (and is countered by) *courage*.

3. *Friendship*: The affected creatures react more positively (e.g., tolerance becomes goodwill). It counters (and is countered by) *hate*.

4. *Happiness*: This effect creates joy and a feeling of complacent well-being, adding +4 to all reaction rolls and making attack unlikely unless the creatures are subject to extreme provocation. It counters (and is countered by) *sadness*.

5. *Hate*: The affected creatures react more negatively (e.g., tolerance becomes negative neutrality). It counters (and is countered by) *friendship*.

6. *Hope*: The effect of hope is to raise morale, saving throw rolls, attack rolls, and damage caused by +2. It counters (and is countered by) *hopelessness*.

7. *Hopelessness*: The affected creatures submit to the demands of any opponent: surrender, get out, etc. Otherwise, the creatures are 25% likely to do nothing in a round, and 25% likely to turn back or retreat. It counters (and is countered by) *hope*.

8. *Sadness*: This creates unhappiness and a tendency toward maudlin introspection. This emotion increases chances of being surprised by −1 and adds +1 to initiative rolls. It counters (and is countered by) *happiness*.

All creatures in the area at the instant the spell is cast are affected unless successful saving throws vs. spell are made, adjusted for Wisdom. The spell lasts as long as the wizard continues to concentrate on projecting the chosen emotion. Those who fail the saving throw against *fear* must roll a new saving throw if they return to the affected area.

Enchanted Weapon (Enchantment)

Range: Touch
Components: V, S, M
Duration: 5 rounds/level
Casting Time: 1 turn
Area of Effect: Weapon(s) touched
Saving Throw: None

This spell turns an ordinary weapon into a magical one. The weapon is the equivalent of a +1 weapon, with +1 to attack and damage rolls. Thus arrows, axes, bolts, bows, daggers, hammers, maces, spears, swords, etc., can be made into temporarily enchanted weapons. Two small (arrows, bolts, daggers, etc.) or one large (axe, bow, hammer, mace, etc.) weapon can be affected by the spell. The spell functions on existing magical weapons as long as the total combined bonus is +3 or less.

Missile weapons enchanted in this way lose their enchantment when they successfully hit a target, but otherwise the spell lasts its full duration. This spell is often used in combination with the *enchant an item* and *permanency* spells to create magical weapons, with this spell being cast once per desired plus of the bonus.

The material components of this spell are powdered lime and carbon.

Enervation (Necromancy)

Range: 10 yards/level
Components: V, S
Duration: 1d4 hours + 1 hour/level
Casting Time: 4
Area of Effect: 1 creature
Saving Throw: Neg.

This spell temporarily suppresses the subject's life force. The necromancer points his finger and utters the incantation, releasing a black bolt of crackling energy. The subject must roll a saving throw vs. spell, adjusted for Dexterity, to avoid the bolt. Success means the spell has no effect. Failure means the subject is treated exactly as if he had been drained of energy levels by a wight, one level for every four levels of the caster. Hit Dice, spells, and other character details dependent on level are lost or reduced. Those drained to 0th level must make a system shock check to survive and are helpless until the spell expires. The spell effect eventually wears off, either after 1d4 hours plus one hour per caster level, or after six hours of complete and undisturbed rest. Level abilities are regained, but lost spells must be rememorized. Undead are immune to this spell.

Evard's Black Tentacles (Conjuration/Summoning)

Range: 30 yards
Components: V, S, M
Duration: 1 hour/level
Casting Time: 1 round
Area of Effect: 30 sq. ft./level
Saving Throw: None

This spell creates many rubbery, black tentacles in the area of effect. These waving members seem to spring forth from the earth, floor, or whatever surface is underfoot—including water. Each tentacle is 10 feet long, AC 4, and requires as many points of damage to destroy as the level of the wizard who cast the spell. There are 1d4 such tentacles, plus one per experience level of the spellcaster.

Any creature within range of the writhing tentacles is subject to attack as determined by the DM. The target of a tentacle attack must roll a saving throw vs. spell. If this succeeds, the subject suffers 1d4 points of damage from

contact with the tentacle, and then the tentacle is destroyed. Failure to save indicates that the damage inflicted is 2d4 points, the ebon member is wrapped around its subject, and damage will be 3d4 points on the second and succeeding rounds. Since these tentacles have no intelligence to guide them, there is the possibility that they entwine any object—a tree, post, pillar, even the wizard himself—or continue to squeeze a dead opponent. A grasping hold established by a tentacle remains until the tentacle is destroyed by some form of attack or until it disappears at the end of the spell's duration.

The component for this spell is a piece of tentacle from a giant octopus or giant squid.

Extension I (Alteration)

Range: 0
Components: V
Duration: Special
Casting Time: 2
Area of Effect: Special
Saving Throw: None

By use of an *extension I* spell, the wizard prolongs the duration of a previously cast 1st-, 2nd-, or 3rd-level spell by 50%. Thus, a *levitation* spell can be made to function 15 minutes/level, a *hold person* spell made to work for three rounds/level, etc. Naturally, the spell affects only spells that have durations. This spell must be cast immediately after the spell to be extended, either by the original caster or another wizard. If a complete round or more elapses, the extension fails and is wasted.

Fear (Illusion/Phantasm)

Range: 0
Components: V, S, M
Duration: Special
Casting Time: 4
Area of Effect: 60' long cone, 30' diameter
                  at end, 5' at base
Saving Throw: Neg.

When a *fear* spell is cast, the wizard sends forth an invisible cone of terror that causes creatures within its area of effect to turn away from the caster and flee in panic. Affected creatures are likely to drop whatever they are holding when struck by the spell; the base chance of this is 60% at 1st level (or at 1 Hit Die), and each level (or Hit Die) above this reduces the probability by 5%. Thus at 10th level there is only a 15% chance, and at 13th level no chance, of dropping items. Creatures affected by fear flee at their fastest rate for a number of melee rounds equal to the level of experience of the spellcaster. Undead and creatures that successfully roll their saving throws vs. the spell are not affected.

The material component of this spell is either the heart of a hen or a white feather.

Fire Charm (Enchantment/Charm)

Range: 10 yards
Components: V, S, M
Duration: 2 rounds/level
Casting Time: 4
Area of Effect: 15-foot radius of fire
Saving Throw: Neg.

By means of this spell the wizard causes a normal fire source, such as a brazier, flambeau, or bonfire, to serve as a magical agent, for from this source he causes a gossamer veil of multi-hued flame to encircle the fire at five feet distance. Any creatures observing the fire or the dancing circle of flame around it must successfully roll a saving throw vs. spell or be charmed into remaining motionless and gazing, transfixed, at the flames. While so charmed, creatures are subject to suggestions of 12 or fewer words, saving vs. spell with a −3 penalty, adjusted for Wisdom. The caster can give one such suggestion to each creature, and the suggestions need not be the same. The maximum duration for such a suggestion is one hour, regardless of the caster's level.

The fire charm is broken if the charmed creature is physically attacked, if a solid object comes between the creature and the veil of flames so as to obstruct vision, or when the duration of the spell expires. Those exposed to the fire charm again may be affected at the DM's option, although bonuses may also be allowed to the saving throws. Note that the veil of flame is not a magical fire, and passing through it incurs the same damage as would be sustained from passing through its original fire source.

The material component for this spell is a small piece of multi-colored silk of exceptional thinness that the spellcaster must throw into the fire source.

Fire Shield (Evocation, Alteration)

Range: 0
Components: V, S, M
Duration: 2 rounds + 1 round/level
Casting Time: 4
Area of Effect: The caster
Saving Throw: None

This spell can be cast in one of two forms: a warm shield that protects against cold-based attacks, or a chill shield that protects against fire-based attacks. Both return damage to creatures making physical attacks against the wizard. The wizard must choose which variation he memorizes when the spell is selected.

When casting this spell, the wizard appears to immolate himself, but the flames are thin and wispy, shedding no heat, though giving light equal to only half the illumination of a normal torch. The color of

the flames is determined randomly (50% chance of either color)—blue or green if the chill shield is cast, violet or blue if the warm shield is employed. The special powers of each shield are as follows:

A) *Warm shield*. The flames are warm to the touch. Any cold-based attacks are saved against with a +2 bonus; either half normal damage or no damage is sustained. There is no bonus against fire-based attacks, but if the wizard fails to make the required saving throw (if any) against them, he sustains double normal damage.

The material component for this variation is a bit of phosphorus.

B) *Chill shield*. The flames are cool to the touch. Any fire-based attacks are saved against with a +2 bonus; either half normal damage or no damage is sustained. There is no bonus against cold-based attacks, but if the wizard fails to make the required saving throw (if any) against them, he sustains double normal damage.

The material component for this variation is a live firefly or glow worm or the tail portions of four dead ones.

Any creature striking the spellcaster with its body or hand-held weapons inflicts normal damage upon the wizard, but the attacker suffers the same amount of damage. An attacker's magical resistance, if any, is tested when the creature actually strikes the wizard. Successful resistance shatters the spell. Failure means the creature's magic resistance does not affect that casting of the spell.

Fire Trap (Abjuration, Evocation)

Range: Touch
Components: V, S, M
Duration: Permanent until discharged
Casting Time: 1 turn
Area of Effect: Object touched
Saving Throw: ½

Any closeable item (book, box, bottle, chest, coffer, coffin, door, drawer, and so forth) can be warded by a *fire trap* spell. The spell is centered on a point selected by the spellcaster. The item so trapped cannot have a second closure or warding spell placed upon it (if such is attempted, the result is 25% first spell fails, 25% second spell fails, or 50% both spells fail). A *knock* spell does not affect a *fire trap* in any way—as soon as the offending party enters or touches the item, the trap discharges. Thieves and others have only ½ of their normal chance to detect a fire trap (by noticing the characteristic markings required to cast the spell). They have only ½ their normal chance to remove the trap (failure detonates the trap immediately). An unsuccessful dispel does not detonate the spell. The caster can use the trapped object without discharging it, as can any individual to whom the spell was

specifically attuned when cast (the exact method usually involves a keyword). When the trap is discharged, there is an explosion of five-foot radius from the spell's center; all creatures within this area must roll saving throws vs. spell. Damage is 1d4 points plus 1 point per level of the caster; half this (round up) for creatures successfully saving. (Underwater, this ward inflicts half damage and creates a large cloud of steam.) The item trapped is not harmed by this explosion.

To place this spell, the caster must trace the outline of the closure with a bit of sulphur or saltpeter and touch the center of the effect. Attunement to another individual requires a hair or similar object from that person.

Fumble (Enchantment/Charm)

Range: 10 yards/level
Components: V, S, M
Duration: 1 round/level
Casting Time: 4
Area of Effect: 30-foot cube
Saving Throw: Special

When a *fumble* spell is cast, the wizard creates an area in which all creatures suddenly become clumsy and awkward. Running creatures trip and fall, those reaching for an item drop it, those employing weapons likewise awkwardly drop them, etc. Recovery from a fall or to pick up a fumbled object typically requires a successful saving throw and takes one round. Note that breakable items might suffer damage when dropped. A subject succeeding with his saving throw can act freely that round, but if he is in the area at the beginning of the next round, another saving throw is required. Alternatively, the spell can be cast at an individual creature. Failure to save means the creature is affected for the spell's entire duration; success means the creature is slowed (see the 3rd-level spell).

The material component of this spell is a dab of solidified milk fat.

Hallucinatory Terrain (Illusion/Phantasm)

Range: 20 yards/level
Components: V, S, M
Duration: 1 hour/level
Casting Time: 1 turn
Area of Effect: Cube up to 30' per side/level
Saving Throw: None

By means of this spell, the wizard causes an illusion that hides the actual terrain within the area of effect. Thus open fields or a road can be made to look like a swamp, hill, crevasse, or some other difficult or impassable terrain. A pond can be made to look like a grassy meadow, a precipice look like a gentle slope, or a rock-strewn gully made to look like a wide and smooth road. The hallucinatory terrain persists until a *dispel magic* spell is cast upon the area or until the duration expires. Individual creatures may see through the illusion, but the illusion persists, affecting others who observe the scene.

If the illusion involves only a subtle change, such as causing an open wood to appear thick and dark, or increasing the slope of a hill, the effect may be unnoticed even by those in the midst of it. If the change is extreme, a grassy plain covering a seething field of volcanic mudpots, for instance, the illusion will no doubt be noticed the instant one person falls prey to it. Each level of experience expands the dimensions of the area affected, e.g., a 12th-level caster affects a 120 yd. x 120 yd. x 120 yd. area.

The material components of this spell are a stone, a twig, and a bit of green plant—leaf or grass blade.

Ice Storm (Evocation)

Range: 10 yards/level
Components: V, S, M
Duration: Special
Casting Time: 4
Area of Effect: Special
Saving Throw: None

This spell can have one of two effects, at the caster's option: Either great hail stones pound down for one round in a 40-foot-diameter area and inflict 3d10 points of damage to any creatures within the area of effect, or driving sleet falls in an 80-foot-diameter area for one round per caster level. The sleet blinds creatures within its area for the duration of the spell and causes the ground in the area to be icy, thus slowing movement by 50% and making it 50% probable that a creature trying to move in the area slips and falls. The sleet also extinguishes torches and small fires.

Note that this spell will negate a *heat metal* spell.

The material components for this spell are a pinch of dust and a few drops of water.

Illusionary Wall (Illusion/Phantasm)

Range: 30 yards
Components: V, S
Duration: Permanent
Casting Time: 4
Area of Effect: 1' × 10' × 10'
Saving Throw: None

This spell creates the illusion of a wall, floor, ceiling, or similar surface, which is permanent until dispelled. It appears absolutely real when viewed, even magically, as with the clerical spell, *true seeing*, or its equivalent, but physical objects can pass through it without difficulty. When the spell is used to hide pits, traps, or normal doors,

normal demihuman and magical detection abilities work normally, and touch or probing searches reveal the true nature of the surface, though they do not cause the illusion to disappear.

The material component is a rare dust that costs at least 400 gp and requires four days to prepare.

Improved Invisibility
(Illusion/Phantasm)

Range: Touch
Components: V, S
Duration: 4 rounds + 1 round/level
Casting Time: 4
Area of Effect: Creature touched
Saving Throw: None

This spell is similar to the *invisibility* spell, but the recipient is able to attack, either by missile discharge, melee combat, or spellcasting, and remain unseen. Note, however, that there are sometimes telltale traces, a shimmering, so that an observant opponent can attack the invisible spell recipient. These traces are only noticeable when specifically looked for (after the invisible character has made his presence known). Attacks against the invisible character suffer −4 penalties to the attack rolls, and the invisible character's saving throws are made with a +4 bonus. High Hit Dice creatures that might notice invisible opponents will notice a creature under this spell as if they had 2 fewer Hit Dice (they roll saving throws vs. spell; success indicates they spot the character).

Leomund's Secure Shelter
(Alteration, Enchantment)

Range: 20 yards
Components: V, S, M
Duration: 1d4 +1 hours + 1 hour/level
Casting Time: 4 turns
Area of Effect: 30 sq. ft./level
Saving Throw: None

This spell enables the wizard to magically call into being a sturdy cottage or lodge, made of material that is common in the area where the spell is cast—stone, timber, or (at worst) sod. The floor area of the lodging is 30 square feet per level of the spellcaster, and the surface is level, clean, and dry. In all respects the lodging resembles a normal cottage, with a sturdy door, two or more shuttered windows, and a small fireplace.

While the lodging is secure against winds of up to 70 miles per hour, it has no heating or cooling source (other than natural insulation qualities). Therefore it must be heated as a normal dwelling, and extreme heat adversely affects it and its occupants. The dwelling does, however, provide considerable security otherwise, as it is as strong as a

normal stone building, regardless of its material composition, resists flames and fire as if it were stone, and is impervious to normal missiles (but not the sort cast by siege machinery or giants).

The door, shutters, and even chimney are secure against intrusion, the former two being wizard locked and the latter being secured by a top grate of iron and a narrow flue. In addition, these three areas are protected by an *alarm* spell. Lastly, an unseen servant is called up to provide service to the spellcaster.

The inside of the shelter contains rude furnishings as desired by the spellcaster—up to eight bunks, a trestle table and benches, as many as four chairs or eight stools, and a writing desk.

The material components of this spell are a square chip of stone, crushed lime, a few grains of sand, a sprinkling of water, and several splinters of wood. These must be augmented by the components of the *alarm* and *unseen servant* spells if these benefits are to be included (string and silver wire and a small bell).

Magic Mirror (Enchantment, Divination)

Range: Touch
Components: V, S, M
Duration: 1 round/level
Casting Time: 1 hour
Area of Effect: Special
Saving Throw: None

By means of this spell, the wizard changes a normal mirror into a scrying device similar to a crystal ball. The details of the use of such a scrying device are found in the *DMG* under the description for the *crystal ball*.

The mirror used must be of finely wrought and highly polished silver of a minimum cost not less than 1,000 gp. This mirror is not harmed by casting the spell, but the other material components—the eye of a hawk, an eagle, or even a roc, and nitric acid, copper, and zinc—are used up.

The following spells can be cast through a *magic mirror: comprehend languages, read magic, tongues,* and *infravision.* The following spells have a 5% chance per level of the caster of operating correctly: *detect magic, detect good or evil,* and *message.* The base chances for the subject to detect any *crystal ball*-like spell is listed in the *crystal ball* entry in the *DMG* (see the "Miscellaneous Magic" section).

Massmorph (Alteration)

Range: 10 yards/level
Components: V, S, M
Duration: Special
Casting Time: 4
Area of Effect: One 10-foot cube/level
Saving Throw: None

When this spell is cast upon willing creatures of man-size or smaller, up to 10 such creatures per level of the caster can be magically altered to appear as trees of any sort. Thus a company of creatures can be made to appear as a copse, grove, or orchard. Furthermore, these massmorphed creatures can be passed through—and even touched—by other creatures without revealing their true nature. Note, however, that blows to the creature-trees cause damage, and blood can be seen.

Creatures to be massmorphed must be within the spell's area of effect and unwilling creatures are not affected. Affected creatures remain unmoving but aware, subject to normal sleep requirements, and able to see, hear, and feel for as long as the spell is in effect. The spell persists until the caster commands it to cease or until a *dispel magic* spell is cast upon the creatures. Creatures left in this state for extended periods are subject to insects, weather, disease, fire, and other natural hazards.

The material component of this spell is a handful of bark chips from the type of tree the creatures are to become.

Minor Creation (Illusion/Phantasm)

Range: Touch
Components: V, S, M
Duration: 1 hour/level
Casting Time: 1 turn
Area of Effect: Special
Saving Throw: None

This spell enables the wizard to create an item of non-living, vegetable nature—soft goods, rope, wood, etc. The caster actually pulls wisps of material of the plane of Shadow from the air and weaves them into the desired item. The volume of the item created cannot exceed one cubic foot per level of the spellcaster. The item remains in existence for only as long as the spell's duration.

The spellcaster must have at least a tiny piece of matter of the same type of item he plans to create by means of the *minor creation* spell—a bit of twisted hemp to create rope, a splinter of wood to create a door, and so forth.

Minor Globe of Invulnerability (Abjuration)

Range: 0
Components: V, S, M
Duration: 1 round/level
Casting Time: 4
Area of Effect: 5-foot-radius sphere
Saving Throw: None

This spell creates an immobile, faintly shimmering magical sphere around the caster that prevents any 1st-, 2nd-, or 3rd-level spell effects from penetrating (i.e., the area of effect of any such spells does not include the area of the minor globe of invulnerability). This includes innate abilities and effects from devices. However, any type of spell can be cast out of the magical sphere, and these pass from the caster of the globe to their subject without affecting the minor globe. Fourth and higher level spells are not affected by the globe. The globe can be brought down by a successful *dispel magic* spell. The caster can leave and return to the globe without penalty. Note that spell effects are not actually disrupted by the globe unless cast directly through or into it: The caster would still see a mirror image created by a wizard outside the globe. If that wizard then entered the globe, the images would wink out, to reappear when the wizard exited the globe. Likewise, a wizard standing in the area of a *light* spell would still receive sufficient light for vision, even though that part of the *light* spell volume in the globe would not be luminous.

The material component of the spell is a glass or crystal bead that shatters at the expiration of the spell.

Monster Summoning II (Conjuration/Summoning)

Range: 40 yards
Components: V, S, M
Duration: 3 rounds + 1 round/level
Casting Time: 4
Area of Effect: Special
Saving Throw: None

This spell is much like the 3rd-level *monster summoning I* spell, except that this spell summons 1d6 2nd-level monsters. These appear anywhere within the spell range and attack the caster's opponents, until he commands them to cease, the spell duration expires, or the monsters are slain. These creatures do not check morale; they vanish when slain. If no opponent exists to fight and the wizard can communicate with them, the summoned monsters can perform other services for the summoning wizard.

The material components of this spell are a tiny bag and a small (not necessarily lit) candle.

Otiluke's Resilient Sphere (Alteration, Evocation)

Range: 20 yards
Components: V, S, M
Duration: 1 round/level
Casting Time: 4
Area of Effect: 1-foot diameter/level
Saving Throw: Neg.

When this spell is cast, the result is a globe of shimmering force that encloses the subject creature—if it is small enough to fit within the diameter of the sphere and it fails to successfully save vs. spell. The resilient sphere contains its subject for the spell's duration, and it is not subject to damage of any sort except from a *rod of cancellation*, a *wand of negation*, or a *disintegrate* or *dispel magic* spell. These cause it to be destroyed without harm to the subject. Nothing can pass through the sphere, inside or out, though the subject can breathe normally. The subject may struggle, but all that occurs is a movement of the sphere. The globe can be physically moved either by people outside the globe or by the struggles of those within.

The material components of the spell are a hemispherical piece of diamond (or similar hard, clear gem material) and a matching hemispherical piece of gum arabic.

Phantasmal Killer (Illusion/Phantasm)

Range: 5 yards/level
Components: V, S
Duration: 1 round/level
Casting Time: 4
Area of Effect: 1 creature
Saving Throw: Special

When this spell is cast, the wizard creates the illusion of the most fearsome thing imaginable to the victim, simply by forming the fears of the victim's subconscious mind into something that its conscious mind can visualize—the most horrible beast. Only the spell recipient can see the phantasmal killer (the caster sees only a shadowy shape), but if it succeeds in scoring a hit, the subject dies from fright. The beast attacks as a 4 Hit Dice monster. It is invulnerable to all attacks, and it can pass through any barriers. Once cast, it inexorably pursues the subject, for it exists only in the subject's mind.

The only defenses against a phantasmal killer are an attempt to disbelieve (which can be tried but once), slaying or rendering unconscious the wizard who cast the spell, or rendering unconscious the target of the spell for its duration. To disbelieve the killer, the subject must specifically state the attempt and then roll an Intelligence check. This roll has a −1 penalty for every four levels of the caster.

Special modifiers apply to this attack:

Condition	Modifier
Surprise	−2
Subject previously attacked by this spell	+1/
Subject is an illusionist	+2
Subject is wearing a *helm of telepathy*	+3

Magic resistance, bonuses against fear, and Wisdom adjustments also apply. Magic resistance is checked first to determine spell operation, and then the fear/Wisdom bonus applies as a minus to the dice roll to match or score less than Intelligence.

If the subject of a phantasmal killer attack succeeds in disbelieving, and he is wearing a *helm of telepathy*, the beast can be turned upon the wizard, who must then disbelieve it or be subject to its attack and possible effects.

If the subject ignores the killer to perform other actions, such as attacking the caster, the killer may, at the DM's option, gain bonuses to hit (for flank or rear attacks, etc.). Spells such as *remove fear* and *cloak of bravery*, cast after the killer has attacked, grant another check to disbelieve the effect.

Plant Growth (Alteration)

Range: 10 yards/level
Components: V, S
Duration: Permanent
Casting Time: 4
Area of Effect: An area 10′ per side/level
Saving Throw: None

When a *plant growth* spell is cast, the wizard causes normal vegetation to grow, entwine, and entangle to form a thicket or jungle that creatures must hack or force a way through at a movement rate of 1 per round (or 2 if larger than man-sized). The area must contain brush and trees for this spell to work. Briars, bushes, creepers, lianas, roots, saplings, thistles, thorn, trees, vines, and weeds become thick and overgrown so as to form a barrier. The area of effect is 10 feet on a side per level of experience of the caster, in any square or rectangular shape that the caster desires. Thus an 8th-level wizard can affect an 80′ × 80′ square, a 160′ × 40′ rectangle, a 640′ × 10′ rectangle, etc. Individual plant girth and height is generally affected less than thickness of brush, branch, and undergrowth. The spell's effects persist in the area until it is cleared by labor, fire, or such magical means as a *dispel magic* spell.

Polymorph Other (Alteration)

Range: 5 yards/level
Components: V, S, M
Duration: Permanent
Casting Time: 4
Area of Effect: 1 creature
Saving Throw: Neg.

The *polymorph other* spell is a powerful magic that completely alters the form and ability, and possibly the personality and mentality, of the recipient. Of course, while a creature with a lower Intelligence can be polymorphed in form into something with a higher Intelligence, it will not gain that creature's mental ability. The reverse—polymorphing a higher Intelligence creature into one of significantly lower Intelligence—results in a creature much more intelligent than appearances would lead one to believe. The polymorphed creature must succeed on a system shock (see Table 3) roll to see if it survives the change. After this, it must make a special Intelligence check to see if it retains its personality (see following).

The polymorphed creature acquires the form and physical abilities of the creature it has been polymorphed into, while retaining its own mind. Form includes natural Armor Class (that due to skin toughness, but not due to quickness, magical nature, etc.), physical movement abilities (walking, swimming, flight with wings, but not plane shifting, blinking, teleporting, etc.), and attack routines (claw/claw/bite, swoop, rake, constriction, but not petrification, breath weapons, energy drain, etc.). Hit points and saving throws do not change from the original form. Noncorporeal forms cannot be assumed. Natural shapeshifters (lycanthropes, dopplegangers, higher level druids, etc.) are affected for but one round, and can then resume their normal form.

If slain, the polymorphed creature reverts to its original form (it's still dead, though). (Note that most creatures generally prefer their own form and will not willingly stand the risk of being subjected to this spell!) As class and level are not attributes of form, abilities derived from either cannot be gained by this spell, nor can exact ability scores be specified.

When the polymorph occurs, the creature's equipment, if any, melds into the new form (in particularly challenging campaigns, the DM may allow protective devices, such as a *ring of protection*, to continue operating effectively). The creature retains its mental abilities, including spell use, assuming the new form allows completion of the proper verbal and somatic components and the material components are available. Creatures not used to a new form might be penalized at the DM's option (e.g., −2 to attack rolls) until they practice sufficiently to master it.

When the physical change occurs, there is a base 100% chance that the subject's personality and mentality change into that of new form (i.e., a roll of 20 or less on 1d20). For each 1 point of Intelligence of the subject, subtract 1 from the base chance on 1d20. Additionally, for every Hit Die of difference between the original form and the form it is assuming, add or subtract 1 (depending on whether polymorphed form has more Hit Dice [or levels] or fewer Hit Dice [or levels] than original, respectively). The chance for assumption of the personality and mentality of the new form is checked daily until the change takes place.

A subject acquiring the mentality of the new form has effectively become the creature whose form was assumed and comes under the control of the DM until recovered by a *wish* spell or similar magic. Once this final change takes place, the creature acquires the new form's full range of magical and special abilities.

Example: If a 1 Hit Die orc of 8 Intelligence is polymorphed into a white dragon with 6 Hit Dice, for example, it is 85% (20 - 8 Intelligence + 5 level difference [6-1] = 17 out of 20 = 85%) likely to actually become one in all respects, but in any case it has the dragon's physical and mental capabilities. If it does not assume the personality and mentality of a white dragon, it knows what it formerly knew as well.

The wizard can use a *dispel magic* spell to change the polymorphed creature back to its original from, and this requires a system shock roll. Those who have lost their individuality and are then converted back maintain the belief that they are actually the polymorphed creature and attempt to return to that form. Thus the orc who comes to believe he is a white dragon, when converted back to his orc form, steadfastly maintains he is really a white dragon polymorphed into the shape of an orc. His companions will most likely consider him mad.

The material component of this spell is a caterpillar cocoon.

Polymorph Self (Alteration)

Range: 0
Components: V
Duration: 2 turns/level
Casting Time: 4
Area of Effect: The caster
Saving Throw: None

When this spell is cast, the wizard is able to assume the form of any creature, save those that are noncorporeal, from as small as a wren to as large as a hippopotamus. Furthermore, the wizard gains its physical mode of locomotion and breathing as well. No system shock roll is required. The spell does not give the new form's other abilities (attack, magic, special movement, etc.), nor does it run the risk of changing personality and mentality.

When the polymorph occurs, the caster's equipment, if any, melds into the new form (in particularly challenging campaigns, the DM may allow protective devices, such as a *ring of protection*, to continue operating effectively). The caster retains all mental abilities, including spell use, assuming the new form allows completion of the proper verbal and somatic components and the material components are available. A caster not used to a new form might be penalized at the DM's option (e.g., −2 penalty to attack rolls) until he practices sufficiently to master it.

Thus a wizard changed into an owl could fly, but his vision would be human; a change to a black pudding would enable movement under doors or along halls and ceilings, but not the pudding's offensive (acid) or defensive capabilities. Naturally, the strength of the new form is sufficient to enable normal movement. The spellcaster can change his form as often as desired for the duration of the spell, each change requiring a round. The wizard retains his own hit points, attack rolls, and saving throws. The wizard can end the spell at any time; when voluntarily returning to his own form and ending the spell, he regains 1d12 hit points. The wizard also will return to his own form when slain or when the effect is dispelled, but no hit points are restored in these cases.

Rainbow Pattern
(Alteration, Illusion/Phantasm)

Range: 10 yards
Components: S, M
Duration: Special
Casting Time: 4
Area of Effect: 30-foot cube
Saving Throw: Neg.

By means of this spell, the wizard creates a glowing, rainbow-hued band of interweaving patterns. Any creature caught in it may become fascinated and gaze at it as long as the effect lasts. The spell can captivate a maximum of 24 levels, or Hit Dice, of creatures—24 creatures with 1 Hit Die each, 12 with 2 Hit Dice, etc. All creatures affected must be within the area of effect, and each is entitled to a saving throw vs. spell. An attack on an affected creature that causes damage frees it from the spell immediately. Creatures that are restrained and removed from the area still try to follow the pattern.

Once the rainbow pattern is cast, the wizard need only gesture in the direction he desires, and the pattern of colors moves slowly off in that direction, at the rate of 30 feet per round. It persists without further attention from the spellcaster for 1d3

rounds. All affected creatures follow the moving rainbow of light. If the pattern leads its subjects into a dangerous area (through flame, off a cliff, etc.), allow a second saving throw. If the view of the lights is completely blocked (by an *obscurement* spell, for instance), the spell is negated.

The wizard need not utter a sound, but he must gesture appropriately while holding a crystal prism and the material component, a piece of phosphor.

Rary's Mnemonic Enhancer
(Alteration)

Range: 0
Components: V, S, M
Duration: 1 day
Casting Time: 1 turn
Area of Effect: The caster
Saving Throw: None

By means of this spell, the wizard is able to memorize, or retain the memory of, three additional spell levels (three 1st-level spells, or one 1st and one 2nd, or one 3rd-level spell). The wizard has two options:

A) Memorize additional spells. This option is taken at the time the spell is cast. The additional spells must be memorized normally and any material components must be acquired.

B) Retain memory of any spell (within the level limits) cast the round prior to starting to cast this spell. The round after a spell is cast, the enhancer must be successfully cast. This restores the previously cast spell to memory. Any material components must be acquired by the caster, however.

The material components of the spell are a piece of string, an ivory plaque of at least 100 gp value, and ink consisting of squid secretion with either black dragon's blood or giant slug digestive juice. These disappear when the spell is cast.

Remove Curse (Abjuration)
Reversible

Range: Touch
Components: V, S
Duration: Permanent
Casting Time: 4
Area of Effect: Special
Saving Throw: Special

Upon casting this spell, the wizard is usually able to remove a curse—whether it is on an object, or a person, or in the form of some undesired sending or evil presence. Note that the *remove curse* spell cannot affect a cursed shield, weapon, or suit of armor, for example, although it usually enables a person afflicted with a cursed item to be rid of it. Certain special curses may not be countered by this spell, or may be countered only by a caster of a certain level or

more. A caster of 12th level or more can cure lycanthropy with this spell by casting it on the animal form. The were-creature receives a saving throw vs. spell and, if successful, the spell fails and the wizard must gain a level before attempting the remedy again.

The reverse of the spell is not permanent; the *bestow curse* lasts for one turn for every experience level of the wizard casting the spell. It causes one of the following effects (roll percentile dice):

D100 Roll	Result
1-50	Lowers one ability of the subject to 3 (the DM determines which by random selection)
51-75	Worsens the subject's attack rolls and saving throws by −4
76-00	Makes the subject 50% likely per turn to drop whatever it is holding (or simply do nothing, in the case of creatures not using tools)

It is possible for a wizard to devise his own curse, and it should be similar in power to those given (the DM has final say). The subject of a *bestow curse* spell must be touched. If the subject is touched, a saving throw is still applicable; if it is successful, the effect is negated. The bestowed curse cannot be dispelled.

Shadow Monsters (Illusion/Phantasm)

Range: 30 yards
Components: V, S
Duration: 1 round/level
Casting Time: 4
Area of Effect: 20-foot cube
Saving Throw: Special

A wizard casting the *shadow monsters* spell uses material from the plane of Shadow to shape semi-real illusions of one or more monsters. The total Hit Dice of the shadow monster or monsters thus created cannot exceed the level of experience of the wizard; thus a 10th-level wizard can create one creature that has 10 Hit Dice, two that have 5 Hit Dice, etc. All shadow monsters created by one spell must be of the same sort. The actual hit point total for each monster is 20% of the hit point total it would normally have. (To determine this, roll the appropriate Hit Dice and multiply the hit points by .2. Any remainder less than .4 is dropped—in the case of monsters with 1 or fewer Hit Dice, this indicates the monster was not successfully created—and scores between .4 and 1 are rounded up to 1 hit point.)

Those viewing the shadow monsters are allowed to disbelieve as per normal illusions, although there is a −2 penalty to the attempt. The shadow monsters perform as the real monsters with respect to Armor

Class and attack forms. Those who believe in the shadow monsters suffer real damage from their attacks. Special attack forms such as petrification or level drain do not actually occur, but a subject who believes they are real will react appropriately.

Those who roll successful saving throws see the shadow monsters as transparent images superimposed on vague shadowy forms. These are Armor Class 10 and inflict only 20% of normal melee damage (biting, clawing, weapon, etc.), dropping fractional damage less than .4 as done with hit points.

Example: A shadow monster griffon attacks a person who knows it is only quasi-real. The monster strikes with two claw attacks and one bite, hitting as a 7-Hit Die monster. All three attacks hit, and the normal damage dice are rolled, multiplied by .2 separately, rounded up or down, then added together to get total damage. Thus if the attacks score 4, 2, and 11 points, then a total of 4 points of damage is inflicted (4 × .2 = .8 [rounded to 1], 2 × .2 = .4 [rounded to 1], 11 × .2 = 2.2 [rounded to 2]. The sum is 1 + 1 + 2 = 4).

Shout (Evocation)

Range: 0
Components: V,M
Duration: Instantaneous
Casting Time: 1
Area of Effect: 10-foot × 30-foot cone
Saving Throw: Special

When a *shout* spell is cast, the wizard gives himself tremendous vocal powers. The caster can emit an ear-splitting noise that has a principal effect in a cone shape radiating from his mouth to a point 30 feet away. Any creature within this area is deafened for 2d6 rounds and suffers 2d6 points of damage. A successful saving throw vs. spell negates the deafness and reduces the damage by half. Any exposed brittle or crystal substance subject to sonic vibrations is shattered by a shout, while those brittle objects in the possession of a creature receive the creature's saving throw. Deafened creatures suffer a −1 penalty to surprise rolls, and those that cast spells with verbal components are 20% likely to miscast them.

The *shout* spell cannot penetrate the 2nd-level clerical spell, *silence, 10' radius*. This spell can be employed but once per day, for otherwise the caster might permanently deafen himself.

The material components for this spell are a drop of honey, a drop of citric acid, and a small cone made from a bull or ram horn.

Solid Fog (Alteration)

Range: 30 yards
Components: V, S, M
Duration: 2d4 rounds + 1 round/level
Casting Time: 4
Area of Effect: 20' × 10' × 10' volume/ level of caster
Saving Throw: None

When this spell is cast, the wizard creates a billowing mass of misty vapors similar to a *wall of fog* spell. The caster can create less vapor if desired, as long as a rectangular or cubic mass at least 10 feet on a side is formed. The fog obscures all sight, normal and infravision, beyond two feet. However, unlike normal fog, only a very strong wind can move these vapors, and any creature attempting to move through the solid fog progresses at a rate of but one foot per movement rate of 1 per round. A *gust of wind* spell cannot affect it. A fireball, flame strike, or a wall of fire can burn it away in a single round.

The material components for the spell are a pinch of dried, powdered peas combined with powdered animal hoof.

Stoneskin (Alteration)

Range: Touch
Components: V, S, M
Duration: Special
Casting Time: 1
Area of Effect: 1 creature
Saving Throw: None

When this spell is cast, the affected creature gains a virtual immunity to any attack by cut, blow, projectile, or the like. Even a *sword of sharpness* cannot affect a creature protected by *stoneskin*, nor can a rock hurled by a giant, a snake's strike, etc. However, magical attacks from such spells as *fireball, magic missile, lightning bolt,* and so forth have their normal effects. The spell blocks 1d4 attacks, plus one attack per two levels of experience the caster has achieved. This limit applies regardless of attack rolls and regardless of whether the attack was physical or magical. For example, a *stoneskin* spell cast by a 9th-level wizard would protect against from five to eight attacks. An attacking griffon would reduce the protection by three each round; four magic missiles would count as four attacks in addition to inflicting their normal damage.

The material components of the spell are granite and diamond dust sprinkled on the recipient's skin.

Vacancy (Alteration, Illusion/Phantasm)

Range: 10 yards/level
Components: V, S, M
Duration: 1 hour/level
Casting Time: 4
Area of Effect: 10-foot radius/level
Saving Throw: None

When a *vacancy* spell is cast, the wizard causes an area to appear to be vacant, neglected, and unused. Those who behold the area see dust on the floor, cobwebs, dirt, and other conditions typical of a long-abandoned place. If they pass through the area of effect, they seem to leave tracks, tear away cobwebs, and so on. Unless they actually contact some object cloaked by the spell, the place appears empty. Merely brushing an invisible object does not cause the *vacancy* spell to be disturbed: Only forceful contact grants a chance to note that all is not as it seems.

If forceful contact with a cloaked object occurs, those creatures subject to the spell can penetrate the spell only if they discover several items that they cannot see; each being is then entitled to a saving throw vs. spell. Failure means they believe that the objects are invisible. A *dispel magic* spell cancels this spell so that the true area is seen. A *true seeing* spell, a *gem of seeing,* and similar effects can penetrate the deception, but a *detect invisibility* spell cannot.

This spell is a very powerful combination of invisibility and illusion, but it can cloak only nonliving things. Living things are not made invisible, but their presence does not otherwise disturb the spell.

The wizard must have a square of the finest black silk to cast this spell. This material component must be worth at least 100 gp and is used up during spellcasting.

Wall of Fire (Evocation)

Range: 60 yards
Components: V, S, M
Duration: Special
Casting Time: 4
Area of Effect: Special
Saving Throw: None

The *wall of fire* spell brings forth an immobile, blazing curtain of magical fire of shimmering color—violet or reddish-blue. The spell creates either an opaque sheet of flame up to one 20-foot square per level of the spellcaster, or a ring with a radius of up to 10 feet + five feet per two levels of experience of the wizard. In either form, the wall of fire is 20 feet high.

The wall of fire must be cast so that it is vertical with respect to the caster. One side of the wall, selected by the caster, sends forth waves of heat, inflicting 2d4 points of damage upon creatures within 10 feet and 1d4 points of damage upon those within 20 feet. In addition, the wall inflicts 2d6 points of damage, plus 1 point of damage per level of the spellcaster, upon any creature passing through it. Creatures especially subject to fire may take additional damage, and undead always take twice normal damage. Note that attempting to catch a moving creature with a newly-created wall of fire is difficult; a successful saving throw enables the creature to avoid the wall, while its rate and direction of movement determine which side of the created wall it is on. The wall of fire lasts as long as the wizard concentrates on maintaining it, or one round per level of experience of the wizard, in the event he does not wish to concentrate upon it.

The material component of the spell is phosphorus.

Wall of Ice (Evocation)

Range: 10 yards/level
Components: V, S, M
Duration: 1 turn/level
Casting Time: 4
Area of Effect: Special
Saving Throw: None

This spell can be cast in one of three ways: as an anchored plane of ice, as a hemisphere, or as a horizontal sheet to fall upon creatures with the effect of an ice storm.

A) *Ice plane.* When this spell is cast, a sheet of strong, hard ice is created. The wall is primarily defensive, stopping pursuers and the like. The wall is one inch thick per level of experience of the wizard. It covers a 10-foot-square area per level (a 10th-level wizard can create a wall of ice up to 100 feet long and 10 feet high or 50 feet long and 20 feet high, etc.). Any creature breaking through the ice suffers 2 points of damage per inch of thickness of the wall. Fire-using creatures suffer 3 points of damage per inch, while cold-using creatures suffer only 1 point of damage per inch when breaking through. The plane can be oriented in any fashion as long as it is anchored along one or more sides.

B) *Hemisphere.* This casting of the spell creates a hemisphere whose maximum radius is equal to three feet plus one foot per caster level. Thus a 7th-level caster can create a hemisphere 10 feet in radius. The hemisphere lasts until it is broken, dispelled, or melted. Note that it is possible, but difficult, to trap mobile opponents under the hemisphere.

C) *Ice sheet.* This casting of the spell causes a horizontal sheet to fall upon opponents. The sheet covers a 10-foot-square area per caster level. The sheet has the same effect as an ice storm's hail stones—3d10 points of damage inflicted to creatures beneath it.

A wall of ice cannot form in an area occupied by physical objects or creatures; its surface must be smooth and unbroken when created. Magical fires such as fireballs and fiery dragon breath melt a wall of ice in one round, though this creates a great cloud of steamy fog that lasts one turn. Normal fires or lesser magical ones do not hasten the melting of a wall of ice.

The material component of this spell is a small piece of quartz or similar rock crystal.

Wizard Eye (Alteration)

Range: 0
Components: V, S, M
Duration: 1 round/level
Casting Time: 1 turn
Area of Effect: Special
Saving Throw: None

When this spell is employed, the wizard creates an invisible sensory organ that sends him visual information. The wizard eye travels at 30 feet per round if viewing an area ahead as a human would (i.e., primarily looking at the floor), or 10 feet per round if examining the ceiling and walls as well as the floor ahead. The wizard eye can see with infravision up to 10 feet, and with normal vision up to 60 feet away in brightly lit areas. The wizard eye can travel in any direction as as long as the spell lasts. It has substance and a form that can be detected (by a *detect invisibility* spell, for instance). Solid barriers prevent the passage of a wizard eye, although it can pass through a space no smaller than a small mouse hole (one inch in diameter).

Using the eye requires the wizard to concentrate. However, if his concentration is broken the spell does not end—the eye merely becomes inert until the wizard again concentrates, subject to the duration of the spell. The powers of the eye cannot be enhanced by other spells or items. The caster is subject to any gaze attack met by the eye. A successful dispel cast on the wizard or eye ends the spell. With respect to blindness, magical darkness, and so on, the wizard eye is considered an independent sensory organ of the caster.

The material component of this spell is a bit of bat fur.

Fifth-Level Spells

Advanced Illusion (Illusion/Phantasm)

Range: 60 yards + 10 yards/level
Components: V, S, M
Duration: 1 round/level
Casting Time: 1 round
Area of Effect: One 40-foot cube + a 10-foot cube/level
Saving Throw: Special

This spell is essentially a *spectral forces* spell that operates through a program (similar to a *programmed illusion* spell) determined by the caster. It is thus unnecessary for the wizard to concentrate on the spell for longer than the round of casting it, as the program has then started and will continue without supervision. The illusion has visual, audio, olfactory, and thermal components. If any viewer actively attempts to disbelieve the spell, he gains a saving throw vs. spell. If any viewer successfully disbelieves and communicates this fact to other viewers, each such viewer gains a saving throw vs. spell with a +4 bonus.

The material components are a bit of fleece and several grains of sand.

Airy Water (Alteration)

Range: 0
Components: V, S, M
Duration: 1 turn/level
Casting Time: 5
Area of Effect: 10' radius sphere or
              15' radius hemisphere
Saving Throw: None

The *airy water* spell turns normal liquid, such as water or water-based solutions, into a less dense, breathable substance. Thus, if the wizard wanted to enter an underwater place, he would step into the water, cast the spell and sink downward in a globe of bubbling water. He and any companions in the spell's area of effect can move freely and breathe just as if the bubbling water were air. The globe is centered on and moves with the caster. Water-breathing creatures avoid a sphere (or hemisphere) of airy water, although intelligent ones can enter it if they are able to move by means other than swimming. No water-breathers can breathe in an area affected by this spell. There is only one word that needs to be spoken to actuate the magic, thus it can be cast underwater. The spell does not filter or remove solid particles of matter.

The material component of the spell is a small handful of alkaline or bromine salts.

Animal Growth (Alteration)
Reversible

Range: 60 yards
Components: V, S, M
Duration: 1 round/level
Casting Time: 5
Area of Effect: Up to 8 animals in a 20' cube
Saving Throw: None

When this spell is cast, the wizard causes all designated animals, up to a maximum of eight, within a 20-foot-square area to grow to twice their normal size. The effects of this growth are doubled Hit Dice (with improvement in attack rolls) and doubled damage in combat. The spell lasts for one round for each level of experience of the wizard casting the spell. Only natural animals, including giant forms, can be affected by this spell.

The reverse, *shrink animal*, reduces animal size by half and likewise reduces Hit Dice, attack damage, etc.

The component of both versions of the spell is a pinch of powdered bone.

Animate Dead (Necromancy)

Range: 10 yards
Components: V, S, M
Duration: Permanent
Casting Time: 5 rounds
Area of Effect: Special
Saving Throw: None

This spell creates the lowest of the undead monsters—skeletons or zombies—usually from the bones or bodies of dead humans, demihumans, or humanoids. The spell causes existing remains to become animated and obey the simple verbal commands of the caster. The skeletons or zombies can follow the caster, remain in an area and attack any creature (or just a specific type of creature) entering the place, etc. The undead remain animated until they are destroyed in combat or are turned; the magic cannot be dispelled. The following types of dead creatures can be animated:

A) *Humans, demihumans, and humanoids with 1 Hit Die.* The wizard can animate one skeleton for each experience level he has attained, or one zombie for every two levels. The experience levels, if any, of the slain are ignored; the body of a newly dead 9th-level fighter is animated as a zombie with 2 Hit Dice, without special class or racial abilities.

B) *Creatures with more than 1 Hit Die.* The number of undead animated is determined by the monster Hit Dice (the total Hit Dice cannot exceed the wizard's level). Skeletal forms have the Hit Dice of the original creature, while zombie forms have one more Hit Die. Thus, a 12th-level wizard could animate four zombie gnolls (4 × [2 + 1 Hit Dice] = 12), or a single fire giant skeleton. Such undead have none of the special abilities they had in life.

C) *Creatures with less than 1 Hit Die.* The caster can animate two skeletons per level or one zombie per level. The creatures have their normal Hit Dice as skeletons and an additional Hit Die as zombies. Clerics receive a +1 bonus when trying to turn these.

This spell assumes that the bodies or bones are available and are reasonably intact (those of skeletons or zombies destroyed in combat won't be!).

It requires a drop of blood and a pinch of bone powder or a bone shard to complete the spell. The casting of this spell is not a good act and only evil wizards use it frequently.

Avoidance (Abjuration, Alteration)
Reversible

Range: 10 yards
Components: V, S, M
Duration: Permanent until dispelled
Casting Time: 5
Area of Effect: Up to 3-foot cube
Saving Throw: Special

By means of this spell, the caster sets up a natural repulsion between the affected object and all other living things except himself. Thus any living creature attempting to touch the affected object is repulsed (unable to come closer than one foot), or repulses the affected object, depending on the relative mass of the two (a halfling attempting to touch an iron chest with an *avoidance* spell upon it will be thrown back, while the chest will skitter away from a giant-sized creature as the creature approaches).

The material component for the spell is a magnetized needle. The spell cannot be cast upon living things; any attempt to cast avoidance upon the apparel or possessions of a living creature entitles the subject creature to a saving throw vs. spell.

The reverse of this spell, *attraction*, uses the same material components and sets up a natural attraction between the affected object and all living things. A creature is drawn to the object if the creature is smaller, or the object slides toward the creature if the creature is larger. A successful bend bars roll must be rolled to remove the enchanted object once it has adhered to an object or creature.

Bigby's Interposing Hand (Evocation)

Range: 10 yards/level
Components: V, S, M
Duration: 1 round/level
Casting Time: 5
Area of Effect: Special
Saving Throw: None

Bigby's interposing hand is a man-sized to gargantuan-sized magical hand that appears between the spellcaster and his chosen opponent. This disembodied hand then moves to remain between the two, regardless of what the spellcaster does or how the opponent tries to get around it. Neither invisibility nor polymorph fools the hand once a creature has been chosen. The hand does not pursue an opponent, nor does it move more than ten feet away from the caster.

The size of the hand is determined by the wizard, and it can be human-sized (five feet) all the way up to titan-sized (25 feet). It provides cover for the caster against the selected opponent, with all the attendant combat adjustments. It has as many hit points as the caster in full health and has an Armor Class of 0.

Any creature weighing less than 2,000 pounds trying to push past it is slowed to 1/2 normal movement. If the original opponent is slain, the caster can designate a new opponent for the hand. The caster can command the hand out of existence at any time.

The material component of the spell is a soft glove.

Chaos (Enchantment/Charm)

Range: 5 yards/level
Components: V, S, M
Duration: 1 round/level
Casting Time: 5
Area of Effect: Up to 40-foot cube
Saving Throw: Special

This spell is similar to the 4th-level *confusion* spell, but only the following beings receive a saving throw: fighters, wizards specialized in enchantments, monsters that use no magic and have an Intelligence of 4 or less, creatures of 21 Intelligence or higher, and creatures with more levels or Hit Dice than the caster's level.

The spell causes disorientation and severe perceptual distortion, creating indecision and the inability to take effective action. The spell affects 1d4 creatures, plus one creature per caster level. Those allowed saving throws roll them vs. spell with −2 penalties, adjusted for Wisdom. Those who successfully save are unaffected by the spell. Affected creatures react as follows:

D10 Roll	Action
1	Wander away (unless prevented) for duration of spell
2-6	Stand confused one round (then roll again)
7-9	Attack nearest creature for one round (then roll again)
10	Act normally for one round (then roll again)

The spell lasts one round for each level of the caster. Those affected are checked by the DM for actions each round for the duration of the spell, or until the "wander away for the duration of the spell" result occurs.

Wandering creatures move as far from the caster as possible using their most typical mode of movement (characters walk, fish swim, bats fly, etc.). Saving throws and actions are checked at the beginning of each round. Any confused creature that is attacked perceives the attacker as an enemy and acts according to its basic nature.

The material component for this spell is a small disc of bronze and a small rod of iron.

Cloudkill (Evocation)

Range: 10 yards
Components: V, S
Duration: 1 round/level
Casting Time: 5
Area of Effect: 40' wide, 20' high, 20' deep cloud
Saving Throw: None

This spell generates a billowing cloud of ghastly yellowish green vapors that is so toxic as to slay any creature with fewer than 4 + 1 Hit Dice, cause creatures with 4 + 1 to 5 + 1 Hit Dice to roll saving throws vs. poison with −4 penalties or be slain, and creatures up to 6 Hit Dice (inclusive) to roll unmodified saving throws vs. poison or be slain. Holding one's breath has no effect on the lethality of the spell. Those above 6th level (or 6 Hit Dice) must leave the cloud immediately or suffer 1d10 points of poison damage each round while in the area of effect.

The cloudkill moves away from the spellcaster at 10 feet per round, rolling along the surface of the ground. A moderate breeze causes it to alter course (roll for direction), but it does not move back toward its caster. A strong wind breaks it up in four rounds, and a greater wind force prevents the use of the spell. Very thick vegetation will disperse the cloud in two rounds. As the vapors are heavier than air, they sink to the lowest level of the land, even pour down den or sinkhole openings; thus the spell is ideal for slaying nests of giant ants, for example. It cannot penetrate liquids, nor can it be cast underwater.

Cone of Cold (Evocation)

Range: 0
Components: V, S, M
Duration: Instantaneous
Casting Time: 5
Area of Effect: Special
Saving Throw: 1/2

When this spell is cast, it causes a cone-shaped area of extreme cold, originating at the wizard's hand and extending outward in a cone five feet long and one foot in diameter per level of the caster. It drains heat and causes 1d4 + 1 points of damage per level of experience of the wizard. For example, a 10th-level wizard would cast a cone of cold 10 feet in diameter and 50 feet long, causing 10d4 + 10 points of damage.

Its material component is a crystal or glass cone of very small size.

Conjure Elemental (Conjuration/Summoning)

Range: 60 yards
Components: V, S, M
Duration: 1 turn/level
Casting Time: 1 turn
Area of Effect: Special
Saving Throw: None

There are actually four spells in the *conjure elemental* spell. The wizard is able to conjure an air, earth, fire, or water elemental with this spell—assuming he has the material component for the particular elemental. (A considerable fire source must be in range to conjure a fire elemental; a large amount of water must be available to conjure a water elemental.) Conjured elementals have 8 Hit Dice.

It is possible to conjure up successive elementals of different types if the spellcaster has memorized two or more of these spells. The type of elemental to be conjured must be decided upon before memorizing the spell. Each type of elemental can be conjured only once per day.

The elemental conjured up must be controlled by the wizard—the spellcaster must concentrate on the elemental doing his commands—or it turns on the wizard and attacks. The elemental will not break off a combat to do so, but it will avoid creatures while seeking its conjurer. If the wizard is wounded or grappled, his concentration is broken. There is always a 5% chance that the elemental turns on its conjurer regardless of concentration. This check is made at the end of the second and each succeeding round. An elemental that breaks free of its control can be dispelled by the caster, but the chance of success is only 50%. The elemental can be controlled up to 30 yards away per level of the spellcaster. The elemental remains until its form on this plane is destroyed due to damage or until the spell's duration expires. Note that water elementals are destroyed if they are ever more than 60 yards from a large body of water.

The material component of the spell (besides the quantity of the element at hand) is a small amount of one of the following:

Air Elemental—burning incense
Earth Elemental—soft clay
Fire Elemental—sulphur and phosphorus
Water Elemental—water and sand

Special protection from uncontrolled elementals is available by means of a *protection from evil* spell.

Contact Other Plane (Divination)

Range: 0
Components: V
Duration: Special
Casting Time: 1 turn
Area of Effect: Special
Saving Throw: None

When this spell is cast, the wizard sends his mind to another plane of existence in order to receive advice and information from powers there. As these powers resent such contact, only brief answers are given. (The DM answers all questions with "yes," "no," "maybe," "never," "irrelevant," etc.) Any questions asked are answered by the power during the spell's duration. The character can contact an elemental plane or some plane farther removed. For every two levels of experience of the wizard, one question may be asked. Contact with minds far removed from the plane of the wizard increases the probability of the spellcaster going insane or dying, but the chance of the power knowing the answer, as well as the probability of the being telling the correct answer, are likewise increased by moving to distant planes. Once the outer planes are reached, the Intelligence of the power contacted determines the effects.

The random table given here is subject to DM changes, development of extraplanar NPC beings, and so on.

If insanity occurs, it strikes as soon as the first question is asked. This condition lasts for one week for each removal of the plane contacted (see the *DMG* or *Manual of the Planes*), to a maximum of ten weeks. There is a 1% chance per plane that the wizard dies before recovering, unless a *remove curse* spell is cast upon him. A surviving wizard can recall the answer to the question.

On rare occasions, this divination may be blocked by the action of certain lesser or greater powers.

Optional Rule

Optionally, the DM may allow a specific outer plane to be contacted (see *Manual of the Planes*); in this case, the difference in alignment between the caster and the plane contacted alters the maximum Intelligence that can be contacted—each difference in moral or ethical alignment lowers the maximum Intelligence that can be contacted by 1 (e.g., an 18th-level lawful good caster could contact the plane of the Seven Heavens (LG) on the "Intelligence 20" line, or the plane of Elysium (NG) on the "Intelligence 19" line).

Demi-Shadow Monsters (Illusion/Phantasm)

Range: 30 yards
Components: V, S
Duration: 1 round/level
Casting Time: 5
Area of Effect: 20-foot cube
Saving Throw: Special

This spell is similar to the 4th-level spell, *shadow monsters*, except that the monsters created are effectively 40% of normal hit points. If the saving throw is made, their damage potential is only 40% of normal and their Armor Class is 8. The monsters have none of the special abilities of the real creatures, although victims may be deluded into believing this to be so.

Dismissal (Abjuration)

Range: 10 yards
Components: V, S, M
Duration: Permanent
Casting Time: 1 round
Area of Effect: 1 creature
Saving Throw: Neg.

By means of this spell, a wizard on the Prime Material plane seeks to force or to enable a creature from another plane of existence to return to its proper plane. Magic resistance, if any, is checked if this spell is used to force a being home. If the resistance fails, the caster's level is compared to the creature's level or Hit Dice. If the wizard's level is higher, the difference is subtracted from the creature's die roll for its saving throw vs. spell. If the creature's level or Hit Dice is higher, the difference is added to the saving throw roll.

If the creature desires to be returned to its home plane, no saving throw is necessary (it chooses to fail the roll).

If the spell is successful, the creature is instantly whisked away, but the spell has a 20% chance of actually sending the subject to a plane other than its own.

The material component is any item that is distasteful to the subject creature.

Distance Distortion (Alteration)

Range: 10 yards/level
Components: V, S, M
Duration: 2 turns/level
Casting Time: 5
Area of Effect: One 10-foot cube per level
Saving Throw: None

This spell can be cast only in an area completely surrounded or enclosed by earth, rock, sand, or similar materials. The wizard must also cast a *conjure elemental* spell to summon an earth elemental. The elemental serves without attempting to break free when the spellcaster announces that his intent is to cast a *distance distortion* spell. The spell places the earth elemental in the area of effect, and the elemental then causes the area's dimensions to be either doubled or halved for those traveling over it (spellcaster's choice of which). Thus a 10' × 100' corridor could seem to be either five feet wide and 50 feet long or 20 feet wide and 200 feet long. When the spell duration has elapsed, the elemental returns to its own plane.

The true nature of an area affected by distance distortion is undetectable to any creature traveling along it, but the area dimly radiates magic, and a *true seeing* spell can reveal that an earth elemental is spread within the area.

The material needed for this spell is a small lump of soft clay.

Plane	Chance of Insanity *	Chance of Knowledge	Chance of Veracity **
Elemental	20%	55% (90%)	62% (75%)
Inner Plane	25%	60%	65%
Astral Plane	30%	65%	67%
Outer Plane, Intelligence 19	35%	70%	70%
O.P., Intelligence 20	40%	75%	73%
O.P., Intelligence 21	45%	80%	75%
O.P., Intelligence 22	50%	85%	78%
O.P., Intelligence 23	55%	90%	81%
O.P., Intelligence 24	60%	95%	85%
O.P., Intelligence 25	65%	98%	90%

* For every point of Intelligence over 15, the wizard reduces insanity chance by 5%.

** If the being does not know an answer, and the chance of veracity is not made, the being will emphatically give an incorrect answer. If the chance of veracity is made, the being will answer "unknown."

Percentages in parentheses are for questions that pertain to the appropriate elemental plane.

Domination (Enchantment/Charm)

Range: 10 yards/level
Components: V, S
Duration: Special
Casting Time: 5
Area of Effect: 1 person
Saving Throw: Neg.

The *domination* spell enables the caster to control the actions of any person until the spell is ended by the subject's Intelligence (see the *charm person* spell). Elves and half-elves resist this enchantment as they do all *charm*-type spells. When the spell is cast, the subject must roll a saving throw vs. spell at a penalty of −2, but Wisdom adjustments apply. Failure means the wizard has established a telepathic link with the subject's mind. If a common language is shared, the wizard can generally force the subject to perform as the wizard desires, within the limits of the subject's body structure and Strength. Note that the caster does not receive direct sensory input from the subject.

Subjects resist this control, and those forced to take actions against their natures receive a new saving throw with a bonus of +1 to +4, depending on the type of action required. Obviously self-destructive orders are not carried out. Once control is established, there is no limit to the range at which it can be exercised, as long as the caster and subject are on the same plane.

A *protection from evil* spell can prevent the caster from exercising control or using the telepathic link while the subject is so warded, but it cannot prevent the establishment of domination.

Dream (Invocation, Illusion/Phantasm)
Reversible

Range: Touch
Components: V, S
Duration: Special
Casting Time: 1 turn
Area of Effect: 1 creature
Saving Throw: None

The *dream* spell enables the caster, or a messenger touched by the caster, to send messages to others in the form of dreams. At the beginning of the spell, the caster must name the recipient or identify him by some title that leaves no doubt as to his identity.

As the caster completes the spell, the person sending the spell falls into a deep trance-like sleep, and instantaneously projects his mind to the recipient. The sender then enters the recipient's dream and delivers the message unless the recipient is magically protected. If the recipient is awake, the message sender can choose to remain in the trance-like sleep. If the sender is disturbed during this time, the spell is immediately cancelled and the sender comes out of the trance. The whereabouts and current activities of the recipient cannot be learned through this spell.

The sender is unaware of his own surroundings or the activities around him while he is in his trance. He is totally defenseless, both physically and mentally (i.e., he always fails any saving throw) while in the trance.

Once the recipient's dreams are entered, the sender can deliver a message of any length, which the recipient remembers perfectly upon waking. The communication is one-way, the recipient cannot ask questions or offer information. Nor can the sender gain any information by observing the dreams of the recipient. Once the message is delivered, the sender's mind returns instantly to his body. The duration of the spell is the time required for the sender to enter the recipient's dream and deliver the message.

The reverse of this spell, *nightmare*, enables the caster to send a hideous and unsettling vision to the recipient, who is allowed a saving throw vs. spell to avoid the effect. The nightmare prevents restful sleep and causes 1d10 hit points of damage. The nightmare leaves the recipient fatigued and unable to regain spells for the next day. A *dispel evil* spell cast upon the recipient stuns the caster of the nightmare for one turn per level of the cleric countering this evil sending.

Extension II (Alteration)

Range: 0
Components: V
Duration: Special
Casting Time: 4
Area of Effect: Special
Saving Throw: None

This spell is the same as the 4th-level *extension I* spell, except it extends the duration of 1st- through 4th-level spells by 50%.

Fabricate (Enchantment, Alteration)

Range: 5 yards/level
Components: V, S, M
Duration: Permanent
Casting Time: Special
Area of Effect: 1 cubic yd./level
Saving Throw: None

By means of this spell, the wizard is able to convert material of one sort into a product that is of the same material. Thus the spellcaster can fabricate a wooden bridge from a clump of trees, a rope from a patch of hemp, clothes from flax or wool, and so forth. Magical or living things cannot be created or altered by a *fabricate* spell. The quality of items made by this spell is commensurate with the quality of material used as the basis for the new fabrication. If a mineral is worked with, the area of effect is reduced by a factor of 27—one cubic foot per level instead of one cubic yard.

Articles requiring a high degree of craftsmanship (jewelry, swords, glass, crystal, etc.) cannot be fabricated unless the wizard otherwise has great skill in the appropriate craft.

Casting requires one full round per cubic yard (or foot) or material to be affected by the spell.

False Vision (Divination)

Range: 0
Components: V, S, M
Duration: 1d4 rounds + 1 round/level
Casting Time: 5
Area of Effect: 30-foot radius
Saving Throw: None

When this spell is cast, the wizard is able to confound any attempt to scry (by means of either a spell or a magical device) any point within the area of effect of the spell. To use the spell, he must be aware of the scrying attempt, although knowledge of the scryer or the scryer's location is not necessary. Upon casting the spell, the caster and all he desires within the radius of the spell become undetectable to the scrying. Furthermore, the caster is able to send whatever message he desires, including vision and sound, according to the medium of the scrying method. To do this, the caster must concentrate on the message he is sending. Once concentration is broken, no further images can be sent, although the caster remains undetectable for the duration of the spell.

The material component for this spell is the ground dust of an emerald worth at least 500 gp, which is sprinkled into the air when the spell is cast.

Feeblemind (Enchantment/Charm)

Range: 10 yards/level
Components: V, S, M
Duration: Permanent
Casting Time: 5
Area of Effect: 1 creature
Saving Throw: Neg.

This spell is used solely against people or creatures who use magic spells. *Feeblemind* causes the subject's intellect to degenerate to that of a moronic child. The subject remains in this state until a *heal* or *wish* spell is used to cancel the effects. Magic-using beings are very vulnerable to this spell, thus their saving throws suffer the following penalties:

Spell Use of Target	Saving Throw Adjustment
Priest	+1
Wizard (human)	−4
Combination or nonhuman	−2

Wisdom adjustments apply to the saving throw.

The material component of this spell is a handful of clay, crystal, glass, or mineral spheres, which disappears when the spell is cast.

Hold Monster (Enchantment/Charm)

Range: 5 yards/level
Components: V, S, M
Duration: 1 round/level
Casting Time: 5
Area of Effect: 1 to 4 creatures in a 40-foot cube
Saving Throw: Neg.

This spell immobilizes from one to four creatures of any type within spell range and in sight of the spellcaster. He can opt to hold one, two, three, or four creatures. If three or four are attacked, each saving throw is normal; if two are attacked, each saving throw suffers a −1 penalty; if only one is attacked, the saving throw suffers a −3 penalty.

The material component for this spell is one hard metal bar or rod for each monster to be held. The bar or rod can be as small as a three-penny nail.

Leomund's Lamentable Belaborment (Enchantment, Evocation)

Range: 10 yards
Components: V
Duration: Special
Casting Time: 5
Area of Effect: 1 or more creatures in a 10-foot radius
Saving Throw: Special

This devious spell distracts the subject creatures by drawing them into an absorbing discussion on topics of interest to them. A chain of responses occurs during the next 11 rounds, with additional saving throws as described later. These responses are conversation (rounds 1-3), possible confusion (rounds 4-6), then either rage or lamentation (rounds 7-11). All saving throws are affected by the creatures' Intelligences, as noted later. The subject creatures must be able to understand the language in which the spellcaster speaks.

Upon casting the spell, the wizard begins discussion of some topic germane to the creature or creatures to be affected. Those making a successful saving throw vs. spell are unaffected. Affected creatures immediately begin to converse with the spellcaster, agreeing or disagreeing, all most politely. As long as the spellcaster chooses, he can maintain the spell by conversing with the subject(s). If the caster is attacked or otherwise distracted, the subject creatures do not notice.

Intelligence	Saving Throw Modifier
2 or less	Spell has no effect
3 to 7	−1
8 to 10	0
11 to 14	+1
15 or higher	+2

The wizard can leave at any time after the casting and the subject(s) continue on as if the caster were still present. As long as they are not attacked, the creatures ignore all else going on around them, spending their time talking and arguing to the exclusion of other activities. However, when the caster leaves, each subject completes only the stage of the spell that it is currently in, and then the spell is broken.

If the caster maintains the spell for more than three rounds, each affected creature can roll another saving throw vs. spell. Those failing to save wander off in confusion for 1d10 + 2 rounds, staying away from the spellcaster. Those who make this saving throw continue to talk and roll saving throws each round the caster continues the spell, up through the sixth round, to avoid the confusion effect.

If the spell is maintained for more than six rounds, each subject must roll a successful saving throw vs. spell to avoid going into a rage, attacking all other subjects of the spell with intent to kill. This rage lasts for 1d4 + 1 rounds. Those who successfully save against the rage effect realize that they have been deceived and collapse to the ground, lamenting their foolishness, for 1d4 rounds unless attacked or otherwise disturbed.

Leomund's Secret Chest (Alteration, Conjuration/Summoning)

Range: Special
Components: V, S, M
Duration: 60 days
Casting Time: 1 turn
Area of Effect: 1 chest of about 2' × 2' × 3' size
Saving Throw: None

This spell enables a specially constructed chest to be hidden deep within the Ethereal plane, to be summoned using a small model of the chest. The large chest must be exceptionally well-crafted and expensive, constructed for the caster by master craftsmen. If made principally of wood, it must be ebony, rosewood, sandalwood, teak, or the like, and all of its corner fittings, nails, and hardware must be platinum. If constructed of ivory, the metal fittings of the chest must be gold. If the chest is fashioned from bronze, copper, or silver, its fittings must be electrum or silver. The cost of such a chest is never less than 5,000 gp. Once it is constructed, the wizard must have a tiny replica (of the same materials and perfect in every detail) made, so that the miniature of the chest appears to be a perfect copy. One wiz-

ard can have but one pair of these chests at any given time—even *wish* spells do not allow exceptions! The chests themselves are nonmagical, and can be fitted with locks, wards, and so on just as any normal chest.

While touching the chest and holding the tiny replica, the caster chants the spell. This causes the large chest to vanish into the Ethereal plane. The chest can contain one cubic foot of material per level of the wizard no matter what its apparent size. Living matter makes it 75% likely that the spell fails, so the chest is typically used for securing valuable spell books, magical items, gems, etc. As long as the spellcaster has the small duplicate of the magical chest, he can recall the large one from the Ethereal plane whenever the chest is desired. If the miniature of the chest is lost or destroyed, there is no way, not even a *wish* spell, that the large chest can return, although an expedition might be mounted to find it.

While the chest is in the Ethereal plane, there is a 1% cumulative chance per week that some being finds it. This chance is reset to 1% whenever the chest is recalled and the spell recast to return it to the Ethereal plane. If the chest is found, the DM must work out the encounter and decide how the being reacts to the chest (for example, it might ignore the chest, fully or partially empty it, or even exchange or add to the items present!).

Whenever the secret chest is brought back to the Prime Material plane, an ethereal window is opened and for a variable amount of time, usually about one turn, slowly diminishes in size. When this hole opens between the planes, check for an ethereal encounter to see if a monster is drawn through.

If the large chest is not retrieved before the spell duration lapses, there is a cumulative chance of 5% per day that the chest is lost.

Magic Jar (Necromancy)

Range: 10 yards/level
Components: V, S, M
Duration: Special
Casting Time: 1 round
Area of Effect: 1 creature
Saving Throw: Special

The *magic jar* spell enables the caster to shift his life force into a special receptacle (a gem or large crystal). From there the caster can force an exchange of life forces between the receptacle and another creature, thus enabling the wizard to take over and control the body of another creature, while the life force of the host is confined in the receptacle. The special life force receptacle must be within spell range of the wizard's body at the time of spellcasting. The wizard's life force shifts into the receptacle in the round in which the casting is completed, allowing no other actions.

While in the magic jar, the caster can sense and attack any life force within a 10-foot-per-level radius (on the same plane); however, the exact creature types and relative physical positions cannot be determined. In a group of life forces, the caster can sense a difference of four or more levels/Hit Dice and can determine whether a life force is positive or negative energy. For example, if two 10th-level fighters are attacking a hill giant and four ogres, the caster could determine that there are three stronger and four weaker life forces within range, all with positive life energy. The caster could try to take over either a stronger or a weaker creature, but he has no control over exactly which creature is attacked.

An attempt to take over a host body requires a full round. It is blocked by a *protection from evil* spell or similar ward. It is successful only if the subject fails a saving throw vs. spell with a special modifier (see following). The saving throw is modified by subtracting the combined Intelligence and Wisdom scores of the target from those of the wizard (Intelligence and hit dice in nonhuman or nonhumanoid creatures). This modifier is added to (or subtracted from) the die roll.

Difference	Die Adjustment
−9 or less	+4
−8 to −6	+3
−5 to −3	+2
−2 to 0	+1
+1 to +4	0
+5 to +8	−1
+9 to +12	−2
+13 or more	−3

A negative score indicates that the wizard has a lower total than the target, thus the host has a saving throw bonus. Failure to take over the host leaves the wizard's life force in the magic jar.

If successful, the caster's life force occupies the host body and the host's life force is confined in the magic jar receptacle. The caster can call upon rudimentary or instinctive knowledge of the subject creature, but not upon its real or acquired knowledge (i.e., the wizard does not automatically know the language or spells of the creature). The caster retains his own attack rolls, class knowledge and training, and any adjustments due to his Intelligence or Wisdom. If the host body is human or humanoid, and the necessary spell components are available, the wizard can even use his memorized spells. The host body retains its own hit points and physical abilities and properties. The DM decides if any additional modifications are necessary; for example, perhaps clumsiness or inefficiency occurs if the caster must become used to the new form. The alignment of the host or receptacle is that of the occupying life force.

The caster can shift freely from the host to the receptacle if within the 10-feet/level range. Each attempt to shift requires one round. The spell ends when the wizard shifts from the jar to his own body.

A successful *dispel magic* spell cast on the host can drive the caster of the *magic jar* spell back into the receptacle and prevent him from making any attacks for 1d4 rounds plus 1 round per level of the caster of the dispel. The base success chance is 50%, +/− 5% per level difference between the casters. A successful *dispel magic* cast against the receptacle forces the occupant back into his own body. If the wizard who cast the *magic jar* is forced back into his own body, the spell ends.

If the host body is slain, the caster returns to the receptacle, if within range, and the life force of the host departs (i.e., it is dead). If the host body is slain beyond the range of the spell, both the host and the caster die.

Any life force with nowhere to go is treated as slain unless recalled by a *raise dead*, *resurrection*, or similar spell.

If the body of the caster is slain, his life force survives if it is in either the receptacle or the host. If the receptacle is destroyed while the caster's life force occupies it, the caster is irrevocably slain.

Major Creation (Illusion/Phantasm)

Range: 10 yards
Components: V, S, M
Duration: Special
Casting Time: 1 turn
Area of Effect: Special
Saving Throw: None

Like the *minor creation* spell, *major creation* enables the wizard to pull wisps of material from the plane of Shadow to create an item of nonliving, vegetable nature—soft goods, rope, wood, etc. The wizard can also create mineral objects—stone, crystal, metal, etc. The item created cannot exceed one cubic foot per level of the spellcaster in volume. The duration of the created item varies with its relative hardness and rarity:

Vegetable matter	2 hours/level
Stone or crystal	1 hour/level
Precious metals	2 turns/level
Gems	1 turn/level
Mithral *	2 rounds/level
Adamantite	1 round/level

* Includes similar rare metals.

Attempting to use any of these as material components in a spell will cause the spell to fail. The spellcaster must have at least a tiny piece of matter of the same type as the item he plans to create—a bit of twisted hemp to create rope, a chip of stone to create a boulder, and so on.

Monster Summoning III
(Conjuration/Summoning)

Range: 50 yards
Components: V, S, M
Duration: 4 rounds + 1 round/level
Casting Time: 5
Area of Effect: Special
Saving Throw: None

This spell is much like the 3rd-level *monster summoning I* spell, except that this spell summons 1d4 3rd-level monsters. These appear within spell range and attack the caster's opponents, until either he commands them to cease, the spell duration expires, or the monsters are slain. These creatures do not check morale and vanish when slain. If no opponent exists to fight, and the wizard can communicate with them, the summoned monsters can perform other services for the wizard.

The material components of this spell are a tiny bag and a small candle.

Mordenkainen's Faithful Hound
(Conjuration/Summoning)

Range: 10 yards
Components: V, S, M
Duration: Special
Casting Time: 5
Area of Effect: Special
Saving Throw: None

By means of this spell, the wizard summons up a phantom watchdog that only he can see. He may then command it to perform as guardian of a passage, room, door, or similar space or portal. The phantom watchdog immediately commences a loud barking if any creature larger than a cat approaches the place it guards. As the faithful hound is able to detect invisible creatures and ward against the approach of ethereal creatures, it is an excellent guardian. It does not react to illusions that are not at least quasi-real.

If the intruding creature exposes its back to the watchdog, the dog delivers a vicious attack as if it were a 10-Hit Dice monster, striking for 3d6 points of damage. It is able to hit opponents of all types, even those normally subject only to magical weapons of +3 or greater. Creatures without backs are not attacked (ochre jellies, for instance). The faithful hound cannot be attacked, but it can be dispelled. The spell lasts for a maximum of one hour plus 1/2 hour per caster level, but once it is activated by an intruder, it lasts only one round per caster level. If the spellcaster is ever more than 30 yards distant from the area that the watchdog guards, the spell ends.

The material components of this spell are a tiny silver whistle, a piece of bone, and a thread.

Passwall (Alteration)

Range: 30 yards
Components: V, S, M
Duration: 1 hour + 1 turn/level
Casting Time: 5
Area of Effect: Special
Saving Throw: None

A *passwall* spell enables the spellcaster to open a passage through wooden, plaster, or stone walls, but not other materials. The spellcaster and any associates can simply walk through. The spell causes a 5′ wide × 8′ high × 10′ deep opening. Several of these spells can form a continuing passage so that very thick walls can be pierced. If dispelled, the passwall closes away from the dispelling caster, ejecting those in the passage.

The material component of this spell is a pinch of sesame seeds.

Seeming (Illusion/Phantasm)

Range: 10-foot radius
Components: V, S
Duration: 12 hours
Casting Time: 5
Area of Effect: 1 person/2 levels
Saving Throw: None

This spell enables the caster to alter the appearance of one person for every two levels of experience he has attained. The change includes clothing and equipment. The caster can make the recipients appear as any generally man-shaped bipedal creature, each up to one foot shorter or taller than his normal height, and thin or fat or in between. All those affected must resemble the same general type of creature: human, orc, ogre, etc. Each remains a recognizable individual. The effect fails for an individual if the illusion chosen by the caster cannot be accomplished within the spell parameters (for example, a halfling could not be made to look like a centaur, but he might be made to look like a short, young ogre). Unwilling persons receive saving throws vs. spell to avoid the effect. Affected persons resume their normal appearances if slain. The spell is not precise enough to duplicate the appearance of a specific individual.

Sending (Evocation)

Range: Special
Components: V, S, M
Duration: Special
Casting Time: 1 turn
Area of Effect: 1 creature
Saving Throw: None

By means of this spell, the caster can contact a single creature with whom he is familiar and whose name and appearance are known. If the creature in question is not on the same plane of existence as the spellcast-er, there is a base 5% chance that the sending does not arrive. Local conditions on other planes may worsen this chance considerably at the option of the DM. The sending, if successful, can be understood even by a creature with an Intelligence as low as 1 (animal Intelligence).

The wizard can send a short message of 25 words or less to the recipient. Also the recipient can answer in like manner immediately. Even if the sending is received, the subject creature is not obligated to act upon it in any manner.

The material component for this spell consists of two tiny cylinders, each with one open end, connected by a short piece of fine copper wire.

Shadow Door (Illusion/Phantasm)

Range: 10 yards
Components: S
Duration: 1 round/level
Casting Time: 2
Area of Effect: Special
Saving Throw: None

By means of this spell, the wizard creates the illusion of a door. The illusion also permits the wizard to appear to step through this "door" and disappear. In reality he has darted aside and can flee, totally invisible, for the spell duration. Creatures viewing this are deluded into seeing or entering an empty 10′ × 10′ room if they open the "door." A *true seeing* spell, a *gem of seeing*, or similar magical means can discover the wizard. Certain high Hit Dice monsters might also notice the wizard (see the *invisibility* spell), but only if making an active attempt to do so.

Shadow Magic (Illusion/Phantasm)

Range: 50 yards + 10 yards/level
Components: V, S
Duration: Special
Casting Time: 5
Area of Effect: Special
Saving Throw: Special

The *shadow magic* spell enables the wizard to tap energy from the Shadow plane to cast a quasi-real wizard evocation spell of 3rd level or less. For example, this spell can be *magic missile*, *fireball*, *lightning bolt*, or so on, and has normal effects upon creatures in the area of effect if they fail their saving throws vs. spell. Thus a creature failing to save against a shadow magic fireball must roll another saving throw, suffering half of the normal fireball damage if successful and full normal fireball damage if the saving throw is failed. If the first saving throw was successful, the shadow magic nature is detected and only 20% of the rolled damage is received (rounding down below fractions below .4 and rounding up fractions of .4 and above).

Stone Shape (Alteration)

Range: Touch
Components: V, S, M
Duration: Permanent
Casting Time: 1 round
Area of Effect: 1 cubic foot/level
Saving Throw: None

By means of this spell, the wizard can form an existing piece of stone into a shape that suits his purposes. For example, a stone weapon can be made, a special trapdoor fashioned, or an idol sculpted. This spell can also enable the spellcaster to reshape a stone door so as to escape imprisonment, providing the volume of stone involved was within the limits of the area of effect. While stone coffers can be thus formed and stone doors made, the fineness of detail is not great. If the construction involves small moving parts, there is a 30% chance they do not function.

The material component of this spell is soft clay that must be worked into roughly the desired shape of the stone object and then touched to the stone when the spell is uttered.

Summon Shadow
(Conjuration/Summoning, Necromancy)

Range: 10 yards
Components: V, S, M
Duration: 1 round + 1 round/level
Casting Time: 5
Area of Effect: 10-foot cube
Saving Throw: None

When this spell is cast, the wizard conjures up one shadow (see the *Monstrous Compendium*) for every three levels of experience he has attained. These monsters are under the control of the spellcaster and attack his enemies on command. The shadows remain until slain, turned, or the spell duration expires.

The material component for this spell is a bit of smoky quartz.

Telekinesis (Alteration)

Range: 10 yards/level
Components: V, S
Duration: Special
Casting Time: 5
Area of Effect: Special
Saving Throw: Neg.

By means of this spell, the wizard is able to move objects by concentrating on moving them mentally. The spell can provide either a gentle, sustained force or a single short, violent thrust.

A sustained force enables the wizard to move a weight of up to 25 pounds a distance up to 20 feet per round. The spell lasts two rounds, plus one round per caster level. The weight can be moved vertically, horizontally, or both. An object moved beyond the caster's range falls or stops. If the caster ceases concentration for any reason, the object falls or stops. The object can be telekinetically manipulated as if with one hand. For example, a lever or rope can be pulled, a key can be turned, an object rotated and so on, if the force required is within the weight limitation. The caster might even be able to untie simple knots, at the discretion of the DM.

Alternatively, the spell energy can be expended in a single round. The caster can hurl one or more objects within range, and within a ten-foot cube, directly away from himself at high speed, to a distance of up to ten feet per caster level. This is subject to a maximum weight of 25 pounds per caster level. Damage caused by hurled objects is decided by the DM, but cannot exceed 1 point of damage per caster level. Opponents who fall within the weight capacity of the spell can be hurled, but they are allowed a saving throw vs. spell to avoid the effect. Furthermore, those able to employ as simple a counter-measure as an *enlarge* spell, for example (thus making the body weight go over the maximum spell limit), can easily counter the spell. The various *Bigby's hand* spells also counter this spell.

Teleport (Alteration)

Range: Touch
Components: V
Duration: Instantaneous
Casting Time: 2
Area of Effect: Special
Saving Throw: None

When this spell is used, the wizard instantly transports himself, along with a certain amount of additional weight that is on or being touched by the spellcaster, to a well-known destination. Distance is not a factor, but interplanar travel is not possible by means of a *teleport* spell. The spellcaster is able to teleport a maximum weight of 250 pounds, plus an additional 150 pounds for each level of experience above the 10th (a 13th-level wizard can teleport up to 700 pounds). If the destination area is very familiar to the wizard (he has a clear mental picture through actual proximity to and study of the area), it is unlikely that there is any error in arriving, although the caster has no control over his facing upon arrival. Lesser known areas (those seen only magically or from a distance) increase the probability of error. Unfamiliar areas present considerable peril (see table).

Destination Is:	Probability of Teleporting: On		
	High	Target	Low
Very familiar	01-02	03-99	00
Studied carefully	01-04	05-98	99-00
Seen casually	01-08	09-96	97-00
Viewed once	01-16	17-92	93-00
Never seen	01-32	33-84	85-00

Teleporting high means the wizard arrives ten feet above the ground for every 1% he is below the lowest "On Target" probability; this could be as high as 320 feet if the destination area was never seen. Any low result means the instant death of the wizard if the area into which he teleports is solid. A wizard cannot teleport to an area of empty space—a substantial surface must be there, whether a wooden floor, a stone floor, natural ground, etc. Areas of strong physical or magical energies may make teleportation more hazardous or even impossible.

Transmute Rock to Mud (Alteration)
Reversible

Range: 10 yards/level
Components: V, S, M
Duration: Special
Casting Time: 5
Area of Effect: One 20-foot cube/level
Saving Throw: None

This spell turns natural rock of any sort into an equal volume of mud. The depth of the mud can never exceed one-half its length or breadth. If it is cast upon a rock, for example, the rock affected collapses into mud. Creatures unable to levitate, fly, or otherwise free themselves from the mud sink at the rate of ten feet per round and suffocate, except for light-weight creatures that could normally pass across such ground. Brush thrown atop the mud can support creatures able to climb on top of it, with the amount of brush required subject to the DM's discretion. The mud remains until a *dispel magic* spell or a reverse of this spell, *mud to rock*, restores its substance—but not necessarily its form. Evaporation turns the mud to normal dirt, at the rate of 1d6 days per ten cubic feet. The *mud to rock* reverse can harden normal mud into soft stone (sandstone or similar mineral) permanently unless magically changed.

The material components for the spell are clay and water (or sand, lime, and water for the reverse).

Wall of Force (Evocation)

Range: 30 yards
Components: V, S, M
Duration: 1 turn + 1 round/level
Casting Time: 5
Area of Effect: Up to 10-foot square/level
Saving Throw: None

A *wall of force* spell creates an invisible barrier in the locale desired by the caster, up to the spell's range. The wall of force cannot move and is totally unaffected by most spells, including *dispel magic*. But a *disintegrate* spell will immediately destroy it, as will a *rod of cancellation* or a sphere of annihilation. Likewise, the wall of force is not affected by blows, missiles, cold, heat, electricity, etc. Spells and breath weapons cannot pass through it in either direction, although *dimension door*, *teleport*, and similar effects can bypass the barrier.

The wizard can, if desired, form the wall into a spherical shape with a radius up to one foot per level or to an open hemispherical shape of 1.5-foot radius per caster level. The wall of force must be continuous and unbroken when formed; if its surface is broken by any object or creature, the spell fails. The caster can end the spell on command.

The material component for this spell is a pinch of powdered diamond worth 5,000 gp.

Wall of Iron (Evocation)

Range: 5 yards/level
Components: V, S, M
Duration: Permanent
Casting Time: 5
Area of Effect: 15 square feet/level or special
Saving Throw: None

When this spell is cast, the wizard causes a vertical iron wall to spring into being. This wall can be used to seal off a passage or close a breach, for the wall inserts itself into any surrounding nonliving material if its area is sufficient to do so. The wall of iron is 1/4 inch thick per level of experience of the spellcaster. The wizard is able to create an area of iron wall up to 15 square feet for each of his experience levels, so at 12th level a wall of iron 180 square feet in area can be created. The wizard can double the wall's area by halving its thickness.

If the caster desires, the wall can be created vertically resting on a flat surface, so that it can be tipped over, to fall on and crush any creature beneath it. The wall is 50% likely to tip in either direction. This chance can be modified by a force of not less than 30 Strength and 400 pounds mass—each pound over 400 or Strength point over 30 alters the chance by 1% in favor of the stronger side. Creatures with room to flee the falling wall may do so by making successful saving throws vs. death. Those who fail are killed. Huge and gargantuan creatures cannot be crushed by the wall.

The wall is permanent, unless successfully dispelled, but it is subject to all forces a normal iron wall is subject to—rust, perforation, etc.

The material component of this spell is a small piece of sheet iron.

Wall of Stone (Evocation)

Range: 5 yards/level
Components: V, S, M
Duration: Permanent
Casting Time: 5
Area of Effect: Special
Saving Throw: None

This spell creates a wall of granite rock that merges into adjoining rock surfaces. It is typically employed to close passages, portals, and breaches against opponents. The wall of stone is 1/4 inch thick and up to 20 square feet per level of experience of the wizard casting the spell. Thus, a 12th-level wizard can create a wall of stone three inches thick and up to 240 square feet in surface area (a 12-foot-wide and 20-foot-high wall, for example, to completely close a 10' × 16' passage). The wall created need not be vertical nor need it rest upon any firm foundation (see the *wall of iron* spell); however, it must merge with and be solidly supported by existing stone. It can be used to bridge a chasm, for instance, or as a ramp. For this use, if the span is more than 20 feet, the wall must be arched and buttressed. This requirement reduces the area of effect by half. Thus, a 20th-level caster can create a span with a surface area of 200 square feet. The wall can be crudely shaped to allow crenelations, battlements, and so forth by likewise reducing the area. The stone is permanent unless destroyed by a *dispel magic* spell or a *disintegrate* spell, or by normal means such as breaking or chipping.

The material component is a small block of granite.

Sixth-Level Spells

Anti-Magic Shell (Abjuration)

Range: 0
Components: V, S
Duration: 1 turn/level
Casting Time: 1
Area of Effect: 1'/level diameter sphere
Saving Throw: None

By means of this spell, the wizard surrounds himself with an invisible barrier that moves with him. The area within this barrier is totally impervious to all magic and magical spell effects, thus preventing the passage of spells or their effects. Likewise it prevents the functioning of any magical items or spells within its confines. The area is also impervious to breath weapons, gaze or voice attacks, and similar special attack forms.

The anti-magic shell also hedges out charmed, summoned, or conjured creatures. It cannot, however, be forced against any creature that it would keep at bay; any attempt to do so creates a discernible pressure against the barrier, and continued pressure will break the spell. Normal creatures (a normally encountered troll rather than one conjured up, for instance) can enter the area, as can normal missiles. Furthermore, while a magical sword does not function magically within the area, it is still a sword. Note that creatures on their home plane are normal creatures there. Thus on the elemental plane of Fire, a randomly encountered fire elemental cannot be kept at bay by this spell. Artifacts, relics, and creatures of

demigod or higher status are unaffected by mortal magic such as this.

Should the caster be larger than the area enclosed by the barrier, parts of his person may be considered exposed, at the referee's option. A *dispel magic* spell does not remove the spell; the caster can end it upon command.

Bigby's Forceful Hand (Evocation)

Range: 10 yards/level
Components: V, S, M
Duration: 1 round/level
Casting Time: 6
Area of Effect: Special
Saving Throw: None

Bigby's forceful hand is a more powerful version of Bigby's interposing hand. It creates a man-sized (five feet) to gargantuan-sized (21 feet) hand that places itself between the spellcaster and a chosen opponent. This disembodied hand then moves to remain between the two, regardless of what the spellcaster does or how the opponent tries to get around it. However, the forceful hand also pushes on the opponent. This force can push away a creature weighing 500 pounds or less, slow movement to 10 feet per round if the creature weighs between 500 and 2,000 pounds, or slow movement by 50% if the creature weighs more than 2,000 pounds.

A creature pushed away is pushed to the range limit, or until pressed against an unyielding surface. The hand itself inflicts no damage. The forceful hand has an Armor Class of 0, has as many hit points as its caster in full health, and vanishes when destroyed. The caster can cause it to retreat (to release a trapped opponent, for example) or dismiss it on command.

The material component is a glove.

Chain Lightning (Evocation)

Range: 40 yards + 5 yards/level
Components: V, S, M
Duration: Instantaneous
Casting Time: 5
Area of Effect: Special
Saving Throw: 1/2

This spell creates an electrical discharge that begins as a single stroke of lightning, 2 1/2 feet wide, commencing from the fingertips of the caster. Unlike a *lightning bolt* spell, chain lightning strikes one object or creature initially, then arcs to a series of other objects or creatures within range, losing energy with each jump.

The bolt initially inflicts 1d6 points of damage per level of the caster, to a maximum of 12d6 (half damage if the object or creature rolls a successful saving throw vs. spell). After the first strike, the lightning arcs to the next nearest object or creature.

Each jump reduces the strength of the lightning by 1d6. Each creature or magical object hit receives a saving throw vs. spell. Success on this save indicates the creature suffers only half damage from the bolt.

The chain can strike as many times (including the first object or creature) as the spell caster has levels, although each creature or object can be struck only once. Thus, a bolt cast by a 12th-level wizard can strike up to 12 times, causing less damage with each strike. The bolt continues to arc until it has struck the appropriate number of objects or creatures, until it strikes an object that grounds it (interconnecting iron bars of a large cell or cage, a large pool of liquid, etc.), or until there are no more objects or creatures to strike.

Direction is not a consideration when plotting chain lightning arcs. Distance is a factor—an arc cannot exceed the spell's range. If the only possible arc is greater than the spell's range, the stroke fades into nothingness. Creatures immune to electrical attack can be struck, even though no damage is taken. Note that it is possible for the chain to arc back to the caster!

The material components are a bit of fur, a piece of amber, glass, or crystal rod, and one silver pin for each experience level of the caster.

Conjure Animals
(Conjuration/Summoning)

Range: 30 yards
Components: V, S
Duration: 1 round/level
Casting Time: 6
Area of Effect: Special
Saving Throw: None

The conjure animals spell enables the wizard to magically create one or more mammals to attack his opponents. The total Hit Dice of the mammals cannot exceed twice his level, if determined randomly, or his level if a specific animal type is requested (see the Dungeon Master's Guide). Thus, a wizard of 12th level could randomly conjure two mammals with 12 Hit Dice, four with 6 Hit Dice each, six with 4 Hit Dice each, eight with 3 Hit Dice each, twelve with 2 Hit Dice each, or 24 with 1 Hit Die each. Count every +1 hit point bonus of a creature as 1/4 of a Hit Die, thus a creature with 4+3 Hit Dice equals a 4 3/4 Hit Dice creature. The conjured animal(s) remain for one round for each level of the conjuring wizard, or until slain. They follow the caster's verbal commands. Conjured animals unfailingly attack the wizard's opponents, but they resist being used for any other purpose.

Contingency (Evocation)

Range: 0
Components: V, S, M
Duration: 1 day/level
Casting Time: 1 turn
Area of Effect: The caster
Saving Throw: None

By means of this spell, the wizard is able to place another spell upon his person so that the latter spell will come into effect under the conditions dictated during the casting of the contingency spell. The contingency spell and the spell it is to bring into effect are cast at the same time (the one-turn casting time indicated is the total for both castings).

The spell to be brought into effect by the prescribed contingency must be one that affects the wizard's person (feather fall, levitation, fly, feign death, etc.) and is of a spell level no higher than 1/3 of the caster's experience level (rounded down), but not higher than the 6th spell level.

Caster Level	Contingency Spell Level
12th-14th	4th
15th-17th	5th
18th +	6th

Only one contingency spell can be placed on the spellcaster at any one time; if a second is cast, the first one (if still active) is cancelled. The conditions needed to bring the spell into effect must be clear, although they can be rather general. For example, a contingency spell cast with an airy water spell might prescribe that any time the wizard is plunged into or otherwise engulfed in water or similar liquid, the airy water spell will instantly come into effect. Or a contingency could bring a feather fall spell into effect any time the wizard falls more than two feet. In all cases, the contingency immediately brings into effect the second spell, the latter being "cast" instantaneously when the prescribed circumstances occur. Note that if complicated or convoluted conditions are prescribed, the whole spell complex (the contingency spell and the companion magic) may fail when called upon.

The material components of this spell are (in addition to those of the companion spell) 100 gp worth of quicksilver and an eyelash of an ogre mage, ki-rin, or similar spell-using creature. In addition, the spell requires a statuette of the wizard carved from elephant ivory (which is not destroyed, though it is subject to wear and tear), which must be carried on the person of the spell-caster for the contingency spell to perform its function when called upon.

Control Weather (Alteration)

Range: 0
Components: V, S, M
Duration: 4d6 hours
Casting Time: 1 turn
Area of Effect: 4d4 square miles
Saving Throw: None

The control weather spell enables a wizard to change the weather in the local area. The spell affects the weather for 4d6 hours in an area of 4d4 square miles. It requires one turn to cast the spell, and an additional 1d4 turns for the weather conditions to occur. The current weather conditions are decided by the DM, depending on the climate and season. Weather conditions have three components: precipitation, temperature, and wind. The spell can change these conditions according to the following chart.

The upper-cased headings represent the existing weather conditions. The small headings beneath each large heading are the new conditions to which the caster can change the existing conditions. Furthermore, the caster can control the direction of the wind. For example, a day that is clear and warm with moderate wind can be controlled to become hazy, hot, and calm. Contradictions are not possible—fog and strong wind, for example. Multiple control weath-

Precipitation	Temperature	Wind
CLEAR WEATHER	HOT	CALM
Very clear	Sweltering heat	Dead calm
Light clouds or hazy	Warm	Light wind
PARTLY CLOUDY	WARM	Moderate wind
Clear weather	Hot	MODERATE WIND
Cloudy	Cool	Calm
Mist/light rain/small hail	COOL	Strong wind
Sleet/Light snow	Warm	STRONG WIND
CLOUDY	Cold	Moderate Wind
Partly cloudy	COLD	Gale
Deep clouds	Cool	GALE
Fog	Arctic cold	Strong wind
Heavy rain/large hail		Storm
Driving sleet/heavy snow		STORM
		Gale
		Hurricane-typhoon

er spells can be used only in succession.

The material components for this spell are burning incense and bits of earth and wood mixed in water. Obviously, this spell functions only in areas where there are appropriate climatic conditions.

Death Fog (Alteration, Evocation)

Range: 30 yards
Components: V, S, M
Duration: 1d4 rounds + 1/level
Casting Time: 6
Area of Effect: Two 10-foot cubes/level
Saving Throw: None

The casting of a *death fog* spell creates an area of solid fog that has the additional property of being highly acidic. The vapors are deadly to living things, so that vegetation exposed to them will die—grass and similar small plants in two rounds, bushes and shrubs in four, small trees in eight, and large trees in 16 rounds. Animal life not immune to acid suffers damage according to the length of time it is exposed to the vapors of a death fog, as follows:

1st round: 1 point
2nd round: 2 points
3rd round: 4 points
4th and each succeeding round: 8 points

The death fog otherwise resembles the 2nd-level *fog cloud*: rolling, billowing vapors that can be moved only by a very strong wind. Any creature attempting to move through the death fog progresses at a rate of but one foot per unit of normal movement rate per round. A *gust of wind* spell cannot affect it. A fireball, flame strike, or a wall of fire can burn it away in a single round.

The material components are a pinch of dried and powdered peas, powdered animal hoof, and strong acid of any sort (including highly distilled vinegar or acid crystals), which must be obtained from an alchemist.

Death Spell (Necromancy)

Range: 10 yards/level
Components: V, S, M
Duration: Instantaneous
Casting Time: 6
Area of Effect: One 30-foot cube/level
Saving Throw: None

When a *death* spell is cast, it snuffs out the life forces of creatures in the area of effect instantly and irrevocably. Such creatures cannot be raised or resurrected, but an individual slain in this manner might be brought back via a *wish*. The number of creatures that can be slain is a function of their Hit Dice.

Creatures' Hit Dice	Maximum # of Creatures Affected
Under 2	4d20
2 to 4	2d20
4+1 to 6+3	2d4
6+4 to 8+3	1d4

If creatures of differing Hit Dice are attacked with a *death* spell, roll the dice (4d20) to determine how many creatures of under 2 Hit Dice are affected. If the number rolled is greater than the actual number of sub-2 Hit Dice creatures, apply the remainder of the roll to the higher Hit Dice creatures by consulting the following table.

Creature's Hit Dice	Conversion Factor (CF)
Under 2	1
2 to 4	2
4+1 to 6+3	10
6+4 to 8+3	20

In other words, from the 4d20 roll subtract the number of creatures of less than 2 Hit Dice (these creatures die). If there are any remaining points from the 4d20 roll, subtract 2 for each creature of 2 to 4 Hit Dice (these creatures also die). If this still doesn't use up all the 4d20 roll, subtract 10 for each creature of 4+1 to 6+3 Hit Dice, and so on. Stop when all the creatures are dead, all the 4d20 roll is used up, or the remainder is less than ½ of the CF of any remaining creatures. (If the remainder is ½ or more of the CF of a creature, that creature dies.)

Example: A mixed group of 20 goblins, eight gnolls, and four ogres, led by a hill giant, are caught in the area of a *death* spell. The 4d20 roll gives a total of 53 points; 20 of this eliminates the goblins (20 × 1 CF), 16 kills the gnolls (8 × 2 CF), and the remaining 17 kills two ogres (10 points to kill one ogre, and the remaining 7 points are enough to kill one more ogre). The other two ogres and the hill giant are unharmed.

A *death* spell does not affect lycanthropes, undead creatures, or creatures from planes other than the Prime Material.

The material component of this spell is a crushed black pearl with a minimum value of 1,000 gp.

Demi-Shadow Magic (Illusion/Phantasm)

Range: 60 yards + 10 yards/level
Components: V, S
Duration: Special
Casting Time: 6
Area of Effect: Special
Saving Throw: Special

This spell is similar to the 5th-level *shadow magic* spell, but this spell enables the casting of partially real 4th- and 5th-level evocations (*cone of cold, wall of fire, wall of ice, cloudkill,* etc.). If recognized as demi-shadow magic (if a saving throw vs. spell is successful), damaging spells inflict only 40% of normal damage, with a minimum of 2 points per die of damage. A demi-magic cloudkill slays creatures with fewer than 2 Hit Dice and inflicts 1d2 points of damage per round.

Disintegrate (Alteration)

Range: 5 yards/level
Components: V, S, M
Duration: Instantaneous
Casting Time: 6
Area of Effect: Special
Saving Throw: Neg.

This spell causes matter to vanish. It affects even matter (or energy) of a magical nature, such as Bigby's forceful hand, but not a globe of invulnerability or an antimagic shell. Disintegration is instantaneous, and its effects are permanent. Any single creature can be affected, even undead. Nonliving matter, up to a 10' × 10' × 10' cube, can be obliterated by the spell. The spell creates a thin, green ray that causes physical material touched to glow and vanish, leaving traces of fine dust. Creatures that successfully save vs. spell have avoided the ray (material items have resisted the magic) and are not affected. Only the first creature or object struck can be affected.

The material components are a lodestone and a pinch of dust.

Enchant an Item (Enchantment, Invocation)

Range: Touch
Components: V, S, M
Duration: Special
Casting Time: Special
Area of Effect: 1 item
Saving Throw: Neg.

This is a spell that must be used by a wizard planning to create a magical item. The *enchant an item* spell prepares the object to accept the magic. The item must meet the following tests: 1) it must be in sound and undamaged condition; 2) the item must be the finest possible, considering its nature, i.e., crafted of the highest quality material and with the finest workmanship; 3) its cost or value must reflect the second test, and in most cases the item must have a raw-materials cost in excess of 100 gp. With respect to requirement 3, it is not possible to apply this test to items such as ropes, leather goods, cloth, and pottery not normally embroidered, bejeweled, tooled, carved, or engraved. If such work or materials can be added to an item without weakening or harming its normal functions, however,

these are required for the item to be enchanted.

The wizard must have access to a workshop or laboratory, properly equipped and from which contaminating magic can be screened. Any magical item not related to the fabrication process (such as most protective devices) and within 30 feet of the materials is a source of contaminating magic and will spoil the process.

The item to be prepared must be touched by the spell caster. This touching must be constant and continual during the casting time, which is a base 16 hours plus an additional 8d8 hours (as the wizard may never work more than eight hours per day, and *haste* or any other spells will not alter the time required in any way, this effectively means that casting time for this spell is two days + 1d8 days). All work must be uninterrupted, and during rest periods the item being enchanted must never be more than one foot distant from the spellcaster, for if it is, the whole spell is spoiled and must be begun again. (Note that during rest periods absolutely no other form of magic can be performed, and the wizard must remain quiet and in isolation or the enchantment is ruined.)

At the end of the spell, the caster will know that the item is ready for the final test. He will then pronounce the final magical syllable, and if the item makes a saving throw (which is exactly the same as that of the wizard) vs. spell, the spell is completed. The spellcaster's saving throw bonuses also apply to the item, up to +3. A result of 1 on the 1d20 roll always results in failure, regardless of modifications. Once the spell is finished, the wizard can begin to place the desired spell upon the item. The spell he plans to place must be cast within 24 hours or the preparatory spell fades, and the item must be enchanted again.

Each spell subsequently cast upon an object bearing an *enchant an item* spell requires 2d4 hours per spell level of the magic being cast. Again, during casting the item must be touched by the wizard, and during the rest periods it must always be within one foot of his person. This procedure holds true for any additional spells placed upon the item, and each successive spell must be begun within 24 hours of the last, even if the prior spell failed.

No magic placed on an item is permanent unless a *permanency* spell is used as a finishing touch. This always runs a 5% risk of draining 1 point of Constitution from the wizard casting the spell. Also, while it is possible to tell when the basic spell (*enchant an item*) succeeds, it is not possible to tell if successive castings actually work, for each must make the same sort of saving throw as the item itself made. Naturally, items that are charged—rods, staves, wands, *javelins of lightning, ring of wishes,* etc.—can never

be made permanent. Magical devices cannot be used to *enchant an item* or cast magic upon an object so prepared, but scrolls can be used for this purpose.

The materials needed for this spell vary according to both the nature of the item being enchanted and the magic to be cast upon it. For example, a *cloak of displacement* might require the hides of one or more displacer beasts, a sword meant to slay dragons could require the blood and some other part of the type(s) of dragon(s) it will be effective against, and a *ring of shooting stars* might require pieces of meteorites and the horn of a ki-rin. These specifics, as well as other information pertaining to this spell, are decided by your Dungeon Master and must be discovered or researched in play.

Ensnarement (Conjuration/Summoning)

Range: 10 yards
Components: V, S, M
Duration: Special
Casting Time: 1 turn
Area of Effect: Special
Saving Throw: Neg.

Casting this spell attempts a dangerous act: to lure a powerful creature from another plane to a specially prepared trap, where it will be held until it agrees to perform one service in return for freedom from the *ensnarement* spell. The type of creature to be ensnared must be known and stated, and if it has a specific, proper, or given name, this must be used in casting the *ensnarement* spell. The spell causes an awareness of a *gate*-like opening on the plane of the creature to be ensnared. A special saving throw is then made to determine if the creature detects the nature of the planar opening as a trap or believes it to be a *gate*. To save, the creature must roll equal to or less than its Intelligence score on 1d20. The score is modified by the difference between the creature's Intelligence and that of the spellcaster. If the creature has a higher score, the difference is subtracted from its dice roll to save. If the spellcaster has a higher score, the difference is added to the dice roll.

If the saving throw succeeds, the creature ignores the spell-created opening, and the spell fails. If the saving throw fails, the creature steps into the opening and is ensnared.

When so trapped, the other-planar creature can freely attack the ensnaring wizard, unless the caster has created a warding circle. Such circles may be temporary (drawn by hand) or permanent (inlaid or carved). Even with such protection, the entrapped creature may break free and wreak its vengeance upon the spellcaster.

A hand-drawn circle has a base failure chance of 20%, while one inlaid or carved has a base of 10% (and that is for the first

time it is used, to determine whether or not the job was done properly). The base chance is modified by the difference between the wizard's combined Intelligence and experience level and the Intelligence and the experience level or Hit Dice of the creature ensnared. If the spellcaster has a higher total, that difference in percentage points is subtracted from the chance for the creature to break free. If the creature has a higher total, that difference is added to its chance to break free.

The chance can be further reduced by careful preparation of the circle. If the hand-made circle is drawn over a longer period of time, using specially prepared pigments (1,000 gp value per turn spent drawing), the chance of breaking free is reduced by 1% for every turn spent in preparation. This can bring the base chance to 0%.

Similarly, an inlaid or carved design can be brought to a 0% chance of the creature breaking free by inlaying with various metals, minerals, etc. This cost will require a minimum of one full month of time and add not less than 50,000 gp to the basic cost of having the circle inlaid or carved into stone. Any break in the circle spoils the efficacy of the spell and enables the creature to break free automatically. Even a straw dropped across the line of a magic circle destroys its power. Fortunately, the creature within cannot so much as place a straw upon any portion of the inscribed ward, for the magic of the barrier absolutely prevents it.

Once safely ensnared, the creature can be kept for as long as the spellcaster dares. (Remember the danger of something breaking the ward!) The creature cannot leave the circle, nor can any of its attacks or powers penetrate the barrier. The caster can offer bribes, use promises, or make threats in order to exact one service from the captive creature.

The DM will then assign a value to what the wizard has said to the ensnared creature, rating it from 0 to 6 (with 6 being the most persuasive). This rating is then subtracted from the Intelligence score of the creature. If the creature rolls a successful Intelligence check against its adjusted Intelligence, it refuses service. New offers, bribes, etc., can be made, or the old ones re-offered 24 hours later, when the creature's Intelligence has dropped by 1 point due to confinement. This can be repeated until the creature promises to serve, until it breaks free, or until the caster decides to get rid of it by means of some riddance spell. Impossible demands or unreasonable commands are never agreed to.

Once the single service is completed, the creature need only so inform the spellcaster to be instantly sent from whence it came. The creature might later seek revenge.

Extension III (Alteration)

Range: 0
Components: V
Duration: Special
Casting Time: 6
Area of Effect: Special
Saving Throw: None

This spell is the same as the 4th-level *extension I* spell, except that it will extend 1st- through 3rd-level spells to double duration and will extend the duration of 4th- or 5th-level spells by 50%.

Eyebite (Enchantment/Charm, Illusion/Phantasm)

Range: 20 yards
Components: V, S
Duration: 1 round/3 levels
Casting Time: 6
Area of Effect: 1 creature
Saving Throw: Special

An *eyebite* spell enables the caster to merely meet the gaze of a creature and speak a single word to cause an effect. This gaze attack is in addition to any other attacks allowed the wizard. The wizard selects one of four possible gaze attacks at the time the spell is cast, and this attack cannot be changed. For example, a 12th-level caster who chose *fear* would have four opportunities to make gaze attacks causing *fear*, one for each round of the spell's duration. Any gaze attack is negated by a successful saving throw vs. spell, with Wisdom adjustments. The four effects of the spell are as follows:

Charm: The wizard can charm a single person or monster by gaze and by uttering a single word. The effect is to make the *charmed* subject absolutely loyal and docile to the caster, even to the point of personal danger. It is otherwise the same as a *charm monster* spell. All creatures other than humans, demihumans, and humanoids save with +2 bonuses.

Fear: The wizard can cause fear by gaze and by speaking a single word. The subject flees in blind terror for 1d4 rounds. After this, the creature refuses to face the caster and cowers or bolts for the nearest cover if subsequently confronted by the caster (50% chance of either). The latter effect lasts one turn per caster level. This attack can be negated by spells that counter *fear*.

Sicken: This power enables the caster to merely gaze, speak a word, and cause sudden pain and fever to sweep over the subject's body. Creatures with ability scores function at half effectiveness, others inflict only one-half damage with physical attacks. Movement is at one-half normal rate. The subject remains stricken for one turn per level of the caster, after which all abilities return at the rate of one point per turn of complete rest or one point per hour of moderate activity. The effects cannot be negated by a *cure disease* or *heal* spell, but a *remove curse* or successful *dispel magic* spell is effective. Creatures other than humans, demihumans, and humanoids save with +2 bonuses versus this attack.

Sleep: The wizard can cause any individual to fall into a comatose slumber by means of a gaze and a single word, unless the subject successfully rolls its saving throw vs. spell. Creatures normally subject to a 1st-level *sleep* spell save with −2 penalties. An affected creature must be shaken or otherwise shocked back to consciousness.

In all cases, the gaze attack has a speed factor of 1. This gaze does not affect undead of any type, or extend beyond the plane occupied by the caster. Note that the caster is subject to the effects of his reflected gaze, and is allowed any applicable saving throw. In the case of a reflected *charm* gaze, the caster is paralyzed until it wears off or is countered.

Geas (Enchantment/Charm)

Range: 10 yards
Components: V
Duration: Special
Casting Time: 4
Area of Effect: 1 creature
Saving Throw: None

A *geas* spell places a magical command upon a creature (usually human or humanoid) to carry out some service, or to refrain from some action or course of activity, as desired by the spellcaster. The creature must be intelligent, conscious, under its own volition, and able to understand the caster. While a geas cannot compel a creature to kill itself or to perform acts that are likely to result in certain death, it can cause almost any other course of action. The geased creature must follow the given instructions until the geas is completed. Failure to do so will cause the creature to grow sick and die within 1d4 weeks. Deviation from or twisting of the instructions causes corresponding loss of Strength points until the deviation ceases. A geas can be done away with by a *wish* spell, but a *dispel magic* or *remove curse* spell will not negate it. Your DM will decide any additional details of a geas, for its casting and fulfillment are tricky, and an improperly cast geas is ignored.

Glassee (Alteration)

Range: Touch
Components: V, S, M
Duration: 1 round/level
Casting Time: 1 round
Area of Effect: Special
Saving Throw: None

By means of this spell, the wizard is able to make a section of metal, stone, or wood as transparent as glass to his gaze, or even make it into transparent material as explained hereafter. Normally, up to four inches of metal can be seen through, stone up to six inches thick can be made transparent, and 20 inches of wood can be affected by the *glassee* spell. The spell will not work on lead, gold, or platinum. The wizard can opt to make the glassee work only for himself for the duration of the spell, or he can actually make a transparent area, a one-way window, in the material affected. Either case gives a viewing area 3' wide by 2' high. If a window is created, it has the strength of the original material.

The material component of the spell is a small piece of crystal or glass.

Globe of Invulnerability (Abjuration)

Range: 0
Components: V, S, M
Duration: 1 round/level
Casting Time: 1 round
Area of Effect: 5-foot-radius sphere
Saving Throw: None

This spell creates an immobile, faintly shimmering, magical sphere around the caster that prevents any 1st-, 2nd-, 3rd-, or 4th-level spell effects from penetrating. Thus the area of effect of any such spell does not include the area of the globe of invulnerability. This includes innate spell-like abilities and effects from devices. However, any type of spell can be cast out of the magical sphere, and these pass from the caster of the globe to the subject without effect upon the globe. Fifth and higher level spells are not affected by the globe. The globe can be brought down by a successful *dispel magic* spell.

The material component of the spell is a glass or crystal bead that shatters at the expiration of the spell.

Guards and Wards (Evocation, Alteration, Enchantment/Charm)

Range: 0
Components: V, S, M
Duration: 1 hour/level
Casting Time: 3 turns
Area of Effect: Special
Saving Throw: None

This special and powerful spell is primarily used to defend the wizard's stronghold. The ward protects a one-storey stronghold, with a base dimension of 400' × 400'. The wizard can ward a multi-storey area by reducing the base area proportionately. The following take place in the warded area upon casing of the spell:

1. All corridors become misty, and visibility is reduced to 10 feet.
2. All doors are *wizard locked*.
3. Stairs are filled with webs from top to bottom. These act as the 2nd-level *web* spell, except that they regrow within one turn if destroyed.
4. Where there are choices in direction— such as a cross or side passage—a minor confusion-type spell functions so as to make it 50% probable that intruders believe they are going in the exact opposite direction.
5. The whole area radiates magic. The normal use of the *detect magic* spell becomes impossible for those of less than the caster's level and difficult for others.
6. One door per level of experience of the wizard is covered by an illusion to appear as if it were a plain wall.
7. The wizard can place one of the following additional magical effects:
   A. *Dancing lights* in four corridors
   B. *Magic mouth* in two places
   C. *Stinking cloud* in two places
   D. *Gust of wind* in one corridor or room
   E. *Suggestion* in one place.

Note that items 6 and 7 function only when the wizard is totally familiar with the area of the spell's effect. *Dispel magic* can remove one effect, at random, per casting. A *remove curse* spell will not work.

The material components of the spell are burning incense, a small measure of sulphur and oil, a knotted string, a small amount of umber hulk blood, and a small silver rod.

Invisible Stalker (Conjuration/Summoning)

Range: 10 yards
Components: V, S, M
Duration: Special
Casting Time: 1 round
Area of Effect: Special
Saving Throw: None

This spell summons an invisible stalker from the elemental plane of Air. This 8 Hit Dice monster obeys and serves the spellcaster in performing whatever tasks are set before it. It is a faultless tracker within one day of the quarry's passing. The invisible stalker follows instructions even if they send him hundreds or thousands of miles away and, once given an order, follows through unceasingly until the task is accomplished. However, the creature is bound to serve; it does not do so from loyalty or desire. Therefore, it resents prolonged missions or complex tasks, and it attempts to pervert instructions accordingly. Invisible stalkers understand common speech but speak no language save their own.

The material components of this spell are burning incense and a piece of horn carved into a crescent shape.

Legend Lore (Divination)

Range: 0
Components: V, S, M
Duration: Special
Casting Time: Special
Area of Effect: Special
Saving Throw: None

The *legend lore* spell is used to determine legendary information regarding a known person, place, or thing. If the person or thing is at hand, or if the wizard is in the place in question, the likelihood of the spell producing results is far greater and the casting time is only 1d4 turns. If only detailed information on the person, place, or thing is known, casting time is 1d10 days. If only rumors are known, casting time is 2d6 weeks.

During the casting, the wizard cannot engage in activities other than the routine: eating, sleeping, etc. When completed, the divination reveals if legendary material is available. It often reveals where this material is—by place name, rhyme, or riddle. It sometimes gives certain information regarding the person, place, or thing (when the object of the *legend lore* is at hand), but this data is always in some cryptic form (rhyme, riddle, anagram, cipher, sign, etc.).

The spell is cast with incense and strips of ivory formed into a rectangle, but some item of value to the caster must be sacrificed in addition—a potion, magical scroll, magical item, etc.

Naturally, *legend lore* reveals informa-tion only if the person, place, or thing is noteworthy or legendary.

Suppose Delsenora came across an extremely well-made sword. It radiates magic, but when she used an *identify* spell, she could not learn any information. Even giving it to a trusted fighter didn't work as the sword did not reveal any special powers. Finally, she casts a *legend lore* spell, hoping to gain more information. Since the sword is at hand, she completes the spell in three turns. In her mind comes the message, "Once this was the sword of he who waits till Albion's time of greatest peril, when unto his hand it shall fly again. Fair was the hand that gave me and fair was the hand that reclaimed me." Clearly, Delsenora realizes, this must be a very powerful item, since her spell gave only a cryptic answer. But who is he who waits? And where is Albion? For more information, Delsenora is going to have to cast more spells. But now the process will take much longer, since she has only the vaguest of clues to follow.

Lower Water (Alteration)
Reversible

Range: 80 yards
Components: V, S, M
Duration: 5 rounds/level
Casting Time: 1 turn
Area of Effect: 10-foot square area/level.
Saving Throw: None

The wizard casting a *lower water* spell causes water or similar fluid in the area of effect to sink away. The water can be lowered up to two feet for every experience level of the wizard, to a minimum depth of one inch. The water is lowered within a square area whose sides are 10 feet long per caster level. Thus, a 12th-level wizard affects a volume 24' × 120' × 120', a 13th-level caster a volume 26' × 130' × 130', and so on. In extremely large and deep bodies of water, such as deep ocean, the spell creates a whirlpool that sweeps ships and similar craft downward, putting them at risk and rendering them unable to leave by normal movement for the duration of the spell. When cast on water elementals and other water-based creatures, this spell acts as a *slow* spell: the creature moves at half speed and makes half the number of attacks each round. It has no effect on other creatures.

The material component of this spell is a small vial of dust.

Its reverse, *raise water*, causes water or similar fluids to return to their highest natural level: spring flood, high tide, etc. This can make fords impassable, float grounded ships, and may even sweep away bridges at the referee's option. It negates *lower water* and vice versa.

The material component of the *raise water* spell is a small vial of water.

Mass Suggestion

(Enchantment/Charm)

Range: 30 yards
Components: V, M
Duration: 4 turns + 4 turns/level
Casting Time: 6
Area of Effect: 1 creature/level
Saving Throw: Neg.

The *mass suggestion* spell enables the wizard to influence the actions of one or more chosen creatures in the same way as the *suggestion* spell. Up to one creature per experience level of the caster can be influenced, provided that all subject creatures are within the 30-yard range. Undead are not subject to this spell. The *suggestion* must be reasonably worded and understood by the creatures, and must be the same for all hearing it. Creatures successfully saving vs. spell are unaffected. Saving throws against the spell suffer a penalty of −1, and if a single creature is to be affected, its saving throw suffers a −4 penalty. Note that a very reasonable mass suggestion can cause the saving throw to be made with an additional penalty (such as −1, −2, etc.) at the discretion of your DM. A mass suggestion can continue in effect for a considerable duration, at the DM's discretion. Conditions that will trigger a special action can also be specified; if the condition is not met before the spell expires, then the action will not be performed.

The material components of this spell are a snake's tongue and either a bit of honeycomb or a drop of sweet oil.

Mirage Arcana

(Illusion/Phantasm, Alteration)

Range: 10 yards/level
Components: V, S,(M optional)
Duration: Special
Casting Time: Special
Area of Effect: 10 feet/level radius
Saving Throw: None

The magic of this spell is similar to that of the *vacancy* spell, only this is more powerful and elaborate. The spell enables the caster to make an area appear to be something other than it is, a setting he has personally seen. The spell remains as long as the caster maintains a minimal concentration upon it. Even after this, the spell persists for a total of one hour plus one additional turn for each experience level of the caster. (Note: Minimal concentration can be maintained during normal conversation but not while spellcasting, in melee, or if harmed by an attack.) If the caster actually uses a small bit of anything connected with the place to create this spell, then it takes on a quasi-reality.

In its basic form, forceful contact is necessary to have any hope of discovering the

magic, short of a detection device or spell. In its more complex form, where a material component is used, detection is possible only by some magical means, whether device, item, or spell. Either form of mirage arcana is subject to the *dispel magic* spell.

As with all powerful illusions, the mind of the believer urges appropriate effects upon the viewer's body. Under the influence of the spell, the viewer could possibly walk across a bed of hot coals thinking it was a shallow stream of water that was cooling his feet (and thus suffer no damage), dine upon imaginary food and actually be satisfied, or rest comfortably upon a bed of sharp stones, thinking it a featherbed. Gravity is not affected by the spell, however, so that an envisioned bridge spanning a deep chasm does not support the believer. Those who witness the event see it as a sudden disappearance of the individual. They do not connect it with an illusion unless they are otherwise aware of some magic at work.

Mislead (Illusion/Phantasm)

Range: 10 yards
Component: S
Duration: 1 round/level
Casting Time: 1
Area of Effect: Special
Saving Throw: None

When a *mislead* spell is cast by the wizard, he actually creates an illusory double at the same time that he is cloaked by *improved invisibility* magic (see the 4th-level spell). The wizard is then free to go elsewhere while his double seemingly moves away. The spell enables the illusion of the wizard to speak and gesture as if it were real, and there are full olfactory and touch components as well. A *true seeing* spell or a *gem of seeing* will reveal the illusion for what it is. A *detect invisibility* or *true seeing* spell, or items such as a *gem of seeing* or *robe of eyes* can detect the invisible wizard (see the 5th-level wizard spell, *shadow door*).

Monster Summoning IV

(Conjuration/Summoning)

Range: 60 yards
Components: V, S, M
Duration: 5 rounds + 1 round/level
Casting Time: 6
Area of Effect: Special
Saving Throw: None

This spell is much like the 3rd-level *monster summoning I* spell, except that this spell summons 1d3 4th-level monsters. These appear within spell range and attack the caster's opponents, until he commands them to cease, the spell duration expires, or the monsters are slain. These creatures do not

check morale; they vanish when slain. If no opponent exists to fight, summoned monsters can, if the wizard can communicate with them, and if they are physically capable, perform other services for the summoning wizard.

The material components of this spell are a tiny bag and a small (not necessarily lit) candle.

Mordenkainen's Lucubration

(Alteration)

Range: 0
Components: V, S
Duration: Instantaneous
Casting Time: 1
Area of Effect: The caster
Saving Throw: None

By use of this spell, the wizard is able to instantly recall any 1st- through 5th-level spell he has used during the past 24 hours. The spell must have been memorized and actually used during that time period. *Mordenkainen's lucubration* allows the recovery of only one spell. If the recalled spell requires material components, these must be provided by the caster; the recovered spell is not usable until the material components are available.

Move Earth (Alteration)

Range: 10 yards/level
Components: V, S, M
Duration: Permanent
Casting Time: Special
Area of Effect: Special
Saving Throw: None

When cast, the *move earth* spell moves dirt (clay, loam, sand) and its other components. Thus embankments can be collapsed, hillocks moved, dunes shifted, etc. However, in no event can rock prominences be collapsed or moved. The area to be affected dictates the casting time; for every 40 yd. × 40 yd. surface area and 10 feet of depth, one turn of casting time is required. The maximum area that can be affected is 240 yd. × 240 yd., which takes four hours. If terrain features are to be moved—as compared to simply caving in banks or walls of earth—it is necessary that an earth elemental be subsequently summoned to assist. All spell casting or summoning must be completed before any effects occur. As any summoned earth elemental will perform most of its work underground, it is unlikely that it will be intercepted or interrupted. Should this occur, however, the movement of the earth requiring its services must be stopped until the elemental is once again available. Should the elemental be slain or dismissed, the *move earth* spell is limited to collapsing banks or walls of earth.

The spell cannot be used for tunneling, and is generally too slow to trap or bury creatures; its primary use is for digging or filling moats or for adjusting terrain contours before a battle.

The material components for this spell are a mixture of soils (clay, loam, sand) in a small bag and an iron blade.

Note: This spell does not violently break the surface of the ground. Instead it creates wave-like crests and troughs, with the earth reacting with glacier-like fluidity until the desired result is achieved. Trees, structures, rock formations, and so on, are relatively unaffected, save for changes in elevation and relative topography.

Otiluke's Freezing Sphere
(Alteration, Evocation)

Range: Special
Components: V, S, M
Duration: Special
Casting Time: 6
Area of Effect: Special
Saving Throw: Special

Otiluke's Freezing Sphere is a multi-purpose spell of considerable power. If the caster opts, he may create any of the following:

A) *Frigid globe*. A small globe of matter at absolute zero temperature that spreads upon contact with water, or a liquid that is principally water, freezing it to a depth of six inches over an area equal to 100 square feet per level of the mage casting the spell. This ice lasts for one round per level of the caster.

The material component is a thin sheet of crystal about an inch square.

B) *Cold ray*. The spell can also be used as a thin ray of cold that springs from the caster's hand to a distance of 10 yards per level of the wizard; this ray inflicts 1d4 + 2 points of damage per level of the caster upon the first creature struck. A saving throw vs. spell is applicable; all damage is negated if it is successful (as the ray is so narrow a save indicates it missed). If the first creature is missed, the path of the ray is plotted to its full distance, and anything else in its path must save (if applicable) or suffer appropriate damage.

The material component is a white sapphire of not less than 1,000 gp value.

C) *Globe of cold*. This creates a small globe about the size of a sling stone, cool to the touch, but not harmful. This globe can be hurled, either by hand to a distance of 40 yards (considered short range), or as a sling bullet. The globe shatters upon impact, inflicting 6d6 points of cold damage upon all creatures within a 10-foot radius (one-half damage if a saving throw vs. spell is

successful). Use the *Dungeon Master's Guide* Grenade-Like Missile Table to find where misses strike. Note that if the globe is not thrown or slung within one round per level of the spell-caster, it shatters and causes cold damage as stated above. This timed effect can be employed against pursuers, although it can prove hazardous to the spellcaster and his associates as well.

The material component is a 1,000-gp diamond.

Part Water (Alteration)

Range: 10 yards/level
Components: V, S, M
Duration: 5 rounds/level
Casting Time: 1 turn
Area of Effect: Special
Saving Throw: None

By employing a *part water* spell, the wizard is able to cause water or similar liquid to move apart, thus forming a 20-foot-wide trough. The depth and length of the trough are dependent upon the level of the wizard, and a trough three feet deep by 10 yards long is created per level. For example, at 12th level the wizard would part water 36 feet deep by 20 feet wide by 120 yards long. The trough remains as long as the spell lasts or until the wizard who cast it opts to end its effects. If cast underwater, this spell creates an air cylinder of appropriate length and diameter. If cast directly on a water elemental or other water-based creature, the creature receives 4d8 damage and must roll a successful saving throw vs. spell or flee in panic for 3d4 rounds.

The material components for the spell are two small sheets of crystal or glass.

Permanent Illusion (Illusion/Phantasm)

Range: 10 yards/level
Components: V, S, M
Duration: Permanent
Casting Time: 6
Area of Effect: 20' cube + 10' cube/level
Saving Throw: Special

When this spell is cast, the wizard creates an illusion with visual, auditory, olfactory, and thermal elements. The spell can create the illusion of any object, creature, or force, as long as it is within the boundaries of the spell's area of effect. It affects all creatures that view the illusion, even to the extent of them suffering damage from falling into an illusory pit full of sharp spikes.

Creatures that attempt to disbelieve the illusion gain a saving throw vs. spell and, if successful, they see it for what it is and add + 4 bonuses to associates' saving throws, if this knowledge can be communicated effectively. Creatures not sensing the spell effect are immune until they become aware of it. The permanent illusion is subject to a *dispel*

magic spell, of course.

The material component of the spell is a bit of fleece.

Programmed Illusion
(Illusion/Phantasm)

Range: 10 yards/level
Components: V, S, M
Duration: Special
Casting Time: 6
Area of Effect: 20' cube + 10' cube/level
Saving Throw: Special

This spell creates a *spectral force* spell that activates upon command or when a specific condition occurs. The illusion has visual, auditory, olfactory, and thermal elements. It can be of any object, creature, or force, as long as it remains within the boundaries of the spell's area of effect.

The occurrence that begins the illusion can be as general or as specific and detailed as desired, such as the following: "Begin only when a venerable female human carrying a sack of groat clusters sits cross-legged within one foot of this spot." Such visual triggers can react to a character using the *disguise* ability. Command range is five yards per level of the wizard, so a 12th-level mage can command the programmed illusion to occur at a maximum encounter range of 60 yards. A programmed illusion cannot distinguish invisible creatures, nor alignment, level, Hit Dice, or class, except by external garb. If desired, the effect can be keyed to a specific noise or spoken word. The spell lasts until the illusion occurs, thus the spell duration is variable. The illusion will last for a maximum of one round per level of the spellcaster.

Creatures that attempt to disbelieve the illusion gain a saving throw vs. spell and, if successful, they see it for what it is and add + 4 bonuses to associates' saving throws, if this knowledge can be communicated effectively. Creatures not sensing the spell effect are immune until they become aware of it. The illusion is subject to a *dispel magic* spell.

The material component of the spell is a bit of fleece.

Project Image
(Alteration, Illusion/Phantasm)

Range: 10 yards/level
Components: V, S, M
Duration: 1 round/level
Casting Time: 6
Area of Effect: Special
Saving Throw: None

By means of this spell, the wizard creates a nonmaterial duplicate of himself, projecting it to any spot within spell range. This image performs actions decided by the wizard—walking, speaking, spellcasting—conforming to the actual actions of the wizard unless he concentrates on making it act differently (in which case the wizard is limited to half movement and no attacks).

The image can be dispelled only by means of a successful *dispel magic* spell (or upon command from the spellcaster); attacks pass harmlessly through it. The image must be within view of the wizard projecting it at all times, and if his sight is obstructed, the spell is broken. Note that if the wizard is invisible at the time the spell is cast, the image is also invisible until the caster's invisibility ends, though the wizard must still be able to see the image (by means of a *detect invisibility* spell or other method) to maintain the spell. If the wizard uses *dimension door, teleport, plane shift,* or similar spell that breaks his line of vision, the *project image* spell ends.

The material component of this spell is a small replica (doll) of the wizard.

Reincarnation (Necromancy)

Range: Touch
Components: V, S, M
Duration: Permanent
Casting Time: 1 turn
Area of Effect: Person touched
Saving Throw: None

With this spell, the wizard can bring back to life a person who died no more than one day per level of experience of the wizard before the casting of the spell. The essence of the dead person is transferred to another body, possibly one very different from his former body. Reincarnation does not require any saving throw, system shock, or resurrection survival roll. The corpse is touched, and a new incarnation of the person will appear in the area in 1d6 turns. The person reincarnated recalls the majority of his former life and form, but the character class, if any, of the new incarnation might be different indeed. The new incarnation is determined on the following table. If a player character race is indicated, the character must be created.

D100 Roll	Incarnation
01-05	Bugbear
06-11	Dwarf
12-18	Elf
19-23	Gnoll
24-28	Gnome
29-33	Goblin
34-40	Half-elf
41-47	Halfling
48-54	Half orc
55-59	Hobgoblin
60-73	Human
74-79	Kobold
80-85	Orc
86-90	Ogre
91-95	Ogre mage
96-00	Troll

Note: Very good or very evil persons will not be reincarnated as creatures whose general alignment is the opposite.

The material components of the spell are a small drum and a drop of blood.

Repulsion (Abjuration)

Range: 10 yards/level
Components: V, S, M
Duration: 1 round/2 levels
Casting Time: 6
Area of Effect: Creatures in a 10-foot-wide path
Saving Throw: None

When this spell is cast, the wizard is able to cause all creatures in the path of the area of effect to move directly away from his person. Repulsion occurs at the speed of the creature attempting to move toward the spellcaster. The repelled creature continues to move away for a complete round even if this takes it beyond spell range. The caster can designate a new direction each round, but use of this power counts as the caster's principal action in the round. The caster can, of course, choose to do something else instead of using the repulsion attack.

The material component for this spell is a pair of small magnetized iron bars attached to two small canine statuettes, one ivory and one ebony.

Shades (Illusion/Phantasm)

Range: 30 yards
Components: V, S
Duration: 1 round/level
Casting Time: 6
Area of Effect: 20-foot cube
Saving Throw: Special

This spell is related to the *shadow monsters* and *demi-shadow monsters* spells. The *shades* spell uses material from the plane of Shadow to form semi-real illusions of one or more monsters, up to 1 Hit Die per caster level. All shades created by one spell must be of the same sort, and they have 60% of the hit point total the real creatures would have. Those viewing the shades and failing their saving throws vs. spell believe the illusion.

The shades perform as the real monsters with respect to Armor Class and attack forms. Special attack forms such as petrification or level drain do not actually occur, but a subject who believes the shades are real will react appropriately, until the illusion is countered by a *dispel magic* spell or the condition is countered by a *heal* spell. Those who roll successful saving throws see the shades as transparent images superimposed on vague shadowy forms. These are Armor Class 6 and cause only 60% of the true monsters' normal melee damage.

Stone to Flesh (Alteration)
Reversible

Range: 10 yards/level
Components: V, S, M
Duration: Permanent
Casting Time: 6
Area of Effect: 1 creature
Saving Throw: Special

The *stone to flesh* spell turns any sort of stone into flesh. If the recipient stone object was formerly living, this spell restores life (and goods), although the survival of the creature is subject to the usual system shock survival roll. Any formerly living creature, regardless of size, can be thus returned to flesh. Ordinary stone can be turned to flesh in a volume of nine cubic feet per level of experience of the spellcaster. Such flesh is inert, lacking a vital life force, unless a life force or magical energy is available (for example, this spell would turn a stone golem into a flesh golem, but an ordinary statue would become a body). If cast upon stone, the wizard can create a cylinder of fleshy material from one to three feet in diameter and up to 10 feet long, allowing a passage to be made.

The material components are a pinch of earth and a drop of blood.

The reverse, *flesh to stone*, turns flesh of any sort to stone. All possessions on the person of the creature likewise turn to stone. The intended subject of the spell receives a saving throw vs. spell to avoid the effect. If a statue created by this spell is subjected to breakage or weathering, the being (if ever returned to his original, fleshy state) will have similar damage, deformities, etc. The DM may allow such damage to be repaired by various high-level clerical spells, such as *regenerate*.

The material components of the spell are lime, water, and earth.

Tenser's Transformation
(Alteration, Evocation)

Range: 0
Components: V, S, M
Duration: 1 round/level
Casting Time: 6
Area of Effect: The caster
Saving Throw: None

Tenser's transformation is a sight guaranteed to astound any creature not aware of its power, for when the wizard casts the spell, he undergoes a startling transformation. The size and strength of the wizard increase to heroic proportions, so he becomes a formidable fighting machine; the spell causes the caster to become a berserk fighter! The wizard's hit points double, and all damage he sustains comes first from the magical points gained; once these points are elimi-

nated, all subsequent damage (to his true hit points) is doubled. The Armor Class of the wizard is 4 better than that he possessed prior to casing the spell (AC 10 goes to 6, AC 9 to 5, AC 8 to 4, etc.), to a maximum Armor Class of −10.

All attacks are as a fighter of the same level as the wizard (i.e., the wizard uses the combat values normally reserved for fighters). The wizard can use either a dagger or a staff when attacking. A dagger can be used twice per round, and each successful attack inflicts an additional 2 points of damage. A staff can be used only once per round, but with a +2 bonus to attack and damage rolls. The wizard fights in melee in preference to all other forms of attack, and continues attacking until all opponents are slain, he is killed, the magic is dispelled, or the spell duration expires.

The material component for casting this spell is a *potion of heroism* (or *superheroism*) that the wizard must consume during the course of uttering the spell.

Transmute Water to Dust (Alteration)
Reversible

Range: 60 yards
Components: V, S, M
Duration: Permanent
Casting Time: 5
Area of Effect: One 10-foot cube/level
Saving Throw: None (special)

When this spell is cast, the subject area instantly undergoes a change from liquid to powdery dust. Note that if the water is already muddy, the area of effect is doubled, while if wet mud is being transmuted, the area of effect is quadrupled. If water remains in contact with the transmuted dust, the former quickly soaks the latter, turning the dust into silty mud, if a sufficient quantity of water exists to do so, otherwise soaking or dampening the dust accordingly.

Only liquid actually in the area of effect at the moment of spellcasting is affected. Liquids that are only partially water are affected only insofar as the actual water content is concerned, except that potions containing water are rendered useless. Living creatures are unaffected, except for those native to the elemental plane of Water. Such creatures receive saving throws vs. spell. Failure inflicts 1d6 points of damage per caster level upon the subject, while success means the creature receives but half damage. Only one such creature can be affected by any single casting of this spell, regardless of the creature's size or the size of the spell's area of effect.

The reverse of the spell is simply a very high-powered *create water* spell that requires a pinch of normal dust as an additional material component.

For either usage of the spell, other components required are diamond dust of at least 500 gp value and a bit of seashell.

True Seeing (Divination)

Range: Touch
Components: V, S, M
Duration: 1 round/level
Casting Time: 1 round
Area of Effect: 60-foot light range
Saving Throw: None

When the wizard employs this spell, he confers upon the recipient the ability to see all things as they actually are. The spell penetrates normal and magical darkness. Secret doors become plain. The exact location of displaced things is obvious. Invisible things become visible. Illusions and apparitions are seen through. Polymorphed, changed, or enchanted objects are apparent. (The real form appears translucently superimposed on the apparent form: a gold dragon polymorphed to human form would appear human with a ghostly dragon looming over the human form.) Unlike the clerical version of this spell, the recipient cannot determine alignment. The recipient can focus his vision to see into the Ethereal plane or the bordering areas of adjacent planes. The range of vision conferred is 60 feet. True seeing does not penetrate solid objects; it in no way confers X-ray vision or its equivalent. Furthermore, the spell effects cannot be enhanced with magic.

The spell requires an ointment for the eyes that is made from a very rare mushroom powder, saffron, and fat. It costs no less than 300 gp per use and must be aged for 1d6 months.

Veil (Illusion/Phantasm)

Range: 10 yards/level
Components: V, S
Duration: 1 turn/level
Casting Time: 6
Area of Effect: 20-foot cube/level
Saving Throw: None

The *veil* spell enables the wizard to instantly change the appearance of his surroundings and party or to create hallucinatory terrain so as to fool even the most clever creatures unless they have the *true seeing* spell, a *gem of seeing*, or similar magical aid. The veil can make a sumptuous room seem a filthy den and even tactile impressions conform to the visual illusion. Likewise, a party might be made to resemble a mixed band of brownies, pixies, and faeries led by a treant. If hallucinatory terrain is created, touch does not cause it to vanish.

Seventh-Level Spells

Banishment (Abjuration)

Range: 20 yards
Components: V, S, M
Duration: Instantaneous
Casting Time: 7
Area of Effect: 1 or more creatures in a 60-foot radius
Saving Throw: Special

A *banishment* spell enables the caster to force some extraplanar creature out of the caster's home plane. The effect is instantaneous, and the subject cannot come back without some special summoning or means of egress from its own plane to the one from which it was banished. Up to 2 Hit Dice or levels of creature per caster level can be banished.

The caster must both name the type of creature(s) to be sent away and give its name and title as well, if any. In any event, the creature's magic resistance must be defeated for the spell to be effective.

The material components of the spell are substances harmful, hateful, or opposed to the nature of the subject(s) of the spell. For every such substance included in the casting, the subject creature(s) loses 5% from its magic resistance and suffers a −2 penalty to its saving throw vs. spell. For example, if iron, holy water, sunstone, and a sprig of rosemary were used in casting a banishment upon a being that hates those things, its saving throw versus the spell would be made with a −8 penalty (four substances times the factor of −2). Special items, such as hair from the tail of a ki-rin, or couatl feathers, could also be added to bring the factor up to −3 or −4 per item. In contrast, a titan's hair or mistletoe blessed by a druid might lower the factor to −1 with respect to the same creature. If the subject creature successfully rolls its saving throw vs. spell, the caster is stung by a backlash of energy, suffers 2d6 points of damage, and is stunned for one round.

Bigby's Grasping Hand (Evocation)

Range: 10 yards/level
Components: V, S, M
Duration: 1 round/level
Casting Time: 7
Area of Effect: Special
Saving Throw: None

Bigby's grasping hand is a superior version of the 6th-level Bigby's forceful hand. It creates a man-sized (five feet) to gargantuan-sized (21 feet) hand that appears and grasps a creature designated by the caster, regardless of what the spellcaster does or how the opponent tries to escape it. The grasping hand can hold motionless a creature or object of up to 1,000 pounds weight, slow movement to 10 feet per round if the creature weighs between 1,000 and 4,000 pounds, or slow movement by 50% if the creature weighs up to 16,000 pounds. The hand itself inflicts no damage. The grasping hand has an Armor Class of 0, has as many hit points as its caster in full health, and vanishes when destroyed. The caster can order it to release a trapped opponent or can dismiss it on command.

The material component is a leather glove.

Charm Plants (Enchantment/Charm)

Range: 30 yards
Components: V, S, M
Duration: Permanent
Casting Time: 1 turn
Area of Effect: Special
Saving Throw: Neg.

The *charm plants* spell enables the spellcaster to bring under command vegetable life forms and communicate with them. These plants obey instructions to the best of their ability. The spell will charm plants in a 30' × 10' area. While the spell does not endow the vegetation with new abilities, it does enable the wizard to command the plants to use whatever they have in order to fulfill his instructions; if the plants in the area of effect do have special or unusual abilities, these are used as commanded by the wizard. For example, this spell can generally duplicate the effects of the 1st-level priest spell *entangle*, if the caster desires.

The saving throw applies only to intelligent plants, and it is made with a −4 penalty to the die roll.

The material components of the spell are a pinch of humus, a drop of water, and a twig or leaf.

Control Undead (Necromancy)

Range: 60 feet
Components: V, S, M
Duration: 3d4 rounds + 1 round/level
Casting Time: 1 round
Area of Effect: 1d6 undead
Saving Throw: Special

This spell enables the wizard to command 1d6 undead creatures for a short period of time. Upon casting the spell, the wizard selects one point within range of the spell. Those undead nearest to this point are affected, until either undead equal in Hit Dice to the caster's level or six undead are affected. Undead with 3 Hit Dice or less are automatically controlled. Those of greater Hit Dice are allowed a saving throw vs. spell, which if successful negates the attempt to control that creature. Regardless of the success or failure of the saving throw, each creature required to make a check counts toward the Hit Dice limit of the spell.

Those creatures under the control of the wizard can be commanded by the caster if they are within hearing range. There is no telepathic communication between the caster and the controlled undead. There is no language requirement either. Even if communication is impossible, the controlled undead do not attack the spellcaster. At the end of the spell, the controlled undead revert to their normal behaviors. Those not mindless will remember the control exerted by the wizard.

The material component for this spell is a small piece each of bone and raw meat.

Delayed Blast Fireball (Evocation)

Range: 100 yards + 10 yards/level
Components: V, S, M
Duration: Special
Casting Time: 7
Area of Effect: 20-foot-radius globe
Saving Throw: ½

This spell creates a fireball, with a +1 bonus to each of its dice of damage, which releases its blast anywhere from instantly to five rounds later, according to the command given by the wizard. In other respects, the spell is the same as the 3rd-level spell *fireball*.

Drawmij's Instant Summons
(Conjuration/Summoning)

Range: Infinite + special
Components: V, S, M
Duration: Instantaneous
Casting Time: 1
Area of Effect: 1 small object
Saving Throw: None

When this spell is cast, the wizard teleports some desired item from virtually any location directly to his hand. The single object can be no longer in any dimension than a sword, can have no more weight than a shield (about eight pounds), and it must be nonliving. To prepare this spell, the wizard must hold a gem of not less than 5,000 gp value in his hand and utter all but the final word of the conjuration. He then must crush this gem and utter the final word. The desired item is then transported instantly into the spellcaster's right or left hand as he desires. The item must have been previously touched during the initial incantation and specifically named; only that particular item is summoned by the spell. The special gem used to summon the item has a magically created inscription naming the item to be summoned. The inscription is invisible and unreadable, except by means of a *read magic* spell, to all but the wizard who cast the summons.

If the item is in the possession of another creature, the spell does not work, and the caster knows who the possessor is and roughly where he, she, or it is located when the summons is cast. Items can be summoned from other planes of existence, but only if such items are not in the possession (not necessarily the physical grasp) of another creature. For each level of experience above the 14th, the wizard is able to summon a desired item from one plane farther removed from the plane he is in at the time the spell is cast (one plane away at 14th level, two planes away at 15th, etc.) Thus, a wizard of 16th level could cast the spell even if the desired item was on the second layer of one of the outer planes, but at 14th level the wizard would be able to summon the item only if it were no farther than one of the inner planes, the Ethereal plane, or the Astral plane (see *Manual of the Planes*). Note that special wards or barriers, or factors that block the *teleport* or *plane shift* spells, may also block the operation of this spell. Objects in Leomund's secret chest cannot be recovered by using this spell.

Note: If the item is wizard marked, it can be summoned from anywhere on the same plane unless special local conditions apply. Furthermore, the details of the location of the item are more specific, and the item is more easily traceable with other types of scrying magic.

Duo-Dimension (Alteration)

Range: 0
Components: V, S, M
Duration: 3 rounds + 1 round/level
Casting Time: 7
Area of Effect: The caster
Saving Throw: None

A *duo-dimension* spell causes the caster to have only two dimensions, height and width, but no depth. He is thus invisible when turned sideways. This invisibility can be detected only by means of a *true seeing* spell or similar methods. In addition, the duo-dimensional wizard can pass through the thinnest of spaces as long as these have the proper height—going through the space between a door and its frame is a simple matter. The wizard can perform all actions normally. He can turn and become invisible, move in this state, and appear again next round and cast a spell, disappearing on the following round.

Note that when turned, the wizard cannot be affected by any form of attack, but when visible, he is subject to double the amount of damage normal for an attack form, e.g., a dagger thrust would inflict 2d4 points of damage if it struck a duo-dimensional wizard. Furthermore, the wizard has a portion of his existence in the Astral plane when the spell is in effect, and he is subject to possible notice by creatures there. If noticed, it is 25% probable that the wizard is pulled entirely into the Astral plane by any attack from an astral creature. Such an attack (and any subsequent attack received on the Astral plane) inflicts normal damage.

The material components of this spell are a flat ivory likeness of the spellcaster (which must be of finest workmanship, gold filigreed, and enameled and gem-studded at an average cost of 500 to 1,000 gp) and a strip of parchment. As the spell is uttered, the parchment is given a half twist and joined at the ends. The figurine is then passed through the parchment loop, and both disappear forever.

Finger of Death (Necromancy)

Range: 60 yards
Components: V, S
Duration: Permanent
Casting Time: 5
Area of Effect: 1 creature
Saving Throw: Neg.

The *finger of death* spell snuffs out the victim's life force. If successful, the victim can be neither raised nor resurrected. In addition, in human subjects the spell initiates changes to the body such that after three days the caster can, by means of a special ceremony costing not less than 1,000 gp plus 500 gp per body, animate the corpse as a juju zombie under the control of the caster.

The changes can be reversed before animation by a *limited wish* or similar spell cast directly upon the body, while a full *wish* restores the subject to life.

The caster utters the *finger of death* spell incantation, points his index finger at the creature to be slain, and unless the victim succeeds in a saving throw vs. spell, death occurs. A creature successfully saving still receives 2d8 + 1 points of damage. If the subject dies of damage, no internal changes occur and the victim can then be revived normally.

Forcecage (Evocation)

Range: 10 yards per 2 levels
Components: V, S + special
Duration: 6 turns + 1/level
Casting Time: 3-4
Area of Effect: 20-foot cube
Saving Throw: None

This powerful spell enables the caster to bring into being a cube of force, but it is unlike the magical item of that name in one important respect: The forcecage does not have solid walls of force; it has alternating bands of force with 1/2-inch gaps between. Thus, it is truly a cage rather than an enclosed space with solid walls. Creatures within the area of effect of the spell are caught and contained unless they are able to pass through the openings—and of course all spells and breath weapons can pass through the gaps in the bars of force of the forcecage.

A creature with magic resistance has a single attempt to pass through the walls of the cage. If the resistance check is successful, the creature escapes. If it fails, then the creature is caged. Note that a successful check does not destroy the cage, nor does it enable other creatures (save familiars) to flee with the escaping creature. The forcecage is also unlike the solid-walled protective device, cube of force, in that it can be gotten rid of only by means of a *dispel magic* spell or by the expiration of the spell.

By means of special preparation at the time of memorization, a forcecage spell can be altered to a forcecube spell. The cube created is 10 feet on a side, and the spell then resembles that of a cube of force in all respects save that of the differences between a cast spell and the magic of a device, including the methods of defeating its power.

Although the actual casting of either application of the spell requires no material component, the study required to commit it to memory does demand that the wizard powder a diamond of at least 1,000 gp value, using the diamond dust to trace the outlines of the cage or cube he desires to create via spellcasting at some later time. Thus, in memorization, the diamond dust is employed and expended, for upon completion of study, the wizard must then toss the dust into the air and it will disappear.

Limited Wish (Conjuration/Summoning, Invocation/Evocation)

Range: Unlimited
Components: V
Duration: Special
Casting Time: Special
Area of Effect: Special
Saving Throw: Special

The *limited wish* is a very potent but difficult spell. It will fulfill literally, but only partially or for a limited duration, the utterance of the spellcaster. Thus, the actuality of the past, present, or future might be altered (but possibly only for the wizard unless the wording of the spell is most carefully stated) in some limited manner. The use of a limited wish will not substantially change major realities, nor will it bring wealth or experience merely by asking. The spell can, for example, restore some hit points (or all hit points for a limited duration) lost by the wizard. It can reduce opponent hit probabilities or damage, increase duration of some magical effect, cause a creature to be favorably disposed to the spellcaster, mimic a spell of 7th level or less, and so on (see the *wish* spell). Greedy desires usually end in disaster for the wisher. Casting time is based on the time spent preparing the wording for the spell (clever players decide what they want to say before using the spell). Normally the casting time is one round (most of it being taken up by deciding what to say). Casting this spell ages the caster one year per 100 years of regular life span.

Mass Invisibility (Illusion/Phantasm)

Range: 10 yards/level
Components: V, S, M
Duration: Special
Casting Time: 7
Area of Effect: Special
Saving Throw: None

This is a more extensive adaptation of the *invisibility* spell for battlefield use. It can hide creatures in a 60 yd. × 60 yd. area; up to 300 to 400 man-sized creatures, 30 to 40 giants, or six to eight large dragons. The effect is mobile with the unit and is broken when the unit attacks. Individuals leaving the unit become visible. The wizard can end this spell upon command.

The material component of the *mass invisibility* spell are an eyelash and a bit of gum arabic, the former encased in the latter.

Monster Summoning V
(Conjuration/Summoning)

Range: 70 yards
Components: V, S, M
Duration: 6 rounds + 1 round/level
Casting Time: 6
Area of Effect: Special
Saving Throw: None

This spell is much like the 3rd-level *monster summoning I* spell, except that this spell summons 1d3 5th-level monsters. These appear within spell range and attack the caster's opponents until either he commands them to cease, the spell duration expires, or the monsters are slain. These creatures do not check morale, and they vanish when slain. If no opponent exists to fight, summoned monsters can, if the wizard can communicate with them, and if they are physically capable, perform other services for the summoning wizard.

The material components of this spell are a tiny bag and a small (not necessarily lit) candle.

Mordenkainen's Magnificent Mansion (Alteration, Conjuration)

Range: 10 yards
Components: V, S, M
Duration: 1 hour/level
Casting Time: 7 rounds
Area of Effect: 300 sq. ft./level
Saving Throw: None

By means of this spell, the wizard conjures up an extradimensional dwelling, entrance to which can be gained only at a single point of space on the plane from which the spell was cast. From the entry point, those creatures observing the area see only a faint shimmering in the air, in an area four feet wide and eight feet high. The caster of the spell controls entry to the mansion, and the portal is shut and made invisible behind him when he enters. He may open it again from his own side at will. Once observers have passed beyond the entrance, they behold a magnificent foyer and numerous chambers beyond. The place is furnished and contains sufficient foodstuffs to serve a nine-course banquet to as many dozens of people as the spellcaster has levels of experience. There is a staff of near-transparent servants, liveried and obedient, there to wait upon all who enter. The atmosphere is clean, fresh, and warm.

Since the place can be entered only through its special portal, outside conditions do not affect the mansion, nor do conditions inside it pass to the plane beyond. Rest and relaxation within the place is normal, but the food is not. It seems excellent and quite filling as long as one is within the place. Once outside, however, its effects dis-

appear immediately, and if those resting have not eaten real food within a reasonable time span, ravenous hunger strikes. Failure to eat normal food immediately results in the onset of fatigue or starvation penalties as decided by the DM.

The material components of this spell are a miniature portal carved from ivory, a small piece of polished marble, and a tiny silver spoon. These are utterly destroyed when the spell is cast.

(It is worth mentioning that this spell has been used in conjunction with a normal portal, as well as with illusion magic. There is evidence that the design and interior of the space created can be altered to suit the caster's wishes.)

Mordenkainen's Sword (Evocation)

Range: 30 yards
Components: V, S, M
Duration: 1 round/level
Casting Time: 7
Area of Effect: Special
Saving Throw: None

Upon casting this spell, the wizard brings into being a shimmering, sword-like plane of force. The spellcaster is able to mentally wield this weapon (to the exclusion of all activities other than movement), causing it to move and strike as if it were being used by a fighter. The basic chance for Mordenkainen's sword to hit is the same as the chance for a sword wielded by a fighter of one-half the level of the spellcaster, e.g., if cast by a 14th-level wizard, the weapon has the same hit probability as a sword wielded by a 7th-level fighter. The sword has no magical attack bonuses, but it can hit nearly any sort of opponent, even those normally struck only by +3 weapons or those astral, ethereal, or out of phase. It hits any Armor Class on a roll of 19 or 20. It inflicts 5d4 points of damage to opponents of man-size or smaller, and 5d6 to opponents larger than man-sized. It lasts until the spell duration expires, a *dispel magic* is used successfully upon it, or its caster no longer desires it.

The material component is a miniature platinum sword with a grip and pommel of copper and zinc, which costs 500 gp to construct, and which disappears after the spell's completion.

Phase Door (Alteration)

Range: Touch
Components: V
Duration: 1 usage/2 levels
Casting Time: 7
Area of Effect: Special
Saving Throw: None

When this spell is cast, the wizard attunes his body, and a section of wall is affected as if by a *passwall* spell. The phase door is in-

visible to all creatures save the spellcaster, and only he can use the space or passage the spell creates, disappearing when the phase door is entered, and appearing when it is exited. If the caster desires, one other creature of man size or less can be taken through the door; this counts as two uses of the door. The door does not pass light, sound, or spell effects, nor can the caster see through it without using it. Thus the spell can provide an escape route, though certain creatures, such as phase spiders, can follow with ease. A *gem of true seeing* and similar magic will reveal the presence of a phase door but will not allow its use.

The phase door lasts for one usage for every two levels of experience of the spellcaster. It can be dispelled only by a casting of *dispel magic* from a higher level wizard, or by several lower level wizards, casting in concert, whose combined levels of experience are more than double that of the wizard who cast the spell (this is the only instance in which combining dispel effects can be done).

Rumor has it that this spell has been adapted by a certain powerful wizard (or wizards) to create renewable (or permanent) portals, which may (or may not) be keyed to specific individuals (henchmen) or items (such as rings).

Power Word, Stun
(Conjuration/Summoning)

Range: 5 yards/level
Components: V
Duration: Special
Casting Time: 1
Area of Effect: 1 creature
Saving Throw: None

When a *power word, stun* spell is uttered, any creature of the mage's choice is stunned—reeling and unable to think coherently or to act—for a duration dependent on its current hit points. Of course, the wizard must be facing the creature, and the creature must be within the range of five yards per experience level of the caster. Creatures with 1 to 30 hit points are stunned for 4d4 rounds, those with 31 to 60 hit points are stunned for 2d4 rounds, those with 61 to 90 hit points are stunned for 1d4 rounds, and creatures with over 90 hit points are not affected. Note that if a creature is weakened so that its hit points are below its usual maximum, the current number of hit points is used.

Prismatic Spray
(Conjuration/Summoning)

Range: 0
Components: V, S
Duration: Instantaneous
Casting Time: 7
Area of Effect: 70'-long plane, 15' wide at
    end, 5' wide at base
Saving Throw: Special

When this spell is cast, the wizard causes seven shimmering, multi-colored rays of light to flash from his hand. These include all colors of the visible spectrum; each ray has a different power and purpose. Any creature with fewer than 8 Hit Dice struck by a ray is blinded for 2d4 rounds, regardless of any other effect.

Any creature in the area of effect will be touched by one or more of the rays. To determine which ray strikes a creature, roll 1d8.

Prismatic Spray Results

1 = red	5 = blue
2 = orange	6 = indigo
3 = yellow	7 = violet
4 = green	8 = struck by two rays, roll again twice ignoring any 8s

Color of Ray	Order of Ray	Effects of Ray
Red	1st	inflicts 20 hit points of damage, save vs. spell for half
Orange	2nd	inflicts 40 hit points of damage, save vs. spell for half
Yellow	3rd	inflicts 80 hit points of damage, save vs. spell for half
Green	4th	save vs. poison or die, if survive suffer 20 points of poison damage
Blue	5th	save vs. petrification or turned to stone
Indigo	6th	save vs. wand or insane
Violet	7th	save vs. spell or sent to another plane

Reverse Gravity (Alteration)

Range: 5 yards/level
Components: V, S, M
Duration: 1 round/level
Casting Time: 7
Area of Effect: 30 feet × 30 feet
Saving Throw: None

This spell reverses gravity in the area of effect, causing all unattached objects and creatures within it to "fall" upward. The reverse gravity lasts as long as the caster desires or until the spell expires. If some solid object is encountered in this "fall," the object strikes it in the same manner as it would during a normal downward fall. At the end of the spell duration, the affected objects and creatures fall downward. As the spell affects an area, objects tens, hundreds, or even thousands of feet in the air above the area can be affected.

The material components of this spell are a lodestone and iron filings.

Sequester
(Illusion/Phantasm, Abjuration)

Range: Touch
Components: V, S, M
Duration: 1 week + 1 day/level
Casting Time: 7
Area of Effect: 2-foot cube/level
Saving Throw: Special

When cast, this spell not only prevents detection and location spells from working to detect or locate the objects affected by the *sequester* spell, it also renders the affected object(s) invisible to any form of sight or seeing. Thus, a *sequester* spell can mask a secret door, a treasure vault, or whatever. Of course, it does not render the subject proof from tactile discovery or from devices, such as a *robe of eyes* or a *gem of seeing*. If cast upon a creature not desiring to be affected, a normal saving throw vs. spell is given. Living creatures (and even undead types) affected by a *sequester* spell become comatose and are effectively in a state of suspended animation until the spell wears off or is dispelled.

The material components of the spell are a basilisk eyelash, gum arabic, and a dram of whitewash.

Shadow Walk (Illusion, Enchantment)

Range: Touch
Components: V, S
Duration: 6 turns/level
Casting Time: 1
Area of Effect: Special
Saving Throw: None

In order to use the *shadow walk* spell, the wizard must be in an area of heavy shadows. The caster and any creature he touches are then transported to the edge of the Prime Material plane where it borders the plane of Shadow. In this region the wizard can move at a rate of up to seven miles per turn, moving normally on the borders of the plane of Shadow but much more rapidly relative to the Prime Material plane. Thus rapid travel can be accomplished by moving in the plane of Shadow and then stepping from the plane of Shadow to the Prime Material plane. The wizard knows where he will come out on the Prime Material plane.

The *shadow walk* spell can also be used to travel to other planes that border on the plane of Shadow, but this requires the potentially perilous transit of the plane of Shadow to arrive at a border with another plane of reality. Any creatures touched by the wizard when *shadow walk* is cast also make the transition to the borders of the plane of Shadow. They may opt to follow the wizard, wander off into Shadowland, or stumble back into the Prime Material plane (50% chance for either result if they are lost or abandoned by the wizard). Creatures unwilling to accompany the wizard into the plane of Shadow get a saving throw, negating the effect if successful.

Simulacrum (Illusion/Phantasm)

Range: Touch
Components: V, S, M
Duration: Permanent
Casting Time: Special
Area of Effect: 1 creature
Saving Throw: None

By means of this spell, the wizard is able to create a duplicate of any creature. The duplicate appears to be exactly the same as the original, but there are differences: the simulacrum has only 51% to 60% (50% + 1d10%) of the hit points of the real creature, there are personality differences, there are areas of knowledge that the duplicate does not have, and a *detect magic* spell will instantly reveal it as a simulacrum, as will a *true seeing* spell. At all times the simulacrum remains under the absolute command of the wizard who created it. No special telepathic link exists, so command must be exercised in some other manner. The spell creates the form of the creature, but it is only a zombie-like creation. A *reincarnation* spell must be used to give the duplicate a vital force, and a *limited wish* spell must be used to empower the duplicate with 40% to 65% (35% + 5 to 30%) of the knowledge and personality of the original. The level, if any, of the simulacrum is from 20% to 50% of that of the original creature.

The duplicate creature is formed from ice or snow. The spell is cast over the rough form and some piece of the creature to be duplicated must be placed inside the snow or ice. Additionally, the spell requires powdered ruby.

The simulacrum has no ability to become more powerful: it cannot increase its level or abilities. If destroyed, it reverts to snow and melts into nothingness. Damage to the simulacrum can be repaired by a complex process requiring at least one day, 100 gp per hit point, and a fully equipped laboratory.

Spell Turning (Abjuration)

Range: 0
Components: V, S, M
Duration: Up to 3 rounds/level
Casting Time: 7
Area of Effect: The caster
Saving Throw: None

This powerful abjuration causes spells cast against the wizard to rebound on the original caster. This includes spells cast from scrolls and innate spell-like abilities, but specifically excludes the following: area effects that are not centered directly upon the protected wizard, spell effects delivered by touch, and spell effects from devices such as wands, staves, etc. Thus a *light* spell cast to blind the protected wizard could be turned back upon and possibly blind the caster, while the same spell would be unaffected if cast to light an area within which the protected wizard is standing.

From seven to ten spell levels are affected by the turning. The exact number is secretly rolled by the DM; the player never knows for certain how effective the spell is.

A spell may be only partially turned—divide the number of remaining levels that can be turned by the spell level of the incoming spell to see what fraction of the effect is turned—the remainder affects the caster. For example, if an incoming fireball is centered on a wizard with one level of turning left. This means that ⅔ of the fireball affects the protected wizard, ⅓ affects the caster, and each is the center of a fireball effect. If the rolled damage is 40 points, the protected wizard receives 27 points of damage and the caster suffers 13. Both (and any creatures in the respective areas) can roll saving throws vs. spell for half damage. Partially turned *hold* or *paralysis* spells will *slow* those who are 50% or more affected.

If the protected wizard and a spellcasting attacker both have *spell turning* effects operating, a resonating field is created that has the following effects:

D100 Roll	Effect
01-70	Spell drains away without effect
71-80	Spell affects both equally at full damage
81-97	Both turning effects are rendered non-functional for 1d4 turns
98-00	Both casters go through a rift into the Positive Material plane

The material component for the spell is a small silver mirror.

Statue (Alteration)

Range: Touch
Components: V, S, M
Duration: 1 hour/level
Casting Time: 7
Area of Effect: Creature touched
Saving Throw: Special

When a *statue* spell is cast, the wizard or other creature is apparently turned to solid stone, along with any garments and equipment worn or carried. The initial transformation from flesh to stone requires one full round after the spell is cast. During this initial transformation, the creature must roll a saving throw of 82% or less, with −1 deducted from the dice roll for each point of Constitution, so an 18 Constitution grants certain success. Failure indicates system shock and death. Thereafter the creature can withstand any inspection and appear to be a stone statue, although a faint magic is detected from the stone if it is checked for.

Despite being in this condition, the petrified individual can see, hear, and smell normally. Feeling is limited to those sensations that can affect the granite-hard substance of the individual's body—i.e., chipping is equal to a slight wound, but breaking off one of the statue's arms is serious damage.

The individual under the magic of a *statue* spell can return to his normal state instantly, act, and then return to the statue state, if he so desires, as long as the spell duration is in effect.

The material components of this spell are lime, sand, and a drop of water stirred by an iron bar, such as a nail or spike.

Teleport Without Error (Alteration)

Range: Touch
Components: V
Duration: Instantaneous
Casting Time: 1
Area of Effect: Special
Saving Throw: None

This spell is similar to the *teleport* spell. The caster is able to transport himself, along with the material weight noted for a *teleport* spell, to any known location in his home plane with no chance for error. The spell also enables the caster to travel to other planes of existence, but any such plane is, at best, "studied carefully." This assumes that the caster has, in fact, actually been to the plane and carefully perused an area for an eventual *teleportation without error* spell. The table for the *teleport* spell is used, with the caster's knowledge of the area to which transportation is desired used to determine chance of error. (Exception: See the 9th-level wizard spell, *succor*.) The caster can do nothing else the round that he appears from a teleport.

Vanish (Alteration)

Range: Touch
Components: V
Duration: Special
Casting Time: 2
Area of Effect: 1 object
Saving Throw: None

When the wizard employs this spell, he causes an object to vanish (i.e., to be teleported as if by a *teleport* spell) if it weighs no more than 50 pounds per caster level. Thus a 14th-level caster can vanish, and cause to reappear at a desired location, an object up to 700 pounds in weight. The maximum volume of material that can be affected is three cubic feet per level of experience. Thus, both weight and volume limit the spell. An object that exceeds either limitation is unaffected and the spell fails.

If desired, a vanished object can be placed deep within the Ethereal plane. In this case, the point from which the object vanished remains faintly magical until the item is retrieved. A successful *dispel magic* spell cast on the point will bring the vanished item back from the Ethereal plane. Note that creatures and magical forces cannot be made to vanish.

There is a 1% chance that a vanished item will be disintegrated instead. There is also a 1% chance that a creature from the Ethereal plane is able to gain access to the Prime Material plane through the vanished item's connection.

Vision (Divination)

Range: 0
Components: V, S, M
Duration: Special
Casting Time: 7
Area of Effect: The caster
Saving Throw: None

At such time as the wizard wishes to gain supernatural guidance, he casts a *vision* spell, calling upon whatever power he desires aid from, and asking the question for which a vision is to be given in answer. Two six-sided dice are rolled. If they total 2 to 6, the power is annoyed and will cause the wizard, by an ultra-powerful geas or quest, to do some service, and no questions are answered. If the dice total 7 to 9, the power is indifferent, and some minor vision, possibly unrelated to the question, is given. A score of 10 or better indicates that the vision is granted.

The material component of the spell is the sacrifice of something valued by the spellcaster or by the power supplicated. The more precious the sacrifice, the better the chance of spell success. A very precious item grants a bonus of +1 on the dice, one that is extremely precious adds +2, and a priceless item adds +3.

Eighth-Level Spells

Antipathy-Sympathy
(Enchantment/Charm)

Range: 30 yards
Components: V, S, M
Duration: 2 hours/level
Casting Time: 1 hour
Area of Effect: Special
Saving Throw: Special

This spell allows the wizard to set certain vibrations to emanate from an object or location that tend to either repel or attract a specific type of intelligent creature or characters of a particular alignment. The wizard must decide which effect is desired with regard to what creature type or alignment before beginning the spellcasting, for the components of each application differ. The spell cannot be cast upon living creatures.

Antipathy: This spell causes the affected creature or alignment type to feel an overpowering urge to leave the area or to not touch the affected item. If a saving throw vs. spell is successful, the creature can stay in the area or touch the item, but the creature will feel very uncomfortable, and a persistent itching will cause it to suffer the loss of 1 point of Dexterity per round (for the spell's duration), subject to a maximum loss of 4 points and a minimum Dexterity of 3. Failure to save vs. spell forces the being to abandon the area or item, shunning it permanently and never willingly returning to it until the spell is removed or expires.

The material component for this application of the spell is a lump of alum soaked in vinegar.

Sympathy: By casting the sympathy application of the spell, the wizard can cause a particular type of creature or alignment of character to feel elated and pleased to be in an area or touching or possessing an object or item. The desire to stay in the area or touch the object is overpowering. Unless a saving throw vs. spell is successfully rolled the creature or character will stay or refuse to release the object. If the saving throw is successful, the creature or character is released from the enchantment, but a subsequent saving throw must be made 1d6 turns later. If this saving throw fails, the affected creature will return to the area or object.

The material components of this spell are 1,000 gp worth of crushed pearls and a drop of honey.

Note that the particular type of creature to be affected must be named specifically, e.g., red dragons, hill giants, wererats, lammasu, catoblepas, vampires, etc. Likewise, the specific alignment must be named, e.g., chaotic evil, chaotic good, lawful neutral, true neutral, etc.

If this spell is cast upon an area, a 10-foot cube can be enchanted per experience level of the caster. If an object or item is enchanted, only that single thing can be enchanted; affected creatures or characters save vs. the spell with a −2 penalty.

Bigby's Clenched Fist (Evocation)

Range: 5 yards/level
Components: V, S, M
Duration: 1 round/level
Casting Time: 8
Area of Effect: Special
Saving Throw: None

The *Bigby's clenched fist* spell brings forth a huge, disembodied hand that is balled into a fist. This magical member is under the mental control of the spellcaster, who can cause it to strike one opponent each round. No concentration is required once the spell is cast. The clenched fist never misses, but it can only strike as directed by the caster. Thus it can be fooled by invisibility or other methods of concealment and misdirection. The effectiveness of its blows varies from round to round.

D20 Roll	Result
1-12	glancing blow—1d6 hp
13-16	solid punch—2d6 hp
17-19	hard punch—3d6 hp and opponent is stunned next round
20	Crushing blow*—4d6 hp and opponent is stunned for next three rounds

* The wizard adds +4 to the die rolls of subsequent attacks if the opponent is stunned, as the opponent is not capable of dodging or defending against the attack effectively.

The fist has an Armor Class of 0, and is destroyed by damage equal to the hit points of its caster at full health.

The material component of this spell is a leather glove and a small device consisting of four rings joined so as to form a slightly curved line, with an "I" upon which the bottoms of the rings rest, the whole fashioned of an alloy of copper and zinc.

Binding (Enchantment, Evocation)

Range: 10 yards
Components: V, S, M
Duration: Special
Casting Time: Special
Area of Effect: 1 creature
Saving Throw: Special

A *binding* spell creates a magical restraint to hold a creature, usually from another plane of existence. Extraplanar creatures must be confined by a circular diagram; other creatures can be physically confined. The duration of the spell depends upon the form of the binding and the level of the caster(s), as well as the length of time the spell is actually uttered. The components vary according to the form of the spell, but they include a continuous chanting utterance read from the scroll or book page giving the spell; gestures appropriate to the form of binding; and materials such as miniature chains of special metal (silver for lycanthropes, etc.), soporific herbs of the rarest sort, a corundum or diamond gem of great size (1,000 gp value per Hit Die of the subject creature), and a vellum depiction or carved statuette of the subject to be captured.

Magic resistance applies unless the subject's true name is used. A saving throw is not applicable as long as the experience level of the caster is at least twice as great as the Hit Dice of the subject. The caster's level can be augmented by one-third of the levels of each assisting wizard of 9th level or higher, and by one level for each assistant of 4th through 8th level. No more than six other wizards can assist with this spell. If the caster's level is less than twice the Hit Dice of the subject, then the subject gains a saving throw vs. spell, modified by the form of binding being attempted. The various forms of binding are these:

Chaining: The subject is confined by restraints that generate an *antipathy* affecting all creatures who approach the subject, except the caster. Duration is as long as one year per level of the caster(s). The subject of this form of binding (as well as in the slumber and bound slumber versions) remains within the restraining barrier.

Slumber: Brings a comatose sleep upon the subject for a duration of up to one year per level of the caster(s).

Bound Slumber: A combination of chaining and slumber that lasts for up to one month per level of the caster(s).

Hedged Prison: The subject is transported to or otherwise brought within a confined area from which it cannot wander by any means until freed. The spell remains until the magical hedge is somehow broken.

Metamorphosis: Causes the subject to change to some noncorporeal form, save for its head or face. The binding is permanent until some prescribed act frees the subject.

Minimus Containment: The subject is shrunken to a height of one inch or even less and held within the hedged prison of some gem or similar object. The subject of a minimus containment, metamorphosis, or hedged prison radiates a very faint aura of magic.

The type of binding does not modify the saving throw for the chaining form of the spell. Slumber allows the subject a +1 bonus, bound slumber a +2 bonus, hedged prison a +3 bonus, metamorphosis a +4 bonus, and minimus containment a +5 bonus to the saving throw. However, if the subject is magically weakened, the referee can assign a −1, −2, or even −4 penalty to the saving throw. A successful saving throw enables the subject to burst its bonds and do as it pleases.

A *binding* spell can be renewed in the case of the first three forms of the spell, for the subject does not have the opportunity to break the bonds. (If anything has caused a weakening of a chaining or slumber version, such as attempts to contact the subject or magically touch it, a normal saving throw applies to the renewal of the spell.) Otherwise, after one year, and each year thereafter, the subject gains a normal saving throw vs. the spell. Whenever it is successful, the *binding* spell is broken and the creature is free.

Clone (Necromancy)

Range: Touch
Components: V, S, M
Duration: Permanent
Casting Time: 1 turn
Area of Effect: Special
Saving Throw: None

This spell creates a duplicate of a human, demihuman, or humanoid creature. This clone is in most respects the duplicate of the individual, complete to the level of experience, memories, etc. However, the duplicate really *is* the person, so that if the original and a duplicate exist at the same time, each knows of the other's existence; and the original person and the clone will each desire to do away with the other, for such an alter-ego is unbearable to both. If one cannot destroy the other, one will go insane (90% likely to be the clone) and destroy itself, or possibly (2% chance) both will become mad and destroy themselves. These events nearly always occur within one week of the dual existence. Note that the clone is the person as he existed at the

time at which the flesh was taken, and all subsequent knowledge, experience, etc., is totally unknown to the clone. The clone is a physical duplicate, and possessions of the original are another matter entirely. A clone takes 2d4 months to grow, and only after that time is dual existence established. Finally, the clone has one less Constitution point than the body it was cloned from, and the cloning fails if the clone would have a Constitution of 0.

The material component of the spell is a small piece of the flesh from the person to be duplicated.

The DM may, in addition, add other stipulations to the success of a cloning effort, requiring that some trace of life must remain in the flesh sample, that some means of storing and preserving the sample must be devised and maintained, etc.

Demand
(Evocation, Enchantment/Charm)

Range: Special
Components: V, S, M
Duration: Special
Casting Time: 1 turn
Area of Effect: 1 creature
Saving Throw: Special

This spell is very much like the 5th-level wizard spell *sending*, allowing a brief contact with a far distant creature, except that the message can also contain a suggestion (see 3rd-level wizard spell), which the subject will do its best to carry out if it fails its saving throw vs. spell, with a −2 penalty. Of course, if the message is impossible or meaningless according to the circumstances that exist for the subject at the time the demand comes, the message is understood but no saving throw is necessary and the suggestion is ineffective.

The caster must be familiar with the creature contacted and must know its name and appearance well. If the creature in question is not in the same plane of existence as the spellcaster, there is a base 5% chance that the demand does not arrive. Local conditions on other planes may worsen this chance considerably at the option of the DM. The demand, if received, will be understood even if the creature has an Intelligence ability score as low as 1 (animal Intelligence). Creatures of demigod status or higher can choose to come or not, as they please.

The demand message to the creature must be 25 words or less, including the suggestion. The creature can also give a short reply immediately.

The material components of the spell are a pair of cylinders, each open at one end, connected by a thin piece of copper wire and some small part of the subject creature—a hair, bit of nail, etc.

Glassteel (Alteration)

Range: Touch
Components: V, S, M
Duration: Permanent
Casting Time: 8
Area of Effect: Object touched
Saving Throw: None

The *glassteel* spell turns normal, non-magical crystal or glass into a transparent substance that has the tensile strength and unbreakability of actual steel. Only a relatively small volume of material can be affected, a maximum weight of 10 pounds per level of experience of the spellcaster, and it must form one whole object. The Armor Class of the substance is 1.

The material components of this spell are a small piece of glass and a small piece of steel.

Incendiary Cloud
(Alteration, Evocation)

Range: 30 yards
Components: V, S, M
Duration: 4 rounds + 1d6 rounds
Casting Time: 2
Area of Effect: Special
Saving Throw: 1/2

An *incendiary cloud* spell exactly resembles the smoke effects of a *pyrotechnics* spell, except that its minimum dimensions are a cloud of 10-foot height by 20-foot length and breadth. This dense vapor cloud billows forth, and on the third round of its existence it begins to flame, causing 1-2 points of damage per level of the wizard who cast it. On the fourth round it inflicts 1d4 points of damage per level of the caster, and on the fifth round this again drops to 1-2 points of damage per level as its flames burn out. Any successive rounds of existence are simply harmless smoke that obscures vision within its confines. Creatures within the cloud need to make only one saving throw if it is successful, but if they fail the first saving throw, they roll again on the fourth and fifth rounds (if necessary) to attempt to reduce damage sustained by one-half.

In order to cast this spell, the wizard must have an available fire source (just as with a *pyrotechnics* spell), scrapings from beneath a dung pile, and a pinch of dust.

Mass Charm (Enchantment/Charm)

Range: 5 yards/level
Component: V
Duration: Special
Casting Time: 8
Area of Effect: Special
Saving Throw: Neg.

A *mass charm* spell affects either persons or monsters just as a *charm person* spell or a *charm monster* spell. The *mass charm* spell, however, affects a number of creatures whose combined levels of experience or Hit Dice does not exceed twice the level of experience of the spellcaster. All affected creatures must be within the spell range and within a 30-foot cube. Note that the creatures' saving throws are unaffected by the number of recipients (see the *charm person* and *charm monster* spells), but all target creatures are subject to a penalty of −2 on their saving throws because of the efficiency and power of this spell. The Wisdom bonus against charm spells does apply.

Maze (Conjuration/Summoning)

Range: 5 yards/level
Components: V, S
Duration: Special
Casting Time: 3
Area of Effect: 1 creature
Saving Throw: None

An extradimensional space is brought into being upon utterance of a *maze* spell. The subject vanishes into the shifting labyrinth of force planes for a period of time that is totally dependent upon its Intelligence. (Note: Minotaurs are not affected by this spell.)

Intelligence of Mazed Creature	Time Trapped in Maze
under 3	2d4 turns
3 to 5	1d4 turns
6 to 8	5d4 rounds
9 to 11	4d4 rounds
12 to 14	3d4 rounds
15 to 17	2d4 rounds
18 and up	1d4 rounds

Note that *teleport* and *dimension door* spells will not help a character escape a *maze* spell, although a *plane shifting* spell will.

Mind Blank (Abjuration)

Range: 30 yards
Components: V, S
Duration: 1 day
Casting Time: 1
Area of Effect: 1 creature
Saving Throw: None

When the very powerful *mind blank* spell is cast, the creature is totally protected from all devices and spells that detect, influence, or read emotions or thoughts. This protects against *augury, charm, command, confusion, divination, empathy* (all forms), *ESP, fear, feeblemind, mass suggestion, phantasmal killer, possession, rulership, soul trapping, suggestion,* and *telepathy.* Cloaking protection also extends to the prevention of discovery or information gathering by *crystal balls* or other scrying devices, *clairaudience, clairvoyance, communing, contacting other planes,* or wish-related methods (*wish, limited wish*). Of course, exceedingly powerful deities can penetrate the spell's barrier.

Monster Summoning VI (Conjuration/Summoning)

Range: 80 yards
Components: V, S, M
Duration: 7 rounds + 1 round/level
Casting Time: 8
Area of Effect: Special
Saving Throw: None

This spell is much like the 3rd-level *monster summoning I* spell, except that it summons 1d3 6th-level monsters. These appear in 1d3 rounds within the spell range and attack the caster's opponents, until either he commands them to cease, the spell duration expires, or the monsters are slain. These creatures do not check morale, and they vanish when slain. If no opponent exists to fight, summoned monsters can, if the wizard can communicate with them, and if they are physically capable, perform other services for the summoning wizard.

The material components of this spell are a tiny bag and a small (not necessarily lit) candle.

Otiluke's Telekinetic Sphere (Evocation, Alteration)

Range: 20 yards
Components: V, S, M
Duration: 2 rounds/level
Casting Time: 4
Area of Effect: 1-foot-diameter sphere per level
Saving Throw: Neg.

This spell is exactly the same as the 4th-level wizard spell, *Otiluke's resilient sphere,* with the addition that the creatures or objects inside the globe are just about weightless—anything contained within it weighs only $1/16$ of its normal weight. Any subject weighing up to 5,000 pounds can be telekinetically lifted in the sphere by the caster. Range of control extends to a maximum distance of 10 yards/level after the sphere has actually succeeded in encapsulating a subject or subjects. Note that even if more than 5,000 pounds of weight is englobed, the perceived weight is but $1/16$ of actual, so the orb can be rolled without exceptional effort. Because of the reduced weight, rapid motion or falling within the field of the sphere is relatively harmless to the object therein, although it can be disastrous should the globe disappear when the subject inside is high above a hard surface. The caster can dismiss the effect with a word.

In addition to a hemispherical piece of diamond and a matching piece of gum arabic, the caster must also have a pair of small bar magnets as material components for this spell.

Otto's Irresistible Dance (Enchantment/Charm)

Range: Touch
Components: V
Duration: 1d4 + 1 rounds
Casting Time: 5
Area of Effect: Creature touched
Saving Throw: None

When an *Otto's irresistible dance* spell is placed upon a creature, the spell causes the recipient to begin dancing, complete with feet shuffling and tapping. This dance makes it impossible for the victim to do anything other than caper and prance; this cavorting worsens the Armor Class of the creature by −4, makes saving throws impossible except on a roll of 20, and negates any consideration of a shield. Note that the creature must be touched—as if melee combat were taking place and the spellcaster were striking to do damage.

Permanency (Alteration)

Range: Special
Components: V, S
Duration: Permanent
Casting Time: 2 rounds
Area of Effect: Special
Saving Throw: None

This spell affects the duration of certain other spells, making the duration permanent. The personal spells upon which a *permanency* is known to be effective are as follows:

comprehend languages	protection from evil
detect evil	protection from normal missiles
detect invisibility	read magic
detect magic	tongues
infravision	unseen servant
protection from cantrips	

The wizard casts the desired spell and then follows with the *permanency* spell. Each *permanency* spell lowers the wizard's Constitution by 1 point. The wizard cannot cast these spells upon other creatures. This application of permanency can be dispelled only by a wizard of greater level than the spellcaster was when he cast the spell.

In addition to personal use, the *permanency* spell can be used to make the following object/creature or area-effect spells permanent:

enlarge	*prismatic sphere*
fear	*stinking cloud*
gust of wind	*wall of fire*
invisibility	*wall of force*
magic mouth	*web*

Additionally, the following spells can be cast upon objects or areas only and rendered permanent:

alarm	*wall of fire*
audible glamer	*distance distortion*
dancing lights	*teleport*
solid fog	

These applications to other spells allow it to be cast simultaneously with any of the latter when no living creature is the target, but the entire spell complex then can be dispelled normally, and thus negated.

The *permanency* spell is also used in the fabrication of magical items (see the 6th-level *enchant an item* spell). At the DM's option, permanency might become unstable or fail after a long period, at least 1,000 years. Unstable effects might operate intermittently or fail altogether.

The DM may allow other selected spells to be made permanent. Researching this possible application of a spell costs as much time and money as independently researching the selected spell. If the DM has already determined that the application is not possible, the research automatically fails. Note that the wizard never learns what is possible, except by the success or failure of his research.

Polymorph Any Object (Alteration)

Range: 5 yards/level
Components: V, S, M
Duration: Variable
Casting Time: 1 round
Area of Effect: Special
Saving Throw: Special

This spell changes one object or creature into another. When used as a *polymorph other* or *stone to flesh* spell, simply treat the spell as a more powerful version, with saving throws made with −4 penalties to the die roll. When it is cast in order to change other objects, the duration of the spell will depend on how radical a change it is from the original state to its enchanted state, as well as how different it is in size. This will be determined by your Dungeon Master by using the following guidelines:

Kingdom	Animal, vegetable, mineral
Class	Mammals, bipeds, fungi, metals, etc.
Relationship	Twig is to tree, sand is to beach, etc.
Size	Smaller, equal, larger
Shape	Comparative resemblance of the original to the polymorphed state
Intelligence	Particularly with regard to a change in which the end product is more intelligent

A change in *kingdom* makes the spell work for hours or turns—i.e., hours if one removed, turns if two removed. Other changes likewise affect spell duration. Thus, changing a lion to an androsphinx would be permanent, but turning a turnip to a purple worm would be a change of only hours duration; turning a tusk into an elephant would be permanent, but turning a twig into a sword would be a change of only several turns duration. All polymorphed objects radiate a strong magic, and if a *dispel magic* spell is successfully cast upon them, they return to their natural form. Note that a *stone to flesh*, or its reverse, will affect objects under this spell. As with other polymorph spells, damage sustained in the new form can result in the injury or death of the polymorphed creature. It is possible to polymorph a creature into rock and grind it to dust, causing damage, perhaps even death. If the creature was changed to dust to start with, more creative methods to damage it would have to be applied—perhaps using a *gust of wind* spell to scatter the dust far and wide. In general, damage occurs when the new form is altered through physical force, although the DM will have to adjudicate many of these situations.

The system shock roll must be applied to living creatures, as must the restrictions noted regarding the *polymorph others* and *stone to flesh* spells. Also note that a polymorph effect often detracts from an item's or creature's powers, but does not add new powers—except possibly movement capabilities not present in the old form. Thus, a *vorpal sword* polymorphed into a dagger would not retain vorpal capability. Likewise, valueless items cannot be made into permanent valuable items.

The material components of this spell are mercury, gum arabic, and smoke.

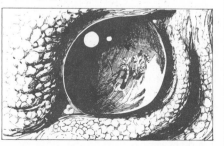

Power Word, Blind (Conjuration/Summoning)

Range: 5 yards/level
Components: V
Duration: Special
Casting Time: 1
Area of Effect: 15-foot-radius sphere
Saving Throw: None

When a *power word, blind* spell is cast, one or more creatures within the area of effect become sightless. The spellcaster selects one creature as the target center, and the effect spreads outward from the center, affecting creatures with the lowest hit point totals first; alternatively, the spell can be focused to affect only an individual creature. Creatures with a current hit point total over 100 hit points are not affected and do not count against the number of creatures affected. The spell affects up to 100 hit points of creatures, but the duration depends upon how many hit points are affected. If 25 or fewer hit points are affected, the blindness is permanent until cured. If 26 to 50 hit points are affected, the blindness lasts for 1d4 + 1 turns, if 51 to 100 hit points of creatures are affected, the spell duration is but 1d4 + 1 rounds. An individual creature cannot be partially affected; if all of its current hit points are affected, it is blinded, otherwise, it is not. Blindness can be removed by a *cure blindness* or *dispel magic* spell.

Prismatic Wall (Conjuration/Summoning)

Range: 10 yards
Components: V, S
Duration: 1 turn/level
Casting Time: 7
Area of Effect: Special
Saving Throw: Special

This spell enables the wizard to conjure up a vertical, opaque wall—a shimmering, multi-colored plane of light that gives him protection from all forms of attack. This scintillating wall flashes all colors of the visible spectrum. Seven of the colors have distinct powers and purposes. Any creature with fewer than 8 Hit Dice that is within 20 feet of the wall and that does not shield its vision is blinded for 2d4 rounds by the colors of the wall. The wall is immobile. The spellcaster can pass through the wall without harm, however. Each color in the wall has a special effect. Each color can also be negated by a specific magical effect, but the colors must be negated in the precise order of the spectrum. The colors and effects (on a being trying to attack the caster) of the *prismatic wall* spell, as well as what will negate each color, are as follows (see next page):

Color	Order of Color	Prismatic Wall Effects — Effects of Color	Spell Negated By
Red	1st	Stops nonmagical missiles—inflicts 20 points of damage, save for half	cone of cold
Orange	2nd	Stops magical missiles—inflicts 40 points of damage, save for half	gust of wind
Yellow	3rd	Stops poisons, gases, and petrification—inflicts 80 points of damage, save for half	disintegrate
Green	4th	Stops breath weapons—save vs. poison or die, survivors suffer 20 points of damage	passwall
Blue	5th	Stops location/detection and mental attacks—save vs. petrification or turned to stone	magic missile
Indigo	6th	Stops magical spells—save vs. wand or insane	continual light
Violet	7th	Force field protection—save vs. spell or sent to another plane	dispel magic

The wall's maximum proportions are 40 feet wide per level of experience of the caster and 20 feet high per level of experience. A *prismatic wall* spell cast to materialize in a space occupied by a creature is disrupted and the spell is wasted.

Screen (Divination/Illusion)

Range: 0
Components: V, S
Duration: 1 hour/level
Casting Time: 1 turn
Area of Effect: 30-foot cube/level
Saving Throw: Special

This spell combines several elements to create a powerful protection from scrying and direct observation. When the spell is cast, the wizard dictates what will and will not be observed in the area of effect. The illusion created must be stated in general terms. Thus the caster could specify the illusion of him and another playing chess for the duration of the spell, but he could not have the illusionary chess players take a break, make dinner, and then resume their game. He could have a crossroads appear quiet and empty even while an army is actually passing through the area. He could specify that no one be seen (including passing strangers), that his troops be undetected, or even that every fifth man or unit should be visible. Once the conditions are set, they cannot be changed.

Attempts to scry the area automatically detect the image stated by the caster with no saving throw allowed. Sight and sound are appropriate to the illusion created. A band of men standing in a meadow could be concealed as an empty meadow with birds chirping, etc. Direct observation may allow a saving throw (as per a normal illusion), if there is cause to disbelieve what is seen. Certainly onlookers in the area would become suspicious if the column of a marching army disappeared at one point to reappear at another! Even entering the area does not cancel the illusion or necessarily allow a saving throw, assuming care is taken by the hidden beings to stay out of the way of those affected by the illusion.

Serten's Spell Immunity (Abjuration)

Range: Touch
Components: V, S, M
Duration: 1 turn/level
Casting Time: 1 round/recipient
Area of Effect: Creature(s) touched
Saving Throw: None

By use of this spell, the wizard is able to confer virtual immunity to certain spells and magical attack forms upon those he touches. For every four levels of experience of the wizard, one creature can be protected by the *Serten's spell immunity* spell, but, if more than one is protected, the duration of the protection is divided among the protected creatures. (Example: A 16th-level wizard can cast the spell upon one creature and it will last 16 turns, or place it upon two creatures for eight turns, or upon four creatures for four turns.) The protection gives a bonus to saving throws, according to spell type and level, as shown in the following table.

Spell level	Wizard Spell	Priest Spell
1st-3rd	+9*	+7
4th-6th	+7	+5
7th-8th	+5	+3

* Includes *beguiling* effects.

The material component of this spell is a diamond of at least 500 gp value, which must be crushed and sprinkled over the spell recipients. Each such creature must also have in its possession a diamond of at least one carat size, intact and carried on its person.

Sink (Enchantment, Alteration)

Range: 10 yards/level
Components: V, S
Duration: Special
Casting Time: 8
Area of Effect: 1 creature or 1 object of 1 cubic foot/level
Saving Throw: Special

By means of this spell, a wizard can force a creature or object into the very earth or floor upon which it stands. When casting the spell, the wizard must chant the spell for the remainder of the round without interruption. At that juncture, the subject creature or object becomes rooted to the spot unless a saving throw vs. spell (for a creature) or a saving throw vs. disintegration (for an object with magical properties) is successful. (Note: "magical properties" include those of magical items as listed in the *Dungeon Master's Guide*, those of items enchanted or otherwise of magical origin, and those of items with protection-type spells or with permanent magical properties or similar spells upon them.) Items of a nonmagical nature are not entitled to a saving throw. The subject becomes of slightly greater density than the surface upon which it stands if its saving throw was not successful.

The spellcaster now has the option of ceasing his spell and leaving the subject as it is, in which case the spell expires in four turns, and the subject returns to normal. If the caster proceeds with the spell (into the next round), the subject begins to sink slowly into the ground. Before any actions are taken in the new round, the subject sinks one-quarter of its height; after the first group acts, another one-quarter; after the second group acts, another; at the end of the round, the victim is totally sunken into the ground.

This entombment places a creature or object into a state of suspended animation. The cessation of time means that the subject does not grow older. Bodily and other functions virtually cease, but the subject is otherwise unharmed. The subject exists in undamaged form in the surface into which it was sunk, its upper point as far beneath the surface as the subject has height—a six-foot-tall victim will be six feet beneath the surface, while a 60-foot-tall subject will have its uppermost point 60 feet below ground level. If the ground around the subject is somehow removed, the spell is broken and the subject returns to normal, but it does not rise up. Such spells as *dig, transmute rock to mud,* and *freedom* (reverse of the 9th-level *imprisonment* spell) will not harm the sunken creature or object and will often be helpful in recovering it. If a *detect magic* spell is cast over an area upon which a *sink* spell was used, it reveals a faint magical aura of undefinable nature, even if the subject is beyond detection range. If the subject is within range of the detection, the spell's schools can be discovered (alteration and enchantment).

Symbol (Conjuration/Summoning)

Range: Touch
Components: V, S, M
Duration: Special
Casting Time: 8
Area of Effect: Special
Saving Throw: Special

A *symbol* spell creates magical runes affecting creatures that pass over, touch, or read the runes, or pass through a portal upon which the symbol is inscribed. Upon casting the spell, the wizard inscribes the symbol upon whatever surface he desires. Likewise, the spellcaster is able to place the symbol of his choice, using any one of the following:

Death	One or more creatures, whose total hit points do not exceed 80, are slain.
Discord	All creatures are affected and immediately fall to loud bickering and arguing; there is a 50% probability that creatures of different alignments attack each other. The bickering lasts for 5d4 rounds, the fighting for 2d4 rounds.
Fear	This symbol creates an extra-strong *fear* spell, causing all creatures to save vs. spell with −4 penalties to the die roll, or panic and flee as if attacked by a *fear* spell.
Hopelessness	All creatures are affected and must turn back in dejection unless they save vs. spell. Affected creatures submit to the demands of any opponent—e.g., surrender, get out, etc.; the hopelessness lasts for 3d4 turns. During this period it is 25% probable that affected creatures take no action during any round, and 25% likely that those taking action turn back or retire from battle, as applicable.
Insanity	One or more creatures whose total hit points do not exceed 120 become insane and remain so, acting as if a *confusion* spell had been placed upon them, until a *heal, restoration,* or *wish* spell is used to remove the madness.
Pain	All creatures are afflicted with wracking pains shooting through their bodies, causing a −2 penalty to Dexterity and a −4 penalty to attack dice for 2d10 turns.
Sleep	All creatures under 8+1 Hit Dice immediately fall into a catatonic slumber and cannot be awakened for 1d12 + 4 turns.
Stunning	One or more creatures whose total hit points do not exceed 160 are stunned and reeling for 3d4 rounds, dropping anything they are holding.

The type of symbol cannot be recognized without being read and thus activating its effects.

The material components of this spell are powdered black opal and diamond dust, worth not less than 5,000 gp each.

Trap the Soul (Conjuration/Summoning)

Range: 10 yards
Components: V, S, M
Duration: Permanent until broken
Casting Time: Special + 1
Area of Effect: 1 creature
Saving Throw: Special

This spell forces the creature's life force (and its material body) into a special prison gem enchanted by the spellcaster. The creature must be seen by the caster when the final word is uttered.

The spell can be triggered in one of two ways. First, the final word of the spell can be spoken when the creature is within spell range. This allows magic resistance (if any) and a saving throw vs. spell to avoid the effect. If the creature's real name is spoken as well, any magic resistance is ignored and the saving throw vs. spell suffers a penalty of −2. If the saving throw is successful, the prison gem shatters.

The second method is far more insidious, for it tricks the victim into accepting a trigger object inscribed with the final spell word, automatically placing the creature's soul into the trap. To use this method, both the creature's true name and the trigger word must be inscribed on the trigger item when the gem is enchanted. A *sympathy* spell can also be placed on the trigger item. As soon as the subject creature picks up or accepts the trigger item, its life force is automatically transferred to the gem, without the benefit of magic resistance or saving throw.

The gem prison will hold the trapped entity indefinitely, or until the gem is broken and the life force is released, allowing the material body to reform. If the creature trapped is a powerful creature from another plane (and this could actually mean a character trapped by some inhabitant of another plane of existence when the character is not on the Prime Material plane), it can be required to perform a service immediately upon being freed. Otherwise the creature can go free once the gem imprisoning it is broken.

Before the actual casting of the *trap the soul* spell, the wizard must prepare the prison, a gem of at least 1,000 gp value for every Hit Die or level of experience possessed by the creature to be trapped (e.g., it requires a gem of 10,000 gp value to trap a 10 Hit Die or 10th-level creature). If the gem is not valuable enough, it shatters when the entrapment is attempted. (Note that while characters have no concept of level as such, the value of the gem needed to trap an individual can be researched. Remember that this value can change over time as characters advance.) Creating the prison gem requires an *enchant an item* spell and the placement of a *maze* spell into the gem, thereby forming the prison to contain the life force.

Ninth-Level Spells

Astral Spell (Evocation)

Range: Touch
Components: V, S
Duration: Special
Casting Time: 9
Area of Effect: Special
Saving Throw: None

By means of the *astral* spell, a wizard can project his astral body into the Astral plane, leaving his physical body and material possessions behind in the Prime Material plane (the plane in which the entire universe and all of its parallels exist). Only magical items can be brought into the Astral plane (although nonmagical items could be rendered temporarily magical through the use of some spells, if the DM allows). As the Astral plane touches upon all of the first levels of the outer planes, the wizard can travel astrally to any of these outer planes as he wills. The caster then leaves the Astral plane, forming a body in the plane of existence he has chosen to enter. It is also possible to travel astrally anywhere in the Prime Material plane by means of the *astral* spell, but a second body cannot be formed in the Prime Material plane. As a general rule, a person astrally projected can be seen only by creatures in the Astral plane.

At all times, the astral body is connected to the material body by a silvery cord. If the cord is broken, the affected person is killed, astrally and materially, but normally only the psychic wind can cause the cord to break. When a second body is formed in a different plane, the silvery cord remains invisibly attached to the new body. If the astral form is slain, the cord simply returns to the original body where it rests in the Prime Material plane, reviving it from its state of suspended animation.

Although astrally projected persons are able to function in the Astral plane, their actions do not affect creatures not existing in the Astral plane. The spell lasts until the wizard desires to end it, or until it is terminated by some outside means (a *dispel magic* spell or destruction of the wizard's body in the Prime Material plane).

The wizard can project the astral forms of up to seven other creatures with him by means of the *astral* spell, providing the creatures are linked in a circle with the wizard. These fellow travelers are dependent upon the wizard and can be stranded. Travel in the Astral plane can be slow or fast according to the wizard's desire. The ultimate destination arrived at is subject to the conceptualization of the mage. (See the *Manual of the Planes* for further information on the Astral plane and astral projection.)

Any magical items can go into the Astral plane, but most become temporarily nonmagical therein, or in any planes removed from the Prime Material plane. Armor and weapons of +3 or better might function in other planes at the DM's option. Artifacts and relics function anywhere. Items drawing their power from a given plane are more powerful in that plane (e.g., a *ring of fire resistance* in the elemental plane of Fire or a *sword of life stealing* in the Negative Material plane).

Bigby's Crushing Hand (Evocation)

Range: 5 yards/level
Components: V, S, M
Duration: 1 round/level
Casting Time: 9
Area of Effect: Special
Saving Throw: None

The *Bigby's crushing hand* spell creates a huge, disembodied hand similar to those of the other *Bigby's hand* spells. The crushing hand is under the mental control of the caster, and he can cause it to grasp and squeeze an opponent. No attack roll is necessary; the hand automatically grasps and inflicts constriction damage any round in which the wizard concentrates. The damage inflicted depends on the number of rounds it acts upon the victim:

1st round	1d10 hit points
2nd and 3rd rounds	2d10 hit points
4th & beyond	4d10 hit points

The crushing hand has an Armor Class of 0, has as many hit points as its caster at full strength, and vanishes when destroyed. The hand is susceptible to normal combat attacks and damaging spells, but if it is struck by an area-effect spell, the person held suffers the same fate as the hand (i.e., if the hand fails its saving throw, the victim automatically fails his). The hand is not effective against noncorporeal or gaseous forms, but it does prevent creatures that are able to slip through small cracks from escaping. If the hand grasps an item or construction, the appropriate saving throw must be made as if squeezed by a Strength of 25.

The material components of the spell are a glove of snake skin and the shell of an egg.

Crystalbrittle (Alteration)

Range: Touch
Components: V, S
Duration: Permanent
Casting Time: 9
Area of Effect: 2 cubic ft./level
Saving Throw: Special

The magic of this spell causes metal, whether as soft as gold or as hard as adamantite, to turn to a crystalline substance as brittle and fragile as crystal. Thus a sword, metal shield, metal armor, or even an iron golem can be changed to a delicate, glass-like material easily shattered by any forceful blow. Furthermore, this change is unalterable short of a *wish* spell; a *dispel magic* will not reverse the spell.

The caster must physically touch the item—if it is an opponent or something an opponent is using or wearing, the wizard must get into melee and roll a successful attack roll. Any single metal item can be affected by the spell. Thus a suit of armor worn by a creature can be changed to crystal, but the creature's shield would not be affected, or vice versa. All items gain a saving throw equal to their magical bonus value or protection (the DM has this information). A +1/+3 sword would get a 10% (average of the two pluses) chance to save; +5 magical armor has a 25% chance to be unaffected; an iron golem has a 15% chance to save (for it is hit only by magical weapons of +3 or better quality). Artifacts and relics constructed of metal may be affected at the discretion of the DM (this is highly unlikely). Affected items not immediately protected are shattered and permanently destroyed if struck by a normal blow from a metal tool or any weighty weapon, including a staff.

Energy Drain (Evocation, Necromancy)

Range: Touch
Components: V, S, M
Duration: Permanent
Casting Time: 3
Area of Effect: 1 creature
Saving Throw: None

By casting this spell, the wizard opens a channel between the plane he is in and the Negative Material plane, the caster becoming the conductor between the two planes. As soon as he touches (equal to a hit if melee is involved) any living creature, the victim loses two levels (as if struck by a spectre). A monster loses 2 Hit Dice permanently, both for hit points and attack ability. A character loses levels, Hit Dice, hit points, and abilities permanently (until regained through adventuring, if applicable).

The material component of this spell is essence of spectre or vampire dust. Preparation requires mere moments, then the material component is cast forth, and upon touching the victim, the wizard speaks the triggering word, causing the spell to take effect instantly.

The spell remains effective for a single round only. Humans or humanoids brought below zero energy levels by this spell can be animated as juju zombies under the control of the caster.

The caster always has a 5% (1 in 20) chance to be affected by the dust, losing one point of Constitution at the same time as the victim is drained. When the number of Constitution points lost equals the caster's original Constitution ability score, the caster dies and becomes a shade.

Foresight (Divination)

Range: 0
Components: V, S, M
Duration: 2d4 rounds + 1 round/level
Casting Time: 1 round
Area of Effect: Special
Saving Throw: None

This spell grants the caster a powerful sixth sense in relation to himself or another. Although cast upon himself, the wizard can specify that he or another is the beneficiary of the spell. Once the spell is cast, the wizard receives instantaneous warnings of impending danger or harm to the object of the spell. Thus, if he were the object of the spell, the wizard would be warned in advance if a thief were about to attempt to backstab him, or if a creature were about to leap out from an unexpected direction, or if an attacker were specifically targeting him with a spell or missile weapon. When the warnings are about him personally, the wizard cannot be surprised and always knows the direction from which any attack on him is made. In addition, the spell gives the wizard a general idea of what action he might take to best protect himself— duck, jump right, close his eyes, etc.—and gives him a defensive bonus of 2 to his Armor Class. When another is the object of the spell, the wizard receives warnings about that person. He must still communicate this to the other to negate any surprise. Shouting a warning, yanking the person back, even telepathically communicating through a *crystal ball* can all be accomplished before the trap is sprung—if the wizard does not hesitate. The object of the spell does not gain the defensive bonus to his Armor Class, however.

The material component for this spell is a hummingbird's feather.

Gate (Conjuration/Summoning)

Range: 30 yards
Components: V, S
Duration: Special
Casting Time: 9
Area of Effect: Special
Saving Throw: None

The casting of a *gate* spell has two effects. First, it causes an interdimensional connection between the plane of existence the wizard is in and the plane in which dwells a specific being of great power, enabling the being to merely step through the gate, or portal, from its plane to that of the caster. Second, the utterance of the spell attracts the attention of the sought-after dweller in the other plane. When casting the spell, the

wizard must name the entity he desires to use the gate and to come to the wizard's aid. There is a 100% certainty that something steps through the gate. Unless the DM has some facts prepared regarding the minions serving the being called forth by the *gate* spell, the being itself comes.

If the matter is trifling, the being might leave, inflict an appropriate penalty on the wizard, or attack the wizard; if the matter is of middling importance, the being can take some positive action to set matters aright, then demand appropriate repayment; and if the matter is urgent, it can act accordingly and ask whatever is its wont thereafter, if appropriate. The actions of the being that comes through depend on many factors, including the alignments of the wizard and the deity, the nature of his companions, and who or what opposes or threatens the wizard. Such beings generally avoid direct conflict with their equals or betters. The being gated in will either return immediately (very unlikely) or remain to take action. Casting this spell ages the wizard five years.

Imprisonment (Abjuration)
Reversible

Range: Touch
Components: V, S
Duration: Permanent
Casting Time: 9
Area of Effect: 1 creature
Saving Throw: None

When an *imprisonment spell* is cast and the victim is touched, the recipient is entombed in a state of suspended animation (see the *temporal stasis* spell) in a small sphere far beneath the surface of the earth. The victim remains there unless a reverse of the spell, with the creature's name and background, is cast. Magical search by *crystal ball*, a *locate object* spell, or similar means will not reveal the fact that a creature is imprisoned. The *imprisonment* spell functions only if the subject creature's name and background are known.

The reverse spell, *freedom*, cast upon the spot at which a creature was entombed and sunk into the earth, causes it to reappear at that spot. If the caster does not perfectly intone the name and background of the creature to be freed, there is a 10% chance that 1 to 100 creatures will be freed from imprisonment at the same time.

Note: The exact details of any creatures freed are up to the DM. A random method of determining this is to roll percentile dice twice (once for imprisoned creature density and once for a base number of creatures at maximum density). The rolls are multiplied and rounded to the nearest whole number. Each released creature has a 10% chance to be in the area of the spellcaster. If monsters are being generated randomly, roll 1d20 for

level, with rolls of 9 + considered 9, and the exact monsters determined by the random encounter tables.

For example, if the initial rolls were 22 and 60, the number of monsters released is .22 X .60 = .1320 = 13 monsters. Since only 10% of these will be in the immediate vicinity of the caster, the wizard may encounter only one or two of them.

Meteor Swarm (Evocation)

Range: 40 yards + 10 yards/level
Components: V, S
Duration: Instantaneous
Casting Time: 9
Area of Effect: Special
Saving Throw: 1/2

A *meteor swarm* is a very powerful and spectacular spell which is similar to the *fireball* spell in many aspects. When it is cast, either four spheres of two-foot diameter or eight spheres of one-foot diameter spring from the outstretched hand of the wizard and streak in a straight line to the distance demanded by the spellcaster, up to the maximum range. Any creature in the straight-line path of these missiles receives the full effect of the missile, or missiles, without benefit of a saving throw. The meteor missiles leave a fiery trail of sparks, and each bursts as a fireball. The large spheres inflict 10d4 points of damage, bursting in a diamond or box pattern. Each has a 30-foot diameter area of effect, and each sphere is 20 feet apart, along the sides of the pattern, so that there are overlapping areas of effect, and the center will be exposed to all four blasts. The eight spheres have one-half the diameter (15 feet) and one-half the damage potential (5d4). They burst in a pattern of a box within a diamond or vice versa, each of the outer sides 20 feet long. Note that the center has four areas of overlapping effect, and there are numerous peripheral areas that have two overlapping areas of effect. A saving throw for each area of effect will indicate whether full damage or half damage is sustained by creatures within each area, except as already stated with regard to the missiles impacting.

Monster Summoning VII
(Conjuration/Summoning)

Range: 90 yards
Components: V, S, M
Duration: 8 rounds + 1 round/level
Casting Time: 9
Area of Effect: Special
Saving Throw: None

This spell is much like the 3rd-level *monster summoning I* spell, except that this spell summons one or two 7th-level monsters that appear one round after the spell is cast, or one 8th-level monster that appears two rounds after the spell is cast.

Mordenkainen's Disjunction
(Alteration, Enchantment)

Range: 0
Components: V
Duration: Instantaneous
Casting Time: 9
Area of Effect: 30-foot radius
Saving Throw: Special

When this spell is cast, all magic and magical items within the radius of the spell, except those on the person of or being touched by the spellcaster, are *disjoined*. That is, spells being cast are separated into their individual components (usually spoiling the effect as a *dispel magic* spell does), and *permanent* and enchanted items must save (vs. spell if actually cast on a creature, or vs. a *dispel magic* spell otherwise) or be turned into normal items. Even artifacts and relics are subject to Mordenkainen's disjunction, although there is only a 1% chance per caster experience level of actually affecting such powerful items. Thus all potions, scrolls, rings, rods, miscellaneous magical items, artifacts and relics, arms and armor, swords, and miscellaneous weapons within 30 feet of the spellcaster can possibly lose all their magical properties when the *Mordenkainen's disjunction* spell is cast. The caster also has a 1% chance per level of destroying an anti-magic shell. If the shell survives the disjunction, no items within it are disjoined.

Note: Destroying artifacts is a dangerous business, and 95% likely to attract the attention of some powerful being who has an interest or connection with the device. Additionally, if an artifact is destroyed, the casting wizard must roll a successful saving throw vs. spell with a −4 penalty or permanently lose all spellcasting abilities.

Power Word, Kill
(Conjuration/Summoning)

Range: 5 yards/two levels
Components: V
Duration: Permanent
Casting Time: 1
Area of Effect: 10-foot radius
Saving Throw: None

When a *power word, kill* spell is uttered, one or more creatures of any type within the spell range and area of effect are slain. The power word slays one creature with up to 60 hit points, or it kills two or more creatures with 10 or fewer hit points, up to a maximum of 120 hit points. The option to attack a single creature, or multiple creatures, must be stated along with the spell range and area of effect center. The current hit points of the creatures are used.

Prismatic Sphere
(Abjuration, Conjuration/Summoning)

Range: 0
Components: V
Duration: 1 turn/level
Casting Time: 7
Area of Effect: 10-foot-radius sphere
Saving Throw: Special

This spell enables the wizard to conjure up an immobile, opaque globe of shimmering, multi-colored light to surround him, giving protection from all forms of attack. This scintillating sphere flashes in all colors of the visible spectrum. Seven of the colors have distinct powers and purposes. Any creature with fewer than 8 Hit Dice is blinded for 2d4 turns by the colors of the sphere. Only the spellcaster can pass in and out of the prismatic sphere without harm, although he can cast it over others to protect them. The sphere can be destroyed, color by color, in consecutive order, by various mag-

ical effects; however, the first must be brought down before the second can be affected, etc. Any creature passing through the barrier receives the effect of every color still remaining. Note that typically the upper hemisphere of the globe is visible, as the spellcaster is at the center of the sphere, so the lower half is usually hidden by the floor surface he is standing upon. The colors and effects of the prismatic sphere, as well as what will negate each globe, are shown on the accompanying table.

Note that a *rod of cancellation* or a *Mordenkainen's disjunction* spell will destroy a prismatic sphere (but an anti-magic shell will fail to penetrate it). Otherwise, anything short of an artifact or relic entering the sphere is destroyed, and any creature is subject to the effects of every color still active—i.e., 70-140 points of damage plus death, petrification, insanity, and instantaneous transportation to another plane.

Color of Globe	Order of Globe	Effects of Globe	Spell Negated By
Red	1st	Stops nonmagical missiles—inflicts 20 points of damage, save vs. spell for half	*cone of cold*
Orange	2nd	Stops magical missiles—inflicts 40 points of damage, save vs. spell for half	*gust of wind*
Yellow	3rd	Stops poisons, gases, and petrification—inflicts 80 points of damage, save vs. spell for half	*disintegrate*
Green	4th	Stops breath weapons—save vs. poison or dead, successful save takes 20 points of poison damage	*passwall*
Blue	5th	Stops location/detection and mental attacks—save vs. petrification or turned to stone	*magic missile*
Indigo	6th	Stops magical spells—save vs. wand or insane	*continual light*
Violet	7th	Force field protection—save vs. spell or sent to another plane	*dispel magic*

Shape Change (Alteration)

Range: 0
Components: V, S, M
Duration: 1 turn/level
Casting Time: 9
Area of Effect: The caster
Saving Throw: None

With this spell, a wizard is able to assume the form of any living thing or creature below demigod status (greater or lesser deity, singular dragon type, or the like). The spellcaster becomes the creature he wishes, and has all of the abilities save those dependent upon Intelligence, innate magical abilities, and magic resistance, for the mind of the creature is that of the spellcaster. Thus he can change into a griffon and fly away, then to an efreet and fly through a roaring flame, and then to a titan to lift up a wagon, etc. These creatures have whatever hit points the wizard has at the time of the shape change. Each alteration in form requires but a second. No system shock is

incurred.

Example: A wizard is in combat and assumes the form of a will o' wisp, and when this form is no longer useful, the wizard changes into a stone golem and walks away. When pursued, the golem-shape is changed to that of a flea, which hides upon a horse until it can hop off and become a bush. If detected as the latter, the wizard can become a dragon, an ant, or just about anything he is familiar with.

A wizard adopting another form also adops its vulnerabilities. For example, a wizard who becomes a spectre is powerless in daylight, and is subject to being turned, controlled, or destroyed by opposing clerics. Unlike similar spells, a wizard who is killed in another form does not revert to his original shape, which may disallow certain types of revivification.

The material component is a jade circlet worth no less than 5,000 gp, which shatters at the end of the spell's duration. In the meantime, the circlet is left in the wake of the shape change, and premature shattering ends the spell immediately.

Succor (Alteration, Enchantment)
Reversible

Range: Touch
Components: V, S, M
Duration: Special
Casting Time: 1 to 4 days
Area of Effect: 1 individual
Saving Throw: None

By casting this spell, the wizard creates a powerful magic in some specially prepared object—a statuette, a jeweled rod, a gem, etc. This object radiates magic, for it contains the power to instantaneously transport its possessor to the abode of the wizard who created it. Once the item is enchanted, the wizard must give it willingly to an individual, at the same time informing him of a command word to be spoken when the item is to be used. To make use of the item, the recipient must speak the command word at the same time that he rends or breaks the item. When this is done, the individual and all that he is wearing and carrying are instantly transported to the abode of the wizard. No other creatures can be affected.

The reversed application of the spell transports the wizard to the immediate vicinity of the possessor of the spelled item, when it is broken and the command word said. The wizard will have a general idea of the location and situation of the item possessor, but has no choice whether or not to go (making this a rare casting indeed!).

The material components used include gemstones totaling not less than 5,000 gp value; whether it is a faceted gem or not is immaterial. The components can be enchanted only once per month (usually on a night of a clear, full moon). At that time, the object is set for the type of succor and its final destination (either the location of the spellcasting or an area well known to the wizard).

Temporal Stasis (Alteration)
Reversible

Range: 10 yards
Components: V, S, M
Duration: Permanent
Casting Time: 9
Area of Effect: One creature
Saving Throw: None

Upon casting this spell, the wizard places the recipient creature into a state of suspended animation. This cessation of time means that the creature does not grow older. Its body functions virtually cease. This state persists until the magic is removed by a *dispel magic* spell or the reverse of the spell (*temporal reinstatement*) is uttered. Note

that the reverse requires only a single word and no somatic or material components.

The material component of a *temporal stasis* spell is a powder composed of diamond, emerald, ruby, and sapphire dust, each crushed stone of at least 100 gp value.

Time Stop (Alteration)

Range: 0
Components: V
Duration: Special
Casting Time: 9
Area of Effect: 15-foot-radius sphere
Saving Throw: None

Upon casting a *time stop* spell, the wizard causes the flow of time to stop for one round in the area of effect. Outside this area the sphere simply seems to shimmer for an instant. Inside the sphere, the caster is free to act for 1d3 rounds of apparent time. The wizard can move and act freely within the area where time is stopped, but all other creatures, except for those of demigod and greater status or unique creatures, are frozen in their actions, for they are literally between ticks of the time clock. (The spell duration is subjective to the caster.) Nothing can enter the area of effect without being stopped in time also. If the wizard leaves the area, the spell is immediately negated. When the spell duration ceases, the wizard is again operating in normal time.

Note: It is recommended that the DM use a stop watch or silently count to time this spell. If the caster is unable to complete the intended action before the spell duration expires, he will probably be caught in an embarrassing situation. The use of a *teleport* spell before the expiration of the *time stop* spell is permissible.

Weird (Illusion/Phantasm)

Range: 30 yards
Components: V, S
Duration: Concentration
Casting Time: 9
Area of Effect: 20-foot radius
Saving Throw: Special

This spell confronts those affected by it with phantasmal images of their most feared enemies, forcing an imaginary combat that seems real, but actually occurs in the blink of an eye. When this spell is cast, the wizard must be able to converse with the victims to bring the spell into being. During the casting, the wizard must call out to the creatures to be affected, informing one or all that their final fate, indeed their doom, is now upon them.

The force of the magic is such that even if the creatures make their saving throws vs. spell, fear will paralyze them for a full round, and they will lose 1d4 Strength points from this fear (the lost Strength will

return in one turn). Failure to save vs. spell causes the creature or creatures to face their nemeses, the opponents most feared and inimical to them. Actual combat must then take place, for no magical means of escape is possible. The foe fought is real for all intents and purposes. Affected creatures that lose, die. If a creature's phantasmal nemesis from the *weird* spell is slain, then the creature emerges with no damage, no loss of items seemingly used in the combat, and no loss of spells likewise seemingly expended. Experience for defeating the weird is gained if applicable. Although each round of combat seems normal, it takes but 1/10 of a round. During the course of the spell, the caster must concentrate fully upon maintaining it. If the combat goes beyond ten rounds, those who saved against the spell can take action. If the caster is disturbed, the *weird* spell ends immediately. Creatures attacked while paralyzed with fear are free of the paralysis immediately.

Wish (Conjuration/Summoning)

Range: Unlimited
Components: V
Duration: Special
Casting Time: Special
Area of Effect: Special
Saving Throw: Special

The *wish spell* is a more potent version of a *limited wish*. If it is used to alter reality with respect to damage sustained by a party, to bring a dead creature to life, or to escape from a difficult situation by lifting the spellcaster (and his party) from one place to another, it will not cause the wizard any disability. Other forms of wishes, however, cause the spellcaster to weaken (−3 on Strength) and require 2d4 days of bed rest due to the stresses the *wish* places upon time, space, and his body. Regardless of what is wished for, the exact terminology of the *wish* spell is likely to be carried out. Casting a *wish* spell ages the caster five years.

This discretionary power of the DM is necessary in order to maintain game balance. As wishing another creature dead would be grossly unfair, for example, your DM might well advance the spellcaster to a future period in which the creature is no longer alive, effectively putting the wishing character out of the campaign.

Priest Spells Note

Following the name of each priest spell, notice that a *magical school* is given in parentheses. This is for reference purposes only. For instance, Wisdom bonuses apply to saving throws vs. enchantment/charm spells. If the appropriate magical school were not listed with priest spells, it would be hard to figure out which spells were considered to be enchantment/charms. There are a few other reasons one might need to know this information. The priest spells are not really organized into magical schools, but rather into *spheres of influence*, as described on page 34 and in Chapter 7: Magic.

See Appendix 2 on page 129 for explanations of what the spell parameters (Range, Components, etc.) mean.

First-Level Spells

Animal Friendship
(Enchantment/Charm)

Sphere: Animal
Range: 10 yards
Components: V, S, M
Duration: Permanent
Casting Time: 1 hour
Area of Effect: 1 animal
Saving Throw: Neg.

By means of this spell, the caster is able to show any animal of animal intelligence to semi-intelligence (i.e., Intelligence 1-4) that he desires friendship. If the animal does not roll a successful saving throw vs. spell immediately when the spell is begun, it stands quietly while the caster finishes the spell. Thereafter, it follows the caster about. The spell functions only if the caster actually wishes to be the animal's friend. If the caster has ulterior motives, the animal always senses them (e.g., the caster intends to eat the animal, send it ahead to set off traps, etc.).

The caster can teach the befriended animal three specific tricks or tasks for each point of Intelligence it possesses. Typical tasks are those taught to a dog or similar pet (i.e., they cannot be complex). Training for each such trick must be done over a period of one week, and all must be done within three months of acquiring the creature. During the three-month period, the animal will not harm the caster, but if the creature is left alone for more than a week, it will revert to its natural state and act accordingly.

The caster can use this spell to attract up to 2 Hit Dice of animal(s) per experience level he possesses. This is also the maximum total Hit Dice of the animals that can be attracted and trained at one time: no more than twice the caster's experience level. Only unaligned animals can be attracted, befriended, and trained.

The material components of this spell are the caster's holy symbol and a piece of food the animal likes.

Bless (Conjuration/Summoning)
Reversible

Sphere: All
Range: 60 yards
Components: V, S, M
Duration: 6 rounds
Casting Time: 1 round
Area of Effect: 50-foot cube
Saving Throw: None

Upon uttering the *bless* spell, the caster raises the morale of friendly creatures and any saving throw rolls they make against *fear* effects by +1. Furthermore, it raises their attack dice rolls by +1. A blessing, however, affects only those not already engaged in melee combat. The caster determines at what range (up to 60 yards) he will cast the spell. At the instant the spell is completed, it affects all creatures in a 50-foot cube centered on the point selected by the caster (thus, affected creatures leaving the area are still subject to the spell's effect; those entering the area after the casting is completed are not).

A second use of this spell is to bless a single item (for example, a crossbow bolt for use against a rakshasa). The weight of the item is limited to one pound per caster level and the effect lasts until the item is used or the spell duration ends.

Multiple *bless* spells are not cumulative. In addition to the verbal and somatic gesture components, the *bless* spell requires holy water.

This spell can be reversed by the priest to a *curse* spell upon enemy creatures that lowers their morale and attack rolls by −1. The curse requires the sprinkling of unholy water.

Combine (Evocation)

Sphere: All
Range: Touch
Components: V, S
Duration: Special
Casting Time: 1 round
Area of Effect: The circle of priests
Saving Throw: None

Using this spell, three to five priests combine their abilities so that one of them casts spells and turns undead at an enhanced level. The highest level priest (or one of them, if two or more are tied for highest) stands alone, while the others join hands in a surrounding circle. The central priest casts the *combine* spell. He temporarily gains one level for each priest in the circle, up to a maximum gain of four levels. The level increase affects turning undead and spell details that vary with the caster's level. Note that the central priest gains no additional spells and that the group is limited to his currently memorized spells.

The encircling priests must concentrate on maintaining the combine effect. They lose all Armor Class bonuses for shield and Dexterity. If any of them has his concentration broken, the *combine* spell ends immediately. If the *combine* spell is broken while the central priest is in the act of casting a spell, that spell is ruined just as if the caster was disturbed. Spells cast in combination have the full enhanced effect, even if the combine is broken before the duration of the enhanced spell ends. Note that the combination is not broken if only the central caster is disturbed.

Command (Enchantment/Charm)

Sphere: Charm
Range: 30 yards
Component: V
Duration: 1 round
Casting Time: 1
Area of Effect: 1 creature
Saving Throw: None

This spell enables the priest to command another creature with a single word. The command must be uttered in a language understood by the creature. The subject will obey to the best of his/its ability only as long as the command is absolutely clear and unequivocal; hence, a command of "Suicide!" is ignored. A command to "Die!" causes the creature to fall in a faint or cataleptic state for one round, but thereafter the creature revives and is alive and well. Typical commands are back, halt, flee, run, stop, fall, go, leave, surrender, sleep, rest, etc. No command affects a creature for more than one round; undead are not affected at all. Creatures with Intelligence of 13 (high) or more, or those with 6 or more Hit Dice (or experience levels) are entitled to a saving throw vs. spell, adjusted for Wisdom. (Creatures with 13 or higher Intelligence *and* 6 Hit Dice/levels get only one saving throw!)

Create Water (Alteration)
Reversible

Sphere: Elemental (Water)
Range: 30 yards
Components: V, S, M
Duration: Permanent
Casting Time: 1 round
Area of Effect: Up to 27 cubic feet
Saving Throw: None

When the priest casts a *create water* spell, up to four gallons of water are generated for every experience level of the caster (e.g., a 2nd-level priest creates up to eight gallons of water, a 3rd-level up to 12 gallons, etc.). The water is clean and drinkable (it is just like rain water). The created water can be dispelled within a round of its creation, otherwise its magic fades, leaving normal water that can be used, spilled, evaporated, etc. Reversing the spell, *destroy water*, obliterates without trace (no vapor, mist, fog, or steam) a like quantity of water. Water can be created or destroyed in an area as small as will actually contain the liquid, or in an area as large as 27 cubic feet (1 cubic yard).

The spell requires at least a drop of water to create, or a pinch of dust to destroy, water.

Note that water can neither be created nor destroyed within a creature. For reference purposes, water weighs about 8 1/2 pounds per gallon, and a cubic foot of water weighs approximately 64 pounds.

Cure Light Wounds (Necromancy)
Reversible

Sphere: Healing
Range: Touch
Components: V, S
Duration: Permanent
Casting Time: 5
Area of Effect: Creature touched
Saving Throw: None

When casting this spell and laying his hand upon a creature, the priest causes 1d8 points of wound or other injury damage to the creature's body to be healed. This healing cannot affect creatures without corporeal bodies, nor can it cure wounds of creatures not living or of extraplanar origin.

The reversed spell, *cause light wounds*, operates in the same manner, inflicting 1d8 points of damage. If a creature is avoiding this touch, an attack roll is needed to determine if the priest's hand strikes the opponent and causes such a wound.

Curing is permanent only insofar as the creature does not sustain further damage; caused wounds will heal—or can be cured—just as any normal injury.

Detect Evil (Divination)
Reversible

Sphere: All
Range: 120 yards
Components: V, S, M
Duration: 1 turn + 5 rounds/level
Casting Time: 1 round
Area of Effect: 10-foot path
Saving Throw: None

This spell discovers emanations of evil, or of good in the case of the reverse spell, from any creature, object, or area. Character alignment, however, is revealed only under unusual circumstances: characters who are strongly aligned, who do not stray from their faith, and who are of at least 9th level might radiate good or evil *if intent upon appropriate actions*. Powerful monsters, such as rakshasas or ki-rin, send forth emanations of evil or good, even if polymorphed. Aligned undead radiate evil, for it is this power and negative force that enable them to continue existing. An evilly cursed object or unholy water radiates evil, but a hidden trap or an unintelligent viper does not.

The degree of evil (faint, moderate, strong, overwhelming) and possibly its general nature (expectant, malignant, gloating, etc.) can be noted. If the evil is overwhelming, the priest has a 10% chance per level of detecting its general bent (lawful, neutral, chaotic). The duration of a *detect evil* (or *detect good*) spell is one turn plus five rounds per level of the priest. Thus a priest of 1st experience level can cast a spell with a 15-round duration, at 2nd level he can cast a 20-round duration spell, etc. The spell has a

path of detection 10 feet wide in the direction in which the priest is facing. The priest must concentrate—stop, have quiet, and intently seek to detect the aura—for at least one round to receive a reading.

The spell requires the use of the priest's holy symbol as its material component, with the priest holding it before him.

Detect Magic (Divination)

Sphere: Divination
Range: 30 yards
Components: V, S, M
Duration: 1 turn
Casting Time: 1 round
Area of Effect: 10-foot path
Saving Throw: None

When the *detect magic* spell is cast, the priest detects magical radiations in a path 10 feet wide and up to 30 yards long, in the direction he is facing. The intensity of the magic can be detected (dim, faint, moderate, strong, overwhelming). The caster has a 10% chance per level to determine the sphere of the magic, but unlike the wizard version of the spell, the type of magic (alteration, conjuration, etc.) cannot be divined. The caster can turn, scanning a 60° arc per round. A stone wall of one foot or more thickness, solid metal of one inch thickness, or a yard or more of solid wood blocks the spell.

The spell requires the use of the priest's holy symbol.

Detect Poison (Divination)

Sphere: Divination
Range: 0
Components: V, S, M
Duration: 1 turn + 1 round/level
Casting Time: 4
Area of Effect: Special
Saving Throw: None

This spell enables the priest to determine if an object has been poisoned or is poisonous. One object, or a 5-foot cubic mass, can be checked per round. The priest has a 5% chance per level of determining the exact type of poison.

The material component is a strip of specially blessed vellum, which turns black if poison is present.

Detect Snares & Pits (Divination)

Sphere: Divination
Range: 0
Components: V, S, M
Duration: 4 rounds/level
Casting Time: 4
Area of Effect: 10-foot path, 40 feet long
Saving Throw: None

Upon casting this spell, the caster is able to detect snares, pits, deadfalls and similar hazards along a 10-foot-wide by 40-foot-long path. Such hazards include simple pits, deadfalls, snares of wilderness creatures (e.g., trapdoor spiders, giant sundews, ant lions, etc.), and primitive traps constructed of natural materials (mantraps, missile trips, hunting snares, etc.). The spell is directional—the caster must face the desired direction to determine if a pit exists or a trap is laid in that direction. The caster experiences a feeling of danger from the direction of a detected hazard, which increases as the danger is approached. The caster learns the general nature of the danger (pit, snare, or deadfall) but not its exact operation, nor how to disarm it. Close examination, however, enables the caster to sense what intended actions might trigger it. The spell detects certain natural hazards—quicksand (snare), sinkholes (pit), or unsafe walls of natural rock (deadfall). Other hazards, such as a cavern that floods during rain, an unsafe construction, or a naturally poisonous plant, are not revealed. The spell does not detect magical traps (save those that operate by pit, deadfall, or snaring; see the 2nd-level spell *trip* and the 3rd-level spell, *snare*), nor those that are mechanically complex, nor does it detect snares or deadfalls that have been rendered safe or inactive.

The caster must have his holy symbol to complete the spell.

Endure Cold/Endure Heat (Alteration)

Sphere: Protection
Range: Touch
Components: V, S
Duration: 1½ hours/level
Casting Time: 1 round
Area of Effect: Creature touched
Saving Throw: None

The creature receiving this spell is protected from normal extremes of cold or heat (depending on which application the priest selects at the time of casting). The creature can stand unprotected in temperatures as low as −30° F. or as high as 130° F. (depending on application) with no ill effect. Temperatures beyond these limits inflict 1 point of damage per hour of exposure for every degree beyond the limit. The spell is immediately cancelled if the recipient is affected by any non-normal heat or cold, such as

magic, breath weapons, and so on. The cancellation occurs regardless of the application and regardless of whether a heat or cold effect hits the character (e.g., an *endure cold* spell is cancelled by magical heat or fire as well as by magical cold). The recipient of the spell does not suffer the first 10 points of damage (after any applicable saving throws) from the heat or cold during the round in which the spell is broken. The spell ends instantly if either *resist fire* or *resist cold* is cast upon the recipient.

Entangle (Alteration)

Sphere: Plant
Range: 80 yards
Components: V, S, M
Duration: 1 turn
Casting Time: 4
Area of Effect: 40-foot cube
Saving Throw: ½

By means of this spell, the caster is able to cause plants in the area of effect to entangle creatures within the area. The grasses, weeds, bushes, and even trees wrap, twist, and entwine about the creatures, holding them fast for the duration of the spell. Any creature entering the area is subject to this effect. A creature that rolls a successful saving throw vs. spell can escape the area, moving at only 10 feet per round until out of the area. Exceptionally large (gargantuan) or strong creatures may suffer little or no distress from this spell, at the DM's option, based on the strength of the entangling plants.

The material component is the caster's holy symbol.

Faerie Fire (Alteration)

Sphere: Weather
Range: 80 yards
Component: V, M
Duration: 4 rounds/level
Casting Time: 4
Area of Effect: 10 sq. feet/level within a 40-foot radius
Saving Throw: None

This spell enables the caster to outline one or more objects or creatures with a pale glowing light. The number of subjects outlined depends upon the number of square feet the caster can affect. Sufficient footage enables several objects or creatures to be outlined by the *faerie fire* spell, but one must be fully outlined before the next is begun, and all must be within the area of effect. Outlined objects or creatures are visible at 80 yards in the dark, 40 yards if the viewer is near a bright light source. Outlined creatures are easier to strike, thus opponents gain a +2 bonus to attack rolls in darkness (including moonlit nights) and a +1 bonus in twilight or better. Note that

outlining can render otherwise invisible creatures visible. However, it cannot outline noncorporeal, ethereal, or gaseous creatures. Nor does the light come anywhere close to sunlight. Therefore it has no special effect on undead or dark-dwelling creatures. The faerie fire can be blue, green, or violet according to the word of the caster at the time of casting. The faerie fire does not cause any harm to the object or creature thus outlined.

The material component is a small piece of foxfire.

Invisibility to Animals (Alteration)

Sphere: Animal
Range: Touch
Components: S, M
Duration: 1 turn + 1 round/level
Casting Time: 4
Area of Effect: 1 creature touched/level
Saving Throw: None

When an *invisibility to animals* spell is cast, the creature touched becomes totally undetectable by normal animals with Intelligences under 6. Normal animals includes giant-sized varieties, but it excludes any with magical abilities or powers. The enchanted individual is able to walk among such animals or pass through them as if he did not exist. For example, this individual could stand before the hungriest of lions or a tyrannosaurus rex and not be molested or even noticed. However, a nightmare, hell hound, or winter wolf would certainly be aware of the individual. For every level the caster has achieved, one creature can be rendered invisible. Any recipient attacking while this spell is in effect ends the spell immediately (for himself only).

The material component of this spell is holly rubbed over the recipient.

Invisibility to Undead (Abjuration)

Sphere: Necromantic
Range: Touch
Components: V, S, M
Duration: 6 rounds
Casting Time: 4
Area of Effect: Creature touched
Saving Throw: Special

This spell causes affected undead to lose track of and ignore the warded creature for the duration of the spell. Undead of 4 or fewer Hit Dice are automatically affected, but those with more Hit Dice receive a saving throw vs. spell to avoid the effect. Note that a priest protected by this spell cannot turn affected undead. The spell ends immediately if the recipient makes any attack, although casting spells such as *cure light wounds*, *augury*, or *chant* does not end the ward.

The material component is the priest's holy symbol.

Light (Alteration)
Reversible

Sphere: Sun
Range: 120 yards
Components: V, S
Duration: 1 hour + 1 turn/level
Casting Time: 4
Area of Effect: 20-foot-radius globe
Saving Throw: Special

This spell causes a luminous glow within 20 feet of the spell's center. The area of light thus caused is equal in brightness to torchlight. Objects in darkness beyond this sphere can be seen, at best, as vague and shadowy shapes. The spell is centered on a point selected by the caster, and he must have a line of sight or unobstructed path to that point when the spell is cast. Light can spring from air, rock, metal, wood, or almost any similar substance. The effect is immobile unless it is specifically centered on a movable object or mobile creature. If this spell is cast upon a creature, any applicable magic resistance and saving throws must be rolled. Successful resistance negates the spell, while a successful saving throw indicates that the spell is centered immediately behind the creature, rather than upon the creature itself. A *light* spell centered on the visual organs of a creature blinds it, reducing its attack and saving throw rolls by 4 and worsening its Armor Class by 4. The caster can extinguish the light at any time by uttering a single word. *Light* spells are not cumulative—multiple castings do not provide a brighter light.

The spell is reversible, causing darkness in the same area and under the same conditions as the *light* spell, but with half the duration. Magical darkness is equal to that of an unlit interior room—pitch darkness. Any normal light source or magical light source of lesser intensity than full daylight does not function in magical darkness. A *darkness* spell cast directly against a *light* spell cancels both, and vice versa.

Locate Animals or Plants
(Divination)

Sphere: Divination (Animal, Plant)
Range: 100 yards + 20 yd./level
Components: V, S, M
Duration: 1 round/level
Casting Time: 1 round
Area of Effect: 20-foot-wide path 20 yards
　　　　　　　　long/level
Saving Throw: None

The caster can find the direction and distance of any one type of animal or plant he desires. The caster, facing in a direction, thinks of the animal or plant, and then knows if any such animal or plant is within range. If so, the exact distance and approxi-

mate number present is learned. During each round of the spell's duration, the caster can face in only one direction, i.e., only a 20-foot-wide path can be known. The spell lasts one round per level of experience of the caster, while the length of the path is 100 yards plus 20 yards per level of experience. (At the DM's option, some casters may be able to locate only those animals [or plants] associated closely with their own mythos.)

The material component is the caster's holy symbol.

While the exact chance of locating a specific type of animal or plant depends on the details and circumstances of the locale, the general frequency of the subject can be used as a guideline: common = 50%, uncommon = 30%, rare = 15%, and very rare = 5%. Most herbs grow in temperate regions, while most spices grow in tropical regions. Most plants sought as spell components or for magical research are rare or very rare. The results of this spell are always determined by the DM.

Magical Stone (Enchantment)

Sphere: Combat
Range: 0
Components: V, S, M
Duration: Special
Casting Time: 4
Area of Effect: Special
Saving Throw: None

By using this spell, the priest can temporarily enchant up to three small pebbles, no larger than sling bullets. The magical stones can then be hurled or slung at an opponent. If hurled, they can be thrown up to 30 yards, and all three can be thrown in one round. The character using them must roll normally to hit, although the magic of the stones enables any character to be proficient with them. The stones are considered +1 weapons for determining if a creature can be struck (those struck only by magical weapons, for instance), although they do not have an attack or damage bonus. Each stone that hits inflicts 1d4 points of damage, 2d4 points against undead. The magic in each stone lasts for but one-half hour or until used.

The material components are the priest's holy symbol and three small pebbles, unworked by tools or magic of any type.

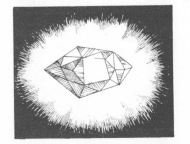

Pass Without Trace
(Enchantment/Charm)

Sphere: Plant
Range: Touch
Components: V, S, M
Duration: 1 turn/level
Casting Time: 1 round
Area of Effect: Creature touched
Saving Throw: None

When this spell is cast, the recipient can move through any type of terrain—mud, snow, dust, etc.—and leave neither footprints nor scent. The area that is passed over radiates magic for 1d6 turns after the affected creature passes. Thus, tracking a person or other creature covered by this spell is impossible by normal means. Of course, intelligent tracking techniques, such as using a spiral search pattern, can result in the trackers picking up the trail at a point where the spell has worn off.

The material component of this spell is a sprig of pine or evergreen, which must be burned and the ashes powdered and scattered when the spell is cast.

Protection From Evil (Abjuration)
Reversible

Sphere: Protection
Range: Touch
Components: V, S, M
Duration: 3 rounds/level
Casting Time: 4
Area of Effect: Creature touched
Saving Throw: None

When this spell is cast, it creates a magical barrier around the recipient at a distance of one foot. The barrier moves with the recipient and has three major effects:

First, all attacks made by evil or evilly enchanted creatures against the protected creature receive a penalty of −2 to each attack roll, and any saving throws caused by such attacks are made by the protected creature with a +2 bonus.

Second, any attempt to exercise mental control over the protected creature (if, for example, it had been charmed by a vampire) or to invade and take over its mind (as by a ghost's magic jar attack) is blocked by this spell. Note that the protection does not prevent a vampire's charm itself, nor end it, but it does prevent the vampire from exercising mental control through the barrier. Likewise, an outside life force is merely kept out, and would not be expelled if in place before the protection was cast.

Third, the spell prevents bodily contact by creatures of an extraplanar or conjured nature (such as aerial servants, elementals, imps, invisible stalkers, salamanders, water weirds, xorn, and others). This causes the natural (body) weapon attacks of such creatures to fail and the creature to recoil if such attacks require touching the protected creature. Animals or monsters summoned or conjured by spells or similar magic are likewise hedged from the character. This protection ends if the protected character makes a melee attack against or tries to force the barrier against the blocked creature.

To complete this spell, the priest uses holy water or burning incense.

This spell can be reversed to become *protection from good*; the second and third benefits remain unchanged.

The material components for the reverse are a circle of unholy water or smoldering dung.

Purify Food & Drink (Alteration)
Reversible

Sphere: All
Range: 30 yards
Components: V, S
Duration: Permanent
Casting Time: 1 round
Area of Effect: 1 cubic foot/level,
          10-foot-square area
Saving Throw: None

When cast, this spell makes spoiled, rotten, poisonous, or otherwise contaminated food and water pure and suitable for eating and drinking. Up to one cubic foot of food and drink per level can be thus made suitable for consumption. This spell does not prevent subsequent natural decay or spoilage. Unholy water and similar food and drink of significance is spoiled by *purify food and drink*, but the spell has no effect on creatures of any type nor upon magical potions.

The reverse of the spell is *putrefy food and drink*. This spoils even holy water. It likewise has no effect upon creatures or potions.

Remove Fear (Abjuration)
Reversible

Sphere: Charm
Range: 10 yards
Components: V, S
Duration: Special
Casting Time: 1
Area of Effect: 1 creature/4 levels
Saving Throw: Special

The priest instills courage in the spell recipient, raising the creature's saving throw rolls against magical *fear* attacks by +4 for one turn. If the recipient has recently (that day) failed a saving throw against such an attack, the spell immediately grants another saving throw, with a +4 bonus to the die roll. For every four levels of the caster, one creature can be affected by the spell (one creature at levels 1 through 4, two creatures

at levels 5 through 8, etc.).

The reverse of the spell, *cause fear*, causes one creature to flee in panic at maximum movement speed away from the caster for 1d4 rounds. A successful saving throw against the reversed effect negates it, and any Wisdom adjustment also applies. Of course, *cause fear* can be automatically countered by *remove fear* and vice versa.

Neither spell has any effect on undead of any sort.

Sanctuary (Abjuration)

Sphere: Protection
Range: Touch
Components: V, S, M
Duration: 2 rounds +1 round/level
Casting Time: 4
Area of Effect: Creature touched
Saving Throw: None

When the priest casts a *sanctuary* spell, any opponent attempting to strike or otherwise directly attack the protected creature must roll a saving throw vs. spell. If the saving throw is successful, the opponent can attack normally and is unaffected by that casting of the spell. If the saving throw is failed, the opponent loses track of and totally ignores the warded creature for the duration of the spell. Those not attempting to attack the subject remain unaffected. Note that this spell does not prevent the operation of area attacks (fireball, ice storm, etc.). While protected by this spell, the subject cannot take direct offensive action without breaking the spell, but may use non-attack spells or otherwise act in any way that does not violate the prohibition against offensive action. This allows a warded priest to heal wounds, for example, or to bless, perform an augury, chant, cast a light in the area (not upon an opponent!), and so on.

The components of the spell include the priest's holy symbol and a small silver mirror.

Shillelagh (Alteration)

Sphere: Combat, Plant
Range: Touch
Components: V, S, M
Duration: 4 rounds + 1 round/level
Casting Time: 2
Area of Effect: 1 normal oaken club
Saving Throw: None

This spell enables the caster to change his own oaken cudgel or unshod staff into a magical weapon that gains a +1 bonus to its attack roll and inflicts 2d4 points of damage on opponents up to man-sized, and 1d4+1 points of damage on larger opponents. The spell inflicts no damage to the staff or cudgel. The caster must wield the shillelagh, of course.

The material components of this spell are a shamrock leaf and the caster's holy symbol.

Second-Level Spells

Aid (Necromancy, Conjuration)

Sphere: Necromantic
Range: Touch
Components: V, S, M
Duration: 1 round + 1 round/level
Casting Time: 5
Area of Effect: Creature touched
Saving Throw: None

The recipient of this spell gains the benefit of a *bless* spell (+1 to attack rolls and saving throws) and a special bonus of 1d8 additional hit points for the duration of the spell. The *aid* spell enables the recipient to actually have more hit points than his full normal total. The bonus hit points are lost first when the recipient takes damage; they cannot be regained by curative magic. Example: A 1st-level fighter has 8 hit points, suffers 2 points of damage (8 − 2 = 6), and then receives an *aid* spell that gives 5 additional hit points. The fighter now has 11 hit points, 5 of which are temporary. If he is then hit for 7 points of damage, 2 normal hit points and all 5 temporary hit points are lost. He then receives a *cure light wounds* spell that heals 4 points of damage, restoring him to his original 8 hit points.

Note that the operation of the spell is unaffected by permanent hit point losses due to energy drain, Hit Die losses, the loss of a familiar, or the operation of certain artifacts; the temporary hit point gain is figured from the new, lower total.

The material components of this spell are a tiny strip of white cloth with a sticky substance (such as tree sap) on the ends, plus the priest's holy symbol.

Augury (Divination)

Sphere: Divination
Range: 0
Components: V, S, M
Duration: Special
Casting Time: 2 rounds
Area of Effect: Special
Saving Throw: None

The priest casting an *augury* spell seeks to divine whether an action in the immediate future (within one-half hour) will be for the benefit of, or harmful to, the party. For example, if a party is considering the destruction of a weird seal that closes a portal, an *augury* spell can be used to find if weal or woe will be the immediate result. If the spell is successful, the DM yields some indication of the probable outcome: "weal," "woe," or possibly a cryptic puzzle or rhyme. The base chance for receiving a meaningful reply is 70%, plus 1% for each level of the priest casting the spell, e.g., 71% at 1st level, 72% at 2nd, etc. Your DM determines any adjustments for the particular conditions of each augury.

For example, if the question is "Will we do well if we venture to the third level?" and a terrible troll guarding 10,000 s.p. and a *shield* +1 lurks near the entrance to the level (which the DM estimates the party could beat after a hard fight) the augury might be: "Great risk brings great reward." If the troll is too strong for the party, the augury might be: "Woe and destruction await!" Likewise, a party casting several auguries about the same action in quick succession might receive identical answers, regardless of the dice rolls.

The material component for augury is a set of gem-inlaid sticks, dragon bones, or similar tokens of at least 1,000 gp value (which are not expended in casting).

Barkskin (Alteration)

Sphere: Protection, Plant
Range: Touch
Components: V, S, M
Duration: 4 rounds + 1 round/level
Casting Time: 5
Area of Effect: Creature touched
Saving Throw: None

When a priest casts the *barkskin* spell upon a creature, its skin becomes as tough as bark, increasing its base Armor Class to AC 6, plus 1 AC for every four levels of the priest: Armor Class 5 at 4th level, Armor Class 4 at 8th, and so on. This spell does not function in combination with normal armor or any magical protection. In addition, saving throw rolls vs. all attack forms except magic gain a +1 bonus. This spell can be placed on the caster or on any other creature he touches.

In addition to his holy symbol, the caster

must have a handful of bark from an oak as the material component of the spell.

Chant (Conjuration/Summoning)

Sphere: Combat
Range: 0
Components: V, S
Duration: Time of chanting
Casting Time: 2 rounds
Area of Effect: 30-foot radius
Saving Throw: None

By means of the *chant* spell, the priest brings special favor upon himself and his party, and causes harm to his enemies. When the *chant* spell is completed, all attack and damage rolls and saving throws made by those in the area of effect who are friendly to the priest gain +1 bonuses, while those of the priest's enemies suffer −1 penalties. This bonus/penalty continues as long as the caster continues to chant the mystic syllables and is stationary. An interruption, however, such as an attack that succeeds and causes damage, grappling the chanter, or a *silence* spell, breaks the spell. Multiple chants are not cumulative; however, if the 3rd-level *prayer* spell is spoken while a priest of the same religious persuasion (not merely alignment!) is chanting, the effect is increased to +2 and −2.

Charm Person or Mammal
(Enchantment/Charm)

Sphere: Animal
Range: 80 yards
Components: V, S
Duration: Special
Casting Time: 5
Area of Effect: 1 person or mammal
Saving Throw: Neg.

This spell affects any single person or mammal it is cast upon. The creature then regards the caster as a trusted friend and ally to be heeded and protected. The term *person* includes any bipedal human, demihuman or humanoid of man-size or smaller, including brownies, dryads, dwarves, elves, gnolls, gnomes, goblins, half-elves, halflings, half-orcs, hobgoblins, humans, kobolds, lizard men, nixies, orcs, pixies, sprites, troglodytes, and others. Thus, a 10th-level fighter is included, while an ogre is not.

The spell does not enable the caster to control the charmed creature as if it were an automaton, but any word or action of the caster is viewed in the most favorable way. Thus a charmed creature would not obey a suicide command, but might believe the caster if assured that the only chance to save the caster's life is for the creature to hold back an onrushing red dragon for "just a round or two" and if the charmed creature's

view of the situation suggests that this course of action still allows a reasonable chance of survival.

The subject's attitudes and priorities are changed with respect to the caster, but basic personality and alignment are not. A request that a victim make itself defenseless, give up a valued item, or even use a charge from a valued item (especially against former associates or allies) might allow an immediate saving throw to see if the charm is thrown off. Likewise, a charmed creature does not necessarily reveal everything it knows or draw maps of entire areas. Any request may be refused, if such refusal is in character and does not directly harm the caster. The victim's regard for the caster does not necessarily extend to the caster's friends or allies. The victim does not react well to the charmer's allies making suggestions such as, "Ask him this question...," nor does the charmed creature put up with verbal or physical abuse from the charmer's associates, if this is out of character.

Note also that the spell does not empower the caster with linguistic capabilities beyond those he normally has. The duration of the spell is a function of the charmed creature's Intelligence, and it is tied to the saving throw. The spell can be broken if a successful saving throw is rolled. This saving throw is checked on a periodic basis according to the creature's Intelligence, even if the caster has not overly strained the relationship.

Intelligence Score	Period Between Checks
3 or less	3 months
4 to 6	2 months
7 to 9	1 month
10 to 12	3 weeks
13 to 14	2 weeks
15 to 16	1 week
17	3 days
18	2 days
19 or more	1 day

If the caster harms, or attempts to harm, the charmed creature by some overt action, or if a *dispel magic* spell is successfully cast upon the charmed creature, the charm is broken automatically.

If the subject of the *charm person/charm mammal* spell successfully rolls its saving throw vs. the spell, the effect is negated.

This spell, if used in conjunction with the *animal friendship* spell, can keep the animal near the caster's home base, if the caster must leave for an extended period.

Detect Charm (Divination)
Reversible

Sphere: Divination
Range: 30 yards
Components: V, S
Duration: 1 turn
Casting Time: 1 round
Area of Effect: 1 creature/round
Saving Throw: None

When used by a priest, this spell can detect if a person or monster is under the influence of a *charm* spell, or similar control such as *hypnosis, suggestion, beguiling, possession*, etc. The creature rolls a saving throw vs. spell and, if successful, the caster learns nothing about that particular creature from the casting. A caster who learns that a creature is being influenced has a 5% chance per level to determine the exact type of influence. Up to 10 different creatures can be checked before the spell wanes. If the creature is under more than one such effect, only the information that the charms exist is gained. The type (since there are conflicting emanations) is impossible to determine.

The reverse of the spell, *undetectable charm*, completely masks all charms on a single creature for 24 hours.

Dust Devil (Conjuration/Summoning)

Sphere: Elemental (Air)
Range: 30 yards
Components: V, S
Duration: 2 rounds/level
Casting Time: 2 rounds
Area of Effect: Special
Saving Throw: None

This spell enables a priest to conjure up a weak air elemental—a dust devil of AC 4, 2 HD, MV 180 feet per round, one attack for 1d4 points of damage, which can be hit by normal weapons. The dust devil appears as a small whirlwind one foot in diameter at its base, five feet tall, and three to four feet across at the top. It moves as directed by the priest, but dissipates if it is ever separated from the caster by more than 30 yards. Its winds are sufficient to put out torches, small campfires, exposed lanterns, and other small, open flames of non-magical origin. The dust devil can hold a gas cloud or a creature in gaseous form at bay or push it away from the caster (though it cannot damage or disperse such a cloud). If skimming along the ground in an area of loose dust, sand, or ash, the dust devil picks up those particles and disperses them in a 10-foot-diameter cloud centered on itself. The cloud obscures normal vision, and creatures caught within are blinded while inside and for one round after they emerge. A spellcaster caught in the dust devil or its cloud while casting must make a saving throw vs.

spell to keep his concentration, or the spell is ruined. Any creature native to the elemental plane of Air—even another dust devil—can disperse a dust devil with a single hit.

Enthrall (Enchantment/Charm)

Sphere: Charm
Range: 0
Components: V, S
Duration: Special
Casting Time: 1 round
Area of Effect: 90-foot radius
Saving Throw: Neg.

A priest using this spell can enthrall an audience that can fully understand his language. Those in the area of effect must save vs. spell or give the caster their undivided attention, totally ignoring their surroundings. Those of a race or religion unfriendly to the caster's have a +4 bonus to the roll. Any Wisdom adjustment also applies. Creatures with 4 or more levels or Hit Dice, or with a Wisdom of 16 or better, are unaffected.

To cast the spell, the caster must speak without interruption for a full round. Thereafter, the enchantment lasts as long as the priest speaks, to a maximum of one hour. Those enthralled take no action while the priest speaks, and for 1d3 rounds thereafter while they discuss the matter. Those entering the area of effect must also save or become enthralled. Those not enthralled are 50% likely every turn to hoot and jeer in unison. If there is excessive jeering, the rest are allowed a new saving throw. The speech ends (but the 1d3 round delay still applies) if the priest is successfully attacked or performs any action other than speaking.

If the audience is attacked, the spell ends and the audience reacts immediately, rolling a reaction check with respect to the source of the interruption, at a penalty of −10.

Note: When handling a large number of saving throws for similar creatures, the DM can assume an average to save time: e.g., a crowd of 20 men with a base saving throw of 16 (25% success chance) will have 15 men enthralled and five not.

Find Traps (Divination)

Sphere: Divination
Range: 30 yards
Components: V, S
Duration: 3 turns
Casting Time: 5
Area of Effect: 10-foot path
Saving Throw: None

When a priest casts a *find traps* spell, all traps—concealed normally or magically—of magical or mechanical nature become apparent to him. Note that this spell is directional, and the caster must face the desired

direction in order to determine if a trap is laid in that particular direction.

A trap is any device or magical ward that meets three criteria: it can inflict a sudden or unexpected result, the spellcaster would view the result as undesirable or harmful, and the harmful or undesirable result was specifically intended as such by the creator. Thus traps include alarms, glyphs, and similar spells or devices.

The caster learns the general nature of the trap (magical or mechanical) but not its exact effect, nor how to disarm it. Close examination will, however, enable the caster to sense what intended actions might trigger it. Note that the caster's divination is limited to his knowledge of what might be unexpected and harmful. The spell cannot predict actions of creatures (hence a concealed murder hole or ambush is not a trap), nor are natural hazards considered traps (a cavern that floods during rain, a wall weakened by age, a naturally poisonous plant). If the DM is using specific glyphs or sigils to identify magical wards (see the *glyph of warding* spell), this spell shows the form of the glyph or mark. The spell does not detect traps that have been disarmed or are otherwise inactive.

Fire Trap (Abjuration, Evocation)

Sphere: Elemental (Fire)
Range: Touch
Components: V, S, M
Duration: Permanent until discharged
Casting Time: 1 turn
Area of Effect: Object touched
Saving Throw: 1/2

Any closeable item (book, box, bottle, chest, coffer, coffin, door, drawer, and so forth) can be warded by a *fire trap* spell. The spell is centered on a point selected by the spellcaster. The item so trapped cannot have a second closure or warding spell placed upon it. A *knock* spell cannot affect a fire trap in any way—as soon as the offending party opens the item, the trap discharges. As with most magical traps, a thief has only half his normal find traps score to detect a fire trap. Failure to remove it successfully detonates it immediately. An unsuccessful *dispel magic* spell will not detonate the spell. When the trap is discharged, there will be an explosion of five-foot radius from the spell's center. All creatures within this area must roll saving throws vs. spell. Damage is 1d4 points plus 1 point per level of the caster; half that total amount for creatures successfully saving. (Underwater, this ward inflicts half damage and creates a large cloud of steam.) The item trapped is not harmed by this explosion.

The caster can use the trapped object without discharging it, as can any individual to whom the spell was specifically attuned when cast (the method usually involves a keyword).

To place this spell, the caster must trace the outline of the closure with a stick of charcoal and touch the center of the effect. Attunement to another individual requires a hair or similar object from the individual.

The material components are holly berries.

Flame Blade (Evocation)

Sphere: Elemental (Fire)
Range: 0
Components: V, S, M
Duration: 4 rounds + 1 round/2 levels
Casting Time: 4
Area of Effect: 3' long, sword-like blade
Saving Throw: None

With this spell, the caster causes a blazing ray of red-hot fire to spring forth from his hand. This blade-like ray is wielded as if it were a scimitar. If the caster successfully hits with the flame blade in melee combat, the creature struck suffers 1d4 + 4 points of damage, with a damage bonus of +2 (i.e., 7-10 points) if the creature is undead or is especially vulnerable to fire. If the creature is protected from fire, the damage inflicted is reduced by 2 (i.e., 1d4 + 2 points). Fire dwellers and those using fire as an innate attack form suffer no damage from the spell. The flame blade can ignite combustible materials such as parchment, straw, dry sticks, cloth, etc. However, it is not a magical weapon in the normal sense of the term, so creatures (other than undead) struck only by magical weapons are not harmed by it. This spell does not function underwater.

In addition to the caster's holy symbol, the spell requires a leaf of sumac as a material component.

Goodberry (Alteration, Evocation)
Reversible

Sphere: Plant
Range: Touch
Components: V, S, M
Duration: 1 day + 1 day/level
Casting Time: 1 round
Area of Effect: 2d4 fresh berries
Saving Throw: None

Casting a *goodberry* spell upon a handful of freshly picked berries makes 2d4 of them magical. The caster (as well as any other caster of the same faith and 3rd or higher level) can immediately discern which berries are affected. A *detect magic* spell discovers this also. Berries with the magic either enable a hungry creature of approximately man-size to eat one and be as well-nourished as if a full normal meal were eaten, or else cure 1 point of physical damage from wounds or other similar causes, sub-

ject to a maximum of 8 points of such curing in any 24-hour period.

The reverse of the spell, *badberry*, causes 2d4 rotten berries to appear wholesome, but each actually delivers 1 point of poison damage (no saving throw) if ingested.

The material component of the spell is the caster's holy symbol passed over the freshly picked, edible berries to be enspelled (blueberries, blackberries, raspberries, currants, gooseberries, etc.).

Heat Metal (Alteration)
Reversible

Sphere: Elemental (Fire)
Range: 40 yards
Components: V, S, M
Duration: 7 rounds
Casting Time: 5
Area of Effect: Special
Saving Throw: Special

By means of the *heat metal* spell, the caster is able to make ferrous metal (iron, iron alloys, steel) extremely hot. Elven chain mail is not affected, and magical metal armor receives an item saving throw vs. magical fire. If this is successful, the *heat metal* spell does not affect it.

On the first round of the spell, the metal merely becomes very warm and uncomfortable to touch (this is also the effect on the last melee round of the spell's duration). During the second and sixth (next to the last) rounds, heat causes blisters and damage; in the third, fourth, and fifth rounds, the metal becomes searing hot, causing damage to exposed flesh, as shown below:

Metal Temperature	Damage per Round
very warm	none
hot	1d4 points
searing*	2d4 points

(*) On the final round of searing, the afflicted creature must roll a successful saving throw vs. spell or suffer one of the following disabilities: hand or foot—unusable for 2d4 days, body—disabled 1d4 days, head—unconscious 1d4 turns. This effect can be completely removed by the 5th-level priest *heal* spell or by normal rest.

Note also that materials such as wood, leather, or flammable cloth smolder and burn if exposed to searing hot metal. Such materials cause searing damage to exposed flesh on the next round. Fire resistance (spell, potion, or ring) or a *protection from fire* spell totally negates the effects of a *heat metal* spell, as does immersion in water or snow, or exposure to a *cold* or *ice storm* spell. This version of the spell does not function underwater. For every two experience levels of the caster, the metal of one man-sized creature can be affected (i.e., arms and

armor, or a single mass of metal equal to 50 pounds weight). Thus, a 3rd-level caster would affect one such creature, a 4th- or 5th-level caster two, etc.

The reverse of the spell, *chill metal*, counters a *heat metal* spell or else causes metal to act as follows:

Metal Temperature	Damage per Round
cold	none
icy	1-2 hit points
freezing*	1d4 hit points

(*) On the final round of freezing, the afflicted creature must roll a successful saving throw vs. spell or suffer from the numbing effects of the cold. This causes the loss of all feeling in a hand (or hands, if the DM rules the saving throw was failed badly) for 1d4 days. During this time, the character's grip is extremely weak and he cannot use that hand for fighting or any other activity requiring a firm grasp.

The *chill metal* spell is countered by a *resist cold* spell, or by any great heat—proximity to a blazing fire (not a mere torch), a magical *flaming sword*, a *wall of fire* spell, etc. Underwater, this version of the spell inflicts no damage, but ice immediately forms around the affected metal, exerting an upward buoyancy.

Hold Person (Enchantment/Charm)

Sphere: Charm
Range: 120 yards
Components, V, S, M
Duration: 2 rounds/level
Casting Time: 5
Area of Effect: 1d4 persons
            in a 20-foot cube
Saving Throw: Neg.

This spell holds 1d4 humans, demihumans, or humanoid creatures rigidly immobile and in place for five or more rounds.

The *hold person* spell affects any bipedal human, demihuman, or humanoid of man-size or smaller, including brownies, dryads, dwarves, elves, gnolls, gnomes, goblins, half-elves, halflings, half-orcs, hobgoblins, humans, kobolds, lizard men, nixies, orcs, pixies, sprites, troglodytes, and others. Thus, a 10th-level fighter could be held, while an ogre could not.

The effect is centered on a point selected by the caster, and it affects persons selected by the caster within the area of effect. If the spell is cast at three persons, each gets a normal saving throw; if only two persons are being enspelled, each rolls his saving throw with a −1 penalty; if the spell is cast at but one person, the saving throw die roll suffers −2 penalty. Saving throws are adjusted for Wisdom. Those who succeed on their saving throws are totally unaffected by the spell. Undead creatures cannot be held.

Held creatures cannot move or speak, but they remain aware of events around them and can use abilities not requiring motion or speech. Being held does not prevent the worsening of the subjects' condition due to wounds, disease, or poison. The priest casting the *hold person* spell can end the spell with a single utterance at any time; otherwise the duration is two rounds at 1st level, four rounds at 2nd level, six rounds at 3rd level, etc.

The spellcaster needs a small, straight piece of iron as the material component of this spell.

Know Alignment (Divination)
Reversible

Sphere: Divination
Range: 10 yards
Components: V, S
Duration: 1 turn
Casting time: 1 round
Area of Effect: 1 creature or object
Saving Throw: Neg.

A *know alignment* spell enables the priest to exactly read the aura of a creature or an aligned object (unaligned objects reveal nothing). The caster must remain stationary and concentrate on the subject for a full round. If the creature rolls a successful saving throw vs. spell, the caster learns nothing about that particular creature from the casting. Certain magical devices negate the power of the *know alignment* spell.

The reverse, *undetectable alignment*, conceals the alignment of an object or creature for 24 hours.

Messenger (Enchantment/Charm)

Sphere: Animal
Range: 20 yards/level
Components: V, S
Duration: 1 day/level
Casting Time: 1 round
Area of Effect: 1 creature
Saving Throw: Neg.

This spell enables the priest to call upon a tiny (size T) creature of at least animal intelligence to act as his messenger. The spell does not affect giant animals and it does not work on creatures of low (i.e., 5) Intelligence or higher. If the creature is within range, the priest, using some type of food desirable to the animal as a lure, can call the animal to come. The animal is allowed a saving throw vs. spell. If the saving throw is failed, the animal advances toward the priest and awaits his bidding. The priest can communicate with the animal in a crude fashion, telling it to go to a certain place, but directions must be simple. The spellcaster can attach some small item or note to the animal. If so instructed, the animal will then wait at that location until the duration of the spell expires. (Note that unless the intended recipient of a message is expecting a messenger in the form of a small animal or bird, the carrier may be ignored.) When the spell's duration expires, the animal or bird returns to its normal activities. The intended recipient of a message gains no communication ability.

Obscurement (Alteration)

Sphere: Weather
Range: 0
Components: V, S
Duration: 4 rounds/level
Casting Time: 5
Area of Effect: Special
Saving Throw: None

This spell causes a misty vapor to arise around the caster. It persists in this locale for four rounds per caster level and reduces the visibility ranges of all types of vision (including infravision) to 2d4 feet. The ground area affected by the spell is a square progression based on the caster's level: a 10' x 10' area at 1st level, a 20' x 20' area at 2nd level, a 30' x 30' area at 3rd level, and so on. The height of the vapor is restricted to 10 feet, although the cloud will otherwise expand to fill confined spaces. A strong wind (such as the 3rd-level wizard spell, *gust of wind*, can cut the duration of an *obscurement* spell by 75%. This spell does not function under water.

Produce Flame (Alteration)

Sphere: Elemental (Fire)
Range: 0
Components: V, S
Duration: 1 round/level
Casting Time: 5
Area of Effect: Special
Saving Throw: None

A bright flame, equal in brightness to a torch, springs forth from the caster's palm when he casts a *produce flame* spell. The flame does not harm the caster, but it is hot and it causes the combustion of flammable materials (paper, cloth, dry wood, oil, etc.). The caster is capable of hurling the magical flame as a missile, with a range of 40 yards (considered short range). The flame flashes on impact, igniting combustibles within a three-foot diameter of its center of impact, and then it goes out. A creature struck by the flame suffers 1d4 +1 points of damage and, if combustion occurs, must spend a round extinguishing the fire or suffer additional damage assigned by the DM until the fire is extinguished. A miss is resolved as a grenade-like missile. If any duration remains to the spell, another flame immediately appears in the caster's hand. The caster can hurl a maximum of one flame per level, but no more than one flame per round.

The caster can snuff out magical flame any time he desires, but fire caused by the flame cannot be so extinguished. This spell does not function under water.

Resist Fire/Resist Cold (Alteration)

Sphere: Protection
Range: Touch
Components: V, S, M
Duration: 1 round/level
Casting Time: 5
Area of Effect: Creature touched
Saving Throw: None

When this spell is placed upon a creature by a priest, the creature's body is toughened to withstand heat or cold, as chosen by the caster. Complete immunity to mild conditions (standing naked in the snow or reaching into an ordinary fire to pluck out a note) is gained. The recipient can somewhat resist intense heat or cold (whether natural or magical in origin), such as red-hot charcoal, a large amount of burning oil, flaming swords, fire storms, fireballs, meteor swarms, red dragon's breath, frostbrand swords, ice storms, *wands of frost*, or white dragon's breath. In all of these cases, the temperature affects the creature to some extent. The recipient of the spell gains a bonus of +3 to saving throws against such attack forms and all damage sustained is reduced by 50%; therefore, if the saving throw is failed, the creature sustains one-half damage, and if the saving throw is successful, only one-quarter damage is sustained. Resistance to fire lasts for one round for each experience level of the priest placing the spell.

The caster needs a drop of mercury as the material component of this spell.

Silence, 15' Radius (Alteration)

Sphere: Guardian
Range: 120 yards
Components: V, S
Duration: 2 rounds/level
Casting Time: 5
Area of Effect: 15-foot-radius sphere
Saving Throw: None

Upon casting this spell, complete silence prevails in the affected area. All sound is stopped: conversation is impossible, spells cannot be cast (or at least not those with verbal components, if the optional component rule is used), and no noise whatsoever issues from or enters the area. The spell can be cast into the air or upon an object, but the effect is stationary unless cast on a mobile object or creature. The spell lasts two rounds for each level of experience of the priest. The spell can be centered upon a creature, and the effect then radiates from the creature and moves as it moves. An unwilling creature receives a saving throw against the spell. If the saving throw is successful, the spell effect is centered about one foot behind the position of the subject creature at the instant of casting. This spell provides a defense against sound-based attacks, such as harpy singing, *horn of blasting*, etc.

Slow Poison (Necromancy)

Sphere: Healing
Range: Touch
Components: V, S, M
Duration: 1 hour/level
Casting Time: 1
Area of Effect: Creature touched
Saving Throw: None

When this spell is placed upon a poisoned individual, it greatly slows the effects of venom, if it is cast upon the victim before the poison takes full effect. (This period, known as the onset time, is known to the DM.) While this spell does not neutralize the venom, it does prevent it from substantially harming the individual for the duration of its magic in hopes that, during that period, a full cure can be accomplished.

The material components of the *slow poison* spell are the priest's holy symbol and a bud of garlic that must be crushed and smeared on the wound (or eaten if poison was ingested).

Snake Charm (Enchantment/Charm)

Sphere: Animal
Range: 30 yards
Components: V, S
Duration: Special
Casting Time: 5
Area of Effect: 30-foot cube
Saving Throw: None

When this spell is cast, a hypnotic pattern is set up that causes one or more snakes to cease all activity except a semi-erect, swaying movement. If the snakes are charmed while in a torpor, the duration of the spell is 1d4+2 turns; if the snakes are not torpid, but are not aroused and angry, the charm lasts 1d3 turns; if the snakes are angry or attacking, the *snake charm* spell lasts 1d4+4 rounds. The priest casting the spell can charm snakes whose total hit points are less than or equal to those of the priest. On the average, a 1st-level priest could charm snakes with a total of 4 or 5 hit points; a 2nd-level priest could charm 9 hit points, etc. The hit points can be those of a single snake or those of several of the reptiles, but the total hit points cannot exceed those of the priest casting the spell. A 23-hit point caster charming a dozen 2-hit point snakes would charm 11 of them. This spell is also effective against any ophidian or ophidianoid monster, such as naga, couatl, etc., subject to magic resistance, hit points, and so forth.

Variations of this spell may exist, allowing other creatures significant to a particular mythos to be affected. Your DM will inform you if such spells exist.

Speak With Animals (Alteration)

Sphere: Animal, Divination
Range: 0
Components: V, S
Duration: 2 rounds/level
Casting Time: 5
Area of Effect: 1 animal within
30-foot radius of priest
Saving Throw: None

This spell empowers the priest to comprehend and communicate with any warm- or cold-blooded normal or giant animal that is not mindless. The priest is able to ask questions and receive answers of the creature, although friendliness and cooperation are by no means assured. Furthermore, terseness and evasiveness are likely in basically wary and cunning creatures (the more stupid ones will instead make inane comments). If the animal is friendly or of the same general alignment as the priest, there is a possibility that the animal will do some favor or service for the priest. This possibility is determined by the DM. Note that this spell differs from the *speak with monsters* spell, for this spell allows conversation only with normal or giant, non-fantastic creatures such as apes, bears, cats, dogs, elephants, and so on.

Spiritual Hammer (Invocation)

Sphere: Combat
Range: 10 yards/level
Components: V, S, M
Duration: 3 rounds + 1 round/level
Casting Time: 5
Area of Effect: Special
Saving Throw: None

By calling upon his deity, the caster of a *spiritual hammer* spell brings into existence a field of force shaped vaguely like a hammer. As long as the caster concentrates upon the hammer, it strikes at any opponent within its range, as desired. Each round the caster can choose to attack the same target as the previous round or switch to a new target that he can see anywhere within his maximum range. The spiritual hammer's chance to successfully hit is equal to that of the caster, without any Strength bonuses. In addition, it strikes as a magical weapon with a bonus of +1 for every six experience levels (or fraction) of the spellcaster, up to a total of +3 to the attack roll and +3 to the damage roll for a 13th-level caster. The base damage inflicted when it scores a hit is exactly the same as a normal war hammer (1d4+1 vs. opponents of man size or smaller, 1d4 upon larger opponents, plus the magical bonus). The hammer strikes in

the same direction as the caster is facing, so if he is behind the target, all bonuses for rear attack are gained along with the loss of any modifications to the target's AC for shield and Dexterity.

As soon as the caster ceases concentration, the *spiritual hammer* spell ends. A *dispel magic* spell that includes either the caster or the force in its area of effect has a chance to dispel the spiritual hammer. If an attacked creature has magic resistance, the resistance is checked the first time the spiritual hammer strikes. If the hammer is successfully resisted, the spell is lost. If not, the hammer has its normal full effect for the duration of the spell.

The material component of this spell is a normal war hammer that the priest must hurl toward opponents while uttering a plea to his deity. The hammer disappears when the spell is cast.

Trip (Enchantment/Charm)

Sphere: Plant
Range: Touch
Components: V, S
Duration: 1 turn/level
Casting Time: 5
Area of Effect: 1 object up to 10 feet long
Saving Throw: Neg.

This magic must be cast upon a normal object—a length of vine, a stick, a pole, a rope, or a similar object. The spell causes the object to rise slightly off the ground or floor it is resting on to trip most creatures crossing it, if they fail their saving throws vs. spell. Note that only as many creatures can be tripped as are actually stepping across the enchanted object. Thus a three-foot-long piece of rope could trip only one man-sized creature. Creatures moving at a very rapid pace (running) when tripped suffer 1 point of damage and are stunned for 1d4+1 rounds if the surface they fall upon is very hard (if it is turf or other soft material, they are merely stunned for the rest of that round). Very large creatures, such as elephants, are not at all affected by a trip. The object continues to trip all creatures passing over it, including the spellcaster, for as long as the spell duration lasts. A creature aware of the object and its potential adds a +4 bonus to its saving throw roll when crossing the object. The enchanted object is 80% undetectable unless a means that detects magical traps is employed or the operation of the spell is observed. This spell does not function under water.

Warp Wood (Alteration)
Reversible

Sphere: Plant
Range: 10 yards/level
Components: V, S
Duration: Permanent
Casting Time: 5
Area of Effect: Special
Saving Throw: Special

When this spell is cast, the priest causes a volume of wood to bend and warp, permanently destroying its straightness, form, and strength. The range of a *warp wood* spell is 10 yards for each level of experience of the caster. It affects approximately a 15-inch shaft of wood of up to one-inch diameter per level of the caster. Thus, at 1st level, a caster might be able to warp an hand axe handle or four crossbow bolts; at 5th level, he could warp the shaft of a typical spear. Note that boards or planks can also be affected, causing a door to be sprung or a boat or ship to leak. Warped missile weapons are useless; warped melee weapons suffer a −4 penalty to their attack rolls.

Enchanted wood is affected only if the spellcaster is of higher level than the caster of the prior enchantment. The spellcaster has a 20% cumulative chance of success per level of difference (20% if one level higher, 40% if two levels higher, etc.). Thus, a door magically held or wizard locked by a 5th-level wizard is 40% likely to be affected by a *warp wood* spell cast by a 7th-level priest. Wooden magical items are considered enchanted at 12th level (or better). Extremely powerful items, such as artifacts, are unaffected by this spell.

The reversed spell, *straighten wood*, straightens bent or crooked wood, or reverses the effects of a *warp wood* spell, subject to the same restrictions.

Withdraw (Alteration)

Sphere: Protection
Range: 0
Components: V, S
Duration: Special
Casting Time: 5
Area of Effect: The caster
Saving Throw: None

By means of a *withdraw* spell, the priest in effect alters the flow of time with regard to himself. While but one round of time passes for those not affected by the spell, the priest is able to spend two rounds, plus one round per level, in contemplation. Thus, a 5th-level priest can withdraw for seven rounds to cogitate on some matter while one round passes for all others. (The DM should allow the player one minute of real time per round withdrawn to ponder some problem or question. No discussion with other play-

ers is permitted.) Note that while affected by the *withdraw* spell, the caster can use only the following spells: any divination spell or any curing or healing spell, the latter on himself only. The casting of any of these spells in a different fashion (e.g., a *cure light wounds* spell bestowed upon a companion) negates the *withdraw* spell. Similarly, the withdrawn caster cannot walk or run, become invisible, or engage in actions other than thinking, reading, and the like. He can be affected by the actions of others, losing any Dexterity or shield bonus. Any successful attack upon the caster breaks the spell.

Wyvern Watch (Evocation)

Sphere: Guardian
Range: 30 yards
Components: V, S, M
Duration: 8 hours or until strike
Casting Time: 5
Area of Effect: 10-foot-radius sphere
Saving Throw: Neg.

This spell is known as *wyvern watch* because of the insubstantial haze brought forth by its casting, which vaguely resembles a wyvern. It is typically used to guard some area against intrusion. Any creature approaching within 10 feet of the guarded area may be affected by the "wyvern." Any creature entering the guarded area must roll a successful saving throw vs. spell or stand paralyzed for one round per level of the caster, until freed by the spellcaster, by a *dispel magic* spell, or by a *remove paralysis* spell. A successful saving throw indicates that the subject creature was missed by the attack of the wyvern-form, and the spell remains in place. As soon as a subject creature is successfully struck by the wyvern-form, the paralysis takes effect and the force of the spell dissipates. The spell force likewise dissipates if no intruder is struck by the wyvern-form for eight hours after the spell is cast. Any creature approaching the space being guarded by the wyvern-form may be able to detect its presence before coming close enough to be attacked; this chance of detection is 90% in bright light, 30% in twilight conditions, and 0% in darkness.

The material component is the priest's holy symbol.

Third-Level Spells

Animate Dead (Necromancy)

Sphere: Necromantic
Range: 10 yards
Components: V, S, M
Duration: Permanent
Casting Time: 1 round
Area of Effect: Special
Saving Throw: None

This spell creates the lowest of the undead monsters, skeletons or zombies, usually from the bones or bodies of dead humans, demihumans, or humanoids. The spell causes these remains to become animated and obey the simple verbal commands of the caster, regardless of how they communicated in life. The skeletons or zombies can follow the caster, remain in an area and attack any creature (or just a specific type of creature) entering the place, etc. The undead remain animated until they are destroyed in combat or are turned; the magic cannot be dispelled.

The priest can animate one skeleton or one zombie for each experience level he has attained. If creatures with more than 1 + Hit Dice are animated, the number is determined by the monster Hit Dice. Skeletal forms have the Hit Dice of the original creature, while zombie forms have 1 more Hit Die. Thus, a 12th-level priest could animate 12 dwarven skeletons (or six zombies), four zombie gnolls, or a single zombie fire giant. Note that this is based on the standard racial Hit Die norm; thus, a high-level adventurer would be animated as a skeleton or zombie of 1 or 2 Hit Dice, and without special class or racial abilities. The caster can, alternatively, animate two small animal skeletons (1-1 Hit Die or less) for every level of experience he has achieved.

The spell requires a drop of blood, a piece of flesh of the type of creature being animated, and a pinch of bone powder or a bone shard to complete the spell. Casting this spell is not a good act, and only evil priests use it frequently.

Call Lightning (Alteration)

Sphere: Weather
Range: 0
Components: V, S
Duration: 1 turn/level
Casting Time: 1 turn
Area of Effect: 360-foot radius
Saving Throw: 1/2

When a *call lightning* spell is cast, there must be a storm of some sort in the area—a rain shower, clouds and wind, hot and cloudy conditions, or even a tornado (including a whirlwind formed by a djinn or air elemental of 7 Hit Dice or more). The caster is then able to call down bolts of lightning. The caster can call down one bolt per turn. The caster need not call a bolt of lightning immediately—other actions, even spellcasting, can be performed; however, the caster must remain stationary and concentrate for a full round each time a bolt is called. The spell has a duration of one turn per caster level. Each bolt causes 2d8 points of electrical damage, plus an additional 1d8 points for each of the caster's experience levels. Thus, a 4th-level caster calls down a 6d8 bolt (2d8 + 4d8).

The bolt of lightning flashes down in a vertical stroke at whatever distance the spellcaster decides, up to 360 yards away. Any creature within a 10-foot radius of the path or the point where the lightning strikes suffers full damage unless a successful saving throw vs. spell is rolled, in which case only one-half damage is taken.

Because it requires a storm overhead, this spell can only be used outdoors. It does not function under ground or under water.

Continual Light (Alteration)
Reversible

Sphere: Sun
Range: 120 yards
Components: V, S
Duration: Permanent
Casting Time: 6
Area of Effect: 60-foot-radius globe
Saving Throw: Special

This spell is similar to a *light* spell, except that it is as bright as full daylight and lasts until negated by magical darkness or by a *dispel magic* spell. Creatures with penalties in bright light suffer them in this spell's area of effect. As with the *light* spell, this can be cast into air, onto an object, or at a creature. In the third case, the continual light affects the space about one foot behind a creature that successfully rolls its saving throw vs. spell (a failed saving throw means the continual light is centered on the creature and

moves as it moves). Note that this spell also blinds a creature if it is successfully cast upon the creature's visual organs. If the spell is cast on a small object that is then placed in a light-proof covering, the spell effects are blocked until the covering is removed.

Continual light brought into an area of magical darkness (or vice versa) cancels the darkness so that the otherwise prevailing light conditions exist in the overlapping areas of effect. A direct casting of a *continual light* spell against a similar or weaker magical darkness cancels both.

This spell eventually consumes the material it is cast upon, but the process takes far longer than the time in a typical campaign. Extremely hard and expensive materials might last hundreds or even thousands of years.

The reverse spell, *continual darkness*, causes complete absence of light (pitch blackness), similar to the *darkness* spell but of greater duration and area.

Create Food & Water (Alteration)

Sphere: Creation
Range: 10 yards
Components: V, S
Duration: Special
Casting Time: 1 turn
Area of Effect: 1 cubic foot/level
Saving Throw: None

When this spell is cast, the priest causes food and water to appear. The food thus created is highly nourishing if rather bland; each cubic foot of the material sustains three human-sized creatures or one horse-sized creature for a full day. The food decays and becomes inedible within 24 hours, although it can be restored for another 24 hours by casting a *purify food and water* spell upon it. The water created by this spell is the same as that created by the 1st-level priest spell *create water*. For each experience level the priest has attained, one cubic foot of food or water is created by the spell. A 2nd-level priest could create one cubic foot of food and one cubic foot of water.

Cure Blindness or Deafness
(Abjuration)
Reversible

Sphere: Necromantic
Range: Touch
Components: V, S
Duration: Permanent
Casting Time: 1 round
Area of Effect: Creature touched
Saving Throw: Special

By touching the creature afflicted, the priest employing the spell can permanently cure some forms of blindness or deafness. This spell does not restore or repair visual or

auditory organs damaged by injury or disease.

Its reverse, *cause blindness or deafness*, requires a successful touch (successful attack roll) on the victim. If the victim rolls a successful saving throw, the effect is negated. If the saving throw is failed, a nondamaging magical blindness or deafness results.

A deafened creature suffers a −1 penalty to surprise rolls, a +1 penalty to its initiative rolls, a 20% chance of spell failure for spells with verbal components, and can react only to what it can see or feel. A blinded creature suffers a −4 penalty to its attack rolls, a +4 penalty to its Armor Class, and a +2 penalty to its initiative rolls.

Cure Disease (Abjuration)
Reversible

Sphere: Necromantic
Range: Touch
Components: V, S
Duration: Permanent
Casting Time: 1 round
Area of Effect: Creature touched
Saving Throw: None

This spell enables the caster to cure most diseases by placing his hand upon the diseased creature. The affliction rapidly disappears thereafter, making the cured creature whole and well in from one turn to 10 days, depending on the type of disease and the state of its advancement when the cure took place. (The DM must adjudicate these conditions.) The spell is also effective against parasitic monsters such as green slime, rot grubs, and others. When cast by a priest of at least 12th level, this spell cures lycanthropy if cast within three days of the infection. Note that the spell does not prevent reoccurrence of a disease if the recipient is again exposed.

The reverse of the *cure disease* spell is *cause disease*. To be effective, the priest must touch the intended victim, and the victim must fail a saving throw vs. spell. The severity of the disease is decided by the priest (debilitating or fatal). The exact details of the disease are decided by the DM, but the following are typical:
* *Debilitating*—The disease takes effect in 1d6 turns, after which the creature loses 1 point of Strength per hour until his Strength is reduced to 2 or less, at which time the recipient is weak and virtually helpless. If a creature has no Strength rating, it loses 10% of its hit points per Strength loss, down to 10% of its original hit points. If the disease also affects hit points, use the more severe penalty. Recovery requires a period of 1d3 weeks.
* *Fatal*—This wasting disease is effective immediately. Infected creatures receive no benefit from *cure wound* spells while the

disease is in effect; wounds heal at only 10% of the natural rate. The disease proves fatal within 1d6 months and can be cured only by magical means. Each month the disease progresses, the creature loses 2 points of Charisma, permanently.

The inflicted disease can be cured by the *cure disease* spell. Lycanthropy cannot be caused.

Dispel Magic (Abjuration)

Sphere: Protection
Range: 60 yards
Components: V, S
Duration: Special
Casting Time: 6
Area of Effect: 30-foot cube or 1 item
Saving Throw: None

When a priest casts this spell, it has a chance to neutralize or negate the magic it comes in contact with as follows:

First, it has a chance to remove spells and spell-like effects (including device effects and innate abilities) from creatures or objects. Second, it may disrupt the casting or use of these in the area of effect at the instant the dispel is cast. Third, it may destroy magical potions (which are treated as 12th level for purposes of this spell).

Each effect or potion in the spell's area is checked to determine if it is dispelled. The caster can always dispel his own magic; otherwise the chance depends on the difference in level between the magical effect and the caster. The base chance of successfully dispelling is 11 or higher on 1d20. If the caster is higher level than the creator of the effect to be dispelled, the difference is *subtracted* from this base number needed. If the caster is lower level, then the difference is *added* to the base. A die roll of 20 always succeeds and a die roll of 1 always fails. Thus, if a caster is 10 levels higher than the magic he is trying to dispel, only a roll of 1 prevents the effect from being dispelled.

A *dispel magic* can affect only a specially enchanted item (such as a magical scroll, ring, wand, rod, staff, miscellaneous item, weapon, shield, or armor) if it is cast directly upon the item. This renders the item nonoperational for 1d4 rounds. An item possessed or carried by a creature has the creature's saving throw against this effect; otherwise it is automatically rendered nonoperational. An interdimensional interface (such as a *bag of holding*) rendered nonoperational is temporarily closed. Note that an item's physical properties are unchanged: a nonoperational magical sword is still a sword.

Artifacts and relics are not subject to this spell, but some of their spell-like effects may be, at the DM's option.

Summary of Dispel Effects

Source of Effect	Resists As	Result of Dispel
Caster	None	Dispel automatic
Other caster/innate ability	Level/HD of other caster	Effect negated
Wand	6th level	Effect negated
Staff	8th level	Effect negated
Potion	12th level	Potion destroyed
Other magical item	12th, unless special	*
Artifact	DM discretion	DM discretion

* Effect negated; if cast directly on item, item becomes nonoperational for 1d4 rounds.

Note that this spell, if successful, will release charmed and similarly beguiled creatures. Certain spells or effects cannot be dispelled; these are listed in the spell descriptions.

Feign Death (Necromancy)

Sphere: Necromantic
Range: Touch
Component: V
Duration: 1 turn + 1 round/level
Casting Time: 1/2
Area of Effect: Person touched
Saving Throw: None

By means of this spell, the caster or any other willing person can be put into a cataleptic state that is impossible to distinguish from actual death. Although the person affected can smell, hear, and know what is going on, no feeling or sight of any sort is possible; thus, any wounding or mistreatment of the body is not felt, no reaction occurs, and damage is only one-half normal. In addition, paralysis, poison, or energy level drain does not affect a person under the influence of this spell, but poison injected or otherwise introduced into the body becomes effective when the spell recipient is no longer under the influence of this spell, although a saving throw is permitted. However, the spell offers no protection from causes of certain death—being crushed under a landslide, etc. Only a willing individual can be affected by a *feign death* spell. The priest is able to end the spell effect at any time, but it requires a full round for bodily functions to begin again.

Note that, unlike the wizard version of this spell, only people can be affected, and that those of any level can be affected by the priest casting this spell.

Flame Walk (Alteration)

Sphere: Elemental (Fire)
Range: Touch
Components: V, S, M
Duration: 1 round + 1/level
Casting Time: 5
Area of Effect: Creature(s) touched
Saving Throw: None

By means of this spell, the caster empowers one or more creatures to withstand nonmagical fires of temperatures up to 2,000° F. (enabling them to walk upon molten lava). It also confers a +2 bonus to saving throws against magical fire and reduces damage from such fires by one-half, even if the saving throw is failed. For every experience level above the minimum required to cast the spell (5th), the priest can affect an additional creature. This spell is not cumulative with *resist fire* spells or similar protections.

The material components of the spell are the priest's holy symbol and at least 500 gp of powdered ruby per affected creature.

Glyph of Warding
(Abjuration, Evocation)

Sphere: Guardian
Range: Touch
Components: V, S, M
Duration: Permanent until discharged
Casting Time: Special
Area of Effect: Special
Saving Throw: Special

A glyph of warding is a powerful inscription magically drawn to prevent unauthorized or hostile creatures from passing, entering, or opening. It can be used to guard a small bridge, to ward an entry, or as a trap on a chest or box.

The priest must set the conditions of the ward; typically any creature violating the warded area without speaking the name of the glyph is subject to the magic it stores. A successful saving throw vs. spell enables the creature to escape the effects of the glyph. Glyphs can be set according to physical characteristics, such as creature type, size, and weight. Glyphs can also be set with respect to good or evil, or to pass those of the caster's religion. They cannot be set according to class, Hit Dice, or level. Multiple glyphs cannot be cast on the same area; although if a cabinet had three drawers, each could be separately warded.

When the spell is cast, the priest weaves a tracery of faintly glowing lines around the warding sigil. For every five square feet of area to be protected, one round is required to trace the warding lines of the glyph. The caster can affect an area equal to a square the sides of which are the same as his level, in feet. The glyph can be placed to conform to any shape up to the limitations of the caster's total square footage. Thus a 6th-level caster could place a glyph on a 6' x 6' square, shape it into a rectangle 4' x 9', a band 2' by 18', or a single strip 1' by 36'. When the spell is completed, the glyph and tracery become invisible.

The priest traces the glyph with incense, which, if the area exceeds 50 square feet, must be sprinkled with powdered diamond (at least 2,000 gp worth).

Typical glyphs shock for 1d4 points of electrical damage per level of the spellcaster, explode for a like amount of fire damage, paralyze, blind, deafen, and so forth. The DM may allow any harmful priest spell effect to be used as a glyph, provided the caster is of sufficient level to cast the spell. Successful saving throws either reduce effects by one-half or negate them, according to the glyph employed. Glyphs cannot be affected or bypassed by such means as physical or magical probing, though they can be dispelled by magic and foiled by high-level thieves using their find-and-remove-traps skill.

The DM may decide that the exact glyphs available to a priest depend on his religion, and he might make new glyphs available according to the magical research rules.

Hold Animal (Enchantment/Charm)

Sphere: Animal
Range: 80 yards
Components: V, S
Duration: 2 rounds/level
Casting Time: 6
Area of Effect: 1 to 4 animals in a
        40-foot cube
Saving Throw: Neg.

By means of this spell, the caster holds one to four animals rigid. Animals affected are normal or giant-sized mammals, birds, or reptiles, but not monsters such as centaurs, gorgons, harpies, naga, etc. Apes, bears, crocodiles, dogs, eagles, foxes, giant beavers, and similar animals are subject to this spell. The hold lasts for two rounds per caster level. The caster decides how many animals can be affected, but the greater the number, the better chance each has to successfully save against the spell. Each animal gets a saving throw: if only one is the subject

of the spell, it has a penalty of −4 to its roll; if two are subject, each receives a penalty of −2 to its roll; if three are subject, each receives a penalty of −1 to its roll; if four are subject, each gets an unmodified saving throw.

A maximum body weight of 400 pounds (100 pounds for nonmammals) per animal per caster level can be affected—e.g., an 8th-level caster can affect up to four 3,200-pound mammals or a like number of 800-pound nonmammals, such as birds or reptiles.

Locate Object (Divination)
Reversible

Sphere: Divination
Range: 60 yards + 10 yd./level
Components: V, S, M
Duration: 8 hours
Casting Time: 1 turn
Area of Effect: 1 object
Saving Throw: None

This spell helps locate a known or familiar object. The priest casts the spell, slowly turns, and will sense when he is facing in the direction of the object to be located, provided the object is within range—e.g., 90 yards for 3rd-level priests, 100 yards for 4th, 110 yards for 5th, etc. The spell locates such objects as apparel, jewelry, furniture, tools, weapons, or even a ladder or stairway. Once the caster has fixed in his mind the item sought, the spell locates only that item. Attempting to find a specific item, such as a kingdom's crown, requires an accurate mental image. If the image is not close enough to the actual item, the spell does not work; in short, desired but unique objects cannot be located by this spell unless they are known by the caster. The spell is blocked by lead.

The casting requires the use of a piece of lodestone.

The reversal, *obscure object*, hides an object from location by spell, crystal ball, or similar means for eight hours. The caster must touch the object being concealed.

Neither application of the spell affects living creatures.

Magical Vestment (Enchantment)

Sphere: Protection
Range: Touch
Components: V, S, M
Duration: 5 rounds/level
Casting Time: 1 round
Area of Effect: The caster
Saving Throw: None

This spell enchants the caster's vestment, providing protection at least the equivalent of chain mail (AC 5). The vestment gains a +1 enchantment for each three levels of the priest beyond 5th level, to a maximum of

AC 1 at 17th level. The magic lasts for five rounds per level of the caster, or until the caster loses consciousness. If the vestment is worn with other armors, only the best AC (either the armor or the vestment) is used—this protection is not cumulative with any other AC protection.

The material components are the vestment to be enchanted and the priest's holy symbol, which are not expended.

Meld Into Stone (Alteration)

Sphere: Elemental (Earth)
Range: 0
Components: V, S, M
Duration: 8 rounds + 1d8 rounds
Casting Time: 6
Area of Effect: Caster
Saving Throw: None

This spell enables the priest to meld his body and possessions into a single block of stone. The stone must be large enough to accommodate his body in all three dimensions. When casting is complete, the priest and not more than 100 pounds of nonliving gear merge with the stone. If either condition is violated, the spell fails and is wasted.

While in the stone, the priest remains in contact, however tenuous, with the face of the stone through which he melded. The priest remains aware of the passage of time. Nothing that goes on outside the stone can be seen or heard, however. Minor physical damage to the stone does not harm the priest, but its partial destruction, if enough so that the caster no longer fits, expels the priest with 4d8 points of damage. The stone's destruction expels the priest and slays him instantly, unless a successful saving throw vs. spell is rolled.

The magic lasts for 1d8 + 8 rounds, the variable part of the duration rolled secretly by the DM. At any time before the duration expires, the priest can step out of the stone through the stone surface he entered. If the duration runs out, or the effect is dispelled before the priest exits the stone, then he is violently expelled and suffers 4d8 points of damage.

The following spells harm the priest if cast upon the stone that he is occupying: *stone to flesh* expels the priest and inflicts 4d8 points of damage; *stone shape* causes 4d4 points of damage, but does not expel the priest; *transmute rock to mud* expels and slays him instantly unless he rolls a successful saving throw vs. spell; *passwall* expels the priest without damage.

Negative Plane Protection (Abjuration)

Sphere: Protection, Necromantic
Range: Touch
Components: V, S
Duration: Special
Casting Time: 1 round
Area of Effect: 1 creature
Saving Throw: None

This spell affords the caster or touched creature partial protection from undead monsters with Negative Material plane connections (such as shadows, wights, wraiths, spectres, or vampires) and certain weapons and spells that drain energy levels. The *negative plane protection* spell opens a channel to the Positive Material plane, possibly offsetting the effect of the negative energy attack. A protected creature struck by a negative energy attack is allowed a saving throw vs. death magic. If successful, the energies cancel with a bright flash of light and a thunderclap. The protected creature suffers only normal hit point damage from the attack and does not suffer any drain of experience or Strength, regardless of the number of levels the attack would have drained. An attacking undead creature suffers 2d6 points of damage from the Positive plane energy; a draining wizard or weapon receives no damage.

This protection is proof against only one such attack, dissipating immediately whether or not the saving throw was successful. If the saving throw is failed, the spell recipient suffers double the usual physical damage, in addition to the loss of experience or Strength that normally occurs. The protection lasts for one turn per level of the priest casting the spell, or until the protected creature is struck by a negative energy attack. This spell cannot be cast on the Negative Material plane.

Plant Growth (Alteration)

Sphere: Plant
Range: 160 yards
Components: V, S, M
Duration: Permanent
Casting Time: 1 round
Area of Effect: Special
Saving Throw: Special

The *plant growth* spell enables the caster to choose either of two different uses. The first causes normal vegetation to grow, entwine, and entangle to form a thicket or jungle that creatures must hack or force a way through at a movement rate of 10 feet per round (or 20 feet per round for larger-than-man-sized creatures). Note that the area must have brush and trees in it in order for this spell to take effect. Briars, bushes, creepers, lianas, roots, saplings, thistles, thorn, trees, vines, and weeds become so thick and overgrown in the area of effect as to form a barrier. The area of effect is a square 20 feet on a side per level of experience of the caster, in any square or rectangular shape that the caster decides upon at the time of the spellcasting. Thus an 8th-level caster can affect a maximum area of 160' × 160' square, a 320' × 80' rectangle, a 640' × 40' rectangle, a 1,280' × 20' rectangle, etc. The spell's effects persist in the area until it is cleared by labor, fire, or such magical means as a *dispel magic* spell.

The second use of the spell affects a one-mile square area. The DM secretly makes a saving throw (based on the caster's level) to see if the spell takes effect. If successful, the spell renders plants more vigorous, fruitful, and hardy, increasing yields by 20% to 50% ([1d4 + 1] × 10%), given a normal growing season. The spell does not prevent disaster in the form of floods, drought, fire, or insects, although even in these cases the plants survive better than expected. This effect lasts only for the life cycle of one season, the winter "death" marking the end of a life cycle even for the sturdiest of trees. In many farming communities, this spell is normally cast at planting time as part of the spring festivals.

Prayer (Conjuration/Summoning)

Sphere: Combat
Range: 0
Components: V, S, M
Duration: 1 round/level
Casting Time: 6
Area of Effect: 60-foot radius
Saving Throw: None

By means of the *prayer* spell, the priest brings special favor upon himself and his party and causes harm to his enemies. Those in the area at the instant the spell is completed are affected for the duration of the spell. When the spell is completed, all attack and damage rolls and saving throws made by those in the area of effect who are friendly to the priest gain +1 bonuses, while those of the priest's enemies suffer −1 penalties. Once the *prayer* spell is uttered, the priest can do other things, unlike a *chant*, which he must continue to make the spell effective. If another priest of the same religious persuasion (not merely the same alignment) is chanting when a prayer is cast, the effects combine to +2 and −2, as long as both are in effect at once.

The priest needs a silver holy symbol, prayer beads, or a similar device as the material component of this spell.

Protection From Fire (Abjuration)

Sphere: Protection, Elemental (Fire)
Range: Touch
Components: V, S, M
Duration: Special
Casting Time: 6
Area of Effect: Creature touched
Saving Throw: None

The effect of a *protection from fire* spell differs according to the recipient of the magic—either the caster or some other creature. In either case, the spell lasts no longer than one turn per caster level.

* If the spell is cast upon the caster, it confers complete invulnerability to normal fires (torches, bonfires, oil fires, and the like) and to exposure to magical fires such as fiery dragon breath, spells such as *burning hands, fireball, fire seeds, fire storm, flame strike, meteor swarm*, hell hound or pyro-hydra breath, etc., until the spell has absorbed 12 points of heat or fire damage per level of the caster, at which time the spell is negated.

* If the spell is cast upon another creature, it gives invulnerability to normal fire, gives a bonus of +4 to saving throw die rolls vs. fire attacks, and it reduces damage sustained from magical fires by 50%.

The caster's holy symbol is the material component.

Pyrotechnics (Alteration)

Sphere: Elemental (Fire)
Range: 160 yards
Components: V, S, M
Duration: Special
Casting Time: 6
Area of Effect: 10 or 100 times
        a single fire source
Saving Throw: Special

A *pyrotechnics* spell draws on an existing fire source to produce either of two effects, at the option of the caster.
* First, it can produce a flashing and fiery burst of glowing, colored aerial fireworks that lasts one round. This effect temporarily blinds those creatures in, under, or within 120 feet of the area that also have an unobstructed line of sight to the effect, for 1d4 + 1 rounds unless the creatures roll successful saving throws vs. spell. The fireworks fill a volume ten times greater than the original fire source.
* Second, it can cause a thick, writhing stream of smoke to arise from the source and form a choking cloud that lasts for one round per experience level of the caster. This covers a roughly hemispherical volume from the ground or floor up (or conforming to the shape of a confined area) that totally obscures vision beyond two feet. The smoke

fills a volume 100 times that of the fire source.

The spell uses one fire source within the area of effect, which is immediately extinguished. An extremely large fire can be used as the source, and it is only partially extinguished by the casting. Magical fires are not extinguished, although a fire-based creature (such as a fire elemental) used as a source suffers 1d4 points of damage, plus 1 point of damage per caster level. This spell does not function under water.

Remove Curse (Abjuration)
Reversible

Sphere: Protection
Range: Touch
Components: V, S
Duration: Permanent
Casting Time: 6
Area of Effect: Special
Saving Throw: Special

Upon casting this spell, the priest is usually able to remove a curse on an object, on a person, or in the form of some undesired sending or evil presence. Note that the *remove curse* spell does not remove the curse from a cursed shield, weapon, or suit of armor, for example, although the spell typically enables the person afflicted with any such cursed item to get rid of it. Certain special curses may not be countered by this spell, or may be countered only by a caster of a certain level or more. A caster of 12th level or more can cure lycanthropy with this spell by casting it on the animal form. The were-creature receives a saving throw vs. spell and, if successful, the spell fails and the priest must gain a level before attempting the remedy on this creature again.

The reverse of the spell is not permanent; the *bestow curse* spell lasts for one turn for every experience level of the priest using the spell. The curse can have one of the following effects (roll percentile dice): 50% of the time it reduces one ability of the victim to 3 (the DM randomly determines which ability); 25% of the time it lowers the victim's attack and saving throw rolls by −4; 25% of the time it makes the victim 50% likely to drop whatever he is holding (or do nothing, in the case of creatures not using tools)—roll each round.

It is possible for a priest to devise his own curse, and it should be similar in power to those given here. Consult your DM. The subject of a *bestow curse* spell must be touched. If the victim is touched, a saving throw is still applicable; if it is successful, the effect is negated. The bestowed curse cannot be dispelled.

Remove Paralysis (Abjuration)

Sphere: Protection
Range: 10 yards/level
Components: V, S
Duration: Permanent
Casting Time: 6
Area of Effect: 1d4 creatures in a 20′ cube
Saving Throw: None

By the use of this spell, the priest can free one or more creatures from the effects of any paralyzation or from related magic (such as a ghoul touch, or a *hold* or *slow* spell). If the spell is cast on one creature, the paralyzation is negated. If cast on two creatures, each receives another saving throw vs. the effect that afflicts it, with a +4 bonus. If cast on three or four creatures, each receives another saving throw with a +2 bonus. There must be no physical or magical barrier between the caster and the creatures to be affected, or the spell fails and is wasted.

Snare (Enchantment/Charm)

Sphere: Plant
Range: Touch
Components: V, S, M
Duration: Permanent until triggered
Casting Time: 3 rounds
Area of Effect: 2′ diameter circle plus 1/6′ per level of the spellcaster
Saving Throw: None

This spell enables the caster to make a snare that is 90% undetectable without magical aid. The snare can be made from any supple vine, a thong, or a rope. When the *snare* spell is cast upon it, the cord-like object blends with its surroundings. One end of the snare is tied in a loop that contracts around one or more of the limbs of any creature stepping inside the circle (note that the head of a worm or snake could be thus ensnared).

If a strong and supple tree is nearby, the snare can be fastened to it. The magic of the spell causes the tree to bend and then straighten when the loop is triggered, inflicting 1d6 points of damage to the creature trapped, and lifting it off the ground by the trapped member(s) (or strangling it if the head/neck triggered the snare). If no such sapling or tree is available, the cord-like object tightens upon the member(s), then wraps around the entire creature, causing no damage, but tightly binding it. Under water, the cord coils back upon its anchor point. The snare is magical, so for one hour it is breakable only by cloud giant or greater Strength (23); each hour thereafter, the snare material loses magic so as to become 1 point more breakable per hour—22 after two hours, 21 after three, 20 after four—until six full hours have elapsed. At that time, 18 Strength will break the bonds. Af-

ter 12 hours have elapsed, the materials of the snare lose all magical properties and the loop opens, freeing anything it held. The snare can be cut with any magical weapon, or with any edged weapon wielded with at least a +2 attack bonus (from Strength, for example).

The caster must have a snake skin and a piece of sinew from a strong animal to weave into the cord-like object from which he will make the snare. Only the caster's holy symbol is otherwise needed.

Speak With Dead (Necromancy)

Sphere: Divination
Range: 1
Components: V, S, M
Duration: Special
Casting Time: 1 turn
Area of Effect: 1 creature
Saving Throw: Special

Upon casting a *speak with dead* spell, the priest is able to ask several questions of a dead creature in a set period of time and receive answers according to the knowledge of that creature. Of course, the priest must be able to converse in the language that the dead creature once used. The length of time the creature has been dead is a factor, since only higher level priests can converse with a long-dead creature. The number of questions that can be answered and the length of time in which the questions can be asked depend on the level of experience of the priest. Even if the casting is successful, such creatures are as evasive as possible when questioned. The dead tend to give extremely brief and limited answers, often cryptic, and to take questions literally. Furthermore, their knowledge is often limited to what they knew in life.

A dead creature of different alignment or of higher level or Hit Dice than the caster's level receives a saving throw vs. spell. A dead creature that successfully saves can refuse to answer questions, ending the spell. At the DM's option, the casting of this spell on a given creature might be restricted to once per week.

The priest needs a holy symbol and burning incense in order to cast this spell upon the body, remains, or a portion thereof. The remains are not expended. This spell does not function under water.

Caster's Level of Experience	Maximum Length of Time Dead	Time Questioned	Number of Questions
up to 7th	1 week	1 round	2
7th-8th	1 month	3 rounds	3
9th-12th	1 year	1 turn	4
13th-15th	10 years	2 turns	5
16th-20th	100 years	3 turns	6
21st and up	1,000 years	1 hour	7

Spike Growth (Alteration, Enchantment)

Sphere: Plant
Range: 60 yards
Components: V, S, M
Duration: 3d4 turns + 1/level
Casting Time: 6
Area of Effect: 10-foot square/level
Saving Throw: None

Wherever any type of plant growth of moderate size or density is found, this spell can be used. The ground-covering vegetation or roots and rootlets in the area becomes very hard and sharply pointed. In effect the ground cover, while appearing to be unchanged, acts as if the area were strewn with caltrops. In areas of bare ground or earthen pits, roots and rootlets act in the same way. For each 10 feet of movement through the area, the victim suffers 2d4 points of damage. He must also roll a saving throw vs. spell. If this saving throw is failed, the victim's movement rate is reduced by 1/3 from its current total (but a creature's movement rate can never be less than 1). This penalty lasts for 24 hours, after which the character's normal movement rate is regained.

Without the use of a spell such as *true seeing*, similar magical aids, or some other special means of detection (such as *detect traps* or *detect snares and pits*), an area affected by *spike growth* is absolutely undetectable as such until a victim enters the area and suffers damage. Even then, the creature cannot determine the extent of the perilous area unless some means of magical detection is used.

The components for this spell are the priest's holy symbol and either seven sharp thorns or seven small twigs, each sharpened to a point.

Starshine (Evocation, Illusion/Phantasm)

Sphere: Sun
Range: 10 yd/level
Components: V, S, M
Duration: 1 turn/level
Casting Time: 6
Area of Effect: 10-foot square/level
Saving Throw: None

A *starshine* spell enables the caster to softly illuminate an area as if it were exposed to a clear night sky filled with stars. Regardless of the height of the open area in which the spell is cast, the area immediately beneath it is lit by starshine. Vision ranges are the same as those for a bright moonlit night—movement noted out to 100 yards; stationary creatures seen up to 50 yards; general identifications made at 30 yards; recognition at 10 yards. The spell creates shadows and has no effect on infravision. The area of effect actually appears to be a night sky, but disbelief of the illusion merely enables the disbeliever to note that the "stars" are actually evoked lights. This spell does not function under water.

The material components are several stalks from an amaryllis plant (especially Hypoxis) and several holly berries.

Stone Shape (Alteration)

Sphere: Elemental (Earth)
Range: Touch
Components: V, S, M
Duration: Permanent
Casting Time: 1 round
Area of Effect: 3' cube plus 1' cube/level
Saving Throw: None

By means of this spell, the caster can form an existing piece of stone into any shape that suits his purposes. For example, a stone weapon can be made, a special trapdoor fashioned, or a crude idol sculpted. By the same token, it enables the spellcaster to reshape a stone door, perhaps so as to escape imprisonment, providing the volume of stone involved was within the limits of the area of effect. While stone coffers can be thus formed, stone doors made, etc., the fineness of detail is not great. If the shaping has moving parts, there is a 30% chance they do not work.

The material component of this spell is soft clay that must be worked into roughly the desired shape of the stone object, and then touched to the stone when the spell is uttered.

Summon Insects
(Conjuration/Summoning)

Sphere: Animal
Range: 30 yards
Components: V, S, M
Duration: 1 round/level
Casting Time: 1 round
Area of Effect: 1 creature
Saving Throw: None

The *summon insects* spell attracts a cloud or swarm of normal insects to attack the foes of the caster. Flying insects appear 70% of the time, while crawling insects appear 30% of the time. The exact insects called are bees, biting flies, hornets, or wasps, if flying insects are indicated; biting ants or pinching beetles, if crawling insects are indicated. A cloud of the flying type, or a swarm of the crawling sort, appears after the spell is cast. This gathers at a point chosen by the caster, within the spell's range, and attacks any single creature the caster points to.

The attacked creature sustains 2 points of damage if it does nothing but attempt to flee or fend off the insects during the time it is attacked; it suffers 4 points of damage per round otherwise. If the insects are ignored, the victim fights with a −2 penalty to his attack roll and a +2 penalty to his Armor

Class. If he attempts to cast a spell, an initiative roll should be made for the insects to see if their damage occurs before the spell is cast. If it does, the victim's concentration is ruined and the spell is lost.

The insects disperse and the spell ends if the victim enters thick smoke or hot flames. Besides being driven off by smoke or hot flames, the swarm might possibly be outrun, or evaded by plunging into a sufficient body of water. If evaded, the summoned insects can be sent against another opponent, but there will be at least a 1 round delay while they leave the former opponent and attack the new victim. Crawling insects can travel only about 10 feet per round (maximum speed over smooth ground) and flying insects travel 60 feet per round. The caster must concentrate to maintain the swarm; it dissipates if he moves or is disturbed.

It is possible, in underground situations, that the caster might summon 1d4 giant ants by means of the spell, but the possibility is only 30% unless giant ants are nearby. This spell does not function under water.

The materials needed for this spell are the caster's holy symbol, a flower petal, and a bit of mud or wet clay.

Tree (Alteration)

Sphere: Plant
Range: 0
Components: V, S, M
Duration: 6 turns + 1 turn/level
Casting Time: 6
Area of Effect: The caster
Saving Throw: None

By means of this spell, the caster is able to assume the form of a small living tree or shrub or that of a large dead tree trunk with but a few limbs. Although the closest inspection cannot reveal that this plant is actually a person, and for all normal tests he is, in fact, a tree or shrub, the caster is able to observe all that goes on around him just as if he were in normal form. The Armor Class and hit points of the plant are those of the caster. The caster can remove the spell at any time, instantly changing from plant to his normal form and having full capability for any action normally possible (including spellcasting). Note that all clothing and gear worn or carried change with the caster.

The material components of this spell are the priest's holy symbol and a twig from a tree.

Water Breathing (Alteration)
Reversible

Sphere: Elemental (Water, Air)
Range: Touch
Components: V, S
Duration: 1 hour/level
Casting Time: 6
Area of Effect: Creature touched
Saving Throw: None

The recipient of a *water breathing* spell is able to breathe under water freely for the duration of the spell—i.e., one hour for each experience level of the caster. The priest can divide the base duration between multiple characters. Thus an 8th-level priest can confer this ability to two characters for four hours, four for two hours, eight for one hour, etc., to a minimum of ½ hour per character.

The reverse, *air breathing*, enables water-breathing creatures to survive comfortably in the atmosphere for an equal duration. Note that neither version prevents the recipient creature from breathing in its natural element.

Water Walk (Alteration)

Sphere: Elemental (Water)
Range: Touch
Components: V, S, M
Duration: 1 turn + 1 turn/level
Casting Time: 6
Area of Effect: Special
Saving Throw: None

By means of this spell, the caster is able to empower one or more creatures to tread upon any liquid as if it were firm ground; this includes mud, quicksand, oil, running water, and snow. The recipient's feet do not touch the surface of the liquid, but oval depressions of his appropriate foot size and two inches deep are left in the mud or snow. The recipient's rate of movement remains normal. If cast underwater, the recipient is borne toward the surface.

For every level of the caster above the minimum required to cast the spell (5th level), he can affect another creature.

The material components for this spell are a piece of cork and the priest's holy symbol.

Fourth-Level Spells

Abjure (Abjuration)

Sphere: Summoning
Range: 10 yards
Components: V, S, M
Duration: Special
Casting Time: 1 round
Area of Effect: 1 creature
Saving Throw: Special

This spell can send an extraplanar creature back to its own plane of existence. The spell fails against entities of demigod status or greater, but their servants or minions can be abjured. If the creature has a specific (proper) name, then that must be known and used. Any magic resistance of the subject must be overcome, or the spell fails. The priest has a 50% chance of success (a roll of 11 or better on 1d20). The roll is adjusted by the difference in level or Hit Dice between the caster and the creature being abjured: the number needed is decreased if the priest has more Hit Dice and increased if the creature has more Hit Dice. If the spell is successful, the creature is instantly hurled back to its own plane. The affected creature must survive a system shock check. If the creature does not have a Constitution score, the required roll is 70% + 2%/Hit Die or level. The caster has no control over where in the creature's plane the abjured creature arrives. If the attempt fails, the priest must gain another level before another attempt can be made on that particular creature.

The spell requires the priest's holy symbol, holy water, and some material inimical to the creature.

Animal Summoning I
(Conjuration, Summoning)

Sphere: Animal, Summoning
Range: 1 mile radius
Components: V, S
Duration: Special
Casting Time: 7
Area of Effect: Special
Saving Throw: None

By means of this spell, the caster calls up to eight animals that have 4 Hit Dice or less, of whatever sort the caster names when the summoning is made. Only animals within range of the caster at the time the spell is cast will come. The caster can try three times to summon three different types of animals—e.g., suppose that wild dogs are first summoned to no avail, then hawks are unsuccessfully called, and finally the caster calls for wild horses that may or may not be within summoning range. Your DM must determine the chance of a summoned animal type being within the range of the spell. The animals summoned aid the caster by whatever means they possess, staying until a fight is over, a specific mission is finished, the caster is safe, he sends them away, etc. Only normal or giant animals can be summoned; fantastic animals or monsters cannot be summoned by this spell (no chimerae, dragons, gorgons, manticores, etc.).

Call Woodland Beings
(Conjuration/Summoning)

Sphere: Summoning
Range: 100 yards/level
Components: V, S, M
Duration: Special
Casting Time: Special
Area of Effect: Special
Saving Throw: Neg.

By means of this spell, the caster is able to summon certain woodland creatures to his location. Naturally, this spell works only outdoors, but not necessarily only in wooded areas. The caster begins the incantation and continues uninterrupted until some called creature appears or two turns have elapsed. (The verbalization and somatic gesturing are easy, so this is not particularly exhausting to the spellcaster.) Only one type

of the following sorts of beings can be summoned by the spell. They come only if they are within the range of the call.

The caster can call three times, for a different type each time. Once a call is successful, no other type can be called without another casting of the spell. (Your DM will consult his outdoor map or base the probability of any such creature being within spell range upon the nature of the area the caster is in at the time of spellcasting.)

The creature(s) called by the spell are entitled to a saving throw vs. spell (with a −4 penalty) to avoid the summons. Any woodland beings answering the call are favorably disposed to the spellcaster and give whatever aid they are capable of. However, if the caller or members of the caller's party are of evil alignment, the creatures are entitled to another saving throw vs. spell (this time with a +4 bonus) when they come within 10 yards of the caster or another evil character with him. These beings immediately seek to escape if their saving throws are successful. In any event, if the caster requests that the summoned creatures engage in combat on his behalf, they are required to roll a loyalty reaction check based on the caster's Charisma and whatever dealings he has had with them.

This spell works with respect to neutral or good woodland creatures, as determined by the DM. Thus the DM can freely add to or alter the list as he sees fit.

If the caster personally knows a certain individual woodland being, that being can be summoned at double the normal range. If this is done, then no other woodland creatures are affected.

The material components of this spell are a pine cone and eight holly berries.

If a percentage chance is given, druids and other nature-based priests add 1% per caster level. These chances can be used if no other campaign information on the area is available.

Cloak of Bravery
(Conjuration/Summoning)
Reversible

Sphere: Charm
Range: Touch
Components: V, S, M
Duration: Special
Casting Time: 6
Area of Effect: Creature touched
Saving Throw: Neg.

The *cloak of bravery* spell can be cast upon any willing creature. The protected individual gains a bonus to his saving throw against any form of fear encountered (but not awe—an ability of some Lesser and Greater Powers). When cast, the spell can affect one to four creatures (caster's choice). If only one is affected, the saving throw bonus is +4. If two are affected, the bonus is +3, and so forth, until four creatures are protected by a +1 bonus. The magic of the *cloak of bravery* spell works only once and then the spell ends, whether or not the creature's saving throw is successful. The spell ends after eight hours if no saving throw is required before then.

The reverse of this spell, *cloak of fear*, empowers a single creature touched to radiate a personal aura of fear, at will, out to a three-foot radius. All other characters and creatures within this aura must roll successful saving throws vs. spell or run away in panic for 2d8 rounds. Affected individuals may or may not drop items, at the DM's option.

The spell has no effect upon undead of any sort. The effect can be used but once, and the spell expires after eight hours if not brought down earlier. Members of the recipient's party are not immune to the effects of the spell.

The material component for the *cloak of bravery* spell is the feather of an eagle or hawk. The reverse requires the tail feathers of a vulture or chicken.

Control Temperature, 10' Radius
(Alteration)

Sphere: Weather
Range: 0
Components: V, S, M
Duration: 4 turns + 1 turn/level
Casting Time: 7
Area of Effect: 10-foot radius
Saving Throw: None

When this spell is cast, the temperature surrounding the caster can be altered by 10 degrees Fahrenheit, either upward or downward, per level of experience of the spellcaster. Thus, a 10th-level caster could raise or lower the surrounding temperature from 1 to 100 degrees. The spell can be used to ensure the comfort of the caster and those with him in extreme weather conditions.

Creature Type Called	——— Type of Woodlands ———		
	Light	Moderate/Sylvan	Dense/Virgin
2d8 brownies	30%	20%	10%
1d4 centaurs	5%	30%	5%
1d4 dryads	1%	25%	15%
1d8 pixies	10%	20%	10%
1d4 satyrs	1%	30%	10%
1d6 sprites	0%	5%	25%
1 treant	—	5%	25%
1 unicorn	—	15%	20%

The party could stand about in shirt sleeves during the worst blizzard (although it would be raining on them) or make ice for their drinks during a scorching heat wave.

The spell also provides protection from intense normal and magical attacks. If the extreme of temperature is beyond what could be affected by the spell (a searing blast of a *fireball* or the icy chill of a white dragon), the spell reduces the damage caused by 5 points for every level of the caster. Normal saving throws are still allowed, and the reduction is taken after the saving throw is made or failed. Once struck by such an attack, the spell immediately collapses.

The material component for this spell is a strip of willow bark (to lower temperatures) or raspberry leaves (to raise temperatures).

Cure Serious Wounds (Necromancy)
Reversible

Sphere: Healing
Range: Touch
Components: V, S
Duration: Permanent
Casting Time: 7
Area of Effect: Creature touched
Saving Throw: None

This spell is a more potent version of the *cure light wounds* spell. When laying his hand upon a creature, the priest heals 2d8 +1 points of wound or other injury damage to the creature's body. This healing cannot affect noncorporeal, nonliving, or extraplanar creatures.

Cause serious wounds, the reverse of the spell, operates similarly to the *cause light wounds* spell, the victim having to be touched first. If the touch is successful, 2d8 +1 points of damage are inflicted.

Detect Lie (Divination)
Reversible

Sphere: Divination
Range: 30 yards
Components: V, S, M
Duration: 1 round/level
Casting Time: 7
Area of Effect: 1 creature
Saving Throw: Neg.

A priest who casts this spell is immediately able to determine if the subject creature deliberately and knowingly speaks a lie. It does not reveal the truth, uncover unintentional inaccuracies, or necessarily reveal evasions. The subject receives a saving throw vs. spell, which is adjusted only by the Wisdom of the *caster*—e.g., if the caster has a Wisdom of 18, the subject's saving throw roll is reduced by 4 (see Table 5).

The material component for the *detect lie* spell is one gp worth of gold dust.

The spell's reverse, *undetectable lie,* prevents the magical detection of lies spoken by the creature for 24 hours.

The reverse requires brass dust as its material component.

Divination (Divination)

Sphere: Divination
Range: 0
Components: V, S, M
Duration: Special
Casting Time: 1 turn
Area of Effect: Special
Saving Throw: None

A *divination* spell is used to garner a useful piece of advice concerning a specific goal, event, or activity that will occur within a one-week period. This can be as simple as a short phrase, or it might take the form of a cryptic rhyme or omen. Unlike the *augury* spell, this gives a specific piece of advice. For example, if the question is "Will we do well if we venture to the third level?" and a terrible troll guarding 10,000 gp and a *shield +1* lurks near the entrance to the level (the DM estimates the party could beat the troll after a hard fight) the divination response might be: "Ready oil and open flame light your way to wealth." In all cases, the DM controls what information is received and whether additional divinations will supply additional information. Note that if the information is not acted upon, the conditions probably change so that the information is no longer useful (in the example, the troll might move away and take the treasure with it).

The base chance for a correct divination is 60%, plus 1% for each experience level of the priest casting the spell. The DM makes adjustments to this base chance considering the actions being divined (if, for example, unusual precautions against the spell have been taken). If the dice roll is failed, the caster knows the spell failed, unless specific magic yielding false information is at work.

The material components of the *divination* spell are a sacrificial offering, incense, and the holy symbol of the priest. If an unusually important *divination* is attempted, sacrifice of particularly valuable gems, jewelry, or magical items may be required.

Free Action (Abjuration, Enchantment)

Sphere: Charm
Range: Touch
Components: V, S, M
Duration: 1 turn/level
Casting Time: 7
Area of Effect: Creature touched
Saving Throw: None

This spell enables the creature touched to move and attack normally for the duration of the spell, even under the influence of

magic that impedes movement (such as *web* or *slow* spells) or while under water. It even negates or prevents the effects of paralysis and *hold* spells. Under water, the individual moves at normal (surface) speed and inflicts full damage, even with such cutting weapons as axes and swords and with such smashing weapons as flails, hammers, and maces, provided that the weapon is wielded in the hand rather than hurled. The *free action* spell does not, however, allow *water breathing* without further appropriate magic.

The material component is a leather thong, bound around the arm or similar appendage, which disintegrates when the spell expires.

Giant Insect (Alteration)
Reversible

Sphere: Animal
Range: 20 yards
Components: V, S, M
Duration: Special
Casting Time: 7
Area of Effect: 1 to 6 insects
Saving Throw: None

By means of this spell, the priest can turn one or more normal-sized insects into larger forms resembling the giant insects described in the *Monstrous Compendium*. Only one type of insect can be altered at one time (i.e., a single casting cannot affect both an ant and a fly) and all insects affected must be grown to the same size. The number of insects and the size to which they can be grown depend upon the priest's level:

Priest's Level	Insect Hit Dice	Maximum Total HD
7-9	3	9
10-12	4	12
13 +	6	15

For example, an 8th-level priest can grow three insects to 3 Hit Dice, four insects to 2 Hit Dice, or nine insects to 1 hit die. Flying insects of 3 Hit Dice or more can carry a rider of human size (assume that such can carry 80 pounds per Hit Die).

If the casting is interrupted for any reason, or if the insects are currently subject to any other magical effect (including this one), the insects die and the spell is ruined. The DM decides how many normal insects of what type are available; this is often a greater limitation on the spell than the limits above.

If the insect created by this spell matches an existing monster description, use the monster description. Otherwise, unless the DM creates a special description, the giant form has an Armor Class of between 8 and 4, one attack, and inflicts 1d4 points of damage per Hit Die.

Example: A 14th-level priest uses the *giant insect* spell to enlarge one beetle (all that is available) to 6 HD size. The DM decides the beetle has AC 5 and bites once for 6d4 points of damage.

Note that the spell works only on actual insects. Arachnids, crustaceans, and other types of small creatures are not affected. Any giant insects created by this spell do not attempt to harm the priest, but the priest's control of such creatures is limited to simple commands ("attack," "defend," "guard," and so forth). Orders to attack a certain creature when it appears or guard against a particular occurrence are too complex. Unless commanded to do otherwise, the giant insects attempt to attack whoever or whatever is near them.

The reverse of the spell, *shrink insect*, reduces any giant insect to normal insect size. The number of Hit Dice affected by the priest is subtracted from the number of Hit Dice of the insects, and any insect reduced to 0 Hit Dice has been shrunk. Partial shrinking is ignored; an insect is either shrunk or unaffected. Thus, a 9th-level priest attacked by giant ants could shrink three warrior ants or four worker ants to normal insect size with no saving throw. This spell has no effect on intelligent insect-like creatures.

The priest must use his holy symbol for either version of the spell.

Hallucinatory Forest
(Illusion/Phantasm)
Reversible

Sphere: Plant
Range: 80 yards
Components: V, S
Duration: Permanent
Casting Time: 7
Area of Effect: 40-foot square/level
Saving Throw: None

When this spell is cast, a hallucinatory forest comes into existence. The illusionary forest appears to be perfectly natural and is indistinguishable from a real forest. Priests attuned to the woodlands—as well as such creatures as centaurs, dryads, green dragons, nymphs, satyrs, and treants—recognize the forest for what it is. All other creatures believe it is there, and movement and order of march are affected accordingly. Touching the illusory growth neither affects the magic nor reveals its nature. The hallucinatory forest remains until it is magically dispelled by a reverse of the spell or a *dispel magic* spell. The area shape is either roughly rectangular or square, in general, and at least 40 feet deep, in whatever location the caster desires. The forest can be of less than maximum area if the caster wishes. One of its edges can appear up to 80 yards away from the caster.

Hold Plant (Enchantment/Charm)

Sphere: Plant
Range: 80 yards
Components: V, S
Duration: 1 round/level
Casting Time: 7
Area of Effect: Special
Saving Throw: Neg.

The *hold plant* spell affects vegetable matter as follows: 1) it causes ambulatory vegetation to cease moving; 2) it prevents vegetable matter from entwining, grasping, closing, or growing; 3) it prevents vegetable matter from making any sound or movement that is not caused by wind. The spell effects apply to all forms of vegetation, including parasitic and fungoid types, and those magically animated or otherwise magically empowered. It affects such monsters as green slime, molds of any sort, shambling mounds, shriekers, treants, etc. The duration of a *hold plant* spell is one round per level of experience of the caster. It affects 1d4 plants in a 40' × 40' area—or a square four to 16 yards on a side of small ground growth such as grass or mold. If but one plant (or four yards square) is chosen as the target for the spell by the caster, the saving throw of the plant (or area of plant growth) is made with a −4 penalty to the die roll; if two plants (or eight yards square) are the target, saving throws suffer a −2 penalty; if three plants (or 12 yards square) are the target, saving throws suffer a −1 penalty; and if the maximum of four plants (or 16 yards square) are the target, saving throws are unmodified.

Imbue With Spell Ability
(Enchantment)

Sphere: Charm
Range: Touch
Components: V, S, M
Duration: Special
Casting Time: 1 turn
Area of Effect: Person touched
Saving Throw: None

By the use of this spell, the priest can transfer a limited number and selection of his currently memorized spells, and the ability to cast them, to another person. Only non-spellcasters (including rangers under 8th level and paladins under 9th level) can receive this bestowal; the *imbue with spell ability* enchantment does not function for those belonging to spellcasting classes, for unintelligent monsters, nor for any individual with less than 1 full Hit Die. In addition, the person thus imbued must have a Wisdom score of 9 or higher. Only priest spells of an informational or defensive nature or a *cure light wounds* spell can be transferred. Transferring any other spell type negates the entire attempt, including any allowable spells that were chosen. Higher level persons can receive more than one spell at the priest's option:

Level of Recipient	Spells Imbued
1	One 1st-level spell
3	Two 1st-level spells
5 +	Two 1st- and one 2nd-level spells

The transferred spell's variable characteristics (range, duration, area of effect, etc.) function according to the level of the priest originally imbuing the spell.

A priest who casts *imbue with spell ability* upon another character loses the number of 1st- and 2nd-level spells he has imbued until the recipient uses the transferred spells or is slain. For example, a 7th-level priest with five 1st- and four 2nd-level spells imbues a 10th-level fighter with a *cure light wounds* spell and a *slow poison* spell. The cleric now can have only four 1st-level spells memorized until the cure is cast and only three 2nd-level spells until the *slow poison* is cast, or until the fighter is killed. In the meantime, the priest remains responsible to his ethos for the use to which the spell is put.

The material components for this spell are the priest's holy symbol, plus some minor item from the recipient that is symbolic of his profession (a lockpick for a thief, etc.). This item, and any material component for the imbued spell, is consumed when the *imbue with spell ability* spell is cast.

Lower Water (Alteration)
Reversible

Sphere: Elemental (Water)
Range: 120 yards
Components: V, S, M
Duration: 1 turn/level
Casting Time: 1 turn
Area of Effect: Special
Saving Throw: None

The *lower water* spell causes water or similar fluid in the area of effect to sink away to a minimum depth of one inch. The depth can be lowered by up to two feet for every experience level of the priest. The water is lowered within a square area whose sides are 10 feet long per caster level. Thus, an 8th-level priest affects a volume up to 16' × 80' × 80', a 9th-level caster affects a volume up to 18' × 90' × 90', and so on. In extremely large and deep bodies of water, such as deep ocean, the spell creates a whirlpool that sweeps ships and similar craft downward, putting them at risk and rendering them unable to leave by normal movement for the duration of the spell. When cast on water elementals and other water-based creatures, this spell acts as a *slow* spell: the creature moves at half speed and makes half its usual number of attacks each round. The spell has no effect on other creatures.

Its reverse, *raise water*, causes water or similar fluids to return to their highest natural level: spring flood, high tide, etc. This can make fords impassable, float grounded ships, and may even sweep away bridges at the DM's option. It negates *lower water* and vice versa.

The material components of this spell are the priest's holy (or unholy) symbol and a pinch of dust.

Neutralize Poison (Necromancy)
Reversible

Sphere: Healing
Range: Touch
Components: V, S
Duration: Permanent
Casting Time: 7
Area of Effect: Creature touched or 1 cubic foot of substance/2 levels
Saving Throw: None

By means of a *neutralize poison* spell, the priest detoxifies any sort of venom in the creature or substance touched. Note that an opponent, such as a poisonous reptile or snake (or even an envenomed weapon of an opponent) unwilling to be so touched requires the priest to roll a successful attack in combat. This spell can prevent death in a poisoned creature if cast before death occurs. The effects of the spell are permanent only with respect to poison existing in the touched creature at the time of the touch, thus creatures (and objects) that generate new poison are not permanently detoxified.

The reversed spell, *poison*, likewise requires an attack roll that succeeds, and the victim is allowed a saving throw vs. poison. If the latter is unsuccessful, the victim is incapacitated and dies in one turn unless the poison is magically neutralized or slowed.

Plant Door (Alteration)

Sphere: Plant
Range: Touch
Components: V, S, M
Duration: Special
Casting Time: 7
Area of Effect: Special
Saving Throw: None

The *plant door* spell opens a magical portal or passageway through trees, undergrowth, thickets, or any similar growth—even growth of a magical nature. The plant door is open to the caster who cast the spell, casters of a higher level, or dryads; others must be shown the location of the door. The door even enables the caster to enter a solid tree

trunk and remain hidden there until the spell ends. The spell also enables the passage or hiding of any man-sized or smaller creature; hiding is subject to space considerations. If the tree is cut down or burned, those within must leave before the tree falls or is consumed, or else they are killed also. The duration of the spell is one turn per level of experience of the caster. If the caster opts to stay within an oak, the spell lasts nine times longer, if in an ash tree, it lasts three times longer than normal. The path created by the spell is up to four feet wide, eight feet high, and 12 feet long per level of experience of the caster. This spell does not function on plant-based monsters—e.g., shambling mounds, molds, slimes, treants, etc.

The material components for this spell are a piece of charcoal and the caster's holy symbol.

Produce Fire (Alteration)
Reversible

Sphere: Elemental (Fire)
Range: 40 yards
Components: V, S, M
Duration: 1 round
Casting Time: 7
Area of Effect: 12-foot square
Saving Throw: None

By means of this spell, the caster causes a common fire of up to 12 feet per side in area. Though it lasts but a single round, unless it ignites additional flammable material, the fire produced by the spell inflicts 1d4 points of damage plus 1 point per caster level (1d4 + 1/level) upon creatures within its area. It ignites combustible materials, such as cloth, oil, paper, parchment, wood, and the like, so as to cause continued burning.

The reverse, *quench fire*, extinguishes any normal fire (coals, oil, tallow, wax, wood, etc.) within the area of effect.

The material component for either version is a paste of sulfur and wax, formed into a ball and thrown at the target.

Protection From Evil, 10' Radius (Abjuration)
Reversible

Sphere: Protection
Range: Touch
Components: V, S, M
Duration: 1 turn/level
Casting Time: 7
Area of Effect: 10-foot-radius sphere
Saving Throw: None

The globe of protection of this spell is identical in all respects to that of a *protection from evil* spell, except that it encompasses a much larger area and its duration is greater. The effect is centered on and moves with the creature touched. Any protected

creature within the circle will break the warding against enchanted/summoned monsters if he attacks those monsters. A creature unable to fit completely into the area of effect (for example, a 21-foot-tall titan) remains partially exposed and subject to whatever penalties the DM decides. If such a creature is the recipient of the spell, the spell acts as a normal *protection from evil* spell for that creature only.

The reverse, *protection from good, 10' radius*, wards against good creatures.

To complete this spell, the priest must trace a circle 20 feet in diameter using holy (or unholy) water and incense (or smoldering dung), according to the *protection from evil* spell.

Protection From Lightning (Abjuration)

Sphere: Protection, Weather
Range: Touch
Components: V, S, M
Duration: Special
Casting Time: 7
Area of Effect: Creature touched
Saving Throw: None

The effect of a *protection from lightning* spell changes depending on who is the recipient of the magic—the caster or some other creature. In either case, the spell lasts no longer than one turn per caster level.

* If the spell is cast upon the caster, it confers complete invulnerability to electrical attack such as dragon breath, or magical lightning such as *lightning bolt, shocking grasp*, storm giant, will 'o wisp, etc., until the spell has absorbed 10 points of electrical damage per level of the caster, at which time the spell is negated.

* If the spell is cast upon another creature, it gives a bonus of +4 to the die roll for saving throws made vs. electrical attacks, and it reduces the damage sustained from such attacks by 50%.

The caster's holy symbol is the material component.

Reflecting Pool (Divination)

Sphere: Divination
Range: 10 yards
Components: V, S, M
Duration: 1 round/level
Casting Time: 2 hours
Area of Effect: Special
Saving Throw: None

This spell enables the caster to cause a pool of normal water found in a natural setting to act as a scrying device. The pool can be of no greater diameter than two feet per level of the caster. The effect is to create a scrying device similar to a *crystal ball*. The scrying can extend only to those planes of existence that are coexistent with or border on the Prime Material plane—the inner planes (including the para-elemental planes, plane of Shadow, etc.). General notes on scrying, detection by the subject, and penalties for attempting to scry beyond the caster's own plane are given in the *DMG*, as well as a description of the *crystal ball* item.

The following spells can be cast through a reflecting pool, with a 5% per level chance for operating correctly: *detect magic, detect snares and pits, detect poison*. Each additional detection attempt requires a round of concentration, regardless of success. Infravision, if available, operates normally through the reflecting pool.

The image is nearly always hazy enough to prevent the reading of script of any type.

The material component is the oil extracted from such nuts as the hickory and the walnut, refined, and dropped in three measures upon the surface of the pool. (A measure need be no more than a single ounce of oil.)

At the DM's option, the casting of this spell may be limited to once per day.

Repel Insects (Abjuration, Alteration)

Sphere: Animal, Protection
Range: 0
Components: V, S, M
Duration: 1 turn/level
Casting Time: 1 round
Area of Effect: 10-foot radius
Saving Throw: None

When this spell is cast, the priest creates an invisible barrier to all sorts of insects, and normal insects do not approach within 10 feet of the caster while the spell is in effect. Giant insects with Hit Dice less than 1/3 of the caster's experience level are also repelled (e.g., 2 Hit Dice for 7th- to 9th-level casters, 3 Hit Dice at 10th through 12th level, etc.). Insects with more Hit Dice can enter the protected area if the insect is especially aggressive and, in addition, rolls a successful saving throw vs. spell. Those that do sustain 1d6 points of damage from passing of the magical barrier. Note that the spell does not in any way affect arachnids, myriapods, and similar creatures—it affects only true insects.

The material components of the *repel insects* spell include any one of the following: several crushed marigold flowers, a whole crushed leek, seven crushed stinging nettle leaves, or a small lump of resin from a camphor tree.

Speak With Plants (Alteration)

Sphere: Plant
Range: 0
Components: V, S, M
Duration: 1 round/level
Casting Time: 1 turn
Area of Effect: 30-foot radius
Saving Throw: None

When cast, a *speak with plants* spell enables the priest to converse, in very rudimentary terms, with all sorts of living vegetables (including fungi, molds, and plant-like monsters, such as shambling mounds) and to exercise limited control over normal plants (i.e., not monsters or plant-like creatures). Thus, the caster can question plants as to whether or not creatures have passed through them, cause thickets to part to enable easy passage, require vines to entangle pursuers, and command similar services. The spell does not enable plants to uproot themselves and move about, but any movements within the plants' normal capabilities are possible. Creatures entangled by the 1st-level spell of that name can be released. The power of the spell lasts for one round for each experience level of the casting priest. All vegetation within the area of effect is affected by the spell.

The material components for this spell are a drop of water, a pinch of dung, and a flame.

Spell Immunity (Abjuration)

Sphere: Protection
Range: Touch
Components: V, S, M
Duration: 1 turn/level
Casting Time: 1 round
Area of Effect: Creature touched
Saving Throw: None

By means of this spell, the priest renders a creature touched immune to the effects of a specified spell of 4th level or lower. It protects against spells, spell-like effects of magical items, and innate spell-like abilities of creatures. It does not protect against breath weapons or gaze attacks of any type. The spell has additional limitations. First, the caster must have directly experienced the effect of the spell specified. For example, if the caster has been attacked by a *fireball* spell at some time, then he can use spell immunity to provide protection from a fireball. Second, the spell cannot affect a creature already magically protected by a potion, protective spell, ring, or other device. Third, only a particular spell can be protected against, not a certain sphere of spells or a group of spells that are similar in effect; thus, a creature given immunity to the *lightning bolt* spell is still vulnerable to a *shocking grasp* spell.

The material component for spell immunity is the same as that for the spell to be protected against.

Sticks to Snakes (Alteration)
Reversible

Sphere: Plant
Range: 30 yards
Components: V, S, M
Duration: 2 rounds/level
Casting Time: 7
Area of Effect: 1d4 sticks + 1 stick/level in a 10-foot cube
Saving Throw: None

By means of this spell, the caster can change 1d4 sticks, plus one stick per experience level, into snakes; thus a 9th-level priest can change 10-13 sticks into an equal number of snakes. These snakes attack as commanded by the priest. There must, of course, be sticks or similar pieces of wood (such as torches, spears, etc.) to turn into snakes. Such a stick cannot be larger than a staff. Sticks held by creatures are allowed a saving throw equal to that of the possessor (i.e., a spear held by an orc must fail the orc's saving throw vs. polymorph). Magical items, such as staves and enchanted spears, are not affected by the spell. Only sticks within the area of effect are changed. The type of snake created varies, but a typical specimen has 2 Hit Dice, Armor Class 6, a movement rate of 9, and either constricts for 1d4+1 points of damage per round or bites for 1 point plus poison (if any). The chance of a snake thus changed being venomous is 5% per caster level, if the spellcaster desires. Thus, an 11th-level priest has a maximum 55% chance that any snake created by the spell is poisonous. The spell lasts for two rounds for each experience level of the spellcaster.

The material components of the spell are a small piece of bark and several snake scales.

The reverse changes normal-sized snakes to sticks for the same duration, or it negates the *sticks to snakes* spell according to the level of the priest countering the spell (e.g., a 10th-level priest casting the reverse spell can turn 11-14 snakes back into sticks).

Tongues (Alteration)
Reversible

Sphere: Divination
Range: 0
Components: V, S
Duration: 1 turn
Casting Time: 7
Area of Effect: The caster
Saving Throw: None

This spell enables the caster to speak and understand additional languages, whether they are racial tongues or regional dialects, but not communications of animals or mindless creatures. When the spell is cast, the spellcaster selects the language or languages to be understood. The spell then empowers the caster with the ability to speak and understand the language desired with perfect fluency and accent. The spell enables the priest to be understood by all speakers of that language within hearing distance, usually 60 feet. This spell does not predispose the subject toward the caster in any way. The priest can speak one additional tongue for every three levels of experience.

The reverse of the spell cancels the effect of the *tongues* spell or confuses verbal communication of any sort within the area of effect.

Fifth-Level Spells

Air Walk (Alteration)

Sphere: Elemental (Air)
Range: Touch
Components: V, S, M
Duration: 1 hour + 1 turn/level
Casting Time: 8
Area of Effect: Creature touched
Saving Throw: None

This spell enables a creature, which can be as large as the largest giant, to tread upon air just as if it were solid ground. Moving upward is similar to walking up a hill; a maximum upward angle of 45 degrees is possible at one-half the creature's movement rate. Likewise, a maximum downward

angle of 45 degrees at the normal movement rate is possible. An air-walking creature is always in control of its movement rate, save when a wind is blowing. In this case the creature gains or loses 10 feet of movement for every 10 miles per hour of wind velocity. The creature may, at the DM's option, be subject to additional penalties, loss of control, and possible damage in exceptionally strong or turbulent winds.

The spell can be placed upon a trained mount, so it can be ridden through the air. Of course, a mount not accustomed to such movement would certainly need careful and lengthy training, the details of which are up to the DM.

The material components for the spell are the priest's holy symbol and a bit of thistledown.

Animal Growth (Alteration)
Reversible

Sphere: Animal
Range: 80 yards
Components: V, S, M
Duration: 2 rounds/level
Casting Time: 8
Area of Effect: Up to 8 animals in a 20-foot-square area
Saving Throw: None

When this spell is cast, the caster causes all animals, up to a maximum of eight, within a 20-foot-square area to grow to twice their normal size. The effects of this growth are doubled Hit Dice (with resultant improvement in attack potential), doubled hit points (except hit points added to Hit Dice), and doubled damage in combat. Movement and AC are not affected. The spell lasts for two rounds for each level of the caster. The spell is particularly useful in conjunction with a *charm person or mammal* spell.

The reverse reduces animal size by one-half, and likewise reduces Hit Dice, hit points, attack damage, etc.

The material component for this spell and its reverse is the caster's holy symbol and a scrap of food.

Animal Summoning II
(Conjuration/Summoning)

Sphere: Animal, Summoning
Range: 60 yards/level
Components: V, S
Duration: Special
Casting Time: 8
Area of Effect: Special
Saving Throw: None

By means of this spell, the caster calls up to six animals that have 8 Hit Dice or less, or 12 animals of 4 Hit Dice or less, of whatever sort the caster names. Only animals within

range of the caster at the time the spell is cast will come. The caster can try three times to summon three different types of animals—suppose that wild dogs are first summoned to no avail, then hawks are unsuccessfully called, and finally the caster calls for wild horses that may or may not be within summoning range. Your DM will determine the chance of a summoned animal type being within range of the spell. The animals summoned aid the caster by whatever means they possess, staying until a fight is over, a specific mission is finished, the caster is safe, he sends them away, etc. Only normal or giant animals can be summoned; fantastic animals or monsters cannot be summoned by this spell (no chimerae, dragons, gorgons, manticores, etc.).

Anti-Plant Shell (Abjuration)

Sphere: Plant, Protection
Range: 0
Components: V, S
Duration: 1 turn/level
Casting Time: 8
Area of Effect: 15' diameter hemisphere
Saving Throw: None

The *anti-plant shell* spell creates an invisible, mobile barrier that keeps out all creatures or missiles of living vegetable material. Thus, the caster (and any creatures within the shell) is protected from attacking plants or vegetable creatures such as shambling mounds or treants. Any attempt to force the barrier against such creatures shatters the barrier immediately. The spell lasts for one turn for each experience level of the caster.

Atonement (Abjuration)

Sphere: All
Range: Touch
Components: V, S, M
Duration: Permanent
Casting Time: 1 turn
Area of Effect: 1 person
Saving Throw: None

This spell is used by the priest to remove the burden of unwilling or unknown deeds from the person who is the subject of the atonement. The spell removes the effects of magical alignment change as well. The person seeking the *atonement* spell must either be truly repentant or not have been in command of his own will when the acts to be atoned for were committed. Your DM will judge this spell in this regard, noting any past instances of its use upon the person. Deliberate misdeeds and acts of knowing and willful nature cannot be atoned for with this spell (see the *quest* spell). A character who refuses to accept an atonement is automatically considered to have committed a willful misdeed.

The priest needs his religious symbol, prayer beads or wheel or book, and burning incense.

Commune (Divination)

Sphere: Divination
Range: 0
Components: V, S, M
Duration: Special
Casting Time: 1 turn
Area of Effect: Special
Saving Throw: None

By use of a *commune* spell, the priest is able to contact his divinity—or agents thereof—and request information in the form of questions that can be answered by a simple "yes" or "no." The priest is allowed one such question for every experience level he has attained. The answers given are correct within the limits of the entity's knowledge ("I don't know" is a legitimate answer, as powerful outer planar beings are not necessarily omniscient). Optionally, the DM may give a single short answer, of five words or less. The spell will, at best, provide information to aid character decisions. Entities communed with structure their answers to further their own purposes. It is probable that the DM will limit the use of *commune* spells to one per adventure, one per week, or even one per month, for the greater powers dislike frequent interruptions. Likewise, if the caster lags, discusses the answers, or goes off to do anything else, the spell immediately ends.

The material components necessary to a *commune* spell are the priest's religious symbol, holy (unholy) water, and incense. If a particularly potent commune is needed, a sacrifice proportionate with the difficulty of obtaining the information is required, and if the offering is insufficient, only partial or no information is gained.

Commune With Nature (Divination)

Sphere: Divination
Range: 0
Components: V, S
Duration: Special
Casting Time: 1 turn
Area of Effect: Special
Saving Throw: None

This spell enables the caster to become one with nature in the area, thus being empowered with knowledge of the surrounding territory. For each level of experience of the caster, he can "know" one fact: the ground ahead, left or right; the plants ahead, left or right; the minerals ahead, left or right; the water courses/bodies of water ahead, left or right; the people dwelling ahead, left or right; the general animal population, left or right; the presence of woodland creatures, left or right; etc. The

presence of powerful unnatural creatures can also be detected, as can the general state of the natural setting. The spell is most effective in outdoor settings, operating in a radius of one-half mile for each level of the caster. In natural underground settings—caves, caverns, etc.—the range is limited to 10 yards per caster level. In constructed settings (dungeons and towns), the spell will not function. The DM may limit the casting of this spell to once per month.

Control Winds (Alteration)

Sphere: Weather
Range: 0
Components: V, S
Duration: 1 turn/level
Casting Time: 8
Area of Effect: 40-foot/level radius
Saving Throw: None

By means of a *control winds* spell, the caster is able to alter wind force in the area of effect. For every three levels of experience, the caster can increase or decrease wind force by one level of strength. Wind strengths are as follows:

Wind Force	Miles Per Hour
Light Breeze	2-7
Moderate Breeze	8-18
Strong Breeze	19-31
Gale	32-54
Storm	55-72
Hurricane	73-176

Winds in excess of 19 miles per hour drive small flying creatures (those eagle-sized and under) from the skies, severely affect missile accuracy, and make sailing difficult. Winds in excess of 32 miles per hour drive even man-sized flying creatures from the skies and cause minor ship damage. Winds in excess of 55 miles per hour drive all flying creatures from the skies, uproot trees of small size, knock down wooden structures, tear off roofs, etc., and endanger ships. Winds in excess of 73 miles per hour are of hurricane force.

An "eye" of 40-foot radius, in which the wind is calm, exists around the caster. Note that while the spell can be used in underground places, the eye shrinks one foot for every foot of confinement, if the spell is cast in an area smaller than the area of effect. (For example, if the area of effect is a 360-foot radius, and the space only allows a 350-foot area, the eye shrinks by 10 feet to a 30-foot radius; a space under 320 feet in radius would eliminate the eye and subject the spellcaster to the effects of the wind.)

Once the spell is cast, the wind force increases (or decreases) by 3 miles per hour per round until the maximum (or minimum) speed is attained. The caster, with one round of complete concentration, can stabilize the wind at its current strength, or set it

to increase or decrease, although the rate of the change cannot be altered. The spell remains in force for one turn for each level of experience of the caster. When the spell is exhausted, the force of the wind wanes (or waxes) at the same rate, until it reaches the level it was at before the spell took effect. Another caster can use a *control winds* spell to counter the effects of a like spell up to the limits of his own ability.

Cure Critical Wounds (Necromancy)
Reversible

Sphere: Healing
Range: Touch
Components: V, S
Duration: Permanent
Casting Time: 8
Area of Effect: Creature touched
Saving Throw: None

The *cure critical wounds* spell is a very potent version of the *cure light wounds* spell. The priest lays his hand upon a creature and heals 3d8+3 points of damage from wounds or other damage. The spell does not affect creatures without corporeal bodies, those of extraplanar origin, or those not living.

The reversed spell, *cause critical wounds*, operates in the same fashion as other *cause wounds* spells, requiring a successful touch to inflict the 3d8+3 points of damage. Caused wounds heal via the same methods as do wounds of other sorts.

Dispel Evil (Abjuration)
Reversible

Sphere: Protection, Summoning
Range: Touch
Components: V, S, M
Duration: 1 round/level
Casting Time: 8
Area of Effect: Creature touched
Saving Throw: Neg.

The priest using this spell causes a summoned creature of evil nature, an evil creature from another plane, or a creature summoned by an evil caster, to return to its own plane or place when the caster successfully strikes it in melee combat. (Examples of such creatures are aerial servants, djinn, efreet, elementals, and invisible stalkers.) An evil enchantment (such as a *charm* spell cast by an evil creature) that is subject to a normal *dispel magic* spell can be automatically dispelled by the *dispel evil* spell. Note that this spell lasts for a maximum of one round for each experience level of the caster, or until expended. While the spell is in effect, all creatures that could be affected by it attack with a −7 penalty to their attack rolls when engaging the spellcaster.

The reverse of the spell, *dispel good*, functions against summoned or enchanted creatures of good alignment or creatures that have been sent to aid the cause of good.

The material components for this spell are the priest's religious object and holy (or unholy) water.

Flame Strike (Evocation)

Sphere: Combat
Range: 60 yards
Components: V, S, M
Duration: Instantaneous
Casting Time: 8
Area of Effect: 5-foot radius
by 30-foot-high column
Saving Throw: ½

When the priest calls down a *flame strike* spell, a vertical column of fire roars downward in the exact location called for by the caster. Any creature within the area of effect of a flame strike must roll a saving throw vs. spell. Failure means the creature sustains 6d8 points of damage; otherwise, the damage is halved.

The material component of this spell is a pinch of sulphur.

Insect Plague (Conjuration/Summoning)

Sphere: Combat
Range: 120 yards
Components: V, S, M
Duration: 2 rounds/level
Casting Time: 1 turn
Area of Effect: 180' diameter, 60' high cloud
Saving Throw: None

When this spell is cast by the priest, a horde of creeping, hopping, and flying insects gather and swarm in a thick cloud. (In an environment free of normal insects, the spell fails.) The insects obscure vision, limiting it to 10 feet. Spellcasting within the cloud is impossible. Creatures in the insect plague sustain 1 point of damage for each round they remain within, due to the bites and stings of the insects, regardless of Armor Class. Invisibility is no protection. All creatures with 2 or fewer Hit Dice will automatically move at their fastest possible speed in a random direction until they are more than 240 yards away from the insects. Creatures with fewer than 5 Hit Dice must check morale; failure means they run as described above.

Heavy smoke drives off insects within its bounds. Fire also drives insects away; a wall of fire in a ring shape keeps a subsequently cast insect plague outside its confines, but a fireball simply clears insects from its blast area for one round. A single torch is ineffective against this vast horde of insects. Lightning, cold, or ice are likewise ineffective, while a strong wind that covers the entire plague area disperses the insects and ends

the spell. The plague lasts two rounds for each level of the caster, and thereafter the insects disperse.

The insects swarm in an area that centers around a summoning point determined by the spellcaster; the point can be up to 120 yards away from the priest. The insect plague does not move thereafter for as long as it lasts. Note that the spell can be countered by a *dispel magic* spell.

The material components of this spell are a few grains of sugar, some kernels of grain, and a smear of fat.

Magic Font (Divination)

Sphere: Divination
Range: Touch
Components: V, S, M
Duration: Special
Casting Time: 1 hour
Area of Effect: Special
Saving Throw: None

The spell causes a holy water font to serve as a scrying device. The spell does not function unless the priest is in good standing with his deity. The basin of holy water becomes similar to a *crystal ball*. For each vial of capacity of the basin, the priest may scry for one round, up to a maximum of one hour; thus, the duration of the *magic font* spell is directly related to the size of the holy water receptacle. The DM will know the chances of a character being able to detect scrying.

The priest's holy symbol and the font and its trappings are not consumed by the spell.

Moonbeam (Evocation, Alteration)

Sphere: Sun
Range: 60 yards + 10 yards/level
Components: V, S, M
Duration: 1 round/level
Casting Time: 7
Saving Throw: None
Area of Effect: 5-foot-radius sphere
(plus special)
Saving Throw: None

By means of this spell, the caster is able to cause a beam of soft, pale light to strike downward from overhead and illuminate whatever area he is pointing at. The light is exactly the same as moonlight, so that colors other than shades of black, gray, or white are vague. The spellcaster can easily make the moonbeam move to any area that he can see and point to. This makes the spell an effective way to spotlight something, an opponent, for example. While the *moonbeam* spell does not eliminate all shadows, a creature centered in a moonbeam is most certainly visible. The reflected light from this spell enables dim visual perception 10 yards beyond the area of effect, but it does not shed a telltale glow that would negate

surprise. The light does not adversely affect infravision. The caster can dim the beam to near darkness if desired. The beam has, in addition, all the properties of true moonlight and can induce a lycanthropic change (while in the beam), unless your DM rules otherwise.

The material components are several seeds of any moonseed plant and a piece of opalescent feldspar (moonstone).

Pass Plant (Alteration)

Sphere: Plant
Range: Touch
Components: V, S, M
Duration: Special
Casting Time: 8
Area of Effect: Special
Saving Throw: None

By using this spell, the caster is able to enter a tree and move from inside it to inside another tree of the same type that lies in approximately the direction desired by the spell user and is within the range shown in the following table.

Type of Tree	Range of Area of Effect
Oak	600 yards
Ash	540 yards
Yew	480 yards
Elm	420 yards
Linden	360 yards
deciduous	300 yards
coniferous	240 yards
other	180 yards

The tree entered and that receiving the caster must be of the same type, must both be living, and of girth at least equal to that of the caster. Note that if the caster enters a tree, an ash, for example, and wishes to pass north as far as possible (540 yards), but the only appropriate ash in range is to the south, the caster will pass to the ash in the south. The *pass plant* spell functions so that the movement takes only one round. The caster can, at his option, remain within the receiving tree for a maximum of one round per level of experience. Otherwise, he can step forth immediately. Should no like tree be in range, the caster simply remains within the tree, does not pass elsewhere, and must step forth in the appropriate number of rounds. If the occupied tree is chopped down or burned, the caster is slain if he does not exit before the process is complete.

Plane Shift (Alteration)

Sphere: Astral
Range: Touch
Components: V, S, M
Duration: Permanent
Casting Time: 8
Area of Effect: Creature touched (special)
Saving Throw: Neg.

When the *plane shift* spell is cast, the priest moves himself or some other creature to another plane of existence. The recipient of the spell remains in the new plane until sent forth by some like means. If several persons link hands in a circle, up to eight can be affected by the plane shift at the same time.

The material component of this spell is a small, forked metal rod—the exact size and metal type dictating to which plane of existence (including sub-planes and alternate dimensions) the spell sends the affected creatures. (Your DM will determine specifics regarding how and what planes are reached.)

An unwilling victim must be touched (successful attack roll) in order to be sent; in addition, the creature is also allowed a saving throw. If the saving throw is successful, the effect of the spell is negated. Note that pinpoint accuracy is rarely achieved; arriving a random distance from an intended destination is common.

The metal rod is not expended when the spell is cast. Forked rods keyed to certain planes may be difficult to come by, as decided by the DM.

Quest (Enchantment/Charm)

Sphere: Charm
Range: 60 yards
Components: V, S, M
Duration: Until fulfilled
Casting Time: 8
Area of Effect: 1 creature
Saving Throw: Neg.

The *quest* spell enables the priest to require the affected creature to perform a service and return to the priest with proof that the deed was accomplished. The quest can, for example, require that the creature locate and return some important or valuable object, rescue a notable person, release some creature, capture a stronghold, slay a person, deliver some item, and so forth. If the quest is not properly followed, due to disregard, delay, or perversion, the creature affected by the spell loses 1 from its saving throw rolls for each day of such action. This penalty is not removed until the quest is properly pursued or the priest cancels it. (There are certain circumstances that will temporarily suspend a quest, and others that will discharge or cancel it; your DM will give you appropriate information as the

need to know arises.)

If cast upon an unwilling subject, the victim is allowed a saving throw. However if the person quested agrees to a task, even if the agreement is gained by force or trickery, no saving throw is allowed. If a quest is just and deserved, a creature of the priest's religion cannot avoid it, and any creature of the priest's alignment saves with a −4 penalty to the saving throw, in any case. A quest cannot be dispelled but can be removed by a priest of the same religion or of higher level than the caster. Some artifacts and relics might negate the spell, as can direct intervention by a deity. Likewise, an unjust or undeserved quest grants bonuses to its saving throws, or might even automatically fail!

The material component of this spell is the priest's holy symbol.

Rainbow (Evocation, Alteration)

Sphere: Weather, Sun
Range: 120 yards
Components: V, S, M
Duration: 1 round/level
Casting Time: 7
Area of Effect: Special
Saving Throw: None

In order to cast this spell, the priest must be in sight of a rainbow of any sort, or have a special component (see below). The *rainbow* spell has two applications, and the priest can choose the desired one at the time of casting. These applications are as follows:

Bow: The spell creates a shimmering, multi-layered short composite bow of rainbow hues. It is light and easy to pull, so that any character can use it without penalty for non-proficiency. It is magical: Each of its shimmering missiles is the equivalent of a +2 weapon, including attack and damage bonuses. Magic resistance can negate the effect of any missile fired from the bow. The bow fires seven missiles before disappearing. It can be fired up to four times per round. Each time a missile is fired, one hue leaves the bow, corresponding to the color of arrow that is released. Each color of arrow has the ability to cause double damage to certain creatures, as follows:

Red—fire dwellers/users and fire elementals
Orange—creatures or constructs of clay, sand, earth, stone or similar materials, and earth elementals
Yellow—vegetable opponents (including fungus creatures, shambling mounds, treants, etc.)
Green—aquatic creatures and water elementals
Blue—aerial creatures, electricity-using creatures, and air elementals.
Indigo—acid-using or poison-using creatures

Violet—metallic or regenerating creatures

When the bow is drawn, an arrow of the appropriate color magically appears, nocked and ready. If no color is requested, or a color that has already been used is asked for, then the next arrow (in the order of the spectrum) appears.

Bridge: The caster causes the rainbow to form a seven-hued bridge up to three feet wide per level of the caster. It must be at least 20 feet long and can be as long as 120 yards, according to the caster's desire. It lasts as long as the spell duration or until ordered out of existence by the caster.

The components for this spell are the priest's holy symbol and a vial of holy water. If no rainbow is in the vicinity, the caster can substitute a diamond of not less than 1,000 gp value, specially prepared with *bless* and *prayer* spells while in sight of a rainbow. The holy water and diamond disappear when the spell is cast.

Raise Dead (Necromancy)
Reversible

Sphere: Necromantic
Range: 30 yards
Components: V, S
Duration: Permanent
Casting Time: 1 round
Area of Effect: 1 person
Saving Throw: Special

When the priest casts a *raise dead* spell, he can restore life to a dwarf, gnome, half-elf, halfling, or human (other creatures may be allowed, at the DM's option). The length of time that the person has been dead is of importance, as the priest can raise persons dead only up to a limit of one day for each experience level of the priest (i.e., a 9th-level priest can raise a person who has been dead for up to nine days).

Note that the body of the person must be whole, or otherwise missing parts are still missing when the person is brought back to life. Likewise, other ills, such as poison and disease, are not negated. The raised person must roll a successful resurrection survival check to survive the ordeal (see Table 3: Constitution) and loses 1 point of Constitution. Furthermore, the raised person is weak and helpless in any event, and he needs a minimum of one full day of rest in bed for each day or fraction he was dead. The person has but 1 hit point when raised and must regain the rest by natural healing or curative magic.

Note that a character's starting Constitution is an absolute limit to the number of times the character can be revived by this means.

The somatic component of the spell is a pointed finger.

The reverse of the spell, *slay living*,

grants the victim a saving throw vs. death magic, and if it is successful, the victim sustains damage equal only to that of a *cause serious wounds* spell—i.e., 2d8+1 points. Failure means the victim dies instantly.

Spike Stones (Alteration, Enchantment)

Sphere: Elemental (Earth)
Range: 30 yards
Components: V, S, M
Duration: 3d4 turns + 1/level
Casting Time: 6
Area of Effect: 10-foot square per level, 1 spike per 1-foot sq.
Saving Throw: None

The *spike stones* spell causes rock to shape itself into long, sharp points that tend to blend into the background. It is effective on both natural rock and worked stone. The spike stones serve to impede progress through an area and to inflict damage. If an area is carefully observed, each observer is 25% likely to notice the sharp points of rock. Otherwise, those entering the spell's area of effect suffer 1d4 points of damage per round. The success of each attack is determined as if the caster of the spell were actually engaging in combat. Those entering the area are subject to attack immediately upon setting foot in the area and for each round spent in the area thereafter. The initial step enables the individual to become aware of some problem only if the initial attack succeeds; otherwise movement continues and the spike stones remain unnoticed until damage occurs. Charging or running victims suffer two attacks per round.

Those falling into pits affected by spike stones suffer six such attacks for every 10 feet fallen, each attack having a +2 bonus to the attack roll. In addition, the damage inflicted by each attack increases by +2 for every 10 feet fallen. Finally, the creatures also suffer any normal falling damage.

The material component of this spell is four tiny stalactites.

Transmute Rock to Mud (Alteration)
Reversible

Sphere: Elemental (Earth, Water)
Range: 160 yards
Components: V, S, M
Duration: Special
Casting Time: 8
Area of Effect: 20-foot cube/level
Saving Throw: None

This spell turns natural rock of any sort into an equal volume of mud. If it is cast upon a rock, for example, the rock affected collapses into mud. Magical or enchanted stone is not affected by the spell. The depth of the mud created cannot exceed 10 feet.

Creatures unable to levitate, fly, or otherwise free themselves from the mud sink at the rate of 1/3 of their height per round and eventually suffocate, save for lightweight creatures that could normally pass across such ground. Brush thrown atop the mud can support creatures able to climb on top of it, with the amount required decided by the DM. Creatures large enough to walk on the bottom can move through the area at a rate of 10 feet per round.

The mud remains until a successful *dispel magic* or *transmute mud to rock* spell restores its substance—but not necessarily its form. Evaporation turns the mud to normal dirt at a rate of 1d6 days per 10 cubic feet. The exact time depends on exposure to the sun, wind, and normal drainage.

The reverse, *transmute mud to rock*, hardens normal mud or quicksand into soft stone (sandstone or similar mineral) permanently unless magically changed. Creatures in the mud are allowed a saving throw to escape before the area is hardened to stone. Dry sand is unaffected.

The material components for the spell are clay and water (or sand, lime, and water for the reverse).

True Seeing (Divination)
Reversible

Sphere: Divination
Range: Touch
Components: V, S, M
Duration: 1 round/level
Casting Time: 8
Area of Effect: Creature touched
Saving Throw: None

When the priest employs this spell, he confers upon the recipient the ability to see all things as they actually are. The spell penetrates normal and magical darkness. Secret doors become plain. The exact location of displaced things is obvious. Invisible things become quite visible. Illusions and apparitions are seen through. Polymorphed, changed, or enchanted things are apparent. Even the aura projected by creatures becomes visible, so that alignment can be discerned. Furthermore, the recipient can focus his vision to see into the Ethereal plane or the bordering areas of adjacent planes. The range of vision conferred is 120 feet. *True seeing*, however, does not penetrate solid objects; it in no way confers X-ray vision or its equivalent. Furthermore, the spell effects cannot be further enhanced with known magic.

The spell requires an ointment for the eyes that is made from very rare mushroom powder, saffron, and fat and costs no less than 300 gp per use.

The reverse, *false seeing*, causes the person to see things as they are not: rich is poor, rough is smooth, beautiful is ugly. The oint-

ment for the reverse spell is concocted of oil, poppy dust, and pink orchid essence.

For both spells, the ointment must be aged for 1d6 months.

Wall of Fire (Conjuration/Summoning)

Sphere: Elemental (Fire)
Range: 80 yards
Components: V, S, M
Duration: Special
Casting Time: 8
Area of Effect: Special
Saving Throw: None

The *wall of fire* spell brings forth an immobile, blazing curtain of magical fire of shimmering color—yellow-green or amber (different from the 4th-level wizard version). The spell creates an opaque sheet of flame up to one 20-foot square per level of the spellcaster, or a ring with a radius of up to 10 feet + five feet for every two levels of experience of the wizard, and 20 feet high.

The wall of fire must be cast so that it is vertical with respect to the caster. One side of the wall, selected by the caster, sends forth waves of heat, inflicting 2d4 points of damage upon creatures within 10 feet and 1d4 points of damage upon those within 20 feet. In addition, the wall inflicts 4d4 points of damage, plus 1 point of damage per level of the spellcaster, to any creature passing through it. Creatures especially subject to fire may take additional damage, and undead always take twice normal damage. Note that attempting to directly catch moving creatures with a newly created wall of fire is difficult; a successful saving throw enables the creature to avoid the wall, while its rate and direction of movement determine which side of the created wall it is on. The wall of fire lasts as long as the priest concentrates on maintaining it, or one round per level of experience of the priest in the event he does not wish to concentrate upon it.

The material component of the spell is phosphorus.

Sixth-Level Spells

Aerial Servant
(Conjuration/Summoning)

Sphere: Summoning
Range: 10 yards
Components: V, S
Duration: 1 day/level
Casting Time: 9
Area of Effect: Special
Saving Throw: None

This spell summons an invisible aerial servant to find and bring back an object or creature described to it by the priest. Unlike an elemental, an aerial servant cannot be commanded to fight for the caster. When it is summoned, the priest must have cast a *protection from evil* spell, be within a protective circle, or have a special item used to control the aerial servant. Otherwise, it attempts to slay its summoner and return from whence it came.

The object or creature to be brought must be such as to allow the aerial servant to physically bring it to the priest (an aerial servant can carry at least 1,000 pounds). If prevented, for any reason, from completing the assigned duty, the aerial servant becomes insane and seeks out and attempts to destroy the caster. The aerial servant returns to its own plane whenever the spell lapses, its duty is fulfilled, it is dispelled, the priest releases it, or the priest is slain. The spell lasts for a maximum of one day for each level of experience of the priest who cast it.

If the creature to be fetched cannot detect invisible objects, the aerial servant attacks, automatically gaining surprise. If the creature involved can detect invisible objects, it still suffers a −2 penalty to all surprise rolls caused by the aerial servant. Each round of combat, the aerial servant must roll to attack. When a hit is scored, the aerial servant has grabbed the item or creature it was sent for. A creature with a Strength rating is allowed an evasion roll, equal to twice its *bend bars* chance, to escape the hold. If the creature in question does not have a Strength rating, roll 1d8 for each Hit Die the aerial servant and the creature grabbed have. The higher total is the stronger. Once seized, the creature cannot free itself by Strength or Dexterity and is flown to the priest forthwith.

Animal Summoning III
(Conjuration, Summoning)

Sphere: Animal, Summoning
Range: 100 yards/level
Components: V, S
Duration: Special
Casting Time: 9
Area of Effect: Special
Saving Throw: None

This spell is the same in duration and effect as the 4th-level *animal summoning I* spell, except that up to four animals of no more than 16 Hit Dice each can be summoned, or eight of no more than 8 Hit Dice, or 16 creatures of no more than 4 Hit Dice. Only animals within range of the caster at the time the spell is cast will come. The caster can try three times to summon three different types of animals—e.g., suppose that wild dogs are first summoned to no avail, then hawks are unsuccessfully called, and finally the caster calls for wild horses that may or may not be within summoning range. Your DM will determine the chance of a summoned animal type being within range of the spell. The animals summoned will aid the caster by whatever means they possess, staying until a fight is over, a specific mission is finished, the caster is safe, he sends them away, etc. Only normal or giant animals can be summoned; fantastic animals or monsters cannot be summoned by this spell (no chimerae, dragons, gorgons, manticores, etc.).

Animate Object (Alteration)

Sphere: Creation, Summoning
Range: 30 yards
Components: V, S
Duration: 1 round/level
Casting Time: 9
Area of Effect: 1 cubic foot/level
Saving Throw: None

This powerful spell enables the priest casting it to imbue inanimate objects with mobility and a semblance of life. The animated object, or objects, then attacks whomever or whatever the priest first designates. The animated object can be of any nonmagical material whatsoever—wood, metal, stone, fabric, leather, ceramic, glass, etc. Attempting to animate an object in someone's possession grants that person a saving throw to prevent the spell's effect. The speed of movement of the object depends on its means of propulsion and its weight. A large wooden table would be rather heavy, but its legs would give it speed. A rug could only slither along. A jar would roll. Thus a large stone pedestal would rock forward at 10 feet per round, a stone statue would move at 40 feet per round, a wooden statue 80 feet per round, an ivory stool of light weight would move at

120 feet per round. Slithering movement is about 10 feet to 20 feet per round; rolling is 30 feet to 60 feet per round. The damage caused by the attack of an animated object depends on its form and composition. Light, supple objects can only obscure vision, obstruct movement, bind, trip, smother, etc. Light, hard objects can fall upon or otherwise strike for 1d2 points of damage or possibly obstruct and trip, as do light, supple objects. Hard, medium-weight objects can crush or strike for 2d4 points of damage, while larger and heavier objects may inflict 3d4, 4d4, or even 5d4 points of damage.

The frequency of attack of animated objects depends on their method of locomotion, appendages, and method of attack. This varies from as seldom as once every five melee rounds to as frequently as once per round. The Armor Class of the object animated is basically a function of material and movement ability. Damage depends on the type of weapon and the object struck. A sharp cutting weapon is effective against fabric, leather, wood, and like substances. Heavy smashing and crushing weapons are useful against wood, stone, and metal objects. Your DM will determine all of these factors, as well as how much damage the animated object can sustain before being destroyed. The priest can animate one cubic foot of material for each experience level he has attained. Thus, a 14th-level priest could animate one or more objects whose solid volume did not exceed 14 cubic feet—a large statue, two rugs, three chairs, or a dozen average crocks.

Anti-Animal Shell (Abjuration)

Sphere: Animal, Protection
Range: 0
Components: V, S, M
Duration: 1 turn/level
Casting Time: 1 round
Area of Effect: 20' diameter hemisphere
Saving Throw: None

By casting this spell, the caster brings into being a hemispherical force field that prevents the entrance of any sort of living creature that is wholly or partially animal (not magical or extraplanar). Thus a sprite, a giant, or a chimera would be kept out, but undead or conjured creatures could pass through the shell of force, as could such monsters as aerial servants, imps, quasits, golems, elementals, etc. The anti-animal shell functions normally against crossbreeds, such as cambions, and lasts for one turn for each level of experience the caster has attained. Forcing the barrier against creatures strains and ultimately collapses the field.

The spell requires the caster's holy symbol and a handful of pepper.

Blade Barrier (Evocation)

Sphere: Guardian, Creation
Range: 30 yards
Components: V, S
Duration: 3 rounds/level
Casting Time: 9
Area of Effect: Special
Saving Throw: Special

The priest employs this spell to set up a wall of circling, razor-sharp blades. These whirl and flash around a central point, creating an immobile barrier. Any creature that attempts to pass through the blade barrier suffers 8d8 points of damage in doing so. The plane of rotation of the blades can be horizontal, vertical, or in between. Creatures within the area of the barrier when it is invoked are entitled to a saving throw vs. spell. If this is successful, the blades are avoided and no damage is suffered; the creature escapes the area of the blade barrier by the shortest possible route. The barrier remains for three rounds for every experience level of the priest casting it. The barrier can cover any area from as small as five feet square to as large as 60 feet square.

Conjure Animals
(Conjuration/Summoning)

Sphere: Summoning
Range: 30 yards
Components: V, S
Duration: 2 rounds/level
Casting Time: 9
Area of Effect: Special
Saving Throw: None

The *conjure animals* spell enables the priest to magically create one or more mammals to attack his opponents. The total Hit Dice of the mammals cannot exceed twice his level, if the creature conjured is determined randomly, or his level, if a specific animal type is requested. The DM selects the type of animal that appears if it is randomly called. Thus, a priest of 12th level could randomly conjure two mammals with 12 Hit Dice each, four with 6 Hit Dice each, six with 4 Hit Dice each, eight with 3 Hit Dice each, 12 with 2 Hit Dice each, or 24 with 1 Hit Die each. Count every +1 hit point added to a creature's Hit Dice as ¼ of a Hit Die. Thus a creature with 4+3 Hit Dice equals a 4¾ Hit Dice creature. The conjured animals remain for two rounds for each level of the conjuring priest, or until slain, and they follow the caster's verbal commands. Conjured animals unfailingly attack the priest's opponents, but resist being used for any other purpose; they do not like it, become noticeably more difficult to control, and may refuse any action, break free, or turn on the caster, depending on the nature of the creature and the details

of the situation. The conjured animals disappear when slain.

Conjure Fire Elemental
(Conjuration/Summoning)
Reversible

Sphere: Elemental (Fire)
Range: 80 yards
Components: V, S
Duration: 1 turn/level
Casting Time: 6 rounds
Area of Effect: Special
Saving Throw: None

Upon casting a *conjure fire elemental* spell, the caster opens a special gate to the elemental plane of Fire, and a fire elemental is summoned to the vicinity of the spellcaster. It is 65% likely that a 12 Hit Dice elemental appears, 20% likely that a 16 Hit Dice elemental appears, 9% likely that two to four salamanders appear, 4% likely that an efreeti appears, and 2% likely that a huge fire elemental of 21 to 24 Hit Dice appears. The conjuring caster need not fear that the elemental force summoned will turn on him, so concentration upon the activities of the fire elemental (or other creatures summoned) or protection from the creature is not necessary. The elemental summoned helps the caster however possible, including attacking opponents of the caster. The fire elemental or other creature summoned remains for a maximum of one turn per level of the caster, or until it is slain, sent back by a *dispel magic* spell, the reverse of this spell (*dismiss fire elemental*), or similar magic.

Find the Path (Divination)
Reversible

Sphere: Divination
Range: Touch
Components: V, S, M
Duration: 1 turn/level
Casting Time: 3 rounds
Area of Effect: Creature touched
Saving Throw: None

The recipient of this spell can find the shortest, most direct physical route that he is seeking, be it the way into or out of a locale. The locale can be outdoors or under ground, a trap, or even a *maze* spell. Note that the spell works with respect to locales, not objects or creatures within a locale. Thus, the spell could not find the way to "a forest where a green dragon lives" or to the location of "a hoard of platinum pieces." The location must be in the same plane as the caster.

The spell enables the subject to sense the correct direction that will eventually lead him to his destination, indicating at the appropriate times the exact path to follow (or physical actions to take—for example,

with concentration the spell enables the subject to sense trip wires or the proper word to bypass a glyph). The spell ends when the destination is reached or when one turn for each caster level has elapsed. The spell frees the subject, and those with him, from a *maze* spell in a single round, and will continue to do so as long as the spell lasts.

Note that this divination is keyed to the caster, not his companions, and that, like the *find traps* spell, it does not predict or allow for the actions of creatures.

The spell requires a set of divination counters of the sort favored by the priest—bones, ivory counters, sticks, carved runes, or whatever.

The reverse spell, *lose the path*, makes the creature touched totally lost and unable to find its way for the duration of the spell, although it can be led, of course.

Fire Seeds (Conjuration)

Sphere: Elemental (Fire)
Range: Touch
Components: V, S, M
Duration: Special
Casting Time: 1 round/seed
Area of Effect: Special
Saving Throw: ½

The *fire seeds* spell creates special missiles or timed incendiaries that burn with great heat. The spell can be cast to create either fire seed missiles or fire seed incendiaries, as chosen when the spell is cast.

* Fire seed missiles: This casting turns up to four acorns into special grenade-like missiles that can be hurled up to 40 yards. An attack roll is required to strike the intended target, and proficiency penalties are considered. Each acorn bursts upon striking any hard surface, causing 2d8 points of damage and igniting any combustible materials within a 10-foot diameter of the point of impact. If a successful saving throw vs. spell is made, a creature within the burst area receives only one-half damage, but a creature struck directly suffers full damage (i.e., no saving throw).

* Fire seed incendiaries: This casting turns up to eight holly berries into special incendiaries. The holly berries are most often placed, being too light to make effective missiles (they can be tossed up to six feet away). They burst into flame if the caster is within 40 yards and speaks a word of command. The berries instantly ignite, causing 1d8 points of damage to any creature and igniting any combustible within a five-foot-diameter burst area. Creatures within the area that successfully save vs. spell suffer half damage.

All fire seeds lose their power after a duration equal to one turn per experience level of the caster—e.g., the seeds of a 13th-level caster remain potent for a maximum of

13 turns after their creation.

No other material components beyond acorns or holly berries are needed for this spell.

Forbiddance (Abjuration)

Sphere: Protection
Range: 30 yards
Components: V, S, M
Duration: Permanent
Casting Time: 6 rounds
Area of Effect: One 60-foot cube/level
Saving Throw: Special

This spell can be used to secure a consecrated area (see *DMG*). The spell seals the area from teleportation, plane shifting, and ethereal penetration. At the option of the caster, the ward can be locked by a password, in which case it can be entered only by those speaking the proper words. Otherwise, the effect on those entering the enchanted area is based on their alignment, relative to the caster's. The most severe penalty is used.

Alignment identical: No effect. If password locked, cannot enter area unless password is known (no saving throw).

Alignment different with respect to law and chaos: Save vs. spell to enter the area; if failed, suffer 2d6 points of damage. If password locked, cannot enter unless password is known.

Alignment different with respect to good and evil: Save vs. spell to enter this area; if failed, suffer 4d6 points of damage. If word locked, cannot enter unless password is known. The attempt does cause damage if the save is failed.

Once a saving throw is failed, an intruder cannot enter the forbidden area until the spell ceases. The ward cannot be dispelled by a caster of lesser level than the one who established it. Intruders who enter by rolling successful saving throws feel uneasy and tense, despite their success.

In addition to the priest's holy symbol, components include holy water and rare incenses worth at least 1,000 gp per 60-foot cube. If a password lock is desired, this also requires the burning of rare incenses worth at least 5,000 gp per 60-foot cube.

Heal (Necromancy)
Reversible

Sphere: Healing
Range: Touch
Components: V, S
Duration: Permanent
Casting Time: 1 round
Area of Effect: Creature touched
Saving Throw: None

The very potent *heal* spell enables the priest to wipe away disease and injury in the creature who receives the benefits of the spell. It completely cures all diseases or blindness of the recipient and heals all points of damage suffered due to wounds or injury. It dispels a *feeblemind* spell. It cures those mental disorders caused by spells or injury to the brain. Naturally, the effects can be negated by later wounds, injuries, and diseases.

The reverse, *harm*, infects the victim with a disease and causes loss of all but 1d4 hit points, if a successful touch is inflicted. For creatures that are not affected by the *heal* (or *harm*) spell, see the *cure light wounds* spell.

Heroes' Feast (Evocation)

Sphere: Creation
Range: 10 yards
Components: V, S, M
Duration: 1 hour
Casting Time: 1 turn
Area of Effect: 1 individual/level
Saving Throw: None

This spell enables the priest to bring forth a great feast that serves as many creatures as the priest has levels of experience. The spell creates a magnificent table, chairs, service, and all the necessary food and drink. The feast takes one full hour to consume, and the beneficial effects do not set in until after this hour is over. Those partaking of the feast are cured of all diseases, are immune to poison for 12 hours, and are healed of 1d4 + 4 points of damage after imbibing the nectar-like beverage that is part of the feast. The ambrosia-like food that is consumed is equal to a *bless* spell that lasts for 12 hours. Also, during this same period, the people who consumed the feast are immune to fear, hopelessness, and panic. If the feast is interrupted for any reason, the spell is ruined and all effects of the spell are negated.

The material components of the spell are the priest's holy symbol and specially fermented honey taken from the cells of bee larvae destined for royal status.

Liveoak (Enchantment)

Sphere: Plant
Range: Touch
Components: V, S, M
Duration: 1 day/level
Casting Time: 1 turn
Area of Effect: 1 oak tree
Saving Throw: None

This spell enables the caster to charm a healthy oak tree (or other type if the DM allows) to cause it to serve as a protector. The spell can be cast on a single tree at a time. While a *liveoak* spell cast by a particular caster is in effect, he cannot cast another such spell. The tree upon which the spell is cast must be within 10 feet of the caster's dwelling place, within a place sacred to the caster, or within 100 yards of something that the caster wishes to guard or protect.

The *liveoak* spell can be cast upon a healthy tree of small, medium, or large size, according to desire and availability. A triggering phrase of up to a maximum of one word per level of the spellcaster is then placed upon the targeted oak; for instance, "Attack any persons who come near without first saying 'sacred mistletoe'" is an 11-word trigger phrase that could be used by a caster of 11th level or higher casting the spell. The *liveoak* spell triggers the tree into animating as a treant of equivalent size, an Armor Class of 0 and with two attacks per round, but with only a 30-foot-per-round movement rate.

Tree Size	Height	Hit Dice	Damage per Attack
Small	12'-14'	7-8	2d8
Medium	16'-19'	9-10	3d6
Large	20'-23' +	11-12	4d6

A tree enchanted by this spell radiates a magical aura (if checked for), and can be returned to normal by a successful casting of a *dispel magic* spell, or upon the desire of the caster who enchanted it. If dispelled, the tree takes root immediately. If released by the caster, it tries to return to its original location before taking root. Damage to the tree can be healed with a *plant growth* spell, which restores 3d4 points of damage. A *plant growth* spell used in this fashion does not increase the size or hit points of the liveoak beyond the original value.

The caster needs his holy symbol to cast this spell.

Part Water (Alteration)

Sphere: Elemental (Water)
Range: 20 yards/level
Components: V, S, M
Duration: 1 turn/level
Casting Time: 1 turn
Area of Effect: Special
Saving Throw: None

By employing a part water spell, the priest is able to cause water or similar liquid to move apart, thus forming a trough. The depth and length of the trough created by the spell depends on the level of the priest. A trough three feet deep per caster level, by 30 yards wide, by 20 yards long per level is created. Thus at 12th level, the priest would part water 36 feet deep by 30 yards wide by 240 yards long. The trough remains as long as the spell lasts or until the priest who cast it opts to end its effects. Existing currents appear to flow through the parted water, although swimming creatures and physical objects such as boats do not enter the rift without strenuous and deliberate effort. If cast underwater, this spell creates an air cylinder of appropriate length and diameter. If cast directly on a water elemental or other water-based creature, the creature receives 4d8 points of damage and must roll a successful saving throw vs. spell or flee in panic for 3d4 rounds.

The material component of this spell is the priest's holy symbol.

Speak With Monsters (Alteration)

Sphere: Divination
Range: 30 yards
Components: V, S
Duration: 2 round/level
Casting Time: 9
Area of Effect: The caster
Saving Throw: None

When cast, the *speak with monsters* spell enables the priest to converse with any type of creature that has any form of communicative ability (including empathic, tactile, pheromonic, etc.). That is, the monster understands, in its own language or equivalent, the intent of what is said to it by the priest and vice versa. The creature thus spoken to is checked by your DM in order to determine reaction. All creatures of the same type as that chosen by the priest can likewise understand if they are within range. The priest can speak to different types of creatures during the spell duration, but he must speak separately to each type. The spell lasts for two rounds per caster level.

Stone Tell (Divination)

Sphere: Elemental (Earth), Divination
Range: Touch
Components: V, S, M
Duration: 1 turn
Casting Time: 1 turn
Area of Effect: 1 cubic yard of stone
Saving Throw: None

When the priest casts a *stone tell* spell upon an area, the very stones speak and relate to the caster who or what has touched them as well as telling what is covered, concealed, or simply behind them. The stones relate complete descriptions, if asked. Note that a stone's perspective, perception, and knowledge may hinder this divination; such details, if any, are decided by the DM.

The material components for this spell are a drop of mercury and a bit of clay.

Transmute Water to Dust (Alteration)
Reversible

Sphere: Elemental (Water, Earth)
Range: 60 yards
Components: V, S, M
Duration: Permanent
Casting Time: 8
Area of Effect: 1 cubic yard/level
Saving Throw: Special

When this spell is cast, the subject area instantly undergoes a change from liquid to powdery dust. Note that if the water is already muddy, the area of effect is doubled, while if wet mud is present, the area of effect is quadrupled. If water remains in contact with the transmuted dust, the former quickly permeates the latter, turning the dust into silty mud, if a sufficient quantity of water exists to do so, otherwise soaking or dampening the dust accordingly.

Only the liquid actually in the area of effect at the moment of spellcasting is affected. Potions that contain water as a component part are rendered useless. Living creatures are unaffected, except for those native to the elemental plane of Water. Such creatures must roll a successful saving throws vs. death or be slain; however, only one such creature can be affected by any single casting of this spell, regardless of the creature's size or the size of the spell's area of effect.

The reverse of this spell is simply a very high-powered *create water* spell that requires a pinch of normal dust as an additional material component.

For either usage of the spell, other components required are diamond dust of at least 500 gp value, a bit of seashell, and the caster's holy symbol.

Transport Via Plants (Alteration)

Sphere: Plant
Range: Touch
Components: V, S
Duration: Special
Casting Time: 4
Area of Effect: Special
Saving Throw: None

By means of this spell, the caster is able to enter any large plant (human-sized or larger) and pass any distance to a plant of the same species in a single round, regardless of the distance, separating the two. The entry plant must be alive. The destination plant need not be familiar to the caster, but it also must be alive. If the caster is uncertain of the destination plant, he need merely determine direction and distance, and the *transport via plants* spell moves him as close as possible to the desired location. There is a basic 20% chance, reduced by 1% per level of experience of the caster, that the transport delivers the caster to a similar species of plant from 1 to 100 miles away from the desired destination plant. If a particular destination plant is desired, but the plant is not living, the spell fails and the caster must come forth from the entrance plant within 24 hours. Note that this spell does not function with plant-like creatures—e.g., shambling mounds, treants, etc. The destruction of an occupied plant slays the caster (see the *plant door* spell).

Turn Wood (Alteration)

Sphere: Plant
Range: 0
Components: V, S
Duration: 1 round/level
Casting Time: 9
Area of Effect: 120-foot-wide path,
        20 feet long/level
Saving Throw: None

When this spell is cast, waves of force roll forth from the caster, moving in the direction he faces, and causing all wooden objects in the path of the spell to be pushed away from the caster to the limit of the area of effect. Wooden objects above three inches in diameter that are fixed firmly are not affected, but loose objects (movable mantles, siege towers, etc.) move back. Objects under three inches in diameter that are fixed splinter and break, and the pieces move with the wave of force. Thus, objects such as wooden shields, spears, wooden weapon shafts and hafts, and arrows and bolts are pushed back, dragging those carrying them with them. If a spear is planted in order to prevent this forced movement, it splinters. Even magical items with wooden sections are turned, although an anti-magic shell blocks the effects. A successful *dispel magic* spell ends the effect. Otherwise, the *turn wood* spell lasts for one round for each experience level of the caster.

The waves of force continue to sweep down the set path for the spell's duration, pushing back wooden objects in the area of effect at a rate of 40 feet per melee round. The length of the path is 20 feet per level of the caster, thus a 14th-level caster casts a *turn wood* spell with an area of effect 120 feet wide by 280 feet long, and the spell lasts for 14 rounds. Note that after casting the spell, the path is set and the caster can then do other things or go elsewhere without affecting the spell's power.

Wall of Thorns
(Conjuration/Summoning)

Sphere: Plant, Creation
Range: 80 yards
Components: V, S
Duration: 1 turn/level
Casting Time: 9
Area of Effect: One 10-foot cube/level
Saving Throw: None

The *wall of thorns* spell creates a barrier of very tough, pliable, tangled brush bearing needle-sharp thorns as long as a person's finger. Any creature breaking through (or crashing into) the wall of thorns suffers 8 points of damage, plus an additional amount of damage equal to the creature's AC. Negative ACs subtract from the base 8 points of damage, but no adjustment is made for Dexterity. Any creature within the area of effect of the spell when it is cast crashes into the *wall of thorns*, and must break through to move. The damage is based on each 10-foot thickness of the barrier.

If the wall of thorns is chopped at, it takes at least four turns to cut a path through a 10-foot thickness. Normal fire cannot harm the barrier, but magical fires burn away the barrier in two turns, creating a wall of fire effect while doing so (see *wall of fire* spell). In this case, the cool side of the wall is that closest to the caster of the thorn wall.

The nearest edge of the wall of thorns appears up to 80 yards distant from the caster, as he desires. The spell lasts for one turn for each level of experience of the caster, covers one 10-foot cube per level of the caster in whatever shape the caster desires. Thus a 14th-level caster could create a wall of thorns up to 70 feet long by 20 feet high (or deep) by 10 feet deep (or high), a 10-foot-high by 10-foot-wide by 140-foot-long wall to block a dungeon passage, or any other sort of shape that suited his needs. The caster can also create a wall of five-foot thickness, which inflicts half damage but can be doubled in one of the other dimensions. Note that those with the ability to pass through overgrown areas are not hindered by this barrier. The caster can dismiss the barrier on command.

Weather Summoning
(Conjuration/Summoning)

Sphere: Weather
Range: 0
Components: V, S
Duration: Special
Casting Time: 1 turn
Area of Effect: Special
Saving Throw: None

By this spell, the caster calls forth weather appropriate to the climate and season of the area he is in at the time. Thus, in spring a tornado, thunderstorm, cold, sleet storm, or hot weather could be summoned. In summer a torrential rain, heat wave, hail storm, etc., can be called for. In autumn, hot or cold weather, fog, sleet, etc., could be summoned. Winter enables great cold, blizzard, or thaw conditions to be summoned. Hurricane-force winds can be summoned near coastal regions in the late winter or early spring. The summoned weather is not under the control of the caster. It might last but a single turn, in the case of a tornado, or for hours or even days in other cases. The area of effect likewise varies from about one square mile to 100 square miles. Note that several casters can act in concert to greatly affect weather, controlling winds, and working jointly to summon very extreme weather conditions.

Within four turns after the spell is cast, the trend of the weather to come is apparent—e.g., clearing skies, gusts of warm or hot air, a chill breeze, overcast skies, etc. Summoned weather arrives 1d12+5 turns after the spell is cast. Note that the new weather condition cannot be changed by the caster once it has been summoned. Once the weather is fully summoned, it cannot be dispelled. If the summoning is successfully dispelled before it has been completed, the weather slowly reverts to its original condition.

Word of Recall (Alteration)

Sphere: Summoning
Range: 0
Components: V
Duration: Special
Casting Time: 1
Area of Effect: Special
Saving Throw: None

The *word of recall* spell takes the priest instantly back to his sanctuary when the word is uttered. The sanctuary must be specifically designated in advance by the priest and must be a well-known place. The actual point of arrival is a designated area no larger than 10' × 10'. The priest can be transported any distance, from above or below ground. Transportation by the *word of recall* spell is safe within a plane, but for each plane the priest is removed, there is a

10% cumulative chance that the priest is irrevocably lost. The priest is able to transport, in addition to himself, 25 pounds of weight per experience level. Thus, a 15th-level priest could transport his person and an additional 375 pounds weight. This extra matter can be equipment, treasure, or even living material, such as another person. Exceeding this limit causes the spell to fail. Note that unusually strong physical fields (e.g., magnetic, gravitational) or magical forces can, at the DM's option, make the use of this spell hazardous or impossible.

Seventh-Level Spells

Animate Rock (Alteration)

Sphere: Elemental (Earth)
Range: 40 yards
Components: V, S, M
Duration: 1 round/level
Casting Time: 1 round
Area of Effect: 2 cubic feet/level
Saving Throw: None

By employing an *animate rock* spell, the caster causes a stone object of up to the indicated size to move (see the 6th-level *animate object* spell.) The animated stone object must be separate (not a part of a huge boulder or the like). It follows the desire of the caster—attacking, breaking objects, blocking—while the magic lasts. It has no intelligence or volition of its own, but it follows instructions exactly as spoken. Note that only one set of instructions for one single action (the whole being simply worded and very brief—12 words or so) can be given to the animated rock. The rock remains animated for one round per experience level of the caster. The volume of rock that can be animated is also based on the experience level of the caster—two cubic feet of stone per level—e.g., 24 cubic feet, a mass of about man-sized, at 12th level.

While the exact details of the animated rock are decided by the DM, its Armor Class is no worse than 5, and it has 1d3 hit

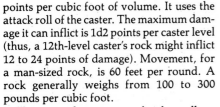

points per cubic foot of volume. It uses the attack roll of the caster. The maximum damage it can inflict is 1d2 points per caster level (thus, a 12th-level caster's rock might inflict 12 to 24 points of damage). Movement, for a man-sized rock, is 60 feet per round. A rock generally weighs from 100 to 300 pounds per cubic foot.

The material components for the spell are a stone and drop of the caster's blood.

Astral Spell (Alteration)

Sphere: Astral
Range: Touch
Components: V, S
Duration: Special
Casting Time: ¹/₂ hour
Area of Effect: Special
Saving Throw: None

By means of the *astral* spell, a priest is able to project his astral body into the Astral plane, leaving his physical body and material possessions behind on the Prime Material plane. As the Astral plane touches upon the first levels of all the outer planes, the priest can travel astrally to the first level of any of these outer planes as he wills. The priest then leaves the Astral plane, forming a body on the plane of existence he has chosen to enter. It is also possible to travel astrally anywhere in the Prime Material plane by means of the *astral* spell (however, a second body cannot be formed on the Prime Material plane; see following).

As a general rule, a person astrally projected can be seen only by creatures on the Astral plane. The astral body is connected at all times to the material body by a silvery cord. If the cord is broken, the affected person is killed, astrally and materially, but generally only the psychic wind can cause the cord to break. When a second body is formed on a different plane, the silvery cord remains invisibly attached to the new body. If the second body or astral form is slain, the cord simply returns to the caster's body where the body rests on the Prime Material plane, reviving it from its state of suspended animation. Although astral projections are able to function on the Astral plane, their actions affect only creatures existing on the Astral plane; a physical body must be materialized on other planes.

The spell lasts until the priest desires to end it, or until it is terminated by some outside means (such as a *dispel magic* spell or destruction of the priest's body on the Prime Material plane [which kills the priest]). The priest can project the astral forms of up to seven other creatures with himself by means of the *astral* spell, providing the creatures are linked in a circle with the priest. These fellow travelers are dependent upon the priest and can be stranded if something happens to the priest. Travel in the Astral plane

can be slow or fast, according to the priest's desire. The ultimate destination arrived at is subject to the desire of the priest.

Changestaff (Evocation, Enchantment)

Sphere: Plant, Creation
Range: Touch
Components: V, S, M
Duration: Special
Casting Time: 4
Area of Effect: The caster's staff
Saving Throw: None

By means of this spell, the caster is able to change a specially prepared staff into a treant-like creature of the largest size (about 24 feet tall). When the priest plants the end of the staff in the ground and speaks a special command and invocation, the staff turns into a treant-like creature with 12 Hit Dice, 40 hit points, and Armor Class 0. It attacks twice per round, inflicting 4d6 points of damage with every successful attack. The staff-treant defends the caster and obeys any spoken commands. However, it is by no means a true treant; it cannot converse with actual treants or control trees. The transformation lasts either for as many turns as the caster has experience levels, until the caster commands the staff to return to its true form, or until the staff is destroyed, whichever occurs first. If the staff-treant is reduced to 0 hit points or less, it crumbles to a sawdust-like powder and the staff is destroyed. Otherwise, the staff can be used again after 24 hours and the staff-treant is at full strength.

To cast a *changestaff* spell, the caster must have either his holy symbol or leaves (ash, oak, or yew) of the same sort as the staff.

The staff for the *changestaff* spell must be specially prepared. The staff must be a sound limb cut from an ash, oak, or yew tree struck by lightning no more than 24 hours before the limb is cut. The limb must then be cured by sun drying and special smoke for 28 days. Then it must be shaped, carved, and polished for another 28 days. The caster cannot adventure or engage in other strenuous activity during either of these periods. The finished staff, engraved with woodland scenes, is then rubbed with the juice of holly berries, and the end of it is thrust into the earth of the caster's grove while he casts a *speak with plant* spell, calling upon the staff to assist in time of need. The item is then charged with a magic that will last for many changes from staff to treant and back again.

Chariot Of Sustarre (Evocation)

Sphere: Elemental (Fire), Creation
Range: 10 yards
Components: V, S, M
Duration: 12 hours
Casting Time: 1 turn
Area of Effect: Special
Saving Throw: None

When this spell is cast, it brings forth a large, flaming chariot pulled by two fiery horses from the elemental plane of Fire. These appear in a clap of thunder amid a cloud of smoke. The vehicle moves at 24 on the ground, 48 flying, and can carry the caster and up to seven other creatures of man-size or less (the passengers must be touched by the caster to protect them from the flames of the chariot). Creatures other than the caster and his designated passengers sustain 2d4 points of fire damage each round if they come within five feet of the horses or chariot. Such creatures suffer no damage if they evade the area by rolling successful saving throws vs. petrification, with Dexterity adjustments.

The caster controls the chariot by verbal command, causing the flaming steeds to stop or go, walk, trot, run or fly, and turn left or right as he desires. Note that the chariot of Sustarre is a physical manifestation and can sustain damage. The vehicle and steeds are struck only by magical weapons or by water (one quart of which inflicts 1 point of damage), they are Armor Class 2, and each requires 30 points of damage to dispel. Naturally, fire has absolutely no effect upon either the vehicle or its steeds, but magical fires other than those of the chariot can affect the riders. Other spells, such as a successful *dispel magic* or *holy word*, will force the chariot back to its home plane, without its passengers. The chariot can be summoned only once per week.

The material components are a small piece of wood, two holly berries, and a fire source at least equal to a torch.

Confusion (Enchantment/Charm)

Sphere: Charm
Range: 80 yards
Components: V, S, M
Duration: 1 round/level
Casting Time: 1 round
Area of Effect: 1d4 creatures within a 40' by 40' square
Saving Throw: Special

This spell causes confusion in one or more creatures within the area, creating indecision and the inability to take effective action. The spell affects 1d4 creatures, plus one creature per two caster levels. Thus, seven to ten creatures can be affected by a 12th- or 13th-level caster, eight to 11 by a 14th- or 15th-level caster, etc. These creatures are allowed saving throws vs. spell with −2 penalties, adjusted for Wisdom. Those successfully saving are unaffected by the spell. Confused creatures react as follows (roll 1d10):

D10
Roll Reaction
1 Wander away (unless prevented) for duration of spell
2-6 Stand confused one round (then roll again)
7-9 Attack nearest creature for one round (then roll again)
10 Act normally for one round (then roll again)

The spell lasts one round for each level of the caster. Those who fail their saving throws are checked by the DM for actions each round, for the duration of the spell, or until the "wander away for the duration of the spell" result occurs.

Wandering creatures move as far from the caster as possible in their most typical mode of movement (characters walk, fish swim, bats fly, etc.). This is not panicked flight. Wandering creatures also have a 50% chance of using any special innate movement abilities (plane shift, burrowing, flight, etc.). Saving throws and actions are checked at the beginning of each round. Any confused creature that is attacked perceives the attacker as an enemy and acts according to its basic nature.

The material component of this spell is a set of three nut shells.

Note: If there are many creatures involved, the DM may decide to assume average results. For example, if there are 16 orcs affected and 25% could be expected to successfully roll the saving throw, then four are assumed to have succeeded, one wanders away, four attack the nearest creature, six stand confused and the last acts normally but must check next round. Since the orcs are not near the party, the DM decides that two who are supposed to attack the nearest creature attack each other, one attacks an orc that saved, and one attacks a confused orc, which strikes back. The next round, the base is 11 orcs, since four originally saved and one wandered off. Another one wanders off, five stands confused, four attack, and one acts normally.

Conjure Earth Elemental
(Conjuration/Summoning)
Reversible

Sphere: Elemental (Earth), Summoning
Range: 40 yards
Components: V, S
Duration: 1 turn/level
Casting Time: 1 turn
Area of Effect: Special
Saving Throw: None

A caster who performs a *conjure earth elemental* spell summons an earth elemental to do his bidding. The elemental is 60% likely to have 12 Hit Dice, 35% likely to have 16 Hit Dice, and 5% likely have 21 to to 24 Hit Dice (20 + 1d4). Furthermore, the caster needs but to command it, and it does as desired, for the elemental regards the caster as a friend to be obeyed. The elemental remains until destroyed, dispelled, sent away by dismissal or a *holy word* spell (see the *conjure fire elemental* spell), or the spell duration expires.

Control Weather (Alteration)

Sphere: Weather
Range: 0
Components: V, S, M
Duration: 4d12 hours
Casting Time: 1 turn
Area of Effect: 4d4 square miles
Saving Throw: None

The *control weather* spell enables a priest to change the weather in the local area. The spell affects the weather for 4d12 hours in an area of 4d4 square miles. It requires one turn to cast the spell, and an additional 1d4 turns for the effects of the spell to be felt. The current weather conditions are decided by the DM, depending on the climate and season. Weather conditions have three components: precipitation, temperature, and wind. The spell can change these conditions according to the following chart:

The upper-case headings represent existing weather conditions. The lower-case headings below each upper-case heading are the new conditions to which the caster can change the existing conditions. Furthermore, the caster can control the direction of the wind. For example, a day that is clear, warm, and with moderate wind can be controlled to become hazy, hot, and calm. Contradictions are not possible—fog and strong wind, for example. Multiple *control weather* spells can be used only in succession.

The material components for this spell are the priest's religious symbol, incense, and prayer beads or similar prayer object. Obviously, this spell functions only in areas where there are appropriate climatic conditions.

If Weather is a major sphere for the priest (as it is for druids), duration and area are doubled, and the caster can change the prevailing weather by *two* places (e.g., he can cause precipitation to go from partly cloudy to heavy sleet, temperature to go from cool to arctic, and wind to go from calm to strong).

Creeping Doom
(Conjuration/Summoning)

Sphere: Animal, Summoning
Range: 0
Components: V, S
Duration: 4 rounds/level
Casting Time: 1 round
Area of Effect: Special
Saving Throw: None

When the caster utters the spell of *creeping doom*, he calls forth a mass of from 500 to 1,000 ([1d6 +4] × 100) venomous, biting and stinging arachnids, insects, and myriapods. This carpet-like mass swarms in an area 20 feet square. Upon command from the caster, the swarm creeps forth at 10 feet per round toward any prey within 80 yards, moving in the direction in which the caster

Precipitation	Temperature	Wind
CLEAR WEATHER	HOT	CALM
Very clear	Sweltering heat	Dead calm
Light clouds or hazy	Warm	Light wind
PARTLY CLOUDY	WARM	Moderate wind
Clear weather	Hot	MODERATE WIND
Cloudy	Cool	Calm
Mist/Light rain/small hail	COOL	Strong wind
Sleet/Light snow	Warm	STRONG WIND
CLOUDY	Cold	Moderate wind
Partly cloudy	COLD	Gale
Deep clouds	Cool	GALE
Fog	Arctic cold	Strong wind
Heavy rain/large hail		Storm
Driving sleet/heavy snow		STORM
		Gale
		Hurricane-typhoon

commands. The creeping doom slays any creature subject to normal attacks, as each of the small horrors inflicts 1 point of damage (each then dies after its attack), so that up to 1,000 points of damage can be inflicted on creatures within the path of the creeping doom. If the creeping doom goes more than 80 yards away from the summoner, it loses 50 of its number for each 10 yards beyond 80 yards (e.g., at 100 yards, its number has shrunk by 100). There are a number of ways to thwart or destroy the creatures forming the swarm. The solutions are left to the imaginations of players and DMs.

Earthquake (Alteration)

Sphere: Elemental (Earth)
Range: 120 yards
Components: V, S, M
Duration: 1 round
Casting Time: 1 turn
Area of Effect: 5-foot diameter/level
Saving Throw: None

When this spell is cast by a priest, a local tremor of fairly high strength rips the ground. The shock is over in one round. The earthquake affects all terrain, vegetation, structures, and creatures in its area of effect. The area of effect of the *earthquake* spell is circular, with a diameter of five feet for every experience level of the priest casting it. Thus a 20th-level priest casts an *earthquake* spell with a 100-foot-diameter area of effect.

Solidly built structures with foundations reaching down to bedrock sustain one-half damage; one-quarter damage if they score above 50% on a saving throw. An earth elemental opposed to the caster in the area of effect can negate 10% to 100% (roll 1d10, 0 = 100%) of the effect. Other magical protections and wards allowed by the DM may also reduce or negate this effect. If cast undersea, this spell may, at the discretion of the DM, create a tsunami or tidal wave.

The material components for this spell are a pinch of dirt, a piece of rock, and a lump of clay.

Exaction (Evocation, Alteration)

Sphere: Charm, Summoning
Range: 10 yards
Components: V, S, M
Duration: Special
Casting Time: 1 round
Area of Effect: 1 creature
Saving Throw: None

When this spell is employed, the priest confronts some powerful creature from another plane (including devas and other powerful minions, for instance, but not demigods or deities of any sort) and requires of it some duty or quest. A creature of an alignment opposed to the priest (e.g., evil if the priest is good, chaotic if the priest is lawful) cannot be ordered around unless it is willing. Note that an absolute (true) neutral creature is effectively opposed to both good and evil, and both law and chaos.

The spellcaster must know something about the creature to exact service from it, or else he must offer some fair trade in return for the service. That is, if the priest is aware that the creature has received some favor from someone of the priest's alignment, then the *exaction* spell can name this as cause; if no balancing reason for service is known, then some valuable gift or service must be pledged in return for the exaction. The service exacted must be reasonable with respect to the past or promised favor or reward, and with the being's effort and risk. The spell then acts, subject to a magic resistance roll, as a quest upon the being that is to perform the required service. Immediately upon completion of the service, the being is transported to the vicinity of the priest, and the priest must then and there return the promised reward, whether it is irrevocable cancellation of a past debt or the giving of some service or other material reward. After this is done, the creature is instantly freed to return to its own plane.

The DM adjudicates when an equitable arrangement has been reached. If the caster requests too much, the creature is free to depart or to attack the priest (as if the agreement were breached) according to its nature. If circumstances leave the situation unbalanced (for example, the creature dies while achieving a result that was not worth the creature dying), then this might create a debt owed by the caster to the creature's surviving kith and kin, making the caster vulnerable to a future *exaction* from that quarter. Agreeing to a future exaction or release in the event of catastrophic failure or death are common caster pledges in securing an exaction.

Failure to fulfill the promise to the letter results in the priest being subject to exaction by the subject creature or by its master, liege, etc., at the very least. At worst, the creature may attack the reneging priest without fear of any of his spells affecting it, for the priest's failure to live up to the bargain gives the creature total immunity from the priest's spell powers.

The material components of this spell are the priest's holy symbol, some matter or substance from the plane of the creature from whom an exaction is expected, and knowledge of the creature's nature or actions that is written out on a parchment that is burned to seal the pledge.

Earthquake Effects:

TERRAIN

	Cave or cavern	—Collapses roof
	Cliffs	—Crumble, causing landslide
	Ground	—Cracks open, causing the following fractions of creatures to fall in and die: —Size S: 1 in 4 —Size M: 1 in 6 —Size L: 1 in 8
	Marsh	—Drains water off to form muddy, rough ground.
	Tunnel	—Caves in

VEGETATION

	Small growth	—No effect
	Trees	—1 in 3 are uprooted and fall

STRUCTURES

	All structures	—Sustain 5d12 points of structural damage; those suffering full damage are thrown down in rubble.

CREATURES

	See "TERRAIN" entry	

Fire Storm (Evocation)
Reversible

Sphere: Elemental (Fire)
Range: 160 yards
Components: V, S
Duration: 1 round
Casting Time: 1 round
Area of Effect: 20-foot cube/level, mini-
mum 16 10-foot cubes
Saving Throw: ½

When a *fire storm* spell is cast, the whole
area is shot through with sheets of roaring
flame that equal a *wall of fire* spell in effect.
Creatures within the area of fire and 10 feet
or less from the edge of the affected area
receive 2d8 points of damage plus additional damage equal to the caster's level (2d8 +
1/level). Creatures that roll successful saving throws vs. spell suffer only one-half
damage. The damage is inflicted each round
the creature stays in the area of effect. The
area of effect is equal to two 10' x 10' cubes
per level of the caster—e.g., a 13th-level
caster can cast a fire storm measuring 130' x
20' x 10'. The height of the storm is 10 or 20
feet; the balance of its area must be in length
and width.

The reverse spell, *fire quench*, smothers
twice the area of effect of a fire storm with
respect to normal fires, and the normal area
of effect with respect to magical fires. Fire-
based creatures, such as elementals, salamanders, etc., of less than demigod status
have a a 5% chance per experience level of
the caster of being extinguished. If cast only
against a *flametongue* sword, the sword
must roll a successful saving throw vs.
crushing blow or be rendered nonmagical.
Such a sword in the possession of a creature
first receives the creature's saving throw,
and if this is successful, the second saving
throw is automatically successful.

Gate (Conjuration/Summoning)

Sphere: Summoning
Range: 30 yards
Components: V, S
Duration: Special
Casting Time: 5
Area of Effect: Special
Saving Throw: None

Casting a *gate* spell has two effects: it
causes an interdimensional connection
between the plane of existence the priest is in
and the plane in which dwells a specific
being of great power. The result of this connection is that the sought-after being can
step through the gate or portal, from its
plane to that of the priest. Uttering the spell
attracts the attention of the dweller on the
other plane. When casting the spell, the
priest must name the entity he desires to
make use of the gate and to come to his aid.

There is a 100% chance that *something*
steps through the gate. The actions of the
being that comes through depend on many
factors, including the alignment of the
priest, the nature of those accompanying
him, and who or what opposes or threatens
the priest. Your DM will decide the exact
result of the spell, based on the creature
called, the desires of the caster and the needs
of the moment. The being gated in either
returns immediately or remains to take
action. Casting this spell ages the priest five
years.

Holy Word (Conjuration/Summoning)
Reversible

Sphere: Combat
Range: 0
Components: V
Duration: Special
Casting Time: 1
Area of Effect: 30-foot radius
Saving Throw: None

Uttering a *holy word* spell creates magic
of tremendous power. It drives off evil creatures from other planes, forcing them to
return to their own planes of existence, provided the speaker is in his home plane. Creatures so banished cannot return for at least a
day. The spell further affects creatures of
differing alignment as shown on the following table:

Effects of Holy Word

Creature's Hit Dice or Level	General	Move	Attack Dice	Spells
Less than 4	Kills	–	–	–
4 to 7 +	Paralyzes 1d4 turns	–	–	–
8 to 11 +	Slows 2d4 rounds	–50%	–4*	–
12 or more	Deafens 1d4 rounds	–25%	–2	50% chance of failure

* Slowed creatures attack only on even-numbered rounds until the effect wears off.

Affected creatures are those within the
30-foot-radius area of effect, which is centered on the priest casting the spell. The side
effects are negated for deafened or silenced
creatures, but such are still driven off if
other-planar.

The reverse, *unholy word*, operates
exactly the same way but affects creatures
of good alignment.

Regenerate (Necromancy)
Reversible

Sphere: Necromantic
Range: Touch
Components: V, S, M
Duration: Permanent
Casting Time: 3 rounds
Area of Effect: Creature touched
Saving Throw: None

When a *regenerate* spell is cast, body
members (fingers, toes, hands, feet, arms,
legs, tails, or even the heads of multi-headed
creatures), bones, and organs grow back.
The process of regeneration requires but one
round if the severed member(s) is (are)
present and touching the creature, 2d4 turns
otherwise. The creature must be living to
receive the benefits of this spell. If the severed member is not present, or if the injury
is older than one day per caster level, the
recipient must roll a successful system shock
check to survive the spell.

The reverse, *wither*, causes the member
or organ touched to shrivel and cease functioning in one round, dropping off into dust
in 2d4 turns. Creatures must be touched for
the harmful effect to occur.

The material components of this spell are
a prayer device and holy water (or unholy
water for the reverse).

Reincarnate (Necromancy)

Sphere: Necromantic
Range: Touch
Components: V, S
Duration: Permanent
Casting Time: 1 turn
Area of Effect: Person touched
Saving Throw: None

With this spell, the priest can bring back a
dead person in another body, if death
occurred no more than one week before the
casting of the spell. Reincarnation does not
require any saving throw, system shock, or
resurrection survival roll. The corpse is
touched, and a new incarnation of the person appears in the area in 1d6 turns. The
person reincarnated recalls the majority of
his former life and form, but the character
class, if any, of the new incarnation might

be very different indeed. The new incarnation is determined on the following table or by DM choice. If a player character race is indicated, the character must be created. At the DM's option, certain special (expensive) incenses can be used that may increase the chance for a character to return as a specific race or species. A *wish* spell can restore a reincarnated character to its original form and status.

D100 Roll	Incarnation
01–03	Badger
04–08	Bear, black
09–12	Bear, brown
13–16	Boar, wild
17–19	Centaur
20–23	Dryad
24–28	Eagle
29–31	Elf
32–34	Faun/satyr
35–36	Fox
37–40	Gnome
41–44	Hawk
45–58	Human
59–61	Lynx
62–64	Owl
65–68	Pixie
69–70	Raccoon
71–75	Stag
76–80	Wolf
81–85	Wolverine
86–00	DM's choice

If an unusual creature form is indicated, the DM can (at his option only) use the guidelines for new player character races to allow the character to earn experience and advance in levels, although this may not be in the same class as before. If the reincarnated character returns as a creature eligible to be the same class as he was previously (i.e., a human fighter returns as an elf), the reincarnated character has half his previous levels and hit points. If the character returns as a new character class, his hit points are half his previous total, but he must begin again at 1st level. If the character returns as a creature unable to have a class, he has half the hit points and saving throws of his previous incarnation.

Restoration (Necromancy)
Reversible

Sphere: Necromantic
Range: Touch
Components: V, S
Duration: Permanent
Casting Time: 3 rounds
Area of Effect: Creature touched
Saving Throw: None

When this spell is cast, the life energy level of the recipient creature is raised by one. This reverses any previous life energy level drain of the creature by a force or monster. Thus, if a 10th-level character had been struck by a wight and drained to 9th level, the *restoration* spell would bring the character up to exactly the number of experience points necessary to restore him to 10th level once again, restoring additional Hit Dice (or hit points) and level functions accordingly. Restoration is effective only if the spell is cast within one day of the recipient's loss of life energy, per experience level of the priest casting it. A *restoration* spell restores the intelligence of a creature affected by a *feeblemind* spell. It also negates all forms of insanity. Casting this spell ages both the caster and the recipient by two years.

The reverse, *energy drain*, draws away one life energy level (see such undead as spectre, wight, and vampire, in the *Monstrous Compendium*). The energy drain requires the victim to be touched. Casting this form of the spell does not age the caster.

Resurrection (Necromancy)
Reversible

Sphere: Necromantic
Range: Touch
Components: V, S, M
Duration: Permanent
Casting Time: 1 turn
Area of Effect: Creature touched
Saving Throw: None

The priest employing this spell is able to restore life and complete strength to any living creature, including elves, he bestows the *resurrection* spell upon. The creature can have been dead up to 10 years per level of the priest casting the spell. Thus a 19th-level priest can resurrect the bones of a creature dead up to 190 years. The creature, upon surviving a resurrection survival check, is immediately restored to full hit points and can perform strenuous activity. The spell cannot bring back a creature that has reached its allotted life span (i.e., died of natural causes). Casting this spell makes it impossible for the priest to cast further spells or engage in combat until he has had one day of bed rest for each experience level or Hit Die of the creature brought back to life. The caster ages three years upon casting this spell.

The reverse, *destruction*, causes the victim of the spell to be instantly dead and turned to dust. A *wish* spell or equivalent is required for recovery. Destruction requires a touch, either in combat or otherwise, and does not age the caster. In addition, the victim is allowed a saving throw (with a −4 penalty). If the save is successful, the victim receives 8d6 points of damage instead.

The material components of the spell are the priest's religious symbol and holy water (unholy water for the reverse spell). The DM may reduce the chances of successful resurrection if little of the creature's remains are available.

Succor (Alteration, Enchantment)
Reversible

Sphere: Summoning
Range: Touch
Components: V, S, M
Duration: Special
Casting Time: 1 day
Area of Effect: Special
Saving Throw: None

By casting this spell, the priest creates a powerful magic in some specially prepared object—a string of prayer beads, a small clay tablet, an ivory baton, etc. This object radiates magic, for it contains the power to instantaneously transport its possessor to the sanctuary of the priest who created its magic. Once the item is enchanted, the priest must give it willingly to an individual, at the same time informing him of a command word to be spoken when the item is to be used. To make use of the item, the recipient must speak the command word at the same time that he rends or breaks the item. When this is done, the individual and all that he is wearing and carrying (up to the maximum encumbrance limit for the character) are instantly transported to the sanctuary of the priest, just as if the individual were capable of speaking a *word of recall* spell. No other creatures can be affected.

The reversed application of the spell causes the priest to be transported to the immediate vicinity of the possessor of the item when it is broken and the command word said. The priest has a general idea of the location and situation of the item's possessor, and can choose not to be affected by this summons. This decision is made at the instant when the transportation is to take place, but if he chooses not to go, then the opportunity is gone forever and the spell is wasted.

The cost of preparing the special item (for either version of the spell) varies from 2,000 to 5,000 gp. The more costly items can transport the subject from one plane of existence to another, if the DM allows. Note that the same factors that can prevent the operation of the *plane shift* and *teleport* spells can also prevent the use of this spell.

Sunray (Evocation, Alteration)

Sphere: Sun
Range: 10 yards/level
Components: V, S, M
Duration: 1 + 1d4 rounds
Casting Time: 4
Area of Effect: 5-foot-radius sphere
(plus special)
Saving Throw: Special

With this spell, the caster can evoke a dazzling beam of light each round in which no action other than movement is performed. The sunray is like a ray of natural sunlight. All creatures in the 10-foot-diameter area of effect must roll successful saving throws vs. spell or be blinded for 1d3 rounds, those using infravision at the time for 2d4 rounds. Creatures to whom sunlight is harmful or unnatural suffer permanent blindness if the saving throw is failed, and are blinded for 2d6 rounds if the saving throw is successful. Those within its area of effect, as well as creatures within 20 feet of its perimeter, lose any infravision capabilities for 1d4 + 1 rounds.

Undead caught within the sunray's area of effect receive 8d6 points of damage, one-half if a saving throw vs. spell is successful. Those undead 20 feet to either side of the sunray's area of effect receive 3d6 points of damage, no damage if a save is successful. In addition, the ray may result in the total destruction of those undead specifically affected by sunlight, if their saving throws are failed. The ultraviolet light generated by the spell inflicts damage on fungoid creatures and subterranean fungi just as if they were undead, but no saving throw is allowed.

The material components are an aster seed and a piece of aventurine feldspar (sunstone).

Symbol (Conjuration/Summoning)

Sphere: Guardian
Range: Touch
Components: V, S, M
Duration: 1 turn/level
Casting Time: 3
Area of Effect: Special
Saving Throw: Neg.

The priest casting this spell inscribes a glowing symbol in the air or upon any surface, according to his desire. Any creature looking at the completed symbol within 60 feet must roll a successful saving throw vs. spell or suffer the effect. The symbol glows for one turn for each experience level of the caster. The particular symbol used is selected by the caster at the time of casting. The caster will not be affected by his own symbol. One of the following effects is chosen by the caster:

Hopelessness: Creatures seeing it must turn back in dejection or surrender to capture or attack unless they roll successful saving throws vs. spell. Its effects last for 3d4 turns.
Pain: Creatures affected suffer −4 penalties to their attack rolls and −2 penalties to their Dexterity ability scores due to wracking pains. The effects last for 2d10 turns.
Persuasion: Creatures seeing the symbol become of the same alignment as and friendly to the priest who scribed the symbol for 1d20 turns unless a saving throw vs. spell is successful.

The material components of this spell are mercury and phosphorus (see 8th-level wizard spell, *symbol*).

Transmute Metal to Wood (Alteration)

Sphere: Elemental (Earth)
Range: 80 yards
Components: V, S, M
Duration: Permanent
Casting Time: 1 round
Area of Effect: 1 metal object
Saving Throw: Special

The *transmute metal to wood* spell enables the caster to change an object from metal to wood. The volume of metal cannot exceed a maximum weight of 10 pounds per experience level of the priest. Magical objects made of metal are 90% resistant to the spell, and those on the person of a creature receive the creature's saving throw as well. Artifacts and relics cannot be transmuted. Note that only a *wish* spell or similar magic can restore a transmuted object to its metallic state. Otherwise, for example, a metal door changed to wood would be forevermore a wooden door.

Wind Walk (Alteration)

Sphere: Elemental (Air)
Range: Touch
Components: V, S, M
Duration: 1 hour/level
Casting Time: 1 round
Area of Effect: Special
Saving Throw: None

This spell enables the priest, and possibly one or two other persons, to alter the substance of his body to a cloud-like vapor. A magical wind then wafts the priest along at a movement rate of 60, or as slow as 6, as the spellcaster wills. The *wind walk* spell lasts as long as the priest desires, up to a maximum duration of six turns (one hour) per experience level of the caster. For every 8 levels of experience the priest has attained, up to 24, he is able to touch another person and carry that person, or those persons, along on the wind walk. Persons wind walking are not invisible, but rather appear misty and translucent. If fully clothed in white, they are 80% likely to be mistaken for clouds, fog, vapors, etc. The priest can regain his physical form as desired, each change to and from vaporous form requiring five rounds. While in vaporous form, the priest and companions are hit only by magic or magical weaponry, though they may be subject to high winds at the DM's discretion. No spellcasting is possible in vaporous form.

The material components of this spell are fire and holy water.

Abjuration

Alarm (1st)
Cantrip (1st)
Protection From Evil (1st)
Protection From Cantrips (2nd)
Dispel Magic (3rd)
Non-Detection (3rd)
Protection From Evil, 10' Radius (3rd)
Protection From Normal Missiles (3rd)
Fire Trap (4th)
Minor Globe of Invulnerability (4th)
Remove Curse (4th)
Avoidance (5th)
Dismissal (5th)
Anti-Magic Shell (6th)
Globe of Invulnerability (6th)
Repulsion (6th)
Banishment (7th)
Sequester (7th)
Spell Turning (7th)
Mind Blank (8th)
Serten's Spell Immunity (8th)
Imprisonment (9th)
Prismatic Sphere (9th)

Alteration

Affect Normal Fires (1st)
Burning Hands (1st)
Cantrip (1st)
Color Spray (1st)
Comprehend Languages (1st)
Dancing Lights (1st)
Enlarge (1st)
Erase (1st)
Feather Fall (1st)
Gaze Reflection (1st)
Hold Portal (1st)
Jump (1st)
Light (1st)
Mending (1st)
Message (1st)
Shocking Grasp (1st)
Spider Climb (1st)
Wizard Mark (1st)
Alter Self (2nd)
Continual Light (2nd)
Darkness, 15' Radius (2nd)
Deeppockets (2nd)
Fog Cloud (2nd)
Fools' Gold (2nd)
Irritation (2nd)
Knock (2nd)
Levitate (2nd)
Magic Mouth (2nd)
Pyrotechnics (2nd)
Rope Trick (2nd)
Shatter (2nd)
Strength (2nd)
Whispering Wind (2nd)
Wizard Lock (2nd)
Blink (3rd)
Delude (3rd)
Explosive Runes (3rd)
Fly (3rd)

Gust of Wind (3rd)
Haste (3rd)
Infravision (3rd)
Item (3rd)
Leomund's Tiny Hut (3rd)
Melf's Minute Meteors (3rd)
Secret Page (3rd)
Slow (3rd)
Tongues (3rd)
Water Breathing (3rd)
Wind Wall (3rd)
Wraithform (3rd)
Dimension Door (4th)
Extension I (4th)
Fire Shield (4th)
Leomund's Secure Shelter (4th)
Massmorph (4th)
Otiluke's Resilient Sphere (4th)
Plant Growth (4th)
Polymorph Other (4th)
Polymorph Self (4th)
Rainbow Pattern (4th)
Rary's Mnemonic Enhancer (4th)
Solid Fog (4th)
Stoneskin (4th)
Vacancy (4th)
Wizard Eye (4th)
Airy Water (5th)
Animal Growth (5th)
Avoidance (5th)
Distance Distortion (5th)
Extension II (5th)
Fabricate (5th)
Leomund's Secret Chest (5th)
Passwall (5th)
Stone Shape (5th)
Telekinesis (5th)
Teleport (5th)
Transmute Rock to Mud (5th)
Control Weather (6th)
Death Fog (6th)
Disintegrate (6th)
Extension III (6th)
Glassee (6th)
Guards and Wards (6th)
Lower Water (6th)
Mirage Arcana (6th)
Mordenkainen's Lucubration (6th)
Move Earth (6th)
Otiluke's Freezing Sphere (6th)
Part Water (6th)
Project Image (6th)
Stone to Flesh (6th)
Tenser's Transformation (6th)
Transmute Water to Dust (6th)
Duo-Dimension (7th)
Mordenkainen's Magnificent Mansion (7th)
Phase Door (7th)
Reverse Gravity (7th)
Statue (7th)
Teleport Without Error (7th)
Vanish (7th)
Glassteel (8th)
Incendiary Cloud (8th)
Otiluke's Telekinetic Sphere (8th)
Permanency (8th)
Polymorph Any Object (8th)

Sink (8th)
Crystalbrittle (9th)
Mordenkainen's Disjunction (9th)
Shape Change (9th)
Succor (9th)
Temporal Stasis (9th)
Time Stop (9th)

Conjuration/Summoning

Armor (1st)
Cantrip (1st)
Find Familiar (1st)
Grease (1st)
Mount (1st)
Unseen Servant (1st)
Glitterdust (2nd)
Melf's Acid Arrow (2nd)
Summon Swarm (2nd)
Flame Arrow (3rd)
Monster Summoning I (3rd)
Phantom Steed (3rd)
Sepia Snake Sigil (3rd)
Evard's Black Tentacles (4th)
Monster Summoning II (4th)
Conjure Elemental (5th)
Leomund's Secret Chest (5th)
Monster Summoning III (5th)
Mordenkainen's Faithful Hound (5th)
Summon Shadow (5th)
Conjure Animals (6th)
Ensnarement (6th)
Invisible Stalker (6th)
Monster Summoning IV (6th)
Drawmij's Instant Summons (7th)
Limited Wish (7th)
Monster Summoning V (7th)
Mordenkainen's Magnificent Mansion (7th)
Power Word, Stun (7th)
Prismatic Spray (7th)
Maze (8th)
Monster Summoning VI (8th)
Power Word, Blind (8th)
Prismatic Wall (8th)
Symbol (8th)
Trap the Soul (8th)
Gate (9th)
Monster Summoning VII (9th)
Power Word, Kill (9th)
Prismatic Sphere (9th)
Wish (9th)

Enchantment/Charm

Cantrip (1st)
Charm Person (1st)
Friends (1st)
Hypnotism (1st)
Sleep (1st)
Taunt (1st)
Bind (2nd)
Deeppockets (2nd)
Forget (2nd)
Ray of Enfeeblement (2nd)
Scare (2nd)

Tasha's Uncontrollable Hideous
 Laughter (2nd)
Hold Person (3rd)
Suggestion (3rd)
Charm Monster (4th)
Confusion (4th)
Emotion (4th)
Enchanted Weapon (4th)
Fire Charm (4th)
Fumble (4th)
Leomund's Secure Shelter (4th)
Magic Mirror (4th)
Chaos (5th)
Domination (5th)
Fabricate (5th)
Feeblemind (5th)
Hold Monster (5th)
Leomund's Lamentable Belaborment (5th)
Enchant an Item (6th)
Eyebite (6th)
Geas (6th)
Guards and Wards (6th)
Mass Suggestion (6th)
Charm Plants (7th)
Shadow Walk (7th)
Antipathy-Sympathy (8th)
Binding (8th)
Demand (8th)
Mass Charm (8th)
Otto's Irresistible Dance (8th)
Sink (8th)
Mordenkainen's Disjunction (9th)
Succor (9th)

Illusion/Phantasm

Audible Glamer (1st)
Cantrip (1st)
Change Self (1st)
Nystul's Magical Aura (1st)
Phantasmal Force (1st)
Spook (1st)
Ventriloquism (1st)
Blindness (2nd)
Blur (2nd)
Deafness (2nd)
Fools' Gold (2nd)
Hypnotic Pattern (2nd)
Improved Phantasmal Force (2nd)
Invisibility (2nd)
Leomund's Trap (2nd)
Mirror Image (2nd)
Misdirection (2nd)
Whispering Wind (2nd)
Illusionary Script (3rd)
Invisibility, 10' Radius (3rd)
Phantom Steed (3rd)
Spectral Force (3rd)
Wraithform (3rd)
Fear (4th)
Hallucinatory Terrain (4th)
Illusionary Wall (4th)
Improved Invisibility (4th)
Minor Creation (4th)
Phantasmal Killer (4th)
Rainbow Pattern (4th)

Shadow Monsters (4th)
Vacancy (4th)
Advanced Illusion (5th)
Demi-Shadow Monsters (5th)
Dream (5th)
Major Creation (5th)
Seeming (5th)
Shadow Door (5th)
Shadow Magic (5th)
Demi-Shadow Magic (6th)
Eyebite (6th)
Mirage Arcana (6th)
Mislead (6th)
Permanent Illusion (6th)
Programmed Illusion (6th)
Project Image (6th)
Shades (6th)
Veil (6th)
Mass Invisibility (7th)
Sequester (7th)
Shadow Walk (7th)
Simulacrum (7th)
Screen (8th)
Weird (9th)

Invocation/Evocation

Alarm (1st)
Cantrip (1st)
Magic Missile (1st)
Shield (1st)
Tenser's Floating Disc (1st)
Wall of Fog (1st)
Flaming Sphere (2nd)
Stinking Cloud (2nd)
Web (2nd)
Fireball (3rd)
Lightning Bolt (3rd)
Melf's Minute Meteors (3rd)
Dig (4th)
Fire Shield (4th)
Fire Trap (4th)
Ice Storm (4th)
Otiluke's Resilient Sphere (4th)
Shout (4th)
Wall of Fire (4th)
Wall of Ice (4th)
Bigby's Interposing Hand (5th)
Cloudkill (5th)
Cone of Cold (5th)
Dream (5th)
Leomund's Lamentable Belaborment (5th)
Sending (5th)
Wall of Force (5th)
Wall of Iron (5th)
Wall of Stone (5th)
Bigby's Forceful Hand (6th)
Chain Lightning (6th)
Contingency (6th)
Death Fog (6th)
Enchant an Item (6th)
Guards and Wards (6th)
Otiluke's Freezing Sphere (6th)
Tenser's Transformation (6th)
Bigby's Grasping Hand (7th)
Delayed Blast Fireball (7th)

Forcecage (7th)
Limited Wish (7th)
Mordenkainen's Sword (7th)
Bigby's Clenched Fist (8th)
Binding (8th)
Demand (8th)
Incendiary Cloud (8th)
Otiluke's Telekinetic Sphere (8th)
Astral Spell (9th)
Bigby's Crushing Hand (9th)
Energy Drain (9th)
Meteor Swarm (9th)

Lesser/Greater Divination

Cantrip (1st)
Detect Magic (1st)
Detect Undead (1st)
Identify (1st)
Read Magic (1st)
Detect Evil (2nd)
Detect Invisibility (2nd)
ESP (2nd)
Know Alignment (2nd)
Locate Object (2nd)
Clairaudience (3rd)
Clairvoyance (3rd)
Detect Scrying (4th)
Magic Mirror (4th)
Contact Other Plane (5th)
False Vision (5th)
Legend Lore (6th)
True Seeing (6th)
Vision (7th)
Screen (8th)
Foresight (9th)

Necromancy

Cantrip (1st)
Chill Touch (1st)
Detect Undead (1st)
Spectral Hand (2nd)
Feign Death (3rd)
Hold Undead (3rd)
Vampiric Touch (3rd)
Contagion (4th)
Enervation (4th)
Animate Dead (5th)
Magic Jar (5th)
Summon Shadow (5th)
Death Spell (6th)
Reincarnation (6th)
Control Undead (7th)
Finger of Death (7th)
Clone (8th)
Energy Drain (9th)

All

Bless (1st)
Combine (1st)
Detect Evil (1st)
Purify Food & Drink (1st)
Atonement (5th)

Animal

Animal Friendship (1st)
Invisibility to Animals (1st)
Locate Animals or Plants (1st)
Charm Person or Mammal (2nd)
Messenger (2nd)
Snake Charm (2nd)
Speak With Animals (2nd)
Hold Animal (3rd)
Summon Insects (3rd)
Animal Summoning I (4th)
Call Woodland Beings (4th)
Giant Insect (4th)
Repel Insects (4th)
Animal Growth (5th)
Animal Summoning II (5th)
Animal Summoning III (6th)
Anti-Animal Shell (6th)
Creeping Doom (7th)

Astral

Plane Shift (5th)
Astral Spell (7th)

Charm

Command (1st)
Remove Fear (1st)
Enthrall (2nd)
Hold Person (2nd)
Cloak of Bravery (4th)
Free Action (4th)
Imbue With Spell Ability (4th)
Quest (5th)
Confusion (7th)
Exaction (7th)

Combat

Magical Stone (1st)
Shillelagh (1st)
Chant (2nd)
Spiritual Hammer (2nd)
Prayer (3rd)
Flame Strike (5th)
Insect Plague (5th)
Holy Word (7th)

Creation

Create Food & Water (3rd)
Animate Object (6th)
Blade Barrier (6th)
Heroes' Feast (6th)
Wall of Thorns (6th)
Changestaff (7th)
Chariot of Sustarre (7th)

Divination

Detect Magic (1st)
Detect Poison (1st)
Detect Snares & Pits (1st)
Locate Animals or Plants (1st)
Augury (2nd)
Detect Charm (2nd)
Find Traps (2nd)
Know Alignment (2nd)
Speak With Animals (2nd)
Locate Object (3rd)
Speak With Dead (3rd)
Detect Lie (4th)
Divination (4th)
Reflecting Pool (4th)
Tongues (4th)
Commune (5th)
Commune With Nature (5th)
Magic Font (5th)
True Seeing (5th)
Find the Path (6th)
Speak With Monsters (6th)

Elemental

Create Water (1st)
Dust Devil (2nd)
Fire Trap (2nd)
Flame Blade (2nd)
Heat Metal (2nd)
Produce Flame (2nd)
Flame Walk (3rd)
Meld Into Stone (3rd)
Protections From Fire (3rd)
Pyrotechnics (3rd)
Stone Shape (3rd)
Water Breathing (3rd)
Water Walk (3rd)
Lower Water (4th)
Produce Fire (4th)
Air Walk (5th)
Spike Stones (5th)
Transmute Rock to Mud (5th)
Wall of Fire (5th)
Conjure Fire Elemental (6th)
Fire Seeds (6th)
Part Water (6th)
Stone Tell (6th)
Transmute Water to Dust (6th)
Animate Rock (7th)
Chariot of Sustarre (7th)
Conjure Earth Elemental (7th)
Earthquake (7th)
Fire Storm (7th)

Transmute Metal to Wood (7th)
Wind Walk (7th)

Guardian

Silence, 15' Radius (2nd)
Wyvern Watch (2nd)
Glyph of Warding (3rd)
Blade Barrier (6th)
Symbol (7th)

Healing

Cure Light Wounds (1st)
Slow Poison (2nd)
Cure Serious Wounds (4th)
Neutralize Poison (4th)
Cure Critical Wounds (5th)
Heal (6th)

Necromantic

Invisibility to Undead (1st)
Aid (2nd)
Animate Dead (3rd)
Cure Blindness or Deafness (3rd)
Cure Disease (3rd)
Feign Death (3rd)
Negative Plane Protection (3rd)
Raise Dead (5th)
Regenerate (7th)
Reincarnate (7th)
Restoration (7th)
Resurrection (7th)

Plant

Entangle (1st)
Pass Without Trace (1st)
Shillelagh (1st)
Barkskin (2nd)
Goodberry (2nd)
Trip (2nd)
Warp Wood (2nd)
Plant Growth (3rd)
Snare (3rd)
Spike Growth (3rd)
Tree (3rd)
Hallucinatory Forest (4th)
Hold Plant (4th)
Plant Door (4th)
Speak With Plants (4th)
Sticks to Snakes (4th)
Anti-Plant Shell (5th)
Pass Plant (5th)
Liveoak (6th)
Transport Via Plants (6th)
Turn Wood (6th)
Wall of Thorns (6th)
Changestaff (7th)

Protection

Endure Cold/Endure Heat (1st)
Protection From Evil (1st)
Sanctuary (1st)
Barkskin (2nd)
Resist Fire/Resist Cold (2nd)
Withdraw (2nd)
Dispel Magic (3rd)
Magical Vestment (3rd)
Negative Plane Protection (3rd)
Protection From Fire (3rd)
Remove Curse (3rd)
Remove Paralysis (3rd)
Protection From Evil, 10' Evil (4th)
Protection From Lightning (4th)
Repel Insects (4th)
Spell Immunity (4th)
Anti-Plant Shell (5th)
Dispel Evil (5th)
Anti-Animal Shell (6th)

Summoning

Abjure (4th)
Animal Summoning I (4th)
Call Woodland Beings (4th)
Animal Summoning II (5th)
Dispel Evil (5th)
Aerial Servant (6th)
Animal Summoning III (6th)
Animate Object (6th)
Conjure Animals (6th)
Wall of Thorns (6th)
Weather Summoning (6th)
Word of Recall (6th)
Conjure Earth Elemental (7th)
Creeping Doom (7th)
Exaction (7th)
Gate (7th)
Succor (7th)

Sun

Light (1st)
Continual Light (3rd)
Starshine (3rd)
Moonbeam (5th)
Rainbow (5th)
Sunray (7th)

Weather

Faerie Fire (1st)
Obscurement (2nd)
Call Lightning (3rd)
Control Temperature, 10' Radius (4th)
Protection From Lightning (4th)
Control Winds (5th)
Rainbow (5th)
Weather Summoning (6th)
Control Weather (7th)

Table 1: STRENGTH

Ability Score	Hit Prob.	Damage Adj.	Weight Allow.	Max. Press	Open Doors	Bend Bars/ Lift Gates	Notes
1	−5	−4	1	3	1	0%	
2	−3	−2	1	5	1	0%	
3	−3	−1	5	10	2	0%	
4-5	−2	−1	10	25	3	0%	
6-7	−1	None	20	55	4	0%	
8-9	Normal	None	35	90	5	1%	
10-11	Normal	None	40	115	6	2%	
12-13	Normal	None	45	140	7	4%	
14-15	Normal	None	55	170	8	7%	
16	Normal	+1	70	195	9	10%	
17	+1	+1	85	220	10	13%	
18	+1	+2	110	255	11	16%	
18/01-50	+1	+3	135	280	12	20%	
18/51-75	+2	+3	160	305	13	25%	
18/76-90	+2	+4	185	330	14	30%	
18/91-99	+2	+5	235	380	15(3)	35%	
18/00	+3	+6	335	480	16(6)	40%	
19	+3	+7	485	640	16(8)	50%	Hill Giant
20	+3	+8	535	700	17(10)	60%	Stone Giant
21	+4	+9	635	810	17(12)	70%	Frost Giant
22	+4	+10	785	970	18(14)	80%	Fire Giant
23	+5	+11	935	1,130	18(16)	90%	Cloud Giant
24	+6	+12	1,235	1,440	19(17)	95%	Storm Giant
25	+7	+14	1,535	1,750	19(18)	99%	Titan

Table 2: DEXTERITY

Ability Score	Reaction Adj.	Missile Attack Adj.	Defensive Adj.
1	−6	−6	+5
2	−4	−4	+5
3	−3	−3	+4
4	−2	−2	+3
5	−1	−1	+2
6	0	0	+1
7	0	0	0
8	0	0	0
9	0	0	0
10-14	0	0	0
15	0	0	−1
16	+1	+1	−2
17	+2	+2	−3
18	+2	+2	−4
19	+3	+3	−4
20	+3	+3	−4
21	+4	+4	−5
22	+4	+4	−5
23	+4	+4	−5
24	+5	+5	−6
25	+5	+5	−6

Table 3: CONSTITUTION

Ability Score	Hit Point Adjustment	System Shock	Resurrection Survival	Poison Save	Regeneration
1	-3	25%	30%	-2	Nil
2	-2	30%	35%	-1	Nil
3	-2	35%	40%	0	Nil
4	-1	40%	45%	0	Nil
5	-1	45%	50%	0	Nil
6	-1	50%	55%	0	Nil
7	0	55%	60%	0	Nil
8	0	60%	65%	0	Nil
9	0	65%	70%	0	Nil
10	0	70%	75%	0	Nil
11	0	75%	80%	0	Nil
12	0	80%	85%	0	Nil
13	0	85%	90%	0	Nil
14	0	88%	92%	0	Nil
15	+1	90%	94%	0	Nil
16	+2	95%	96%	0	Nil
17	+2 (+3)*	97%	98%	0	Nil
18	+2 (+4)*	99%	100%	0	Nil
19	+2 (+5)*	99%	100%	+1	Nil
20	+2 (+5)**	99%	100%	+1	1/6 turns
21	+2 (+6)***	99%	100%	+2	1/5 turns
22	+2 (+6)***	99%	100%	+2	1/4 turns
23	+2 (+6)****	99%	100%	+3	1/3 turns
24	+2 (+7)****	99%	100%	+3	1/2 turns
25	+2 (+7)****	100%	100%	+4	1/1 turn

* Parenthetical bonus applies to warriors only. All other classes receive maximum bonus of +2 per die.
** All 1s rolled for Hit Dice are considered 2s.
*** All 1s and 2s rolled for Hit Dice are considered 3s.
**** All 1s, 2s, and 3s rolled for Hit Dice are considered 4s.

Table 4: INTELLIGENCE

Ability Score	# of Lang.	Spell Level	Chance to Learn Spell	Max. # of Spells/Lvl	Spell Immunity
1	0*	—	—	—	—
2	1	—	—	—	—
3	1	—	—	—	—
4	1	—	—	—	—
5	1	—	—	—	—
6	1	—	—	—	—
7	1	—	—	—	—
8	1	—	—	—	—
9	2	4th	35%	6	—
10	2	5th	40%	7	—
11	2	5th	45%	7	—
12	3	6th	50%	7	—
13	3	6th	55%	9	—
14	4	7th	60%	9	—
15	4	7th	65%	11	—
16	5	8th	70%	11	—
17	6	8th	75%	14	—
18	7	9th	85%	18	—
19	8	9th	95%	All	1st-lvl illusions
20	9	9th	96%	All	2nd-lvl illusions
21	10	9th	97%	All	3rd-lvl illusions
22	11	9th	98%	All	4th-lvl illusions
23	12	9th	99%	All	5th-lvl illusions
24	15	9th	100%	All	6th-lvl illusions
25	20	9th	100%	All	7th-lvl illusions

* While unable to speak a language, the character can still communicate by grunts and gestures.

Table 5: WISDOM

Ability Score	Magical Defense Adjustment	Bonus Spells	Chance of Spell Failure	Spell Immunity
1	−6	—	80%	—
2	−4	—	60%	—
3	−3	—	50%	—
4	−2	—	45%	—
5	−1	—	40%	—
6	−1	—	35%	—
7	−1	—	30%	—
8	0	—	25%	—
9	0	0	20%	—
10	0	0	15%	—
11	0	0	10%	—
12	0	0	5%	—
13	0	1st	0%	—
14	0	1st	0%	—
15	+1	2nd	0%	—
16	+2	2nd	0%	—
17	+3	3rd	0%	—
18	+4	4th	0%	—
19	+4	1st, 4th	0%	Cause fear, Charm person, Command, Friends, Hypnotism
20	+4	2nd, 4th	0%	Forget, Hold person, Ray of enfeeblement, Scare
21	+4	3rd, 5th	0%	Fear
22	+4	4th, 5th	0%	Charm monster, Confusion, Emotion, Fumble, Suggestion
23	+4	5th, 5th	0%	Chaos, Feeblemind, Hold monster, Magic jar, Quest
24	+4	6th, 6th	0%	Geas, Mass suggestion, Rod of rulership
25	+4	6th, 7th	0%	Antipathy/sympathy, Death spell, Mass charm

Table 6: CHARISMA

Ability Score	Maximum # of Henchmen	Loyalty Base	Reaction Adjustment
1	0	-8	-7
2	1	-7	-6
3	1	-6	-5
4	1	-5	-4
5	2	-4	-3
6	2	-3	-2
7	3	-2	-1
8	3	-1	0
9	4	0	0
10	4	0	0
11	4	0	0
12	5	0	0
13	5	0	+1
14	6	+1	+2
15	7	+3	+3
16	8	+4	+5
17	10	+6	+6
18	15	+8	+7
19	20	+10	+8
20	25	+12	+9
21	30	+14	+10
22	35	+16	+11
23	40	+18	+12
24	45	+20	+13
25	50	+20	+14

Table 7: RACIAL ABILITY REQUIREMENTS

Ability	Dwarf	Elf	Gnome	Half-Elf	Halfling
Strength	8/18	3/18	6/18	3/18	7/18 *
Dexterity	3/17	6/18	3/18	6/18	7/18
Constitution	11/18	7/18	8/18	6/18	10/18
Intelligence	3/18	8/18	6/18	4/18	6/18
Wisdom	3/18	3/18	3/18	3/18	3/17
Charisma	3/17	8/18	3/18	3/18	3/18

* Halfling fighters do not roll for exceptional Strength.

Table 8: RACIAL ABILITY ADJUSTMENTS

Race	Adjustments
Dwarf	+1 Constitution; −1 Charisma
Elf	+1 Dexterity; −1 Constitution
Gnome	+1 Intelligence; −1 Wisdom
Halfling	+1 Dexterity; −1 Strength

Table 9: CONSTITUTION SAVING THROW BONUSES

Constitution Score	Saving Throw Bonus
4-6	+1
7-10	+2
11-13	+3
14-17	+4
18-19	+5

Table 13: CLASS ABILITY MINIMUMS

Character Class	Str	Dex	Con	Int	Wis	Cha
Fighter	9	—	—	—	—	—
Paladin *	12	—	9	—	13	17
Ranger *	13	13	14	—	14	—
Mage	—	—	—	9	—	—
Specialist*	Var	Var	Var	Var	Var	Var
Cleric	—	—	—	—	9	—
Druid *	—	—	—	—	12	15
Thief	—	9	—	—	—	—
Bard *	—	12	—	13	—	15

* Optional character class. Specialist includes illusionist.

Table 18: RANGER ABILITIES

Ranger Level	Hide in Shadows	Move Silently	Casting Level	Priest Spell Levels 1	2	3
1	10%	15%	—	—	—	—
2	15%	21%	—	—	—	—
3	20%	27%	—	—	—	—
4	25%	33%	—	—	—	—
5	31%	40%	—	—	—	—
6	37%	47%	—	—	—	—
7	43%	55%	—	—	—	—
8	49%	62%	1	1	—	—
9	56%	70%	2	2	—	—
10	63%	78%	3	2	1	—
11	70%	86%	4	2	2	—
12	77%	94%	5	2	2	1
13	85%	99% *	6	3	2	1
14	93%	99%	7	3	2	2
15	99% *	99%	8	3	3	2
16	99%	99%	9	3	3**	3

* Maximum percentile score
** Maximum spell ability

Table 21: WIZARD SPELL PROGRESSION

Wizard Level	1	2	3	4	5	6	7	8	9
1	1	—	—	—	—	—	—	—	—
2	2	—	—	—	—	—	—	—	—
3	2	1	—	—	—	—	—	—	—
4	3	2	—	—	—	—	—	—	—
5	4	2	1	—	—	—	—	—	—
6	4	2	2	—	—	—	—	—	—
7	4	3	2	1	—	—	—	—	—
8	4	3	3	2	—	—	—	—	—
9	4	3	3	2	1	—	—	—	—
10	4	4	3	2	2	—	—	—	—
11	4	4	4	3	3	—	—	—	—
12	4	4	4	4	4	1	—	—	—
13	5	5	5	4	4	2	—	—	—
14	5	5	5	4	4	2	1	—	—
15	5	5	5	5	5	2	1	—	—
16	5	5	5	5	5	3	2	1	—
17	5	5	5	5	5	3	3	2	—
18	5	5	5	5	5	3	3	2	1
19	5	5	5	5	5	3	3	3	1
20	5	5	5	5	5	4	3	3	2

Table 22: WIZARD SPECIALIST REQUIREMENTS

Specialist	School	Race	Minimum Ability Score	Opposition School(s)
Abjurer	Abjuration	H	15 Wis	Alteration & Illusion
Conjurer	Conj./Summ.	H, ½ E	15 Con	Gr. Divin. & Invocation
Diviner	Gr. Divin.	H, ½ E, E	16 Wis	Conj./Summ.
Enchanter	Ench./Charm	H, ½ E, E	16 Cha	Invoc./Evoc. & Necromancy
Illusionist	Illusion	H, G	16 Dex	Necro., Invoc./Evoc., Abjur.
Invoker	Invoc./Evoc.	H	16 Con	Ench./Charm & Conj./Summ.
Necromancer	Necromancy	H	16 Wis	Illusion & Ench./Charm
Transmuter	Alteration	H, ½ E	15 Dex	Abjuration & Necromancy

Table 27: THIEVING SKILL RACIAL ADJUSTMENTS

Skill	Dwarf	Elf	Gnome	Half-elf	Halfling
Pick Pockets	—	+5%	—	+10%	+5%
Open Locks	+10%	−5%	+5%	—	+5%
Find/Remove Traps	+15%	—	+10%	—	+5%
Move Silently	—	+5%	+5%	—	+10%
Hide in Shadows	—	+10%	+5%	+5%	+15%
Detect Noise	—	+5%	+10%	—	+5%
Climb Walls	−10%	—	−15%	—	−15%
Read Languages	−5%	—	—	—	−5%

Table 24: PRIEST SPELL PROGRESSION

Priest Level	1	2	3	4	5	6*	7**
1	1	—	—	—	—	—	—
2	2	—	—	—	—	—	—
3	2	1	—	—	—	—	—
4	3	2	—	—	—	—	—
5	3	3	1	—	—	—	—
6	3	3	2	—	—	—	—
7	3	3	2	1	—	—	—
8	3	3	3	2	—	—	—
9	4	4	3	2	1	—	—
10	4	4	3	3	2	—	—
11	5	4	4	3	2	1	—
12	6	5	5	3	2	2	—
13	6	6	6	3	2	2	—
14	6	6	6	5	3	2	1
15	6	6	6	6	4	2	1
16	7	7	7	6	4	3	1
17	7	7	7	7	5	3	2
18	8	8	8	8	6	4	2
19	9	9	8	8	6	4	2
20	9	9	9	8	7	5	2

* Usable only by priests with 17 or greater Wisdom.

** Usable only by priests with 18 or greater Wisdom.

Table 26: THIEVING SKILL BASE SCORES

Skill	Base Score
Pick Pockets	15%
Open Locks	10%
Find/Remove Traps	5%
Move Silently	10%
Hide in Shadows	5%
Detect Noise	15%
Climb Walls	60%
Read Languages	0%

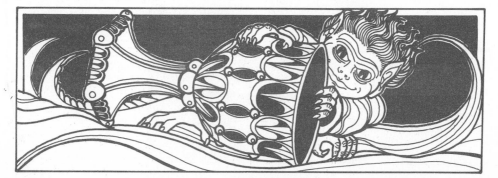

Table 28: THIEVING SKILL DEXTERITY ADJUSTMENTS

Dexterity	Pick Pockets	Open Locks	Find/ Remove Traps	Move Silently	Hide in Shadows
9	−15%	−10%	−10%	−20%	−10%
10	−10%	−5%	−10%	−15%	−5%
11	−5%	—	−5%	−10%	—
12	—	—	—	−5%	—
13-15	—	—	—	—	—
16	—	+5%	—	—	—
17	+5%	+10%	—	+5%	+5%
18	+10%	+15%	+5%	+10%	+10%
19	+15%	+20%	+10%	+15%	+15%

Table 29: THIEVING SKILL ARMOR ADJUSTMENTS

Skill	No Armor	Elven Chain*	Padded or Studded Leather
Pick Pockets	+5%	−20%	−30%
Open Locks	—	−5%	−10%
Find/Remove Traps	—	−5%	−10%
Move Silently	+10%	−10%	−20%
Hide in Shadows	+5%	−10%	−20%
Detect Noise	—	−5%	−10%
Climb Walls	+10%	−20%	−30%
Read Languages	—	—	—

* Bards (only) in non-elven chain mail suffer an additional −5% penalty.

Table 34: PROFICIENCY SLOTS

	Weapon Proficiencies			Nonweapon Proficiencies	
Group	Initial	#Levels	Penalty	Initial	#Levels
Warrior	4	3	−2	3	3
Wizard	1	6	−5	4	3
Priest	2	4	−3	4	3
Rogue	2	4	−3	3	4

Table 35: SPECIALIST ATTACKS PER ROUND

Fighter Level	Melee Weapon	Light X-bow	Heavy X-bow	Thrown Dagger	Thrown Dart	Other (Non-bow) Missiles
1-6	3/2	1/1	1/2	3/1	4/1	3/2
7-12	2/1	3/2	1/1	4/1	5/1	2/1
13+	5/2	2/1	3/2	5/1	6/1	5/2

Table 30: BACKSTAB DAMAGE MULTIPLIERS

Thief's Level	Damage Multiplier
1-4	× 2
5-8	× 3
9-12	× 4
13+	× 5

Table 33: BARD ABILITIES

Climb Walls	Detect Noise	Pick Pockets	Read Languages
50%	20%	10%	5%

Table 36: SECONDARY SKILLS

D100 Roll	Secondary Skill
01-02	Armorer (make, repair, & evaluate armor and weapons)
03-04	Bowyer/Fletcher (make, repair, & evaluate bows and arrows)
05-10	Farmer (basic agriculture)
11-14	Fisher (swimming, nets, and small boat handling)
15-20	Forester (basic wood lore, lumbering)
21-23	Gambler (knowledge of gambling games)
24-27	Groom (animal handling)
28-32	Hunter (basic wood lore, butchering, basic tracking)
33-34	Jeweler (appraisal of gems and jewelry)
35-37	Leather worker (skinning, tanning)
38-39	Limner/Painter (map making, appraisal of art objects)
40-42	Mason (stone-cutting)
43-44	Miner (stone-cutting, assaying)
45-46	Navigator (astronomy, sailing, swimming, navigation)
47-49	Sailor (sailing, swimming)
50-51	Scribe (reading, writing, basic math)
52-53	Shipwright (sailing, carpentry)
54-56	Tailor/Weaver (weaving, sewing, embroidery)
57-59	Teamster/Freighter (animal handling, wagon-repair)
60-62	Trader/Barterer (appraisal of common goods)
63-66	Trapper/Furrier (basic wood lore, skinning)
67-68	Weaponsmith (make, repair, & evaluate weapons)
69-71	Woodworker/Carpenter (carpentry, carving)
72-85	No skill of measureable worth
86-00	Roll twice (reroll any result of 86-00)

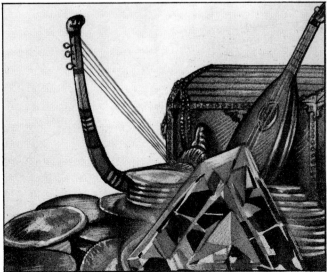

Go Beyond The Game

Playing the AD&D® game, playing any role-playing game, isn't enough anymore To get the most out of your gaming hobby, join the RPGA™ Network, an international organization of role-playing game enthusiasts.

All members receive a special introductory kit and the award-winning, bimonthly POLYHEDRON® Newszine. The Newszine is packed with gaming advice, news about the industry, and features for a variety of role-playing games, including the AD&D game and AD&D 2nd Edition game. In addition, there is an exciting adventure in every issue.

Through the POLYHEDRON Newszine and the RPGA Network, members learn how to contact other gamers, form gaming clubs, and improve their playing techniques.

The Network features an international ranking system for players and judges who compete in top-notch gaming tournaments at conventions throughout the world.

The Network also offers a club program where gaming groups can take part in hobby-related competitions.

Playing the game just isn't enough anymore. Discover that there is more to the role-playing hobby than just the rule books.

Discover the adventure in the RPGA Network.

To request a membership form, contact:

**RPGA Network
P.O. Box 515
Lake Geneva, WI 53147
USA**